THE PENGUIN DICTIONARY OF POPULAR Canadian Quotations

Also by John Robert Colombo

Colombo's Canadian Quotations

Colombo's Concise Canadian Quotations

Colombo's New Canadian Quotations

The Dictionary of Canadian Quotations

Colombo's All-Time Great Canadian Quotations

John Robert Colombo's Famous Lasting Words

Colombo's Canadian References

Canadian Literary Landmarks

1001 Questions About Canada

999 Questions About Canada

1000 Questions About Canada

The Penguin Book of Canadian Jokes

The Penguin Book of More Canadian Jokes

The Monster Book of Canadian Monsters

The Native Series

All the Poems of John Robert Colombo

THE PENGUIN DICTIONARY OF POPULAR

Canadian Quotations

EDITED BY

JOHN ROBERT COLOMBO

PENGUIN
CANADA

PENGUIN CANADA

Published by the Penguin Group

Penguin Group (Canada), 90 Eglinton Avenue East, Suite 700, Toronto, Ontario, Canada M4P 2Y3
(a division of Pearson Canada Inc.)

Penguin Group (USA) Inc., 375 Hudson Street, New York, New York 10014, U.S.A.
Penguin Books Ltd, 80 Strand, London WC2R 0RL, England
Penguin Ireland, 25 St Stephen's Green, Dublin 2, Ireland (a division of Penguin Books Ltd)
Penguin Group (Australia), 250 Camberwell Road, Camberwell, Victoria 3124, Australia
(a division of Pearson Australia Group Pty Ltd)
Penguin Books India Pvt Ltd, 11 Community Centre, Panchsheel Park, New Delhi – 110 017, India
Penguin Group (NZ), cnr Airborne and Rosedale Roads, Albany, Auckland 1310, New Zealand
(a division of Pearson New Zealand Ltd)
Penguin Books (South Africa) (Pty) Ltd, 24 Sturdee Avenue, Rosebank, Johannesburg 2196,
South Africa

Penguin Books Ltd, Registered Offices: 80 Strand, London WC2R 0RL, England

First published 2006

1 2 3 4 5 6 7 8 9 10 (WEB)

Manufactured in Canada.

LIBRARY AND ARCHIVES CANADA CATALOGUING IN PUBLICATION

The Penguin dictionary of popular Canadian quotations / [compiled by] John Robert Colombo.

Includes index.
ISBN-13: 978-0-14-305369-9
ISBN-10: 0-14-305369-8

1. Quotations, Canadian (English). 2. Canada—Quotations, maxims, etc.
I. Colombo, John Robert, 1936–

PN6084.C15P46 2006 C818'.02 C2005-907764-6

Visit the Penguin Group (Canada) website at **www.penguin.ca**

Special and corporate bulk purchase rates available; please see
www.penguin.ca/corporatesales or call 1-800-399-6858, ext. 477 or 474

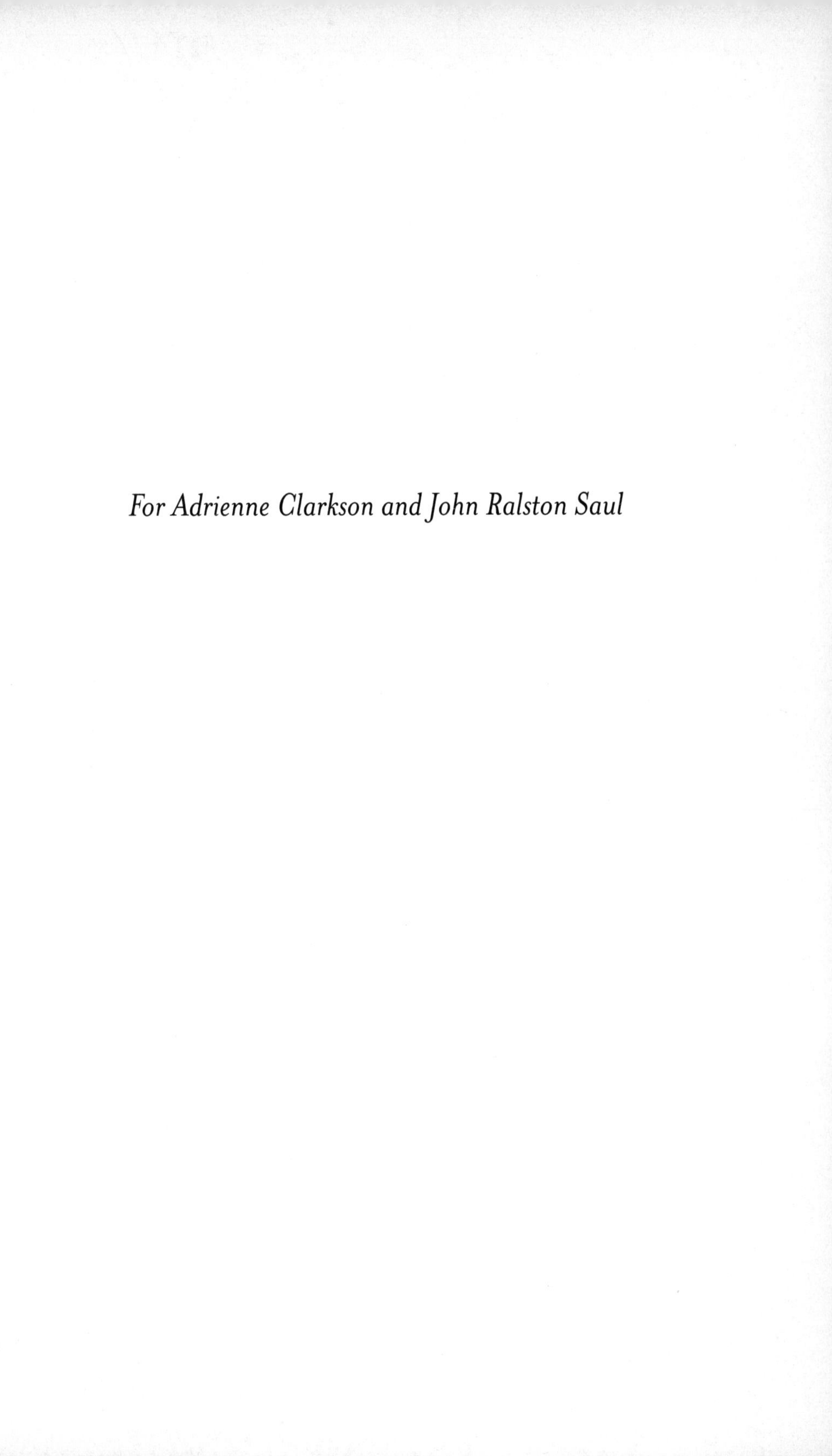

For Adrienne Clarkson and John Ralston Saul

Preface

The Penguin Dictionary of Popular Canadian Quotations is a compilation of the observations and opinions of Canadians about all subjects under the sun and of non-Canadians about this country and its customs. In these pages are more than 4000 quotations (comments and opinions) on over 900 subjects (themes and topics) from more than 1400 contributors. Although each quotation is brief and stands alone, the collection of quoted matter will impress the reader, browser, or user as a collective effort to define a country, a world, and a people. This dictionary of quotations presents a national mosaic of attitudes, insights, information, and opinions. Here is a book for reading as well as reference that may launch a thousand editorials and presentations, as well as settle arguments about who said what and when and why!

The adjective *popular* in the title is taken to mean *familiar*—as in Bartlett's *Familiar Quotations*—and also *quotable*—as in the regular "Quotable Quotes" feature of *The Reader's Digest.* It is true that not every quotation that appears here is truly familiar; indeed, the average reader is likely to recognize only a few of them as familiar. It is also true that not every quotation is quotable in the sense that its syllables "stick like burrs in the mind," as a quotation collector once described memorability. Yet the present compiler believes that these quotations deserve to be better known than they are today. These clutches of words are expressions of opinion and insight, distillations of experience, and sometimes tiny dramas, individually held or commonly shared.

Like Caesar's Gaul, each quotation appears in three parts: a head, a body, and a tail. The *head* is the key word, and these key or subject words are arranged alphabetically. The headings have been chosen to be inclusive rather than exclusive. To help students interested in the ramifications of a particular subject, there are approximately 500 "see" and "see also" entries to lead them to similar or associated entries. The *body* is the quotation proper. The 4000 "quotable quotes" are arranged under each head in chronological order—occasionally with related remarks clustered together to highlight a common concern. The *tail* is the all-important source note. Each of these may consist of the following elements: the contributor's name, identification of the speaker or writer at the time the remark was made, the venue or occasion (article, book, speech, address, quip, email, letter), and, as required, further interpretive, explanatory details. The index presents a summary of the dictionary's contents arranged according to contributor, then by remark according to page and column.

"What is new about this dictionary of quotations?" is a question that readers, browsers, and users might well ask. The answer lies in the essential characteristics of the work. It is a contemporary compilation. Quotations from the past have been included according to the amount of light they shed on current preoccupations. As a topical collection, this book offers numerous entries on subjects of considerable and current interest to Canadians. Some of these subjects are, at random, Canada & United States, Health Care, Media, and Same-sex Marriage.

The dictionary also includes those 200 or so "classic" quotations recorded over the centuries without which no collection of Canadian quotations could be complete. These classic quotations, of particular value for students and teachers, should be familiar to Canadians of all backgrounds, wherever they live.

Finally, and inevitably, a collection of Canadian quotations is, in part, a book about Canada. Yet this dictionary is more than a book about a country; it encompasses all aspects of life—everything under the sun and beyond, to sections on space and stars! This dictionary of quotations offers the reader a Canadian perspective on human nature and the world.

Readers and browsers will find in these pages a blend of old and new, the conventional and the provocative. The collection is the seventh dictionary of quotations that the editor has compiled. Indeed, each of those compilations has its own emphasis. They include *Colombo's Canadian Quotations* (1974), *Colombo's Concise Canadian Quotations* (1976), *Colombo's New Canadian Quotations* (1987), *The Dictionary of Canadian Quotations* (1991), *Colombo's All-Time Great Canadian Quotations* (1994), and *John Robert Colombo's Famous Lasting Words* (2000). These six—plus this, the seventh—compendia complement one another, as each volume has its individual focus. The first two collections were necessarily historical in orientation, to "catch up" with what had happened in the past. The next two were more topical in interest, to convey the emphasis on currency. The fifth was unique, as a historically arranged survey of statements made across time, ranging from 2500 B.C. to the near future! The sixth presents an up-to-date collection as of the year 2000. The seventh volume, the present one, a book while yet a dictionary, is the most topical in nature, in its emphasis on currency and contemporarity.

The majority of the quotations in this collection represent the interests or the expressions of the last decade and a half, so this makes it very much a twenty-first-century publication. Approximately one-third of the quotations refer to subjects of national interest and two-thirds to subjects of specific human interest. Perhaps 15 percent of the total come from francophone sources; the rest are derived from sources that are anglophone and allophone. Included are some quotations of historical interest—Sir Wilfrid Laurier's "The twentieth century belongs to Canada"—and of current interest—Roy MacGregor's "Saskatchewan is where medicare came from; Alberta may be where it is going." Some quotations reflect attitudes—Marshall McLuhan's "The medium is the message"—and others, dramas—"I shook hands with the devil." Although pains have been taken to represent minority interests—including ethnic and religious issues and concerns—the orientation of the collection is intentionally pan-Canadian. Previous collections have endorsed the maxim of the Toronto editor J. Castell Hopkins: "Canada only needs to be known in order to be great." (There, I have included it here, too!) Those 11 words were written in 1901, and they remain as true today as they were more than a century ago. Only through self-knowledge and national knowledge may we become capable of greatness as individuals and as inhabitants of this land.

Acknowledgments

A publication of this sweep may be the labour of one person but it consists of the contributions of many people. For assistance that I received in the past, I am pleased to acknowledge the help of my researcher M. Alice Neal and special librarian Philip Singer. For assistance in the present, I am indebted to Ed Butts, Donna Dunlop, and Dwight Whalen, as well as to innumerable researchers, writers, colleagues, and correspondents. Useful contributions were made by Tom Ban, Joel Bonn, Cyril Greenland, Tony Hawke, Robert Priest, Robert J. Sawyer, Barry Shainbaum, Bill Sherk, Milan Somborac, and George A. Vanderburgh.

The quoted matter comes from innumerable sources. Some of the remarks were first heard by members of The Empire Club of Canada; I am grateful to the officers of that club for permission to reproduce these speakers' words. Other quotations are largely matters of public record that sometimes come from the columns of three of the country's leading newspapers, *The Globe and Mail*, the *Toronto Star*, and the *National Post.* Magazines such as *Maclean's* and *Saturday Night* and programs produced by CBC Radio and CBC-TV are also cited frequently as sources. I have drawn on the full range of printed materials—newspapers, magazines, reviews, journals, books—as well as the media—notably television and the internet. (However did researchers manage before the invention of the World Wide Web and the search engine Google.com?)

I am indebted to the patient and helpful librarians of the Metropolitan Toronto Reference Library (Metro Central), the Locke and Frum branches of the Toronto Public Library System, the John P. Robarts Research Library of the University of Toronto, and the CBC Reference Library. The librarians of the Calgary Public Library were also generous. No subsidies or grants were requested for the preparation of the present work, though I hasten to acknowledge the receipt of subventions in the past from the Canada Council of the Arts as well as the Multiculturalism Directorate and the Department of the Secretary of State of the Government of Canada.

Confidence in this publication was expressed by a dedicated and talented trio of editors at Penguin Canada: Andrea Crozier, Helen Reeves, and Tracy Bordian. Eliza Marciniak kept the production firmly on schedule. The editing was undertaken with talent and tact by Kathleen Richards, whose thoroughness improved every page. I am indebted to David A. Gotlib for a state-of-the-art computer and to Felice and Frank Spitzer for technical assistance and discussions about specific ways that technology may be used to lighten the load of mankind. I remain in the debt of my wife, Ruth, for her encouragement as well as for her knack of drawing to my attention remarks that I would otherwise have overlooked. The book is dedicated, with permission, to a remarkable couple who have raised the national Plimsoll line of grace, intelligence, and integrity.

This book is a public expression of values and concerns as well as an expression of personal interests and tastes. The resulting compilation is a one-person production that aims to be inclusive and objective without sacrificing enthusiasm and special interest. Readers may detect here and there a taste for the bizarre and the unexpected. Finally, this is a roundabout way of saying that the interpretations and emphases are my own and that any errors of omission or commission may be laid directly at my door. Such matters, brought to my attention, will be rectified in future editions.

Readers wishing to draw my attention to quotations that could be included in future editions may reach me through my email address at *jrc@ca.inter.net*, through my website *www.colombo.ca*, or through the editorial department of Penguin Canada, the address of which appears on the copyright page.

Chimo!

John Robert Colombo
Toronto, 1 December 2005

THE PENGUIN DICTIONARY OF POPULAR Canadian Quotations

a

AARDVARKIAN

Aardvarkian, *noun.*

A person who always likes to come first.

Noun coined by **Bill Sherk**, logophile, during a sudden attack of aardvarkitis, brought on by his failure to coin the first entry in his first book, *Brave New Words* (1979). "Aardvarkian" became the first entry in its sequel, *More Brave New Words* (1981).

ABILITIES *See also* Disabilities; Talent

Here am I, / Yes, it is I, / Fresh and alert, / Ready to answer!

Piuvkaq, Inuit singer, "Song Deriding Another Hunter," translated from the Inuktitut by Knud Rasmussen, *The Netsilik Eskimos: Social Life and Spiritual Culture* (1931), translated from the Danish by W.E. Calvert.

People are always ready to admit a man's ability after he gets there.

Bob Edwards, publisher, *Calgary Eye Opener*, 27 January 1912.

We must not be so heavenly minded that we are no earthly good.

Lindsay King, minister, characteristic saying, Happy Valley United Church, Goose Bay, Labrador, December 1953.

The common man is capable.

J.T. Tompkins, adult educator and a founder of the Antigonish Movement, as recalled by Harvey (Pablo) Steele, *Agent for Change: The Story of Pablo Steele* (1973), as told to Gary MacEoin.

Let's not concentrate on disabilities, let's focus on abilities.

Rick Hansen, wheelchair athlete, quoted by Paula Todd, *Toronto Star*, 29 June 1986.

ABORIGINAL RIGHTS *See also* Nationhood; Native Peoples; Rights

We pride ourselves too much on our sterling human-rights record. It is not so shining. If there is a common denominator in the history of the northern half of North America, it is the continuing inability to deal seriously with aboriginal rights.

John Fraser, author, "Diary," *Saturday Night*, November 1989.

We advocate recognition of Aboriginal nations within Canada as political entities through which Aboriginal people can express their distinctive identity within the context of their Canadian citizenship.

René Dussault and **Georges Erasmus**, co-chairs, *Report of the Royal Commission on Aboriginal Peoples* (1996), Volume 5, *Renewal.*

The Government of Canada today formally expresses to all Aboriginal people in Canada our profound regret for past actions of the federal government which have contributed to these difficult pages in the history of our relationship together.

"Statement of Reconciliation: Learning from the Past," read by **Jane Stewart**, minister of Indian Affairs, Ottawa, 7 January 1999, published in *The Globe and Mail*, 8 January 1999.

Self-government is seen by the First Peoples as the way out of their internal colonial status; it is their response to inequality and social injustice. It is their way of establishing their presence as equals and as self-governing entities within the Canadian Confederation. Seen in this light, self-government is a fight for justice and equality, the logical extension of democracy and democratic rule in Canada.

Anver Saloojee, political scientist, "Social Cohesion and the Limits of Multiculturalism in Canada," *Racism, Eh? A Critical Inter-Disciplinary Anthology of Race and Racism in Canada* (2004), edited by Camille A. Nelson and Charmaine A. Nelson.

The vision of a multiracial, multiethnic polity at the national level is one that "democratizes democracy." The democratization of democracy in Canada must also involve the full implementation of the inherent right of the first Nations to govern themselves.

Anver Saloojee, political scientist, "Social Cohesion and the Limits of Multiculturalism in Canada," *Racism, Eh? A Critical Inter-Disciplinary Anthology of Race and Racism in Canada* (2004), edited by Camille A. Nelson and Charmaine A. Nelson.

The country has embarked on an experiment in aboriginal self-government that the rest of the world is watching. In this experiment, both aboriginal and non-aboriginal peoples have said no to paternalism and dependency, yes to self-reliance and self-government.

Michael Ignatieff, commentator, address, biennial policy conference of the Liberal Party, Ottawa, 3 March 2005, excerpted as "A Generous Helping of Liberal Brains," *The Globe and Mail*, 4 March 2005.

ABORTION *See also* Women's Rights

By fighting for reproductive freedom, I am contributing to a more caring and loving society based on the ideals of peace, justice and freedom, and devoted to the full realization of human potential. Having known myself the depth of human depravity and cruelty, I wish to do whatever I can to replace hate with love, cruelty with kindness, and irrationality with reason.

Henry Morgentaler, physician, address, "The Continuing Controversies of Abortion," Toronto, 12 April 1990, The Empire Club of Canada.

Abortion is a decision between a woman, her doctor, and God.

Ralph Klein, Calgary mayor, quoted in *The Globe and Mail*, 7 April 1995.

The abortion-rights argument bears the same urgent relationship to the ideological maintenance of egalitarian democracy as the right to own slaves did to the maintenance of ancient democracy.

William D. Gairdner, athlete, academic, businessman, author, and commentator, *The Trouble with Democracy: A Citizen Speaks Out* (2001).

People who are pro-choice want to make sure that abortion is done safely, early, and rarely.

Rebecca Cook, specialist in reproductive law, University of Toronto, in Heather Sokoloff, "Focus Groups Used for Rebranding Abortion Rights," *National Post*, 11 January 2002.

Henry Morgentaler is undoubtedly Canada's best known abortionist. Under the newspeak of the orthodoxy, it is no longer permissible to say abortionist. Morgentaler is now to be described as an "abortion provider." I presume, further, that if one wished to refer to abortionists collectively, it would be necessary to speak of the "abortion provider community."

Robert Ivan Martin, law professor, *The Most Dangerous Branch: How the Supreme Court of Canada Has Undermined Our Law and Our Democracy* (2003).

I believe every woman should have the right to a safe abortion, no questions asked.

Henry Morgentaler, physician, characteristic remark, repeated in the biographical TV movie *Choice: The Henry Morgentaler Story* (2005), aired on Global Television, 5 January 2005.

ABUSE: SEXUAL *See also* Pornography; Victims & Victimhood; Women's Rights

There is no quicker way for a profession to lose public respect than to cover up, institutionally, for members who have done arrant wrong, a lesson that priesthoods are learning once again, and this could mean that the Roman Catholic priesthood's self-regulating rules about celibacy and the gender of members need revision.

Jane Jacobs, urban planning critic, *Dark Age Ahead* (2004).

ACADIANS

Images of division and enmity marked my first contact, albeit indirect, with Nova Scotia—the common experience of so many

American schoolchildren, grappling with the unpopular assignment of Longfellow's epic poem *Evangeline*, centred on the expulsion of the Acadians in 1755.

Stephen Jay Gould, paleontologist and author, "An Ode to Human Decency," *The Globe and Mail*, 20 September 2001.

It is impossible to visit Nova Scotia—or to grow up here, as I did—without being acutely aware of the deportation of the Acadians. This province was built on the ruins of the Acadie....

Dean Jobb, journalist, *The Acadians: A People's Story of Exile and Triumph* (2005), published to mark the 250th anniversary of the expulsion of the Acadians and their dispersal across British North America.

ACCENT *See also* Language; Public Speaking; Speech

"But I thought Australians had a queer accent, like the English."

"They've all kinds of accents, but you can never mistake their voice. It's got the sun in it. Canadians have got grinding ice in theirs, and Virginians have got butter. So have the Irish. In Britain there are no voices, only speaking tubes."

Discussion between Glaswegian merchant Dickson McCunn and pompous poet John Heritage in **John Buchan**'s novel *Huntingtower* (1922).

The Canadians speak with a stronger American accent. That is the main distinction. Their American accent is sometimes quite virulent. The lower orders really let themselves go, trumpeting away through their noses for all they are worth.

Wyndham Lewis, English author, one-time Toronto resident, *America, I Presume* (1940).

I don't agree he was an American. Something of a student in accents, I detected in his speech the typically Canadian "*ou*" as a diphthong, the Canadian (unless of course, he comes from any French-Canadian district) makes a separate sound for each letter. The word "about," for instance, he pronounces as "*aboh-oot.*" ...

Passage from the mystery novel *The List of Adrian Messenger* (1960) by novelist and screenwriter **Philip MacDonald**. The action of the novel, later filmed, takes place in London. The villain's accent is being discussed.

Students will be shown how to eliminate undesirable qualities of the Canadian accent (tight lower back-jaw, nasality, vowel lift, monotonous tones) while at the same time improving diction.

Bill Vincent, voice coach, description of some of the benefits of course instruction at his Voice and Company Studio, website, 23 June 2002.

Look. One of the things that always happens is, if you meet somebody who's speaking with a North American accent, basically the rule is, you say, "Are you a Canadian?" Because if you say, "Are you an American?" and they turn out to be Canadian, they'll be very upset and you'll be off to a bad start. If you say, "Are you a Canadian?" Americans on the whole, don't take offence. I kind of wish you didn't always have to deal with Canadians by making it quite clear that you understand they're not Americans.

David Malouf, Australian author, interviewed in Sydney by Paul Wells, "That Déjà-Vu Feeling," *Maclean's*, 1 March 2004.

ACCOUNTABILITY *See also* Responsibility

I do not advocate secret deals around green baize tables in a dim light with all the curtains drawn. No democratic state—as I have already said—can or should countenance commitments secretly entered into, or adopt policies or make engagements without the people knowing about them and the legislature passing on them.

Lester B. Pearson, diplomat, Fletcher School of Law and Diplomacy, Tufts University, Medford, Mass., *Diplomacy in the Nuclear Age* (1959). This lecture, delivered at the William L. Clayton Centre for International Economic Affairs, is the origin of the widely quoted—and condemned—phrase about "secret deals" and "commitments secretly entered into."

Accountability is a relationship based on obligations to demonstrate, review and take responsibility for performance, both the results achieved in light of agreed expectations and the means used.

Sheila Fraser, attorney general, in Jeffrey Simpson, "The Nation," *The Globe and Mail*, 6 December 2002.

We will open the front doors of City Hall for the people of Toronto. We will padlock the back doors to deal-makers and influence-peddlers.

David Miller, Toronto mayor-elect, victory speech, 10 November 2003, recalled in "Inside City Hall," *The Globe and Mail*, 2 January 2004.

The definition of madness is loss of connection with reality. By that definition, this was accounting gone mad; in olden times it would have been said that transgressing members of the profession had sold their souls to the devil.

Jane Jacobs, urban planning critic, on accountancy practices that hid the true state of U.S. corporate giant Enron's finances, *Dark Age Ahead* (2004).

ACHIEVEMENT *See also* Success

The biggest things are always the easiest to do because there is no competition.

Sir William C. Van Horne, railroad builder, observation made about 1890, in Peter C. Newman, *Flame of Power* (1959).

If you don't care who gets the credit, you can accomplish anything.

Harry "Red" Foster, founder of Foster Advertising Ltd., in Maggie Siggins, Toronto *Telegram*, 19 June 1969.

I did the best that I could be expected to do.

Saul Bellow, Lachine-born, Chicago-based novelist, in James Atlas, "Last Days of a Ladies' Man," *Saturday Night*, 14 October 2000.

ACID RAIN *See also* Environmentalism; Pollution

Canada is a country whose main exports are hockey players and cold fronts. Our main imports are baseball players and acid rain.

Attributed to Prime Minister **Pierre Elliott Trudeau** in an address he delivered in the United States in the 1970s.

Acid rain? It's not an act of nature; it's the byproduct of industry, a man-made gift of death from the United States to Canada, from Great Britain to Norway, and from Germany's industrial heartland to its farthest reaches. We cannot defend against this deadly rain. Everywhere it falls, it destroys forests, lakes, agricultural lands, washing away human lives and the dreams on which they're built.

Anita Gordon and **David Suzuki**, science broadcasters, *It's a Matter of Survival* (1990).

ACQUIRED IMMUNE DEFICIENCY SYNDROME (AIDS)

I've got gay cancer. I'm going to die and so are you.

Gaetan Dugas, flight attendant and early carrier of AIDS, who boasted of having infected at least 2500 men across North America during the last decade of his life. He died of HIV complications in Quebec City in 1984, according to Randy Shilts, *And the Band Played On: Politics, People and the AIDS Epidemic* (1987).

I've come to the point where as though saving one human life is what it's all about. In the beginning there were these huge numbers and you wanted to drive everything forward. Now I think, "Can we somehow save those five lives in Zanzibar? Can we somehow keep those ten people alive in Malawi?" ... In a sense, the human carnage is just beginning. That's why I feel so frantic.

Stephen Lewis, UN special envoy for HIV/AIDS in Africa, on the paucity of progress and the magnitude of the plight, interviewed by Bob Hepburn, "Stephen Lewis's Quiet Despair," *Toronto Star*, 14 May 2005.

ACTION

There is more action in motion.

Tom Daly, producer and director, "It's the Mind That Moves," *Pot-Pourri* (National Film Board), summer 1977.

One must inhibit thought at some point in order to act.

Frank Zingrone, theorist, *The Media Symplex: At the Edge of Meaning in the Age of Chaos* (2001).

An old folk tale has two birds listening to a hunter singing as he walks through the forest below their tree. "What a beautiful voice," one bird says. "Forget the voice," the other replies, "watch his hands."

Guy Gavriel Kay, columnist and novelist, "'Sorry' Seems to Be the Easiest Word," *National Post*, 16 January 2003.

ACTIVISM

Politicians, take note. There is a power out there in suburbia, so far harnessed only to charity drives, campaigns and PTAs, which, if ever properly brought to bear on the great problems of the day, will have an impact so great the result of its being detonated (like the Amchitka A-bomb test) cannot be predicted.

Robert Hunter, environmentalist and activist, noting the potential of ordinary people, such as the Vancouverites who established the Don't Make a Wave Committee to protest the U.S. bomb testing at Amchitka off the west coast of Alaska, interviewed in 1969, as noted by Michael Brown and John May, *The Greenpeace Story* (1989). The committee became the Greenpeace Foundation.

Do one outrageous act every day.

June Callwood, activist and journalist, quoted by Judy Steed, *The Globe and Mail*, 5 June 1987.

No police, Canadian or international security or intelligence agents, investigators, reporters or those reporting to or working for the aforementioned may apply or attend unless invited.

The caution attached to the "Alberta Action Camp Application Form" for an invitation to attend a training session for activists, sponsored by the Co-Motion Action Camp (Number 403), which teaches Canadians the Art of Non-Violent Civil Disobedience; website, August 2000.

If you drop the bomb, you blow me up.

David McTaggart, ecologist and activist, warning issued to French forces threatening to bomb his Greenpeace vessel, *Rainbow Warrior*, in Ted Turner, interviewed by Ned Martel, "The Radical Do-Gooder," *The New York Times Magazine*, 30 December 2001.

To be truly radical, you must make hope possible, not despair convincing. To get the results you never had, you must do the things you have never done.

Pierre Ducasse, leadership candidate, NDP leadership convention, Toronto, 25 January 2003, in Paul Wells, *National Post*, 27 January 2003.

ACTORS & ACTING *See also* Accent; Arts & Artists; Celebrities; Cinema; Hollywood; Language; Theatre

Remember, there are no small parts, just small actors.

Marie Dressler, Cobourg-born stage and screen personality, interviewed in Boston in 1890, according to Charles Foster, *Stardust and Shadows: Canadians in Early Hollywood* (2000).

Olivier continued, "I played a French Canadian myself during the war, in a film called *The 49th Parallel*."

I knew that too, and bloody well he'd done it.

"I learned the part phonetically with the help of a wonderful little book by a man called Drummond, written entirely in French Canadian dialect."

"Leetle Bateese," I said.

"That's the one."

Conversation between the great English actor **Sir Laurence Olivier** and the light-comedy star **Bernard Braden** that refers to Olivier's role of "Johnny the Trapper" in the amazing 1942 wartime movie as well as to the under-appreciated habitant poems composed in dialect by William Henry Drummond, as noted by Bernard Braden in his memoirs, *The Kindness of Strangers* (1990).

Hellooo—there!

Bernard Braden, Vancouver-born English comic actor and radio personality, *The Kindness of Strangers* (1990). "Then there's Braden's

'Uncle Gabby,' the garrulous old-timer whose mighty 'Hellooo—there!' has echoed across the Atlantic and penetrated into the corner of homes all over the British Isles" (*BBC Year Book, 1950*). Scriptwriter Eric Nicol, then a resident of London, created the character and wrote the monologues.

This country lacks the audacity to adore.

William Hutt, actor, in Keith Garebian, *William Hutt: A Theatre Portrait* (1988).

I wanted to be lost in a foreign land, in a country where I didn't speak the language. So I went to England.

Al Waxman, actor, leaving Toronto for London to study acting in 1960, *That's What I Am* (1999).

I was British by accident of birth. I became Canadian by act of choice.

Barry Morse, veteran actor, remark, CBC Radio's *Ideas*, 29 October 2001.

What's the difference between an optimist and a pessimist? Ask someone to name a great Canadian actor and the optimist says Christopher Plummer and the pessimist says William Shatner.

Adapted from a remark made by **Kate Taylor**, drama critic, "Artistic Licence," *The Globe and Mail*, 23 May 2002.

Trust your gut instincts. There's a lot to do down the road; there's always more. In small matters trust your mind, but in the important decisions of life … trust your heart.

Various pieces of advice from **Al Waxman**, described as "actor, director, humanitarian (1935–2001)" on the stone inscription at the foot of the life-size bronze statue created by sculptor Ruth Abernethy, erected in his honour as "King of Kensington," Belleville Park, Kensington Market, Toronto, unveiled 23 June 2002.

Acting is something you have to love to do because there's no other reason to do it.

Eugene Levy, comic and actor, interviewed by Gayle MacDonald, "Levy's Guide to La-La Land," *The Globe and Mail*, 24 September 2002.

Obituary? I don't want it to read "Actor Starred in *The Sound of Music*."

Christopher Plummer, stage and screen actor, interviewed by Richard Ouzounian, "Plummer's Life 'Just like Lear,'" *Toronto Star*, 3 March 2004.

ADDICTION *See also* Health

My name is Paul and I'm an alcoholic.

Paul Okalik, Nunavut premier, one-time drinker, lawyer, addressing an addictions conference in Montreal, as noted by Christie Blatchford, "A Royal Glimpse of the True North," *National Post*, 5 October 2002.

It would seem that the most addictive drug on earth causes persistent addiction in no more than one user in one hundred.

Bruce Alexander, researcher, referring to his studies of crack addiction conducted at Simon Fraser University, in Lauren Slater, "Pack Rat," *Opening Skinner's Box: Great Psychological Experiments of the Twentieth Century* (2004).

ADOLESCENCE *See also* Age; Children; Youth

Adolescence is a difficult phase in modern life because we have made it so by artificially extending childhood beyond puberty.

Marcel Danesi, semiotician, *Forever Young: The "Teen-Aging" of Modern Culture* (2003).

Eliminating adolescence, thus, entails three obvious things: (1) eliminating our social-scientific view of it; (2) restoring worth to the family as an institution; and (3) imbuing media representations of adolescence and family life with more dignity.

Marcel Danesi, semiotician, *Forever Young: The "Teen-Aging" of Modern Culture* (2003).

Adolescence is almost as undesirable a condition as dotage, except that it has a better prognosis.

George Jonas, columnist, "Put Them under a Barrel," *National Post*, 6 May 2005.

ADOPTION *See also* Family

Remember that these situations are the norm in many families and other families face similar challenges. You are not alone.

> **Marie Adams**, educator, advice to parents, *Our Son, a Stranger: Adoption Breakdown and Its Effects on Parents* (2002).

It is estimated that one in five people in this country have been touched by adoption in some way. For many, it is a joyful experience to build a family through adoption, but for birth families and communities who have lost their children through traditional adoption practices or for adult adoptees denied access to information about their identity because of dated legislation, the grief and anger can be overwhelming. By its very nature, traditional adoption is a bittersweet institution.

> **Sandra Scarth**, president, Adoption Council of Canada, "Time for Straight Talk about Adoption," council statement issued August 2003.

While over 20,000 Canadian children remain in care, only 2,000 are placed for adoption annually.

> **C.C. Speirs** et al., "Adoptable but Still in Limbo: The Forgotten Children in Canada," Child and Youth Care Forum 2003, Volume 32, Number 2.

ADSCAM *See* Sponsorship & Advertising Scandal

ADULTERY *See also* Sex

Adultery is the same the world over; it's only the method of approach that varies.

> **Sir James Lougheed**, chairman of the Senate Divorce Committee, remark made in 1889, in Robert M. Hamilton, *Canadian Quotations and Phrases* (1952).

ADVENTURE

Only the Air-Spirits know / What lies beyond the hills, / Yet I urge my team farther on. / Drive on and on, / On and on!

> Traditional **Inuit hunter's song** collected in the Central Arctic in 1923 by the Arctic explorer Knud Rasmussen and inscribed on his memorial outside Copenhagen, Denmark, in 1963.

I would not know how to instill a taste for adventure in those who have not acquired it. (Anyway, who can ever prove the necessity for the gypsy life?)

> **Pierre Elliott Trudeau**, canoeist, "Exhaustion and Fulfilment: The Ascetic in a Canoe" (1944), *Wilderness Canada* (1970), edited by Borden Spears.

Life is an adventure, or it is nothing.

> **David Walker**, author, *Where the Night Winds Blow* (1960).

ADVERTISING *See also* Consumerism; Merchandising; Shopping; Television

As a child of Empire, my vision of Canada—"Our Lady of the Snows," as Kipling called it in one of his imperial odes—derived from tales of the rugged outdoors I read in *Boy's Own Annual*s and from an advertisement on Australian radio. Out of the roaring blizzard came a voice intoning: for coughs and colds, do as the Mounties do in the frozen wastes of the Canadian north. Take Buckley's Canadiol Mixture.

> **David Malouf**, Australian man of letters, referring to growing up in Australia in the 1940s, "Wisdom from a Tale of Two Nations," *Maclean's*, 22 March 2004.

The advertising myths are still dehabilitating. They picture a promised land of satisfaction and social smoothness from soft drinks to beauty aids which hoodwinks all too many of us.

> **Lawren Harris**, artist, musing in the early 1940s, in Lisa Christensen, *A Hiker's Guide to the Rocky Mountain Art of Lawren Harris* (2000).

It reminds me of Toronto where we have two sections to the paper so that both Eaton's and Simpsons can carry back page ads.

> **Kate Aitken**, "Mrs. A.," newspaperwoman, referring to the two capitals of South Africa, address, "By Jet to Jo'burg," Toronto, 22 January 1952, The Empire Club of Canada.

Stop looking at this sign ... and come to Canada.

Words that conclude the eight-minute sequence of images associated with Canadian tourism that flashed from the New York Lightboard in 1961 in New York City's Times Square, produced and directed by the National Film Board's **Norman McLaren** for the Department of Northern Affairs, as in Maynard Collins, *Norman McLaren* (1976). The NFB also released *New York Light Record* (1961), an eight-minute documentary film that records the reactions of New Yorkers to the innovative commercial billboard.

New, Free Discovery / Saves You Money. / Proven Health, Love, Safety. / Results Guaranteed.

Martin Myers, advertising executive, "Twelve Most Persuasive Words in the English Language," *Marketing*, 26 November 1979. Myers took the dozen words, selected by Yale University as the most persuasive, and created advertising copy with them.

Intellectibles.

Word devised by **Maury Bay**, proprietor of the Hungry Mind Bookshop: Books for Extraordinary Times, and displayed on a street sign, Winnipeg, 21 October 2001.

Brag Tag. / Practise Safe Sun. / Prepare—for Adventure. / Washing Instructions: Give 'em Hell. / Sewn with Canadian Persnicketeyness.

Some slogans and advertising matter associated with Tilley Endurables, a line of sports and adventure wear created by manufacturer **Alex Tilley**, in Judy Steed, "Design Works," *Toronto Star*, 18 February 2002.

I wasn't born with a silver knife in my back. I was a funny-looking, short, skinny kid, always the butt of jokes, and I learned to defend myself with my wit.

Jerry Goodis, advertising executive, in Catherine Porter, "Obit," *Toronto Star*, 10 November 2002.

I think we've been so busy telling everyone else's story that we forgot to tell our own.

David Powell, husband of the late Judy Elder, accepting on her behalf the posthumous honour of induction into the Marketing Hall of Legends, in Tony Wong, "Drive and Charisma Define First Inductees," *Toronto Star*, 28 January 2005.

AFFECTION *See also* Love

Let's hear it for hugs. A good hug gives you emotional reassurance, physical support, and a spiritual life.

Betty Jane Wylie, author, *obiter dictum*, May 1990.

AFGHAN WAR *See also* War

Who, on September 10, 2001, believed Canada today would have troops in Afghanistan helping to winkle al-Qaeda out of the caves? (Parenthetically, who could believe that, once having begged the United States to let us into the Afghan War, Canadians would then tell the Americans how to run their operations?)

J.L. Granatstein, historian, "Defence Free-loading Imperils Sovereignty," *National Post*, 22 February 2002.

AFRICA *See also* Acquired Immune Deficiency Syndrome; Libya; Rwanda

Legally, Biafra doesn't exist. To ask, "Where's Biafra?" is tantamount to asking, "Where is Laurentia?"

Pierre Elliott Trudeau, prime minister, explaining to journalist Peter C. Newman why he had uttered the offensive retort "Where's Biafra?" when asked about starving people in that African country, as recalled by Newman, *Here Be Dragons: Telling Tales of People, Passion, and Power* (2004). In April 1970 Trudeau compared recognizing the breakaway province of Nigeria to Laurentia, the notional independent state of Quebec.

In fact, I've been to Africa about seven times now, and I've got to know some of the lions fairly well. They all have different faces, just as different as the faces in this room.

Robert Bateman, artist, address, "My Art and My Life," Toronto, 13 November 1986, The Empire Club of Canada.

I am deeply moved by the warmth and courage of the Canadian people which I felt so strongly during my recent visit to your country. Your support of the struggle against apartheid restored me in my journey home and reassured me that many just people around the world are with us.

Attributed to **Desmond Tutu**, archbishop, during his visit to Canada, February 2000.

The 21st century will be a century when Africa will fully become part of the international community.

Jean Chrétien, prime minister, address, Dakar, Senegal, 12 April 2002, "21st Century Is Yours, P.M. Tells Africa," *Toronto Star*, 13 April 2002.

What the hell do I want to go to a place like Mombassa? Snakes just scare the hell out of me. I'm sort of scared about going there, but the wife is really nervous. I just see myself in a pot of boiling water with all these natives dancing around me.

Mel Lastman, Toronto mayor, declining a trip to Mombasa, Kenya, to lobby on behalf of Toronto's 2008 bid at the Association of National Olympic Committees of Africa, interviewed by Chris Atchison on 8 June 2001 in Barcelona, Spain, as noted in the *Toronto Star*, 21 June 2001. Lastman considered it a private joke, but the remark doomed the Toronto bid. "I don't want to end up in a cooking pot" is the way it is frequently quoted, notably by travel writer Paul Theroux, *Dark Star Safari: Overland from Cairo to Cape Town* (2003).

AGE *See also* Adolescence; Maturity; Youth

Tomorrow is my nineteenth birthday. My life is slipping away so fast. I shall be an old man before I have accomplished anything.

Charles Ritchie, diplomat and diarist, diary entry, 22 September 1924, *An Appetite for Life: The Education of a Young Diarist, 1924–1927* (1977).

Old age with nothing to look back upon, nothing to lean upon, is poor stuff as compared with the old age that renews its youth and life and interests in its children and grandchildren. Ask a few lonely old people going out with the tide.

Stephen Leacock, humorist, *Last Leaves* (1945).

Take care of yourself until you're old enough to do your best work. That's when everything becomes clearer, what's important and what's less important, and how to proceed.

Henry Brant, Montreal-born, Santa Barbara–based composer, winner at the age of 88 of the Pulitzer Prize for an avant-garde composition, *Ice Field*, in Colin Eatcock, "Career High Note for a 'Musical Original,'" *The Globe and Mail*, 13 April 2002.

I have reached the dreary age when every farewell could well be the last, one of those bleak universal truths that cannot be made palatable with a greeting card bromide.

Remark of a character from **Edward O. Phillips**'s novel *A Voyage on Sunday* (2004).

The Institute of Actuaries told the Romanow Commission that "between 30 and 50 percent" of patient costs are incurred in the last six months of life.

Ivor Shapiro, researcher, "Life, at What Price?" *The Walrus*, November 2004.

There's a sticker on my computer which reads, "We do not stop playing because we are old. We grow old because we stop playing." That's my credo.

Peter C. Newman, journalist and author, "Going Strong," *Maclean's*, 8 November 2004.

Eighty is the new sixty-five. Honestly, I know so many eighty-year-olds. Here in West Vancouver, sixty per cent of the population is over sixty-five. Actual fact.

Douglas Coupland, author and artist, interviewed by Alexandra Gill, "Mirror, Mirror on the Page," *The Globe and Mail*, 30 December 2004.

Life is shorter than you think. There is never a way to tell people how fast the years go by after sixty-five.

Observation made by the elderly child psychiatrist, in **Catherine Gildiner**'s novel *Seduction* (2005).

There is a sign, outside a plastic-surgery office in west-end Toronto, that reads, "Aging is treatable."

Christie Blatchford, columnist, "For All of Us, a Life Force," *The Globe and Mail*, 9 April 2005.

AGRICULTURE *See also* Farmers & Farming

I do not mean to compare the Canadian North to Iowa or Ontario where cereals flourish, but I do mean to compare the North favourably with the semi-arid grazing lands anywhere.

Vilhjalmur Stefansson, Arctic explorer, address, "The Canadian Arctic Region," Toronto, 11 November 1918, The Empire Club of Canada.

I am particularly interested in the agricultural side of Ontario, because I have become a farmer in a small way myself and have bought a ranch in southern Alberta where I hope to start in very soon and ultimately make good. As you know, farmers in the West think themselves a very important community and I see that the farmers have recently been asserting themselves in Ontario too; but let me assure you that I intend to be a very simple sort of farmer who will not go in for politics or try to upset your ideas in any way.

Edward, Prince of Wales, address, "An Address," Toronto, 2 November 1919, The Empire Club of Canada.

With the emergence of agriculture, the world was never again as it had previously been. Almost everywhere, the pristine economies and their cultures went down to defeat and memory loss.

Jane Jacobs, urban planning critic, *Dark Age Ahead* (2004).

AID, FOREIGN *See* Foreign Aid

AIDS *See* Acquired Immune Deficiency Syndrome

AIR *See also* Earth; Environmentalism; Pollution

After the tragic fire of 1986 at the Chernobyl nuclear plant, radio-isotopes were detected over Sweden within minutes and over Canada's Arctic in hours. It was a grim reminder that the air is a global commodity, a planetary system. No one nation has its own supply of air any more than any one of us has a private stock of it. The air of the Earth is finite and shared by all life forms.

Anita Gordon and **David Suzuki**, science broadcasters, *It's a Matter of Survival* (1990).

AIR FORCE *See* Canadian Armed Forces

ALASKA *See also* Continentalism

A Canadian "Polish Corridor" separates the State of Alaska from the main body of the continental United States; and this zone of Canadian territory has come to be of first-class strategic importance for the United States now that the North Pole has come to be a military front between the United States and the Soviet Union.

Arnold J. Toynbee, English historian, "The Case for a Bilingual Canada," *Temper of the Times: An Anthology of Assorted Contemporary Literature* (1969), edited by Ralph Greenfield and Ronald Side.

ALBERTA

Tomorrow we arrive at Edmonton, the Capital of Alberta, and thereafter leave the corn belt for the rising slopes of the Rocky mountains. This region, twenty Switzerlands rolled into one, also stands between us and the beautiful luxuriant Pacific Coast.

Winston Churchill, British statesman, letter written to his wife, 12 September 1929, in David Dilks, *"The Great Dominion": Winston Churchill in Canada* 1900–1954 (2005).

Always in Alberta there is a fresh wind blowing.

Nellie McClung, pioneer and early feminist, *The Stream Runs Fast: My Own Story* (1945).

Monroe meets Mitchum in the most savage wilderness of all the Americas!

Advertising copy on the movie poster of the film *River of No Return* (1954), set in northern Alberta, the sole Western movie directed by **Otto Preminger**.

This is Canada's Alabama. In the next few years, we may have there, on a lesser scale, what the U.S. has had in the past few years in the South.

Peter Gzowski, journalist, comparing the plight of Native Canadians in Alberta with the plight of black Americans in Alabama, *Maclean's*, 6 July 1963.

It has always been good political sport in the West for a western politician to go East and tell the East how to run their affairs for the benefit of the West. You might not like what I say but I assure you that this approach is very well received in Okotoks.

Peter Lougheed, Alberta Conservative leader, address, "Where Canada?" Toronto, 17 March 1966, The Empire Club of Canada.

That faith, courage and greatness of heart of all our early settlers live on in the way of life that makes Alberta the good land it is today.

John Patrick Gillese, writer, quoted in *The Albertans* (1981).

Though the distance from Calgary to Athabasca was little more than three hundred miles, the journey took a traveller to the borders of another world. North of here the highways were few, the inhabitants fewer still. The rich prairie lands of the province steadily gave way to forest, marshland, and wilderness.

Description of northern Alberta from British author **Clive Barker**'s novel *Cabal* (1988). To quote the jacket copy of the Poseidon edition, the book describes a "necropolis" situated in "the wilds of Canada, beneath which all the great monsters of the world—the nightbreed—are in hiding."

I am a Canadian first and an Albertan by choice, for it is like no other place in all the world.

Andy Russell, outdoorsman, *Alberta on My Mind* (1990).

Few people actually dare to come out and say, "I'm from Alberta." The very admission is a social gaffe. Albertans are regarded as creatures from the swamp, Neanderthals, figures of fun, fools and daredevils, lunatic Bible-thumpers, gun-toting renegades, and crazy oilmen who really don't appreciate their tolerated position within this great nation.

Aritha van Herk, author, *Mavericks: An Incorrigible History of Alberta* (2002).

There's no doubt that Alberta is Canada's SF capital.... Ultimately, though, I think it's the stunning prairie night skies—the Milky Way arching from horizon to horizon, the aurora weaving back and forth. You can't help thinking about your place in the universe with that canopy overhead.

Robert J. Sawyer, science-fiction author, "Alberta Bound," *Prairie Books Now*, spring 2004.

What does this story of cartels and government interference in the marketplace have to do with Alberta? Merely everything. *These are the forces that created modern Alberta.*

Bill Longstaff, researcher, "Alberta's Oil Riches Created by OPEC, Not by Politicians or CEOs," *The CCPA Monitor*, February 2005.

In the shadow of the Rocky Mountains rests one of the most breathtaking and majestic golf courses in the world. It has two levels of greens fees—one for Albertans and a higher one for all others. The rationale is that because Albertans have used their tax dollars to develop the property, they "deserve" to benefit from their investment. This justification has nothing to do with golf. Rather, it is a reflection of a mindset and belief system that speaks to a sense of entitlement and proprietary exclusions.

Allan Gregg, commentator, "Quebec's Final Victory," *The Walrus*, February 2005.

ALCOHOL *See also* Food & Drink; Prohibition

Americans are plagued with organized crime. We have provincial liquor boards.

Dave Broadfoot, comedian, "Dave Broadfoot's Canada," Toronto, 9 March 1978, The Empire Club of Canada.

It is absurd that throughout Canada no independent liquor stores are permitted. Consequently, prices are high and choice is poor.... Perhaps eventually the Canadians will treat their citizens as adults.

Stephen Brock, English travel writer, *Maple Leaf Rag: Travels across Canada* (1987).

It's a Canadian Thing in 151 countries.

Advertising slogan for Seagram's Premium Canadian Club whisky, billboard, downtown Toronto, 27 June 2003.

ALIENS *See also* Science Fiction; Space; Unidentified Flying Objects; Universe

The existence of other worlds in the sky, more or less analogous to Earth, are confirmed periodically by animal tracks found on fresh snow which appear to start from nowhere. The inference is that the animal has fallen from the sky.

John MacDonald, researcher, Igloolik Research Centre, *The Arctic Sky: Inuit Astronomy, Star Lore, and Legend* (1998).

I know, I know—it seemed crazy that the alien had come to Toronto. Sure, the city is popular with tourists, but you'd think a being from another world would head for the United Nations—or maybe Washington. Didn't Klaatu go to Washington in Robert Wise's movie *The Day the Earth Stood Still*?

Speech of the narrator in **Robert J. Sawyer**'s science-fiction novel *Calculating God* (2000), following first contact with an alien landing in Toronto.

As the archetypes of our dreams have kept pace with technology, so has our folklore. Now we have nightmares about nuclear wars and lane crashes, and in the last half of the twentieth century, a new mythology of alien technology has risen. The onset of this collective myth was sudden.

Christopher Dewdney, poet and author, referring to flying saucers and UFOs, which first attracted widespread attention in 1947, *Acquainted with the Night: Excursions through the World after Dark* (2004).

ALPHABET *See also* Printing; Typography

Alphabets are often created by fiat, but it is usually in tiny increments that real typographic style evolves.

Robert Bringhurst, author and typographer, *The Elements of Typographic Style* (2nd ed., 1996).

AMBITION *See also* Desire

If you want something badly enough, you will find a way to get it.

John Kim Bell, orchestra founder and conductor, quoted on a poster distributed by the Kahnawake Social Services Resource Centre, Que., 1987.

AMERICA *See also* Americans; Canada & United States; Canadians & Americans; Mexico; North America

O my America! My new-found-land.

John Donne, poet, referring specifically to Newfoundland, "Elegie XIX" (1633), *Complete Poetry and Selected Prose* (1932), edited by John Hayward. The elegy was written as early as 1590, seven years after Sir Humphrey Gilbert's landfall.

Here is thy America, here or nowhere!

Exclamation made by the wanderer in **J.W. von Goethe**'s two-part novel *Wilhelm Meister* (1795, 1829), once the character comes to the realization that life at hand is greater than life in the abstract.

The inhabitants of the United States insist upon referring to themselves as "Americans," whereas an inhabitant of Mexico is termed a "Mexican," and the term "American" is denied to the people of Canada.

Wyndham Lewis, English author, one-time Toronto resident, *America, I Presume* (1940).

The U.S.A. is the most powerful human creation of all time.

James Laxer, political scientist, in Andrew Cohen, "Planet America," *The Globe and Mail*, 14 October 2000.

Signing deals with weaker countries like Canada, Mexico, and the rest of the Americas will not prevent the U.S. from acting unilaterally to protect its interests whenever it feels the need to do so. What we really need is a summit of the Americas to figure out what to do about the unilateralist United States.

James Laxer, political scientist, "Unilateralism Sweeps Washington," referring to the upcoming Summit of the Americas (excluding Cuba) to be held in Quebec City, *Toronto Star*, 9 April 2001.

Why don't they change it to "One nation under Canada"?

Robin Williams, U.S. actor, responding to an editor from *The New Yorker* magazine for an alternative to the phrase "One nation under God," after the Court of the United States Court of Appeals for the Ninth Circuit ruled in July 2002 that it is unconstitutional to require school children to recite the "Pledge of Allegiance" because it contains the phrase "one nation under God."

If you were from outer space and were shown a topographical map of North America and then told to come up with the stupidest way possible to slice it up, you'd probably say, "Let's put a straight line right across the middle which totally ignores all ecosystems, biospheres and geological formations—that way we can permanently warp and cripple the citizens of both sides of the border." That is what happened.

Douglas Coupland, novelist and essayist, "Strong and Free," *Maclean's*, 25 November 2002.

The world has long watched the United States with a mixture of envy, admiration, resentment, fear, and disgust. Perhaps nowhere are these feelings more potent—or the watching more constant—than in Canada.

Michael Adams, consultant, *Fire and Ice: The United States, Canada and the Myth of Converging Values* (2003), with Amy Langstaff and David Jamieson.

Al Gore … seemed to be running for Prime Minister of Canada (where he would have won by a landslide) rather than the United States … [where he] failed to touch the nerves of either American idealism or self-interested pragmatism.

Michael Adams, consultant, referring to the U.S. vice-president, defeated by George W. Bush, *Fire and Ice: The United States, Canada and the Myth of Converging Values* (2003), with Amy Langstaff and David Jamieson.

He understands I want to make sure our relations with our most important neighbour to the north of us, the Canadians, is strong….

George W. Bush, U.S. presidential candidate, interpreting the endorsement of "Canadian Prime Minister Jean Poutine" suggested by comedian Rick Mercer during a campaign stop on CBC-TV's *This Hour Has 22 Minutes* in 2000, in Michael Adams, *Fire and Ice* (2003), with Amy Langstaff and David Jamieson.

You have always wanted to be a city upon a hill, a light to all nations, and for a while you were. Give me your tired, your poor, you sang, and for a while you meant it.

Margaret Atwood, author, "A Letter to America," *The Globe and Mail*, 28 March 2003.

Remember the old joke that when Nixon looked at Canada he saw 30,000,000 Democrats.

Margaret MacMillan, historian, "Just Good Friends or Something More?" *National Post*, 30 April 2003.

The U.S. has the best damn government money can buy.

Paul Watson, environmental activist, interviewed by John F. Schumaker, "Earth Warrior," *The CCPA Monitor*, December 2003.

Those looking for ideology in the White House should consider this: For the men who rule our world, rules are for other people. The truly powerful feed ideology to the masses like fast food while they dine on the most rarified delicacy of all: impunity.

Naomi Klein, columnist and author, "No Neo-Con, Just Plain Greed," *The Globe and Mail*, 20 December 2003.

AMERICANS *See also* America; Anti-Americanism; Canada & United States; Canadians & Americans; Colonialism

Seventeen brilliant books analyse them every month: they don't read them.

Stephen Leacock, humorist, *Back to Prosperity: The Great Opportunity of the Empire Conference* (1932).

The Americans are a queer people: they don't give a damn. All the world criticizes them and they don't give a damn.... The Americans don't give a damn: don't need to: never did need to. That is their salvation.

Stephen Leacock, humorist, *Back to Prosperity: The Great Opportunity of the Empire Conference* (1932).

The Americans are our best friends, whether we like it or not.

Robert Thompson, national leader, Social Credit Party (1961–1967), well-known malapropism, recalled by Peter C. Newman, *Home Country* (1973).

The Americans might not always be right. But they are always right next door.

Thomas Walkom, columnist, referring to the Cold War and the War on Terrorism, "Return of the Old, Cold War," *Toronto Star*, 28 September 2002.

AMERICANS & CANADIANS *See* America; Americans; Canadians & Americans

AMIEL, BARBARA

And now I have an extravagance that knows no bounds.

Barbara Amiel, Lady Black, wife of capitalist Conrad Black, referring to her resolve to spend following an incident in her youth when she was snubbed for wearing recycled clothes, in Julia Reed, "Being Bold," *Vogue*, August 2002.

Now anyone who criticizes Lady Black runs the risk of looking jealous or Canadian or both.

Judith Timson, journalist, "Our Fair Lady: Barbara Amiel and Her Not-so-secret Ambitions," *Chatelaine*, November 2002.

Only a few hundred women in the world can afford to dress like Mrs. Black, and Mrs. Black may not be among them.

Margaret Wente, columnist, "Lord Black Walks the Plank," *The Globe and Mail*, 18 November 2003.

The only foolish remark that Oborne cites which I did make and which has been quoted ad infinitum by now is the remark to the *Vogue* writer, Julia Reed, that "My extravagance knows no bounds." I have been saying that wryly about myself all my life in every economic circumstance. I think I must have heard it in a bad radio play once. I didn't know whether I used it in conversation with Reed in reference to handkerchiefs, hand cream, or hand bags but it certainly was the most ill-timed throwaway comment I could have made.

Barbara Amiel, columnist, "Letters," *National Post*, 9 February 2004. The reference is to Peter Oborne, whose column "The Ballad of Connie and Babs" appeared in *The Spectator*, 24 January 2004, and was reprinted in the *National Post* as "In a World of Their Own Making," 31 January 2004. Amiel recalled the original remark herself in her *Maclean's* column after it appeared in an interview published earlier in *Vogue*.

I've always thought if I hadn't been given some good looks and cursed with loving clothes, I would have achieved more as a writer because I would have had more time. It's been a distraction. Clothes and decent looks are a handicap because they don't coexist well with the life of a writer.

Barbara Amiel, columnist, interviewed by Joan Crockatt and Arlene Bynon, "Being Barbara," *Toronto Star*, 6 February 2005.

When I said to (the writer) "my extravagance knows no bounds," I was being ironic about myself. I was making a joke. I became my own Marie Antoinette. "Let them eat cake." (I did [it] as a favour and it boomeranged on me.)

Barbara Amiel, columnist, interviewed by Joan Crockatt and Arlene Bynon, "Being Barbara," *Toronto Star*, 6 February 2005.

ANCESTRY *See also* Heritage; History; Pioneers

Your forefathers have been able to win their way into the heart of wild nature as pioneers taming the savage wilderness and forest, facing fearful odds with amazing heroism and with undying energy of purpose, searching out lonely tracks along the banks of unknown rivers as they have flowed toward the Arctic north. They have threaded their railways across mountains which were once thought to be inaccessible, they have thrown their bridges over mighty chasms, thus linking the whole continent.

Rabindranath Tagore, Bengali sage, farewell message delivered to the Southam newspaper chain, Fourth Triennial Conference of the National Council of Education, Vancouver, 8–13 April 1929, quoted in "Tagore," *The Canadian Theosophist*, May 1929.

The neat thing about worshipping your ancestors is that you live your life knowing you too will become an ancestor one day.

Observation of a character in the one-woman show *Afrika Solo* (1990) by playwright **Djanet Sears**.

ANGELS *See also* Religion; Spiritualism

To learn to talk with angels is really learning to talk with ourselves and with each other in new and profoundly deeper ways. It is learning how to communicate with our universe more openly and how to be more in tune with our role as co-creators and participate in its evolution.

Dorothy Maclean, medium, *To Hear the Angels Sing: An Odyssey of Co-Creation with the Devic Kingdom* (1980).

ANGER

Do not be afraid to recognize your anger and to acknowledge it. Say, "I am very angry right now, so I am not prepared to discuss this any further."

Marie Adams, educator, advice to parents, *Our Son, a Stranger: Adoption Breakdown and Its Effects on Parents* (2002).

Anger can be described as frustrated hopes.

Michael Fullan, educator, observation, in Alanna Mitchell, "School of Britannia," *Toronto Star*, 1 May 2004.

ANIMAL RIGHTS *See also* Animals

Have the wild things no moral or legal rights? What right has man to inflict such long and fearful agony on a fellow-creature, simply because that creature does not speak his language?

Ernest Thompson Seton, artist and naturalist, "Redruff," *Wild Animals I Have Known* (1898).

Animal liberation is human liberation! It's a concept often lost on all but the most reflective animal liberationists.

Viki Miller, president, Toronto Humane Society, editorial, *Ark II*, summer 1986.

Many people envision a time when animals will no longer be looked upon as human property. Through education or policy reform, activists and lawyers are slowly chipping away at the property status of animals, hoping to establish recognition that animals have interests and do not exist merely to serve humans.

John Mulcahy and **Diana Goodrich**, animal activists, "What Is a Sanctuary?" *Fauna Foundation Newsletter*, January 2001.

ANIMALS *See also* Animal Rights; Bears; Beavers; Birds; Buffalo; Cats; Conservation; Dogs; Seal Hunt; Snakes; Whales; Wildlife; Wolves; Zoos

The life of a wild animal always has a tragic end.

Ernest Thompson Seton, naturalist and author, *Wild Animals I Have Known* (1898).

From contemporary records we learn that persons who attached themselves to a Dog developed the greatest fidelity towards it, following it around all day, and walking great distances after it, often through broken country.

Stephen Leacock, humorist, written as if "From a Young People's Encyclopedia of Useful Knowledge, A.D. 4026," *Short Circuits* (1928).

Some people say the animals see the straight path and flee from it in fear, for they know that it was built by man.

James Houston, naturalist and novelist, *The White Dawn* (1971).

We have five hundred years of tenure as the most lethal animal ever to have appeared upon this wasting planet.

Farley Mowat, naturalist and author, *Sea of Slaughter* (1984).

ANTARCTICA *See also* Arctic Regions; North Pole

But Canada's most enduring legacy to the Antarctic has been the handful of early explorers who opened up the mysterious continent with frozen fingers, aching backs, and pounding hearts.

Dean Beeby, author, *In a Crystal Land: Canadian Explorers in Antarctica* (1994). Beeby studied the feats of endurance of 15 Canadian explorers.

ANTHEM, NATIONAL *See* National Anthem

ANTHROPOLOGY

The animals of the Burgess Shale are the world's most important fossils, in part because they have revised our view of life, but also because they are objects of such exquisite beauty....

Stephen Jay Gould, paleontologist and author, *Wonderful Life: The Burgess Shale and the Nature of History* (1989). Paleontologists and biologists have long recognized the unique importance of the marine-animal fossils found in the Burgess Shale, Yoho National Park, B.C., first recognized in 1909 and now a World Heritage Site.

And so, if you wish to ask the question of the ages—why do humans exist?—a major part of the answer, touching those aspects of the issue that science can treat at all, must be: because Pikaia survived the Burgess decimation.

Stephen Jay Gould, paleontologist and author, *Wonderful Life: The Burgess Shale and the Nature of History* (1989). Gould, the Harvard scientist and essayist, argued that Pikaia, a fossil found at the Burgess Shale, Yoho National Park, B.C., is the world's first known chordate, "a member of our own phylum—in fact, the first recorded member of our immediate ancestry." Not all paleontologists accept his findings.

ANTI-AMERICANISM *See also* Americans; Canada & United States

We have discovered after two centuries that you can't make a country out of anti-Americans.

J.L. Granatstein, historian, in Steven Pearlstein, "O Canada! A National Swan Song?" *The Washington Post*, 5 September 2000.

Anti-Americanism holds a cherished place in the Canadian imagination, right beside hockey, health care, and poutine. It is our birthright, and it is what we have instead of a foreign policy.

Robert Fulford, columnist, "Fantasy Informs Our Foreign Policy," *National Post*, 7 September 2002.

Fermez la Bush!

Bilingual placard at a protest against U.S. President George W. Bush, Toronto, 18 September 2002.

In a pinch, globally, Canada-bashing can be a kind of snack until a banquet of America-bashing arrives.

Douglas Coupland, novelist and essayist, "Strong and Free," *Maclean's*, 25 November 2002.

As far as I can tell, a very large number of Canadians define themselves not for what they are, but what they are not—namely Americans. How else to explain that aside from ice hockey, the CBC and a passionate disdain for Toronto there are few national institutions and experiences that Albertans, Manitobans, Nova Scotians and Quebecers share?

Clifford Krauss, Toronto-based correspondent for *The New York Times*, "Soul Search," *Maclean's*, 25 November 2002.

Damn the Americans, I hate those bastards!

Carolyn Parrish, Member of Parliament, addressing reporters following a scrum, Centre Block, Parliament Hill, 26 February 2003, in Daniel LeBlanc, "Parrish Says She Regrets Remark Made 'in the Heat of the Moment,'" *The Globe and Mail*, 27 February 2003. A few hours after uttering the insult, Parrish, a government backbencher, lamely attempted to play down her outburst by distinguishing between her view of the Bush administration and her view of the American people as well as the Chrétien administration's view of either one or the other or both: "My comments do not reflect my personal opinion of the American people and they certainly do not reflect the views of the government of Canada."

Of course, Carolyn Parrish should not have called Americans "bastards." Not when there are many more colourful insults available. Jackals or jackasses, to quote H.L. Mencken. Goons and grandees, courtesy of Norman Mailer. "A squalid nuisance," Winston Churchill said of one of his opponents.

Catherine Ford, journalist, "Parrish's Sin Was Lack of Imagination," Montreal *Gazette*, 6 March 2003.

Screw the Americans!

Attributed to **Laurier LaPierre**, senator and former broadcaster, Senate, 26 March 2003, in Jack Aubry, "LaPierre Accused of Anti-U.S. Remark," *National Post*, 27 March 2003. LaPierre denied making the remark, which is attributed to him in the Senate's Debates. He did speak the day following U.S. Ambassador Paul Cellucci's criticism of Canada's response to the Iraq war, but he maintained that what he said with respect to the Americans' selling arms to Iraq, as the Russians had done, was "So did the Americans!"

ANTI-SEMITISM *See also* Jewish Culture; Judaism

None is too many.

Attributed to an unnamed senior government official with the Department of Immigration who was explaining to journalists in early 1945 how many Jews would be allowed into Canada at the end of World War II. The remark—though not the sentiment—is erroneously attributed to F.C. Blair, director of Immigration, who did write, in a letter to Undersecretary of State O.D. Skelton, 16 June 1939: "The line must be drawn somewhere." Noted by Irving Abella and Harold E. Troper, *None Is Too Many: Canada and the Jews of Europe, 1933–1948* (1982).

I am a separatist as you are a Jew. It took your people 2,000 years to have your homeland in Israel. If it takes us ten, fifty, or one hundred years more, I can wait.

Yves Michaud, shareholder-rights activist and prospective Parti Québécois candidate, recalling an observation he made to Liberal Senator Leo Kolber, radio interview, 12 December 2000, in Rhéal Séguin, "Péquiste's Anti-Jewish Remarks Condemned," *The Globe and Mail*, 15 December 2000.

Michaud's prospective candidacy created a crisis in the Parti Québécois. Here is what Michaud told the host of CKAC-AM Radio in Montreal, 5 December: "I went to my barber about a month ago. A Liberal senator was there, whom I won't name … he represents a French-speaking riding, and he asks me: 'Are you still a separatist, Yves?' I said, 'Yes, yes, I am a separatist just like you are Jewish. It took your people 2,000 years to have their own country in Israel,' I said. 'As far as I'm concerned, whether it takes ten years, fifty years, or one hundred more years, I can wait.' So he tells me, 'It's not the same thing.' It's never the same for them. So I said, 'What isn't the same? The Armenians didn't suffer, the Palestinians don't suffer, the Rwandans don't suffer?' I said, 'It's always about you. You are the only people in the world who have suffered in the history of mankind.'" Noted by Rhéal Séguin, "End Intolerance, Bouchard Urges," *The Globe and Mail*, 21 December 2000.

Only a single country will resist for one more century, that where the priests rule, the most tedious of all lands.... but I'll go there, I'll serve at mass. I'll teach the catechism, there's no other choice if you want to save your ... and that I'm determined to do.

Louis-Ferdinand Céline, French novelist, fascist, and anti-Semite, writing in his fractured fashion about the province of Quebec, which he visited in 1936 and where he and his sentiments were lauded, as in Daniel Poliquin, *In the Name of the Father: An Essay on Quebec Nationalism* (2001), translated by Don Winkler.

Today André Laurendeau and Henri Bourassa are being let off the hook for their follies on the grounds that they were but products of their time. With such pusillanimous reasoning, one will soon be exonerating Adolf Hitler. It is claimed as well that they didn't know, couldn't have known.

Daniel Poliquin, commentator and novelist, *In the Name of the Father: An Essay on Quebec Nationalism* (2001), translated by Don Winkler.

To allow their violence and intimidation to succeed in silencing an important voice should be unacceptable to a university which promotes the values of freedom of speech and open exchange of ideas. Failure to do so will only embolden those who see violence as the only way to achieve results.

Simon Wiesenthal, Vienna-based "Nazi-hunter," in an open letter to Frederick Lowry, rector of Concordia University in Montreal, urging the institution to re-schedule the address of Israeli diplomat Benjamin Netanyahu since its disruption by Palestinian sympathizers in September 2002. In Graeme Hamilton, "Nazi-hunter Criticizes Actions of Concordia," *National Post*, 16 October 2002.

Several years ago I attended a presentation by The Women of Colour Collective in Calgary. The purpose of the workshop was to raise awareness and sensitivity about one's own racist attitudes. The presenters encouraged participation and feedback from the audience, and the workshop seemed to be very effective. However, when I mentioned my experience of anti-Semitism, I was told that my experience did not really count as racism. I knew that from their point of view I did not look like a member of a "visible" minority; but the feeling of being silenced was painful, nonetheless. My experience did count for me.

Melanie Fogel, Faculty of Communication and Culture, University of Calgary, "Racism between Jews: Israeli Women in Calgary," *Racism, Eh? A Critical Inter-Disciplinary Anthology of Race and Racism in Canada* (2004), edited by Camille A. Nelson and Charmaine A. Nelson. The Women's Studies course "Contemporary Issues in Feminism" was held on the Calgary campus in July 1993.

"Following the speech, Mr. Parker requested an interview and asked Mr. Ahenakew to clarify what he meant. Mr. Ahenakew said Adolf Hitler was right to kill Jews during the Holocaust because they 'damn near owned all of Germany prior to the war. That's why he fried six million of those guys, you know. Jews would have owned the god-damned world.'

"When asked by Mr. Parker how he could justify the killing of six million Jews, Mr. Ahenakew responded, 'How do you get rid of a disease like that, that's going to take over everything.'

"The pair debated the subject until Mr. Ahenakew ended the conversation by saying, 'To Hell with the Jews. I can't stand them and that's it. Don't talk about the Jews,' according to the taped interview."

Account of an interview given by **David Ahenakew**, chief, Assembly of First Nations, following an address to the Federation of Saskatchewan Indian Nations, Saskatoon, 13 December 2002, as noted by reporter James Parker, the Saskatoon *StarPhoenix*. Two years later, Ahenakew was tried in a Saskatoon Provincial Court for hate-mongering, found guilty, and fined. The paraphrase above appeared in Darren Bernhardt's dispatch "Comments Never Expected to Be Widely Heard: Ahenakew," *The Globe and Mail*, 5 April 2005. Bernhardt's subsequent report, "Ahenakew Tells Judge Jews to Blame for WWII," *National Post*, 6 April 2005, included the following testimony: Crown prosecutor Brent Klause: "So you still believe today, in 2005, that the Jewish people started the Second World War?" Ahenakew: "Yes." Klause: "You stand by your comments?" Ahenakew: "Yeah."

Anti-Semitism is born in ignorance and nurtured in envy. It is the stepchild of delusion and evil.

Brian Mulroney, former prime minister, address, conference, Anti-Semitism: The Politicization of Prejudice in the Contemporary World, University of Toronto, published in *National Post*, 10 February 2003.

This is not my Canada. This is not our Canada.

Paul Martin, prime minister, speech, Burlington, Ont., 5 April 2004, in Susan Delacourt, "'Not Our Canada,'" *Toronto Star*, 6 April 2004. He was denouncing the act of arson that incinerated the library of the United Talmud Torah School, Montreal, calling it "an act of violence directed at all Canadians."

I am now forced to choose between freedom of speech and the Order of Canada. I choose free speech.

David Ahenakew, former chief, Assembly of First Nations, news conference, quoted in the *Toronto Star*, 12 July 2005. Expelled from the Order of Canada, he blamed the expulsion on a "Jewish conspiracy" and refused to return the "snowflake" insignia. Subsequently a court of law found him guilty of hate-mongering and subjected him to a fine.

APHORISMS *See also* Words

The obvious is the opposite of the commonplace. The aphorism represents most clearly the stage at which the idea is able to pass into a power.

Northrop Frye, cultural critic, aphorism, "Notebook 3" (1946–1948), *Northrop Frye Newsletter*, fall 2000.

APOCALYPSE

A really great apocalypse has the ability to be forever read and misread.

Donald Harman Akenson, historian, referring specifically to the Book of Daniel in the Bible, Queen's University, Kingston, Ont., *Surpassing Wonder: The Invention of the Bible and the Talmuds* (1998).

APPRECIATION *See* Gratitude

ARCHAEOLOGY *See also* Discovery

What archaeologist will dare assert that the same hand which planned the Pyramids of Egypt, Karnak, and the thousand ruins now crumbling to oblivion on the sandy banks of the Nile, did not erect the monumental Nagkon-Wat of Cambodia? or trace the hieroglyphics on the obelisks and doors of the deserted Indian village, newly discovered in British Columbia by Lord Dufferin? or those on the ruins of Palenque and Uxmal, of Central America?

H.P. Blavatsky, theosophist, Chapter VII, *Isis Unveiled: A Master-Key to the Mysteries of Ancient and Modern Science and Theology* (1877). The reference is to Lord Dufferin, governor general of Canada from 1872 to 1878, but the reference to "obelisks and doors" is obscure.

An archaeological site constitutes any locality that exhibits the material remains of a former people.

R.G. Forbis and **W.C. Noble**, archaeologists, "Archaeology," *The Canadian Encyclopedia* (2nd ed., 1988).

ARCHITECTURE *See also* Cities & Towns; Design; Heritage; Planning

The real purpose of architecture, I think, as with any art, is to somehow interpret our environment to us.

Arthur Erickson, architect, address, "Seeing Is Believing," Toronto, 23 November 1967, The Empire Club of Canada.

The wigwam, like the triangle, is not an enclosed space and is merely the most economical means of anchoring a vertical plane or object.

Marshall McLuhan, media philosopher, address, "The End of the Work Ethic," Toronto, 16 November 1972, The Empire Club of Canada.

I looked around. You have Victoriana in Toronto. There's a lot of Richardson Romanesque: Queen's Park is very good, I like that building. I decided that if the government buildings could be monumental, who's the CBC not to be? I was Post-Modern in those days, so I decided to make it as monumental as we possibly could. I had looked for a contextual peg [in the neighbourhood], you know, and there wasn't anything there. Just the Convention Centre—a great big nothing. It's boring: as a foil, it's great. So we said, 'Let people be contextual with what we've built.'"

Philip Johnson, New York–based architect, designer of the facade of the CBC Broadcast Centre in Toronto, interviewed by David Lasker, "CBC Sets Tone with New Centre," *The Globe and Mail*, 10 September 1992.

Architects cannot solve everything, but we can and must ask the right questions.

Moshe Safdie, architect, *The City after the Automobile: An Architect's Vision* (1997), with Wendy Kohn.

Frank Gehry ... designs all of Toronto's imaginary buildings.

Robert Fulford, arts commentator, referring to Toronto-raised, award-winning architect who had yet to design a building in Toronto, "Dreams of the Waterfront," *National Post*, 22 September 2001.

Hitler with all his bombs has managed to do, relatively speaking, less damage to London buildings than a mixture of Toronto developers, politicians, and just downright greed has done to the fragile heritage of Toronto.

Attributed to architect and conservator **Eric Arthur** by his son, the designer Paul Arthur, *Eric Ross Arthur: Conservation in Context* (2002), edited by Alec Keefer.

The form of the building emerges out of a myriad of spiritual adventures, becomes quantifiable, and materializes as it rejoins the issues of everyday life.

Daniel Libeskind, Polish-born architect, quoted by James Adams, "What Makes an Architect Also an Artist?" *The Globe and Mail*, 27 February 2002. The remark was recalled when Libeskind, once a professor in Toronto, won the Renaissance ROM commission to design an addition to the Royal Ontario Museum.

ARCTIC REGIONS *See also* Antarctica; Discovery; Exploration; North; North Pole; Northern Lights

The whole region I have been describing has excessively hard winters, for eight months of the year the cold is intolerable ... even apart from the eight months' winter, the remaining four months are cold.

Herodotus, ancient Greek historian, writing about 430 B.C., as noted by Aubrey de Selincourt, translator, *Herodotus: The Histories* (1954).

The Imperishable Sacred Land. The reason for the name is that it is stated that: this "Imperishable Sacred Land" never shared the fate of the other Continents, because it is the only one whose destiny it is to last from the beginning to the end of the Manvantara throughout each round. It is the cradle of the first man and the dwelling of the last divine mortal, chosen as a Shishta for the future seed of humanity. Of this mysterious and sacred land very little can be said, except, perhaps, according to a poetical expression in one of the Commentaries, that the "Pole-star has its watchful eye upon it, from the dawn to the close of the twilight of a Day of the Great Breath."

H.P. Blavatsky, theosophist, *The Secret Doctrine: The Synthesis of Science, Religion and Philosophy*, Volume II (1888; 3rd ed., 1902).

I first took possession of Baffin Land for Canada in the presence of several Eskimo, and after firing 19 shots I instructed an Eskimo to fire the 20th, telling him that he was now a Canadian.

J.-E. Bernier, captain, address, "Our Northern Heritage," Toronto, 7 October 1926, The Empire Club of Canada.

I suggested that unless they wanted to keep the whole Arctic as imaginary as its leading imaginary tenant, Santa Claus, the Americans had better take some steps to bring their text books into conformity with the information in which William Shakespeare and Queen Elizabeth believed three hundred years ago and in which their Weather Bureau believes today.... As late as ten years ago, every series of school geographies in common use in the United States said that "North of the Arctic Circle it is always cold" (except one or two which said, "North of the Arctic Circle it is never warm"—they gave you that much choice). (Laughter.)

Vilhjalmur Stefansson, Arctic explorer, address, "Abolishing the Arctic," Toronto, 25 October 1928, The Empire Club of Canada.

Freud in the Arctic is even more amusing and more terrible than in Vienna.

Denis Saurat, Anglo-French critic, reviewing Joseph Velter's novel *La Baie de Trépassés*, about six Soviet scientists marooned in the Arctic, "Recent French Novels," *The Listener*, 6 March 1935.

The more northern sections of the continent reflect light from the surfaces of uncounted lakes and shallow tundra ponds hollowed out by glacial action. Looking down from a height on the broken landscape, one can often have the impression that there is more water than solid ground in the scene before one.

Marjorie Spock, student of anthroposophy, "North America under a Light Sky," *The Golden Blade* (1971), edited by Arnold Freeman and Charles Waterman.

You all know the Arctic from reading about it in books, and some of you know it personally from your own experience. It is a place of myth and preconception, but also a theatre of exciting opportunity.

Joseph MacInnis, Arctic marine explorer, address, "Diving under the North Pole," Toronto, 26 February 1976, The Empire Club of Canada.

If it is not already too late, the high Arctic could conceivably become the world's Walden Pond—a last remnant of this planet that could be protected and remain undisturbed by man, inviolate, as the place from which a sane view of ourselves and the world we have made and are making is still possible.

Eli Bornstein, sculptor, "Notes on Art and Nature" (1987), *Eli Bornstein: Art toward Nature* (1996), edited by Jonneke Fritz-Jobse.

On the whitening blue-white, where landmarks / aren't made of land, and vanish, / she can live without help.

Lines about a bear on polar ice from the poem "The Ice Indigene," by the Australian poet **Les Murray**, *Conscious and Verbal* (2001).

The Arctic is still a place that is seen primarily through the eyes of outsiders, a territory known to the world from explorers' narratives rather than from the writings, drawings and films of its own people. To most southerners the Arctic remains what it was to their counterparts centuries and perhaps even millennia ago: the ultimate otherworld.

Robert McGee, anthropologist, *The Last Imaginary Place: A Human History of the Arctic World* (2003).

It is a wonderful thing to see a living history.

Paul Martin, prime minister, five-day tour of the North, speech, Pond Inlet, Baffin Island, 11 August 2004, in Alexander Panetta, "P.M. Reaffirms Sovereignty over Arctic during Visit," *The Globe and Mail*, 12 August 2004.

The Arctic Circle is a threshold in the mind, not its circumference. North is where all the parallels converge to open out ... into the mystery surrounding us.

Henry Beissel, poet, in Peter Davidson, "The Idea of North," *Harper's Magazine*, March 2005.

ARGENTINA

The country imagined by my ancestors, the extraordinary country that educated me and made me who I am, no longer exists among its ruins. Argentina is no longer, and the bastards who destroyed it are still alive.

Alberto Manguel, Canadian author, born in Argentina, "No Money, No Vision, No Faith," *The Globe and Mail*, 27 December 2001.

My passport said "Buenos Aires"; in my dreams I was not so certain.

Alberto Manguel, Canadian author, born in Argentina, "Destination Ithaka," *Passages: Welcome Home to Canada* (2002), with a preface by Rudyard Griffiths.

ARISTOCRACY *See also* Class System; Society

Canada has never had an aristocracy, and indeed anything that could be called an "upper class," and consequently has felt the lack of the spirit of adventure and moral experiment that these elements give to a population.

Robertson Davies, man of letters, letter, 31 January 1977, *For Your Eye Alone: Letters, 1976–1995* (1999).

ARMED FORCES *See* Canadian Armed Forces

ARMS RACE *See also* Disarmament; Nuclear Warfare; War

Remember your humanity, and forget the rest.

Exhortation in the declaration signed by **Albert Einstein** and **Bertrand Russell** during the Cold War era that drew together "concerned scientists" from the East and the West to the first Pugwash Conference, held in Nova Scotia and other locations from 1957 to 1997. Scientist and peace activist Sir Joseph Rothblat accepted the 1995 Nobel Peace Prize for work on behalf of Pugwash, a Canadian initiative. In Holcomb Noble, "Joseph Rothblat, Physicist and Peacemaker, 1908–2005," *The Globe and Mail*, 7 September 2005.

ARMY *See* Canadian Armed Forces

ARTS & ARTISTS *See also* Beauty; Cartoon Art; Civilization; Crafts; Creativity; Critics & Criticism; Dance; Group of Seven; Ideas; Land; Language; Music; Sculpture; Theatre

"What a wonderful picture!" she murmured half to herself, half aloud, and half not aloud and half not to herself.

Stephen Leacock, humorist, *Moonbeams from the Larger Lunacy* (1915).

I own a slide depicting Cézanne's portrait of his wife. It is absolutely point blank or full face—and the lady has only one ear. It is pretty obvious that neither of these gentlemen made their living by painting portraits.

Wylie Grier, critic, address, "Two Views of Canadian Art," Toronto, 26 February 1925, Association of Canadian Clubs of Canada.

There are a great many people interested in Canadian art today, more than ever before. That interest is sometimes like that of the old lady who was hurrying rapidly out of one of our Group exhibitions, and when asked why she was in such a hurry she explained, "I hate these pictures, but I am afraid if I stay around here longer I am going to like them."

A.Y. Jackson, artist, address, "Two Views of Canadian Art," Toronto, 26 February 1925, The Empire Club of Canada.

The truth is that works of art test the spectator much more than the spectator tests them.

Lawren Harris, artist, "Modern Art and Its Aesthetic Reactions" (1927), in Lisa Christensen, *A Hiker's Guide to the Rocky Mountain Art of Lawren Harris* (2000).

When art becomes obscure it has forgotten the fact that the reason for avoiding the commonplace is to discover the obvious. There can be no such thing as the revelation of a mystery, and everyone knows that perfect simplicity is the only way of expressing complex and original ideas.

Northrop Frye, cultural and literary critic, aphorism, "Notebook 3" (1946–1948), *Northrop Frye Newsletter*, fall 2000.

I myself am inclined to drift, to accept a lesser situation rather than strive for a greater, and yet, I know that character in life and art is only made by an effort that is quite beyond one's ordinary everyday acceptance of things as they are.

Lawren Harris, artist, letter to Catharine Whyte in 1949, in Lisa Christensen, *A Hiker's Guide to the Rocky Mountain Art of Lawren Harris* (2000).

It is not the Canadian artist who is not good enough; it is the Canadian public which is not good enough for the artist.

Mavor Moore, theatre personality, "The Canadian Theatre" (1950), *Reinventing Myself: Memoirs* (1994).

I stared. A huge animal with crested back and horned head. There was no mistaking him. And there, a man on a horse—and there four suns—and there, canoes. I felt the shivers coursing my back from nape to tail—the Schoolcraft site! Inscription Rock! My fourteen months' search was over.

Selwyn Dewdney, Native art specialist, *Indian Rock Paintings of the Great Lakes* (1967). Dewdney is referring to the summer of 1958 when he succeeded in locating the fabled Agawa site of "rock art" in northwestern Ontario, described a century earlier by Indian agent H.R. Schoolcraft. It is now a provincial historic site. Two years later, in 1960, at Beardmore, Ont., Dewdney donated painting supplies to a fledgling Native artist named Norval Morrisseau.

However, unlike Gertrude Stein, who wrote, "A rose is a rose is a rose," an Indian would be more likely to say, "A bird is a loon is an eagle is a man is a manitou!"

Selwyn Dewdney, Native art specialist, *Indian Rock Paintings of the Great Lakes* (1967).

It's nice to have the avant-garde behind you.

Marshall McLuhan, media philosopher, after dozing through a private screening of Stanley Kubrick's film *2001: A Space Odyssey* in 1968, in W. Terrence Gordon, *Marshall McLuhan: Escape into Understanding: A Biography* (1997).

Art can be viewing this world and looking for the something more that this world reveals, and reveals, so to speak, in silent speech, reveals by a presence that cannot be defined or got hold of. In other words, there is to art an interpretative significance as a possibility.

Bernard Lonergan, theologian, *Topics in Education* (1959, 1993), in *The Lonergan Reader* (1997), edited by Mark D. Morelli and Elizabeth A. Morelli.

Art is man's nature: free acts are disciplined acts; free speech is cultivated speech.

Northrop Frye, literary and cultural critic, Item 103, "Notebook 18" (1962–1963), *Northrop Frye Newsletter*, winter 2001–2002.

I sat down and looked at them, attempting to conjure up a vision of the people who had made them, trying to divine the meaning they once had held for the people of this region. And the masks looked back at me, mute, mysterious, impassive, yet with a strange, nearly mesmeric power, regarding me fixedly across the unfathomable gap of centuries.

Fred Bruemmer, photographer and writer, "The Petroglyphs of Hudson Strait," *The Beaver*, summer 1973. The so-called devils' heads or devils' faces were carved in rock at sites near the village of Wakeham Bay on the south shore of Hudson Strait in the Eastern Arctic by the Dorset people, predecessors of today's Inuit, perhaps a thousand years ago. The heads are notable for their sense of menace.

In fact, I think of myself as a twelve- or thirteen-year-old kid. I don't think I have changed any of my basic standards in life, or what I want out of life, which is to get out there and have adventures in nature and put it down in paint. I was always totally driven to paint. I never thought I would support myself with my art. That never was a goal, and it is still not a goal, believe it or not. I just paint for myself and I'm totally amazed that people want to pay money for my paintings nowadays.

Robert Bateman, artist, address, "My Art and My Life," Toronto, 13 November 1986, The Empire Club of Canada.

The Albright–Knox Gallery is a high-toned, beautiful little gallery, an avant-garde snob art gallery with all the Andy Warhols, Frank Stellas, Rosenbergs and Rosenquists. It has Picassos and Matisses and, if you haven't seen it, that's one reason for going to Buffalo. I can't think of another one, but that is one reason for going to Buffalo and a very good reason. But, at any rate, they had the guts to have a show of Andrew Wyeth.

Robert Bateman, artist, address, "My Art and My Life," Toronto, 13 November 1986, The Empire Club of Canada.

It's the best money we ever wasted.

Barney Danson, Member of Parliament, response at a public meeting to a constituent who complained of the "waste" of public money on construction of Ottawa's National Arts Centre, election of 1979, recalled by Danson in correspondence, 25 October 2003.

I was fortunate enough to have my first retrospective in Provence in the south of France in 1991. I'm happy to say that the French treat artists the way Canadians treat hockey players. It's a country with such a grand tradition of admiration for what artists do. It touched me so deeply going there that I was almost in disbelief at the kind of reverence that I got for the kind of work that I was doing. It was just a very, very moving experience to be there and to enjoy all of that. I happen to have an uncanny resemblance to Cézanne so I managed to avail myself of that a bit and did a self portrait in the same vein.

Charles Pachter, artist, address, "A Romance with Canada," Toronto, 23 June 1994, The Empire Club of Canada.

English-Canadian artists are a strange lot. Probably because of the fact that their country is so profoundly hostile to art, they feel the need to hide themselves behind a façade of absolute banality. Alex Colville looks, speaks, and dresses like the C.E.O. of a large accounting firm. Glenn Gould could easily have been mistaken for a slightly dishevelled Presbyterian minister. David Cronenberg could pass for an Oshawa engineer. And yet what strange passions lurk behind these inscrutable masks. I have always found great English-Canadian artists to be incredibly lonely, disturbed, and dangerous people. That is why they are so interesting.

Denys Arcand, Quebec film director, foreword to the screenplay, *Thirty-two Short Films about Glenn Gould* (1995), by François Girard and Don McKellar.

The masters of the art, it seems to me, are those who never stop apprenticing.

Robert Bringhurst, poet, translator, and typographer, referring specifically to typographers, interviewed by Delve Withrington in 1997, on the website www.typebooks.org, May 2004.

There's nothing wrong with a completely emotional poem, or a completely intellectual dissertation, or a completely physical sculpture—that's all good. But it could be greater, within the same film length, if it had all those elements together.

Tom Daly, producer and director, "The Growth of a Craft: My Debt to Legg and Grierson," *John Grierson and the NFB* (1984), produced by the John Grierson Project.

Back in No Time.

Characteristic notice left on door of the Paris flat of **Brion Gysin** before he departed on long journeys and esthetic adventures, *Back in No Time: The Brion Gysin Reader* (2001), edited by Jason Weiss. Raised in Edmonton, Gysin was an expatriate writer, artist, theorist, and resident of New York, Tangiers, and Paris. He co-developed William Burroughs's "cut-up" technique and, rumour has it, supplied the recipe for hash fudge to Gertrude Stein.

The arts are no more elitist than education or health care. We all participate in some way or other. We sing and dance, quilt or work with wood, encourage and attend our children's performances in a school play or band. Some of us make artistic practice a career, and operate at a professional level far beyond common engagement. Whatever we do, the arts feed all of us: They feed pleasure, creativity, our economy, the reputation that our towns, provinces and country enjoy far and wide.

Donna Scott, arts administrator, resigning as CEO from the Ontario Arts Council, "Arts Funding Crisis," *The Globe and Mail*, 4 December 2000.

To our national credit, most Canadian cities, even small ones, have an art scene. It's one of those subtle but potent things that spring to my mind, at least when I suck in some air and say to myself, I am so glad that I am not American.

Douglas Coupland, author and artist, "Critical Mass," *The Globe and Mail*, 12 May 2001.

The explosion of colours is my rebellion in the face of sadness, death, and anguish.

Rita Letrendre, artist who paints with bright abstract colours, quoted by Simon Blais, in Hedwidge Asselin, *Rita Letendre: Les Eléments / The Elements* (2001).

Without dance, without music, without words and ideas, a country cannot have a soul, or a dream.

Charles, Prince of Wales, notes on the program distributed at a Toronto gala, 30 April 2001, in Michael Valpy, "A Prince's Gala," *The Globe and Mail*, 1 May 2001.

It's not difficult to become one of the best painters in Canada because everybody else quits.

Paterson Ewen, painter, in Ron Graham, "Heaven and Hell," *Maclean's*, 4 March 2002.

Above all, every Inuit print and every Inuit sculpture will always bear the mark of James Houston.

Douglas M. Gibson, publisher, paying tribute to artist and arts administrator James Houston, memorial service, Mystic, Conn., "The Man Who Invented Inuit Art," *Toronto Star*, 22 May 2005.

There are really just two kinds of art, that which appeals to one and that which doesn't.

Ken Danby, artist, characteristic observation, 6 July 2005.

The arts are the parklands of the mind. That's where we go to refresh our sensibilities—our sensitiveness to other human beings and other kinds of experience.

William Hutt, actor, adapted from a remark quoted by John Bemrose, "Farewell Flourish," *Performance Magazine*, autumn 2005.

ASIA *See also* China; Tibet

Strengthening Canada's position in the competitive world of international commerce is a priority for the entire country. The Pacific Gateway Strategy reaches beyond British Columbia—it is a pan-Western initiative which will benefit all of Canada.

Transport Canada, "Canada's Pacific Gateway Strategy," Transport Canada's website, October 2005.

ASTROLOGY *See also* Belief; Destiny; Science

The ancients visualized a ladder linking heaven and earth, its main rungs the seven planetary spheres, but in our time the best image is that of a labyrinth. Now one journeys *within* to find the self, encountering archetypal beings or situations that correspond to planetary energies.

Priscilla Costello, Toronto astrologer, "Ladder to Labyrinth: The Spiritual and Psychological Dimensions of Astrology" (1996), *The Inner West: An Introduction to the Hidden Wisdom of the West* (2004).

Astrology is part of our past, but astrologers have given no plausible reason why it should have a role in our future except for its undeniable historical value.

Ivan W. Kelly, psychologist, University of Saskatchewan, "The Concepts of Modern Astrology: A Critique," *Psychological Reports*, Number 81, 1997.

ASTRONOMY *See also* Earth; Space; Stars; Universe

There appears to be life on the planet Mars. A few years ago this statement was commonly regarded as fantastic. Now it is commonly accepted.

Simon Newcomb, Nova Scotia–born astronomer and leading American spokesman for science in his day, *Astronomy for Everybody*, "the astronomy text of my childhood," in Carl Sagan, *Pale Blue Dot: A Vision of the Human Future in Space* (1994). Sagan added ruefully, "Not 'intelligent life,' he was quick to add, but green plants."

Astronomy is terrifying. It describes a hell in which we seem to be the only inhabitants.

Louis Dudek, poet and aphorist, *Epigrams* (1975).

Stargazers, amateur astronomers, astronomy enthusiasts—whatever we call ourselves—are naturalists of the night. We appreciate what so many ignore.

Terence Dickinson, preface, *NightWatch: An Equinox Guide to Viewing the Universe* (1983, 1989).

ATHEISM *See also* Belief; Faith

Such a faith was the equivalent of The Three Bears. They never think that religion might be a poetic approach to some important questions, and that of all poetry, only about a third is good poetry.

Robertson Davies, man of letters, referring to atheists "who have rejected the Faith They Learned at Mother's Knee," letter, 18 November 1984, *For Your Eye Alone: Letters, 1976–1995* (1999).

If one wished to sum up in one word the central evil of the modern age, one could do so with the word "atheism."

William Stoddart, Traditionalist thinker, critic of Modernity, "Inter-religious Conflict or 'Communalism' in the Light of Tradition," *Sacred Web: A Journal of Tradition and Modernity*, July 2002.

ATLANTIC PROVINCES *See also* New Brunswick; Newfoundland & Labrador; Nova Scotia; Prince Edward Island

Maps don't always tell the whole truth. There's a sense in which the Atlantic Provinces aren't where the atlas would have you believe they are. Culturally speaking, they're a group of islands in the North Atlantic, about half way between the Gaspé Peninsula and the west coast of Ireland.

Alden Nowlan, poet and writer, *Weekend Magazine*, 15 January 1977.

Atlantic Canada's culture of defeat will be hard to overcome as long as Atlantic Canada is actually physically trailing the rest of the country. When that starts to change, the culture will start to change too.

Stephen Harper, leader, Canadian Alliance, address, 29 May 2002, in Brian Laghi, "Premiers Tell Harper His Attack Was Wrong," *The Globe and Mail*, 30 May 2002.

There is a tendency in the region that breeds a culture of defeatism. Nobody's to blame for it, but it is the responsibility of parties to offer alternatives, and we have a program that says that Atlantic Canada can be as wealthy as any other region.

Stephen Harper, leader, Canadian Alliance, address, 29 May 2002, in Brian Laghi, "Premiers Tell Harper His Attack Was Wrong," *The Globe and Mail*, 30 May 2002.

ATOMIC ENERGY *See also* Nuclear Warfare; Power

The United States has only very poor ores of uranium in moderate quantities. There is some good ore in Canada and the former Czechoslovakia, while the most important source of uranium is Belgian Congo.

Letter drafted by **Leo Szilard**, signed by physicist **Albert Einstein**, and addressed to

U.S. President Franklin D. Roosevelt, dated 2 August 1939. This reference to Canada appears in this, the most important letter written in modern times, reproduced by J. Bronowski, *The Ascent of Man* (1973). It resulted in the establishment of the Manhattan Project and the crash program to produce the world's first atomic bomb.

ATTENTION *See also* Consciousness

I now have come to the conclusion that attention and the study of attention is very important to our life itself. Did you ever stop to think that you cannot know anything, remember anything, or even be aware of experiencing anything, unless your attention has fallen on it at the time?

Tom Daly, producer and director, "The Growth of a Craft: My Debt to Legg and Grierson," *John Grierson and the NFB* (1984), produced by the John Grierson Project.

ATTITUDE

Drift. Capture accidents. Ask stupid questions. Don't be cool. Cool is conservative fear dressed in black.

Bruce Mau, designer, maxims from "An Incomplete Manifesto for Growth," in Sarah Scott, "Getting Better All the Time, *National Post*, 28 June 2003.

Every work of art that is important has a strong idea behind it. It's what grabs us immediately—at least that's how I see what good art is.... The films that remain with us are those that reveal some insight into human nature. These are the best kinds of films.

Norman Jewison, TV floor director and later movie director, 8 September 1952, *This Terrible Business Has Been Good to Me: An Autobiography* (2004).

ATWOOD, MARGARET

I was informed by one of the Toronto newspapers this fall that I am the Barbra Streisand of Canadian literature. I'm not sure what the points of comparison are. To me Barbra Streisand is someone with a long nose and a very loud voice and I certainly have the wrong nose and I am gradually developing the loud voice but I had always thought of myself rather as the Mary Pickford of Canadian literature. Spreading joy.

Margaret Atwood, author, address, "Getting Out from Under," Toronto, 5 April 1973, The Empire Club of Canada.

Margaret Atwood has achieved apotheosis. Were there such things as secular saints, she'd be one now: the Blessed Margaret at least.

Scott Symons, author, "Atwood-as-Icon" (1990), *Dear Reader: Selected Scott Symons* (1998), edited by Christopher Elson.

Atwood is Icon because we have none. A nation in disarray. A case of Real Absence because we've lost any sense of Real Presence. She can reign until we break the bondage—hers, and ours.

Scott Symons, author, "Atwood-as-Icon" (1990), *Dear Reader: Selected Scott Symons* (1998), edited by Christopher Elson.

Having met her, I can report that she is that precious specimen—an interesting Canadian.

Jasper Gerard, journalist with London's *Sunday Times*, on the Booker Prize–winning author, quoted in "N.B.," *The Times Literary Supplement*, 17 November 2000.

AURORA BOREALIS *See* Northern Lights

AUSTRALIA

They have common ambitions, and they are being welded and fused into an undeniable nation; I do not think anyone can miss the sense of that. A distinct Australian type is emerging. One of the characteristics of the nation is that they feel that the rest of the world is not a patch on Australia. Australian superiority is not a matter of discussion at all; they admit it. They have a national literature crude, but Australian. They read their own publications, they are protected by the wide Pacific from the flood of American literature which we get, and from some literature from

England which is just about as objectionable. They grow their own literature, and against their will they are developing, and if they do not look out will have, a national language.

John W. Dafoe, publisher, address, "Australian Politics," Toronto, 11 March 1926, The Empire Club of Canada.

Without a colossal neighbour or a profound cultural schism, which are the chief political realities of Canada, Australia has developed a distinct nationality.... Remote and relaxed, inhabited sparsely by bronzed and attractive people from every imaginable ethnic provenance, Australia is a strangely romantic concept that does not disappoint expectations.

Conrad Black, publisher and historian, *A Life in Progress* (1993).

I think Canada is a place where you can re-experience Australia again. I feel that more strongly in Canada than I would in the United States. Because the United States is too big and too different and so much of its energy comes from sheer numbers of people—which is not true of us, and it's not true of Canada.

David Malouf, Australian author, interviewed in Sydney by Paul Wells, "That Déjà-Vu Feeling," *Maclean's*, 1 March 2004.

This is our kind of history. One not of great men or heroes but of work done, houses and cities built, many small lives that have left their own small mark. A country imagined, but also held in the memory, remembered, and carried forward as a present reality to be dealt with and drawn on.

David Malouf, Australian author comparing Canadian and Australian history in terms of practicalities rather than heroics, "Wisdom from a Tale of Two Nations," *Maclean's*, 22 March 2004.

AUTHENTICITY *See also* Honesty; Reality; Truth

What we owe to our phonies! The solemn-minded souls cannot understand how enriching they are.

Robertson Davies, man of letters, letter, 20 November 1994, *For Your Eye Alone: Letters, 1976–1995* (1999).

AUTHORITY *See also* Freedom; Leadership; Power

There is barely an area in our daily life untouched by authorities of one kind or another, instructing us on the use of both mind and body; we are subsumed by an army of specialists, hired to protect us from the hardening of our arteries and the softening of our minds.

Irvine Schiffer, psychoanalyst, *Charisma: A Psychoanalytic Look at Mass Society* (1973).

Freedom even precedes authority, because what comes from the Creator's hands is a free human being. And since we must harmonize freedoms, we create society, and thereby authority. Authority follows freedom.

Georges-Henri Lévesque, sociologist, interviewed by Max Nemni and Monique Nemni, *Cité libre*, fall 1999.

AUTHORS *See also* Canadian Literature; Literature; Science Fiction; Writers & Writing

All the characters in this book are fictitious including the author.

Disclaimer carried in the first and all subsequent editions of **Paul Hiebert**'s popular work of humour, *Sarah Binks* (1947).

Being an author is a state of mind, and it cannot be changed.... It is possible to learn to write well, and even very well, as hundreds of thousands of writers of technical and scientific and informative books have shown. But ... I am talking about writers of two sorts: poets and story-tellers.... [I]f you happen to be born one, you cannot escape. You need not write, but ... you have something to say that will not let you alone. You may be good and you may be bad ... but you are not likely to be silent. Your urge to communicate is overpoweringly strong, and if you resist it the urge may take a very ugly turn, by which I mean that your fantasy life may get the better of your external life, and that can lead in only one direction.

Robertson Davies, author, address, "How the Author Reaches His Public," Toronto, 2 March 1972, The Empire Club of Canada.

Yes, I love to be *une de mes soeurs, un de mes frères canadiennes.* As a matter of fact I think that I have only one real wish and that is to be one of the breed of those writers we call "*fraternels*" or, as you say, brotherly. Others may be greater but my beloved writers we call "*les fraternels.*"

Gabrielle Roy, novelist, unpublished letter to translator David Lobdell, Quebec, 19 September 1974.

A Note about the Author / Anne Carson lives in Canada.

Terse (if officious or ominous) biographical note in **Anne Carson**'s book of poems *Men in the Off Hours* (2000).

I'd like to claim that the remarkable success of *Renegade* [*in Power* (1963, 1973)] changed me not a bit, that I remained the unassuming, unpretentious, charmingly clumsy, generic no-name writer I was meant to be. But I can't.

Peter C. Newman, journalist and memoirist, *Here Be Dragons: Telling Tales of People, Passion, and Power* (2004).

AUTOMOBILES *See also* Traffic; Transportation; Travel

Our motor car is our supreme form of privacy when away from home.

Marshall McLuhan, media theorist, address, Mohawk College, Hamilton, Ont., 17 May 1977.

Canada doesn't invest in creativity. We rip off fashions from New York and Europe. Canada is the fifth-largest auto manufacturer in the world, yet we're not using that capability to create a national statement: a car of our own. What a wasted opportunity. Think of what the Ferrari represents to Italians, the Citroën to the French, the Volvo to the Swedes. Imagine a Canadian car—not a Bricklin, but a 4x4. Something uniquely Canadian in look and spirit. I can see the Japanese lining up already.

Paul Lavoie, president, TAXI Advertising & Design, "How to Reinvent the Brand," *The Globe and Mail*'s *Report on Business*, May 2001.

In Canada, minivans outsell SUVs by a ratio of two to one. In the United States, SUVs outsell minivans two to one. This is a stark difference whose roots can be traced directly to the differing values of our two countries.

Michael Adams, consultant, *Fire and Ice: The United States, Canada and the Myth of Converging Values* (2003), with Amy Langstaff and David Jamieson.

Not TV or illegal drugs but the automobile has been the chief destroyer of American communities.

Jane Jacobs, urban planning critic, *Dark Age Ahead* (2004).

AUTUMN *See also* Seasons

Canada does a good job of fall. It's one of the reasons we have a national flag that pays homage to a tree. After a spring of unyielding sugar and a summer of providing shade, the sugar maple gives itself a standing ovation in the fall by turning into a beacon of gold and red. Its beauty is echoed by different maples across the country and by many other plants that refused to go gently into that good night of winter.

Jennifer Bennett, writer, "Fairest of the Fall," *Canadian Living*, November 2005.

AVIATION *See also* Transportation; Travel

Flying is something which anybody can do.... The sooner people get out of their minds the bugbear that they are not properly equipped for flying, the better. There is no doubt it is easier than driving a motor car. The real danger is hitting the ground the wrong way.

William A. Bishop, aviator, address, "British Aviation in War and Peace," Toronto, 16 October 1930, The Empire Club of Canada.

Perhaps we can get into the situation of today via the remark of the little boy on his first aeroplane ride. Once they had taken off, he said: "Daddy, when do we start to get smaller?" The little boy's question is rather complex since it is plain that the plane gets smaller, while the cabin does not. The little boy would never have asked such a question in an open cockpit plane, for not only does the plane get smaller, but the occupants also feel increasingly insignificant. However, the enclosed space of the cabin of the plane presents a very special kind of structure, namely, a visual space; that is, a space or figure without a ground.

Marshall McLuhan, media philosopher, address, "The End of the Work Ethic," Toronto, 16 November 1972, The Empire Club of Canada.

People spend twice as much on the phone as they do on the airlines, and we wonder why the airlines are having trouble finding passengers.

Dian Cohen, columnist, address, "Making It in the New Economy," Toronto, 6 February 1992, The Empire Club of Canada.

Now, anybody who has ever flown knows the unwritten rule: The person who travels in the centre seat gets both arm-rests. It's a bit like the consolation prize at a Sadie Hawkins dance, an olive branch to the poor sap who is travelling "monkey in the middle," if you will.

Stephen Quesnelle, Edmonton-based airline passenger, "Testosterone and Chip Diplomacy," *The Globe and Mail*, 22 February 2005.

AWARDS & HONOURS *See also* Nobel Prize

Awards are, of course, a lot of crap, but they awe the simple.

Robertson Davies, man of letters, letter to Mordecai Richler, 12 February 1990, *For Your Eye Alone: Letters, 1976–1995* (1999).

This award is not about winners, but about writers, writers who are working away at home. Nobody ever writes a book in a pressed suit.

Michael Ondaatje, novelist, acceptance speech, joint winner (with David Adams Richards) of Giller Prize for Literature, 2 November 2000, Toronto, in Sandra Martin, "Giller Prize Drama Ends in a Tie," *The Globe and Mail*, 3 November 2000.

I hate when people cop attitude. It's why I can't stand the world's-best-piper tag. I was the best piper, but just for one day.

Bruce Gandy, Halifax-based bagpiper, winner of the Gold Medal at Inverness, the Scottish pipe competition that began in 1841, in September 2002, in Shawna Richer, "The World's Best Bagpiper Won't Blow His Own Horn," *The Globe and Mail*, 20 November 2002.

If there were a writing Olympics, our men and women would be on the podium all the time, and our national anthem would be played so often that even non-Canadians would know the words.

Douglas M. Gibson, publisher, McClelland & Stewart Ltd., letter to the editor, noting the frequency with which Canadian fiction writers are contenders for international book awards, *The Globe and Mail*, 26 September 2002.

Don't tell the guys I cried, eh?

Mike Myers, Scarborough, Ontario–born comedian and actor, during a city council ceremony held in June 2003 to unveil a Scarborough street named in his honour (Mike Myers Drive), "Inside City Hall," *The Globe and Mail*, 2 January 2004.

It changes your life, the Oscar. For about six months. After that few people remember who won or who was nominated. But at that moment I was immensely grateful. The Academy had been good to me.

Norman Jewison, floor director and later movie director, *This Terrible Business Has Been Good to Me: An Autobiography* (2004). In 1999, the Academy of Motion Picture Arts and Sciences presented Jewison with its prestigious Irving Thalberg Award.

BALLET *See also* Dance; Music

I don't think ballet need only be about the women's dreams. I don't see myself as a hairdresser.

James Kudelka, director of the National Ballet of Canada, about his imbroglio with prima ballerina Kimberly Glasco, in Heather Mallick, "Et Tutu, Brute," *The Globe and Mail,* 25 July 2000.

BANKS & BANKING *See also* Finance

I do not intend to imply that Canadian bankers are greater scoundrels than, say, Canadian journalists. But they are not lily-white, never have been.

Walter Stewart, journalist, address, "Canadian Banks—Myth and Reality," Toronto, 3 March 1983, The Empire Club of Canada.

Canadians *believe* in banking; there are nearly as many bank branches as taverns in this country.

Peter C. Newman, author, *Debrett's Illustrated Guide to the Canadian Establishment* (1983).

BASEBALL

In the beginning was the word, & the word was "Play Ball!"

Line from the title poem of **George Bowering**'s book *Baseball, A Poem in the Magic Number 9* (1967).

Within the context of this weltanschauung, baseball was viewed as an interior republican game suited for southern climes. The manly sports of lacrosse, cricket, and later ice hockey were the proper diversions for the hardy Men of the North.

John Bell, editor, discussing baseball's status in North America, introduction, *The Grand-Slam Book of Canadian Baseball Writing* (1993).

When the Toronto Blue Jays won the World Series two years in a row in 1992 and 1993, Torontonians were thrilled to have broken the U.S. hold on baseball's highest honour, despite the fact that the whole team consisted of Dominicans and Americans.

Varda Burstyn, cultural critic, *The Rites of Men: Manhood, Politics, and the Culture of Sport* (1999).

I wish you won the World Series. I'm always in favour of the smallest. You're a big country but your population is not as large as other countries. So I favour you for this.

Fidel Castro, president of Cuba, impromptu press conference, Vancouver, during a stopover between Japan and Cuba, 4 March 2003, in Jason Proctor, "Leader Muses on Baseball, Salmon, War and Health," *National Post,* 5 March 2003.

BASKETBALL

I strongly believe the Toronto Raptors Basketball Club can be right alongside the Leafs as Toronto's team of the 21st century.

Richard Peddie, CEO, The Toronto Raptors Basketball Club, address, "The Future of Basketball in Toronto," Toronto, 19 February 1998, The Empire Club of Canada.

It's more important that you're a good person—because you can be a good person a lot longer than you can be a good basketball player.

Jack Donohue, college basketball coach, characteristic remark, recalled by Roy MacGregor, "This Country," *The Globe and Mail,* 22 April 2003.

BEARS

There's an old trapper's tale that says the best way to defend yourself against a polar bear attack is to shoot your buddy and run like hell.

Jeff MacInnis, adventurer, recalling northern lore, *Polar Passage: The Historic First Sail through the Northwest Passage* (1989), with Wade Rowland.

More than any species, grizzlies represent wilderness. If the grizzly bear, with its wide-ranging habitats, can survive, then many other species will survive.

Statement, "Eastern Slopes Grizzly Bear Project," 1994, website for June 2005.

Charles Dickens was the first to use the term "polar bear," reports Britain's *Daily Express* newspaper. Before him, it was called "white bear."

Curious fact noted by **Michael Kesterton**, "Social Studies," *The Globe and Mail,* 1 July 2005.

BEAUTY *See also* Arts & Artists; Fashion; Perception

Beauty's whatever / makes the adrenalin run.

Lines from **John Newlove**'s poem "The Double-Headed Snake," *Black Night Window* (1968).

My point is: you really don't need to go to Niagara Falls or the Rocky Mountains or Hawaii to see beauty. You have it right outside your back door. You are stumbling over it all the time, if you are tuned in and sensitive enough to nature. The amazing thing about nature is that you can walk fifty feet and get a totally different viewpoint, a totally different image.

Robert Bateman, artist, address, "My Art and My Life," Toronto, 13 November 1986, The Empire Club of Canada.

The most lonely places are the most lovely.

Thomas A. Clark, poet, "In Praise of Walking," *Wild Culture: Specimens from* The Journal of Wild Culture (1992), edited by Whitney Smith and Christopher Lowry.

Being will be here. / Beauty will be here. / But this beauty that visits us now will be gone.

Lines from the poem "New World Suite No. 3," in **Robert Bringhurst**'s *The Calling: Selected Poems, 1970–1995* (1995).

In the truly advanced civilization, we would all go boldly forward as we are, saying, "Love me for who I have become." Thank God I don't live in that world. I would be unemployed.

R. Stephen Mulholland, Toronto-based plastic surgeon, quoted by Matthew McKinnon in "Mulholland's Drive," *Toro,* August–September 2003.

If I encounter a beautiful face, it's like being overcome by a wave of religious awe. To stroll the streets is to risk being swept up in serial unpredictable epiphanies.

Robert Priest, poet and columnist, "The Phrase 'Just a Pretty Face' Has No Meaning for Me," *Now,* 16 December 2004.

BEAVERBROOK, LORD (MAX AITKEN)

Make a star or break a star, I'm not interested in anything in between.

Advice attributed to **Lord Beaverbrook**, publisher of the *Daily Express* (London), by John Barber, theatre critic, as noted by Laurence Olivier, *Confessions of an Actor* (1982).

He did not care in which direction the car was travelling, so long as he remained in the driver's seat.

Attributed to **Lord Beaverbrook** about David Lloyd George by Leo Rosten, *Carnival of Wit* (1994).

Of course I believe in the devil. How else could I explain Lord Beaverbrook?

Attributed to English novelist **Evelyn Waugh** in the CBC-TV documentary *The Various Lives of Max Aitken* (2001), narrated by Patrick Watson.

Here I must say, in my eighty-sixth year, I do not feel greatly different from when I was eighty-five. This is my final word. It is time for me to become an apprentice once more. I have not settled in which direction. But somewhere, sometime soon.

Max Aitken, **Lord Beaverbrook**, memorable parting words he delivered at the impressive banquet held in his honour on his eighty-fifth birthday by Roy Thomson, Lord Thomson of

Fleet, London, 25 May 1964. The Ontario-born publisher and public figure died two week later.

BEAVERS

The function of the beaver is to retain water; in areas where the beaver has been removed there is a shortage of water. There is a shortage of water in the West, mainly owing to the fact that the beaver have been ruthlessly removed.

Grey Owl, author and conservationist, address, "A Plea for the Canadian Northland," Toronto, 12 November 1936, The Empire Club of Canada.

Canada was built on dead beavers.

Margaret Atwood, author, interview, *Arts Report*, National Public Radio, 19 September 1988.

Canada is the only country founded on the relentless pursuit of the rodent.

Preston Manning, former Reform Party leader, address, IdeaCity conference, Toronto, 20 June 2002.

To see a beaver industriously building a dam shows that much hard work is to be expected before you eventually realize your goals. If the beaver is in distress, or has trouble with his building, this is indicative of a need to change your career as the goal you have set may be unrealistic.

Dream Interpretation Services, entry for "Beaver," internet, 27 May 2003.

BEER

Working families need care. They need care that is regulated, safe and secure, and that's what we're building here. Don't give people $25 a day to blow on beer and popcorn.

Scott Reid, Liberal communications director, interviewed on CBC-TV, 11 December 2005. He committed this gaffe trying to dismiss the Conservative pre-election plan to distribute $1,200 a year to parents of young children to help defray daycare expenses. Reid was subsequently reprimanded by Liberal Prime Minister Paul Martin and, offering an apology, noted, "I put the *jack* in *jackass*." Jim Brown in "Liberals Scramble over 'Beer, Popcorn' Comment," *Toronto Star*, 11 December 2005.

BELIEF

See also Atheism; Buddhism; Catholicism; Christianity; Creation; Creationism; Faith; Ghosts; Gods; Mysticism; Myths & Mythology; Philosophy; Prayer; Religion; Science; Souls; Spirit; Spiritualism

In despite of our vaunted material common-sense, there is a perfect craving abroad for belief in something beyond the compass of the believable.

Stephen Leacock, humorist, *Essays and Literary Studies* (1919).

I remember a perplexed curate of the Church of England telling me that he felt that "after all, there must be a kind of something." That's just exactly how I feel about it. There must be something to believe in, life must have its Santa Claus.

Stephen Leacock, humorist, *My Remarkable Uncle* (1942).

For the sake of their own souls most men live by pretending to believe in something they secretly know isn't true.

Morley Callaghan, author and memoirist, referring especially to Ernest Hemingway's estimation of his own boxing prowess, *That Summer in Paris* (1963).

In our society the very significant assumption is generally made that all events—without exception—can be contained and managed within the conventional system of beliefs. We tolerate the unexplained but not the inexplicable.

Erving Goffman, psychologist, *Frame Analysis: An Essay on the Organization of Experience* (1974).

But what I really believe—it is a continuing quest toward an ever-fleeing goal. What I cannot put up with is the brash certainties of the atheists, who reject all poetry, all beauty, all humility and decent dubiety, and who are so often desolated when something happens to them that cannot be healed with their astringent medicine. They are a pompous, humourless, self-honouring lot, and I like to disconcert them whenever I can.

Robertson Davies, man of letters, letter, 18 November 1984, *For Your Eye Alone: Letters, 1976–1995* (1999).

Belief follows behaviour. Thereafter behaviour follows belief.

Peter Urs Bender, business motivator, characteristic remark, 20 May 2000.

I think that our world will be a better place if we all continue to believe whatever we wish, but behave as if we were the sole arbiters of our fate.

Robert Buckman, physician and humanist, *Can We Be Good without God? Biology, Behaviour and the Need to Believe* (2002).

As human beings we have clearly believed whatever we wish for at least the past 100,000 years.

Robert Buckman, physician and humanist, *Can We Be Good without God? Biology, Behaviour and the Need to Believe* (2002).

BERMUDA

Just in what precise way Bermuda is a "colony" is a subject only understood by advanced metaphysicians. Bermuda has in fact been self-governing a great deal longer than Canada; some 355 years to be exact. And Bermudians are very much, as Mr. Vincent Massey once pointed out about Canadians, the more British in that they passionately adhere to that most British of all human characteristics, the determination to do everything in their own sweet way!

Sir Edwin Leather, governor of Bermuda, address, "Bermuda Calling," Toronto, 12 December 1974, The Empire Club of Canada.

BERTON, PIERRE

I'd much rather be thought of as an iconoclast than as an icon.

Adapted from an interview with media personality **Pierre Berton**, "Behind the Scenes," *Maclean's*, 21 July 2003.

We should celebrate Pierre Berton's ongoing accomplishments. The Big Foot of CanLit is truly a national treasure.

Peter C. Newman, columnist, "Big Foot of CanLit," *Maclean's*, 22 October 2001.

Pierre Berton gave us our story. He knew what we had to know about ourselves.

Adrienne Clarkson, governor general, tribute to the late Pierre Berton, CBC-TV, 7 December 2004, in Martin Knelman, "A Glowing Farewell," *Toronto Star*, 8 December 2004.

Without Pierre Berton there would scarcely be any Canadian history left.

J.L. Granatstein, historian, paying tribute to the narrative historian, in Sandra Martin, "A Voice of Canada Is Gone as Pierre Berton Dies at Eighty-four," *The Globe and Mail*, 1 December 2004.

BETTING *See* Games & Gambling

BIBLE *See also* Christianity

When God began to create the heaven and the earth—

Opening words of Genesis 1:1, as translated by **W. Gunther Plaut** et al., *The Torah: A Modern Commentary* (1961, 1967, 1981). As Plaut, rabbi emeritus of the Holy Blossom Congregation in Toronto, explains in the notes, "Other translations render this, 'In the beginning God created.' Both translations are possible, but we cannot be sure that this difference is more than stylistic." The suggestion is that the act of creation is continuing and not completed. Interestingly, too, Adam is described as an "earthling."

Any careful reader of the Bible realizes that, often, stones speak louder than words.

Donald Harman Akenson, historian, first sentence, *God's Peoples: Covenant and Land in South Africa, Israel, and Ulster* (1991).

If you don't count Jehovah's injunctions, there are no humorists in the Bible.

Attributed to **Mordecai Richler**, essayist, by Leo Rosten, *Carnival of Wit* (1994).

BIG FOOT *See* Sasquatch

BILINGUALISM *See also* Canada; French Canada; French Language; Language

We have spent nearly two billion dollars to make this country bilingual, only to pronounce it a total failure and an utter disaster. Quebec renounced bilingualism and went unilingual in a valiant attempt to protect its language and culture. Why not Quebec French? Why not the rest of Canada English? Why can't we build a nation on that basis? Only James Richardson of all the politicians had the courage to say, "Yes, we have one regional language in Quebec, and let's respect it. And we have one official language in the rest of Canada." I'm a firm believer in learning a second and a third language. I speak three of them. It's a culture devoutly to be fostered. I am bilingual. French was my first tongue. I also speak Italian. But you cannot legislate bilingualism. You can only foster it effectively through the educational system, slowly. It may take twenty-five years, but that's the way to go.

Laura Sabia, journalist, address, "Canada, the Crown, and Chauvinism," Toronto, 19 October 1978, The Empire Club of Canada.

BIRDS

In England the nighthawk is the poor-will. Lévi-Strauss says in imitation of its cry: "Five notes, three of which are not heard."

Wayne Grady, author, *The Bone Museum: Travels in the Lost Worlds of Dinosaurs and Birds* (2000).

In no one museum in the country are the birds of even a small locality well represented. There are a few creditable private collections, but none of these contains a sufficient series of skins to show the variations in plumage of all the species—the variations of sex and age and seasons, to say nothing of individual and geographical variation.

Montague Chamberlain, ornithologist, *A Systematic Table of Canadian Birds* (1888).

Birder originally meant "bird-killer." Birdwatcher is still my preferred term. It's watching birds.

Adapted from a remark made by **Graeme Gibson**, novelist and amateur ornithologist, interviewed by Michael Enright, CBC Radio's *Sunday Morning*, 27 November 2005. He added, "A bird independent of its habitat becomes a curious thing."

BIRTH

The first human statement is a scream.

Robin Skelton, poet and aphorist, *A Devious Dictionary* (1991).

I had no say in anything connected with my birth. Had I known what lay ahead I might have declined the invitation.

Mavor Moore, theatre personality, opening sentences, *Reinventing Myself: Memoirs* (1994).

BIRTH CONTROL *See also* Abortion

Children have a right to be born with a reasonable chance to legitimately earn a living, but I fear that the percentage of those who can qualify for very little more than the permanently unemployed is rapidly increasing, and will constitute an unbearable relief burden, or become a menace to society.

A.R. Kaufman, founder, Parents' Information Bureau, "Bulletin" (1938), in Angus McLaren and Arlene Tigar McLaren, *The Bedroom and the State: The Changing Practices and Politics of Contraception and Abortion in Canada, 1880–1980* (1986).

If women had been running the world back when the wheel was invented, they would have invented the pill instead.

Doris Anderson, editor of *Chatelaine*, in conversation, 1 February 1976.

The Pill was such a little thing. But the bang it made was bigger than the atom bomb.

Margaret Wente, columnist, "The Pill Changed Everything," *The Globe and Mail*, 10 April 2004.

BIRTHDAYS

Every day can be your birthday if you want it to be.

Leonard Wasser, businessman, in Nancy Wasser, "Lives Lived," *The Globe and Mail*, 19 November 2003.

BLACK, CONRAD

I may make mistakes but right now I can't think of any.

Conrad Black, on acquiring ownership of *The Daily Telegraph*, in journalist Max Hastings, *The Sunday Times*, 15 December 1985, before Hastings's appointment as the *Telegraph*'s editor, *Editor: An Inside Story of Newspapers* (2002). The London daily was known as "The Daily Torygraph."

Interest in Canada is like Canadian art—it has no market outside the country.

Conrad Black, Lord Black of Crossharbour, address, Fraser Institute, Vancouver, 15 November 2001, in Greg Joye, "Black Hails His Own 'Act of Patriotism,'" *The Globe and Mail*, 16 November 2001.

In extending and exploring my own horizons, I have not deserted my country. It is possible to transcend nationality.... If no such renewal comes, I will be consolable, a partial, voluntary, comfortable, and trans-national exile. If it does come, I will rejoice and be present.

Conrad Black, publisher, requiring "a spark of national self-esteem and renewal" as a condition for his continued residence in Canada, *A Life in Progress* (1993). These are the final sentences of his memoirs, and they discharge a Gaullist air. Black was granted British citizenship in 2001.

Lord Almost.

Facetious title conferred by columnist **Dalton Camp** upon publisher Conrad Black when the latter initially failed to secure his peerage, thanks to the intervention of Prime Minister Jean Chrétien, June 1999.

I've only met Black briefly, but I like his style. He's smart, and he's every inch the capitalist: It's too bad we can't clone him to help Canada compete in this highly competitive world.

Ken Walker, physician and medical columnist (aka Dr. Gifford-Jones), *"You're Going to Do What?" The Memoirs of Dr. W. Gifford-Jones* (2000).

Canada, despite his strictures, can boast of having produced a giant for the world.

William Johnson, columnist, "Not Everyone Hates Conrad Black," *The Globe and Mail*, 22 November 2001.

It will be Conrad's first opportunity to meet ordinary people.

John Fraser, commentator, tongue-in-cheek reference to Black's entering Britain's House of Lords, shorn of its hereditary peers and enhanced by Labour appointees, in Calvin Trillin, "Paper Baron," *The New Yorker*, 17 December 2001.

It has been written that he never uses one word when six will do, and among the six there will probably be a couple of words like "puerile" or "febrile," or even "rumbustious."

Calvin Trillin, essayist, "Paper Baron," *The New Yorker*, 17 December 2001.

It was also oddly familiar. Where had I seen it before, a large, handsome man with a supercilious and condescending manner and a baroque vocabulary? Of course: Orson Welles in *Citizen Kane*.

Robert Fulford, commentator, recalling his meeting with publisher Conrad Black, as noted by essayist Calvin Trillin, "Paper Baron," *The New Yorker*, 17 December 2001.

I've heard about people making it in Toronto after failing in New York, but not vice versa.

Unidentified commentator, interview in *The Guardian*, as noted in "Who Said What," *Toronto Star*, 30 December 2001.

Canadian citizenship was merely an impediment to my progress in another, more amenable jurisdiction.

Conrad Black, publisher and historian, on attaining the title Lord Black of Crossharbour,

"Who Said What," *Toronto Star*, 30 December 2001.

I made 50 million bucks yesterday. That's a flameout I could get used to.

Conrad Black, former president of Hollinger, Toronto, disclaiming any irregularities and claiming profits on rises in share value, in Siri Agrell, *National Post*, 17 November 2003. Peter Foster observed in "Stranger Than Fiction," *National Post*, 19 November 2003: "He also noted that he had made $50-million on Monday. Unfortunately, that was the increase in the value of his shares following the announcement that he was stepping down as CEO. The market had spoken, and it had clearly disagreed with him."

Conrad had turned himself into a latter day Citizen Kane. He looked like a young Orson Welles and behaved like an old William Randolph Hearst.

Peter C. Newman, journalist and memoirist, *Here Be Dragons: Telling Tales of People, Passion, and Power* (2004).

There has not been an occasion for many months when I got on our plane without wondering whether it was really affordable. But I'm not prepared to re-enact the French Revolutionary renunciation of the rights of nobility. We have to find a balance between an unfair taxation on the company and a reasonable treatment of the founder-builders-managers. We are proprietors, after all, beleaguered though we may be.

Conrad Black, founder of the Hollinger empire, private email to Hollinger executive Peter Atkinson, 5 August 2002, reprinted in *The Globe and Mail*, 26 January 2004.

His message was brutally clear: Lord Black of Crossharbour, Thesaurus Rex, Defender of the Divine Right of Things, Master of the Non-Compete Clause, was toast.

Peter C. Newman, journalist and memoirist, summarizing the effect of the decision of a Delaware judge in 2004 on Black's financial dealings, *Here Be Dragons: Telling Tales of People, Passion, and Power* (2004).

The tragedy here is not what happened to the Blacks; maybe they deserved most of their troubles, maybe they didn't. But for a short period, a really interesting, attached and intelligent proprietor owned and operated some of the English-speaking world's great publishing titles. It was exciting. Now, lesser folk are in charge.

John Fraser, former editor of *Saturday Night* magazine, a publication once owned by Conrad Black, reviewing two studies of the financial and social woes of Conrad Black and Barbara Amiel Black, "Back to Black," *The Globe and Mail*, 6 November 2004.

Black's is a humdrum scandal. There are no ice statues urinating vodka, *à la* Tyco; no scent of insider trading *à la* Michael Milken or Martha Stewart; no legions of unemployed Sun Belters, *à la* Enron. Reading newspaper accounts at the time, you got the sense you'd already seen this movie, and it was more entertaining the first time. Black seemed just one more corporate Garfield who overindulged, got called on it and was exiled to his Palm Beach mansion amid the usual flurry of lawsuits. What do you expect from Canada? Even its scandals are boring.

Bryan Burrough, correspondent at *Vanity Fair*, "Board Game," *The New York Times Book Review*, 2 January 2005. This is a review of two biographies of Conrad Black, subtitled "Conrad Black took millions out of Hollinger while his socially prominent directors looked the other way."

I have no doubt that mothers in America use my name to frighten their children into finishing their vegetables. But this is not a permanent state of affairs.

Conrad Black, capitalist, interviewed in *Fortune*, in David Olive, "Not His Finest Hour So Far," *Toronto Star*, 27 May 2005.

BLOC QUÉBÉCOIS

See also Canada & Quebec; Political Parties; Referenda on Quebec Sovereignty; Separatism; Sovereignty-Association

Why is the Bloc Québécois so popular? Essentially, because it is a French-Canadian party that speaks only French in the House of

Commons and talks almost exclusively about Quebec. Many Quebeckers feel at home with the Bloc. Those are realities against which it is extremely difficult to fight.

Lysiane Gagnon, columnist, "Tory Flirting Won't Work in Quebec," *The Globe and Mail*, 14 March 2005.

What's so beautiful about the Liberals and the Bloc in Quebec is that they so badly need each other. The Bloc needs the Liberals to be corrupt, and the Liberals need the Bloc to be separatists, because the only way that people will vote for corruption is the threat of separation and the only way that people will vote for separation is the threat of corruption. They are in a strange way each other's best friend.

Stephen Harper, Conservative Party leader, interviewed by the editors of *Maclean's*, 9 May 2005.

BOOKS *See also* Authors; Libraries; Literature; Reading; Writers & Writing

It is necessary for one deeply interested in books to acquire the detachment from one's reading that ordinary people have who are not much interested in them: to have something of their massive indifference which is not blown about by every wind of doctrine.

Northrop Frye, literary and cultural critic, aphorism, "Notebook 3" (1946–1948), *Northrop Frye Newsletter*, fall 2000.

Each page of a book is a city. Each line is a street. Each word is a dwelling. My eyes run along a street, opening each door and entering each dwelling in turn.

Line from **Réjean Ducharme**'s novel *L'avalée des avalés* (1966), on display at Bibliothèque nationale du Québec, Montreal, May 2005, anonymously translated.

Writing books is easy work: publicizing them is ditch-digger's work, and rather ignominious.

Robertson Davies, man of letters, letter, referring to the collection he edited, *Feast of Stephen* (1970), *For Your Eye Alone: Letters, 1976–1995* (1999).

Every book eventually becomes the creation of its reader.

Alberto Manguel, man of letters, foreword, *The Pleasure of Reading* (1992), edited by Antonia Fraser.

Reproductions, of course, are fine as far as they go, but you will never know what a fifteenth-century manuscript or printed book is like until you touch one, smell one, hold one in your hands.

Robert Bringhurst, author and typographer, *The Elements of Typographic Style* (2nd ed., 1996).

Like all my other books, this one seems to be made up essentially of missing pages.

Alberto Manguel, man of letters, *Reading Pictures: A History of Love and Hate* (2000).

Perfect proof reading occurs only after publication.

Hugh Arscott, aphorist, *Hugh's Views: Volume 4* (2000).

One day a book will open you.

Robert Priest, poet and columnist, "Enough Free Books for an Emperor," *Now*, 27 May 2000.

I'm still not in danger of making a living.... It's a wonderful way of making not much of a living.

David Mason, proprietor, David Mason Books, thoughts on 40 years in the antiquarian trade in Toronto, 8 August 2001.

My greatest wish—other than salvation—was to have a book. A long book with a never-ending story. One I could read again and again, with new eyes and a fresh understanding each time.

Thoughts of the castaway on board a lifeboat, in **Yann Martel**'s *The Life of Pi: A Novel* (2002).

A great book may only be read by a small number, but those people ultimately become influencers, the movers and shakers of society. If people don't want to be shaken out of their everyday lives, nobody can help that.

But the people who do get involved, they are the ones … that change the world.

John Calder, Canadian-born, London-based publisher, interviewed by Craig Taylor, "A True Friend to Writers," *National Post*, 12 January 2002.

See, it's easier to sell your first novel than it is your sixth. With a first novel, the publisher doesn't know if you're going to be the next Asimov, and so they're willing to take a chance. By the time your fifth novel is out, they do know—and I wasn't. A publisher would be better off buying a new novel, for less money, from a first-timer, than another book from me. I decided it was time for drastic action.

Robert J. Sawyer, science-fiction author, "Autobiography" (2004), *Relativity: Stories and Essays* (2004). The author is referring to the ups and downs of his career writing and publishing SF. There will never be another Isaac Asimov, nor another Robert J. Sawyer, whose career then developed rocket power.

Watch the movies, read the books, even buy the toys. And realize that whilst *The Da Vinci Code* is an adult book for those with the minds of children, the Narnia stories are children's books for those with minds.

Michael Coren, biographer, "From a Man of Faith, a World of Fantasy," *National Post*, 15 March 2005.

BORDER, CANADA–UNITED STATES

See also America; Canada & United States; Terrorism

Thank God, we are once more on British soil.

Winston Churchill, future statesman, first words on alighting from the train from Boston, Windsor Station, Montreal, 23 December 1900.

The very thought of that long borderland stretching from the mouth of the St. Lawrence out to Vancouver— … for I tell you, my friends, it is good to have a good neighbor, and it is not necessary that all neighbors should always marry (laughter). That long borderland along which I myself have tramped, fished, and shot—without a fort and without an army of defence on either side—the thought of that magnificent inland sea without a battle-fleet or a war-vessel … is one of the most inspiring thoughts in our modern life.

Henry Van Dyke, American essayist and diplomat, address, "Canada and the United States," Toronto, 25 October 1929, The Empire Club of Canada.

My curiosity at being in a new country was mildly appeased by the difference—the almost imperceptible difference—between the Canadian and the inhabitant of the States.

Wyndham Lewis, English author, one-time Toronto resident, *America, I Presume* (1940).

The 49th parallel is much more than the most open border in the world. It marks a continental divide. A friendly divide to be sure. But one that marks some fundamental differences. Differences that our intense closeness has not weakened or diluted. Nor will it in the future.

Jean Chrétien, prime minister, address at Duke University, N.C., December 2000, in Lawrence Martin, "Mulroney: He Haunts Us Still," *The Globe and Mail*, 15 October 2001.

We casually call it the 49th parallel, yet the boundary that divides Canada from the United States runs along that oft-cited latitude only from Middleboro, Man., to White Rock in British Columbia.

Peter C. Newman, columnist, "The Defining Border," *Maclean's*, 31 December 2001.

I also want to apologize for the border. It's an awful long one, George, and it's hard to patrol. It must be costing you a pile of money to keep the riff-raff and the terrorists out. Here's an amazing coincidence that you may not have noticed. The border is just as long on our side as on yours.… Here's something else: Did you know that, over the years, more armed Americans have tried to get into Canada than armed Canadians have tried to get into the States?

Colin Mochrie, actor-comedian, "A Canadian Apologizes," routine posted on a website as mock letter addressed to U.S. President George W. Bush, 8 June 2002.

It's an undefended border, and it always will be.

Wesley Wark, historian, referring to the tightening of security along the Canada-U.S. border, in Clifford Krauss, *The New York Times*, 23 March 2003.

If the forty-ninth parallel does sometimes appear to be the boundary between self-confident and self-conscious, it's not surprising—you would have to be particularly thick to grow up thinking Canada was all that mattered in the world.

Steve Burgess, columnist, "They Really Like Us, Eh?" *Maclean's*, 13 October 2003.

BOUCHARD, LUCIEN

See also Bloc Québécois; Referenda on Quebec Sovereignty; Separatism

Let clever politicians, those arsonists disguised as firemen, those sorcerer's apprentices, come and tell us here in Ottawa, before the people, before past, present and future generations, whether or not they repudiate signatures that were freely given, at that time of grace in the national life of this country, at sunrise on June 3, 1987.

Mr. Speaker, enough of this hypocrisy! Let the real culprits take off their masks, or if they cannot stand the light of day or fear the judgment that history will pass on them, let them be inspired by Macdonald and Cartier and look to the future, our children's future, and then reach out to the fraternal hand Quebec still offers, perhaps for the last time.

Lucien Bouchard, Member of Parliament for Lac-Saint-Jean, changing his party affiliation, House of Commons, 22 May 1990.

Mr. Speaker, I entered politics late in life, under trying circumstances, but with the best of intentions. Two reasons prompted me to go into the lions' den. The first is the attraction of the beau risque, the worthy risk of co-operating with Mr. Mulroney. The second, Mr. Mulroney himself. In Sept-Îles, on a warm day in August 1984, he made the solemn commitment to bring this country together. I knew as well that he had met this commitment by having all provincial premiers sign the 1987 Accord which would enable Quebec to endorse formally the 1982 patriation.

Lucien Bouchard, Member of Parliament for Lac-Saint-Jean, changing his party affiliation, House of Commons, 22 May 1990.

When I first read the accord I had the impression that Quebec had made light of the fact that it had been humiliated and that it was justifiably indignant. Still, convinced that nothing better could be achieved, I finally concluded that we had to pull ourselves out of the ghetto and prostration where Pierre Trudeau's arrogant deception had confined us. I said to myself that we had to take that opportunity to turn the page on the bitterness of the recent past and, with Brian Mulroney, begin to write a glorious chapter highlighted by acts of faith, tolerant gestures and open dialogues.

Lucien Bouchard, Member of Parliament for Lac-Saint-Jean, changing his party affiliation, House of Commons, 22 May 1990. According to Hansard, Bouchard said "out of the ghetto and prostration"; the phrase is remembered as "the ghetto of frustration."

Every time he appeared I imagined ... that he was accompanied by a bass-trombone orchestra, playing the brooding score from a Verdi opera. He was a basso profundo—a swarthy villain, intent on defiling the coloratura diva's lily whites.

Peter C. Newman, columnist, referring to the television appearances of Quebec premier Lucien Bouchard, "Adieu to Separatism?" *Maclean's*, 12 May 2003.

Bouchard didn't get out of his limousine any more than Parizeau got off the train.

Daniel Poliquin, commentator and novelist, *In the Name of the Father: An Essay on Quebec Nationalism* (2001), translated by Don Winkler. Poliquin is considering how ignorant of

Canada west of Ottawa Lucien Bouchard and Jacques Parizeau were before they assumed the premiership of Quebec. Bouchard visited Toronto for the first time as premier, much preferring his stint as ambassador to France, and Parizeau made one train trip to the Rockies and back (which, he later maintained, turned him into a separatist).

Whining Conditions.

Pun on Quebec premier **Lucien Bouchard**'s oft-quoted remark about holding the third Quebec referendum on sovereignty only when there are "winning conditions," Aislin's cartoon, Montreal *Gazette*, 12 January 2001.

Bouchard is what every francophone male wants to be: A guy who reads Proust and who's married to a blonde Californian.

Attributed to pollster **Michael Adams** by Richard Gwyn, "Home and Away," *Toronto Star*, 13 January 2001.

Lucien Bouchard's dream is my worst nightmare.

Roy Romanow, Saskatchewan premier, on learning of the resignation of Quebec premier Lucien Bouchard, CBC Radio's *The National*, 22 January 2001.

I think there's no way I could have known about Bouchard. No way. I trusted him too much. You've got to understand, I had his goddamned wedding reception in my house. That's how close he was.

Brian Mulroney, prime minister, in Peter C. Newman, *The Secret Mulroney Tapes: Unguarded Confessions of a Prime Minister* (2005).

BOXING

You don't just work on your ability to administer punishment. You have to work on your ability to withstand it. I worked on both.

George Chuvalo, boxer, in Pamela Wallin, according to Gil Kezer, *Forever Young*, December 2001.

BRITAIN *See* British Empire; Canada & United Kingdom

BRITISH COLUMBIA

In 1825 the Hudson's Bay Company had established Fort Vancouver in what is now the State of Washington. The company's description of the future British Columbia was hardly flattering.... "A vast wilderness area west of the Rocky Mountains tenanted by wild beasts and still wilder savages." Mr. President, I do apologize to any British Columbians who are present here today.

Viscount Amory, former H.B.C. governor, address, "Three Hundred Years," Toronto, 4 March 1971, The Empire Club of Canada.

Those who are convicts and those who ought to be.

Attributed to **Sir Arthur Edward Kennedy**, last royal governor of Vancouver Island (1863–1867), describing the class structure of the British colony on the Pacific.

Victoria is 3,000 miles from Ottawa whereas Ottawa is 30,000 miles from Victoria.

Edward G. Prior, British Columbia premier, remark made in 1903, in Kenneth Coates, *Canada's Colonies: A History of the Yukon and Northwest Territories* (1985).

We spoke of the racing tides off Vancouver, and the lonely pine-clad ridges running up to the snow-peaks of the Selkirks, to which we had both travelled once upon a time in search of sport.

Narrator recalling fishing and hunting expeditions with friends in **John Buchan**'s short story "The Kings of Orion" (1906), *The Moon Endureth* (1912).

British Columbia is a large body of land entirely surrounded by envy.

Eric Nicol, humorist, one of his favourite aphorisms, letter, December 1976.

British Columbia has long suffered from its reputation as a slightly wing-nutty province. Though investors have been attracted by our weather, they've always been wary of our climate.

Norman Spector, columnist, "Here in B.C. We're Not the Wing Nuts We Used to Be," *The Globe and Mail*, 16 May 2005.

BRITISH EMPIRE *See also* Canada & United Kingdom; Colonialism

As for myself, my course is clear. A British subject I was born—a British subject I will die.

Sir John A. Macdonald, first prime minister, born a British subject in Scotland in 1815, died a British subject in Canada in 1891. He appealed to the British connection in his final address in the House of Commons, 7 February 1891. Only with the passage of the Canadian Citizenship Act in 1947 did Canadians officially became "citizens" of Canada, while retaining their status as British "subjects."

A Canadian who attends the debates in the House of Commons may wait for days before one imperial consideration emerges, and may see the Government which controls his destinies turned out of office on some business of English education.

Complaint by fictional Lord Arpin, former prime minister of Great Britain, in **John Buchan**'s novel *A Lodge in the Wilderness* (1906).

Thy blessing, Lord, on Canada, / Young giant of the West, / Still upward lay her broadening way, / And may her feet be blessed!

Verse from "A Hymn of Empire," written by **Sir Arthur Conan Doyle** for the coronation of George V, 1911.

It is no real concern of mine whether liberal or conservative is in power in Canada, or whether labour or liberal is in power in Australia or whether Jahn Smuts or Jahn Hertzog governs South Africa—nor is it any real concern of mine whether Mr. Baldwin or Mr. Lloyd George or Mr. Macdonald is Prime Minister of Britain, but there is one thing of the most vital concern to all of us, and that is, that whatever party and whatever leader may be in power in any dominion or in the mother country, that party and that leader shall accept the Empire as a basis of all policy, and shall be fully resolved to do nothing to impair the corporate spirit or weaken the unity of our great British League of Nations. (Great applause.)

John Buchan, barrister, author, and future governor general, address, "Some New Elements in British Politics," Toronto, 23 October 1924, The Empire Club of Canada.

Gentlemen, the British Government has promised that the Dominions shall be consulted and that Parliament shall know what their views are before it has to take the decision which will be asked of it in the autumn. And I would venture to say this: it seems a long way from Toronto to Cairo, but Canada has an interest as a partner in the Empire in the decision of these great matters. Anything that happens injuriously to the interests of Australia and New Zealand must affect Canadian interests and Canadian sentiment. (Hear, hear.) Anything that affects the welfare of the whole affects the welfare of every part. Canada should have her opinion upon this subject of Egypt too. (Applause.)

Winston Churchill, statesman, on possible Imperial crisis, "British Imperial Interests," Toronto, 13 August 1929, The Empire Club of Canada.

BRITISH MONARCHY *See also* Royal Tours

I'm like that with my underlying Jeffersonian republicanism: back I slip to such crazy ideas as that all men are equal, and that hereditary rights (still saving out the British monarchy) are hereditary wrongs.

Stephen Leacock, humorist, *The Boy I Left Behind Me* (1946).

If the Queen of Canada really was *the Queen of Canada*, I think she should have a summer palace at Niagara-on-the-Lake and a winter palace at Banff.

Charles Pachter, artist celebrated for his "Queen on Moose" series of paintings, remark made in May 1976.

Scrap the Queen, indeed! We need the monarchy more now than we have ever done before. I, for one, want the Queen and not a political appointee as Head of State. She is above the political fray and the machinations of discredited political Judas Iscariots. She is a symbol of statehood. She is responsible, disciplined, gracious—virtues we would do well to emulate. Our Prime Minister finally got the message that he did not have the mandate nor the approval of the people of Canada to tamper with the Queen's place in Confederation. The Speech from the Throne last week went out of its way to assure us that the Queen was safe—for now, anyway. After an election, God only knows.

Laura Sabia, journalist, address, "Canada, the Crown, and Chauvinism," Toronto, 19 October 1978, The Empire Club of Canada.

The expression "monarch of the north" also used to confuse me as a child and it was one of the reasons why as a young boy growing up in Toronto I used to wonder if there was any difference between the moose and the Queen, given that they were both monarchs. And the only way I could solve this was by bringing them together. In 1972 I began to think about how the whole phenomenon appears to a child. That fascinating person, dripping in finery and with a foreign accent and jewels and furs, who came here once in a while was our version of Hollywood. Canadians used to fall on bended knee much differently than they do today. It shows how times have changed over the decades.

Charles Pachter, artist, address, "A Romance with Canada," Toronto, 23 June 1994, The Empire Club of Canada.

Here's the rub: We don't seem to want her, but we can't seem to do without her.

John Fraser, columnist, referring to the monarchy during the Jubilee celebrations for Queen Elizabeth II, "In Between Two Portraits," *National Post*, 5 June 2002.

But she sails on, our old Queen. She sails on dutifully, determined to do the right thing as best she can, to hold firm to her Coronation oath of service and commitment.

John Fraser, columnist, referring to Queen Elizabeth II in her Jubilee year marking 50 years of her reign, "In Between Two Portraits," *National Post*, 5 June 2002.

I have always thought of the King as Elvis, Mr. Speaker.

John Manley, deputy prime minister, House of Commons, 7 October 2002. He was responding to Joe Clark's baiting him as "John King" because of previous remarks critical of the monarchy, if not the visit, of the present Queen.

The monarch's time will expire in Canada some day, but, alas, not for a very long time.

Jeffrey Simpson, columnist, during Queen Elizabeth's Royal Jubilee visit, "The Nation," *The Globe and Mail*, 8 October 2002.

I treasure my place in the life of Canada and my bond with Canadians everywhere.

Elizabeth II, Queen of Canada, address, Royal Jubilee visit, her twenty-second official visit to Canada, Vancouver, 7 October 2002, *National Post*, 8 October 2002.

Never underestimate The House of Windsor. The firm, as it's known, hasn't stayed in business this long without understanding its market.

Anne Kingston, columnist, referring to the future wedding announcement of Prince Charles and Camilla Parker Bowles, "The House of Windsor Gets Its Way," *National Post*, 18 February 2005.

BRITISH CHARACTER *See also* British Empire; Canada & United Kingdom

The passion to be left alone, if only to one's own foolishness, lies deep rooted in the British character.

Stephen Leacock, humorist, *Here Are My Lectures and Stories* (1937).

BROADCASTING *See also* Canadian Broadcasting Corporation; Communications; Radio; Television

It is essential that broadcasting be surrounded with such safeguards as will prevent the air becoming what might be described as an atmospheric billboard.

Sir Henry Thornton, public broadcasting pioneer, prophetic warning about the designs of commercial advertising on radio both public and private, address, Advertising Clubs of the World, Philadelphia, 21 June 1926, as in E. Austin Weir, *The Struggle for National Broadcasting in Canada* (1965).

Resolution re A National Policy for exploitation of the Radio:

That in the interests of Canadian national life and culture, it is imperative to proceed at once with the organisation of radio broadcasting on a basis of public service, with Dominion and Provincial co-operation.

Recommendations, *Education and Leisure: Addresses Delivered at the Fourth Triennial Conference on Education Held at Victoria and Vancouver, Canada, April 1929* (1929), edited by S.E. Lang.

The question is, the State or the United States?

Graham Spry, chairman, Canadian Radio League, address before the Parliamentary Committee on Broadcasting, 18 April 1932, expressing the need for government intervention to ensure a Canadian presence on the airwaves. In the 1960s, cultural nationalists turned these nine words into something of a mantra.

There are two kinds of Russian place names, Mavor: long ones like O-O-O-OMSK and short ones like DnieperpetrOVSK.

Attributed to **Lorne Greene**, CBC Radio news announcer, quoted by writer and broadcaster Mavor Moore during World War II, *Reinventing Myself: Memoirs* (1994). For his dramatic delivery, Greene, whose parents were born in Russia, was dubbed the "Voice of Doom."

For God's sake. Either we have a country or we don't. Let's decide!

Attributed to **Pierre Juneau**, chair, Canadian Radio-television and Telecommunications Commission, trying to balance the demands of private broadcasters and the needs of public broadcasting in defence of the CBC's mandate, during an appearance before the Senate Committee on Communications, October 1974.

Good morning, or afternoon, or evening even.

Greeting of broadcaster **Peter Gzowski**, host of CBC Radio's *Morningside*, 1971 to 1997, which was broadcast and re-broadcast in whole or part at various hours of the day and night in Canada and over CBC Radio Canada International and over the internet. His more common greeting was "Hello, I'm Peter Gzowski, and this is 'Morningside.'"

I like to feel I play the king of instruments, the phonograph.

Clyde Gilmour, broadcaster, host of CBC Radio's *Gilmour's Albums*, interview, *Today Magazine*, 3 October 1981.

People came up to me and said, "You know, I thought I heard you say ... but ... ," then they blamed themselves.

Pamela Wallin, broadcaster, explaining that after identifying West German chancellor Helmut Schmidt as "Helmut Shit" on CTV's *Canada A.M.* viewers did not believe their own ears, as noted by Joan Green, Lynda Palazzi, and Marguerite Senecal, *Northern Lights: Outstanding Canadian Women* (2004).

What you try to do is to speak truth to power.

Lister Sinclair, veteran writer and radio broadcaster, defining his aim and that of other communicators, *Ideas*, CBC Radio, 29 October 2001.

Our job is to help us to locate ourselves in the universe.

Attributed to veteran broadcaster **Lister Sinclair** during a two-hour tribute, CBC Radio's *Ideas*, 29 October 2001.

Nevertheless, while the Canadian broadcasting system has slowly shifted from dualistic to pluralistic, the question of ethnic and third-language broadcasting's proper place in the public service is still up in the air.

Ryan Edwardson, historian, concluding sentence, "Other Canadian Voices: The Development of Ethnic Broadcasting in

Canada," *Racism, Eh? A Critical Inter-Disciplinary Anthology of Race and Racism in Canada* (2004), edited by Camille A. Nelson and Charmaine A. Nelson.

Si la tendance se maintient ...

Characteristic expression, of **Bernard Derome**, Radio-Canada's *Le Téléjournal*, French-language equivalent of CBC-TV's *The National*. As Paul Wells wrote in "Return of a Legend," *Maclean's*, 29 March 2004, "His unflappable calm seems indispensable. In millions of households, the highlight of any election night was the moment when Derome would project the winner using an otherwise unremarkable catchphrase he first employed in 1973: '*Si la tendance se maintien....*' ('if the trend holds ...')."

BUDDHISM *See also* Religion; Zen

So Zen and Buddhism and Yoga are to electronic technology what Wordsworth was to the railroads—the necessary Yeatsian complement to create a real, full culture. I don't think you can humanize electronic technology with anything less. Being a good Presbyterian or Anglican is just not powerful enough to handle the forces of the electronic world—computers, space travel, the disintegration of the natural order as we have been defining it.

William Irwin Thompson, theorist, "Mind Jazz," *Wild Culture: Specimens from* The Journal of Wild Culture (1992), edited by Whitney Smith and Christopher Lowry.

BUDGETS *See also* Finance; Politics

Unfortunately, budgets in Canada are an excessively political topic. They are almost the only political topic. The budget is almost the only thing that a political party can do in Canada in the way of influencing votes, and after all, influencing votes is the chief business of politicians. (Laughter.)

B.K. Sandwell, editor and economist, address, "Budget," Toronto, 23 February 1928, The Empire Club of Canada.

The thing you have to remember about federal budgets is that they don't actually mean anything. That isn't to say they mean nothing: that would be far too specific. They aren't devoid of meaning, they're beside it. They exist in a world where the very concept of meaning is meaningless.

Andrew Coyne, columnist, "Budgets Would Make Kafka Blush," *National Post*, 24 February 2005.

The way this Parliament is supposed to work is that what the Liberals don't steal the NDP gets to spend.

Stephen Harper, Opposition leader, criticizing an agreement between the minority Liberal government under Paul Martin and the NDP under Jack Layton to alter expenditures in the budget, CBC Radio, *News*, 27 April 2005.

BUFFALO

The buffalo / as they stand in a circle / I join them.

Ojibwa poem, "Buffalo," *Songs of the Great Land* (1989), edited by John Robert Colombo.

The meat of the buffalo tastes the same on both sides of the border.

Attributed to **Sitting Bull**, chief of the Sioux nation, who crossed "the line" into Canada following the battle of Little Big Horn in 1876, by John Newlove in 1965.

BUREAUCRACY *See also* Government; Public Service

So ... how would you like your open-heart surgery done by a civil servant? Or how would you like your baby delivered by the same folks who deliver the mail? Or your gall bladder done by a bureaucrat?

Headline prepared by the National Citizens Coalition, a conservative group, the slogan of which is "For more freedom through less government"; open letter from its president, Colin Brown, 19 March 1984.

The country has become more and more institutionalized and bureaucratized. But institutions do not create products, and bureaucrats do not create wealth. That is something we seem to have forgotten.

Frank Stronach, manufacturer, Magna International, address, "Operating within a Global Economy," Toronto, 10 February 1994, The Empire Club of Canada.

Bureaucracy: The triumph of policy over intelligence.

Hugh Arscott, aphorist, *Hugh's Views: Volume 5* (2001).

BUSH, GEORGE W. *See also* Anti-Americanism; Canada & United States; Defence; Terrorism

He's not a moron at all. He is a friend.

Jean Chrétien, prime minister, referring to U.S. President George W. Bush, NATO Summit, Prague, Czech Republic, 21 November 2002, in Daniel Leblanc and Jeff Sallot, "P.M. Urged to Fire Aide for Insult to Bush," *The Globe and Mail*, 22 November 2002. Chrétien was under pressure to distance himself from the injudicious remark made by Françoise Ducros, director of communications in the Prime Minister's Office, when she described Bush as a "moron" in a private conversation with a journalist, overheard by another journalist, Prague, 20 November 2002. She had in mind Bush's attempt to dominate the NATO agenda. The first journalist has been identified as Robert Fife, bureau chief for the *National Post* and Southam News; the second, Chris Hall, parliamentary correspondent, CBC Radio. The next day, 21 November, Chrétien explained, "It's a word she uses regularly," according to Shawn McCarthy and Jeff Shallot, "A Style That Grates on Enemies—and Friends," *The Globe and Mail*, 23 November 2002.

What a moron. Of course, our official position is that he is not trying to hijack the summit.

Françoise Ducros, director of communications in the Prime Minister's Office, referring to U.S. President George W. Bush as a "moron" during a private conversation with a journalist that was overheard by another journalist, Prague, 20 November 2002. She shared a popular view of Bush as well as his determination to place on the NATO agenda the issue of Iraq's "weapons of mass destruction."

I told Paul that I really have only one regret about this visit to Canada. There's a prominent citizen who endorsed me in the 2000 election, and I wanted a chance to finally thank him for that endorsement. I was hoping to meet Jean Poutine.

George W. Bush, U.S. president, address, Pier 21, Halifax, 1 December 2004, in Gloria Galloway, "Evoking World War II, Bush Prods Canadians," *The Globe and Mail*, 2 December 2004.

BUSINESS *See also* Commerce; Corporations; Entrepreneurship; Executives; Finance; Free Trade; Globalism & Globalization; Growth; Industry; Manufacturing; Trade

Good business comes where good business is invited.

Frank T. Sherk, first Canadian-born president of H.J. Heinz Company of Canada, address, Leamington Chamber of Commerce, Leamington, Ont., 23 February 1961.

Life at the top is financially rewarding, spiritually draining, physically exhausting, and short.

Peter C. Newman, author, *The Canadian Establishment: Volume One* (1975).

You can hire better than you can sire.

Alfred McInroy Cudd, founder, Cuddy International Corp., on finding a successor among family or employees, in Gordon Pitts, *In the Blood: Battles to Succeed in Canada's Family Businesses* (2000).

It's not easy letting go of our past. The heart is more stubborn than the head.

Edgar Bronfman Jr., corporate executive, on the merger of the Seagram Corporation, established by his grandfather Samuel Bronfman in 1924, with the giant French water utility Vivendi, final shareholders' meeting, Montreal, 5 December 2000, in David Olive, "How Edgar Jr. Rid Seagram of Liquor," *National Post*, 6 December 2000. One unidentified shareholder grumbled, "It's the shortest funeral I was ever at."

To many people, Canadian Tire is a proxy for Canada. Indeed, a letter to the editor [of the

Cornwall *Standard-Freeholder*], written during the last federal election, brought that connection home to me in an amusing fashion: "Wouldn't we be better off," the writer asked, "if we just hired Canadian Tire to run the country? They're pretty well national, they know what they are doing, they don't believe in deficits, they are efficient, they are honest, they are innovators—everything that politicians are not." To that list of qualities, I would add, "We also have our own currency."

Martha Billes, CEO of Canadian Tire, address, "The Ethics of Self-Reliance," Toronto, 8 February 2001, The Empire Club of Canada.

We already have some unique and hugely successful products we can boast about, whether it's Research in Motion's BlackBerry, Bombardier's Ski-Doo, John Fluevog's shoes, Nortel's many innovations or Cirque du Soleil's brilliance. But does the world know they are Canadian?

Paul Lavoie, president, TAXI Advertising & Design, "How to Reinvent the Brand," *The Globe and Mail*'s *Report on Business*, May 2001.

Administration is an activity where the urgent preempts the important.

C.C. (Kelly) Gotlieb, computer scientist, characteristic remark first made in the 1970s, recorded 7 November 2001.

I do not wish to live in a society in which the only standpoint is profit and everything else is other people's business.... But I also take great joy and comfort from the groundswell of young people who say, "We do not wish to live in a world in which there is no standpoint other than profit."

Ursula Franklin, scientist and social justice activist, "Legitimate Expectations," *Canadian Perspectives*, winter 2001.

If you want to start something, it takes just as much effort to run a corner store as it does to run a multi-billion-dollar multinational. You're going to work 18 hours a day anyway, so choose your battle. Make it big. Make sure it's going to be a huge market and build your plan to be the number-one company in that market.

Glenn Ballman, entrepreneur, founder of online retailer/portal Onvia, interviewed by Leonard Brody et al., *Innovation Nation: Canadian Leadership from Java to Jurassic Park* (2002).

Politics is about compromise; business is about doing.

Attributed to **Paul Martin**, businessman and politician, quoted on CBC Radio, 22 September 2003.

Self-policing and self-regulation have never been typical business responsibilities.

Jane Jacobs, urban planning critic, *Dark Age Ahead* (2004).

C

CALGARY

The city of Calgary has more college-educated citizens per capita than any other Canadian city.

Linda Frum, journalist, *Linda Frum's Guide to Canadian Universities* (1987).

Calgary isn't at all what I thought it would be. It isn't at all the city our Eastern media present as some latter-day American boomtown. Calgary is a sane, quiet, polite, essentially British North American City. A transplant from some Ontario we've betrayed or sold. One of Leacock's "sunshine towns," set on the Prairies, and come of age as a rising metropolis.

Scott Symons, author, "Calgary" (1979), *Dear Reader: Selected Scott Symons* (1998), edited by Christopher Elson.

Even Calgary, young as it is, has a history. We should be aware that today will be history in the eyes, memories and chronicles of those who will be here long after we have gone.

Jack Peach, commentator, preface, *Days Gone By: Jack Peach on Calgary's Past* (1993).

There can be nothing more ludicrous than a grown man with a paunch teetering around Calgary on the high heels and pointed toes of cowboy boots, attempting to capture some primitive cachet from some distant past.

Allan Fotheringham, columnist, *Fictionary of Facts and Follies* (2001).

CALIFORNIA

Parts of Los Angeles give me the feeling I'm living in a parking lot with neon signs.

Al Waxman, actor, in Laura Berthold Monteros, *The Herald Examiner* (Los Angeles), 26 June 1977.

Los Angeles *is* the apocalyptic landscape, both geologically and socially. There you find a decay of the Western psyche, of that hierarchy of the soul.

Lines from the title song of **Leonard Cohen**'s album *The Future* (1992).

Los Angeles is full of Canadians. According to the Los Angeles chamber of the Academy of Canadian Cinema and Television, L.A. is now the third largest Canadian city.

Lesley Ellen Harris, screenwriter, "Made in L.A.," *The Canadian Forum*, November 1993.

CAMPBELL, KIM

And then there is Kim Campbell, who has an unerring instinct for her own jugular.

Peter C. Newman, author, address, "The Canadian Revolution," Toronto, 30 November 1995, The Empire Club of Canada.

CANADA *See also* Canada & France; Canada & Quebec; Canada & United Kingdom; Canada & United States; Canada & the World; Canadians; Canadians & Americans; Confederation; Dominion; French Canada

The sayd men did moreover certify unto us, that there was the way and beginning of the great river of Hochelaga and ready way to Canada, which river the further it went the narrower it came, even unto Canada.

Jacques Cartier, explorer, journal entry, 26 July 1535, "A Shorte and Briefe Narrative" (1535), *The Principal Navigations, Voyages, Traffiques and Discoveries of the English Nation* (1598), compiled by Richard Hakluyt. This is the first reference in print to the word *Canada*, which in Algonkian means "huts."

The simultaneous creation of a new nationality.

Lord Monck, subsequently appointed first governor general, Throne Speech, Parliament of Canada, Quebec, 19 January 1865. The concept of "a new nationality" (as distinct from the American ideal of "a new nation") originated in 1858 with the Montreal lawyer Alexander Morris, later appointed lieutenant-governor of Manitoba.

I protest against the local Independence man calling himself the only true Canadian. I would retort: "Little he knows of Canada, who only Canada knows." I claim to be an Imperialist not only from the heart, but also from the head, and one of my strongest claims for Imperialism is that I believe it the only means by which there will ever be a real Canadian nation.

W. Wilfred Campbell, poet and imperialist, address, "Imperialism in Canada," Toronto, 23 November 1904, The Empire Club of Canada.

So long Canada has remained to me a geographical fact and not anything representing a national personality with a full revelation of her life. I am afraid my present visit to these shores will hardly help me in vivifying my schoolbook knowledge into a deeper relation.

Rabindranath Tagore, Bengali sage, "Farewell to Canada," 13 April 1929, *Education and Leisure: Addresses Delivered at the Fourth Triennial Conference on Education Held at Victoria and Vancouver, Canada, April 1929* (1929), edited by S.E. Lang.

Get your bags packed, everybody, and put in plenty of woollen kit. I've never been to Canada, but I seem to have heard that the winters there are inclined to be chilly.

Decision of character Major James Bigglesworth in *Biggles Flies North* (1939) in the once-popular British boys' series by Captain **W.E. Johns**. For his sole Canadian adventure, Biggles heads for "Fort Beaver," Mackenzie, North-West Territories, Canada, to clear up difficulties connected with the disappearance of an English pilot and problems with "Arctic Airways."

Nowadays, in fact, a wonderful thing about your country is that there is hardly any part of it where something new and very valuable may not spring to life any day either on the surface of the soil or underneath it. It is a very large field but well worth looking at very carefully.

Winston Churchill, British statesman, radio broadcast from Ottawa, 30 June 1954, in David Dilks, *"The Great Dominion": Winston Churchill in Canada 1900–1954* (2005).

Canada could have enjoyed: / English government, / French culture, / And American know-how. // Instead it ended up with: / English know-how, French government, / And American culture.

Free-verse poem by **John Robert Colombo**, "O Canada" (1965), first published in *The New Romans* (1968), edited by Al Purdy.

The genius of Canada remains essentially a deflationary genius.

Jan Morris, Anglo-Welsh travel writer, "On the Confederation Special," *Travels* (1976).

It is part of the civic genius—part of the Canadian genius, too—to reduce the heroic to the banal.

Jan Morris, Anglo-Welsh travel writer, "Suddenly Saskatoon," *Saturday Night*, July–August 1990.

Canada is distinctly not boring, and it is largely its own fault that the world sees it so.... Canada really is one of the best of all countries—perhaps the best—and that it is boring is only because it says it is.

Jan Morris, Anglo-Welsh travel writer, "In Praise of Canada," *Toronto Star*, 15 June 1992.

The French, the English following, ventured westward from Acadia and the valley of the St. Lawrence in the quest for furs and places to plant their flags. They savaged the Indians, quelled rebellions and threw back American invaders. They never grew to like each other much, yet in the end they stopped shooting and left the key under the mat for dreamers from other lands beyond the sea.

Rae Corelli, newspaperman, "The Tracks of History," *Maclean's*, 6 July 1992.

We flew over Canada of course and this is one of the first areas I saw of Canada. There was blue ice off the coast, this is Labrador. There were other areas too covered by ice and this is how you'd see it in space flight as we travelled from west to east. This is James Bay and, down from the top to the right, is the Moose River in Moosonee and further over the Albany River. When we take all these pictures, the people on the ground make us look good. We had over 3,000 frames from our flight of which 2,700 were taken of the earth. So when we came back we had to have some really smart people figure out where we were. We knew what we were looking at from space because we had a computer telling us where we were, but when we come back that's a different story.

Roberta Bondar, astronaut, address, "The Adventure of Space," Toronto, 22 September 1992, The Empire Club of Canada.

Put bluntly, the nation-state called Canada has become an empty shell of its former self. If you hold Canada to your ear, you can hear the ocean.

John Gray, author, *Lost in North America* (1994).

Too often—as a nation and as individuals—we decry what we lack, instead of celebrating what we already have. Yet to most of the world's troubled citizens, Canada appears blessed with the mandate of heaven.

Peter C. Newman, columnist and author, "Canada Is the Solution, Not the Problem," *Defining Moments: Dispatches from an Unfinished Revolution* (1997).

In a thousand years, Canada won't be the same country it is now, nor will it probably be the same in five hundred, a hundred, fifty or even ten. My own hunch is that Vancouver will eventually evolve into a city state going as far north as Whistler, as far east as the Fraser Canyon and then to the U.S. border.

Douglas Coupland, author, *City of Glass: Douglas Coupland's Vancouver* (2000).

Lately, I often have the strong feeling that my country, Canada, is fading away. We are collectively imagining a different place.

Clive Doucet, Acadian poet, "Farewell to the Place Called Home," *The Globe and Mail*, 15 July 2000.

The country never fought a revolution or a civil war, pioneered no great social or political movement, produced no great world leader and committed no memorable atrocities—as one writer put it, Canada has no Lincolns, no Gettysburgs, and no Gettysburg addresses.

Steven Pearlstein, former Canadian correspondent, *The Washington Post*, "O Canada! A National Swan Song?" *The Washington Post*, 5 September 2000. Reprinted as "The Eternal Question: Will Canada Survive?" in *Toronto Star*, 9 September 2000. Pearlstein ignores the Rebellions of 1837–1838, the Antigonish Movement, the Pugwash Conferences, Greenpeace, and medicare.

For all this, Canada in 2000 is potentially an imagined community of real communities which I would call post-nationalist communities. Each has its distinctive inheritance and outlook, but each is capable of membership in a wider community of shared civic values.

Ramsay Cook, historian, "Canada 2000: Towards a Post-Nationalist Canada," *Cité libre*, fall 2000.

If Canada is already an object of envy around the world, imagine what it would be like when all of us—Francophones, Anglophones, Allophones and Native Peoples—decide to accept one another as we are and finally learn to live together harmoniously.

Guy Bertrand, advocate and lawyer, "Let's Turn Over a New Page," *Cité libre*, fall 2000.

We have been able to manage division, encourage commonality, accept difference, and achieve prosperity, all without bloodshed.

Ken Dryden, hockey personality, lawyer, and author, address, Charles R. Bronfman Lecture in Canadian Studies, University of Ottawa, "The Canadian Way," *Maclean's*, 13 November 2000.

Canada had seemed to me a tolerable society but also without resolution.

Ted Honderich, Grote professor of mind and logic, University College London, born in Baden, Ont., *Philosopher: A Kind of Life* (2001).

Canadians may have it wrong when they focus on the founding nations rather than on the nation they founded, a nation where English and French have accommodated each other for more than two centuries, a nation respected around the world for its fairness and honesty, a nation that has fought many wars but is known for keeping the peace. And now a nation that has proved it is willing to stop hiding behind its borders.

Anthony DePalma, former correspondent for Canada and Mexico, *The New York Times*, *Here: A Biography of the New American Continent* (2001).

I sometimes think of Canada as the first post-modern nation-state, invented 150 years before the idea of post-modernity.

John Ralston Saul, philosopher, "My Canada Includes the North," *The Globe and Mail*, 9 March 2001.

My sense of the Canada of the imagination, as a powerful space between old worlds and new, increased.

Pico Iyer, traveller and writer, "Mongrel Beauties," *Saturday Night*, 31 March 2001.

And so Canada, although you are not my home or native land, we will always share this bond of your unstinting hospitality to people who descended upon you as frightened strangers, and received nothing but solace and solidarity in your embrace of goodness. So Canada, because we beat as one heart, from Evangeline in Louisiana to the intrepid Mr. Sukanen of Moose Jaw, I will stand on guard for thee.

Stephen Jay Gould, zoologist, "An Ode to Human Decency," *The Globe and Mail*, 20 September 2001. Gould and his family had their Milan–New York City flight diverted to Halifax on 11 September 2001 in the aftermath of the World Trade Center disaster.

A plain vanilla place....

Conrad Black, Lord Black of Crossharbour, publisher and historian, describing the blandness of Canada, address, Fraser Institute, Vancouver, 15 November 2001, in Greg Joye, "Black Hails His Own 'Act of Patriotism,'" *The Globe and Mail*, 16 November 2001.

O Canada, as the anthem goes, / scene of my boyhood summers, / you are the pack of Sweet Caporals on the table, / you are the dove-soft train-whistle in the night, / you are the empty chair at the end of the empty dock.

Lines from the poem "Canada," by **Billy Collins**, Poet Laureate of the Library of Congress, found on his website bigsnap.com, 25 June 2002.

Rather, like one of those places whose existence we assume because of a name on a sign above a platform, glimpsed at as our train stops and then rushes on, the word "Canada" awoke no echoes, inspired no images, lent no meaning to my port of destination.

Alberto Manguel, Canadian author, born in Argentina, "Destination Ithaka," *Passages: Welcome Home to Canada* (2002), with preface by Rudyard Griffiths.

Canada is like an intelligent, thirty-five-year-old woman.

Douglas Adams, novelist and humorist, curious statement, *The Salmon of Doubt: Hitchhiking the Galaxy One Last Time* (2002).

The best thing about Canada is that it is not this. It is this and that.

George Bowering, poet, characteristic remark, in Erin Anderssen, "Irreverent Bowering Named Poet Laureate," *The Globe and Mail*, 12 November 2002.

My name is Bono and I am a rock star.... I'm a fan of Canada. The world needs more Canada.

Bono, lead singer with U2, performing at the Liberal Convention, 15 November 2003, in Heather Sokoloff, "'I Believe the World Needs More Canada,'" *National Post*, 15 November 2003.

"What is Canada really like?" she asked, her remark prompted not by the desire for a response but a wish to show she came in peace.

"Canada is knowing where your wallet is," I replied.

Dialogue from **Edward O. Phillips**'s novel *A Voyage on Sunday* (2004).

Canada is a country that works in practice, but not in theory.

Stéphane Dion, Quebec political scientist and Cabinet minister, in Peter C. Newman, *Here Be Dragons: Telling Tales of People, Passion, and Power* (2004).

A place belongs to whoever claims it most ardently. That's why I spent a good deal of my energy proclaiming Canada as my turf.

Peter C. Newman, journalist and memoirist, *Here Be Dragons: Telling Tales of People, Passion, and Power* (2004).

I don't see any cosmic problem in Canada. I'm optimistic. Canada will endure beyond all expectations. The days of staying up all night agonizing are long gone. People will say it's going to hell in a hand basket, and that the politicians are all bad—but really, this is a spectacularly successful country. Canada's a good idea, it's as simple as that. There are some things that are just us. And it's more than just being American.

Keith Spicer, former first Official Languages Commissioner and former chair of Citizens' Forum on Canada's Future, in Roy MacGregor, "This Country," *The Globe and Mail*, 16 November 2004.

Some time, not too long ago, while no one was watching, Canada became the world's most successful country.

John Ibbitson, columnist and author, opening sentence, *The Polite Revolution: Perfecting the Canadian Dream* (2005).

CANADA DAY *See* Holidays: Canada Day

CANADA & FRANCE *See also* Canada; Canada & Quebec; France

But as to merit, I know / For sure, yes, yes, I swear … / The likes of us you will not find / From Paris to Canada, / From Paris to Canada, / From Paris to Canada.

Reference to Canada in lines from the libretto for **Wolfgang A. Mozart**'s opera *Così Fan Tutte* (1790), with Italian lyrics composed by **Lorenzo da Ponte**. The reference appears in Guglielmo's Aria, which is included in Canadian productions and generally dropped from productions elsewhere. The second act of Mozart's next opera, *The Magic Flute* (1791), commences with four notes that recall the opening notes of "O Canada," the national anthem, composed by Calixa Lavallée some 90 years later.

Children of Canada.

Attributed to **Charles de Gaulle**, president of France, by Daniel Poliquin, *In the Name of the Father* (2001), who wrote, "General de Gaulle arrived at Expo 67, opened wide his arms, and pronounced the words we now know so well. Over and over he called us his 'children of Canada.' Very sweet, that Pierre Bourgault would claim thirty years later that he was decolonized in a flash. Guy Bouthillier would say much the same. They were both wrong. The General's declaration would have just the opposite effect. Quebec nationalism would recolonize itself with unprecedented zeal."

I really think that Canada is a country of the 21st century because it incarnates the values of the 21st century—its information, communications, environment and open spaces, its diversity and tolerance.

Jean-Pierre Raffarin, prime minister of France, interviewed before a four-day trip to Ottawa, Montreal, and Quebec City, by Alan Freeman, "French P.M. Prepared to Challenge Status Quo," *The Globe and Mail*, 17 May 2003.

There is enough closeness so that we can understand each other and enough difference that we can learn from each other.

Jean-Pierre Raffarin, prime minister of France, interviewed before a four-day trip to Ottawa, Montreal, and Quebec City, by Alan Freeman,

"French P.M. Prepared to Challenge Status Quo," *The Globe and Mail*, 17 May 2003.

CANADA & QUEBEC *See also* French Canada; French Canadians; Quebec; Referenda on Quebec Sovereignty; Separatism; Sovereignty-Association; Two Solitudes

For your information, Quebec is a province with the longest undefended border in Canada.

Dalton Camp, columnist, *Toronto Star*, 22 January 1976.

All we want is an independent Quebec within a strong and united Canada.

Yvon Deschamps, entertainer, associated with one of his comic routines, in Peter C. Newman, *Maclean's*, 13 November 1978.

A number of Quebecers have often looked at Canada as a threat or a yoke. Canada has often seen Quebec as a dreadful pain in the neck that prevented Canadians to be the Canadians they wanted to be. René Lévesque used to compare the Two Solitudes to two scorpions in a bottle. Let's get the scorpions out of the bottle. They might even learn to live side by side in harmony.

Jacques Parizeau, Quebec Opposition leader, address, "What Does Sovereignty-Association Mean?" Toronto, 11 December 1990, The Empire Club of Canada.

English Canada will not make concessions—and we are not even sure of that—unless it has a knife to its throat.

Léon Dion, constitutional expert, adviser to the Bourassa administration, testimony, Bélanger–Campeau Commission on the future of Quebec, 12 December 1990. He suggested that the knife should be Quebec's threat to English Canada to hold a referendum on independence.

Quebec must stop being coy and accept or reject Canada. Canada will embrace either Quebec or, failing Quebec, the United States. North America will be divided geographically or linguistically.

Conrad Black, publisher, *A Life in Progress* (1993).

People always ask when are we finally going to settle this French–English stuff, this perpetual regional tension? The answer is never. That's not the problem. That's the point.

Gene Allen, history adviser, in Mark Starowicz, "The Death of History," *The Globe and Mail*, 20 September 2000.

I am not only convinced that it has no usefulness, but that it has been harmful. You can't say I'm not being frank here. And it is the result of forty years of reflection that leads me to say this.

Bernard Landry, Quebec premier, interview, referring to the influence of Canada on Quebec, CBC-Radio, 14 March 2001, in Rhéal Séguin, "Federation 'Harmful,' Landry Says," *The Globe and Mail*, 15 March 2001.

Quebec is a nation of seven and a half million people. We are the Latinos of the north. Quebec is a Latin nation.

Bernard Landry, Quebec premier, speech delivered in French, Spanish, and English, anticipating the free-trade conference to be held in Quebec City, 16 April 2001, in Graeme Hamilton, "People's Summit Speech," *National Post*, 17 April 2001.

English Canada is once again at war with Quebec. Since the referendum it dreams of a New Battle of the Plains of Abraham. It dreams to finish with Quebec.

Norman Lester, broadcaster and commentator, *Le Livre Noir du Canada Anglais* (2001), as translated by Graham Fraser, "Quebec Book Stirs Nationalist Plot," *Toronto Star*, 1 December 2001.

In Canada, "French" and "English" are our first names. Our surname is "Canada."

Jean Lesage, Quebec premier, in Roméo Dallaire, *Shake Hands with the Devil: The Failure of Humanity in Rwanda* (2003).

There is no such thing as a best country in the world. Canadians can live in Canada, Italians can live in Italy, and the best country for Quebeckers is Quebec.

Attributed in so many words to **Gilles Duceppe**, Bloc Québécois leader, countering the charge of the party's divisive and exclusionary nature, campaigning in Thetford Mines, Que., in Daniel LeBlanc, "Bloc Excludes English, Minorities, Pettigrew Charges," *The Globe and Mail*, 27 May 2004.

CANADA & UNITED KINGDOM *See also* British Empire; Canada; Colonialism

There is no place in Canadian government for over-washed Englishmen, who are utterly ignorant of the country and full of crochets as all Englishmen are.

Sir John A. Macdonald, first prime minister (1857–1858, 1864, 1867–1873, 1878–1891), in Arthur Herman, *How the Scots Invented the Modern World* (2001). (Herman spells "Macdonald" as "MacDonald.")

Standing there on this little sacred plot of ground which is called the House of Commons, and seeing Lloyd George, Chamberlain and Stanley Baldwin, and the rest—well, there you are. There is the confession of the Toronto boy to you. I felt, "I am in the Big League, boys!"

Beverley Baxter, Canadian-born newspaperman and Member of the British Parliament, address, "From the Heart of Things," Toronto, 9 September 1937, The Empire Club of Canada.

Englishmen were not the most popular people in Canada and advertisements for jobs sometimes brazenly stated "no Englishman need apply." This was the result of an influx of colonially minded Englishmen who came close to sneering at the Canadian way of life and became known as broncos because they were always kicking the Canadians.

Vincent Brome, biographer, *Ernest Jones: Freud's Alter Ego* (1983). He is referring to the period in Toronto in 1908–1913 when the psychiatrist and psychoanalyst Ernest Jones held a professorship in the department of psychiatry, University of Toronto.

A Nation spoke to a Nation, / A Throne sent word to a Throne: / "Daughter am I in my mother's house, / But mistress in my own."

Lines from British author and poet **Rudyard Kipling**'s verse from "Our Lady of the Snows," subtitled "Canadian Preferential Tariff, 1897," published in the London *Times*, 27 April 1897. Canada and its relationship with Great Britain, the "mother country," were given images in the title and these lines, widely relished and subsequently resented.

Therefore, I would end my talk to you with these words and I say this as one who in his affection puts Canada first. To me Canada is my native land and I shall be very unhappy if anything ever severs me from my close association with my own people here, but I say this as a Canadian to Canadians, I urge you to trust the spirit of Britain. I urge you, Gentlemen, to strengthen the spirit of Britain for, believe me, the burden that Britain carries is very great. (Prolonged cheers.)

Beverley Baxter, Canadian-born newspaperman and Member of the British Parliament, address, "From the Heart of Things," Toronto, 9 September 1937, The Empire Club of Canada.

When I travel about Canada, nothing delights me more than to hear England spoken of affectionately as "the Old Country." I notice that on this side of the Atlantic people have a peculiar aptitude for finding words and expressions to describe exactly and vividly some quite familiar object but I have not come across any expression which so accurately reflects the sentiments of those who use it as the expression "the Old Country."

Earl of Athlone, governor general, address, "An Address," Toronto, 20 January 1941, The Empire Club of Canada.

I am told that in the Lester B. Pearson building in Ottawa this tribute to Mr. Pearson appears: "Sooner and better than his contemporaries he had come to understand that the world, for all of its diversity, was one … that no nation, even the most powerful, could escape a common creaturehood and a common peril." This is one of the challenges of our time, and it is a challenge which we in Canada and Britain can and shall meet. The other challenge, perhaps an even greater one, is to keep faith with the liberties and freedoms our forefathers won.

Margaret Thatcher, U.K. Opposition leader, address, "The Heirs of Runnymede," Toronto, 25 September 1975, The Empire Club of Canada.

Canada is a country which excites the imagination of the British people. There are few in Britain who do not have relatives or friends who have come to live here.

James Callaghan, prime minister of Great Britain, address, "Britain Today," Toronto, 14 September 1976, The Empire Club of Canada.

Without the French, English Canadians would have to accept that profound distinctions with the United States do not exist and that we should cease trying to invent them.

Conrad Black, publisher, *A Life in Progress* (1993).

For the past half century, though, Canada's efforts to assume its place in the world as an important and independent nation required that it separate itself from the United Kingdom—at least, until those efforts more urgently required that it separate itself from the United States.

Calvin Trillin, essayist, "Paper Baron," *The New Yorker*, 17 December 2001.

As Yann Martel once put it, our experiment in becoming one of the world's great multicultural hotels continues to be working. There are worse fates, no doubt, than evolving into a confederation of shopping centres next door to Holiday Inns.

Michael Bliss, historian and columnist, writing more in sorrow than in anger, "A Country Going to Pieces," *National Post*, 22 October 2004.

CANADA & UNITED STATES *See also* Border, Canada–United States; Canada

If today he should choose to say he thinks it necessary to invade Canada to prevent the British from invading us, how could you stop him? You may say to him, "I see no probability of the British invading us," but he would say to you, "I see it if you don't."

Abraham Lincoln, later U.S. president, objecting to President James Polk's planned invasion of Mexico, 1848, in Ed Finn, "Hail Caesar!" *The CCPA Monitor*, February 2003.

The day of annexation to the United States is past. Our future lies elsewhere. Be it said without concealment and without bitterness. They have chosen their lot; we have chosen ours. Let us go our separate ways in peace. Let them still keep their perennial Independence Day, with its fulminating fireworks and its Yankee Doodle. We keep our Magna Carta and our rough-and-ready Rule Britannia, shouting as lustily as they! The propaganda of Annexation is dead. Citizens we want, indeed, but not the prophets of an alien gospel.

Stephen Leacock, economist and humorist, address, "Education and Empire Unity," Toronto, 19 March 1907, The Empire Club of Canada.

I see no argument for the union of Canada with the United States. There is excellent feeling between the two countries, but they could no more join at this period of their history than a great oak could combine with a well-rooted pine to make one tree.

Sir Arthur Conan Doyle, author and traveller, following his 1914 tour of the United States and Canada, based on articles published in *Cornhill* magazine the following year, collected by Christopher Redmond, *Western Wanderings* (1994).

We share common values from thc past, a common defence line at present, and common aspirations for the future, and indeed the future of all mankind. Geography has made us neighbours. History has made us friends. Economics has made us partners. And necessity has made us allies. Those whom nature hath so joined together, let no man put asunder. What unites us is far greater than what divides us.

John F. Kennedy, U.S. president, address, joint sitting, Senate and the House of Commons, 17 May 1961.

Canada is generally referred to as "America" by my fellow countrymen, back in Bulgaria, implying by this the United States; and only when I came to Canada and lived here awhile did I realize how right my fellow countrymen were in their mistaken identification of Canada and the United States.

Nikola Roussanoff, Bulgarian-born, Toronto-based teacher and writer since 1956, observation made in December 1976.

You speak first, my friend, because if you speak first I might be able to agree with you. But if I speak first, you would be compelled to disagree.

Dean Rusk, U.S. Secretary of State (1961–1969), suggesting to Paul Martin Sr. that this was the Canadian way of conversing, in Drew Fagan, "Home and Abroad," *The Globe and Mail*, 25 March 2003.

Living next to you is in some ways like sleeping with an elephant. No matter how friendly and even-tempered the beast, one is affected by every twitch and grunt.

Pierre Elliott Trudeau, prime minister, speech, National Press Club, Washington, D.C., 25 March 1969. Lawrence Martin in *The Presidents and the Prime Ministers* (1982) attributed authorship of the speech and the remark to Trudeau's adviser Ivan Head.

Canada is an almost perfect illustration of the workings of the new imperialism. She is well on the way to becoming a political, economic and cultural colony of the greatest of these modern empires, the United States. Her fate may be a portent for the future of the world. If she roused herself and took the lead in a movement of national self-assertion by the smaller states, she could not only break the monolithic front which North America now presents to the world, but she might also help to inspire other dependent nations to recover their independence from other imperial masters. It is a great role, upon which the fate of humanity may hang; but the tragic fact is that Canada may not be strong enough to play it.

Donald G. Creighton, historian, address, "Coming Defeat of Canadian Nationalism," Toronto, 16 November 1970, The Empire Club of Canada.

As J.K. Galbraith said not long ago in Toronto, the only way to get away from the influence of the American economy would be to float our half of the continent off somewhere else.

Robert M. MacIntosh, general manager, Bank of Nova Scotia, debate, "Canadian Independence," Toronto, 3 February 1972, The Empire Club of Canada.

Quebec is part of Canada as much as a cat in the mouth of a crocodile is part of the crocodile.

Yves Beauchemain, novelist, quoted by Alberto Manguel in *Books in Canada*, May 1983.

Think of your children pledging allegiance to the Maple Leaf. Mayonnaise on everything. Winter eleven months of the year. Anne Murray—all day, every day. The Canadians. They walk among us. William Shatner. Michael J. Fox. Monty Hall. Mike Myers. Alex Trebek. All of them Canadians. All of them here.

Despairing thoughts of the U.S. president (played by Alan Alda) in the movie *Canadian Bacon* (1994), written and directed by **Michael Moore**. To revive their economy, the Americans launch a Cold War on Canada, and so suffer the consequences.

On the fifth or sixth try, I worded the question differently: "Excuse me, do you have a minute for Canadian television?"

"You have a TV station in Canada? Sure, what do you want to know?"

Rick Mercer, television comedian, "Talking about *Talking to Americans*," *Elm Street*, February–March 2001. He is explaining the origins of his popular TV series *Talking to*

Americans in an interview in Washington, D.C., in 1998.

If the United States is the indispensable nation, I like to think of Canada as the value-added nation. Human security is the application abroad of the talents of accommodation, tolerance and mutual respect—talents that we have used to build a strong, unified country where all Canadians can thrive and prosper.

Lloyd Axworthy, minister of Foreign Affairs, address, "Canada's Actions against Land Mines," Toronto, 28 June 1999, The Empire Club of Canada.

The core problem with the U.S.-Canadian relationship, of course, is that the U.S. doesn't know there is a problem. The U.S. barely knows there's a Canada.

Bruce McCall, humorist and cartoonist for *The New Yorker*, born in Simcoe, Ont., address in Toronto, Writers' Trust, *Toronto Star*, 3 June 2000.

Several years ago, when Christopher Wren was the *New York Times*' correspondent in Canada, he found himself on a television panel, being roundly criticized for the lack of interest that the American media show in Canada.

"That's not true at all—we're very interested in Canada," he said, adding mischievously: "It's just the first hundred miles we're not very interested in."

Graham Fraser, columnist, "Jean Malaurie's Arctic Obsession," *Toronto Star*, 27 August 2000.

I left Canada at eighteen so I couldn't vote there.... I have an immigrant's love for the country.... Canada is a little neater but I like it messy.

Michael J. Fox, Canadian-born Hollywood actor, on becoming a U.S. citizen (in order to vote in the upcoming U.S. elections), interviewed in *George* magazine, in *Toronto Star*, 3 October 2000.

Canada needs to fulfill the role of a sanctuary. When things get really bad in the States, you can always go north to Canada.

Bill Bryson, American travel writer, interviewed in *The Globe and Mail*, 9 December 2000.

Canadians know almost everything there is to know about America. We're inundated with every sordid little detail about their culture. Americans know nothing about Canada. Granted, none of us expect the elephant to be an expert on the mouse, but a little bit of knowledge can only help. In my own little way I'm trying to fix that.

Rick Mercer, television comedian, "Talking about *Talking to Americans*," *Elm Street*, February–March 2001.

To the Americans, and increasingly to ourselves, we have become not so much a great nation as a vague necklace of northern provinces, the prosperous and peaceful northern fringe of the continent.

Michael Bliss, historian and columnist, "Sept. 11: The End of Canadian Nationalism," *National Post*, 29 September 2001.

The path of U.S. foreign policy is soaked in blood.

Sunera Thobani, academic, speech, Women's Resistance Conference, Ottawa, 15 October 2001, "Thobani 'Rant' Called Hateful," quoted by Mary Vallis and Mark Hume, *National Post*, 17 October 2001.

We do not bear the burden of our neighbours to the south. They have a mixed blessing. And whether they choose it or not, they have either to act as custodian or policeman or they have to retreat into their massive shell. We don't have that. The idea of Canada is that we are not here to rule but I do think, however, that we are here to exemplify.

Rex Murphy, broadcaster, address, "Canada after September 11," Toronto, 6 December 2001, The Empire Club of Canada.

Homer: Why should we leave America to visit America junior?

Marg: It's clean and bland.

Dialogue between two characters on the TV special of *The Simpsons* titled "The Bart

Wants What It Wants," aired on Global TV, 17 February 2002. Homer visits Canada in the episode written by Tim Long, formerly of Exeter, Ont., and Joel Cohen, a native of Calgary, Alta.

More people live in Illinois, Michigan and Ohio combined than in Canada. Imagine if you told these three states that they had to protect everything north of the 49th parallel, almost right up to the North Pole, and they had to do so using only their own economies, with no subsidization. They'd obviously call you nuts, and yet this is exactly what Canada has to do.

Douglas Coupland, novelist and essayist, "Strong and Free," *Maclean's*, 25 November 2002.

At the most basic level—the level of our values, the feelings and beliefs that inform our understanding of and interaction with the world around us—Canadians and Americans are markedly different, and are becoming more so.

Michael Adams, consultant, *Fire and Ice: The United States, Canada and the Myth of Converging Values* (2003), with Amy Langstaff and David Jamieson.

Those tin-pot bureaucrats in the State Department are fools. Where do they want red-blooded Americans to travel? Canada? You ever been to Canada? A bunch of hosers skating on the ice and whizzing in the snow after eating Tim Hortons.

Sentiments attributed to **Gordon Bethune**, CEO, Continental Airlines, in a satiric column written and disseminated by travel business columnist Joe Brancatelli on his website, "Joe Sent Me: The Brancatelli File," 27 February 2003. It follows the U.S. State Department's issuing of a travel advisory against unnecessary air travel before the invasion of Iraq.

Canada can't get too far from the United States, but it shouldn't get too close either.

John Manley, Liberal Cabinet minister, in Peter McKenna, "Martin Foreign Policy: Like Father, Like Son," *The Globe and Mail*, 12 May 2003.

One of the besetting sins of Americans is that they don't seem to think that any place outside the United States is totally real; their curiosity about Canada seems almost nonexistent.

Jane Jacobs, urban planning critic, *Dark Age Ahead* (2004).

America is not an elephant. For one thing, elephants never forget, whereas Americans don't really know much to begin with. Ninety per cent of them can't pick out their hometown on an unmarked map. We're bigger than they are and we're on top. If we were in prison, they'd be our bitch.

Rick Mercer, political satirist, CBC-TV's *This Hour Has 22 Minutes*, November 1996, in Jonathon Gatehouse, "Rick's Shtick," *Maclean's*, 16 February 2004.

Thank God for Canadians. They're just like us, only better. They like us. They really do. They just wish we'd read a little more.

Michael Moore, documentary filmmaker, address, Campaign for America's Future, Boston, in Jeffrey Simpson, "There's a Problem, and It's Called Nader," *The Globe and Mail*, 28 July 2004.

One tries to explain that "Who cares what the rest of the world thinks?" is a common American reaction, leaving the poor Canadians to quietly mutter, "Oh dear."

Molly Ivens, U.S. author and columnist, "Tough Sledding in the North," *The CCPA Monitor*, October 2004.

Canada is a very tolerant version of the U.S. It's beautiful, big and by outward appearances as fast-moving as the U.S. But you can whisper the word "liberal" without being strung up.

Roddy Doyle, Irish novelist, interviewed in Winnipeg, "Doyle's Wry Words on Canada," *Toronto Star*, 2 October 2004.

I have a strong feeling that well-being—Canadian or American—is most strongly indicated by the balance between public achievement and private development. The Canadian balance is better than that in the

United States, and there shouldn't be any doubt on that point.

John Kenneth Galbraith, Ontario-born economist and author, interviewed by Shawn McCarthy, "Unmitigated Galbraith," *The Globe and Mail*, 19 February 2005.

Canadian-American relations are to 21st century Canadian politics what Quebec-Canada relations were in the 20th century. That also means that the distinction between foreign and domestic policy has all but collapsed: Everything is "intermestic."

Michael Ignatieff, commentator, in Anne Dawson, "Human Rights Prof Has Great Canadian Genes," *National Post*, 3 March 2005.

I grew up in South Canada—Detroit.

Daniel Okrent, ombudsman, *The New York Times*, interviewed by Michael Enright, CBC Radio's "Sunday Morning," 6 March 2005.

CANADA & THE WORLD *See also*

Canada; Foreign Aid; Foreign Affairs; International Affairs; United Nations; World

Everything one reads today about international affairs discusses over and over again the role of Canada, the varied important roles played by the Middle Powers ... the place where Canada can do something that the United States can't or the United Kingdom can't or Australia can't, and we are all of us who pay any attention to international relations very sensible of Canada's strategic position.

Margaret Mead, ethnologist, address, "How Fast Can Man Change," Toronto, 18 April 1957, The Empire Club of Canada.

If Canada's so great, how come so few people live there? There's enough space in Canada for every single human being on earth, as long as no one wants to lie down, but the population density is only eight per square mile. There are almost 100 times as many Israelis in a given space ... which proves that, if so many people live here, Israel is more livable.

Sam Orbaum, Montreal-born columnist, "I'd Rather Live in Israel," *The Jerusalem Post Magazine*, 13 July 2001.

The land of milk and honey, also the land of deodorant and toiletry ... of prosperity, house, car, CD player, computer, clean air, snow, lakes, mountains in abundance.

Evocation of Canada by a Bombay Parsi in Bombay-born Canadian novelist **Rohinton Mistry**'s novel *Family Matters* (2002), reviewed by John Updike, "Home Care," *The New Yorker*, 30 September 2002. The editors titled the review on the cover "An Indian Tolstoy?"

We like to think we're perceived as a principled middle power. In truth, we're widely seen as woolly-headed moralizers.

Norman Spector, columnist and former diplomat, "Canada's Global Decline," *Ottawa Citizen*, 15 March 2003.

Would anyone notice if Canada disappeared?

Question asked on the cover of *Time Canada*, introducing its lead article "Toward a Canadian Identity," as gleefully noted in an editorial in the *National Post*, 24 May 2003.

CANADIAN ALLIANCE *See also*

Conservative Party of Canada; Political Parties; Reform Party

This is a new century, this is a new party, it's a new day for Canada.

Stockwell Day, former treasurer of Alberta, elected leader of the newly formed Canadian Alliance, and leader of the Official Opposition, acceptance speech, Toronto, 8 July 2000, in Tim Harper, *Toronto Star*, 9 July 2000.

Given that this will be the Alliance's first election, I suggest to you it is building upon a successful Western populist base, that they should be successful in every part of the country, except for the Maritimes, for a real simple reason. People in the eastern provinces believe in handouts and "Give me a cheque for doing nothing." They don't want to do what all our ancestors did, and that was work for a living and go to where the jobs are. So probably the Alliance won't go over as well there.

John Mykytyshyn, pollster, member of the Alliance's National Council, slur on the Maritime work ethic made at a conference on campaigns and elections, Vancouver, 11 August 2000, reproduced in *The Globe and Mail*, 12 August 2000. Three days following the gaffe, Mykytyshyn apologized "for a poor choice of words and any misunderstanding or hurt feelings," and Alliance leader Stockwell Day, disavowing the slur, dropped Mykytyshyn from the National Council, as noted by Campbell Clark and Brian Laghi, *The Globe and Mail*, 15 August 2000.

How can a group of politicians expect Canadians to trust them to bring unity to this nation if they cannot unify themselves?

Brian Mulroney, former prime minister, speech referring to divisions within the Canadian Alliance, Conservative fundraising dinner, Montreal, 23 May 2001, quoted in *The Globe and Mail*, 24 May 2001.

The Reform Party in pantyhose.

Characterization of the Canadian Alliance Party, formerly the Reform Party of Canada, attributed to former Prime Minister **Brian Mulroney**, as noted by Brian Hutchinson, "Cue for Treason," *Saturday Night*, 7 July 2001.

I'm an English teacher. The word *dénouement* comes to mind.

Deborah Grey, Member of Parliament, leading member of the Canadian Alliance Party, expressing her thoughts on her expulsion from the party for criticizing its leader, Stockwell Day, interview on CBC Radio, 14 December 2001.

I think newly elected Alliance leader Stephen Harper, 42, will become Canada's prime minister one day. What's more, I think he'll be a good prime minister.

George Jonas, columnist and prophet, "Harper's Flaws May Prove an Asset," *National Post*, 22 April 2002.

No truck or trade with the morticians of the Alliance Party.

John Crosbie, former Conservative Cabinet minister, address, federal party meeting, Ottawa, 24 August 2002, in Carol Goar, "Glorious, Irrational Solitude," *Toronto Star*, 31 August 2002. The movement to "unite the right" was dismissed in words that recall how continentalism was rejected during the 1911 election: "No truck or trade with the Yankees."

CANADIAN ARMED FORCES *See also* Defence; Peacekeeping; Soldiers; Torture; War

There is a story in my book about a manoeuvre, again in New Brunswick, where there was this army cadet corps. The cadets did not have enough rifles to pass around so they used broomsticks for this particular manoeuvre. At one point though one of the soldiers pointed a broomstick at another and said: "Bang, bang, you're dead." And the other said, "No, no, I'm not, I'm a tank."

Peter C. Newman, author, referring to his book *The Canadian Revolution*, address, "The Canadian Revolution," Toronto, 30 November 1995, The Empire Club of Canada.

It's all very well for the Americans to spend a fortune on defence, they have to defend the free world from terrorism. We only have to defend our own smugness.

Attributed to "a retired Canadian officer" after the tabling of the federal budget on 10 December 2001, according to David Warren, "G.I. Joe Has Never Looked Better," *National Post*, 12 December 2001.

The one certainty in the world of uncertainty is that we do not know the future. The one constant is that whatever it holds, we will require well-equipped professional soldiers, sailors, and airmen. We will certainly require broad-based reserve forces, trained and equipped for a variety of roles, forming our mobilization base and constituting Canada's primary homeland defence.

J.L. Granatstein, historian, "Defence Free-loading Imperils Sovereignty," *National Post*, 22 February 2002.

I regret to say that Canadians are a people who ordinarily expect someone else to do the fighting for us—first France, then Britain, and now the United States. Protected by three oceans and linked with great powers, except in the two world wars and in the unique decades of the early Cold War, Canadians have always been prepared to let someone else make the strategic decisions, pay most of the bills, and do most of the dying. This, by definition, is a colonial attitude. It is an attitude that reflects a weak sense of self, a weak sense of sovereignty, a weak sense of our national interests.

J.L. Granatstein, historian, "Defence Free-loading Imperils Sovereignty," *National Post,* 22 February 2002.

The military is Canada's antique road show.

Adapted from a remark made by **Colin Kenny**, senator, head of a senate committee critical of federal funding of the Armed Forces, as noted by Sheldon Alberts, "Pull Troops Back from Abroad, Say Senators," *National Post,* 13 November 2002.

Gen. MacKenzie said he wished that when the Canadian Forces show up on the horizon, the international commander would say, "Thank God, here come the Canadians." But he said that commander is more like to say, "Here comes a pain in the ass that is going to borrow vehicles, borrow ammunition and borrow food within the first twenty-four hours they are on the ground."

Hugh Winsor, columnist, "The Power Game," *The Globe and Mail,* 10 March 2003, referring to the views of retired Major General Lewis MacKenzie as expressed at a defence conference.

In certain ways the U.S. military may be going down a path that the C.F. have already trodden. There is evidence that American military culture is being transformed in a fashion that could lead to the U.S. forces becoming Canadianized. As they have been downsized, professionalized, and made more subject to more civilian control, American forces have exhibited some of the characteristics of their Canadian cousins.

Allan D. English, research fellow, Canadian Forces Leadership Institute, *Understanding Military Culture: A Canadian Perspective* (2004).

What we require, in effect, are military intellectuals, not just technicians of death.

J.L. Granatstein, historian, "We Must Begin Rebuilding Our Military—Now," *National Post,* 7 February 2004.

Instead of disarming our citizens, we will rearm our military.

Stephen Harper, Conservative Party leader, press conference, Ottawa, 23 May 2004, campaigning, Brockville, Ont., in Brian Laghi, "Federal Election 2004," *The Globe and Mail,* 24 May 2004.

You could fit the entire Canadian army on a football field and still have room for the game.

Caspar Weinberger, former U.S. defence secretary, in Lawrence Martin, "Beware the Day of Reckoning," *The Globe and Mail,* 23 December 2004.

Boy Scouts with guns.

Attributed to former Prime Minister **Jean Chrétien** as a "famous quip" by Paul Koring, "Military Cost-saving Doesn't Cut It in the Big, Bad World," *The Globe and Mail,* 28 January 2005.

CANADIAN BROADCASTING CORPORATION *See also* Broadcasting; Radio; Television

If I were in the middle of, let's say, the Indian Ocean, with no program title or announcer's name or station-break to guide me, I believe I could tell a CBC radio broadcast from any British, U.S., Australian, or probably other Canadian offering, no matter which accent the CBC program happened to have. CBC Radio has a distinctive and unmistakable personality: it hangs loose. If I say non-commercial or non-professional, probably no one will understand that I mean to praise: so I'm back to people. CBC voices may sound British- or French-accented or U.S. or Maritime or Albertan or Upper Canada College: but they sound like people, instead of announcers or experts or entertainers, or other kinds of media-machines.

Judith Merril, science-fiction personality, writing in 1968, *Better to Have Loved: The Life of Judith Merril* (2002), with Emily Pohl-Weary.

The CBC is the backbone and heart of Canadian broadcasting. It's a literal fact, I believe, that without the CBC for the past 50-odd years there would not be a Canada—or at least a Canada we could recognize. With or without the words "national unity" in the Broadcasting Act, national unity is what the CBC inevitably promotes just by being itself at its best, the mirror and echo-chamber of Canada. Even before Lorne Greene and Roger Baulu said: "Here is the CBC news" and "*Voici les nouvelles de Radio-Canada*" in the Second World War, the CBC became synonymous with the idea and ideal of Canada, coast to coast, border to Arctic, and by short-wave around the world. No other broadcaster will or can be what the CBC must be.

Keith Spicer, chair, Canadian Radio-television and Telecommunications Commission, address, "Broadcasting in the Nineties," Toronto, 24 May 1990, The Empire Club of Canada.

I've always said the CBC is like Scotch and olives. You'll like it when you're ready for it.

Arthur Black, broadcaster and author, interviewed by Alexandra Gill, "Fade to Black," *The Globe and Mail*, 26 June 2002.

When CNN proclaims that Armageddon has arrived, it will be helpful to have the CBC.

Michael Valpy, columnist, "The End Is Near, but Only South of the Border," *The Globe and Mail*, 26 April 2003.

CANADIAN ENGLISH *See also* Accent; Language; Speech

Last night, I cashed my pogey and went to buy a mickey of C.C. at the beer parlour, but my skidoo got stuck in the muskeg on my way back to the duplex. I was trying to deke out a deer, you see. Damn chinook, melted everything. And then a Mountie snuck up behind me in a ghost car and gave me an impaired. I was S.O.L., sitting there dressed only in my Stanfields and a toque at the time. And the Mountie, he's all chippy and everything, calling me a "shit disturber" and whatnot. What could I say, except "Chimo!"

William Ferguson and **Ian Ferguson**, writers, *How to Be a Canadian (Even if You Are One)* (2001). "If the person you are talking to nods sympathetically, they're one of us. If, however, they stare at you with blank incomprehension, they are not a real Canadian. Have them reported to the authorities at once."

CANADIAN IDENTITY *See also* Identities

I find when I stand on a street in a Canadian city and look across the street, it couldn't be anywhere but Canada, but how can I prove it? If you take any item in the picture—the front gate or the hedge or the shape of the windows, you could find those in other countries but there is something about the way things are put together that is Canadian. It is a subtle aspect of the pattern rather than any grossly recognizable thing.

Margaret Mead, ethnologist, address, "How Fast Can Man Change," Toronto, 18 April 1957, The Empire Club of Canada.

The huge advantage of Canada is its backwardness.

Attributed to **Marshall McLuhan**, media philosopher, before the emergence of Pierre Elliott Trudeau on the federal political scene in 1968.

The English Canadian is a little like one of those land mines left over from the Second World War, which still turn up from time to time. No trouble if you don't kick it too hard. But like the mine we go off with a considerable bang if detonated. Left alone we tick quietly away, submerged and inoffensive.

Thoughts of an English-speaking Montrealer in **Edward O. Phillips**'s novel *Sunday's Child* (1981).

Canada is the largest country in the world that doesn't exist.

Richard Rodriguez, U.S. social commentator of Mexican-Indian background, interviewed by Neil Bissoondath, *Markings*, TVOntario, 3 July 1995.

Being Canadian is not a nationality. If somebody says they're Swedish or Japanese they define themselves. But being Canadian is an act of faith, something very different, because it is full of potentials that are as yet unrealized.

Peter C. Newman, author, address, "The Canadian Revolution," Toronto, 30 November 1995, The Empire Club of Canada.

We went to a very good restaurant and had a fine dinner, and had a wonderful debate with the professors as to which country was the most boring—Canada or Sweden? They insisted that Sweden, with its longer history, was undoubtedly the winner, but Brenda and I insisted that in Canada we worked harder at being boring and enjoyed worldwide success. It was one of the most delightful evenings I have ever spent, and the professors were certainly among the least boring people I have met—witty and merry. We all got a bit drunk.

Robertson Davies, man of letters, referring to "a marvellous day in Uppsala," Sweden, letter, April 1988, *For Your Eye Alone: Letters, 1976–1995* (1999).

The genius of Canada remains essentially a deflationary genius.

Jan Morris, Anglo-Welsh travel writer, "On the Confederation Special," *Travels* (1976). This astute statement is as true today as it was when it was made three decades ago. For Morris's kindred observations, see "Canadianism" in *John Robert Colombo's Famous Lasting Words* (2000).

We have a rather hazy one of Canada, to be honest, that keeps changing. There used to be this image of a Mountie riding around Jasper or Banff. Now I guess cities like Toronto give us a different image.

Kazuo Ishiguro, English novelist of Japanese descent, who first visited Alberta as a hitchhiker in 1974, commenting on the national image in England today, interviewed by Philip Marchand, "Memories of Shanghai Fuel Intriguing Mystery," *Toronto Star*, 20 May 2000.

The Canadian search for identity has for some decades placed us in chains. To attain a positive and creative nationalism, Canadians need to question the myths that are suffocating the country.

Alain Dubuc, editorialist for *La Presse*, LaFontaine-Baldwin Lecture, published in *The Globe and Mail*, 10 March 2001.

Canadians have often been cold, but not, Pierre Trudeau aside, cool.

Adam Gopnik, columnist, "There Is No End to the Kick-ass Canucks," *National Post*, 2 March 2002.

Tricultural at birth and bilingual to this day, Canada has had to imagine identities protean enough to stretch across five and a half time zones and to accommodate a province constantly negotiating for secession.

Pico Iyer, traveller and essayist, "The Last Refuge," *Harper's Magazine*, June 2002.

More and more Canadians will have dual identities, as both a Canadian citizen and as a member of this or that ethnic group with cultural and often other connections to a "home" country.

Richard Gwyn, columnist, "Being Canadian Is a Work Forever in Progress," *Toronto Star*, 25 March 2005.

CANADIAN LITERATURE *See also* Writers & Writing

For as Earl Grey said when he was Governor General of this Dominion: "Canada has been too busy writing her history with the gun and the axe and the plough to bother about writing it with the pen." Or, to quote his exact words when speaking of Canadians: "Their energies are so much absorbed in this task that it would be unreasonable to expect them to be in the van of movements which aim at the realization of the higher and nobler life."

Arthur Stringer, novelist, address, "The Interpreters of Canada," Toronto, 7 April 1932, The Empire Club of Canada.

I cannot consider that my fellow authors in Canada have shown a proper sense of the gravity of the prosecution to which I have been subjected.

H.G. Wells, English author, letter to Howard Angus Kennedy of the Canadian Authors' Association, 5 December 1932. The CAA had asked Wells to attend its annual convention in "the mother country." Shaw and other notables appeared, but not Wells, who complained that Canadian authors and academics served as appeal witnesses for Florence Deeks, the Toronto spinster who charged Wells with plagiarism with respect to *The Outline of History*, as noted by A.B. McKillop, *The Spinster and the Prophet: Florence Deeks, H.G. Wells, and the Mystery of the Purloined Past* (2000).

Opvarts and at ham, or this ogry Osler will oxmaul us all, sayd he....

Baffling reference to Sir William Osler, renowned and respected Canadian-born physician and surgeon, in **James Joyce**'s literary work *Finnegans Wake* (1939). Osler is the sole Canadian to be mentioned in this omnibus of allusions.

Stick a pin in Canadian literature at random, and nine times out of ten you'll find a victim.

Margaret Atwood, author, *Survival: A Thematic Guide to Canadian Literature* (1972).

Nothing published in Canada before 1945 is worth reading.

Attributed to **John Metcalf**, editor and critic, by Greg Ioannou and Lynne Missen, introduction, *Shivers: An Anthology of Canadian Ghost Stories* (1990).

There is a young French Canadian I know whose brain is seething with just such thoughts. He smells of genius a mile off.... He can write in the tone of a sage, a poet, a madman, or like "Jesus the Second." In one letter he will lift me to the heavens, in the next crush me like a worm.

Henry Miller, American author, *Big Sur and the Oranges of Hieronymous Bosch* (1957). Miller is writing about Gérard Robitaille, the French-Canadian fiction writer and memoirist who served as Miller's secretary first in Paris and then in Big Sur, California.

My wish for the reader of this anthology is that he or she will take away from these pages the image of Canada as a vast sheet of paper with only a few words printed near the top. It is up to the present and future generations to add their own words to these few words, to create works of the literary imagination that are worthy of the vigour and variety of the land and its people.

John Robert Colombo, author, foreword, *Krystal Garden / Kristálykert* (2001), a bilingual (English–Hungarian) anthology of Canadian poetry, edited by Jon Tarnoc and Katalin Thury.

These days, in fact, Canadian literature seems to be enjoying an astonishing resurgence, largely because it's written by newcomers from all the corners of the world, finding themselves, in Canada, surrounded by people from the other three corners, and trying to work out what community can mean when the street is full of strangers.

Pico Iyer, traveller and writer, "Mongrel Beauties," *Saturday Night*, 31 March 2001.

I read this phrase years ago, that Canada was a young country born into the old age of the world; as such, it has a young literature and there is nothing wrong about being young.

Alistair MacLeod, novelist, theme of his acceptance speech, IMPAC Dublin Literary Award, interviewed by Judy Stoffman, "No Great Mischief," *Toronto Star*, 16 June 2001.

The Frankfurt Book Fair has recently been overrun with Koreans and Indians who write in English (the best English novelist in the world is not British at all, but a Mahogany who lives in snowy Toronto and writes of Bombay). Inevitably, the pale conclusion is that brown writers move "between" cultures. I resist "between"; I prefer "among" or "because of." You keep the handicap.

Richard Rodriguez, American commentator, *Brown: The Last Discovery of America* (2002).

The author Rodriguez does not name is the Bombay-born novelist Rohinton Mistry.

It's a vast country, so that inspires you. It's also the greatest hotel on Earth: It welcomes people from everywhere. It's a good country to write from because in many ways Canada is the world.

Yann Martel, novelist, recipient of the 2002 Booker Prize for *The Life of Pi* (2001), acceptance speech, British Library, London, 22 October 2002, in Michael Higgins, *The Globe and Mail*, 23 October 2002.

CANADIANS *See also* Canada; Canadians & Americans; Canadians & the World

There are indeed people who lack a developed persona—"Canadians who know not Europe's sham politeness"—blundering from one social solecism to the next, perfectly harmless and innocent, soulful bores or appealing children, or, if they are women, spectral Cassandras dreaded for their tactlessness, eternally misunderstood, never knowing what they are about, always taking forgiveness for granted, blind to the world, hopeless dreamers. From them we can see how a neglected persona works, and what one must do to remedy the evil.

C.G. Jung, Swiss psychologist, "The Relations between the Ego and the Unconscious" (1916), *Two Essays on Analytic Psychology* (1966), translated from the German by R.F.C. Hull. This is the single most insightful analysis of the Canadian psyche ever penned. It captures national "do-goodism," United Church–basement mentality, borrowing, as it does, the quoted words from the poem "*Der Wilde*" (The Wild One), composed by the German poet Johann Gottfried Seume, who, impressed by the Hessians, served as a British soldier in British North America in the 1780s. The poem, familiar to Europeans but not to North Americans, first appeared in Seume's *Sämmutliche Werke* (1839). It records the thoughtless ingratitude of a European whose life is selflessly saved by one of the Native people.

I remember a tale that has been going around London. A member of one of the clubs there came in with one or two Canadian friends. A little group were sitting at the table, and they invited this member and his Canadian friends to come and have a cup of coffee and cigar with them, which they had, and after they had left, one of the Londoners remarked, "You can always tell a Canadian, can't you?" "Yes," said another, "but you can't tell him much." (Great laughter.) I feel very conscious of that.

Lord Leverhulme, British manufacturer, address, "Education and Commerce," Toronto, 4 December 1919, The Empire Club of Canada.

I don't believe there is such a thing as a Canadian type. We are neither predominantly fair nor dark. We are above the average in height but we are not sons of Anak. There is no distinguishing feature which marks a Canadian for what he is at first glance, a special kind of nose, a recognizable jaw, an exclusive cut of jib generally. When you find yourself in a group exclusively Canadian, nevertheless, you realize the fact. I sometimes attend meetings of the Canadian Society in New York and I am conscious instantly of a racial solidarity. It may not be a physical matter at all. It may instead be similarity of training, of thought and belief and tradition.

Thomas B. Costain, novelist, address, "A Glance at the Future," Toronto, 8 May 1951, The Empire Club of Canada.

A Canadian is what you are when you're not something else.

Attributed to **Max Ferguson**, radio personality in the 1960s.

What is it the Canadian wants to protect? ... He always called him that bloody Canadian, but bloody wasn't the word he used—if you know what I mean.

References to a Canadian murderer of English background (played by Kirk Douglas) in the movie *The List of Adrian Messenger* (1963), directed by John Huston, based on the mystery story written in 1960 by **Philip MacDonald**.

As Canadian as possible—under the circumstances.

Heather Scott, radio listener, who won the CBC Radio contest to complete the statement "As Canadian as possible ..." The contest was held in the early 1960s, and Peter Gzowski hosted it; see his *This Country in the Morning* (1974).

It should be obvious enough that we are a northern people whose culture derives from Europe and whose primary political and economic influence is from the United States.

Robertson Davies, man of letters, letter, 31 January 1977, *For Your Eye Alone: Letters, 1976–1995* (1999).

I am proud to be a Newfoundlander. I'm proud of being part Nova Scotian. I'm proud of my roots in Quebec, and I'm proud of the fact that I have lived most of my life in the province of Ontario. My pride in all these things is a part of my pride in being a Canadian. All these local traditions are subsumed in being a Canadian and in the Canadian tradition.

Eugene Forsey, constitutional specialist, address, "Canada, Quebec, and the Constitution," Toronto, 28 April 1977, The Empire Club of Canada.

They were like people far away, living on other people's land and off the people's brains, and that was all they thought they should do. That was why they were so bored and dull. I thought I would die if I stayed among them.

Thoughts of the narrator about Canadians in **V.S. Naipaul**'s novel *A Bend in the River* (1980).

My name is Joe and I am Canadian!

Concluding line of the 60-second monologue "I Am Canadian" delivered by actor Jeff Douglas, the first of many airings on television, 17 March 2000. Also known as "the Molson rant," it was prepared by the Bensimon-Bryne D'Arcy advertising agency to promote Molson's Canadian beer. The copywriters were **Michael Smith** and **David Swaine** and the text appears in *The Penguin Treasury of Popular Canadian Poems and Songs* (2002), edited by John Robert Colombo.

Adversity is the only way we grow—otherwise we'd all be like Canadians—pasty white, and boring!

Anita Noyes-Smith, South African astrologer and head of Nigher Sources International, in Cara Viereckl, Johannesburg *Star*, 2 June 2000.

I am Canadian, of Coors!

Takeoff on "the Molson rant," following announcement of the merger of Molson Inc. of Montreal with the Adolph Coors Co. of Colorado, by correspondent Michael Derblich, Letters to the Editor, *The Globe and Mail*, 23 July 2004.

I'd like to live in other places for a while. But Canada is home. It's where I want to be. Like Joe, I am a Canadian.

Ken Dryden, hockey personality, lawyer, and author, referring to the Molson "I am a Canadian" commercial, address, Charles R. Bronfman Lecture in Canadian Studies, November, University of Ottawa, "The Canadian Way," *Maclean's*, 13 November 2000.

What our writers and artists sneer at as "typically Canadian" is reality for most of the world. It's not a unique flaw in our character. It doesn't resign us to a second-rate destiny. In our now more global world, in fact, smallness is becoming everybody's reality. And knowing how to live with smallness is becoming an ever more important skill.

Ken Dryden, hockey personality, lawyer, and author, address, Charles R. Bronfman Lecture in Canadian Studies, November, University of Ottawa, "The Canadian Way," *Maclean's*, 13 November 2000.

In search of hyperbole, only a Canadian can say: "As Canadian as a Royal Commission."

Attributed (without citing a source) to **Marshall McLuhan** by William Ferguson and Ian Ferguson, *How to Be a Canadian (Even if You Are One)* (2001).

A Canadian is someone who needs to be re-Canadianized by non-Canadians to become Canadian at last.

David Solway, poet, "Medicine for the CanLit Soul," *National Post*, 6 January 2001.

For someone who has lived in the catholic worlds of Argentina, France, Italy, Spain, French Polynesia, in all their ordinary mad behaviour, the civil awareness and tidy obedience of the Canadian citizen appears as different and far more astounding madness.

Alberto Manguel, Canadian author, born in Argentina, "Destination Ithaka," *Passages: Welcome Home to Canada* (2002), with a preface by Rudyard Griffiths.

There are three things that seem to unite Canadians, or at least the men—beer, wings and hockey nights. See that? Read it again. Beer. Wings. Hockey. You don't need to know your Gretzky from your Trudeau to understand what that really means. Beer, wings and hockey nights—that's the universal lingo for "let's get hosed, stumble home drunk, kick the wife out, take the kids for a walk and sleep with the dog."

Ken Wiwa, columnist, "Am I Canadian?" *The Globe and Mail*, 1 July 2003.

What defines a Canadian best? It must be the lurking fear that somewhere, somehow, you might have offended someone.

Margaret Wente, columnist, *An Accidental Canadian: Reflections on My Home and (Not) Native Land* (2004).

A Canadian is someone who is becoming a Canadian.

Richard Gwyn, columnist, "Being Canadian Is a Work Forever in Progress," *Toronto Star*, 25 March 2005.

CANADIANS & AMERICANS *See also* Americans; Canadians

If we have in a sense become Americanized, it is our own fault as a people. It is because we have failed to develop our inward and Imperial resources apart from the material. It is because we have failed to use those present-day mediums, the press, the platform, the school, the pulpit, the library, the Parliament, as organizations to educate, influence and inspire our people toward Imperial and Canadian ideals. It is necessary to educate through the mediums I have mentioned, or else we as a people will go to the wall.

W. Wilfred Campbell, poet and imperialist, address, "Imperialism in Canada," Toronto, 23 November 1904, The Empire Club of Canada.

The English-speaking Canadians protest that they will never become Americans—they are already Americans without knowing it.

Samuel Moffett, American social scientist, *The Americanization of Canada* (1907).

The Canadians live over the fence from us, but you mix up a Canuck with a Yank in your remarks and you'll get a bat in the eye.

Opinion of the American millionaire John S. Blenkiron in **John Buchan**'s Great War novel *Mr. Standfast* (1919).

Both the Canadians and Americans draw their children [on sleighs] like Eskimos in the winter; both chew gum; both affect the attire of the lumberjack and seek to astonish by the violence of their sports jerseys or their formal freakishness. They are so similar in civilization that what it seems to amount to is that Canadians are just a disloyal and reactionary faction in the original American community, who have gone to live among the snows and the birchbark canoes in order to be free to go on curtseying to the English Royal Family.

Wyndham Lewis, English author, one-time Toronto resident, *America, I Presume* (1940).

Canadians are Americans with no Disneyland.

Margaret Mahy, author, *The Changeover* (1984).

Inside every Canadian, whether she or he knows it or not, there is, in fact, an American.

John Meisel, political scientist, "Escaping Extinction: Cultural Defence of an Undefended Border," *Southern Exposure: Canadian Perspectives on the United States* (1986), edited by D.H. Flaherty and W.R. McKercher.

There is no doubt in my mind that the Americans know less about us than we know about them. The border, as Margaret Atwood has put it, often seems like a one-way mirror. We see the Americans. They see themselves.

Allan Gotlieb, ambassador to the United States, address, "Some Canadian Myths about the U.S.," Toronto, 9 April 1987, The Empire Club of Canada.

Americans have great and noble principles and they go to hell trying to live up to them. Canadians also have great and noble principles but they go to heaven figuring out ways to get around them.

Noam Chomsky, U.S. linguist and social activist, in Christopher Dafoe, *The Globe and Mail*, 13 March 1993.

It's virtually certain that a much larger proportion of Canadians could pass as Americans than the reverse. We know a great deal about them. They, notoriously, know almost nothing about us.

William Watson, analyst, *Globalization and the Meaning of Canadian Life* (1998).

In terms of attitudes and values, however, Canadians and Americans are about as close as any two peoples in the world. What Freud called "the narcissism of minor differences" may fairly describe what separates Canadians from Americans, and yet, for those who hew to them, these "small differences" matter.

Jeffrey Simpson, columnist, *Star-Spangled Canadians: Canadians Living the American Dream* (2000).

If Canada was ordained to be anything, it was to be snowy and reasonable. I wanted to remove myself from American morality plays. I wanted to live a snowy and reasonable life.

Stephen Strauss, science columnist and former American, "Why I Became a Canadian," *The Globe and Mail*, 1 July 2000.

Some Americans are just too nice. That's why they are so concerned when I tell them our national Parliament Buildings are melting. That's why they're so proud of us when I tell them we fly the Stars and Stripes over our president's mansion.

Rick Mercer, television comedian, "Talking about *Talking to Americans*," *Elm Street*, February–March 2001.

I'm an American with a difference, to be sure, but an American still. Being anti-U.S., I have finally figured out, is like being anti-winter. You can whine and bitch all you like, but in the end you have to admit you love it.

Peter Gzowski, journalist and broadcaster, "Being Anti-U.S. Is Like Being Anti-Winter," *The Globe and Mail*, 15 September 2001.

"You seem familiar yet somehow strange—are you by any chance Canadian?"

Spoken by a well-dressed man to an elegantly gowned woman, both diners in a fancy restaurant, in a cartoon signed **D. Reilly**, *The New Yorker*, 19 November 2001.

I am an American, an American with a difference.

Peter Gzowski, author and broadcaster, in conversation with Shelagh Rogers, CBC Radio's *This Morning*, 22 November 2001.

It interests Americans that Canada is clean and empty ... : the largest country in the world that doesn't exit.

Richard Rodriguez, American commentator, *Brown: The Last Discovery of America* (2002).

No thanks! We don't want to become Americans. We can do much better.

Mel Hurtig, publisher and nationalist, chapter heading, *The Vanishing Country: Is It Too Late to Save Canada?* (2002).

Apologies all around, because I'm Canadian, eh? ... I am a Canadian and I want to apologize. I'm not sure for what but I'll think of something. That's what we Candians are like.

Colin Mochrie, actor-comedian, "A Canadian Apologizes," routine posted on a website, 8 June 2002. Mochrie's routine takes the form of a mock letter addressed to U.S. President George W. Bush.

Canadian youth are more "American" than their parents and grandparents, but they remain vastly less American than Americans.

Michael Adams, consultant, *Fire and Ice: The United States, Canada and the Myth of Converging Values* (2003), with Amy Langstaff and David Jamieson.

I was also impressed with just how much Canadians' social values seemed to be diverging from those of Americans. (After all, we are frequently made to feel that we have become nothing more than unarmed Americans with health insurance.)

Michael Adams, consultant, *Fire and Ice: The United States, Canada and the Myth of Converging Values* (2003), with Amy Langstaff and David Jamieson.

I have found Americans to be more deferential to institutions than Canadians. This is counterintuitive. I have found Canadians to be less anomic, aimless, and alienated … than are Americans, who are nominally a more religious people. This too is counterintuitive. And, perhaps most surprising, I have found Canadians to be a more autonomous people than Americans, less outer-directed and less conformist. This too is contrary to the stereotype of Americans as a nation of individualists.

Michael Adams, consultant, *Fire and Ice: The United States, Canada and the Myth of Converging Values* (2003), with Amy Langstaff and David Jamieson.

Americans are the only best friends we have.

Based on a remark made by **L. Ian MacDonald**, "The Back Pages," *Maclean's*, 3 March 2003. He is alluding to the celebrated observation "The Americans are our best friends, whether we like it or not."

Some of us used to be you; some of us want to be you; some of you used to be us.

Margaret Atwood, author, "A Letter to America," *The Globe and Mail*, 28 March 2003.

Being American is not a citizenship. It is a religion.

Being Canadian, on the other hand, varies from region to region and can mean different things to different people.

Diane Francis, columnist, "A Wake Up Call for Canada–U.S. Relations," *National Post*, 12 April 2003.

Having a friend doesn't mean you are kneeling in front of him.

Attributed to **Gilles Duceppe**, Bloc Québécois leader, during the leadership debates, 15 June 2004.

If life in Canada is cheaper, the money saved by extinguishing the ego is one reason.

Bruce McCall, Canadian-born New York humorist, "O Canada! That Fractured, Frosty Land," *The New York Times*, 21 November 2004.

I, frankly, felt that the reception we received on the way in from the airport was very warm and hospitable, and I want to thank the Canadian people who came out to wave—with all five fingers—for the hospitality.

George W. Bush, U.S. president, paying his first "working visit" to Canada, Ottawa news conference, 31 November 2004, in Anne Dawson and Mike Blanchfield, "Bush and Martin Mend the Fences," *National Post*, 1 December 2004.

When all is said and done, we are friends. And we like that.

George W. Bush, U.S. president, address, Pier 21, Halifax, 1 December 2004, in Gloria Galloway, "Evoking World War II, Bush Prods Canadians," *The Globe and Mail*, 2 December 2004.

To an American, a Canadian is … organic, healthy, solid, reliable, boring.

Line about a Canadian character in **Alison Lurie**'s novel *Truth and Consequences* (2005).

When something new appears in the world, the American asks: How can money be made from this? The Canadian asks: How can we regulate it?

Robert Fulford, "The Values Battle," *National Post*, 24 September 2005.

I'm always very happy here in Canada. There are probably about half of my fellow countrymen who want me to stay. And there are times when I've wanted to stay.

Bill Clinton, former U.S. president, address at a motivational seminar, Toronto, 18 October 2005, quoted by Rosie DiManno, "A Clear Voice of Reason amid the Rancour," *Toronto Star*, 19 October 2005.

CANCER *See also* Health; Medicine

It is commonly believed that once cancer has been diagnosed, a patient is helpless before the relentless onslaught of the disease. This misconception fuels the excessive sense of hopelessness and despair that characterizes the word "cancer."

L. Martin Jerry, professor of medicine, "Cancer," *The Canadian Encyclopedia* (2nd ed., 1988).

I don't want to make breast cancer the centre of my life, but it infuses my life and there is a resonance of "I've been through the fire," and people know that. In my meditation I have finally been able to look at the spectre of death and not run away. My mantra is now "Let it break you open." I'm not grateful I had cancer, but it certainly has been an extraordinary teacher.

Esther Myers, Iyenger yoga instructor and cancer survivor, favourite mantra, in Jean Marmoreo, *The New Middle Ages: Women in Midlife* (2002).

Cancer is so limited. It cannot cripple love, it cannot shatter hope, it cannot erode faith, it cannot destroy peace, it cannot kill friendship, it cannot suppress memories, it cannot silence courage, it cannot invade the soul, it cannot steal eternal life, it cannot conquer the spirit.

Poster, Princess Margaret Hospital, Toronto, as noted by Lynda Murtha, "Signs of Hope Span Generations," *The Globe and Mail*, 21 September 2005.

CANOES

"Now, I think that it much better that, as we all go along together, that every man paddle his own canoe. That my thought."

Speech of an Indian character in **Frederick Marryat**'s novel *The Settlers in Canada* (1844). This is said to be the first appearance in print of the folk expression for self-sufficiency "Paddle your own canoe."

Slowly as a cloud we go, / Sky above and sky below…

Couplet from poet **Archibald Lampman**'s lyrical poem "Morning on the Lièvre," a dream-like description of canoeing in late September on the Lièvre River, the second-largest tributary of the Ottawa River in Quebec, *Among the Millet* (1888). The National Film Board documentary *Morning on the Lièvre* (1961) made affecting use of this couplet as a refrain.

What sets a canoeing expedition apart is that it purifies you more rapidly and inescapably than any other. Travel a thousand miles by train and you are a brute; pedal five hundred on a bicycle and you remain basically a bourgeois; paddle a hundred in canoe and you are already a child of nature.

Pierre Elliott Trudeau, canoeist and future prime minister, "Exhaustion and Fulfillment: The Ascetic in a Canoe" (1944) in *Wilderness Canada* (1970), edited by Borden Spears.

A Canadian is somebody who knows how to make love in a canoe.

Pierre Berton, media personality, interviewed by Dick Brown, *The Canadian*, 22 December 1973.

We are a nation of canoeists, and have been since the earliest days, paddling our way up the St. Lawrence, across the lakes, over the portages of the shield, west along the North Saskatchewan through the Yellowhead gap and thence southwest by the Columbia and Fraser rivers to the sea. When someone asks you how Canada could exist as a horizontal country with its plains and mountains running vertically, tell him about the paddlers.

Pierre Berton, historian, *Why We Act Like Canadians* (1982).

When such children read Pauline Johnson's "The Song My Paddle Sings" in their school readers—as they did, until the 1960s—they knew that the paddle in the song was not just Pauline's paddle but their paddle too.

Margaret Atwood, author, referring to generations of Boy Scouts and Girl Guides, "The Grey Owl Syndrome," *Strange Things: The Malevolent North in Canadian Literature* (1995).

Canada is a canoe route.

Attributed to historian **A.R.M. Lower** by Will Ferguson, *Canadian History for Dummies* (2000).

Pierre Berton once declared that a Canadian is someone "who knows how to make love in a canoe." But Pierre was just bragging. Or lying. If average Canadians ever tried to "pull a Berton" they'd end up looking like Mr. Canoe Head. (For those of you unfamiliar with His Canoe-Headedness, Mr. Canoe Head was a superhero whose head was permamently stuck inside a canoe. But it was okay, because he wore disguises to hide it. You know, fake beards and whatnot.)

William Ferguson and **Ian Ferguson**, writers, *How to Be a Canadian (Even if You Are One)* (2001).

Canada is more than a canoe route after all. Canada is a road trip. And like any road trip worthy of the name, it is ultimately about freedom in its purest form.

Will Ferguson, author, *Beauty Tips from Moose Jaw: Travels in Search of Canada* (2004).

CANUCKS

Americans have pulled me aside on several occasions to ask, in the hushest of tones, "Is it, you know, rude to call Canadians Canucks?" When I say that it's perfectly fine, I get a disbelieving stare. So then I say, "There's even a hockey team called the Canucks," and only then do they relax. Yes, it's okay.

Douglas Coupland, novelist and essayist, "Strong and Free," *Maclean's*, 25 November 2002.

CAPE BRETON ISLAND

I have travelled around the globe. I have seen the Canadian and the American Rockies, the Andes and the Alps and the Highlands of Scotland; but for simple beauty Cape Breton Island outrivals them all.

Alexander Graham Bell, inventor and summer resident at Baddeck, Cape Breton Island, N.S., in Wes Rataushk, *Silver Highway: A Celebration of the Trans-Canada Highway* (1888).

Home is Cape Breton, and I'm here to stay.

Rita MacNeil, singer-composer, resident of Big Pond, Cape Breton Island, N.S., in Ann Finlayson, *Maclean's*, 7 November 1988.

CAPITAL PUNISHMENT *See also* Crime; Law

A Canadian told me, "Emo, I can't believe you have capital punishment in the States. It turns the government into a murderer." I said, "How about imprisonment? It turns the government into a gay dungeon-master."

Emo Philips, U.S. comedian, characteristic remark, www.emophilips.com, November 2003.

CAPITALISM *See also* Business; Entrepreneurship; Free Enterprise; Labour; Socialism

What I am saying, then, if I might put it in simple, almost prosy, business-like speech, is this—that we need to get back to a sane capitalism. The "capitalist" is not such a dreadful sinner as some people think. We have called him so many hard names, we have labelled him with such a lot of epithets, that the poor fellow scarcely shows his face. We have got him almost taxed to extinction, and we turn the screw further and further with every annual budget. We have got him to the point now where the best he can do is to hide his wealth and keep himself in the shade, crying out, if he can, "I, too, am poor!"

Stephen Leacock, economist and humorist, address, "The Proper Limits of State Intervention," Toronto, 6 March 1924, The Empire Club of Canada.

Corporate welfare bums.

David Lewis, New Democratic Party leader, speech, New Glasgow, N.S., 3 August 1972. According to Walter Stewart in *Divide and Con* (1973), Lewis branded as "corporate welfare bums" those corporations, large and small, that avoided paying their fair share of business taxes as well as those businesses that pressed all levels of government for additional grants, concessions, subsidies, deferrals, remissions, depreciations, and incentives.

The Third World, as they say, has always existed for the comfort of the First.

Naomi Klein, commentator, *No Logo: Taking Aim at the Brand Name Bullies* (2000).

CARTOON ART *See also* Arts & Artists

They had better start making stronger rope—if they want to hold Canadians captive!

Leo Bachle, artist and creator of Johnny Canuck, eponymous strongman hero of Dime Comics in 1941, a "Canadian White," as noted by Michael Hirsch and Patrick Loubert, *The Great Canadian Comic Books* (1971).

I'm the roughest, toughest, meanest Canuck in the Klondike!

Boast of Blacque Jacques Shellaque, the bully and villain in the Bugs Bunny cartoon *Bonanza Bunny* (1959), set in the Klondike, directed by Robert McKimson with voice by **Mel Blanc**. The character was considered the French-Canadian answer to Yosemite Sam. Shellaque tries to separate the American Bugs from his *carats* (carrots).

We will land within 30 kilometres of their airships ... then we go by snowmobile.

Statement by Captain Canuck, comic-book superhero, to his sidekick in the first issue of *Captain Canuck* (1975), created by illustrator **Richard Comely**. Canuck is probably the only caped superhero to travel by snowmobile, as noted by Christopher Hutsul, "Captain Canuck Clings to Life," *Toronto Star*, 26 June 2005.

We were counting on Canadians feeling superior to the Simpsons as being doltish Americans, but now the secret is out.

Matt Groening, creator of the comic strip *The Simpsons*, admitting to an interviewer that the beer-loving, porkchop-eating Homer was named after his father, who was born in Winnipeg, as noted by CP, "Move over Pooh, Homer's from Winnipeg, Too," *National Post*, 20 July 2002.

The medium's low pretensions keep you from getting too full of yourself.

Gregory Gallant, comic artist who signs his work "Seth," referring to past evaluations of his art form, in Murray Whyte, "Galleries," *Toronto Star*, 25 June 2005.

CATHOLICISM *See also* Belief; Education

We have had enough of confusion, enough of confrontations, enough of dissent. Those who go looking for dissent are not Catholic.

Gerald Emmett Carter, retired cardinal and archbishop of Toronto (1978–1990), statement made in 1979, quoted in his obituary article by Michael Valpy, "Cardinal Felt at Ease with Politics, Power," *The Globe and Mail*, 7 April 2003.

May this Canadian land sing to the Lord from the shores of the Atlantic to those of the Pacific and from the South to the frozen wastelands of the North...

John Paul II, pope, homily, Laval Stadium, Quebec City, 9 September 1984, *The Canadian Catholic Review: The Papal Visit, Oct. 1984.*

I have heard him speak many times, most notably his Magna International–sponsored address to many thousands gathered in the mid-1980s at Toronto's Varsity Stadium, on which occasion St. Michael's College president James McConica smartly quipped that the Cardinal's lecture was a veritable "soul on ice."

Michael Higgins, president, St. Jerome's University, Waterloo, Ont., 14 April 1986, "The New Benedictine Order," *The Globe and Mail*, 20 April 2005. Higgins refers to Joseph Cardinal Ratzinger, the future Pope Benedict XVI.

The shortcomings of excesses of the clergy do not make God's existence and supremacy and entitlement to the adherence of people less clear. I do commend Catholicism to those so inclined. It is not a panacea, but it is sane, rigorous, and consoling, and the human spirit and intelligence can be comfortable within it.

Conrad Black, publisher and Anglican convert to Catholicism, *A Life in Progress* (1993).

Dear young friends. Toronto is waiting for all of you who can make it. In the heart of a multi-faith city ... come, and make the great avenues of Toronto resound with the joyful tidings that Christ loves every person and brings to fulfillment every trace of goodness, beauty, and truth found in the city of man.

John Paul II, pope, inviting Catholic youth to attend World Youth Day, 23–28 July 2002, in Raymond J. de Souza, "Pope Summons World's Youth to Toronto," *National Post*, 31 July 2001.

John Paul Two / We Love You.

Chant of 250 000 Catholic youth, gathered to celebrate World Youth Day in the presence of Pope John Paul II at Exhibition Place, Toronto, CBC Radio, 25 July 2002.

I sometimes wonder if the Pope has ever changed a diaper or been peed on by a toddler who hasn't quite mastered the art of getting to the bathroom on time.

Joanna Manning, Catholic critic, interviewed by Wayne Holst, "Truth Not What It Once Was," *Toronto Star*, 3 August 2002.

Wherever Mary of Canada finds herself in a country, her merciful lack of surprise at any human deed, thought, or failure, and her encompassing tenderness for all creation transcends religious labels, money, status, background, geography, and all that divides us.

Joan Skogan, author, *Mary of Canada: The Virgin Mary in Canadian Culture, Spirituality, History, and Geography* (2003).

One hundred and seventeen old men in dresses who have presumably never had sex are going to select one from among their number who will then make decisions that will profoundly affect the everyday lives (and deaths—from AIDS in Africa and crushing poverty due to lack of birth control in Latin America) of 1.1 billion people. What is even more strange is that the 1.1 billion people are willing to play the game. And people think science fiction is unbelievable.

Bill Gekoski, Montreal correspondent, Letters to the Editor, *The Globe and Mail*, 9 April 2005.

CATS

Or what if it was cats and not humans who invented technology—should cats build scratching-post skyscrapers covered entirely with shag carpeting? Would they have TV shows starring rubber squeak toys?

Thoughts of the narrator in **Douglas Coupland**'s novel *Life after God* (1994).

CBC *See* Canadian Broadcasting Corporation

CELEBRITIES *See also* Actors & Acting; Fame; Hollywood

If you really want the Americans to take notice, for god's sake, start producing Canadian equivalents to Donald Trump, Dennis Rodman, Hillary and Bill Clinton—the worst over-sized public personalities that make the skin crawl. Don Cherry can't do it alone.

Bruce McCall, humorist and cartoonist for *The New Yorker*, born in Simcoe, Ont., Toronto talk for the Writers' Trust, *Toronto Star*, 3 June 2000.

When rulers are ruthless and priests are randy, actors become role models.

Mavor Moore, theatre personality, characteristic observation, 22 December 2002.

No longer does every culture have a self-created pantheon; every culture has Julia Roberts.

Mark Abley, author, *Spoken Here: Travels among Threatened Languages* (2003).

One of the peculiarities of becoming a celebrity in Canada, however minor, is that people are constantly coming up to remind you who you are.

Peter C. Newman, journalist and memoirist, *Here Be Dragons: Telling Tales of People, Passion, and Power* (2004).

Much as I love Canada and Canadians, I am extremely angry that you stole Jane Jacobs from us. (She has been living in Toronto since the 1970s.) While Peter Jennings, Michael J. Fox, Céline Dion, Wayne Gretzky and Emily Carr have all enriched American life, I would trade them all to get Ms. Jacobs back.

Christopher B. Leinberger, U.S. developer and consultant, paying graceful tribute to urban theorist and essayist Jane Jacobs, "Walk This Way," *National Post*, 28 April 2005.

CENSORSHIP *See also* Communications; Freedom of Expression; Media; Political Correctness; Rights

Yes, gentlemen, come what will, while I live, Nova Scotia shall have the blessing of an open and unshackled press.

Joseph Howe, journalist and statesman, impassioned address to the jury in a Halifax courtroom, May 1835. He defended himself from charges of libel and the acquittal marked a turning point in press freedom throughout British North America, later Canada. The speech appears in *The Speeches and Public Letters of The Hon. Joseph Howe* (1858), edited by William Annand.

Resolution *re* Foreign Literature in Canada:

That the National Conference assembled in Vancouver is strongly of the opinion that it is incompatible with the development in Canada of the type of citizenship which Canadians desire that the country should be flooded, as it is flooded, with publications which are undesirable from the point of view of morals, intellectual standards, and a sound nationalism in accord with our British tradition.

The Conference therefore urgently requests the Executive Committee to approach the Canadian Government and ask that steps be taken to prevent the sale of such publications in Canada.

Recommendations, *Education and Leisure: Addresses Delivered at the Fourth Triennial Conference on Education Held at Victoria and Vancouver, Canada, April 1929* (1929), edited by S.E. Lang.

Once when I was very young I found myself on a train with nothing to read, and in desperation bought a thriller from a news agent. It told me, in effect, that practically all the Chinese in North American cities were engaged in drug-running and in kidnapping young white women. It would be against the law to distribute such stuff in Ontario today, and I thoroughly approve of the law.

Northrop Frye, literary and cultural critic, address, "The Authority of Learning," Toronto, 19 June 1984, The Empire Club of Canada.

Our oral tradition is a powerful safeguard against the repressive censors of the right and the left, the pious busybodies who would purge common speech of its irreverence and pungency. I say: Long may loose lips flap!

Bill Casselman, anthologist, *Canadian Sayings: 1,200 Folk Sayings Used by Canadians* (1999).

The law sets out to get the Marquis de Sade, and Customs lands Jane Rule.

Susan Crean, commentator, referring to amendments to the Criminal Code passed by Parliament that Customs authorities so interpreted as to ban the importation of literature rather than pornography, "Customs Should Censor Itself," *The Globe and Mail*, 19 March 2001. The amendments reflected the feminist theories of Andrea Dworkin and Catharine MacKinnon.

CENTRAL CANADA *See* Ontario; Quebec

CHANCE *See also* Destiny; Luck

Statistics is the theory of chance.

Ian Hacking, philosopher, *Logic of Statistical Inference* (1965).

CHANGE *See also* Environmentalism; Progress

We cannot in Canada continue as we are. We must become something greater or something infinitely less.

Stephen Leacock, economist and humorist, address, "Education and Empire Unity," Toronto, 19 March 1907, The Empire Club of Canada.

What's holding us back from moving faster? Basically, I think Canada's held back by a rather large cherished illusion. (A cherished illusion is one that is held even more firmly when we know it is contrary to fact because we find it comforting.) The illusion is that you can deal with challenge by just saying No. In too many powerful places in our society we have evolved a Canadian culture that is a culture of refusal.

Dian Cohen, columnist, address, "Making It in the New Economy," Toronto, 6 February 1992, The Empire Club of Canada.

I came to Rochdale, and for that matter to Canada, for the same reason I had invested the largest part of my adult life in speculative fiction: I wanted to change the world.

Judith Merril, science-fiction personality, who moved from New York to Toronto in 1968, *Better to Have Loved: The Life of Judith Merril* (2002), with Emily Pohl-Weary.

It is obvious that social change would be reflected in changes of language, but what interests me much more is the reverse possibility: that the teaching of language, and the structures of literature in which language is contained, may foster and encourage certain social changes.

Northrop Frye, cultural and literary critic, address, "The Authority of Learning," Toronto, 19 June 1984, The Empire Club of Canada.

If you want to know who is going to change this country, go home and look in the mirror.

Maude Barlow, chair, Council of Canadians, address, League of Canadian Poets, Toronto, 25 May 1991.

Those who were good at living with trees are on their way out, and those who are good at living with video display terminals and silicon tubes will be selected for. So cultures are actually selecting for a new post-natural environment in which the dance may be beyond imagination of what nature may be in the 21st century.

William Irwin Thompson, theorist, "Mind Jazz," *Wild Culture: Specimens from* The Journal of Wild Culture (1992), edited by Whitney Smith and Christopher Lowry.

Economists can talk about globalization and technological change in the abstract all they want, but governments must not.

Paul Martin, finance minister, Budget Speech, House of Commons, 18 February 1997.

With today's rate of accelerating change, any country, corporation, organization, or individual will be affected more by what happens outside their sphere of influence than anything within such a sphere. It is time to appoint a Vice President of External Effects.... As this bulldozer of change rolls over our planet, we all have to learn that if we don't become part of the bulldozer, we'll become part of the road.

Frank Ogden, futurist, characteristic observations, 1 June 2003.

Accept the fact that there are some things that you cannot control, that you cannot change. Life is not always fair.

Marie Adams, educator, offering advice to parents, *Our Son, a Stranger: Adoption Breakdown and Its Effects on Parents* (2003).

To reach an ethical approach that would argue for less adaptation and greater lifestyle change, we must extend our concern for consequences out beyond "humans here and now" to the wider principle of "humans everywhere in the present."

Harold Coward, climatologist, "What Can Individuals Do?" *Hard Choices: Climate Change in Canada* (2004), edited by Harold Coward and Andrew J. Weaver. Coward is using the formulations of philosopher Thomas Hurka to distinguish between "welfarism" and "perfectionism," between short, self-interested views and long, wide-interest views of the need for social and personal change to cope with climate change.

Nobody likes change—but a wet baby.

Michael Fullan, educator, observations, in Alanna Mitchell, "School of Britannia," *Toronto Star*, 1 May 2004.

CHAREST, JEAN

"Certains disent que Charest est démagogue." "Il n'est pas de Magog, il est de Sherbrooke."

Exchange concerning Jean Charest in the editorial cartoon titled *"Nos Voisins," La Tribune* (Sherbrooke, Que.), 11 February 2002. Two neighbours discuss Charest, punning on "demagogue" and Magog, the city in Quebec's Eastern Townships near his birthplace of Sherbrooke.

Leadership matters. Quebec's leadership will make Canada a stronger country.

Jean Charest, leader of the Quebec Liberal Party and premier designate, victory speech, Quebec City, 14 April 2003, in Graham Fraser, "Charest Wins," *Toronto Star*, 15 April 2003.

Jean Charest cannot succeed without us.

Peter C. Newman, columnist, referring to Charest, newly elected Quebec premier, "Adieu to Separatism?" *Maclean's*, 12 May 2003.

Charest was one of only two Tories who survived the general election that followed, prompting the joke on Parliament Hill that his perky wife, Michèle, was sleeping with half the Conservative caucus.

Peter C. Newman, columnist, referring to the federal election of June 1993, "Adieu to Separatism?" *Maclean's*, 12 May 2003.

Patience has become his middle name and he implicitly trusts his own judgment.

Peter C. Newman, columnist, referring to Quebec Premier Jean Charest, "Adieu to Separatism?" *Maclean's*, 12 May 2003.

CHARITY *See also* Philanthropy

There are no pockets in a shroud.

Sigmund Samuel, philanthropist, characteristic remark made before his death at the age of 93 in 1962, in Donald Jones, *Toronto Star*, 20 May 1978.

A man who is handicapped, who is in the throngs of the slums, when he has an empty stomach, all he wants is respect and that his rights for work, expression, life, and medical aid be respected. This is what he wants, respect; and not gushing pity.

Jean Vanier, humanitarian, address, "A World in Violence: Eruption to Hope?" Toronto, 11 February 1971, The Empire Club of Canada.

For God's Sake Care.

Attention-getting slogan adopted by the Salvation Army for use throughout the world, introduced to mark its centenary campaign in 1978, while the Army was under the world leadership of Ontario-born General **Arnold Brown**, as noted in his obituary by Mary Sherwin, "He Led the Salvation Army," *The Globe and Mail*, 18 July 2002.

Give a little, it costs a lot. Give a lot, it costs a little. Give everything, it costs nothing at all.

Joseph Raya, Metropolitan Akko of the Melkite Greek Catholic Church, who died at Barry's Bay, Ont., 10 June 2005, as noted in his obituary by Ron Csillag, *The Globe and Mail*, 21 July 2005.

Nothing is more personal than a personal cheque.

Attributed to **Yechiel Eckstein**, Orthodox rabbi who advocates a rapprochement with and fundraises among U.S. fundamentalists, described as "the son of the chief rabbi of Canada," by Zev Chafets, "The Rabbi Who Loved Evangelicals (and Vice Versa)," *The New York Times Magazine*, 24 July 2005.

CHARLOTTETOWN

The people of Charlottetown, Prince Edward Island, are "neighbourly"—that is, they visit with one another as a form of recreation. At the same time, they don't give strangers their complete confidence. They like to get to know a person gradually before becoming entirely friendly with him.

Charles Paul May, U.S. travel writer, *Great Cities of Canada* (1967).

Thus, though declining in the order of Canadian municipalities in size, Charlottetown offers a quality of life far richer than its small population would suggest.

Peter E. Rider, historian, "Charlottetown," *The Canadian Encyclopedia* (2nd ed., 1988).

CHARLOTTETOWN CONSTITUTIONAL ACCORD

See Distinct Society

CHARTER OF RIGHTS AND FREEDOMS

See also Constitution; Rights; Trudeau, Pierre Elliott

Whereas Canada is founded upon principles that recognize the supremacy of God and the rule of law:

The Canadian Charter of Rights and Freedoms guarantees the rights and freedoms set out in it subject only to such reasonable limits prescribed by law as can be demonstrably justified in a free and democratic society.

Everyone has the following fundamental freedoms: (a) freedom of conscience and religion; (b) freedom of thought, belief, opinion and expression, including freedom of the press and other media of communication; (c) freedom of peaceful assembly; and (d) freedom of association....

The Constitution of Canada is the supreme law of Canada, and any law that is inconsistent with the provisions of the Constitution is, to the extent of the inconsistency, of no force or effect.

Two key provisions of the Canadian Charter of Rights and Freedoms of The Constitution Act, 1982.

This young document, whose implications we have not yet digested, has already been internalized as a central element in the Canadian identity to the point that it is now impossible to deviate from it. There is something suspect about this sudden and absolute adoption that makes us wonder how it was possible to be Canadian a quarter-century ago.

Alain Dubuc, editorialist for *La Presse*, LaFontaine-Baldwin Lecture, published in *The Globe and Mail*, 10 March 2001. The Charter of Rights and Freedoms was introduced by Prime Minister Trudeau in the Constitution Act, 1982.

What has the Charter done for the homeless or the dispossessed?

Alan Hutchinson, law professor, in Kirk Makin, "Rights Gone Wrong?" *The Globe and Mail*, 6 April 2002, as quoted by Robert Ivan Martin, *The Most Dangerous Branch: How the Supreme Court of Canada Has Undermined Our Law and Our Democracy* (2003). Martin sees this as investing the Charter with "magical properties" and explains, "Implicit in Hutchinson's assertion is the belief that the Charter could have done something for the homeless and the dispossessed, but did not. Hutchinson's anthropomorphic assertion appears to bespeak a belief that a collection of legal abstractions, like the Charter, might actually be capable of doing things."

Some will argue that the use of the notwithstanding clause in the Charter is wrong in principle. I must respectfully disagree. The notwithstanding clause was inserted to recognize Parliamentary supremacy and the need for democratic oversight for the courts. No Canadian can say that the courts always get things right. Judges are not elected and are ultimately not accountable for their decisions. Fundamental social change should only occur with the consent of the people through their democratic institutions.

Aloysius Ambrozic, Roman Catholic cardinal, archbishop of the Diocese of Toronto, "An Open Letter: Why the Rush on Same-Sex Marriage?" *The Globe and Mail*, 19 January 2005.

If the notwithstanding clause is increasingly seen as illegitimate by the political class, maybe it's because it never was particularly legitimate in the eyes of the public. And if the public doesn't like it, maybe that's because they see it for what it is: a constitutional hypocrisy, a perpetual invitation to mischief, a dagger pointed at the Charter's heart.

Andrew Coyne, columnist, "The Trouble with 'Notwithstanding,'" *National Post*, 29 January 2005.

CHERRY, DON *See also* Celebrities

It isn't easy to become Don Cherry. For starters, you need to have a mother named Maude and a father named Delmar.

Don Cherry, sports personality, *Quotations from Chairman Cherry* (1991).

CHILDREN *See also* Family

No society is properly organized until every child that is born into it shall have an opportunity in life. Success in life and capacity to live we cannot give. But opportunity we can. We can at least see that the gifts that are laid in the child's cradle by nature are not obliterated by the cruel fortune of the accident of birth: that its brain and body are not stunted by lack of food and air and by the heavy burden of premature toil. The playtime of childhood should be held sacred by the nation.

Stephen Leacock, humorist, *The Unsolved Riddle of Social Justice* (1920).

The fastest way to forgive your parents is to have children of your own.

Hugh Arscott, aphorist, *Hugh's Views: Volume 4* (2000).

It's commonly said that children are the church of tomorrow. That's not true—they are an integral part of the church today. But they will not be around tomorrow, if our congregations persist in using yesterday's methods to educate them.

Donna Sinclair and **Christopher White**, authors, *Jacob's Blessing: Dreams, Hopes, & Visions for the Church* (2000).

If you have children, do your best to like them.

Robert Buckman, physician and humanist, *Can We Be Good without God? Biology, Behaviour and the Need to Believe* (2002).

Remember that you and your children are two separate people.

Marie Adams, educator, offering advice to parents, *Our Son, a Stranger: Adoption Breakdown and Its Effects on Parents* (2002).

One of your key personalities as a parent is to help your child develop an inner compass that will guide her through life, helping her to make the best possible decisions along the way.

Barbara Coloroso, parenting consultant, *Kids Are Worth It* (2002).

Dogs Welcome / Children must be / on a Leash!

Sign in the window of a bookshop, Toronto, May 2002.

There are now more laws protecting children than there are laws protecting adults. There are more books written for or about children than there are on virtually any other topic of human concern. The toy industry has become central to our economy.

Marcel Danesi, semiotician, *Forever Young: The "Teen-Aging" of Modern Culture* (2003).

Two adults who have too little adult companionship besides themselves can easily drift into isolation from society and become lonely, paranoid, resentful, stressed, depressed, and at their wits' ends. Sitcom families and "reality" TV can and do fill isolated hours, but cannot offer the support of live friends and the practical information of varied acquaintances.

Jane Jacobs, urban planning critic, *Dark Age Ahead* (2004).

I want to start a revolution to create a humane and sustainable world by addressing the needs of the very young. It starts with respect for the children as a whole person. That leads us to question everything, from corporate presence in our schools to our selfish stewardship of the planet to the way we measure economic progress.

Raffi (born Raffi Cavoukian), children's performer, embracing the principles and policies of "child-honouring," in Gary Stephen Ross, "Raffi Grows Up," *Saturday Night*, March 2005.

Well-loved children grow into adults who do not build concentration camps, do not rape, and do not murder.

Henry Morgentaler, physician and women's rights activist, convocation address, University of Western Ontario, London, 16 June 2005, in Joseph Hall, "A Good Day for Western,'" *Toronto Star*, 17 June 2005.

Raising kids makes you crazy, but having raised them makes you philosophical.

Judith Timson, columnist, "The Empty Nest Is Anything but Empty," *The Globe and Mail*, 17 September 2005.

CHILE

As a Canadian, you rarely have a chance to live life in the raw. Events just carried us forward.

Marc Dolgin, diplomat, explaining how he and fellow diplomat David Adam, at the Canadian Embassy in Santiago, Chile, against the orders of the ambassador and the policy of the Canadian government, offered asylum and eventually safe passage to Canada for 225 Chileans during the 1973 right-wing coup, as noted by Janice Paskey, "An Inhumane Policy," *National Post*, 27 December 2000.

CHINA

When I came down from Ku Su Terrace, in the East, / I had already arranged for a vessel to float on the sea: / And until now resentment lingers in my mind / That I did not succeed in exploring Fu Sang.

Sentiments of the Chinese Buddhist monk **Huei Shan**, traditionally the explorer of North America in 499 B.C., as expressed by the Chinese poet Tu Fu in his "Poem of Fu Sang" (A.D. 726). According to Chinese tradition, Huei Shan discovered the New World. Tu Fu's words, translated by Florence Ayscouth, are in Hendon Mason Harris, *The Asiatic Fathers of America* (1980). "Fu Sang" means "fir-tree," and some argue that the reference is to the west coast of British Columbia and the interior lands as far east as Writing-on-Stone Provincial Park, Alta., according to Henriette Hertz, *Pale Ink: Two Ancient Records of Chinese Exploration in America* (1953; revised, 1972).

With the emergence of China as an acknowledged great power and the unhappy war in the Indian sub-continent, he is a bold man who would make prophecies about the future of Asia. Nonetheless, I still hold to my opinion that during the next few years we are going to witness a tremendous upsurge in financial and economic development in the Asian countries. Were I twenty-five years younger, I would go to Asia and make my headquarters there, where I am certain I could build and sustain a vast business empire.

Roy Thomson, publisher, address, "The World Today," Toronto, 6 January 1972, The Empire Club of Canada.

What will Western corporations do if and when Chinese workers comprehend their exploitation and start doing something to correct the situation? Will widespread unrest end in another Tiananmen Square slaughter? If so, it is not exactly clear where the next pool of cheap labour is going to come from. Robots perhaps. And they'll be made in China too.

John Fraser, essayist, "Strange Journey," *The Walrus*, February 2005.

Ask anyone here and they will tell you: Shanghai is the future. But that is not so. Shanghai is not the future; it is *every* future, a palimpsest of urban visions, a history of what is to come.

Mark Kingwell, philosopher and commentator, "The City of Tomorrow," *Harper's*, February 2005.

CHIROPRACTIC *See also* Health; Medicine

If no other discovery had been made, this, of itself, should have been hailed with delight.... It was I who combined the science and art and developed the principles thereof. I have answered the time-worn question—what is life?

Daniel David Palmer (1845–1913), founder of the practice of chiropractic (Latin for "done by hand"), born in Brown's Corners (now Audley and part of Ajax), Ont., and raised in nearby Port Perry. He established the Palmer College of Chiropractic in Davenport, Iowa, and wrote *The Chiropractor's Adjuster* (1910).

CHRÉTIEN, JEAN

Not you again!

Exclamation of **Queen Elizabeth II** on seeing Jean Chrétien as minister of Justice at Buckingham Palace during yet another round of negotiations that eventually led to the patriation of the Constitution in April 1982. Quoted by John Fraser, "In Between Two Portraits," *National Post*, 5 June 2002. Fraser went on to explain: "When she said 'Not you again!' the 'you' was for all of us and our constitutional mayhem, and not just the justice minister."

He'll make a good prime minister, but not a great one.

Mitchell Sharp, former Cabinet minister, referring to the election in October 1993 of Jean Chrétien, quoted in "How Jean Chrétien Managed from 1993," editorial, *The Globe and Mail*, 14 November 2003.

Is this a Prime Minister?

Progressive Conservative television advertisement that shows an unflattering close-up of Chrétien's face and posed the rhetorical question, campaign of 1993, immediately withdrawn with later apologies by Prime Minister Kim Campbell, as recalled by columnist John Doyle, *The Globe and Mail*, 1 December 2003.

Canada is a rich country with a talented population. All we lack is leadership. On his past record, there are no grounds to believe Jean Chrétien is of the future rather than of the past, but the people's will will be done, by him, or by others. If he doesn't grasp the real lesson of the fate of the other two traditional parties, he will share that fate. Miracles do occur and after what this country has been through in recent years, we're due for one.

Conrad Black, newspaper magnate, address, "Post-election Prospects in Canada," Toronto, 2 November 1993, The Empire Club of Canada.

His policies and principles can be summed up in two words: whatever works.

Peter C. Newman, columnist and author, "Jean Chrétien's Winning Formula," *Defining Moments: Dispatches from an Unfinished Revolution* (1997).

The little guy from Ottawa who disguises himself as the little guy from Shawinigan.

Characterization of Shawinigan-born Prime Minister Jean Chrétien by **Gilles Duceppe**, Bloc Québécois leader, in James Brooke, "One Battle More for Canada's Old Warrior," *The New York Times*, 26 November 2000.

I'm a problem-solver. It's my life.

Jean Chrétien, prime minister, interviewed by Don Newman, as noted by Jeffrey Simpson, "The Nation," *The Globe and Mail*, 8 September 2001.

Speaking recently of the elements of Chrétien's success, someone who has been close to him said, "The Prime Minister works hard at being humble."

Calvin Trillin, essayist, "Paper Baron," *The New Yorker*, 17 December 2001.

The Prime Minister is often described as being unable to speak either of Canada's official languages.

Calvin Trillin, essayist, "Paper Baron," *The New Yorker*, 17 December 2001.

I took a walk in the snow. And I'm staying. As long as I am Prime Minister, I remain the Prime Minister. Another day, another snowstorm—in July—I might decide to go.

Jean Chrétien, prime minister, announcing a Cabinet shuffle, Ottawa, 15 January 2002, in Tim Harper, "Chrétien Dumps 7, 13 Others Change Jobs," *Toronto Star*, 16 January 2002. The prime minister is alluding to Pierre Trudeau's snowy walk before his resignation in 1984.

The Prime Minister has suggested that "a few million dollars" may have been stolen from the taxpayers of Canada. If it happened, he argues, it was in a good cause—presumably akin to stealing bread on behalf of starving children. What's a few million?

Russell Mills, publisher of *The Ottawa Citizen*, opening paragraph of editorial, 1 June 2002, calling for Chrétien's resignation. It brought about the dismissal of the long-time newspaperman from his post by the Southam paper's new owners, CanWest Global Communications Corp. The editorial concluded: "Mr. Chrétien, we ask you to step down—for the good of your party and of the country. If you will not, we urge the Liberal party to throw you out."

He knew his limitations, which is more than I can say for most of us.

Attributed to **Pierre Elliott Trudeau** regarding Prime Minister Jean Chrétien by James Travers, "In Ottawa," *Toronto Star*, 18 October 2003.

Historians who prefer politicians to be visionaries will not find much to admire in Mr. Chrétien. Nothing he ever said as Prime Minister will nestle in the lexicon of noble Canadian quotations. No speech will make it into the history books. No memorable phrase will ever stick to him. Neither official language became his trumpet.

Jeffrey Simpson, columnist, on Chrétien's expressive powers, "What He Leaves Behind," *The Globe and Mail*, 1 November 2003.

He's cut / Smart to boot / And we salute / Our grand fromage now. / You were the kid / They couldn't beat. // The gays / All sing your praise / For days and days, / Though you wouldn't wed one. // A generous heart / A mighty fist / Once you depart / You'll be missed.

Lyrics from vocal tribute composed by **Paul Anka**, singer-songwriter, to the tune of his song "My Way," which he performed at Chrétien's retirement, Air Canada Centre, Toronto, 13 November 2003, published on the front page of *The Globe and Mail*, 14 November 2003.

Travelling around the world, I have found out that he is admired throughout the world.

Oscar Peterson, jazz pianist, tribute to Chrétien on his retirement, Air Canada Centre, Toronto, 13 November 2003, in Andrew Ryan, "Liberal Convention," *The Globe and Mail*, 14 November 2003.

Vive le Canada!

Jean Chrétien, prime minister, closing words of address, Liberal convention, Toronto, 13 November 2003, in Graham Fraser, *Toronto Star*, 14 November 2003.

Salut, p'tit gars.

Main headline on the impending retirement of Jean Chrétien as prime minister, subheaded "Or, in Canada's other official language: 'Goodbye, Little Guy' (from Shawinigan)," *Toronto Star*, 14 November 2003.

I describe it as skating on thin ice. You never know when there is a big hole that will gobble you up and you will disappear forever. It's a thrill to survive.

Jean Chrétien, prime minister, reviewing his political career, interview by Terence McKenna for the CBC-TV's *Life & Times: Jean Chrétien*, in columnist John Doyle, *The Globe and Mail*, 1 December 2003.

When I entered politics forty-one years ago, there was no medicare, no Canada Pension Plan, no official bilingualism, no national child benefits, no Kyoto, no free trade agreement, no Canadian flag, no Charter of Rights. Our constitution was a British document.

Jean Chrétien, former prime minister, accepting an honorary degree, Queen's University, Kingston, Ont., 27 May 2004, in Mike Blanchfield, "Voting Does Matter, Chrétien Tells Youth," *National Post*, 28 May 2004.

CHRISTIANITY *See also* Belief

I have seen men of every walk of life try it. I have seen lords and ladies and royalty, I have seen congressmen and senators, I have seen university professors give their lives to Christ. It has happened right here in Toronto in the last few days. One of your professors at the University of Toronto shook my hand last night and said: "Billy, for the last five days I have been living! I didn't know what living was. I would have laughed at this whole thing two weeks ago, but my life is different. I can't explain it. Some of my friends laugh at me, but my life is different."

Billy Graham, evangelist, address, "Is There an Answer?" Toronto, 6 October 1955, The Empire Club of Canada.

Christianity is very much to blame for this; the notion that salvation is free and may be attained by the idlest, the dullest, the stupidest is understandably very popular with persons who may be so described.

Robertson Davies, man of letters, letter, 18 November 1984, *For Your Eye Alone: Letters, 1976–1995* (1999).

A goodly portion of the life of Jesus was written well before he was born.

Donald Harman Akenson, historian, *Surpassing Wonder: The Invention of the Bible and the Talmuds* (1998). The passage appears in italics in the original because it highlights the Hebrew foreground and background of the "factional leader" who is credited with the founding of Christianity.

If Hinduism flows placidly like the Ganges, then Christianity bustles like Toronto at rush hour. It is a religion as swift as a swallow, as urgent as an ambulance. It turns on a dime, expresses itself in an instant. In a moment you are lost or saved. Christianity stretches back through the ages, but in essence it exists only at one time: right now.

Thoughts of the narrator in **Yann Martel**'s *The Life of Pi: A Novel* (2002).

A journalist jailed in Iran is likely to get more attention than two million Christians killed or enslaved in Sudan.

Richard John Neuhaus, founder of First Things, born in Pembroke, Ont., Lutheran pastor who became Catholic priest, "Religious Freedom in a Time of War," *First Things: The Journal of Religion and Public Life*, January 2002.

Christianity in particular is, around the world and in almost all its forms, the carrier of democracy and political liberalization.

Richard John Neuhaus, founder of First Things, born in Pembroke, Ont., Lutheran pastor who became Catholic priest, "Religious Freedom in a Time of War," *First Things: The Journal of Religion and Public Life*, January 2002.

Religion and spirituality are supposedly about life—abundant, evolving, transforming, ultimately triumphant life. An empty cross can convey that. But a crucifix symbolizes the opposite.

Tom Harpur, columnist and author, *The Pagan Christ: Recovering the Lost Light* (2004).

Two thousand years after his death, Christ is still huge. Bigger, in fact, than the Beatles.

Robert Priest, poet and columnist, "Cross Examination," *Now*, 8 April 2004.

CHRISTMAS *See also* Holidays

'Twas in the moon of wintertime / When all the birds had fled, / That Mighty Gitchi Manitou / Sent angel choirs instead. / Before their light the stars grew dim, / And wand'ring hunters heard the hymn: / "Jesus, your King, is born: / Jesus is born; In excelsis gloria!"

Jean de Brébeuf, Jesuit missionary, composer of the first Canadian Christmas carol in the Huron language at Sainte-Marie-among-the-Hurons (near present-day Midland, Ont.) in 1641. It has been sung in three languages—Huron, French, English—and the first verse in translation, by J.E. Middleton in 1926, appears here.

I have found that the fancy of the cattle dropping on their knees at midnight on Christmas Eve is very widespread, even among people who ought to know better.

David Boyle, archaeologist, "Canadian Folk-Lore," *The Globe*, 13 November 1897. Boyle found this folk belief common in rural areas, notably in 1837 in South Dumfries, Upper Canada.

On Christmas morning the streets are always bright with snow, not too much of it nor too little, hard-frozen snow, all crystals and glittering in the flood of sunshine that goes with Christmas day.... If there was ever any other Christmas weather I have forgotten it.

Stephen Leacock, humorist, *My Remarkable Uncle* (1942).

Perhaps what Christmas is all about is to help us rediscover the child in all of us, the fact that we have hearts and are capable of loving.

Jean Vanier, founder of L'Arche, in Tom Harpur, *Harpur's Heaven and Hell* (1983).

Christmas takes place in the depth of our northern winter. It is a time for celebration of the birth of the inner Christ in each of us. The inner Christ is the light in the darkness, the spirit in the body, the eternal "I am" that makes possible unconditional love and tolerance.

Alexa Petrenko, columnist and broadcaster, "Food for Thought," *Ontario's Common Ground Magazine*, winter 1990.

CHURCH *See also* Religion

A church is a recognition, in stone and wood and brick, of spiritual awakenings. It nods, to each individual person.... A church reminds us of what we have known. And it tells us that the possibility of the door swinging open again remains.

Margaret Visser, scholar, *The Geometry of Love: Space, Time, Mystery, and Meaning in an Ordinary Church* (2000).

The church exists to worship God. For God's sake, let our worship truly reflect the God we know.

Donna Sinclair and **Christopher White**, authors, *Jacob's Blessing: Dreams, Hopes, & Visions for the Church* (2000).

If your church were to close, would the sidewalks in your community sag from lack of love?

Bruce McLeod, former moderator of the United Church of Canada, in Donna Sinclair and Christopher White, *Jacob's Blessing: Dreams, Hopes, & Visions for the Church* (2000).

Many of our members and clergy still live with the confused idea that we are a fixture in Canadian society, that our participation in and with the state is essential to our identity. Of course, in 21st century secular Canada, this is no longer the case.

Roland De Vries, Presbyterian minister, "Withdrawing from Marriage," *National Post*, 10 December 2004.

I find that the separation of the Church and the state is one of the most beautiful inventions of modern times.

Pierre Pettigrew, minister of Foreign Affairs, interviewed on 27 January 2005 by Elizabeth Thompson and Anne Dawson, "Church Told to Butt Out," *National Post*, 28 January 2005. Pettigrew is responding to the expressed opposition of religious leaders—Roman Catholics, Muslims, Sikhs, Orthodox Jews—to extending marriage to couples of the same sex.

CINEMA *See also* Hollywood

In a Dark Pool with a Bear Behind.

Wording on the card to describe the scene that shows the shapely Dolores (actress Nell Shipman) bathing *au naturel* in an Alberta mountain pool, with her pet bear Brownie behind her, in the silent movie *Back to God's Country* (1919). This melodramatic adventure was Canada's first feature film, as noted by Kay Armatage, "The Girl from God's Country," *Maclean's*, 1 September 2003. Exhibitors were exhorted, "Don't Book Back to God's Country unless You want to prove that the Nude is NOT Rude." The nude scene predated Hedy Lamarr's in *Ecstasy* (1933) by 14 years.

Then there is the problem of the motion picture. Whether we like them or not we have to face the fact that the movies stand for a new art in this mechanized age of ours.... It is the new way of interpreting life, of holding the mirror up to nature. It has captured the world and it would seem the one vehicle that could and should interpret to the world the beauty and splendor of our Dominion.

Arthur Stringer, novelist and sometime Hollywood scriptwriter, address, "The Interpreters of Canada," Toronto, 7 April 1932, The Empire Club of Canada.

Who is that dastardly Canadian?

Words to this effect are spoken by the detective Colonel Anthony Gethryn (played by George C. Scott) about the nationality of a murder suspect in the movie *The List of Adrian Messenger* (1963) directed by John Huston. It is based on the mystery novel *The List of Adrian Messenger* (1960) written by the British novelist and screenwriter **Philip MacDonald**. At one point in the novel the philandering suspect is referred to "as that copulatory Canadian."

Above all, I certainly don't want to solve the riddles of tragedy by the trickery of the magic lantern.

Pierre Perrault, filmmaker, preferring documentary films over feature films, "Film and Reality," *How to Make or Not Make a Canadian Film* (1968), edited by André Pâquet.

A film industry will arise when people want to make films and people want to see them. It will be Canadian if Canadians make them. And that's the long and short of it.

Allan King, filmmaker, distinguishing between American-style and Canadian-made movies, "Canadian—Cinema—Vancouver," *How to Make or Not Make a Canadian Film* (1968), edited by André Pâquet.

I can't tell you what a Canadian film is, or how to make one, though you can spot them when you see them.

Allan King, filmmaker, "Canadian—Cinema—Vancouver," *How to Make or Not Make a Canadian Film* (1968), edited by André Pâquet.

Indeed, the film-makers of the new cinema refuse to admit that conditions for the production of an avant-garde work should be different, or to pay the price of experimentation. Yet for the last five years they have all been clamouring and working for a traditional feature film industry, in which they will never participate themselves and against which, in fact, they make their films. It is an avant-garde determined to create its own rear-guard—which is a very ironic situation indeed.

Jacques Godbout, filmmaker, referring to script-heavy Hollywood-style movies made in Canada, "A Trap: The Script," *How to Make or Not Make a Canadian Film* (1968), edited by André Pâquet.

Meanwhile, mediocre works will continue to be produced in Quebec and the rest of Canada and from time to time, perhaps once every five years, an outstandingly successful film will appear (like a Lelouch). But is it worth it? Would it not be better to try to create a left-wing cinema even if this proved uneconomic for some time to come? The establishment of a feature film industry is a mirage in our desert, but it is only a mirage.

Jacques Godbout, filmmaker, "A Trap: The Script," referring to script-heavy Hollywood-style movies made in Canada, *How to Make or Not Make a Canadian Film* (1968), edited by André Pâquet.

I find that too much is written about our cinema. Basically, we don't have cinema, we have film literature. I have the impression that if you were to collect all the articles, dossiers, briefs, etc., that have already been written on our films, it would take longer to read than to look at the film themselves.

Denys Arcand, filmmaker, "Speaking of Canadian Film," *How to Make or Not Make a Canadian Film* (1968), edited by André Pâquet.

You might like it or you might dislike it, but it is touching you somewhere else, and I think the best of these "other" films are the ones that touch you, in a way that your defences are unable to block out. You may have many mental defences but you may still be quite naked to intuitive thrusts or physical thrusts or emotional thrusts, and that may be where you are defenceless and hurtable, and vulnerable, but also where new things can move you and touch you.

Tom Daly, producer and director, referring particularly to the experimental short films of director Arthur Lipsett, "Running Past Our Habit Patterns," *Pot-Pourri* (National Film Board), September 1973.

You Should Know How Bad This Film Is. After All, You Paid for It.... If using public money to produce films like *The Parasite Murders* is the only way that English Canada can have a film industry, then perhaps English Canada should not have a film industry.

Robert Fulford, writing as Marshall Delaney, review of David Cronenberg's film *Shivers* (aka *The Parasite Murders*), *Saturday Night*, September 1975. As Caelum Vatnsdal noted in *They Came from Within* (2004), "Of course there *were* no films like Cronenberg's at the time, and I can only assume he means any genre project."

When Parisians or Romans or citizens of Toronto, Rio or even Wichita Falls, Texas, go to the movies, they don't say, "Tonight let's go to a Canadian movie, or a French movie, or an American movie." Not at all. What they do say is "Let's go see a really good movie tonight." And to hell with who made it or its origins. That is the way the real world operates.

Jack Valenti, CEO, Motion Picture Association of America, address, "The Cinema Future," 19 October 1989, Toronto, The Empire Club of Canada.

Handmade cinema is like watching thought, if thought could be seen.

Norman McLaren, filmmaker, quoted by director Don McWilliams on the liner notes of his NFB-CBC video documentary *Creative Process: Norman McLaren* (1991).

Without a vibrant feature film industry, we will always and inevitably export our best talent. It is a culturally devastating loss. It is also a preposterous economic waste. Imagine mobilizing our educational system to train doctors, scientists, engineers and entrepreneurs in order to send the most brilliant of them abroad to serve and enrich another economy. That is what we do in film.

Allan King, documentary director, address, "Creating a Healthy Base for Canadian Feature Films," Toronto, 21 January 1999, The Empire Club of Canada.

But this is going to be the best movie ever! It's a foreign film from Canada.

Line of dialogue spoken by the cartoon character Stan in the movie of the musical *South Park: Bigger, Longer & Uncut* (1999).

The Toronto festival was born in Cannes, on the Carlton terrace, where people buy each other ridiculously expensive rounds of Pimm's Royale and do business while pretending not to.

Brian D. Johnson, film commentator, referring to the meeting of Dusty Cohl and Bill Marshall at the Cannes International Film Festival before 1975, which laid the groundwork for the Toronto International Film Festival, *Brave Films, Wild Nights: 25 Years of Festival Fever* (2000).

Toronto for me is like a reaffirmation that it is not a waste of a lifetime to spend it going to movies and writing about them.

Roger Ebert, U.S. movie critic, on the opening of the 26th annual Toronto International Film Festival, "In Autumn, Thoughts Turn to Film," *National Post*, 6 September 2001.

How often when someone's just starting out do you get, "Is she real or is she fake?"

Rachel Roberts, Vancouver-born model, about her film debut as the "model" for the computer simulation of a woman in the movie *Simone* (2002) written and directed by Andrew Niccol. In the film's credits, it reads: "Simone as Herself." Rachel Roberts is to receive acknowledgement in the film's video release. Simone stands for "Simulation One."

Sylvia Plath: I hope you won't think I'm a neurotic American.
Professor Thomas: No, a neurotic Canadian.

Approximate wording of the exchange between **Sylvia Plath** (played by Gwyneth Paltrow) and her compassionate neighbour (Michael Gambon) in the movie *Sylvia* (2003), directed by Christine Jeffs.

I have nothing against films shot in Toronto, a city I love. But if a musical named *O Canada* were currently being filmed in Chicago, how would that make you feel?

Roger Ebert, movie critic, referring to criticism that the U.S. movie musical *Chicago* was actually shot in Toronto, "Answer Man," *National Post*, 25 April 2003.

I didn't object to losing the girl in almost every film that I made, but always hated the fact that I lost because the script made me out to be a big dumb guy. If only one writer had made me lose the girl because I was mean and vicious I would be completely happy today.

Jack Carson, Hollywood actor who specialized in "heavy" roles, born in Carman, Man., interviewed by Charles Foster, *Once Upon a Time in Paradise: Canadians in the Golden Age of Hollywood* (2003).

Whenever I die, I can always say: At least I did the best film I could make given the talent I had.

Denys Arcand, film director, interviewed by J. Kelly Nestruck, "'I Was Made to Be a Filmmaker,'" *National Post*, 20 November 2003.

The multiculturalism that keeps Canadian film in the realm of art cinema is the same multiculturalism that in literature is building an established and popularly accepted literary tradition. It does not do so in Canadian film because Canadian film has been historically inherently "foreign" to Canadians.

George Melnyk, academic, *One Hundred Years of Canadian Cinema* (2004).

It's no exaggeration to say that the history of Canadian fiction film-making is, in the main, one of catastrophe, neglect and wasted potential.

Caelum Vatnsdal, writer, *They Came from Within: A History of Canadian Horror Cinema* (2004).

The reason for making a film is to find out what it was that made you want to make that film in the first place.

David Cronenberg, director, in Jonathan Dee, "David Cronenberg's Body Language," *The New York Times*, 18 September 2005.

There are hundreds of films we have enjoyed or admired. There are a few we really love. That's what is so exciting about film: that it can speak intimately to each one of us, and some stay with us forever.

Norman Jewison, floor director and later movie director, *This Terrible Business Has Been Good to Me: An Autobiography* (2004).

Everyone from Hollywood is here. Wait. This is like the Canadian Oscars.

Billy Crystal, comedian and host, 2004 Academy Awards, Hollywood, California, referring to the film industry's "runaway" productions, in Brad Wheeler, "Oscars 2005," *The Globe and Mail*, 10 February 2005.

Feature films are the literature of our generation. They express the social conscience of our society.

Attributed to movie director **Norman Jewison** by film commentator Risa Shuman, interviewed by Michael Enright on CBC Radio's *Sunday Morning*, 27 February 2005.

Canada could never have produced a movie called *It's a Wonderful Life*. Way too boastful. Had the perennial holiday favourite been made by Canadians, its title would instead have been *It's an All-Right Life*.

Adapted from a remark made by **Lorne Michaels**, creator of SCTV's *Saturday Night Live*, by Scott Feschuk, "Why Are We So Funny?" *The Reader's Digest*, June 2005.

CITIES & TOWNS

See also Architecture; Housing; Places

Big cities should become true great cities. It is up to them henceforth to create a new humanism which will know how to reconcile technological progress and the requirements of the economy with the fundamental needs of mankind. As once said an eminent American sociologist, Lewis Mumford, we are facing the danger of catastrophe, if our great cities become like ant-hills, without regard for the dignity and welfare of the individual. They should become instead the masterpieces of our civilization.

Jean Drapeau, Montreal mayor, address, "For Whom the Big City Toils," Toronto, 19 January 1967, The Empire Club of Canada.

If the other jurisdictions do not want to give up their rights and responsibilities—those two words must always be used together—then they must have the courage to take the ultimate political responsibility of taxing to do the job, or the other side of that which is to take responsibility for not doing the job. In either case the electorate will judge, but that is one of the ways parties and politicians are re-elected or defeated, and that is what democracy is all about. You have to take the basic decision and be responsible to the taxpayers, or else do not act and be responsible for not acting.

Barney Danson, minister of State responsible for urban affairs, House of Commons, 8 December 1969.

Today, at the end of the millennium, the greatest task confronting us is to evolve, invent, and create a new urban environment: a place of meeting and interaction; a place that is adaptable and pluralistic; a place of man-made and natural beauty.

Moshe Safdie, architect, *The City after the Automobile: An Architect's Vision* (1997), with Wendy Kohn.

In thirty years, most North American cities ought to be pretty much the same as they are now. The aura of Lincoln, Nebraska, will remain essentially untouched; Chicago will still be Chicago. Ditto Halifax, Tallahassee and what have you. A few new buildings, a few more people, bigger trees—you get the idea. But Vancouver? We have no idea what this place is going to be like next year, let alone in a few decades.

Douglas Coupland, author, *City of Glass: Douglas Coupland's Vancouver* (2000).

Canada is the only country in the world that thinks it can thrive without the presence of a major metropolis.

Attributed to **Joe Berridge**, Toronto city spokesperson, by John Barber, "Inside Toronto," *The Globe and Mail*, 1 May 2003.

At last guess, there were more than a million Canadians living in greater Los Angeles, making L.A. the fourth largest Canadian city.

Murray White, correspondent, "Hollywood Canuck Pioneers," *Toronto Star*, 20 June 2004.

Whereas the United States had a frontier, and countries like Argentina and France and England have the Capital, one clear, overpowering, political, social and cultural centre—Buenos Aires, Paris and London being the national death stars of their respective countries—Canada has no single central city. It has scattered metropolises of various sizes, regional outposts with their own spheres of influence. There is no London, and that is not necessarily a bad thing.

Will Ferguson, travel writer, "On the Road with Will," *Maclean's*, 15 October 2004.

Art is about passion, and a city without passion is just a big town.

Pier Giorgio Di Cicco, Poet Laureate of the City of Toronto, acceptance speech, City Council, October 2004, quoted in *Scuola & Cultura* (Columbus Centre), spring 2005.

CITIZENSHIP *See also* Immigration; Nationhood

I talked to a young Canadian. He came into my office and he said: "I want to get back to Canada. I have been here between two and three years. I am not improving as a soldier. I left behind me a wife and child, because I believed it was my duty to do something in my trade to help the common cause. I am now getting no better as a soldier and I am deteriorating as a citizen." Those words burned themselves into my conscience. "I am deteriorating as a citizen."

R.B. Bennett, former prime minister, address, "An Address," Toronto, 13 October 1942, The Empire Club of Canada.

One reason I want to be a Canadian citizen is that it seems the closest I can come, in a foolish world, to being a world citizen.

Judith Merril, science-fiction personality, writing in 1968, *Better to Have Loved: The Life of Judith Merril* (2002), with Emily Pohl-Weary.

There should be a law that Canadians would not be granted citizenship until they've crossed this country by car or, if they can find one, by train.

Peter C. Newman, columnist and author, "Love This Land, Not the Constitution," *Defining Moments: Dispatches from an Unfinished Revolution* (1997).

Renouncing my citizenship was the last and most consistent act of dissent I could pose against a public policy which I believe is depriving Canada of its right and duty to be one of the world's greatest countries.

Conrad Black, Lord Black of Crossharbour, address, Fraser Institute, Vancouver, 15 November 2001, published in the *National Post*, 16 November 2001. As a foreign citizen, he could no longer retain ownership of his extensive chain of newspapers. As a Canadian citizen, he was unable to accept British peerage. He resolved the issue by ceasing to be a commoner, a Canadian, and a Canadian "press lord." He was elevated to the peerage on 31 October 2001.

"Are you a journalist?"
"No, just a citizen."

Characteristically modest reply of a young aide to a government minister, made by the late **Neil Morrison**, broadcaster, public servant, and citizen, as recalled by his son Eric Morrison, "Lives Lived," *The Globe and Mail*, 9 December 2002.

Canadians have been seduced into believing that the Constitution and the courts will, magically, take care of everything. In a democracy, however, citizens take care of everything.

Robert Ivan Martin, law professor, *The Most Dangerous Branch: How the Supreme Court of Canada Has Undermined Our Law and Our Democracy* (2003).

No one has yet figured out how to be a citizen of the world and only the world.

Mark Abley, author, *Spoken Here: Travels among Threatened Languages* (2003).

I feel like a North American, like a citizen of the world, but everybody needs a place where they have to take you in.

Robert MacNeil, writer and broadcaster, born in Halifax, based in New York City, interviewed by Noah Richler, "Yes, You Can Go Home Again," *National Post*, 29 May 2003.

Our citizenship is based on an idea of sharing, of the acceptance and accommodation of difference, and of trying to diminish antagonisms.... Our citizenship is not a buffet table. Our citizenship is a fixed menu.

Adrienne Clarkson, governor general, address at a citizenship ceremony, Calgary, March 2003, in Christopher Guly, "Class Act at Rideau Hall," *Forever Young*, July 2003.

Helping individuals become acceptable and fulfilled members of a culture takes generous individual attention to each one, usually from numerous people. Many autobiographies and memoirs attest gratefully to just such life-saving and morale-boosting attention.

Jane Jacobs, urban planning critic, *Dark Age Ahead* (2004).

CIVILIZATION *See also* Arts & Artists; Culture; Golden Ages; Heritage; Humanity; Society

Trench by trench the ramparts of ignorance have had to be conquered, as civilization has spread north.... A civilization as high as that of Ontario is certain to be developed farther north than Ontario, to a distance where it would be foolish for the wisest of us to try to estimate.

Vilhjalmur Stefansson, Arctic explorer, address, "The Canadian Arctic Region,"

Toronto, 11 November 1918, The Empire Club of Canada.

Civilization has made the Indian an outcast in his own country. That sounds like a paradox but it is a fact.

Grey Owl, author and conservationist, address, "A Plea for the Canadian Northland," Toronto, 12 November 1936, The Empire Club of Canada.

Canada is not a constitution. Canada is not a balance sheet. Canada is an ideal of civilization called tolerance. The tribe-torn world we see on our TV screens needs to see Canada succeed. And maybe we can see a better reason to succeed if we look at how badly the world needs Canada.

Keith Spicer, chair, Canadian Radio-television and Telecommunications Commission, address, "Broadcasting in the Nineties," Toronto, 24 May 1990, The Empire Club of Canada.

For me, at least, Canada is the civilized centre of the world.

Pico Iyer, traveller and essayist, introductory comment, address, "Imagining Canada," Hart House, Toronto, 5 April 2001.

Without art, we're handicapped, and living a stifled, barren existence. Art is a necessity. Art is an absolutely essential part of our enlightenment process. We cannot, as a species, as a civilized society, regard ourselves as being enlightened without the arts.

Ken Danby, artist, characteristic observation, 6 July 2005.

CLARK, JOE

What I don't understand is, why was 67 per cent not enough?

Charles, Prince of Wales, questioning Joe Clark, Governor General's Dinner, Ottawa, 20 June 1983, as quoted by Patrick Martin, Allan Gregg, and George Perlin, *Contenders: The Tory Quest for Power* (1983). The prince asked the question nine days after the 1983 Conservative Party's leadership convention at which Clark lost the vote—even with 67 percent support. As Martin, Gregg, and Perlin noted, "To the Clark group at Winnipeg only two scenarios had been thoroughly contemplated: If fewer than 66 per cent of the delegates voted against a leadership convention, then Clark would have no choice but to call for a convention and, of course, run for the leadership himself. If more than 67 per cent voted to retain the present leadership then Clark could feel entitled to stay. What they had not considered was if the vote should fall in between." The result of the ballot was bad luck for Clark: 66.9 percent. At least one placard read: "GO JOE GO ... PLEASE!"

Joe Clark is an able Parliamentarian, a veteran minister, an honest politician, a decent guy, a dogged fighter, and a good Canadian. Does that make him qualified to be Prime Minister?

Michael Bliss, historian and columnist, "Joe Clark for P.M.? Get Serious," *National Post*, 16 June 2001.

Canadians dislike many of this generation's politicians as the kind of men you wouldn't dare try to buy a used car from. You'd lose your shirt in the deal. Canadians came rather to like Joe Clark for exactly the opposite reason: Buy a used car from him and he'd probably lose his shirt in the deal.

Which would be our shirts, and ultimately our country.

Michael Bliss, columnist, "Clark: Never a Winner," *National Post*, 7 August 2002.

This is not the result of a walk in the snow, it has taken longer than that.

Joe Clark, Conservative Party leader, announcing his intention to resign the leadership in six months' time, Ottawa, press conference, Ottawa, 6 August 2002. Clark is alluding to the "walk in the snow" taken by Prime Minister Pierre Trudeau before deciding to retire in 1984.

If you're ever in a fight, Joe Clark will be the first person to offer to hold your coat.

Allan Fotheringham, columnist, "Lost Luggage, Lost Hope," *Maclean's*, 19 August 2002.

On the Tory airplane during a swing through Quebec in the 1979 election, I was sitting beside Val Sears on the Joe Clark plane in Quebec City when the leader, clad in a yellow cardigan, waddled to the back of the plane, looked at Sears, and asked innocently, "How long are you with us, Val?" Sears replied, "As long as it takes."

Robert Lewis, former editor of *Maclean's* magazine, recalled in an email, 14 January 2003.

Joe Clark never made an important political decision that was correct. It is feline to have more than one life. It is unique to Joe Clark to have only recurrent deaths.

Attributed to retired politician **Joe Clark** by Conrad Black, Letters to the Editor, by William E. Lee, Esquimalt, B.C., *National Post*, 20 October 2003.

My worst blunder was to describe Joe Clark, when he proved to be so astonishingly ineffective as prime minister, as acting "like a fawn caught eating broccoli." Even I couldn't fathom the meaning of that one, though Joe immediately dropped me a line promising to stop munching the green stuff.

Peter C. Newman, journalist and memoirist, referring to strained stylistic efforts in his prose, *Here Be Dragons: Telling Tales of People, Passion, and Power* (2004).

I used to call them Flora and Fauna...

Jean Chrétien, prime minister, final speech, House of Commons, 6 November 2003, as reported in "His Final Speech: 2003," *National Post*, 7 November 2003. He was referring to Opposition members Flora MacDonald and Joe Clark in his days as minister for Indian Affairs.

CLARKSON, ADRIENNE

I am Adrienne Clarkson *and you're not.*

Spoof of the style of Adrienne Clarkson, host of CBC-TV's *Adrienne Clarkson Presents*, the program launched in June 1990, and caricatured by the popular comedy team of CBC Radio's *Double Exposure*, before her appointment as governor general. The line brings to mind Laurier LaPierre's droll sign-off on his Montreal-based TV show in the mid-1970s: "I am Laurier LaPierre ... and you are you."

Call me Madame.

Adrienne Clarkson, governor general, establishing the style of address, before her installation as the 26th governor general of Canada, Ottawa, 7 October 1999. She became Her Excellency and her husband, author John Ralston Saul, His Excellency.

I heard that one of the longest waves big championship surfers off the coast of South Africa can ride is about three miles. According to my father, I've done two-and-a-half.

Adrienne Clarkson, governor general, interviewed by Christopher Guly, "Class Act at Rideau Hall," *Forever Young*, July 2003.

CLASS SYSTEM *See also* Society

Now for the first time I said to myself, I was fully in America (though it was only Canada).... I had got—and I saw that I had got—into a classless universe. Its great oddity (for me) was dependent upon that. I shall never forget the sensation. Rather uncanny.

Wyndham Lewis, English author and one-time Toronto resident, *America, I Presume* (1940). He is describing nude bathing in the men-only pool at Hart House, the student union of the University of Toronto.

Being utterly abstract, the human rights perspective denies the existence of classes and, thereby, reinforces class domination. Popular democracy provides the only mechanism through which ordinary people might challenge the dominant clique.

Robert Ivan Martin, law professor, *The Most Dangerous Branch: How the Supreme Court of Canada Has Undermined Our Law and Our Democracy* (2003).

CLIMATE *See also* Environmentalism; Seasons; Weather

The point is, there are two kinds of good climate; there is a good loafing climate and a good working climate. (Laughter and applause.)

I suggest that it is not a good climate where bananas and yams flourish if men decay. Canada, excepting Victoria, B.C., has a working rather than a loafing climate. (Hear, hear, and applause.)

Vilhjalmur Stefansson, Arctic explorer, address, "Abolishing the Arctic," Toronto, 25 October 1928, The Empire Club of Canada.

When the history of global climate change is finally written, it will show that the debate was badly derailed early in the game by three simple words: proof, uncertainty, and risk.

Lydia Dotto, science commentator, *Storm Warning: Gambling with the Climate of Our Planet* (1999).

Climate change is only one of several human-induced environmental—what? ... crises? difficulties? challenges? Any noun I might choose has political spin, defines allegiances, presupposes a point of view.

Jan Zwicky, poet, introduction, *Hard Choices: Climate Change in Canada* (2004), edited by Harold Coward and Andrew J. Weaver.

Our society is currently well adapted, by both where and how we live and work, to the climate of the past century. While there are some potentially positive effects in Canada as these climatic conditions change, many more severe and adverse impacts will be increasingly felt in coming decades.

James P. Bruce and **Stewart J. Cohen**, climatologists, "Impacts of Climate Change in Canada," *Hard Choices: Climate Change in Canada* (2004), edited by Harold Coward and Andrew J. Weaver.

The climate change we are in store for over the next few centuries will be larger and occur faster than at any time in the last 10,000 years.

Harold Coward, climatologist, "What Can Individuals Do?" *Hard Choices: Climate Change in Canada* (2004), edited by Harold Coward and Andrew J. Weaver.

CLONES *See also* Genetic Engineering; Research; Science

It was the same when Louise Brown, the first test-tube baby, was born. It was all Frankenstein and monsters. And now you have hundreds of test-tube babies made every day, and nobody asks anything about it because they know it's not bad. And that's why I am hoping that Clonaid will be the first company to make a cloned baby. And then everyone will see on CNN, maybe *Larry King Live*, a beautiful family, a smiling baby, and we know it will be smiling because it will be a copy of the one we know, and people will say, "Ah, that's beautiful!" and public opinion will change. It was the same at the beginning of fire, and with the steam engine and electricity. All human progress.

Claude Vorilhon, aka Raël, Quebec-based founder of the Raëlian movement, which supports the research group Clonaid to further the cause of human cloning, in Margaret Talbot, "A Desire to Duplicate," *The New York Times Magazine*, 4 March 2001.

The process is going well. A baby will be born twelve to twenty-four months from now.

Claude Vorilhon, aka Raël, cult leader based in Quebec's Eastern Townships, referring to the plans for his company Clonaid to clone a human being; interviewed in London, England, "Cult Head Predicts Human Clone in Two Years," Reuters, 15 February 2002. Raël went on to say, "My mission is to prepare human beings for future technology. Life expectancy is now ninety years; at the beginning of the century it was forty years. Once we have applied this technology to human beings we will soon live seven hundred years."

CLOTHES *See* Fashion

COACHING *See also* Mentoring; Sports

Coachin' beats workin' and it beats non-workin'. It's somewheres in between.

Jack Donohue, college basketball coach, characteristic remark, broadcast in his obituary, CBC Radio, 17 April 2003.

COHEN, LEONARD

Now a man appears on his own, he must be singing although his lips scarcely move, the caption gave the name Leonard Cohen, and the image looks fixedly at Raimundo Silva, the movements of his mouth articulate a question, Why won't you listen to me, lonely man, no doubt adding, Listen to me while you can, before it's too late, one video-clip follows another and, they are never repeated, this isn't a disk you can play over and over again, I might be back but I can't say when, you might miss me, so take your chance, take your chance. Raimundo Silva bent over, turned on the sound.

Description of one of Leonard Cohen's rock-like videos seen on television through the eyes of a proofreader character, Raimundo Silva, in novelist **José Saramago**'s *The History of the Siege of Lisbon* (1996), translated from the Portuguese by Giovanni Pontieio.

Give me a Leonard Cohen afterworld / so I can sigh eternally.

Two lines from rock group Nirvana's singer-songwriter **Kurt Cobain**'s song "Pennyroyal Tea."

COLLECTIVITY *See also* Communities; Socialism; Society

If we bring out what is truly within us, as Canadians—if we have a collective consciousness—we will realize that we are all a part of each other.

Adrienne Clarkson, governor general, interviewed by Richard Addis, "Year 1: 'I Met Canadians,'" *The Globe and Mail*, 19 October 2000.

COLLEGES & UNIVERSITIES *See* Universities & Colleges

COLONIALISM *See also* British Empire; Canada & United States

Many of you at this point are probably saying to yourselves that this sounds very anti-Canadian. Let me quickly add that I have lived in this country for twenty-two years, and of all the colonies, Canada is my favourite.

Ben Wicks, London, U.K.–born cartoonist, address, "Up the Empire," Toronto, 9 November 1978, The Empire Club of Canada.

COLOUR

If white is the presence of all colours, then black is the potential of all colours.

Christopher Dewdney, poet and author, *Acquainted with the Night: Excursions through the World after Dark* (2004).

COMEDY *See also* Humour

If I told him once, I told him a thousand times, I said, "Julie, don't go!"

Famous oft-repeated line from "the Julius Caesar skit," fondly remembered from NBC's *The Ed Sullivan Show*, 4 May 1958. **Johnny Wayne** and **Frank Shuster** wrote and performed the skit and the line was spoken by Calpurnia (actress Sylvia Lennick).

Is there a doctor in the Horse?

Amusing pun from the **Johnny Wayne** and **Frank Shuster** comic skit "Siege of Troy," in the 1950s, recalled by John Saunders, "Comic Shuster Dies at 85," *The Globe and Mail*, 14 January 2002.

Charlie Farquharson thinks a computer is somebody who lives in the country and works in the city. They told him it was a machine that thinks almost like a human being. He said, "That's the kind of person we were having trouble with in the first place. I don't want one of them around. There's only three kinds of computer. There's yer burrows, yer honey well, and yer one-b-m. But I've dug a hole out behind the house fer all that. All that's taken care of."

Don Harron, actor and comedian, address, "Getting Away with It for Forty-four Years," Toronto, 10 April 1980, The Empire Club of Canada.

Hello, my name is Bernard Braden and I'm not an Englishman trying to sound like an American. I'm a Canadian trying to sound like an American.

Opening skit of BBC Radio's light-comedy series *Breakfast with Braden,* starring the Vancouver-born Bernard Braden and his Canadian-born wife Barbara Kelly. Scripts were written by **Denis Norden** and **Frank Muir**, with **Eric Nicol**, as noted by Braden in his memoirs, *The Kindness of Strangers* (1990). The immensely popular series was succeeded by *Bedtime with Braden* and *On the Braden Beat.*

Comedians today are marketing their worst mood. If you're a comedian who is not mad at anything, you can't work in this business today. But I'm not mad. I think you should take life with a grain of salt. I think you should relax, kick back and have some fun. And I just wanted to do something that I would enjoy going to work for.

Steve Smith, comic known for his handyman character Red Green, star of CBC-TV's *The Red Green Show,* in Randall King, *Winnipeg Free Press,* 12 April 2002.

I never even had that idea until you mentioned it. Now it's gonna be igloo, igloo, igloo, igloo! Igloo all the time!

Conan O'Brien, host of the television show *Late Night with Conan O'Brien,* prompted by advice to avoid stereotypes, press conference in Toronto, 15 December 2003, announcing that he will present the talk show from Toronto, 10–13 February 2004, in Michael Posner, "When O'Brien Hits Town, It Will Be 'Igloo All the Time,'" *The Globe and Mail,* 16 December 2003.

Comedy is the province of the outsider, the cry of the intelligent but powerless. Millennia of persecution created the necessary vulnerability and empathy needed to produce first-rate comedy.

Mark Breslin, founder of Yuk Yuk's chain of comedy clubs, "Comedy Stripped," *The Village Post,* June 2005.

COMMERCE *See also* Business

A society that works, an economy that works, a home of choice for global champions: we have the makings of a compelling brand.

Thomas P. d'Aquino and **David Stewart-Patterson**, president and vice president, respectively, of the Business Council on National Issues and authors, *Northern Edge: The Will to Win* (2001).

COMMON SENSE

The four main villains in this loss of common sense in our society, the four horsemen of the modern apocalypse, are the politicians, the academics and intellectuals, the church and the media, not necessarily in that order. The masses, the people who work for a living, have common sense.

Peter Worthington, editor, *Toronto Sun,* address, "Blame the Media," Toronto, 8 March 1979, The Empire Club of Canada.

And this brought me back to something that we were actually taught in my college career: the old idea of the "common sensorium"—commune sensorium—the place where all your senses meet, and where they can all be evaluated relative to one another, to see if they are in harmony or disharmony, or whatever. It's the origin of the term "common sense"—that's where the phrase comes from.

Tom Daly, producer and director, "The Growth of a Craft: My Debt to Legg and Grierson," *John Grierson and the NFB* (1984), produced by the John Grierson Project.

COMMUNICATIONS *See also* Broadcasting; Free Speech; Freedom of Expression; Global Village; Information Technology; Internet; Interviews; Media; Questions; Radio; Rights; Technology; Telephone; Television

Although communication has often been offered as the medicine, it has seldom produced a cure.

Erving Goffman, psychologist, *Strategic Interaction* (1969).

A public that indulges primarily in tragedy, calamity, oddity, conflict, and sex is a public unprepared for intelligent discourse on major issues and knowledgeable decision-making.

Knowlton Nash, journalist, *Trivia Pursuit: How Showbiz Values Are Corrupting the News* (1998).

Guess what, Joel, I'm talking to you on a real cellular phone, walking down the street in New York.

Martin Cooper, Toronto-born, Winnipeg-raised inventor of the cellular telephone and leader of the research team at Motorola making the world's first mobile (cellular) telephone call in downtown Manhattan to his competitor, Joel Engel at Bell Labs, April 2003, in Doug Saunders, "Lord of the Ring," *The Globe and Mail*, 1 February 2003. Cooper reminisced: "When I and my colleagues at Motorola built the first cellular phone in 1973, it weighed ½ pounds. This phone I'm talking on weighs a little over three ounces. That first phone was absolutely wonderful but not very practical. We literally built it to prove a point."

Before you inform, you have to entertain.

David Phillips, climatologist, interviewed by Stephen Strauss, "Canada's Mr. Weather," *The Globe and Mail*, 13 September 2003.

COMMUNISM *See also* Dictatorship; Fascism; Russia

Happiness is driving a taxi in Toronto.

George Gabori, social democrat who was imprisoned by the Communists in his native Hungary, and was driving a taxicab in Toronto, in Ethan Herberman, *Toronto Star*, 27 June 1982.

Nothing so distresses a communist as to discover that the bourgeois state is really what he says it is.

H.S. Ferns, historian, *Reading from Left to Right: One Man's Political History* (1983).

Stalinist communism is dead. The dogmatic, totalitarian state is deader. But we don't know what kind of new totalitarianism will arise or how it will adjust and evolve. So you can't say communism is completely dead.

Franklyn Griffiths, academic, University of Toronto, in *Toronto Star*, 30 September 1989.

COMMUNITIES *See also* Cities & Towns; Civilization; Places; Society

There is too much accent upon the community, particularly upon the community in its organized capacity as a City, as a Province, as a State, and so on, and too little upon the individual man. That I believe to be the main reason why we are pessimistic as to the future. The means whereby we can change our pessimism for optimism is merely by going in for individual work. (Loud applause.)

B.K. Sandwell, professor of English, address, "On Being Sorry for Ourselves," Toronto, 24 January 1924, The Empire Club of Canada.

A national may be considered a community of communities. The nation is an organic entity of goals and resources.

Léon Dion, sociologist, Quebec government adviser, *Quebec: The Unfinished Revolution* (1976), translated by Thérèse Romer. Prime Minister **Joe Clark** was comfortable with the notion that Canada was "a community of communities," but **Pierre Trudeau**, a self-styled federalist, derided the idea as "ten premiers and the Prime Minister as a kind of head waiter to take their orders" and also as "a loose confederation of shopping centres."

My topic today is Canada—A Community of Communities. Joe Clark coined this phrase and I believe that it really sums up what Canada *is* today. Not what some intellectuals and theorists want it to be—but what our country *is* today.

A. Roy Megarry, publisher, address, "Canada—A Community of Communities," Toronto, 9 March 1989, The Empire Club of Canada.

We are not alone, nor are we together.

Line from an untitled prose poem, in **Antonio D'Alfonso**'s *Panick Love* (1992).

For communities to exist, people must encounter one another in person. These encounters must include more than best friends or colleagues at work. They must include diverse people who share the neighbourhood, and often enough share its needs.

Jane Jacobs, urban planning critic, *Dark Age Ahead* (2004).

COMPASSION

In the end all human beings become candidates for compassion, all of us, without exception.

Thoughts of a character in **Rohinton Mistry**'s novel *Family Matters* (2002).

COMPENSATION *See also* Business; Executives

I never met a group of managers or executives who felt overpaid or underworked.

Peter Urs Bender, motivational speaker, characteristic remark, 11 May 2000.

COMPOSERS *See also* Music; Singers & Songs

Will *nobody* write a few songs for Canada?

Thomas Macqueen, first publisher of the *Huron Signal* newspaper in 1848, in Henry J. Morgan, *Bibliotheca Canadensis* (1867).

From about age eight I had the idea I wanted to be a composer—mainly, at that time, in order to become very, very famous.

John Beckwith, composer and teacher, interviewed by *Musicanada*, November 1967.

COMPUTERS *See also* Communications; Global Village; Free Trade; Information Technology; Internet; Offices; Technology; Y2K

Today the hunter, the engineer, the programmer, the researcher, and the aesthete are one.

Marshall McLuhan, media philosopher, address, "The End of the Work Ethic," Toronto, 16 November 1972, The Empire Club of Canada.

Computers may replace men, but they will never replace women.

Louis Dudek, poet, *Epigrams* (1975).

Cooperate on move one; thereafter, do whatever the other player did the previous move.

Two commands that operate TIT FOR TAT, the computer program devised by **Anatol Rapoport**, psychologist and philosopher at the University of Toronto, that sheds light on the nature of international cooperation and the systemic causes of warfare. His program outperformed all other such programs in the scenario known as the Prisoners' Dilemma at an international computer tournament at Indiana University in 1979, and it continues to excel. It initiates and rewards reciprocal cooperation.

We can use wearable computers to enhance our lives, we can create a permanent connection to borderless cyberspace communities, we can permanently interact with the machine, so long as we retain our awareness of how our choices will affect our selves and our world.

Steve Mann, computer specialist, *Cyborg: Digital Destiny and Human Possibility in the Age of the Wearable Computer* (2001), with Hal Niedzviecki.

I just sit on my little chair with my pad and pen. I write longhand on those legal pads on every second line. Sometimes I use exam books from the university. If I was to write it on a computer it would feel as if the fairies wrote it. When I press my ballpoint pen into the legal pad, I know it's me.

Alistair MacLeod, fiction writer, "Q&A," *Maclean's*, 24 March 2003.

I always like to say: As the world speaks English, Internet speaks Java.

James Gosling, Canadian-born developer of the internet programming language known as Java, quoted on the webpage of Sun Microsystems, 20 December 2004.

Most things today complicate life, like your new software package that comes with a 300-page manual.

Red Green, persona of comic actor Steve Smith on *The Red Green Show* about a handyman mad about duct tape, in Jim Coyle, "A Little Duct Tape for the Canadian Soul," *Toronto Star*, 1 September 2005.

CONFEDERATION *See also* Canada; Dominion; Federal–Provincial Relations; Government

Providence Being Their Guide / They Builded Better Than They Knew.

Inscription on the bronze plaque erected in 1917 but not unveiled until 1 July 1927 outside the Legislative Chamber, Providence House, Charlottetown, P.E.I. Here was established the basis for the confederation of the colonies of British North America. The inscription is interesting, being a cento of English and American poetry. "Providence being their guide" comes from the passage in **John Milton**'s *Paradise Lost* (1667) that describes the expulsion of Adam and Eve from the Garden of Eden. "They builded better than they knew" comes from "The Problem," *Poems* (1847), in which **Ralph Waldo Emerson** wrote about the need for belief. The lines remain a powerful pastiche of British thought and American sentiment, and so are completely Canadian.

Confederation had been a political union of several provinces, not a cultural compact between two ethnic communities, English and French.

Donald G. Creighton, historian, distinguishing between two conceptions of Canada—political union versus cultural pact—arguing that the Fathers of Confederation took the Conservative view, envisioning a union, not the Liberal view, opting for a pact. Creighton offers evidence in *Canada's First Century* (1970).

To say precisely at what point Canada began is like deciding where all the sources and all the little tributary streams of a river come together in a single course. One such moment was when the two men who gave their names to this lecture series, LaFontaine and Baldwin, bringing with them their people, their language groups and the experience they represented, made common cause to win responsible government.

David Malouf, Australian man of letters, noting the influence of the French and English statesmen who established its basis almost two decades before the Act of Confederation in 1867, "Wisdom from a Tale of Two Nations," *Maclean's*, 22 March 2004.

CONFIDENTIALITY *See also* Journalism; Privacy

To compel a journalist to break a promise of confidentiality would do serious harm to the constitutional entrenched right of the media to gather and disseminate information.

Madam Justice **Mary Lou Benotto**, Ontario Superior Court, ruling, 21 January 2004, in Robert Fulford, "Commentary," *National Post*, 22 January 2004.

CONFLICT

Canada, David Cronenberg has said, is a country cursed with the ability to see both sides of an issue, so conflict—the essence of drama or so we're told—is not our strong suit. This leaves us with our poor frostbitten insecurities, which, as it happens, are always pretty funny.

Caelum Vatnsdal, writer, referring to the noted director of horror films, *They Came from Within: A History of Canadian Horror Cinema* (2004).

CONFUSION

Lord Ronald said nothing; he flung himself from the room, flung himself upon his horse and rode madly off in all directions.

Lines from humorist **Stephen Leacock**'s parody "Gertrude the Governess" in his self-published collection of parodies *Nonsense Novels* (1911). Ralph Curry in his biography of Leacock notes that the expression "riding madly off in all directions" came into its own when former U.S. President Theodore Roosevelt used it in a political address.

CONQUEST OF 1759 *See* Quebec, Conquest of

CONSCIENCE *See also* Good & Evil; Virtue & Vice

This is where you can feel everything simultaneously without being afraid of the contradictions that you have, but in a kind of objective way, which is exactly similar to the way you feel things about others.

Tom Daly, producer and director, "The Growth of a Craft: My Debt to Legg and Grierson," *John Grierson and the NFB* (1984), produced by the John Grierson Project.

People are at their most brilliant while defending themselves against their own conscience.

Irena F. Karafilly, aphorist, characteristic observation, 7 November 2000.

CONSCIOUSNESS *See also* Attention

Cosmic Consciousness, then, is a higher form of consciousness than that possessed by the ordinary man.

Richard Maurice Bucke, psychiatrist and theorist, *Cosmic Consciousness: A Study in the Evolution of the Human Mind* (1901). He coined the term "cosmic consciousness" in a paper read before the American Medico-Psychological Association meeting in Philadelphia, 18 May 1894.

When I beheld this awe-inspiring vista my consciousness was suddenly swept up as if by an enormous, overpowering wave to a plane far beyond anything I had ever experienced. Words could never describe this state of consciousness.

Sylvia Hellman, Swami Radha, German-born disciple of Swami Sivananda, who immigrated to Canada in 1951, *Radha: Diary of a Woman's Search* (1960), in Andrew Rawlinson, *The Book of Enlightened Masters: Western Teachers in Eastern Traditions* (1997).

My consciousness consists in the existence of a world.

Ted Honderich, Grote professor of mind and logic, University College London, born in Baden, Ont., *Philosopher: A Kind of Life* (2001). This is Honderich's principal contribution to the subject of the nature of consciousness in his series of lectures to the Royal Institute of Philosophy in London in 1996–1997. He is "guided by the idea of consciousness as existence."

CONSCRIPTION *See also* War

Not necessarily conscription, but conscription if necessary.

W.L. Mackenzie King, prime minister, address on the National Resources Mobilization Act, House of Commons, 7 July 1942. King uttered this classical formulation with respect to the need for conscription for military service overseas, based on an unsigned editorial "Mr. King on Conscription," *Toronto Daily Star*, 11 June 1942. The editorialist argued, "But the government says enough are coming forward; that enough may continue to come forward, and that conscription for overseas duty, which it is willing to impose if necessary, may never be necessary at all." According to journalist David MacDonald, the wording was drawn to King's attention by his adviser, J.S. Pickersgill; King eagerly adapted the formula to his own purposes.

CONSERVATION *See also* Environmentalism

I want to arouse in the Canadian people a sense of responsibility, the great responsibility they have for that north country and its inhabitants, human and animal. I thank you. (Hearty applause.)

Grey Owl, author and conservationist, address, "A Plea for the Canadian Northland," Toronto, 12 November 1936, The Empire Club of Canada.

Red Indians and Eskimos who live in the forest and on the tundra are conservationists by deepest instinct, and left to their care the North would remain very much as nature made it.

Marjorie Spock, student of anthroposophy, "North America under a Light Sky," *The Golden Blade* (1971), edited by Arnold Freeman and Charles Waterman.

It occurs to me that the high Arctic is the ultimate remaining watershed for civilization as a retreat for broad reflection, speculation, contemplation or meditation on questions of the human condition.

Eli Bornstein, artist, "Notes on Art and Nature" (1987), *Eli Bornstein: Art Toward Nature* (1996), edited by Jonneke Fritz-Jobse.

To want a better city passionately.

Phrase associated with the Toronto Region Architectural Conservancy movement and attributed to **Eric Arthur**, architect and its prime mover, in Alec Keefer, *Conservation in Context* (1999).

We don't inherit the Earth from our grandparents. We borrow it from our children.

Conservancy saying, recalled by Rose Cross, wife of Alexander (Sandy) Cross, at the dedication of the Cross Conservation Area, Alta., 1989, in Brian Brennan, in Sandy Cross's obituary "He Just Loved That Land," *The Globe and Mail,* 19 January 2004.

Why save what we're losing when all can celebrate what we've already lost, right?

Dwight Whalen, researcher, characteristic observation, private correspondence, 17 May 2004.

CONSERVATISM *See also* Conservative Party of Canada; Red Tory

I find, as I have been interviewed in Canada, in the few brief hours I've been here this time, that all commentators seem to regard one as something of a phenomenon because one set out in politics with convictions. They don't quite understand that. They say, "Well, here we have pragmatism." To this I say, if you are embarking on a great voyage across the oceans, you have to have some stars to steer by, and the stars have to be constant. It's no good steering by shooting stars. So, yes, I had conviction.

Margaret Thatcher, prime minister of Great Britain, address, "The New World Order," Toronto, 8 November 1993, The Empire Club of Canada.

CONSERVATIVE PARTY OF CANADA

See also Canadian Alliance; Conservatism; Conservatives; Political Parties; Progressive Conservative Party; Red Tory; Reform Party

I can tell you—without hesitation, without concern—that the Conservative party founded this country 133 years ago and the Conservative party will be here defending the interests of Canada 133 years from tonight.

Brian Mulroney, former prime minister, address, Conservative gathering, Toronto, 24 October 2000, in Joël-Denis Bellavance, *National Post,* 25 October 2000.

The leader must have a firm vision of Canada, a deep knowledge of its people, a familiarity with its languages, an understanding of its soul, and an unshakable resolve to lead his party to victory. The leader must be part political strategist, part inspirational speaker, part visionary, part fund-raiser, part cheerleader and part parish priest and—I say this only partly with tongue in cheek—all bound together by a strong capacity for self delusion!

Brian Mulroney, former prime minister, speech defining the essential qualities of a Conservative leader, Conservative fundraising dinner, Montreal, 23 May 2001, quoted in *The Globe and Mail,* 24 May 2001.

I am against a merger, I am against the destruction of the Progressive Conservative party.... This new creature, this so-called Conservative Party of Canada, if it goes forward, will be an illegitimate creation conceived in deception and born in betrayal.

David Orchard, prominent Conservative, objecting to the plan to merge the Canadian Alliance and the Progressive Conservative Party, press statement, 17 October 2003, in Tonda MacCharles, "'Born in Betrayal,' Merger Condemned," *Toronto Star,* 18 October 2003.

We're not the government, we're the people who came to fix government.

Characteristic remark of **Mike Harris** while premier of Ontario (1995–2003), as noted by Murray Campbell, "Tory Spending Revelations a Bitter Pill from Harris Era," *The Globe and Mail,* 27 May 2004.

It's not like a death in the family. It's the family dying.... I don't believe in this new party as I see it now ... I may be proven wrong in time, but I don't intend to add my reputation to a venture that on the evidence I see now is not something I would like to see governing the country.

Joe Clark, former prime minister and twice leader of the Progressive Conservative Party of Canada, "Clark Quits the Party He Twice Led," *National Post*, 9 December 2003. Clark is responding to the decision of members of the Canadian Alliance and the PCPC to jointly form the CPC on 7 December 2003.

CONSERVATIVES *See also* Canadian Alliance; Conservative Party of Canada; Conservatism; Red Tory

I am a conservative. That is why I deeply resent the neo-conservatives who are not conservatives at all. They are the opposite: radicals who are destroying cherished institutions and wreaking havoc on our human heritage as well as our natural heritage.

Robert Bateman, artist and naturalist, "I Am a Conservative, I Conserve," *The Globe and Mail*, 13 December 2003.

Now that the Conservatives have reunited, there will be a change of government in our lifetime.

Michael Bliss, columnist, anticipating a contest between Liberal Prime Minister Paul Martin and Conservative leader Stephen Harper, "'Most Important Election' in Canadian History?" *National Post*, 10 May 2004.

The voters of Quebec have three choices: corruption, separatism, or us.

Attributed to Conservative Party leader **Stephen Harper**, in anticipation of a federal election call, after addressing a Quebec constituency, interviewed on Global TV, 11 May 2004.

My Canada will be as Canadian as any other candidate's. You know, in this country, you can be a Canadian without being a Liberal. The government seems to forget that.

Stephen Harper, Conservative Party leader, press conference, Ottawa, 23 May 2004, in Heather Scoffield and Campbell Clark, "Martin Waves the Flag," *The Globe and Mail*, 24 May 2004.

CONSTITUTIONS *See also* Charter of Rights and Freedoms

The B.N.A. Act planted in Canada a living tree capable of growth and expansion within its natural limits.

Lord Sankey, Lord Chancellor of the Privy Council of Great Britain, minting the image of the British North America Act, 1867, and hence the Canadian Constitution, as a "living tree," as noted by Peter W. Hogg, *Constitutional Law of Canada* (1999). Two citations: "Lord Sankey's metaphor would be more generally accepted" (*Edwards* v. *A.-G. Can.* [1930] A.C. 114, at 136). "The Supreme Court of Canada has approved the living tree metaphor in *A-G. Que.* v. *Blaikie* [1979] 2 S.C.R. 1016, at 1029."

The Soviet constitution is the best constitution in the world, and the most meaningless. (It should be a lesson to us when we bring ours home.) It guarantees every citizen the right to pray, and it also guarantees every atheist the right to carry on anti-religious propaganda—which is like having a hockey game when one team can't shoot at the other team's goal. Under those circumstances, I imagine even the Leafs could get a draw with the Canadiens.

Peter Worthington, editor, *Toronto Sun*, address, "Blame the Media," Toronto, 8 March 1979, The Empire Club of Canada.

It is astonishing how many people simply cannot get it into their heads that we now have a very rigid Constitution. It is going to be the devil of a job to get anything new into it, or anything old of any importance out of it.

Eugene Forsey, constitutional specialist, Letters to the Editor, *The Globe and Mail*, 25 April 1987, in J.E. Hodgetts, *The Sound of One Voice: Eugene Forsey and His Letters to the Press* (2000).

The way to the future really only has two paths. One involves the development of a new constitution for all of Canada and the other involves the complete separation of Quebec and the possible breakup of the rest of Canada.

Angus Reid, public opinion analyst, address, "Canada at the Crossroads," Toronto, 28 February 1991, The Empire Club of Canada.

We have never signed. We will never sign. We will sign when it's an agreement between two sovereign nations.

Bernard Landry, Quebec deputy premier, speech announcing his leadership bid, 21 January 2001, ignoring the fact that the Constitution Act requires the "signature" of no province, quoted in *The Globe and Mail*, 2 March 2001.

The reason I am against constitutional change is because it gives people false hope. It would make them think that we have solved all the problems that are out there, when really, the Constitution is just words.

Jean Chrétien, prime minister, justifying the constitutional status quo, expressing an unwillingness to alter the line about "all thy sons command" in the English lyrics of "O Canada," reception at 24 Sussex Drive, Ottawa, 5 June 2001, in Allan Thompson, "P.M. No Fan of Wording in Anthem," *Toronto Star*, 7 June 2001.

To define and protect the rights of individuals is a prime purpose of the constitution of a democratic state.

Attributed to constitutional specialist **F.R. Scott** by Graham Fraser, "The Fight for Canada's Rights," *Toronto Star*, 13 April 2002.

But the real starting point in understanding our orthodoxy is its commitment to relativism—intellectual, cultural, and moral. A paradox is immediately apparent. How can one have an orthodoxy based on relativism?

Robert Ivan Martin, law professor, *The Most Dangerous Branch: How the Supreme Court of Canada Has Undermined Our Law and Our Democracy* (2003). Martin deals with the paradox by noting the fact that the orthodoxies are "shot through with inconsistencies and contradictions" and "the practitioners of the orthodoxy apply it to all ideas except their own." He concludes, "The soundness of relativism is assumed; relativism itself is not subjected to relativistic analysis."

The value of Canada to the world is values and spirit and not structures. What we need in Canada is not another constitution but a simple poetic preamble that explains Canada in 300 to 400 words and kids should memorize.

Keith Spicer, former journalist and retired chair, Citizens' Forum on Canada's Future, interviewed by Alan Freeman, "A Free Man in Paris," *The Globe and Mail*, 12 July 2003.

CONSUMERISM

See also Advertising; Markets & Marketing; Merchandising; Shopping

We are free men today, free to live our individual lives, free to conduct business as we see fit. There is no way to protect the long suffering public from such things as the absurd fashion dictates handed down from Paris, from long movie trailers, from singing commercials, from the loading of our daily mail with printed matter, from long speeches and long sermons, from the present giving racket which has involved us in handing out gifts on every kind of holiday, on St. Valentine's Day, Mother's Day, Father's Day, anniversaries, going away gifts and coming home gifts to those who gave going away gifts, from the tipping evil which is creeping into everything. We are living in a time of tribute, a period of outstretched palms.

Thomas B. Costain, novelist, address, "A Glance at the Future," Toronto, 8 May 1951, The Empire Club of Canada.

The concept of a conserver society arises from the deep concern for the future and the realization that decisions taken today, in areas such as energy and resources, may have irreversible and possibly destructive impact in the medium and long term. The necessity for a conserver society follows from our perception of the world as a finite host to humanity and from our recognition of increasing global interdependence.

Ursula Franklin, scientist, address, "The Conserver Society," Toronto, 30 March 1978, The Empire Club of Canada.

As more people discover the brand-name secrets of the global logo web, their outrage will fuel the next big political movement, a vast wave of opposition squarely targeting transnational corporations, particularly those with very high name-brand recognition.

Naomi Klein, commentator, *No Logo: Taking Aim at the Brand Bullies* (2000).

In our current culture of rights, individual whims and preferences are quickly characterized as rights.... The freedom of choice here seems analogous to the freedom of the consumer in the marketplace. When the citizen is reduced to the consumer, additional damage is inflicted on democracy. A consumer is not active; a consumer simply makes reactive choices about buying goods which are offered for sale by others.

Robert Ivan Martin, law professor, *The Most Dangerous Branch: How the Supreme Court of Canada Has Undermined Our Law and Our Democracy* (2003).

If you preach salvation through shopping instead of salvation through service, the sense of community is weakened and even destroyed.

Robert Bateman, artist and naturalist, "I Am a Conservative, I Conserve," *The Globe and Mail*, 13 December 2003.

CONTINENTALISM *See also* America; Canada & United States; Defence; North America; North American Free Trade Agreement (NAFTA)

The United States will annex Canada, with the exception of Quebec. We don't want Quebec. Even the people in Winnipeg don't want Quebec.

Alan Caruba, founder of the media-monitoring company National Anxiety Center in Maplewood, N.J., New Year's prediction, in Graeme Smith, "Remember, You Read It Here First," *The Globe and Mail*, 1 January 2002.

Can you imagine American conservatives allowing in their midst one huge Massachusetts?

Michael Adams, consultant, *Fire and Ice: The United States, Canada and the Myth of Converging Values* (2003), with Amy Langstaff and David Jamieson.

Grand Bargain.

Term coined by **Allan Gotlieb**, former Canadian ambassador to Washington, to refer in the post-FTA and NAFTA period to "any new scheme to integrate ourselves more closely economically with the U.S.," according to columnist Richard Gwyn, "Surviving Survivalism," *Literary Review of Canada*, December 2004.

CONTRACEPTION *See* Abortion; Birth; Birth Control

CONVERSATION

Sometimes in Canada and Toronto, you feel, when you're talking to somebody, as if you're talking to a pillow, that they will not actually say what they think. But all the while, the civility and politeness is a really nice thing.

Jane Jacobs, urban critic, interviewed by Eleanor Wachtel, *Original Minds* (2003).

COOL *See also* Attitude

Is Canada cool? Indeed, a cautious case can be made that Canada is now rather cool. Just when you had all but forgotten that carbon-based life exists above the 49th parallel, those sly Canadians have redefined their entire nation as Berkeley North.

David Montgomery, journalist, "Is Canada Cool?" *The Economist*, c. 31 September 2003. Quoted by Steve Burgess, "They Really Like Us, Eh?" *Maclean's*, 13 October 2003. The journalist had in mind recent Canadian initiatives on the status of same-sex marriages, decriminalization of marijuana, anti–Iraq war statements, etc.

No, we're not cool. But consider: the current cool list includes the likes of Ben Affleck, Jennifer Lopez, Hilary Duff and Sean (P. Diddy) Combs. Maybe we should leave well enough alone.

Steve Burgess, columnist, "They Really Like Us, Eh?" *Maclean's*, 13 October 2003.

CO-OPERATIVE MOVEMENT *See also* New Democratic Party

We must create the kind of society in which man will be free to free his soul.

M.M. Coady, priest and social activist with the co-operative Antigonish Movement, in J.R. Kidd, "The Social Gospel and Adult Education in Canada," *The Social Gospel in Canada* (1975), edited by Richard Allen.

If competitive individualism is the mark of America, then the co-operation of groups within large institutional structures expresses an essential Canadian value.

William Kilbourn, historian, "The Peaceable Kingdom Still," *Daedalus: Journal of the American Academy of Arts and Sciences*, Fall 1988 (*In Search of Canada* issue).

COPYRIGHT *See also* Symbols

What will they try to trademark next? I guess the word "Canada" is safe, eh? Think so? Did you know that at EXPO 86 in Vancouver, British Columbia, during the preparation of our national pavilion on Canadian soil the federal government of Canada was not allowed to use the maple leaf logo and the name Canada until it had humbly applied for permission from the Ace Novelty Company of Seattle, Washington? The good folks at Ace Novelty had been granted exclusive use of the name Canada and the maple leaf logo at the exposition. Now there's word-watching with a vengeance. Interesting, how in specific venues a country might not own the rights to its own name!

Bill Casselman, writer and broadcaster, *Casselmania: More Wacky Canadian Words & Sayings* (1996).

In my books the word "copyright" means "copy it right."

Peter Urs Bender, motivational speaker, characteristic remark, 11 May 2000.

CORPORATIONS *See also* Business; Executives

Despite our openness to trade, Canada is home to far fewer transnational corporations than Denmark, South Korea, Switzerland or Sweden. Canada is home to two of the top 150 global companies. The Netherlands has six and Switzerland five.

Brian Mulroney, former prime minister, address, Conservative Party gathering, Markham, Ont., 9 June 2000, published in *The Globe and Mail*, 10 June 2000.

We were not born to live in a corporate globe, yet that is the world we are moving towards.

Eric Kierans, economist, a line from his forthcoming *Remembering*, in Richard Gwyn, "Home and Away," *Toronto Star*, 31 January 2001.

Now we are faced with the foolish idea that a corporation should be regarded legally as "a person." In reality, a corporation is simply a pile of money to which a number of persons have sold their moral allegiance.

Robert Bateman, artist and naturalist, "I Am a Conservative, I Conserve," *The Globe and Mail*, 13 December 2003.

By the end of the century, the corporation had become the world's dominant institution. Yet history humbles dominant institutions. Great empires, the church, the monarchy, the Communist parties of Eastern Europe were all overthrown, diminished, or absorbed into new orders. It's unlikely that the corporation will be the first dominant institution to defy history. It has failed to solve, and indeed has worsened, some of the world's most pressing problems: war, environmental destruction, ill-health.

Joel Bakan, law professor, *The Corporation: The Pathological Pursuit of Profit and Power* (2004).

Corporations evade taxes, cook their books, create big toxic messes, and screw their workers for the best possible reasons: because they can; because it pays; because we, the chumps, are willing to pay for it so long as we get our little sliver of the tasty pie.

Lauren Penny, journalist, *Your Call Is Important to Us: The Truth about Bullshit* (2005).

CORRUPTION *See also* Accountability; Crime; Government; Patronage; Sponsorship & Advertising Scandal

These hands are clean!

Caption to the most famous Canadian political cartoon, called "Whither Are We Drifting?" drawn by the noted artist **J.W. Bengough** for the Toronto comic weekly *Grip*, 6 August 1873. It depicts in caricature Prime Minister Sir John A. Macdonald absolving himself of charges of corruption in connection with the Pacific Scandal. The cartoon shows him holding a sign that says "Send me another $10,000."

Elections are not won by prayers alone.

Attributed to **Joseph-Israël Tarte**, minister of Public Works in Sir Wilfrid Laurier's administration, master of patronage, commenting on the election of the Liberals in the election of 1896.

The thing which amazes me is that I know perfectly well, as a historian, that there is corruption in any government—there's always corruption. It's bad when it's more than fifteen percent.

Michel Brunet, historian, interviewed by Ramsay Cook, *The Craft of History* (1973), edited by Eleanor Cook.

Perhaps there were a few million dollars that might have been stolen in the process, but how many millions of millions of dollars have we saved because we have re-established the stability of Canada by keeping it a united country?

Jean Chrétien, prime minister, address, Liberal Party fundraising dinner, Winnipeg, 30 May 2002, in Shawn McCarthy, "Shut Down Campaign, P.M. Orders Martin," *The Globe and Mail*, 31 May 2002. The "process" was the advertising campaign to promote national unity in Quebec. The federal government's failure to account for the funding became a national scandal. The prime minister's high-handed manner brought to mind the rhetorical question attributed to Liberal minister C.D. Howe: "What's a million?"

The root of the problem is that money always looks for power; regrettably, the powerful sometimes violate their public trust in the hope of becoming wealthy. The time for concrete action against political corruption, Ottawa's bipartisan problem, is now.

Norman Spector, columnist, afterword, *A Secret Trial: Brian Mulroney, Stevie Cameron, and the Public Trust* (2004), by William Kaplan.

COUNTRIES *See also* Land; Nationalism; Places

There are countries for children, and others for men, some few only for giants…

Lines from **Jean-Guy Pilon**'s prose poem "The Needs of the Land!" *Recours au pays* (1961), translated by Louis Dudek, *Poetry of Our Time* (1965), edited by Louis Dudek.

A country, after all, is not something you build as the pharaohs built the pyramids, and then leave standing there to defy eternity. A country is something that is built every day out of certain basic shared values. And so it is in the hands of every Canadian to determine how well and wisely we shall build the country of the future.

Pierre Elliott Trudeau, prime minister, in Allan Gregg, "Quebec's Final Victory," *The Walrus*, February 2005.

And if we were going to go beyond the idea of the nation state as occupying a piece of turf, we had to look upon identities coming from living processes and to see people as endosymbionts in a cell, sharing a process, not a turf.

William Irwin Thompson, theorist, "Mind Jazz," *Wild Culture: Specimens from* The Journal of Wild Culture (1992), edited by Whitney Smith and Christopher Lowry. His definition: "*Endosymbiont* is another word for a good neighbour within a cell. The metaphor for this is the mitochondria, the little critters that crawled into our cells ages ago that have their own DNA (their own identity) and produce oxygen for our cells."

A country has to be built by the very forces that tear it apart.

Antonio D'Alfonso, poet and essayist, "The Path to Hope," *In Italics: In Defense of Ethnicity* (1996).

What a place, Canada; they started a country, and no one showed up.

Line of dialogue spoken by the character created by actor **Rodney Dangerfield** in the movie *Meet Wally Sparks* (1997).

A country can be influential in the world by the size of its heart and the breadth of its mind, and this is the role Canada can play.

Attributed to **Pierre Elliott Trudeau** by Jacques Hébert in his tribute at Trudeau's funeral, Notre-Dame Basilica, Montreal, 3 October 2000, printed in *Cité libre*, fall 2000.

To want to found a country on imaginary or outdated grievances is to march into history backwards.

Daniel Poliquin, commentator and novelist, *In the Name of the Father: An Essay on Quebec Nationalism* (2001), translated by Don Winkler.

What is my country? Is it the country I inhabit, or is it the country that inhabits me? In my case it's kind of an amalgam.

Robert MacNeil, Montreal-born, Halifax-raised broadcaster and novelist, interview, "You Can Go Home Again," *Maclean's*, 29 July 2002.

Some time in the last half dozen years, Canadians decided that we had made it as a country.

Richard Gwyn, columnist and essayist, "Surviving Survivalism," *Literary Review of Canada*, December 2004.

COUNTRY LIFE

We could see the roads winding away from the dear old, plain red brick school of our oh-so-short days of youth, and most of us took one of those roads sooner or later. And a country kid's memories are still filtered through the dust thrown up by buggy wheels and the snowskirt swirling between the little horse and his cutter.

Lauchlan MacInnes, teacher, evocative passage about youth and country life, in Norman MacInnes, "Lives Lived," *The Globe and Mail*, 15 January 2002.

COURAGE *See also* Leadership

I look down on people who just give up and become vegetables. You must always have enough courage to tell yourself that you can be important for someone else.

Michel Tremblay, playwright, in Donald Smith, *Voices of Deliverance: Interviews with Quebec and Acadian Writers* (1986), translated by Donald Smith.

CRAFTS *See also* Arts & Artists

As a matter of fact, Greek pottery is one of the greatest design fabrics ever created. It is an artistic miracle.... There is no essential difference between the plan of a Greek vase and the plan of a Greek temple or theatre.

Jay Hambidge, artist, writer, and theorist, born in Simcoe, Ont., *Dynamic Symmetry: The Greek Vase* (1920).

I now realize that the craft itself becomes your teacher, your own teacher, and thereby also a source of help to anyone else, at the point where either you or other teachers disappear—the ones that you had and respected—or where you can't get more from them because it has to become your own understanding.

Tom Daly, producer and director, "The Growth of a Craft: My Debt to Legg and Grierson," *John Grierson and the NFB* (1984), produced by the John Grierson Project.

CREATION *See also* Belief

Very well, God made the world, but Raven made it first.

Reply of Inuit elders to missionaries who offered them the Biblical account of the creation of the world, as noted by Robert F. Spencer, *The North Alaskan Eskimo: A Study in Ecology and Society* (1959), Bulletin Number 171.

A scientific genesis would go something like this: In the beginning there was nothing—no universe, no space, and no time—less than a vacuum. Since there was less than nothing, there was nothing even to compare nothingness with—an inconceivable state. But in this nothingness a unique event occurred: an infinitesimal blip, maybe an intimation, a tiny precognitive echo of the immensity to follow.

Christopher Dewdney, poet and author, contrasting the account of creation described in Genesis with that in scientific literature, *Acquainted with the Night: Excursions through the World after Dark* (2004).

CREATIONISM *See also* Belief; Evolution

I suspect that the creationist has less mystery to explain away than the wholehearted evolutionist. On the balance of the things that I have both read and discovered for myself, I am a creationist, so far as mega-evolution is concerned.

Evan Shute, physician and theorist, *Flaws in the Theory of Evolution* (1961).

CREATIVITY *See also* Ideas

A creative illness succeeds a period of intense preoccupation with an idea and a search for a certain truth. It is a polymorphous condition that can take the shape of depression, neurosis, psychosomatic ailments, or even psychosis.... The subject emerges from his ordeal with a permanent transformation in his personality and the conviction that he has discovered a great truth or a new spiritual world.

Henri F. Ellenberger, Montreal psychiatrist and historian, credited with naming the notion and the ordeal of some creators, *The Discovery of the Unconscious* (1970).

I think the creative process is inherently one of the dance of opposites. It's a complex kind of alchemy. Any other simplifying ideology always falsifies one side of our nature.

William Irwin Thompson, theorist, "Mind Jazz," *Wild Culture: Specimens from* The Journal of Wild Culture (1992), edited by Whitney Smith and Christopher Lowry.

Drift. Allow yourself to wander aimlessly. Explore adjacencies. Lack judgement. Postpone criticism.

Bruce Mau, designer, author of essay "Incomplete Manifesto for Growth," in Sarah Scott, "Shock of the New," *Globe and Mail's Report on Business,* August 2002.

It is the mark of creative activity, in whatever sphere, that it surprises. If it doesn't surprise it is re-creative, a hobby. But in order to surprise it must be given the freedom to do so.

John C. Polanyi, scientist, address, The New Liberalism Conference, Toronto, published as "Fostering Better Science," *Toronto Star*, 30 September 2002.

Creativity and ability to accumulate skills and knowledge are inborn capacities of anatomically modern human beings, much as language is an inborn capacity.

Jane Jacobs, urban planning critic, discussing human beings in pre- and post-agrarian societies, *Dark Age Ahead* (2004).

CRIME *See also* Abuse: Sexual; Capital Punishment; Corruption; Ethics; Good & Evil; Law; Marijuana; Murder; Patronage; Police; Royal Canadian Mounted Police; Victims & Victimhood; Violence; Virtue & Vice

When virtue is at liberty, so to some extent is vice. In a free world there is, alas, more common crime than in a dictatorial system. Dictatorships do cut down on rape, and pillage, not to mention sexual harassment, by the simple expedient of sending people to labour camps for life or cutting off their hands without a trial. The same liberty that protects me also protects members of the Mafia.

Barbara Amiel, journalist, address, "How Canada Does It and Other Social Diseases," Toronto, 4 February 1982, The Empire Club of Canada.

In the U.S. capital of Washington, D.C., the [murder] rate was a whopping 46.6 per 100,000, in contrast to only 0.36—three murders—in 2001 in Canada's capital of Ottawa where, thankfully in this case, nothing much ever happens. (The only U.S. city listed by the Census Bureau whose murder rate is lower than Toronto's is Honolulu.)

Michael Adams, consultant, *Fire and Ice: The United States, Canada and the Myth of Converging Values* (2003), with Amy Langstaff and David Jamieson.

Property theft is about as common as rain in Vancouver. There are 7,000 reports for every 100,000 residents, which puts us near the top of the list of 354 North American cities. Miami, a world-class crime centre, has a lock on top spot at 11,000.

Paul Sullivan, columnist, "The West," *The Globe and Mail*, 25 November 2003.

You never leave a body without giving it a bullet in the head.

Attributed to organized crime boss **Frank Cotroni** as a recipe for a surefire Mafia hit as recalled by mob turncoat Réal Simard and quoted by Miro Cernetig, "Mandolins and Miniskirts: How to Mourn a Mafioso," *Toronto Star*, 22 August 2004.

CRITICS & CRITICISM *See also* Arts & Artists; Language; Writers & Writing

Jones decided that sensitivity to criticism was inbuilt into the Canadian character and he must avoid such indulgences at all costs, simultaneously parading his Welsh, non-English, roots. However he could not accept the Canadian proposition that having escaped the obsolete ways of the Old World they proceeded to avoid the lawless brashness of America and automatically emerged as a superior civilisation. He described the Canadians in a letter to Freud as "naive, childish and [holding] the simplest views of the problems of life. They care for nothing except money-making and sport, they chew gum instead of smoking or drinking and their public meetings are monuments of sentimental platitudes."

Vincent Brome, biographer, *Ernest Jones: Freud's Alter Ego* (1983). Dr. Ernest Jones, the future biographer of Sigmund Freud, held a professorship in the department of psychiatry, University of Toronto, in 1908–1913. His letter to Freud in Vienna is dated 10 December 1908.

Constant abuse of politicians, constant attacks upon the efficiency and the integrity of public men is having a bad effect in this country, resulting in the destroying of public confidence in our representative constitution and instilling in the minds of our younger generation that public life and all politicians are corrupt.

Grattan O'Leary, newspaper editor, address, "The Public and the Politicians," Toronto, 30 March 1933, The Empire Club of Canada.

I still feel that in criticism everything positive stands, everything negative dates.

Northrop Frye, cultural critic, aphorism, "Notebook 3" (1946–1948), *Northrop Frye Newsletter*, fall 2000.

Thinking about art helps us think, too, about exploring the full freedom of our ways of feeling and perceiving.

Bernard Lonergan, theologian, *Topics in Education* (1959, 1993) in *The Lonergan Reader* (1997), edited by Mark D. Morelli and Elizabeth A. Morelli.

Canadians are extremely sensitive about any criticism of themselves, and as a Canadian I am deeply concerned about such things. This sensitivity springs, I think, from a nagging self-doubt; we know in our hearts that we are not the sort of people we pretend to be. This was not always so: I think this trouble dates from 1945, when Canada discovered a new awareness of itself, but mistook what that awareness meant. We set out then on the psychological folly of trying to be like the U.S., in its extreme psychological extroversion and we failed because Canada is, and has always been, an introverted country, as Norway, Sweden and—yes—Russia are introverted. We see the world differently, and experience the world differently, from our great noisy neighbour, and nothing will make us like the U.S.

Robertson Davies, man of letters, letter to Josef Škvorecký, 27 August 1984, *For Your Eye Alone: Letters, 1976–1995* (1999).

Criticism without creativity produces charts.

Mavor Moore, theatre personality, *Reinventing Myself: Memoirs* (1994).

I grew up thinking a lot about the relationship between art and religion, which may explain why I later combined the two and became a critic.

Mavor Moore, theatre personality, *Reinventing Myself: Memoirs* (1994).

CRUELTY *See also* Good & Evil

If we wish to draw out examples from that state in which various philosophers hoped pre-eminently to discover the natural godliness of human nature, namely, from the so-called state of nature, we need but compare with this hypothesis the scenes of unprovoked cruelty in the murder-dramas enacted in Tofoa, New Zealand, and in the Navigator Islands, and the unending cruelty (of which Captain Hearne tells) in the wide wastes of northwestern America, cruelty from which, indeed, not a soul reaps the smallest benefit....

Immanuel Kant, German philosopher, *Religion within the Limits of Reason Alone* (1793), translated by Theodore M. Greene and Hoyt H. Hudson in 1960. This is presumably the sole reference to Canada in the works of the great philosopher. Kant's footnote: "Thus the war ceaselessly waged between the Arathapescaw Indians and the Dog Rib Indians has no other object than mere slaughter. Bravery in war is, in the opinion of savages, the highest virtue. Even in a civilized state it is an object of admiration and a basis for the special regard commanded by that profession in which bravery is the sole merit; and this is not without rational cause." Translator's footnote: "Samuel Hearne ... his account of a *Journey from Prince of Wales's Fort in Hudson's Bay to the Northwest* was published in 1795. Kant evidently had read the brief account of Hearne's travels in Douglas's introduction to Cook's *Third Voyage*, London, 1784."

CUBA

Cuba is going down in flames in the middle of Lake Leman while I descend into the heart of things.

Line from **Hubert Aquin**'s novel *Prochain épisode* (1965). Daniel Poliquin, writing in *In the Name of the Father* (2001), explains: "It is a key passage in the history of the Quebec novel, where the writer links Quebec with Third World freedom-fighting and gives vent to his obsession with bourgeois life and its crippling apathy."

My own life almost exactly divides into a Canadian half and an American half by now, and even though I've spent the past thirty years in New York, the key fact is that I'm still a Canadian citizen and can go to Cuba any damn time I want. As long as they don't stamp my passport, of course.

Bruce McCall, humorist and cartoonist for *The New Yorker*, born in Simcoe, Ont., Toronto, talk for the Writers' Trust, *Toronto Star*, 3 June 2000.

I had taken my first trip to Toronto, the ideal way station for a traveller from California who wanted to go to Cuba.

Pico Iyer, traveller and writer, "Mongrel Beauties," *Saturday Night*, 31 March 2001.

CULTURAL MOSAIC *See also* Diversity; Ethnicity; Multiculturalism

It is indeed a mosaic of vast dimensions and great breadth.

Victoria Hayward, American traveller, *Romantic Canada* (1922). The ethnic composition of Canadian society is characterized here for the first time as a "mosaic." The image is routinely contrasted with the American "melting-pot" which was first used decades earlier by the Anglo-Jewish writer Israel Zangwill.

My intention is not to embarrass you with too rosy a picture of the Canadian mosaic as if it were free of all tension. But you have the experience, an infrastructure grounded in wisdom, and the moral wherewithal to be able to handle challenges to your social and political fabric.

Aga Khan, spiritual leader of the Shia Ismaili Muslims, address, Conference on Leadership and Diversity, Ottawa, 19 May 2004, printed in *The Globe and Mail*, 20 May 2004.

CULTURE *See also* Civilization; Culture: Canadian; Culture; Folklore; Myths & Mythology; Quebec

As I say, all culture originates in remembering the Sabbath.

Northrop Frye, cultural and literary critic, aphorism, "Notebook 3" (1946–1948), *Northrop Frye Newsletter*, fall 2000.

But it is beginning to look like Canadians may choose to have purposes and expressions of their own. The question is will we be willing to pay for them. I hope so. It depends on whether we want to be masters or servants.

Allan King, filmmaker, distinguishing between American-style and Canadian-made movies, "Canadian—Cinema—Vancouver," *How to Make or Not Make a Canadian Film* (1968), edited by André Pâquet.

In the early part of this century, we were a country of weeds and frontiers; of open spaces and empty muskeg (just ask Pierre Berton); a country of unheard echoes, mystery, and isolation. This loneliness made us self-reliant, independent, thoughtful, and suspicious of others (just ask Brian Mulroney). The pioneer mentality developed individuals with courage to face great hardships alone. We became strong but we had little time for thought or culture. Artists were ignored or thought expendable (just ask Robert Goulet). There was no time for the luxury of music, poetry, or artistic expression. We had railroads and cities to build, vast prairies and land to till and tame, forests to cut, minerals to dig. Now, in the latter part of the century, we have begun to change—mature—and, hopefully, we are coming of age.

Norman Jewison, film director, address, "The Power of Film and Its Influence," Toronto, 5 April 1984, The Empire Club of Canada.

I think Canada is in a unique position from which to study the role of language and the humanities in culture. Its political and economic structures may be in something of a shambles, but its culture, and I speak here more particularly of its literary culture, is flourishing and exhilarating. As we study this situation, we begin to see that two different social rhythms are involved. Political and economic movements tend to expand and centralize; cultural ones tend to decentralize, to bring to articulateness smaller and smaller communities. One has to keep the contrast steadily in mind: if we hitch a political development to a cultural one, as in separatism, we get a kind of neo-fascism; if we hitch a cultural development to a political one, we get a pompous, bureaucratic pseudo-culture.

Northrop Frye, cultural and literary critic, address, "The Authority of Learning," Toronto, 19 June 1984, The Empire Club of Canada.

My starting hypothesis is the following: Culture is not the accumulation of history, theology, science, and art, but the self-awareness provoked by the fact that all four activities coexist and progressively coalesce in one single period of time.

Antonio D'Alfonso, poet and essayist, "In the Mouths of People," *In Italics: In Defense of Ethnicity* (1996).

Claiming to have an exclusive proprietorship over what is real and true, the culture offers us little opportunity to explore what is unfamiliar. Those who introduce novel ideas into the culture tend to be pushed to the periphery. Therefore, the culture's consensus reality changes very slowly.

Adam Crabtree, psychotherapist and theorist, *Trace Zero: Breaking the Spell of Conformity* (1997).

A culture is a set of meanings and values informing a common way of life, and there are as many cultures as there are distinct sets of such meanings and values.

Bernard Lonergan, theologian, *Doctrinal Pluralism* (1971) in *The Lonergan Reader* (1997), edited by Mark D. Morelli and Elizabeth A. Morelli.

Every view of the world that fades away, every culture that disappears, diminishes the possibilities of human life.

Wade Davis, explorer and author, "A Dead End for Humanity," *The Globe and Mail*, 28 December 2000.

A culture is determined by its most volatile minority, not its inert majority. When one considers that human beings and apes are 98 per cent similar, one recognizes that small numbers go a long way.

Barabara Amiel, columnist, "Taming the House Cat," *Maclean's*, 14 June 2004.

CULTURE: CANADIAN *See also* Culture

If we are true to ourselves, Canadian unity may well serve as a model for the wider unity of humanity. In the unity of mankind lies the one sure foundation of enduring peace.

W.L. Mackenzie King, prime minister, inaugural broadcast, CBC Radio's International Service, 25 February 1945, in James L. Hall, *Radio Canada International: Voice of a Middle Power* (1997).

The countries in past history that we admire most are not necessarily the economically prosperous ones but those that have made major contributions to our cultural heritage. Our aim should be to make Canada a country that is recognized throughout the world, and throughout history, as a country that has advanced in a significant way the progress of science, art, and literature.

Gerhard Herzberg, convocation address, "The Dangers of Science Policy," York University, Toronto, 7 November 1969, in Boris Stoicheff, *Gerhard Herzberg: An Illustrious Life in Science* (2002).

Canada is often described as a "young" country, culturally speaking. Every time a new arts centre opens, we are discovered by some editorial writer to have "finally come of age." But the notion holds true only in a narrowly middle-class-urban and eurocentric sense.

John Beckwith, composer and teacher, 1977 essay, *Music Papers: Articles and Talks by a Canadian Composer, 1961–1994* (1997).

Having reached the Pacific, Canadians have begun to turn back on themselves, to create that added dimension Teilhard de Chardin calls the noosphere or, to put it more simply, Canadian culture.

D.G. Jones, poet and critic, *Butterfly on Rock: A Study of Themes and Images in Canadian Literature* (1970).

I end up feeling like I have to pay for the rape of Canada. But I didn't have nothin' to do with it.

Keith Richards, Rolling Stones rock performer, *The Biography*, in Antonio D'Alfonso, "Atopia," *In Italics: In Defense of Ethnicity* (1996).

If you define yourself based on culture, you have to find one.... Canadian culture is an invention, but not a very credible invention.

Jacques Parizeau, former Quebec premier, interviewed by Daniel LeBlanc, "Canadian Culture a Fake," *The Globe and Mail*, 2 June 2000.

The history of Canada is the cumulative experience of its constituent peoples. We don't expect a Jew to forget the Holocaust, an Acadian to forget the deportation, a Quebecker to forget the sudden isolation from France, or the Haida, the Mi'kmaq or the Six Nations to forget what shaped their culture and their thought.

Mark Starowicz, TV producer, "The Death of History," *The Globe and Mail*, 20 September 2000.

Indeed the prevalence of this idea that the public sphere is culturally neutral, and that Canada, therefore, has "no official culture," is illustrated by the popular assertion of (and about) Canadians who do not identify with a particular cultural group, that they have "no culture" at all. One recent culture minister in Québec made such an assertion when she claimed that "there is no real Ontario culture."

Jakeet Singh, sociologist and political scientist, "Re-articulating Multiculturalism," *Racism, Eh? A Critical Inter-Disciplinary Anthology of Race and Racism in Canada* (2004), edited by

Camille A. Nelson and Charmaine A. Nelson. "Ontario Has No Culture, Péquiste Declares," appears in *The Globe and Mail*, 9 March 2001.

Without our culture, we are invisible, without faith in ourselves. Canada has defied the odds precisely because we have sufficient faith to have endured in the face of domestic and international storms. It's public policy that has made a telling difference. We have actually had the audacity to invest in our future.

Scott McIntyre, publisher, referring to writers and publishers, "Literary Life Support," *Maclean's*, 3 June 2002.

I like the fact that what we usually call Canadian culture is, in fact, an experiment in world culture. We are just now playing with things that will become a reality for a lot of other parts of the world in the future. That's very exciting.

Christos Hatzis, Greek-born Toronto-based composer, in Robert Crew, "Big 50th for Christos Hatzis," *Toronto Star*, 20 March 2003.

CURIOSITY

Everything has its astonishing, wondrous aspect, if you bring a mind to it that's really your own—a mind that hasn't been smeared and blurred with half-understood muck from schools, or the daily papers, or any other rag-bag of reach-me-down notions.

Line of dialogue from **Robertson Davies**'s novel *World of Wonders* (1975).

Curiosity is the real life force of people and it's not something that passes with age. I find I'm much more curious than I ever was.

Adrienne Clarkson, governor general, interviewed by Christopher Guly, "Class Act at Rideau Hall," *Forever Young*, July 2003.

Polite society is never curious, and the more formal and aristocratic a society is, the more likely its social intercourse is to consist of an exchange of banalities.

Gerald Hannon, journalist, "The Curious Case of Malcolm Gladwell," *Saturday Night*, September 2005.

CURLING

We'll explain the appeal of curling to you if you explain the appeal of the National Rifle Association to us.

Attributed to **Andy Barrie**, CBC Radio host, addressing a group of Americans, 2000.

If you could mix up chess, golf, billiards, and shuffle-board, you would have the sport of curling.

Kevin Martin, curling skip, in Roy MacGregor, "NBC Calls Canada Coolest," *National Post*, 19 February 2002.

CURRENCY

Loonie & Toonie.

Nicknames for, respectively, the one-dollar coin (which features a loon on the reverse side), introduced in 1987, and the two-dollar coin (formed of two metals) introduced in 1995.

I do have to fine you. That will be a thousand dollars Canadian, or ten American dollars if you prefer.

Dialogue spoken by the character created by the actor **Dan Aykroyd** in the movie *Canadian Bacon* (1994).

Why are you so happy? Did you find someone to take that Canadian quarter of yours?

Rhetorical question asked by Jerry of the character George in the episode "They Come Back" of the TV series *Seinfeld* during the 1998 season.

CYCLING *See also* Sports

Any destination is achievable; you just have to keep pedalling every day.

Chris Robertson, cyclist, in Barry Shainbaum, *Hope & Heroes: Portraits of Integrity & Inspiration* (2003), after cycling from Point Pelee in southern Ontario to Tuktoyaktuk in the High Arctic, a distance of 6520 kilometres.

d

DANCE *See also* Ballet; Music

Walk In and Dance Out.

Slogan of the dance school opened in Hollywood in 1918 by 17-year-old vaudeville dancer **Ben Blue**, who had been born Benjamin Bernstein in Montreal and went on to become a movie personality, as noted by Charles Foster, *Once Upon a Time in Paradise: Canadians in the Golden Age of Hollywood* (2003).

The world dances, and we can learn so much about ourselves and the world by studying the movement patterns around us.

Janice Pomer, instructor of movement and dance, *Perpetual Motion: Creative Movement Exercises for Dance and Dramatic Arts* (2001).

When I look back on my career, I realize I had a lot of nerve. I had stride. I had guts. If you really want to be a choreographer, get down to business. Give it all you've got. You've got to prove yourself, honey, and if you do it doesn't matter if you're a man or a woman.

Onna White, dancer and choreographer born in Inverness, N.S., on 24 March 1922, winner of a special Academy Award in 1969 for choreography of the movie *Oliver!* Her words were recalled in an interview just before her death in California, 8 April 2005.

DARKNESS

The stars have twinkled over depravity and mass slaughter, and the moon has illuminated many nocturnal battles.

Christopher Dewdney, poet and author, *Acquainted with the Night: Excursions through the World after Dark* (2004).

DAVIES, ROBERTSON *See also* Authors; Critics & Criticism; Writers & Writing

All my life I have been writing, trying in one way and another to rouse Canadians to some recognition of the truth about their own nature. They are not Americans; history and climate forbid it. But Oh, how despairingly they try to be what they are not!

Robertson Davies, man of letters, letter to Josef Škvorecký, 27 August 1984, *For Your Eye Alone: Letters, 1976–1995* (1999).

I was brought up a Calvinist and have never got over it.

Robertson Davies, man of letters, letter, April 1995, *For Your Eye Alone: Letters, 1976–1995* (1999).

DAY

Day is so powerful, so iconic and illuminated, that night fades quickly in its thrall, as though twilight were a dream, a quirky memory.

Christopher Dewdney, poet and author, *Acquainted with the Night: Excursions through the World after Dark* (2004).

DAY, STOCKWELL *See also* Canadian Alliance; Political Parties; Reform Party

Either the Alliance doesn't have an arts policy, or it does have one and it consists of demolition. He wants to blow up Ottawa, its national arts policy along with much else, and sit on top of the pile of rubble. He wants to be king of the hole in the doughnut.

Margaret Atwood, author, on Canadian Alliance leader Stockwell Day's silence on an arts policy, "Dealing a Blank Card," *The Globe and Mail*, 1 November 2000.

I hope he will survive. He has a great future as leader of the Opposition. We want him to stay there for a long, long time.

Jean Chrétien, prime minister, referring to Canadian Alliance leader and leader of the Opposition Stockwell Day, interviewed by Mike Bullard on CTV's late-night talk show *Open Mike with Mike Bullard*, 17 May 2001, in

Sean Fine and Caroline Mallan, *The Globe and Mail*, 18 May 2001.

Canada does not deserve the fate of a quasi–one party state. We need a single viable alternative that citizens will look to with hope and confidence as a future government. I will do whatever I can, including putting my own leadership on the line to see this happen, because Canada deserves nothing less.

Stockwell Day, leader, Canadian Alliance Party, address, "A Single Democratic Conservative Option," Toronto, 14 June 2001, The Empire Club of Canada.

Noting that the Canadian Alliance platform favoured referenda, Mercer used his TV show to suggest a referendum mandating that Stockwell Day change his first name to Doris. Through E-mail, he got hundreds of thousands of signatures overnight.... Eventually, he became widely known as Stockboy Day, although some people continued to call him Doris.

Calvin Trillin, essayist, referring to comedian Rick Mercer, "Paper Baron," *The New Yorker*, 17 December 2001.

Smite 'em, Lord, smite 'em!

Caption to an editorial cartoon drawn by **Anthony Jenkins** of *The Globe and Mail* representing the thoughts of Stockwell Day, besieged leader of the Canadian Alliance and lay preacher, brow perspiring, head bowed in prayer, recalled at the year's end, "2001: A Cartoon Odyssey," *The Globe and Mail*, 26 December 2001.

In the past day or so, we have learned that Stockwell Day apparently believes that the world is 6,000 years old, Adam and Eve were real people and—my personal favourite—humans walked the earth with dinosaurs. Valerie, I just want to remind Mr. Day that *The Flintstones* was not a documentary. And this is the only dinosaur that recently co-existed with humans.

Warren Kinsella, Liberal political commentator and apologist, referring to the fundamentalist Biblical beliefs of Canadian Alliance leader Stockwell Day, in interview by host Valerie Pringle on CTV's *Canada AM*, 16 November 2001, as noted in his memoir *Kicking Ass in Canadian Politics* (2002).

DEATH *See also* Clones; Epitaphs; Euthanasia; Genocide; Immortality; Murder; Suicide

We are as near to heaven by sea as by land!

Immortal dying words of **Sir Humphrey Gilbert**, the English mariner who had earlier established Newfoundland as England's first overseas colony, 5 August 1583. On the return voyage, near the Azores, his frigate *Squirrel* began to sink, and Sir Humphrey was heard to exhort his crew members with these words, among the most famous in the literature of exploration. The crew aboard his companion ship, *The Golden Hind*, also overheard Gilbert's words.

The dead are lonely. / Only the living / know how lonely / the dead can be.

Final verse of **George Whalley**'s poem "Fragment" (1946), *The Collected Poems of George Whalley* (1986), edited by George Johnston.

In case I die in this mess, I leave all to the wife, Cecil Geo. Harris.

Words scratched with a penknife on a tractor fender by **Cecil Harris**, a dying farmer, whose tractor pinned him down after flipping on him, Bad Hills, Sask., 8 June 1948. A probate court deemed it a valid will. The red fender and the brown-handled knife are on permanent display at the Law Library, University of Saskatchewan, according to Roy MacGregor, "Saskatchewan Turns One Hundred," *The Globe and Mail*, 24 December 2004. MacGregor calls the mementoes "striking reminders of the resilience and ingenuity of this tough little Prairie province."

I am going into overtime, where the most exciting part of the game is played.

Stan Obodiac, hockey personality, characteristic remark made while weak from cancer, honoured at Maple Leaf Gardens by being selected to drop the opening puck, Maple Leaf Gardens, 13 October 1984.

Death is man's problem. Life is woman's problem.

Wilson Duff, anthropologist, random observation, in *Bird of Paradox: The Unpublished Writings of Wilson Duff* (1996), edited by E.N. Anderson.

This is where I came to when my body left its body and my spirit stayed in its spirit home.

Lines written by poet **Al Purdy** that appear on his tombstone in Ameliasburgh, Ont. Purdy died on 21 April 2000, as noted by Geoff Heinricks, "Canada's Honours System Grows Up," *National Post,* 17 February 2001.

It seemed like only yesterday when I'd died, but, of course, it was almost certainly centuries ago.

Opening sentence of **Robert J. Sawyer**'s science-fiction short story "The Shoulders of Giants" (2000), reprinted in *Relativity: Stories and Essays* (2004).

When I die, I want people to say that I inspired them. I don't care so much that they say I was a good man or a kind man or a happy man or a great man. I want them to say that they saw the world filled with a bit more adventure. That they were a little bit less afraid to do something that they truly wanted.... Even if one person stands up at my funeral and says that I inspired them, that will be enough. The world will know I died happily.

Stephen Canning, mountaineer and environmentalist, "Death," article found on his computer following his death from a fall from Mount Logan, Y.T., at the age of 22, in Shandell Susin, "Lives Lived," *The Globe and Mail,* 26 August 2004.

People can die more peacefully when they feel they're leaving a legacy. In other words, we have to make our deaths mean something. And one way you can do that is to make it a heroic death. Heroic deaths leave legacies and so he becomes the hero in the campaign to legalize physician-assisted suicide or euthanasia or whatever.

Margaret Somerville, ethicist, referring to the public decision of Marcel Tremblay of Kanata, Ont., to commit suicide, in Pauline Tam, "Tremblay Case Raises Host of Ethical Questions," *National Post,* 29 January 2005.

Gone to the Sand Hills.

"A southern Alberta euphemism for death," according to **Bill Casselman**, *Canadian Sayings: 1,200 Folk Sayings Used by Canadians* (1999): "The Sand Hills are the Happy Hunting Grounds for the Blood people of the sandy-hill country south of Lethbridge."

If death is an integral part of life, which I believe it to be, then death should be protected as a right under Section 7 of the Constitution. The right to die with dignity should be as well protected as is any other aspect of the right to life.

Peter Cory, justice, Supreme Court of Canada, dissenting decision on the Sue Rodriguez case in 1993, quoted in the editorial "Helping Someone to Die," *The Globe and Mail,* 9 November 2005.

Let's stop being hypocrites. Hospitals are practising euthanasia. They call it protocol.

Claire L'Heureux-Dubé, justice, Supreme Court of Canada, quoted in the editorial "Helping Someone to Die," *The Globe and Mail,* 9 November 2005.

DEBATE

Every minute spent on parry is a minute lost to thrust.

Adapted from an observation made by columnist **John Ibbitson**, "Politics," *The Globe and Mail,* 24 September 2003.

DEFENCE *See also* Canadian Armed Forces; War

There is widely spread in Canada a vague feeling that if anything turns up we shall be protected by a curious combination of the Monroe doctrine and the British navy.

W.L. Grant, historian, address, "The Fallacy of Nationalism," Toronto, 11 April 1912, The Empire Club of Canada.

I give to you assurance that the people of the United States will not stand idly by if domination of Canadian soil is threatened by any other Empire.

Franklin D. Roosevelt, U.S. president, convocation address, Queen's University, Kingston, Ont., 18 August 1938. This is the classic expression of American solidarity with the Dominion and hence with the British Empire.

You may have heard me say that nations don't distrust each other because they are armed. They are armed because they distrust each other. With the longest undefended border in the world, Canada and the United States are proof of the flip side of that—when nations live in trust and friendship, they live in peace.

Ronald Reagan, U.S. president, address, "Relationships," Toronto, 21 June 1988, The Empire Club of Canada.

Washington's pressure tactics to impose its rules threaten to define the limits of our citizenship by demoting Canada to a junior partnership in a political entity known as the NAP—the North American Perimeter.

Peter C. Newman, columnist, "The Defining Border," *Maclean's*, 31 December 2001.

Well-meaning nitwits are trying to brick us all up inside Fortress Canada, with a cask of amontillado perhaps, but with only the most provisional rights or freedoms.

Spider Robinson, science-fiction author, "Forward—Into the Past!" *The Globe and Mail*, 1 January 2002.

Canada is a defence freeloader and, like freeloaders everywhere, we dislike those who carry the burden for us. I am a nationalist, but I like to believe my nationalism is founded on my understanding of Canada's national interests.

J.L. Granatstein, historian, "Defence Freeloading Imperils Sovereignty," *National Post*, 22 February 2002.

Two big oceans and a polar icecap have kept us safe for centuries.

Desmond Morton, historian, address, "National Defence," Toronto, 17 April 2002, The Empire Club of Canada.

Liberal societies cannot be defended by herbivores. We need carnivores to save us.

Michael Ignatieff, essayist, widely quoted aphorism, *The Lesser Evil: Political Ethics in an Age of Terror* (2004).

"We cannot defend our country and save our homes and families by waiting for the enemy to attack us. To remain on the defensive is the surest way to bring the war to Canada. Of course, we should protect our coasts and strengthen our ports and cities against attack ... we must also go out and meet the enemy before he reaches our shores. We must defeat him before he attacks us, before our cities are laid to waste." Mackenzie King was correct then, and we must always remember the wisdom of his words today. In the new era, the threat is different, but our duties are the same.

George W. Bush, U.S. president, quoting a passage from a 1942 wartime speech of former Prime Minister W.L. Mackenzie King, address, Pier 21, Halifax, 1 December 2004, in Brian Laghi and Alan Freeman, "Evoking World War II, Bush Prods Canadians," *The Globe and Mail*, 2 December 2004.

I hope we'll also move forward on ballistic-missile defence co-operation to protect the next generation of Canadians and Americans from the threats we know will arise.

George W. Bush, U.S. president, address, Pier 21, Halifax, 1 December 2004, in Brian Laghi and Alan Freeman, "Evoking World War II, Bush Prods Canadians," *The Globe and Mail*, 2 December 2004.

I'm not taking this position, but some future president is going to say, "Why are we paying to defend Canada?" I don't understand this. Are you saying that if you got up and said this is necessary for the defence of Canada, it wouldn't be accepted?

Attributed to U.S. President **George W. Bush** during a discussion with Prime Minister Paul

Martin in Ottawa in November 2005, as recalled by an unidentified Canadian official and quoted by Nicholas Kohler, "Bush Twists P.M.'s Arm on Missile Defence," *National Post*, 24 January 2005. At stake was continental protection in light of the Chrétien administration's refusal to participate in the U.S. missile-defence system (dubbed Star Wars under President Ronald Reagan) and the Martin administration's reluctance to lobby for its adoption in Parliament. It was originally reported in *The Washington Post*, 23 January 2005. Martin recalled the discussion but no bullying or arm-twisting.

In this situation, security policy north of the 49th parallel was expressed by the doctrine of "Defence against Help"—which maintained that, if Canadians did not defend themselves against the Soviet threat to the satisfaction of the Americans, the Pentagon would defend them anyway, but according to its own lights.

Stephen Clarkson, political scientist, referring to the Cold War when Canada was regarded as a "buffer zone," "Independent 'Security' Policy for Canada Is Not Impossible," *The CCPA Monitor*, February 2005.

Also in the small favours department, Canada announced last week that it would increase its spending on defence, which as a percentage of GDP—1.2% in 2003—is now the lowest in NATO after Luxembourg and Iceland (which has no military). The U.S. spent 3.5% of GDP in 2003.

Editorial, *The Wall Street Journal*, 28 February 2005, reprinted as "Canadian Free Riders," *National Post*, 2 March 2005.

No Sales to Canada / Due to the hatred toward Americans and the American way of life exhibited by the Canadian government, et al., we do not wish to promote or sell our products and services into Canada. Until Canada allows the US to fully deploy our North American Anti-Missile Defense system fully in order to protect BOTH Canada and the United States, we will not sell across the Canadian border nor promote our products therein.

Advisory on the website of Weldtron, Inc., Alice, Texas, drafted by its owner **David Herbert**, as noted in "Canucks Not Welcome," *National Post*, 2 March 2005. Herbert is expressing displeasure with the Paul Martin government's unwillingness to endorse the Bush administration's anti-missile defence scheme.

Governments in Bern know something governments in Ottawa have forgotten. The Alps defend the Swiss because the Swiss defend the Alps. The seas and the longitudes will not defend Canadians unless Canadians defend the longitudes and the seas.

George Jonas, columnist, "A Lesson from the Swiss," *National Post*, 2 May 2005.

DEMOCRACY *See also* Government

The democracy has now become the tyrant. For this reason it is all-important that the people should be warned of the fact that the danger is now to be found in the democratic rather than the aristocratic element, which no longer rules. If the democracy were left to itself, it would soon bring its own destruction, but Imperialism, or the saner constructive period, has taken its place.

W. Wilfred Campbell, poet and imperialist, address, "Imperialism in Canada," Toronto, 23 November 1904, The Empire Club of Canada.

Modern democracy is the best system of government as yet operative in this world of sin.

Stephen Leacock, humorist, *The Unsolved Riddle of Social Justice* (1920).

Democracy of course was inefficient, so it ought to be. Efficiency is an unnatural strain, like Sunday School, or company manners. Democracy was more or less crooked; so is humanity; so are you.

Stephen Leacock, humorist, *The Unsolved Riddle of Social Justice* (1920).

One of the great American newspapers—I believe it was the *New York Times*, wrote that with him "The robes of nobility had become the habits of democracy."

Leonard Brockington, orator, "John Buchan in Canada," in Susan Buchan, *John Buchan by His Wife and Friends* (1947).

So we must look into the future and see what world we are building, for our old age and for the future of our children. We are going through this period of participatory democracy. I hope it is a permanent form of participatory democracy. I favour equally anticipatory democracy because we must see what is ahead of us.

Barney Danson, Member of Parliament, on international affairs, House of Commons, 29 May 1969.

Perhaps letters to the editor may be a useful form of participatory democracy. Perhaps even one voice, shouting a good cause loud enough and long enough, may produce some effect, even on ideas, policies and governments which seem impregnable.

Eugene Forsey, constitutional specialist and author of more than 800 letters to the periodical press, article "When Forsey Writes Letters He Can Cause a Lot of Rows," *The Ottawa Journal*, 2 January 1974, in J.E. Hodgetts, *The Sound of One Voice: Eugene Forsey and His Letters to the Press* (2000).

Today we talk about the deadliness of our system. What on earth do we mean? We have allowed such talk to wander unobstructed, carelessly, into our language. The deadliness of our system? Of liberal democracy? Of a system that in the history of the world has produced a better standard of living for more of its people than any other in the world? Not perfect. Not able to eliminate all the evils of poverty, disease and dirt, but the very best yet, as yet, that human beings have discovered.

Barbara Amiel, journalist, address, "How Canada Does It and Other Social Diseases," Toronto, 4 February 1982, The Empire Club of Canada.

Democracy is a fine thing, but too much democracy is anarchy.

David J. Bercuson, **Robert Bothwell**, and **J.L. Granatstein**, historians, *The Great Brain Robbery: The Decline of Canada's Universities* (1984), excerpted in "Degrading the Degree," *The Globe and Mail*, 8 September 1984.

Sadly, the most important moral, political, and cultural principles and precepts that affect our lives are persistently being eroded by the judiciary and the courts as they remove them from representative democratic control.

Anne C. Cools, senator, foreword to Robert Ivan Martin, *The Most Dangerous Branch: How the Supreme Court of Canada Has Undermined Our Law and Our Democracy* (2003).

Canada is admirably positioned to share with the developing world her experience in humane governance to support pluralism, the development of civil society, and meritocratic premises for action.

Aga Khan, spiritual leader of the Shia Ismaili Muslims, address, Conference on Leadership and Diversity, Ottawa, 19 May 2004, published in *The Globe and Mail*, 20 May 2004.

This may be the genius of mature democracy. What looks like a dichotomy may turn out to be the self-balancing, self-healing capacity of small-l liberalism: A capacity to continue political discourse and maintain a functioning government, no matter how wide, how deep, or how evenly matched the rift may be between two factions in society. Divisions that would lead to civil war in other systems have led (so far) to nothing worse than "third way" politicians in ours. A heroic model it is not. But while it may not be uplifting, it's survivable.

George Jonas, columnist, "The Culture War's Elected Peacemakers," *National Post*, 31 May 2004.

DEPRESSION *See also* Mental Illness; Psychiatry

It is estimated that one in every four Canadians will experience a degree of depression serious enough to require treatment at some time in their lives.

Leslie Beck, nutrition consultant, *Leslie Beck's Nutrition Encyclopedia* (2001).

Okay, remember this like a mantra: Sadness lifts, depression persists.

Sarah Rosenthal, health specialist, *Women of the '60s Turning 50* (2000).

DEPRESSION, ECONOMIC

When the Depression came, our world stopped and we got off.

James H. Gray, historian, in Barry Broadfoot, *Ten Lost Years, 1929–1939: Memoirs of Canadians Who Survived the Depression* (1973).

DESIGN *See also* Architecture; Creativity; Perception; Typography

There is an old law of graphic design which states that those things which are close together will appear to belong together.

Carl Dair, typographer, "Why Typography?" (1968), in Sheila Heti, "The Actual Space," *The Writers' Trust of Canada: Canada Book Week, Issue 2*, "Literary Landscapes," 21–27 April 2003.

The well-made page is now what it was then: a window into history, language and the mind: a map of what is being said and a portrait of the voice that is silently speaking.

Robert Bringhurst, author and typographer, *The Elements of Typographic Style* (2nd ed., 1996).

No longer associated simply with objects and appearances, design is increasingly understood in a much wider sense as the human capacity to plan and produce desired outcomes.

Bruce Mau, designer, "Massive Change" exhibition (2004), in Christopher Hume, "Massive Fraud?" *Toronto Star*, 27 February 2005.

For most of us, design is invisible. Until it fails.

Bruce Mau, designer, opening sentence, *Massive Change* exhibition catalogue (2004), noted by Peter Goddard, "Bruce Mau Delivers Massive Disappointment," *Toronto Star*, 11 March 2005.

One of the most interesting things we did was take the visual out of design.

Bruce Mau, designer, "Designs for Living," *The New York Times Magazine*, 26 September 2004.

DESIRE *See also* Ambition

Desire is everything, not talent. It's the degree of one's desire that will dictate the extent of one's success, in any endeavour.

Ken Danby, artist, characteristic observation, 6 July 2005.

DESPAIR

Unless we take a new and radical form of action, unless we try to really become, each one of us, men of peace and not just the givers of gifts but really begin sharing, deeply sharing, opening our hearts, opening our doors to the afflicted, to the lonely, to the sick, unless we really take a new mode of action, a drastic, rapid serious action, committing ourselves and radically changing our lives to understand the deep friction of the majority of humanity, we will but continue on this downhill road which opens up the world to conflagration or greater despair.

Jean Vanier, humanitarian, address, "A World in Violence: Eruption to Hope?" Toronto, 11 February 1971, The Empire Club of Canada.

In the greatest moments of despair, how do we recognize that the pilot light of our spirit hasn't gone out? What do we cling to?

Brent Carver, actor, interviewed by Richard Ouzounian, "Carver No Stranger to Death's Shadow," *Toronto Star*, 17 October 2004.

DESTINY *See also* Future; Prediction & Prophecy

The potentialities of Canada are immense. The realization rests with her people. Its attainment cannot fail you if you bend to the task with a long pull and a strong pull, as is the Canadian way, and, above all, with a pull all together.

Otto H. Kahn, financier and philanthropist, address, "An International Survey," Toronto, 17 April 1924, The Empire Club of Canada.

Perhaps and perhaps not. For the most difficult of all is to understand how we ourselves came, and where we go on the day we no longer live. Over all beginning and ending there is darkness.

Apákak, elder, in Knud Rasmussen, *The Alaskan Eskimos* (1952), Volume 10, Number 3, "Report of the Fifth Thule Expedition (1921–24)" (1952), edited by H. Ostermann.

Canada is too young to fall victim to the malady of disillusionment and scepticism, and she must believe in great ideals in the face of contradiction—for she has the great gift of youth, she has the direct consciousness of the stir of growth within, which should make her trust her own self, which is the only sure way of trusting the world. Let her feel in the sacred dawn of her life that the expectation of the human destiny is upon her as upon other young sister countries of hers, which have just entered into the cycle of their promise.

Rabindranath Tagore, Bengali sage, "Farewell to Canada," 13 April 1929, *Education and Leisure: Addresses Delivered at the Fourth Triennial Conference on Education Held at Victoria and Vancouver, Canada, April 1929* (1929), edited by S.E. Lang.

Canada's destiny remains circumscribed by a dozen suits bickering over constitutional crumbs in a loopy process that is as relevant to our daily lives as the mating habits of Brazilian killer bees.

Peter C. Newman, columnist and author, "Love This Land, Not the Constitution," *Defining Moments: Dispatches from an Unfinished Revolution* (1997).

DICTATORSHIP *See also* Government; Ideas

As long as men want God on Earth, there will always be a Hitler.

Reg Hartt, cineaste, attributes the remark to an "old woman" who observed him posting a handbill to promote a showing of the famous Nazi documentary-cum-propaganda film *Triumph of the Will* in Toronto in the 1970s.

One sometimes wonders whether some historian in the future will not find a strict cause–effect relationship between the cynicism, bitterness, and moral and aesthetic relativism of the postmodern sensibility and the cynicism, bitterness, and moral relativism of our post-Marxist, post-Soviet, and to many our post-socialist political climate. Or maybe the postmodern sensibility, with its "deconstruction" of all meaning and all values, functions precisely as a psychological defence mechanism, so that we do not have to deal with the bewildering "meaning" of a phenomenon that stares us in the face: our post-Christian century's central experience of the loss of faith in our salvation by society, after the true face of state Dictatorship was revealed under the mask of Messianism.

Erika Gottlieb, scholar, *Dystopian Fiction East and West: Universe of Terror and Trial* (2001).

DIETS *See also* Food & Drink; Obesity; Weight

Most people I know feel that life would be complete if they could just lose ten pounds.

Betty Jane Wylie, author, observation made in 1990.

The bottom line is that to successfully lose weight, you have to find something that fits into your routine and into your lifestyle.

Barbie Casselman, nutritionist, address, "Understanding Healthy Nutrition," Toronto, 11 March 1992, The Empire Club of Canada.

By the time they reach adulthood, nearly half of all North American females have concerns about their weight and many have already begun the vicious cycle of dieting and weight gain.

Leslie Beck, nutrition consultant, *Leslie Beck's Nutrition Encyclopedia* (2001).

DINING *See also* Food & Drink

Keep yer fork, Duke, the pie's acomin'.

Advice of an over-friendly waitress, to the governor general, the Duke of Connaught, as she removed the main-course plates but not all the cutlery at a Board of Trade dinner in a small community in British Columbia's Peace River district between 1911 and 1916. In the popular mind the advice was delivered to **Prince Philip, Duke of Edinburgh**, who has denied the incident ever occurred to him. "No one would dare," Philip told historian James Eayrs. Peter Gzowski, host of CBC Radio's *Morningside*, canvassed listeners about the anecdote and came to the conclusion that the incident did occur but to Connaught and not to Philip.

DINOSAURS

The dinosaurs are indeed dead. The sight of their bronze skeletons in the darkened galleries of our museums seems to call us hauntingly. They too were wonderful, they are dead, and their death recalls to us something of the meaning of living. Their giant skeletons embody the abundance of a long-vanished world. The life of our planet has more than recovered from the forces that destroyed the world in which they lived. Yet, would we have survived had we been in their place?

Dale A. Russell, paleontologist, *A Vanished World: The Dinosaurs of Western Canada* (1977).

DION, CÉLINE

When she accepts the Emmy Award, her aged, unsmiling dungeon master of a husband will be remote-controlling her arm movements from the audience with a small steering wheel. When she gets back to Canada, he'll reward her by letting her jump for a nice three-pack of fresh nylons.

Cintra Wilson, U.S. commentator, referring to the singer's husband and manager René Angelil, *A Massive Swelling: Celebrity Re-examined as a Grotesque, Crippling Disease and Other Cultural Revelations* (2000).

I call her "The Singing Q-tip." She's so f—ing thin. I hate her.

Elton John, British rock and pop singer, performing in the same venue at Caesars Palace in Las Vegas as the slender Quebec singer, in Richard Ouzounian, "A Cranky Elton's Still Got It," *Toronto Star*, 29 July 2005. Dion has delivered 200 sell-out performances a year since 2003.

DIPLOMACY *See also* Canada & the World; Negotiation

It [Canada] must ever hope to be able to win the heart of the world by offering the best that it produces and never by material force or cunning diplomacy—even like what occurred in the golden age of India when her messengers reached far distant alien lands, carrying the gifts of love and wisdom, the message of emancipation, acknowledging common human fellowship at the risk of danger and death.

Rabindranath Tagore, Bengali sage, "Farewell to Canada," 13 April 1929, *Education and Leisure: Addresses Delivered at the Fourth Triennial Conference on Education Held at Victoria and Vancouver, Canada, April 1929* (1929), edited by S.E. Lang.

I believe in intervention and personal responsibility. In fact, to me, diplomacy is getting what you want without actually going to war.

Adrienne Clarkson, agent general for Ontario, address, "Ontario and the French Connection," Toronto, 21 November 1985, The Empire Club of Canada.

DISABILITIES *See also* Abilities

We are all of us deeply handicapped because we take so much for granted and we repose so much in the security of life and position. How to change our hearts, how to change our egoism into universal brotherhood? How to change our desire to acquire and to possess into sharing and oblativity? How to be transformed? How to break down the fear that is in me when I am in front of the afflicted people, the handicapped people? How to welcome them with arms outstretched and without fear? How to change this deep need to possess, in order to dispossess and to give; not in a sort of paternalistic way but realizing that life is only life if we share? Life is not life if we give and think we are someone. Life is real life only if we share deeply, only if we give and receive, only if we spend time, only if we welcome into our hearts and into our homes the afflicted ones.

Jean Vanier, humanitarian, address, "A World in Violence: Eruption to Hope?" Toronto, 11 February 1971, The Empire Club of Canada.

The true measure of a civilization rests upon how it cares for its vulnerable members.

Reva Gerstein, professor of social work, *The Final Report of the Mayor's Action Task Force on Discharged Psychiatric Patients, Toronto* (1984).

This show is so good, I've just got to take it to Las Vegas.

Liberace, U.S. pianist and entertainer, responding to a special performance of the Famous People Players in Toronto, in Diane Dupuis, founder, Famous People Players, "Living the Dream," Toronto, 25 October 1990, The Empire Club of Toronto. "I mean, wow, it was like a dream come true. I said, 'Wait until he finds out who we are. I mean surely that would make a difference.' And when the company came out on stage and took their hoods off and became visible to him, he looked at them and he went back to the microphone, and still looking at them, he said, 'It's not because of who you are that you make people laugh or cry. It's because you're truly talented people who have the same right to be integrated as anybody else and you're going to love Las Vegas.'"

For people who move around in the dark, you turned lights on in our heads.

Alan Alda, American actor, paying tribute to the Famous People Players, as recalled by the group's founder Diane Dupuis, "Living the Dream," Toronto, 25 October 1990, The Empire Club of Toronto.

In August 1964, I founded L'Arche: a network of small homes and communities where we live together, men and women with intellectual disabilities and those who feel called to share their lives with them.

Jean Vanier, humanitarian, *Becoming Human* (1998).

One day a wheelchair will be something we see at a museum.

Rick Hansen, wheelchair athlete and fundraiser, launching the first annual Wheels in Motion event, news conference, Toronto, 21 May 2003, in Fatima Najm, "Hansen Back in Motion," *Toronto Star*, 22 May 2003.

DISARMAMENT *See also* Arms Race; Land Mines; Nuclear Warfare; War

The time, in my view, has come for a small country like Canada to join with other smaller countries in a relentless attack on the insanity of the nuclear terror and on the international military–industrial complex which feeds it.

David Lewis, NDP deputy leader, address, "NATO in the Balance," 27 March 1969, The Empire Club of Canada.

I believe that the question of disarmament is the most pressing, practical, moral and spiritual issue of our times.

Margaret Laurence, novelist, "Foreword," *Canada and the Nuclear Arms Race* (1983), edited by Ernie Regehr.

DISASTERS *See also* Charity

Canadians are fond of a good disaster, specially if it has ice, water, or snow in it.

Margaret Atwood, author, "Concerning Franklin and His Gallant Crew," *Strange Things: The Malevolent North in Canadian Literature* (1995).

There are obvious problems with the way that the international community responds to human disasters.

Lewis MacKenzie, retired major general, in Barry Shainbaum, *Hope & Heroes: Portraits of Integrity & Inspiration* (2003).

Some might argue this is the tribal instinct coming to the fore, the same reflex that permits the headline: "150,000 Dead, Five of Them Canadian."

Anne Kingston, columnist, referring to Western attitudes to the death toll from the Southeast Asian tsunami in December 2004, "It's Always about Us," *National Post*, 4 January 2005.

The last place on earth you'd want to be is the first place you'll find the Red Cross.

Ann Medina, broadcast journalist, endorsing the annual campaign of the Canadian Red Cross, quoted in its fundraising literature, February 2005.

DISCOVERY *See also* Exploration; Research

I shall give this country a name and call it *Helluland.*

Attributed to **Leif Ericsson**, also known as Leif the Lucky, explorer and colonist, referring to Baffin Island in the Eastern Arctic about A.D. 1000 as "Helluland," the equivalent of "slag-land," as preserved in the *Greenlanders' Saga,* translated from *The Vinland Sagas* (1965), in turn translated from the Old Icelandic by Magnus Magnusson and Hermann Palsson. Leif went on to call the Labrador coast *Markland* (or "forest-land") and L'Anse aux Meadows at the northeastern tip of Newfoundland *Vinland* (or "wine-land").

The best known authorities agree that practically all the information that is likely to be obtained on this subject has come to light, and the translation and explanations of the old Saga manuscripts have been deciphered in a manner that leaves very little room for further enquiry on this subject. The only real live question that still awaits explanation and proof is where Wineland really was?

W.A. Munn, cod-liver oil merchant, amateur historian, and researcher, on evidence for determining the site of the Norse settlement of Wineland or Vinland, *Location of Helluland, Markland, and Wineland from the Icelandic Sagas* (1914). Munn argued that Norse landfalls and settlements had probably occurred at Cape Porcupine and Pistolet Bay. A half century later, his speculations would be proved correct. In 1960, the Danish explorer Helge Ingstad located the remains of the first Norse settlement of North America near the remote fishing village of L'Anse aux Meadows at the northeast tip of Newfoundland. Ingstad gives credit to Munn for his account *Westward to Vinland: The Discovery of Pre-Columbian Norse Home-sites in North America* (1969), translated from the Norwegian by Erik J. Friis.

This land he called *Prima vista,* that is to say, *First seen.*

Attributed to **John Cabot**, Italian-born navigator and explorer, naming the historic landfall at Cape Bonavista, Nfld., on 24 June 1497, *terra primum vista* ("first-seen land"), according to Richard Hakluyt, *The Principal Navigations, Voyages, Traffiques and Discoveries of the English Nation* (1598).

In fine I am rather inclined to believe that this is the land God gave to Cain.

Jacques Cartier, explorer, journal entry describing the northern shore of the Gulf of St. Lawrence as he sailed past what would later be named Labrador and Quebec, summer 1534, *"Première Relation," The Voyages of Jacques Cartier* (1924), translated by H.P. Biggar.

In 1534 the Frenchman Jacques Cartier "discovered" the mouth of the St. Lawrence, west of Newfoundland, where he was confounded by "the presence of 1,000 Basque fishing vessels."

Andrew Collins, researcher, *Gateway to Atlantis: The Search for the Source of a Lost Civilization* (2000), quoting Mark Kurlansky, *Cod: A Biography of the Fish That Changed the World* (1997).

It is true that the bottom line is not the same; I must make discoveries, you must make a profit. It is also true, I hope, that you are better at making a profit than I am at making discoveries. (I almost never make a discovery.) But, along the way, the forces with which we must contend are similar.

John C. Polanyi, chemist and professor, discussing research and development (and not as businessmen would have it, development and research), address, "A Scientist and the World He Lives In," Toronto, 27 November 1986, The Empire Club of Canada.

You cannot discover new oceans until you lose sight of the shore.

Peter C. Newman, journalist and memoirist, *Here Be Dragons: Telling Tales of People, Passion, and Power* (2004).

DISEASE *See also* Health

Care more particularly for the individual patient than for the special features of the disease.

Sir William Osler, physician, "Address to the Students of the Albany Medical College," *Albany Medical Annual*, Volume 20 (1899).

I'm also disturbed because the doctors tell me I'm as sound as a dollar.

John G. Diefenbaker, former prime minister, convalescing in Ottawa, in Ken MacGray, *Toronto Star*, 26 April 1975.

VENI VIDI V.D.

Graffiti sprayed on the wall, Toronto General Hospital, April 1980.

DISTINCT SOCIETY *See also* Canada & Quebec

Quebec constitutes, within Canada, a distinct society.

Key provision of the Meech Lake Constitutional Accord, adopted for future provincial ratification at an all-ministers' conference, Ottawa, 3 June 1987. By granting constitutional recognition of the distinctive character of the province of Quebec, the accord sought to provide for "two distinct societies" (*deux nations*) in Canada. Manitoba and Newfoundland did not ratify the Accord.

Quebec constitutes within Canada a distinct society, which includes a French-speaking majority, a unique culture and a civil law tradition.

The most contentious clause of the many contentious clauses of the Charlottetown Constitutional Accord of the First Ministers and Native and Territorial Leaders for Constitutional Reform, 28 August 1992, published in *The Globe and Mail*, 1 September 1992. The referendum itself was held (and failed) on 26 October 1992.

You must know if you really want to understand Quebec that we are not a distinct society. We are a nation.

Bernard Landry, Quebec deputy premier, address announcing his candidacy as Parti Québécois leader and premier, 21 January 2001, in Rhéal Séguin, "Secession at Top of Agenda," *The Globe and Mail*, 22 January 2001.

Ottawa offered something its constitutional idiot savants called the "distinct society" option. It was the perfect Canadian political ploy: almost everyone came out against it, except those who insisted that it was meaningless.

Peter C. Newman, columnist, referring to the Brian Mulroney administration's touting of "distinct society" as an "answer" to Quebec's sovereignty "option," "Adieu to Separatism?" *Maclean's*, 12 May 2003.

Point of fact, there was nothing wrong with Meech Lake except one thing: Trudeau's vanity. He didn't want anybody to succeed where he had failed. Trudeau's contribution was not to build Canada, but to destroy it, and I had to come in and save it.

Brian Mulroney, prime minister, in Peter C. Newman, *The Secret Mulroney Tapes: Unguarded Confessions of a Prime Minister* (2005).

Doesn't mean a goddamned thing. The distinct society clause, as I said to Clyde Wells, all it means is dick to me. Means dick.

Brian Mulroney, prime minister, referring to Newfoundland premier and to the "distinct society" clause in the Meech Lake Accord, in Peter C. Newman, *The Secret Mulroney Tapes: Unguarded Confessions of a Prime Minister* (2005).

Meech was treated as a holdup in a gas station at 6:00 o'clock in the morning.

Mila Mulroney, wife of former Prime Minister Brian Mulroney, castigating the press for dissing the Meech Lake Constitutional Accord, as noted by Peter C. Newman, *The Secret Mulroney Tapes: Unguarded Confessions of a Prime Minister* (2005).

DIVERSITY *See also* Multiculturalism

All the technological innovations and the wars of this bloodstained century will be wiped away in historical memory by the fact that the 21st century was the era in which we stood by and either actively endorsed or passively accepted the massive loss of both cultural and biological diversity. And that will be the hallmark of the coming century.

Mark Abley, author, *Spoken Here: Travels among Threatened Languages* (2003).

Consider the deep diversity in a multi-layered Canada: Neither Aboriginal peoples nor the Québécois can possibly endorse an official multiculturalism that lumps together all diversities, both immigrant and indigenous, as well as the superficial and the deep. Since a culture-blind multiculturalism cannot speak the language of deep diversity, it has proven every bit as controlling as "old fashioned racism."

Augie Fleras, sociologist, "Racializing Culture / Culturalizing Race," *Racism, Eh? A Critical Inter-Disciplinary Anthology of Race and Racism in Canada* (2004), edited by Camille A. Nelson and Charmaine A. Nelson.

The challenge rests in constructing a multicultural Canada that is safe from diversity, safe for diversity. In that Canada's multicultural discourses cannot cope with the challenge of making DIVERSITY safe from Canada as well as safe for Canada, a pattern of multicultural racism is established that is quintessentially part of the "Canadian way."

Augie Fleras, sociologist, "Racializing Culture / Culturalizing Race," *Racism, Eh? A Critical Inter-Disciplinary Anthology of Race and Racism in Canada* (2004), edited by Camille A. Nelson and Charmaine A. Nelson.

DIVORCE *See also* Marriage

Divorce: disunion, disjunction, disconnection, dissolution, separation, severance, breach, split, detachment, disruption, partition. It is all these things at once. The ending of a union once made in love.

Gail Vaz-Oxlade, columnist, *Divorce: A Canadian Woman's Guide* (2000).

I now understand that "Tomorrow is another day" is more than just a sentiment. It is an anthem for a divorcing person, a mantra to be whispered, screamed, howled, ground out between clenched teeth.

Gail Vaz-Oxlade, columnist, *Divorce: A Canadian Woman's Guide* (2000).

I believed we could uncouple our lives and move on in new directions, like cars uncoupling from a train, but I had no idea how to make this happen. I needed wisdom and role models, yet what I found was the toxic energy that surrounds divorce in our culture.

Silken Laumann, athlete, "Starting Over: Rebuilding a Life after Divorce," *Chatelaine*, September 2003.

In the end, we divorced over religious differences: I thought I was God, and she didn't. She haunts me still.

Peter C. Newman, journalist and memoirist, about his marriage to and divorce from Christina McCall, *Here Be Dragons: Telling Tales of People, Passion, and Power* (2004).

DOCTORS *See also* Medicine

The best doctor, like the successful general, is the one who makes the fewest mistakes.

Sir William Osler, physician, "The Pathological Institute of a General Hospital," *Glasgow Medical Journal*, Volume 76, 1911.

Educate your nerve centres so that not the slightest dilator or contractor influence shall pass to the vessels of your face under any professional trial.

Sir William Osler, physician, "Aequanimitas," *Aequanimitas* (1932).

The physician needs a clear head and a kind heart.

Sir William Osler, physician, "Teaching and Thinking," *Aequanimitas* (1932).

DOCUMENTARY *See* Cinema

DOGS

Near this spot / Are deposited the Remains of one / Who possessed Beauty without Vanity, / Strength without Insolence, / Courage without Ferocity, / And all the Virtues of Man, without his Vices. / This Praise, which would be unmeaning Flattery / If inscribed over human ashes, / Is but a just Tribute to the memory of / BOATSWAIN, a Dog, / Who was born at Newfoundland, May, 1803, / And died at Newstead Abbey, November 18, 1808.

Lines inscribed on a memorial marker on his ancestral acres in England by **George Gordon, Lord Byron**, English poet (1788–1824), "Epitaph to a Newfoundland Dog," *A Second Treasury of the Familiar* (1950), edited by Ralph L. Woods.

We dedicate this fountain to mankind's / Most devoted and loyal friend / The Dog. / We wish them fun walks / Happy times / Cool drinks. / Willy, thanks for getting us walking in this beautiful park. / This clear water is for you and all the little fur people. / October 1999 / Drink My Loves. / Daphne Shick & Family.

Inscription on a ground-level fountain, Alexander Muir Park, Toronto, observed, May 2000.

Training dogs is easy; training trainers is hard.

Stanley Coren, psychologist, *How Dogs Think: Understanding the Canine Mind* (2004).

DOMINION *See also* Canada

The simple fact is that we are citizens of a Dominion, just as Americans are citizens of a republic and Englishmen citizens of a kingdom. The British North America Act says twice that we are a Dominion.... That would enhance our status. Then, at last, we should achieve our destiny: neither kingdom nor republic, nor anything else known to political terminology, but just a nameless Something, a sublime Blank!

Eugene Forsey, constitutional specialist, arguing for retaining the word "Dominion," *The Globe and Mail,* 11 December 1951, in J.E. Hodgetts, *The Sound of One Voice: Eugene Forsey and His Letters to the Press* (2000).

Dominion remains the official, constitutional title of our country, and will so remain till it is changed by formal constitutional amendment.

Eugene Forsey, constitutional specialist, *The Globe and Mail,* 16 July 1982, in J.E. Hodgetts, *The Sound of One Voice: Eugene Forsey and His Letters to the Press* (2000). Forsey was noting that despite the private member's bill that replaced the designation "Dominion Day" with "Canada Day" in 1982, according to the BNA Act, 1867, part of the Constitution Act, 1982, Canada is to "form and be one Dominion."

Canada was the first country to be called a dominion.

Wayne Grady, author, *Chasing the Chinook: On the Trail of Canadian Words and Culture* (1998).

DOUGLAS, T.C. (TOMMY) *See also* Health Care; Medicare; New Democratic Party; Socialism

You won't find me very interesting. I never do anything but work.

T.C. (Tommy) Douglas, statesman, admission to his biographer Doris Shackleton, *Tommy Douglas* (1975).

I have often thought that my whole political life—my whole life as a matter of fact—could be summed up in the words "printer, preacher, politician, premier—or the descent of man."

T.C. (Tommy) Douglas, statesman, quoted in *Time,* 27 October 1975.

Courage, my friend, it is not too late to build a better world.

Inscription on the tombstone of statesman **T.C. (Tommy) Douglas** (1904–1986), Beechwood Cemetery, Ottawa, noted by Ed Finn, "The Father of Medicare," *The CCPA Monitor,* February 2005. "Courage, my friends ... 'tis not too late to make a better world" also appears beneath his photograph on the wall of the Saskatoon office of Roy Romanow, subsequent Saskatchewan premier who in April 2001 was appointed sole commissioner of the Royal Commission on the Future of Health Care in Canada, as noted by Roy

MacGregor, "This Country," *The Globe and Mail*, 29 September 2002.

DOUKHOBORS

In Canada, Sulerjitsky lived for a year or two with the Doukhobors, conducting negotiations with the government as the representative of the peasants, leading the peasants and teaching them how to begin their new life. Life in a tent, hard cares, harder work, all this left a mark on his health. I wonder if the rich Doukhobors in Canada know of this, or whether they know that his family and his two children are at present suffering need, hunger and cold in Moscow.

Constantin Stanislavski, theatre director and instructor, *My Life in Art* (1924, 1948), translated from the Russian by Elizabeth Reynolds Hapgood. The reference is to Leopold Antonovich Sulerjitsky, a remarkable Russian and friend of Stanislavski's Moscow Art Theatre. He accepted Leo Tolstoy's commission to help to settle the Doukhobors in Western Canada and subsequently came to grief.

The Doukhobors of Redknife displayed a certain awareness of their nudity by turning their backs on Stani's camera so he soon tired of photographing white cubical rear ends, even though the weatherbeaten necks and forearms helped his compositions.

Narration from actor **David Niven**'s novel *Go Slowly, Come Back Quickly* (1981).

Tolstoy also wished upon Canada the Doukhobors, a primitive rabble of peasant Believers who were transferred here because even Russia could not stand them. They Believe, but not in Education (they burn schools) nor in taxes (they don't pay 'em) nor in any sort of national service. Tolstoy has much to answer for.

Robertson Davies, man of letters, referring to Leo Tolstoy and his role in re-establishing Doukhobor peasants on the Prairies, 8 February 1988, *For Your Eye Alone: Letters, 1976–1995* (1999).

DREAMS *See also* Vision

There was silence in the room. Then a voice, stunning as thunder, clear and common as a train whistle—the voice of a ball-park announcer: "If you build it, he will come."

W.P. Kinsella, fiction writer and sports enthusiast, "Shoeless Joe Jackson Comes to Iowa" (1980), a short story expanded into the novel *Shoeless Joe* (1982), later filmed as *Field of Dreams* (1989), by writer-director Phil Alden Robinson. *Toronto Star* columnist **Joey Slinger** offered an aside: "The field of our dreams is flooded and frozen and has a net at either end."

It's tough to build a country to match a dream.

Pierre Elliott Trudeau, prime minister, farewell speech, Liberal Party, Ottawa, 9 February 1984.

Our hopes are high. Our faith in the people is great. Our courage is strong. And our dreams for this beautiful country will never die.

Pierre Elliott Trudeau, prime minister, farewell speech, Liberal Party, Ottawa, 9 February 1984.

Dare to dream, dare to be different and, above all, dare to take chances.

Diane Dupuis, founder, Famous People Players, address, "Living the Dream," Toronto, 25 October 1990, The Empire Club of Toronto.

We have dreamed as long as we've been human, and probably before that.

Christopher Dewdney, poet and author, *Acquainted with the Night: Excursions through the World after Dark* (2004).

DRINKING *See* Alcohol; Food & Drink

DRUGS & DRUG TRADE *See also* America; Marijuana; Medicine

Turn on, tune in, drop out.

Associated with **Timothy Leary**, psychedelic pioneer, and used by him as the title of a lecture he delivered in 1966; according to Nigel Rees, *Cassell's Companion to Quotations* (1997), the maxim is "summing up his philosophy of 'the game of life.' Leary attributed the phrase to Marshall McLuhan."

I have never, ever knowingly taken illegal drugs, and I would never embarrass my family, my friends, my country, and the kids who love me.

Ben Johnson, champion sprinter billed as "the fastest man in the world," press conference, Toronto, 4 October 1988. After he was stripped of his Olympic gold medal, he later admitted to using banned anabolic steroids. Canadians' ambivalent response to the Johnson affair found classic expression in Frank Edwards's editorial cartoon in *The Kingston Whig-Standard.* Edwards drew three identical caricatures of the sprinter and captioned them in turn "Canadian Wins Gold Medal," "Jamaican-Canadian Accused of Steroid Use," and "Jamaican Stripped of Gold Medal."

Former Marijuana Smuggler / Having successfully completed a ten year sentence, incident-free, for importing 75 tons of marijuana into the United States, I am now seeking a legal and legitimate means to support myself and my family.

First lines of a job-wanted advertisement that appeared in the "Classified" section of *The Financial Post, National Post,* 19 February 2001. Placed by a Newfoundland-born, Toronto-based former international drug smuggler who wanted to use his business experience and knowledge of languages, the ad sparked media interest and produced a number of firm job offers.

Then: I'm going to Canada for Cheap Drugs.
Now: I'm going to Canada for Cheap Drugs.

Captions for adjoining panels showing hippies for "Then" and geriatrics for "Now," drawn by **Mike Peters**, *The Dayton Daily News,* reprinted in *The New York Times,* 9 November 2003.

The Canadians are even more cannabis-tolerant; although they have not legalized the drug, they are loath to stomp out the growers. This illicit industry has emerged as Canada's most valuable agricultural product—bigger than wheat, cattle or timber.

Editors of Forbes, comparing Canadian and American attitudes towards marijuana, "Cash Crop," *Forbes,* 10 November 2003.

When a drug comes in from Canada, I want to make sure it cures you and doesn't kill you.

George W. Bush, U.S. president, on his country's importation of low-cost pharmaceuticals from Canada in a debate with Democratic candidate John Kerry, *The News Hour with Jim Lehrer,* PBS, 8 October 2004.

DUPLESSIS, MAURICE

The bishops eat from my hand.

Maurice Duplessis, Union Nationale Party leader and Quebec premier in the 1940s and 1950s, characteristic remark. Conrad Black in *Duplessis* (1977) suggests that the remark is "possibly Duplessis' most famous line of all, frequently uttered in the Assembly and in conversation, but difficult to find in contemporary newspapers. Everyone who knew Duplessis remembers this."

I never married because I have a mistress, a most demanding, but a wonderful mistress—my Province of Quebec.

Maurice Duplessis, adapted from a remark recalled by Pierre Sévigny, *This Game of Politics* (1965).

DUTY

Mastery of self, conscientious devotion to duty, deep human interest in human beings—these best of all lessons you must learn now or never.

Sir William Osler, physician, "Sir Thomas Browne," *An Alabama Student and Other Biographical Essays* (1908).

To know just what has to be done, then to do it, comprises the whole philosophy of practical life.

Sir William Osler, physician, "British Medicine in Greater Britain," *Aequanimitas* (1932).

When a man discovers his duty do not insult him with freedom.

L.S. Cattarini, aphorist, "The Intimation of Destiny" (2000), *Beyond Sartre and Sterility: Surviving Existentialism* (1986, 2002).

DYING WORDS *See* Epitaphs

e

EARTH *See also* Environmentalism; Exploration; Geography; Space

On Spaceship Earth there are no passengers, but all are crew.

Marshall McLuhan, media philosopher, opening statement, address, "The End of the Work Ethic," 16 November 1972, The Empire Club of Canada.

On land, inevitably surrounded by trees or buildings or hills, it is easy to forget the *size* of the world, but at sea, impossible to ignore. Once out in the ocean, the scale of everything changes as though you had entered a new dimension, a dominion of gigantic beings.

David McTaggart, ecologist and activist, *Greenpeace III: Journey into the Bomb* (1978).

One of the most wonderful things you can do from space is look at the planet earth. I had a wonderful time, when I had a few minutes, looking at our golden planet. It was so beautiful. The light angle changed every time I looked at it, making the atmosphere different colours. Some days it was golden, some days it was a turquoise blue, it was always changing. I can only tell you that we cannot attach the same quality of depth and luxury of colour on this film, as you can see with the human eye in space.

Roberta Bondar, astronaut, address, "The Adventure of Space," Toronto, 22 September 1992, The Empire Club of Canada.

EASTER *See* Holidays: Easter

ECOLOGY *See also* Environmentalism

Ecology is only another name for this acoustic simultaneity and the sudden responsibility for creating ecological environments pressed very suddenly upon Western man on October 17th, 1959. That was the day when Sputnik went into orbit, putting this planet inside a man-made environment for the first time. As soon as the planet went inside a man-made environment, the occupants of the planet began to hum and sing the ecological theme song without any further prompting.

Marshall McLuhan, media philosopher, address, "The End of the Work Ethic," Toronto, 16 November 1972, The Empire Club of Canada.

However, in the age of ecology, the age in which we recognize that everything affects everything, it is no longer possible to remain unaware of the effects of the things we make, on our psychic and social lives. We are living in a situation which has been called "future shock." Future shock, in fact, is "culture lag," that is, the failure to notice what is happening in the present.

Marshall McLuhan, media philosopher, address, "The End of the Work Ethic," Toronto, 16 November 1972, The Empire Club of Canada.

Ecology is studying processes within our horizon. How does a cell work? How does a swamp work? How does a marsh work? How do biological processes enter into a dialogue? How do they interact with human beings?

William Irwin Thompson, theorist, "Mind Jazz," *Wild Culture: Specimens from* The Journal of Wild Culture (1992), edited by Whitney Smith and Christopher Lowry.

The earth, like trees, dies from the top down. The things that are killing the North will kill, if not left unchecked, everything else.

Margaret Atwood, author, "Linoleum Caves," *Strange Things: The Malevolent North in Canadian Literature* (1995).

Our species has demonstrated a singular and ever-expanding ability to eradicate its fellow species, and to erode the support system upon which life depends. We are clever creatures.

Farley Mowat, author, foreword, in Elizabeth May, *At the Cutting Edge: The Crisis in Canada's Forests* (2005).

ECONOMICS *See also* Business; Currency; Depression, Economic; Finance; Food Banks; Free Trade; Globalism & Globalization; Inflation; Stock Market

Articles of which the consumption is not conspicuous are incapable of gratifying this passion.

John Rae, Scottish-born Canadian economist, referring to human vanity, *The Sociological Theory of Capital* (1834). Rae anticipated by 65 years the notion of "conspicuous consumption" identified with Thorstein Veblen, *The Theory of the Leisure Class* (1899).

If Canada is to be at its best fighting weight, it cannot afford to go into the international ring with the fatiguing fat of services and products—or, indeed, of a work force—priced beyond what could be achieved if costs were whittled by efficiency and attuned to realism.

Donald Gordon, chairman, Canadian National Railways, address, "Realism or Fatalism," Toronto, 12 March 1962, The Empire Club of Canada.

I wish to emphasize this point. If economics alone had been considered Canada would not have been created in 1867. If economics only are considered, it is difficult to justify today the continued existence of Canada. Our country was not created and it does not continue to exist for economic reasons.

Robert L. Stanfield, Nova Scotia premier, address, "A Nova Scotian View of Confederation," Toronto, 24 November 1966, The Empire Club of Canada.

Harold Innis once said that the risk of being an economist in Canada was that you might die of laughter.

Robert M. MacIntosh, general manager, Bank of Nova Scotia, debate, "Canadian Independence," Toronto, 3 February 1972, The Empire Club of Canada.

The cause of the current recession cannot be attributed to a single source in Canada or abroad. In many respects we are all to blame: governments, employers, employees, consumers. Our expectations and demands have been too high in relation to our effort. We have not worked together as closely as we should. We have been fearful of adjusting to change.

Thomas d'Aquino, president, Business Council on National Issues, address, Toronto, 13 January 1983, The Empire Club of Canada.

The new economy's a lot bigger than the old one. Your customer's no longer in the neighbourhood or around the comer—she's over the horizon and in another country. Same thing with your competition.

Dian Cohen, columnist, address, "Making It in the New Economy," Toronto, 6 February 1992, The Empire Club of Canada.

I'm not sure why Canadian policy issues are universally regarded as being dull—why the winning entry in the old competition for most boring headline, "Worthwhile Canadian Initiative," still seems so funny (yes, I think it's funny, too). Maybe it has something to do with the way they talk, eh? But when it comes to international monetary matters, Canada has often been a very interesting case—the country that defies the trends, that demonstrates by example the hollowness of the conventional wisdom of the moment.

Paul Krugman, U.S. economist, "O Canada: A Neglected Nation Gets Its Nobel" (1999), *The Great Unraveling: Losing Our Way in the New Century* (2003). Krugman is writing about the economist Robert Mundell, recipient of the Nobel Prize for analyses done in the 1960s based on the effectiveness of Canadian monetary policies and practices.

Individual property rights and open markets bring prosperity and social independence for the largest possible number of people. Collective property rights and government control bring poverty and dependency even as they enrich the small elite that manages the system. The paradox of Canada is that, while individual property and open markets have worked well for our people as a whole, we continue to encourage aboriginal people to travel in collectivist directions that produce more poverty, despair, and political conflict.

Tom Flanagan, political scientist, "Are Aboriginals Canadian?" *Cité libre*, fall 2000.

Canada is the only country that has enshrined regional economic equality as a constitutional objective, thus committing itself to the impossible proposition of moving resources to people instead of the other way round.

Conrad Black, publisher, "Time for an American Takeover," reprinted from *The Wall Street Journal* in *The Globe and Mail*, 1 December 2000.

Things are bad enough so that I haven't noticed any great revival of interest in that book. Perhaps I should have a new edition with a new title. It could be *The Depressed Economy*, and it would face the fact that only a reduced colony of booklovers could afford to buy it.

John Kenneth Galbraith, economist and author, on the eve of his 94th birthday, commenting on the fate of his celebrated book *The Affluent Society* (1958), interviewed by William Keegan, "Man for All Markets," *Guardian Weekly*, 10 October 2002.

Trickle-down theory—the less than elegant metaphor that, if one feeds the horse enough oats, some will pass through to the road for the sparrows.

John Kenneth Galbraith, economist and author, in Kate Harries, "Scotch Hangover Subsidies," *Toronto Star*, 12 October 2003.

To me, the most astonishing aspect of this economic expansion is the continued inability of Canadian economists to credit what is right in front of their eyes if they could only look.

Jane Jacobs, urban planning critic, *Dark Age Ahead* (2004). She is referring to new job creation as the result of "import replacing" and its "multiplier effect," characteristic of metropolitan Canada in the early 2000s, instead of the old standbys, "export-led economic life" and "consumer-led explanation."

It somehow followed that if countries were in financial trouble, they were moral transgressors. They had to discipline themselves. Wear hair shirts. Embrace denial and fasting.

This was the crucifixion theory of economics: you had to be killed economically and socially in order to be reborn clean and healthy.

John Ralston Saul, philosopher, "The Collapse of Globalism and the Rebirth of Nationalism," *Harper's*, March 2004.

EDITORS & EDITING *See also* Publishers & Publishing

The best copy editors are an author's saving grace.

A.B. McKillop, historian, *The Spinster and the Prophet* (2000).

EDMONTON

Edmonton isn't really the end of the world—although you can see it from there.

Ralph Klein, Calgary mayor, address, Olympic Writers Festival, 2 March 1988, as noted in *The Globe and Mail*, 15 March 2001.

Many may be wondering what on Earth I have done to deserve such celebrity. Not a lot; I have quoted an unnamed British athlete as describing the Alberta capital as "Deadmonton," I have remarked on the "visually unappealing" nature of the place, and poked gentle fun at one newspaper headline above a report on the men's marathon which read: 'Gritty Canadian Thrills Crowd with Gusty Run for 42nd Spot.' What puzzles this observer is that if Edmontonians are so confident about their city's greatness, why do they give a monkey's — about what some visiting hack might think? But they do.

Robert Philip, U.K. sports reporter who wrote for *The Daily Telegraph* during a visit to cover the 8th World Championships in Athletics, "How Could I Have Missed the Mall?" *National Post*, 9 August 2001.

I think it's wonderful, the pride of Edmontonians. My opinion is irrelevant. What makes a city is the people and you are great people.

Robert Philip, U.K. sports reporter, viewing the city's greenery from a helicopter, in Robert Remington, "Not Bad from Above, Critic Admits," *National Post*, 10 August 2001.

EDUCATION *See also* Employment; Learning; Medical Research; Research; Teachers & Teaching; Training; Universities & Colleges

Education and life are interchangeable terms: that is as true of the seed breaking into flower and the flower passing into fruit, as it is of the little child blooming into manhood, and manhood exchanging the beauty of the flower full-blown for the beauty of the fruit of wisdom.

Ernest Raymond, conference attendee, Conference Sermon at Christ Church Cathedral, Victoria, B.C., 7 April 1929, *Education and Leisure: Addresses Delivered at the Fourth Triennial Conference on Education Held at Victoria and Vancouver, Canada, April 1929* (1929), edited by S.E. Lang.

Very few people can stand the strain of being educated without getting superior over it.

Stephen Leacock, humorist, *My Remarkable Uncle* (1942).

An educated person is not a past participle: education is a life-long process never finished. It is often said that undergraduate training does nothing more than define the limits of one's ignorance. It also shows us that, no matter how much a good instructor can help us, we are the only ones who can do the work: we have to teach ourselves.

George Whalley, scholar, commencement address, Rothesay College School, N.B., 1959, *George Whalley: Remembrances* (1989), edited by Michael D. Moore.

Anyone who thinks there's a difference between education and entertainment doesn't know the first thing about either.

Attributed to **Marshall McLuhan** by Marc Salem, mentalist, interviewed by Michael Posner, "It's All in the Mind," *The Globe and Mail*, 5 March 2002.

The trouble with cheap specialized education is that you never stop paying for it.

Marshall McLuhan, communications theorist, *Culture Is Our Business* (1970).

Schooling you get in the schoolroom. Education you get in the poolroom.

Attibuted to **Robert Mirvish**, Toronto-born novelist and theatrical agent, brother of impresario Edwin "Honest Ed" Mirvish, *obiter dictum*, 20 April 1977.

We swallowed whole the bolus that if we educated everybody we would end poverty, unemployment and passing racial tensions. If only everybody could have a B.A., we would all be temperate, nice people and listen to Bach and read the *Toronto Sun*. Of course, in order to make sure that everybody got to university or to a post-secondary institution, we had to get everybody to high school: everybody, so we denied excellence as an elitist concept. We refused to fail people who should have been failed, and we cheated and frustrated our students and our teachers. We handed out masses of diplomas but we could not find the necessary white-collar jobs for the possessors of a B.A. who were unfortunately unable to spell, and we wondered why a B.A. had become worthless.

Barbara Amiel, journalist, address, "How Canada Does It and Other Social Diseases," Toronto, 4 February 1982, The Empire Club of Canada.

I think that Catholic education is a waste of money. It is a duplication completely. There is a lot of that effort and money that could be spent in beefing up one publicly supported, tax supported, school system. We all know the stories of Catholic schools with portables bursting at the seams and public schools kept open with only a hundred kids in them. It really bothered me when I had to say goodbye to my little five-year-olds and send them to one school, and their next-door neighbour, their best friends, went to another school. We divide our society like that along religious grounds. It doesn't make sense to me. I'm not trying to be anti-Catholic or anything like that. The cupboard is bare. Let's cut costs, but not fritter away the money.

Diane Francis, columnist, address, "A Look at Canada Incorporated," Toronto, 1 November 1990, The Empire Club of Canada.

Imagine someone who was frozen 400 years ago, came alive today and looked around at an engineering lab or a cockpit in a jumbo jet or a doctor in an operating theatre. He would think: "Wow, has the world ever changed." Technology has been at the heart of very profound changes. If he went into a lecture hall of a typical university he'd say: "Finally something I recognise." Learning has essentially been unchanged for many years.

Don Tapscott, speaker, address, "Growing Up Digital," Toronto, 5 February 1998, The Empire Club of Canada.

Well, I left school at fourteen. I have regretted it all my life. Yes, I have regretted it all my life. I should have left at twelve.

Bud McDougald, capitalist, interviewed by Peter C. Newman, address, "Titans," Toronto, 10 November 1998, The Empire Club of Canada. Newman calls this his favourite interview.

It has long been recognized that getting an education is effective for bettering oneself and one's chances in the world. But a degree and an education are not necessarily synonymous.

Jane Jacobs, urban planning critic, *Dark Age Ahead* (2004).

People only call me a guru because they can't spell charlatan.

Michael Fullan, educator, observation, in Alanna Mitchell, "School of Britannia," *Toronto Star*, 1 May 2004.

People love to talk about excellence in the university system, as long as no one or no university gets too far ahead. Call it the Canadian affliction.

Jeffrey Simpson, "How Bob Rae Rescued Dalton McGuinty," *The Globe and Mail*, 8 February 2005.

We risk romancing mediocrity. From that embrace only decline will follow.

Bob Rae, commissioner, unveiling a government panel's review of post-secondary education, "Ontario: A Leader in Learning," 7 February 2005, noted in the lead editorial in *The Globe and Mail*, 8 February 2005.

The arts are just as important as math and science in education and in our lives.

Ken Danby, artist, characteristic observation, 6 July 2005.

EFFICIENCY

The Peter Principle—In a hierarchy, every employee tends to rise to his level of incompetence.

Laurence J. Peter, psychologist, *The Peter Principle* (1969), with Raymond Hull.

Man cannot live by incompetence alone.

Laurence J. Peter, psychologist, *The Peter Prescription: How to Be Creative, Confident and Competent* (1972).

When a culture is rich enough and inherently complex enough to afford redundancy of nurturers, but eliminates them as an extravagance or loses their cultural services through heedlessness of what is being lost, the consequence is self-inflicted cultural genocide. Then watch the vicious spirals go into action!

Jane Jacobs, urban planning critic, *Dark Age Ahead* (2004).

EFFORT *See also* Ambition

Fight for the highest attainable aim, / But do not put up resistance in vain.

Hans Selye, medical specialist, quoting a jingle that he personally found useful, address, "How to Cope with Stress," Toronto, 29 October 1970, The Empire Club of Canada.

A journey of a single step starts with a thousand excuses.

Chris Gudgeon, author, *You're Not as Good as You Think You Are: A Demotivational Guide* (1997). A new take on the traditional proverb by Lao-tzu, Chinese poet (c. 604–c. 531 B.C.), "A journey of a thousand miles must begin with a single step."

My father was once asked the secret of his success, and he replied: "Striving always to make things better." To me, that is the essence of self-reliance—taking personal responsibility for personal, corporate and national success. That means winning, and winning is what it's all about. Canadians can be winners.

Martha Billes, CEO of Canadian Tire, address, "The Ethics of Self-Reliance," Toronto, 8 February 2001, The Empire Club of Canada.

EGOTISM

The only thing I fear is my mouth.

Mel Lastman, Toronto politician, dismissing other candidates in the election for mayor of Toronto, November 1997, "Quotations from Chairman Mel," *Toronto Star*, 23 September 2003.

There is a fine difference between feeling the universe evolves from within and feeling the universe revolves around you. But there's a big difference in the outcome.

Peter Urs Bender, motivational speaker, *Gutfeeling: Instinct and Spirituality@Work* (2002).

Wind expands to fill the bag available to it.

James Bacque, researcher and novelist, characteristic remark, 27 May 2003.

EH? *See also* Language; Words

"Eh?" is heard all over the English-speaking world and it dates back to the Middle Ages, according to *The Oxford English Dictionary*.... Utterances like "eh?" are the relics of the animal cries from which human speech arose. As instinctive utterances, they have more or less the same meanings in most cultures. If one tribe of people is more addicted to one of these injections, it is solely a matter of cultural identity.

Thomas M. Paikeday, lexicographer and compiler, *The Penguin Canadian Dictionary* (1990), private communication, 1 March 1991.

Texans and other congenital blowhards moving north should learn to speak in a low voice and a tone so mild that even declarative statements sound like questions. (Thus that Canadian habit of appending that "eh?" to every sentence, both a plea for approval and a licence for the hearer to disagree.)

Bruce McCall, Canadian-born New York humorist, "O Canada! That Fractured, Frosty Land," *The New York Times*, 21 November 2004.

ELECTIONS *See also* Politics

In and of itself, a vote is nothing. It neither warms the skin nor fills the stomach. Very often the privilege of a vote confers nothing but the right to express one's opinion as to which of two crooks is the crookeder.

Stephen Leacock, humorist, *Essays and Literary Studies* (1916).

We always support the CCF, except at election time.

Attributed in the 1940s to **Joseph S. Atkinson**, publisher of the *Toronto Daily Star*, a newspaper with a progressive social policy, as recalled by David MacDonald in an unpublished history of that newspaper. Atkinson was commenting on the Co-operative Commonwealth Federation, precursor of the New Democratic Party.

Good morning—prophet.

John G. Diefenbaker, prime minister, post-election news conference, greeting Blair Fraser, whose editorial in *Maclean's* had mistakenly assumed a Liberal victory, as noted by Richard Foot, "Gaffes," *National Post*, 28 November 2000.

In politics, unless your purpose is to win the next election, you have already conceded defeat.

Joe Clark, Progressive Conservative leader, address, Ottawa, in Les Whittington, "I'm Still the Man to Lead the Tories: Clark," *Toronto Star*, 24 April 2002.

My view is: Have precise ideas, tell them before the election, and if you get elected, then you'll have a mandate.

Mario Dumont, Action démocratique du Québec leader, interview, "The Week," *Maclean's*, 7 October 2002.

Nobody returns to Canada just to vote in an election, but Canadians have been known to leave the country to escape an election.

Eric Nicol, humorist, *Canadian Politics Unplugged* (2003), with Peter Whalley.

Mr. McGuinty (this story is instant political folklore) was described by the illuminati running the Tory campaign as "an evil reptilian kitten-eater from another planet." Did it not occur to these same technicians of toss and gore that their main campaign theme—"He's (meaning Mr. McGuinty) not up to the job"—was more boomerang than arrow? That it crystallized with admirable punch, not the contrast between their man and Dalton McGuinty, but between Mike Harris and his pastel successor, Mr. Eves?

Rex Murphy, "Japes of Wrath," *The Globe and Mail*, 4 October 2003. In the Ontario election campaign on 2 October 2003, Ontario Conservative Premier Ernie Eves, successor of Mike Harris, was defeated by Liberal leader Dalton McGuinty. A minor factor behind the landslide victory was the Conservative Party's continued use of invective and insult in their campaign. (The Liberals stuck to their principles and policies.) A party aide's fax that so described McGuinty was leaked to the press and, as Rex Murphy observed, boomeranged.

I campaign every day of the year. I work the same way I do the day before or after I get elected.

Hazel McCallion, long-time mayor of Mississauga, Ont., sixth-largest Canadian city, 82 years of age, re-elected for her 10th term, 10 November 2003, in Nicholas Keung, *Toronto Star*, 11 November 2003.

There came a fork in the "high road." The Liberals took it.

Line from an email bulletin sent from Ontario Conservative Premier **Ernie Eves**'s campaign office, 11 September 2003, during the provincial election campaign that saw Eves's Conservatives trying to diminish the standing of Liberal leader Dalton McGuinty, recalled in *Toronto Star*, 13 September 2003.

Now, all I want to know is what does a controller do?

Mel Lastman, municipal politician, victory speech on being elected controller of North York, Ont., 1969, "Quotations from Chairman Mel," *Toronto Star*, 23 September 2003.

And not voting is never easier than at the start of summer, when excuses are thicker than blackflies.

Roy MacGregor, columnist, "This Country," *The Globe and Mail*, 18 May 2004.

A Canadian election is exactly like a police lineup, except you get to choose who's going to rob you.

Paul Foster, comedian, Radio CJAD-AM, Montreal, 1 May 2005.

ELECTRICAL POWER *See also* Power

If electricity should replace coal as the motive force of the future, a country such as Canada, with her immense water-power, will be far better endowed by nature than England. Or some undreamed-of force may be discovered by science which will make some other colony the predominant industrial power.

Surmise of Mr. Ebenezer Wakefield, "a Canadian Statesman," in **John Buchan**'s novel *A Lodge in the Wilderness* (1906).

I am an advocate of competitive markets in electricity. But my fear is that people take this stuff too literally. It's dangerous when the real market enthusiasts take over.

Mark Jaccard, economist and former chief of the B.C. Utilities Commission, interviewed by

Thomas Walkom, "Confusion Reigns over Electricity," *Toronto Star*, 24 February 2002. He is referring to the Ontario government's move to privatize electric power in the province.

ELITISM

The trouble is, elitism is a dirty word in Canada. It makes us uncomfortable. "Good enough" is good enough for us.

Margaret Wente, columnist, "That Clanging Sound Signals Trouble at U. of T.," *The Globe and Mail*, 8 February 2005.

EMBLEMS, NATIONAL *See* National Emblems

EMIGRATION *See also* Immigration

Because Canadians leave Canada sometimes and go to other countries to make their way, must they be spiritually disfranchised? I don't think that is the highest wisdom or the highest statesmanship. In England they didn't object to electing me to Parliament because I was a Canadian; they are glad to have the Canadian point of view and the Canadian temperament in their discussions. It is very hard to throw off the motherhood of Canada.

Beverley Baxter, political commentator, address, "What I Have Seen Over There and Over Here," Toronto, 6 October 1941, The Empire Club of Canada.

I like to live in countries which you can leave. Without anybody asking. I felt this the first time when I was crossing the bridge at Niagara Falls to enter the U.S. We didn't stop at Canadian customs. We only waved to the Canadians. I said, "That's good." That you can leave.

George Faludy, Hungarian-born poet, refugee, and later Canadian citizen, interviewed by Alan Twigg, *Strong Voices: Conversations with Fifty Canadian Authors* (1988).

In order to migrate to a certain place, you must leave another. This truism is not as simple as it seems. Nothing tells you at what precise point departure ends and arrival begins, what goodbyes are forever, what street signs you are seeing for the last time, what doors you have locked behind you and will never open again. Once your back is turned, the landscape shifts, objects change shape, people take on other voices and other faces.

Alberto Manguel, Argentina-born Canadian citizen and resident of France, "Destination Ithaka," *Passages: Welcome Home to Canada* (2002), with a preface by Rudyard Griffiths.

EMOTIONS

Understatement was the rule in our house. Emotions, even positive ones, were kept firmly under control. It was the Eleventh Commandment, carved on its very own tablet of stone and presented specifically to those of Presbyterian persuasion: Thou Shalt Not Emote.... If someone does or says something that upsets you, you don't say so. Maybe it's another Presbyterian thing; if the Eleventh Commandment is Thou Shalt Not Emote, the Twelfth is Thou Shalt Not Admit to Being Upset, and when it becomes evident to the whole world that you are upset, Thou Shalt on No Account Explain Why. No, you swallow your feelings, force them down inside yourself, where they can feed and grow and swell and expand until you explode, unforgivably, to the utter bewilderment of whoever it was who upset you.

Thoughts of the narrator Kate Morrison in **Mary Lawson**'s novel *Crow Lake* (2000).

If a holistic model of Emotional Intelligence can be described, then self-awareness would be the mind, self-mastery would be the body (or action itself), and inter-personal effectiveness would be the heart.

Daniel Star, speaker on Emotional Intelligence, "Emotional Intelligence at Work," *Contact Point Magazine*, fall 2000.

And remember, if you will, "doom" is only "mood" backwards.

Robert Priest, poet and columnist, "Mood Disorder," *Now*, 2 December 2004.

EMPATHY

Empathy is getting along with people you don't like.

Michael Fullan, educator, observation, in Alanna Mitchell, "School of Britannia," *Toronto Star*, 1 May 2004.

EMPLOYMENT *See also* Compensation; Education; Entrepreneurship; Labour; Pensions; Retirement; Unemployment; Unions; Welfare; Work

As a matter of fact, here in Canada especially, and in the United Kingdom and the United States as well, the employee of yesterday is the employer of tomorrow. We are all made of the same flesh and blood; we have the same ambitions, the same aspirations; and I for one rejoice that the workman today is desiring to rise and better himself, to be enabled to place his wife and family in better social conditions, and even if possible to own his own motor car and take them for joy-rides on a Saturday afternoon. Why not?

Lord Leverhulme, British manufacturer, address, "Education and Commerce," Toronto, 4 December 1919, The Empire Club of Canada.

Many of us have been responding to market signals and the economy is transforming itself from resource dependency to knowledge based. For instance, as *Canadian Business* magazine recently pointed out: More Canadians are now employed in our electronics industry than our pulp and paper industry. More Canadians are now employed in our communications and telecommunications industry than our mining and petroleum industries combined. Regionally, too, some major adjustments have already taken place: More Quebecers work in health and medical care than in construction, textile, clothing, furniture and mining industries combined. More Albertans work in financial services than in oil and gas. More people in B.C. work in communications and telecommunications than the whole forest industries. More Nova Scotians work as teachers and professors than as fish processors, miners, forestry workers, pulp and paper and construction workers combined.

Dian Cohen, columnist, citing research by Nuala Beck, address, "Making It in the New Economy," Toronto, 6 February 1992, The Empire Club of Canada.

The credential is not a passport to a job, as naive graduates sometimes suppose. It is more basic and necessary: a passport to consideration for a job.

Jane Jacobs, urban planning critic, *Dark Age Ahead* (2004).

ENERGY *See also* Power

What's wrong with solar energy? I believe we could have solar energy in this country, and I'm convinced we could get some of it from the sun. The sun shines all day. After sundown, every man for himself. We'll have to get through the night without using any energy at all. Some of us are doing that now. We're not impotent, we're just slightly ahead of our time.

Dave Broadfoot, comedian, "Dave Broadfoot's Canada," Toronto, 9 March 1978, The Empire Club of Canada.

The term "energy" is often used interchangeably with the term "power," but incorrectly so. Energy is defined as the capacity to do work and is measured in joules (J) or watt hours (1 Wh = 3600 J). Power is the work done per unit time and is measured in watts (W), i.e., joules per second.

O.J.C. Runnalls, scientist, "Energy," *The Canadian Encyclopedia* (2nd ed., 1988).

ENGINEERING

Experience, not science, is the basis for engineering.

Witold Rybczynski, architect and author, "How Things Work," *The New York Review of Books*, 9 June 2005.

ENGLAND *See* Canada & United Kingdom

ENTITLEMENTS

You're saying I'm not entitled to my entitlements.

David Dingwall, former head of the Royal Canadian Mint, referring to his executive expenses, perquisites, compensation, severance, and other "entitlements" in response to questions posed by Ed Broadbent, House of Commons operations committee, Ottawa, 19 October 2005, quoted by John Ivison, "Dingwall Gives Tories Much to Chew On," *National Post*, 20 October 2005.

ENTREPRENEURSHIP *See also* Business; Capitalism; Free Enterprise

The genesis of entrepreneurship is recognizing opportunities beyond the reach of resources currently available to the entrepreneur. If adequate resources were available, there would be no need for entrepreneurship, because good managers could do the job. The unique appeal of entrepreneurs is based on how they identify opportunities and how they multiply the effectiveness of their scarce resources in exploiting the opportunities they see.

Donald Rumball, business writer, *The Entrepreneurial Edge: Canada's Top Entrepreneurs Reveal the Secrets of Their Success* (1989).

Take what you've learned and accumulated during your lifetime and then jump off a new cliff.

Ellie Rubin, entrepreneur, co-founder of the Bulldog Group, interviewed by Leonard Brody et al., *Innovation Nation: Canadian Leadership from Java to Jurassic Park* (2002).

Lie No. 1: Being an entrepreneur is fun. / Lie No. 2: Entrepreneurs succeed. / Lie No. 3: You should quit your day job and start your company now. / Lie No. 4: You need venture capital. / Lie No. 5: You need a specific education to be an entrepreneur.

List of five untruths that explain why "most of what you read about entrepreneurship and innovation is a lie" in the words of mentor and management specialist **Paul Kedrosky**, "Afterword," *Innovation Nation: Canadian Leadership from Java to Jurassic Park* (2002), edited by Leonard Brody et al.

ENVIRONMENTALISM *See also* Acid Rain; Air; Change; Conservation; Earth; Ecology; Energy; Forests; Global Warming; Greenhouse Effect; Kyoto Accord; Pollution; Recycling; Resources; Waste Disposal; Wildlife

The moment we realized that the environmental holocaust has nothing to do with good and evil but only with ambiguity, we began to lose hope. We went to sleep one night in Burlington and got up in the morning in Beirut.

David Lees, journalist, "Living in the Nuclear Shadow," *Toronto Life*, November 1989.

We have altered our environment to suit ourselves, and we have found to our amazement and sometimes consternation that this new world also suits a few uninvited species.

Wayne Grady, writer and naturalist, *Toronto the Wild: Field Notes of an Urban Naturalist* (1995).

Ontario voters are like people who drive SUVs to an environmentalists' rally. They want Alabama-style taxes and Swedish-style social services.

Murray Campbell, columnist, "Queen's Park," *The Globe and Mail*, 4 November 2003.

We want to pass on a healthy environment and a sustainable lifestyle to our children and grandchildren. Just as an egalitarian ethical principle argues for equity between nations, so also we must ensure that there will be equity for future peoples—"seven generations into the future" to quote one Aboriginal teaching. Other Aboriginals argue that equity extends from three generations before us (great-grandparents) to three generations after us (great-grandchildren).

Harold Coward, climatologist, "What Can Individuals Do?" *Hard Choices: Climate Change in Canada* (2004), edited by Harold Coward and Andrew J. Weaver.

EPITAPHS *See also* Death

Here it is: Here lie the remains of THOMAS LAMB, / Killed by a great big tree falling upon him, slap, bang.

Nineteenth-century epitaph of one **Thomas Lamb** from a graveyard in Prince Edward Island, according to Michelle Lovric, editor, *Eccentric Epitaphs: Gaffes from Beyond the Grave* (2000).

If they nail the lid down on my coffin tomorrow, the world doesn't owe me much. My epitaph could read, "He passed by and knew happiness. He loved the earth and tried in his own time to make it a better place to live in for all things."

Andy Russell, "the last of the mountain men," statement made in 1984, recalled by Tom Hawthorn, "Andy Russell, Outdoorsman and Author, 1915–2005," *The Globe and Mail*, 3 June 2005.

Richard Needham's tiresome and repetitious columns will no longer appear because he is dead.

Self-selected epitaph of columnist **Richard Needham**, as recalled by Margaret Wente, *An Accidental Canadian: Reflections on My Home and (Not) Native Land* (2004).

It was a wonderful read.

Self-chosen epitaph chosen tongue-in-cheek by **Alberto Manguel**, author of *The History of Reading*, as in Katherine Ashenburg, "Lighting Out for the Territory," *The Globe and Mail*, 30 December 2000.

Stellar Athlete, Baseball Expert, and Jemseg, N.B., Financial Wizard, Seeks Further Success Elsewhere.

Self-chosen epitaph of **Dalton Camp**, political commentator, from 1992, as recalled in the obituary "Dalton Camp, 1920–2002," *Toronto Star*, 19 March 2002.

They have been joined to the sea and the sky / May they rest in peace.

Inscription on the memorial at Peggys Cove, N.S., noted by Sarah Jane Crowe, *Toronto Star*, 2 September 2002. Other lines: "In memory of the 229 men, women and children on the Swissair Flight 111 who perished off these shores, September 2, 1998."

I once was celebrated, / Though always short of cash; / I'm now, alas, translated / To this small pile of ash; / And yet, despite mortality, / And not much hope of Heaven, / My thanks for friends and family, / Especially for Evan.

Verse written in 1996 by **Frances Hyland**, actress, who died in Toronto on 11 July 2004. The lines were published (and re-punctuated) in the *Toronto Star*, 18 July 2004. Evan McCowan is her son by the late director George McCowan.

I would have liked to live forever. Life has been so good to me!

Walter Pidgeon, Hollywood actor born in Saint John, N.B., dying words, Hollywood, 25 September 1984, in Charles Foster, *Once Upon a Time in Paradise: Canadians in the Golden Age of Hollywood* (2003).

EQUALITY *See also* Government; Rights; Socialism

The only way in which the authorities can prevent us from succeeding is by destroying the social equality which is the distinctive characteristic, as much of the populations of Upper Canada as of Lower Canada. This social equality must necessarily bring our political liberty. No privileged caste can exist in Canada beyond and above the mass of its inhabitants.

Louis-Hippolyte LaFontaine, Father of Confederation, joint prime minister in 1842, speech of 1840, announcing the alliance between himself and Robert Baldwin, as quoted by philosopher **John Ralston Saul**, speech, Canadian Club, April, "Education," *Toronto Star*, 8 May 2002. Saul states, "There's a line which I insist on putting in every speech I give.... I think it's maybe the single most important paragraph in Canadian political life."

I think the best definition of when equality will arrive is: "We will have true equality when we have as many incompetent women in positions of power as we have incompetent men." That may take some time.

Peter C. Newman, journalist, address, "Titans: How the New Canadian Establishment Seized Power," Toronto, 10 November 1998, The Empire Club of Canada.

How a nation treats its minorities may be a measure of its sensitivity, but how the majority is treated measures its maturity.

Kevin McKechnie, correspondent, Letters to the Editor, *Toronto Star*, 9 August 2002.

Equality must not only be part of our thinking, it must be part of our living. If we embrace equality as a culture and encourage others to do the same, you will be one step closer to creating a society in which you, your children and your children's children need not fear disempowerment or oppression. That I call justice for all.

Claire L'Heureux-Dubé, justice, Supreme Court of Canada, speech, "Search for Equality" (1998), as quoted by Robert Ivan Martin, *The Most Dangerous Branch: How the Supreme Court of Canada Has Undermined Our Law and Our Democracy* (2003). Martin observed, "If my thoughts were that banal, I would keep them to myself."

One other thing which should be clear from this book is that our national quest has not been for all human rights, but, almost exclusively, for "equality." A central point which de Tocqueville made in *Democracy in America* was that the quest for equality would eventually subvert democracy.

Robert Ivan Martin, law professor, *The Most Dangerous Branch: How the Supreme Court of Canada Has Undermined Our Law and Our Democracy* (2003).

It is easier to run an egalitarian "have-not" province than to run an egalitarian "have" province.

Eric Howe, U.S.-born economist and University of Saskatchewan professor, referring to that province's sudden emergence as a "have" province, in Roy MacGregor, "Saskatchewan Turns One Hundred," *The Globe and Mail*, 24 December 2004.

ERROR *See also* Failure

It is always better to do a thing wrong the first time.

Sir William Osler, physician, in Wilder Penfield, "A Medical Student's Memories of the Regius Professor," Bulletin Number IX, *International Association of Medical Museums and Journal of Technical Methods* (Montreal, 1926).

ESKIMOS *See* Inuit

ETHICS *See also* Good & Evil; Government; Principles; Religion; Values; Virtue & Vice

Acceptance of the belief by wrongdoers that "everybody does it" has become a great enemy of effective self-policing. But fortunately, in reality, everybody does not do wrong. If everyone did, our civilization would have irretrievably collapsed.

Jane Jacobs, urban planning critic, *Dark Age Ahead* (2004).

Ethics is the measurement of the public good. Morality is the weapon of religious and social righteousness.

John Ralston Saul, philosopher, "The Collapse of Globalism and the Rebirth of Nationalism," *Harper's*, March 2004.

Show me a country that sets up an ethics commissioner's office and I'll show you a country that sorely needs one.

George Jonas, columnist, "From Taiwan to Moose Jaw a Dangerous World," *National Post*, 13 December 2004.

We must comprehend *both our knowing and our unknowing* if we are to incorporate the new techno-science into our individual and collective lives in ways that enrich them not only physically, but also morally. The basic questions we must continue to address are who we are as humans and how we should understand ourselves.

Margaret Somerville, ethicist, "The Importance of a Basic Presumption of Respect for the Natural," *Sacred Web: A Journal of Tradition and Modernity*, 13 June 2004.

ETHNICITY *See also* Multiculturalism; Race & Racism; Separatism

The word "ethnic" fascinated me: Canadians—well, Torontonians, at least—seem to use it so wonderfully impartially to grace all manifestations of non-Anglo-Saxon-non-French culture—but one senses so much more of envy than of patronage in its use—as if they think English/French/"Canadian" means acultural—non-ethos?

Judith Merril, science-fiction writer, 1968, *Better to Have Loved: The Life of Judith Merril* (2002), with Emily Pohl-Weary.

There is an ethnic vote against the sovereignty of the Quebec people. If we do not act to integrate our immigrants and to assimilate them, well, we are headed on the slope of the Louisianization, the folklorization of our society.

Yves Michaud, shareholder-rights activist and prospective Parti Québécois candidate, appearing before the Estates-General on Language, 13 December 2000, quoted by Rhéal Séguin, "End Intolerance, Bouchard Urges," *The Globe and Mail*, 21 December 2000.

In God's crucible, as the English author Israel Zangwill famously called America, comes fresh evidence that from time to time, there may be in the great melting pot something akin to a meltdown.

Christie Blatchford, columnist, "Land of the Free—for Good and Bad," *National Post*, 25 October 2002. She is referring to the Washington, D.C., sniper.

EUROPE *See also* Canada & the World; individual countries

The plural and protean identities that Canadians have been juggling, if only in their minds, for decades are only now becoming realities for members of, say, the European Union.

Pico Iyer, traveller and writer, "Mongrel Beauties," *Saturday Night*, 31 March 2001.

The European attitude seems to be, "How do we preserve our culture?" whereas the Canadians say that "our" includes these new people. It's a radically different approach.

Keith Spicer, journalist and former chair, Citizens' Forum on Canada's Future, in Roy MacGregor, "This Country," *The Globe and Mail*, 16 November 2004.

The Europeans have become Canadian in their view of the United States, reliant on the Americans for real security, but simultaneously contemptuous of them for their militarism, like socialist teens who sneer at their industrial father's capitalism, then rush off to the bank to cash his cheques.

Lorne Gunter, commentator, "When Being Right Is a Duty," *National Post*, 13 January 2005.

EUROPEAN UNION

What I am suggesting is that Canada should lead the Commonwealth into association with the Common Market, thereby retaining the inspiration of a multi-racial community of nations, binding the new Europe more usefully into the fabric of the free world, without fear of it becoming a white man's club, and giving the developing countries of the world all the advantages they now possess in the Commonwealth, and more. We would greatly enrich our lives, broaden our trade, and assume a positive role in world leadership.

H.I. Macdonald, dean, University College, University of Toronto, address, "Inside the Common Market," Toronto, 16 November 1961, The Empire Club of Canada.

It is hard to avoid the feeling, while in Brussels, that you are aboard an enormous space station, populated by a sleek and superior race that has only a distant relationship to the faraway Europeans who bred them.

Doug Saunders, columnist, describing the "eurocrats" of the east end of Brussels, headquarters of the European Union, "Europe: Out of the Ashes," *The Globe and Mail*, 11 June 2005.

EUTHANASIA *See also* Suicide

Canada has a tradition of working together to build a caring, compassionate and just society. This tradition includes caring for and loving each disabled, sick and dying member of our community. Compassion means literally "to suffer alongside." Are we a compassionate society? Then we do not kill weak, disabled, sick people.

Euthanasia Prevention Coalition of B.C., "Dutch Legalise Euthanasia: Canada Recommends Caring Not Killing," press release, 29 April 2000.

There's no mercy in killing.... I have seen the future and it stinks of the odour of the morgue.

Michael Coren, author and broadcaster, "There's No Mercy in Killing," *All Things Considered: Collected Columns and Essays* (2001).

Our best approach at this time may be to modify homicide laws to include motivational factors as a legitimate defence. *Just as homicide is acceptable in cases of self-defence, it could be considered acceptable if the motive is mercy.* Obviously, strict parameters would have to be established that would include patients' request and approval, or, in the case of incompetent patients, advance directives in the form of a living will or family and court approval. Euthanasia is homicide. Some homicides are justified.

Robert B. Lane, philosopher, "Assisted Suicide," *Humanist in Canada,* spring 2005.

EVIL *See* Good & Evil

EVOLUTION *See also* Belief; Creationism; Science

All the animals are descended from one another. The horse is really a bird, and is the same animal as the crow. The differences between them are purely superficial. If a crow had two more feet and no feathers it would be a horse except for its size.

Stephen Leacock, humorist, *Winnowed Wisdom* (1926).

Nevertheless the failure of Darwin and his successors to attempt an equitable assessment of the religious issues at stake indicates a regrettable obtuseness and lack of responsibility.

William R. Thompson, entomologist, introduction to the Everyman Library edition of Charles Darwin's *On the Origin of Species* (Dent, 1956), reprinted as a booklet *New Challenging 'Introduction' to* The Origin of Species (Revolution Protest Movement, 1967).

Mega-evolution is really a philosophy dating from the days of biological ignorance; it was a philosophical synthesis built up in a biological kindergarten.

Evan Shute, physician and theorist, *Flaws in the Theory of Evolution* (1961), in Martin Lings, "Signs of the Times," *The Sword of Gnosis* (1974, 1986), edited by Jacob Needleman.

Wind back the tape of life to the early days of the Burgess Shale; let it play again from an identical starting point, and the chance becomes vanishingly small that anything like human intelligence would grace the replay.

Stephen Jay Gould, paleontologist, author and student of British Columbia's Burgess Shale, the fossil quarry formed 530 million years ago, *Wonderful Life: The Burgess Shale and the Nature of History* (1989).

It is hubris to imagine our species can destroy everything, or even everything that matters to it, just as it is hubris to imagine we are what evolution is "for," or that human interests are distinct from and ontologically superior to all others.

Jan Zwicky, poet, introduction, *Hard Choices: Climate Change in Canada* (2004), edited by Harold Coward and Andrew J. Weaver.

EXCELLENCE *See also* Education; Mediocrity; Perfectionism

You soon learn that some individuals seem to have the tendency to a certain kind of excellence that others do not have, and if you feel that a suggested proposal fits well with their kind of perception and talent you may feel that there's a good chance that something worthwhile will come out of that.

Tom Daly, producer and director, "Running Past Our Habit Patterns," *Pot-Pourri* (National Film Board), September 1973.

We'd rather have one hundred centres of mediocrity than one centre of excellence.

Margaret Wente, columnist, "That Clanging Sound Signals Trouble at U. of T.," *The Globe and Mail*, 8 February 2005.

EXECUTIVES *See also* Business; Compensation

An executive is the man who tries to give the impression of hurrying in the direction he is being pushed.

Sidney Smith, academic and politician, in Frank E. Archibald, *Mostly Maritimes* (1972).

The first sign of a company in decline is that the shareholders don't get what they deserve because the executives get what they don't deserve.

James Bacque, researcher and novelist, characteristic remark, 27 May 2003.

EXERCISE *See also* Health; Sports; Walking

Every day I see people walking through Toronto's underground who are intelligent people, but they still haven't learned the ABCs of preventive medicine. Morning after morning 95 per cent of young, healthy workers take the escalator rather than walk up 25 steps, yet these people are going to sit at their desks most of the day. Ida, as Minister of Health, would put a sign at the bottom of every escalator in Toronto's underground that reads: "This escalator is for the disabled. Take it if you want to become obese, have a premature coronary, develop brittle bones, arthritis and other degenerative problems that need not happen."

Kenneth Walker, physician and columnist (aka Dr. Gifford-Jones), address, "The Healthy Barmaid, The New Minister of Health?" Toronto, 11 April 1996, The Empire Club of Canada.

Jogging adds years to your life because you soon feel so much older.

Hugh Arscott, aphorist, *Hugh's Views: Volume 5* (2001).

The churches may be deserted, but the gyms are full of the heaving, sweating faithful mortifying their flesh. Like all religions practised in cold northern climates, healthism requires plenty of strict self-denial. Some people even have a personal trainer, our age's version of a spiritual adviser.

Margaret Wente, columnist, *An Accidental Canadian: Reflections on My Home and (Not) Native Land* (2004).

EXILE *See also* Immigration; Refugees

Listen to me, as when ye heard our father / Sing long ago the song of our shores— / Listen to me, and then in chorus gather / All your deep voices—these hoary woods are grand; / But we are exiles from our fathers' land.

Verse from "Canadian Boat-Song (from the Gaelic)" (1829), which expresses a Highland Scot's lament for exile in the New World, attributed to versifier **David Macbeth Moir** with help from colonist **John Galt**.

Statelessness is a uniquely modern phenomenon, one which forces us to rethink all prior notions of exile. For when the Nazis withdrew citizenship from native German Jews, and then expelled them from the nation's borders, that meant exile in a wholly novel sense. For no state can now be expected to admit citizens without proper papers. Yet Hitler taught us a lesson that we might not like to hear. Under the conditions of contemporary life, the Lockean state of nature has vanished. If the state withdraws citizenship, there may now be no place to go. It turns out that we are more dependent on the state for our liberties than any of us might like to think.

Paul Roazen, historian, York University, "Finding Oneself in Exile," *Queen's Quarterly*, fall 1997.

There is more than one way to be exiled. The most brutal form of exile is the one where language, communities, and relations were extinguished. But you can also be exiled by the spirit of the times, which is constructing a world in which you feel you no longer have a place.

Clive Doucet, Acadian poet, "Farewell to the Place Called Home," *The Globe and Mail*, 15 July 2000.

EXISTENCE

That something exists outside ourselves and our preoccupations, so near, so readily available, is our greatest blessing.

Thomas A. Clark, poet, "In Praise of Walking," *Wild Culture: Specimens from* The Journal of Wild Culture (1992), edited by Whitney Smith and Christopher Lowry.

We live in a time where things do not seem to exist unless they have been captured in an image.

Commentary of the feature documentary film *Picture of Light* (1994), about the attraction of the Northern Lights, written, produced, and directed by **Peter Mettler**.

Are you making a life—or just making a living? Winners make a life, and the spin-off benefit is that they also make an excellent living. People who focus too much time and effort on making a living miss much of their life in the process.

Leslie Bendaly, motivational speaker, *Winner Instinct: The 6 New Laws of Success* (1999).

EXPLORATION *See also* Arctic Regions; Discovery; Space; Universe

I now mixed up some vermillion in melted grease, and inscribed, in large characters, on the South-East face of the rock on which we had slept last night, this brief memorial—"Alexander Mackenzie, from Canada, by land, the twenty-second of July, one thousand seven hundred and ninety-three."

Sir Alexander Mackenzie, explorer, *Voyages from Montreal on the River St. Lawrence, through the Continent of North America, to the Frozen and Pacific Oceans* (1801). The year was 1793 and the trek, largely on foot, took him from Montreal to Dean Channel, Bella Coola River, B.C., where he left this memorial, the most historic graffiti in the country's history.

We drank tea & ate some of our shoes for supper.

Entry in the log kept by Arctic explorer **Sir John Franklin** during his polar expedition of 1820, according to Fergus Fleming, *Tales of Endurance* (2005).

Why cannot I sit here lovingly, quietly and simply thinking of that most delightful man, Champlain, without offending you? Samuel de Champlain, of Brouage, on the Bay of Biscaye, if you remember.

William Carlos Williams, U.S. author and poet, "The Founding of Quebec," *In the American Grain: Essays* (1925). The author found the explorer and colonizer Samuel de Champlain (c. 1567–1635) "the perfection of what we lack."

We may never know what these forgotten folk called themselves but since they appear to have been known to their contemporaries as Albans, this is the name I give them.

Farley Mowat, author, *The Farfarers: Before the Norse* (1998). Albans is Mowat's term for an ostensible pre-Norse, seafaring people (perhaps Picts of early Scotland and Gaul) who left warlike neighbours behind to sail from the British Isles to Iceland, Greenland, and then Newfoundland, where they erected edifices of stone before disappearing from the historical record.

All living things explore.

Chris Hadfield, astonaut, on the imperative of space exploration, "Astronaut Shares the Lessons of Columbia," *National Post*, 10 February 2003.

EXPO 67

I came to the fair a nationalist, full of pride in my adopted Canada. I left a humanist, full of hope for all mankind.

Peter C. Newman, journalist and memoirist, recalling the opening of Expo 67 in Montreal, 1967, *Here Be Dragons: Telling Tales of People, Passion, and Power* (2004).

EXTERNAL AFFAIRS *See* Foreign Affairs

EXTREMISM *See also* Activism

Extremists on our side are more restrained.

Lucien Bouchard, Quebec premier, address, Philadelphia, Penn., 21 May 1998, in Barrie McKenna, "Bouchard Blasts Dogging Tactics of Equity Leader," *The Globe and Mail*, 22 May 1998. Bouchard was reacting to the "extremism" of Don Donderi and Keith Henderson, Equality Party activists, who waved signs and distributed leaflets calling Bouchard a liar when during his image-building speeches in four U.S. cities he claimed that Quebec was "bilingual." Donderi and Henderson wanted to draw attention to the province's oppression of its anglophone minority.

FAILURE *See also* Error; Success

One of the worst stings of defeat is the sympathy that goes with it.

Bob Edwards, publisher, *Calgary Eye Opener*, 8 June 1912.

What is true is that the failure of an individual in a free society hurts more because they cannot ascribe their failure to outside restrictions, or to the unfairness of the ruling classes. Failure in our society becomes more the fault of the individual and we have convinced ourselves that even that is unfair, that people should not be held accountable for their inability to become nuclear physicists, millionaires, or to look like Brooke Shields, and that there must be a committee to legislate equality of results or punish achievement.

Barbara Amiel, journalist, address, "How Canada Does It and Other Social Diseases," Toronto, 4 February 1982, The Empire Club of Canada.

FAITH *See also* Atheism; Belief

Faith in the gods or in the saints cures one, faith in little pills another, hypnotic suggestion a third, faith in a plain common doctor a fourth.

Sir William Osler, physician, "Medicine in the Nineteenth Century," *Aequanimitas* (1932).

In every generation Canadians have had to rework the miracle of their political existence. Canada has been created because there has existed within the hearts of its people a determination to build for themselves an enduring home. Canada is a supreme act of faith.

A.R.M. Lower, historian, oft-quoted opinion, *Colony to Nation: A History of Canada* (1946).

Faith is knowledge born of religious love.

Bernard Lonergan, theologian, *Method in Theology* (1972) in *The Lonergan Reader* (1997), edited by Mark D. Morelli and Elizabeth A. Morelli.

Faith sees God's face in every human face.

Characteristic assertion of **Catherine de Hueck Doherty** (1896–1985), founder of Madonna House, a centre dedicated to Our Lady of Combermere, Ont., characteristic assertion, website, June 21 2005.

FAME *See also* Celebrities

"I'm world-famous," Dr. Parks said, "all over Canada."

Boast made by a character in **Mordecai Richler**'s satiric novel *The Incomparable Atuk* (1963). Everyone is familiar with Andy Warhol's prediction: "In the future everyone will be famous for fifteen minutes." Not everyone knows the Canadian variation: "In the future everyone will be famous for fifteen minutes, thirty in Newfoundland."

Early recognition spoils some writers, but posthumous recognition saves none.

Irena F. Karafilly, aphorist, characteristic expression, 7 November 2000.

FAMILY *See also* Adoption; Children; Education; Fatherhood; Motherhood; Parenting; Society; Youth

The family—the one institution in which the better side of human nature shines with an undimmed light.

Stephen Leacock, humorist, *The Unsolved Riddle of Social Justice* (1920).

The time has come when man must control the course of civilization on this earth. But the time is short, the need for action urgent. Human society cannot survive without the institution of the family. By bringing strength and wisdom to new families in the ever-changing context of modern society and by establishing an accepted code of common morality and teaching reasonable self-discipline and service to others, civilization can be controlled.

Wilder Penfield, neurosurgeon, address, "The World and the Mind of Man," Toronto, 16 January 1969, The Empire Club of Canada.

My family is the snuggest of ships, and one that will carry me to home port.

Peter C. Newman, journalist and memoirist, *Here Be Dragons: Telling Tales of People, Passion, and Power* (2004).

There are more important things than the nuclear family—like conservation of biodiversity, the need to reduce human populations, and the interdependence of species.

Paul Watson, environmental activist, interviewed by John F. Schumaker, "Earth Warrior," *The CCPA Monitor*, December 2003–January 2004.

FARMERS & FARMING *See also* Agriculture; Environmentalism; Food & Drink; Free Trade

Up! be stirring, be alive, / Get upon a farm and thrive! / He's a king upon a throne / Who has acre of his own!

Refrain of the verse "Acres of Your Own," by **Alexander M'Lachlan**, *Songs of the Great Dominion* (1889), edited by William Douw Lighthall.

As a brother farmer, however, I should like to pay a tribute to the farmers of Ontario, who have always been a very wholesome, energetic and respected section of the community. I know they, no less than the rest of the community, will always remember to think of the wider interests of the nation as well as of their own, as it takes all kinds of interests to make a great nation, and Canada cannot afford to be one-sided. I hope, therefore, that Ontario will set a lead by showing how all may pursue their own legitimate interests without forgetting the welfare of the Dominion and of the Empire as a whole.

Edward, Prince of Wales, address, "An Address," Toronto, 2 November 1919, The Empire Club of Canada.

Farmers say little, but they think profoundly.

Sir Andrew MacPhail, essayist, address, "The Farmer," Toronto, 4 March 1920, The Empire Club of Canada.

I do not know about the dairy farmer: I think he faces some "udder" frustrating situations; I suggest he is on the horns of a dilemma.

Barney Danson, Member of Parliament, addressing the issue of food subsidies, House of Commons, 19 June 1972.

Thieves Beware / Our Poultry Are Tattooed / and Marks Registered / with Ontario Gov't. / Provincial Police Have Positive Identification. / Ketchum's, Ottawa.

Wording on the tin notice attached to one of the doors of "Gipsy House," the country home of Roald Dahl, the English writer (1916–1990), Great Missenden, near Oxford, England. The origins of the notice, something of a family joke, are obscure, as it seems to have been commercially manufactured. A photograph appears in Tim Walker's "Welcome to the Dahl House," *The New York Times Magazine*, 18 August 2002.

I don't want to go from raising cattle in Manitoba to raising camels.

Gary Doer, Manitoba premier, address on the subject of global warming, at a premiers' conference, Halifax, 2 August 2002, in Shawn McCarthy, "Premiers Derail Klein Plan," *The Globe and Mail*, 3 August 2002.

An American bull sniffing a Canadian cow doesn't ask for that cow's national identity.

Ralph Klein, Alberta premier, press conference, 29 December 2003, in Dawn Walton, Jim Mahoney, and Graeme Smith, "BSE Contracted in Canada, U.S. Officials Say," *The Globe and Mail*, 30 December 2003.

FASCISM *See also* Communism; Democracy; Dictatorship; Government; World War II

I wish I could take Hitler and Mussolini out bass fishing on Lake Simcoe. They'd come back better men—or they'd never come back.

Stephen Leacock, humorist, *Too Much College, or Education Eating Up Life: With Kindred Essays in Education and Humour* (1939).

Traditional but outdated electoral procedures and new developments in the party structures both within and outside Parliament are opening the way to a quasi-totalitarianism which, for the lack of a better name, I would call five-year fascism.

George Woodcock, social commentator, referring to current Canadian electoral practices and procedures, the maximum period between elections being five years, "Five-Year Fascism," *The Canadian Forum*, December 1990.

FASHION *See also* Beauty; Tuque

The mini-skirt is a form of high-rise.

Attributed to media philosopher **Marshall McLuhan** in the late 1960s.

Canada does have a neo-Canadian look: subdued, restrained, in good taste, not at all American.

Mary McCarthy, U.S. novelist, interviewed by Peter Gzowski, CBC Radio's *Morningside*, 22 October 1982.

I always wondered what happened to beige. Now I know: It's alive and well and living in North York.

Barry Humphries, Australian comedian performing in Toronto in the guise of Dame Edna Everage, in Richard Ouzounian, "Last Review," *Toronto Star*, 8 November 2000.

Canadian fashion design identity languishes unacknowledged, especially when compared to France, America, Italy, Britain, or Spain, and any success by Canadians tends to become subsumed under the more identifiable American fashion scene. In fact, even this recognition denotes real achievement.

Alexandra Palmer, museum curator, introduction, *Fashion: A Canadian Perspective* (2004).

FATHERHOOD *See also* Family

A wise father doesn't see everything.

W.A.C. Bennett, one-time B.C. premier, advice recalled by his son B.C. Premier Bill Bennett, *Today Magazine*, 9 August 1980.

FEAR

I am afraid of the worst, but I am not sure what that is.

Abraham Rotstein, political economist, characteristic remark, aphorism dating from December 1972.

The prescription for fear is action.

Silken Laumann, champion rower, in Barry Shainbaum, *Hope & Heroes: Portraits of Integrity & Inspiration* (2003).

FEDERAL–PROVINCIAL RELATIONS

See also Confederation; Government; Prime Ministers; Provinces

While the ship of state now sails on larger ventures and into foreign waters she still retains the watertight compartments which are an essential part of her original structure.

Celebrated judgement of **Lord Atkin**, Judicial Committee of the Privy Council, in the Labour Conventions case of 1936–1937, concerning the interpretation and implementation within Canada of international treaties concluded by the federal government, as noted by P. Macklem et al., editors, *Canadian Constitutional Law* (2nd ed., 1997).

The problem with asymmetrical federalism is that greed is perfectly symmetrical. It is, always and everywhere, bottomless.

Paul Wells, columnist, "The Back Page," *Maclean's*, 14 February 2005.

FEMINISM *See also* Women; Women's Rights

When women place themselves in situations for which they are not qualified by their nature to fill with obvious advantage, they become a ridiculous caricature of themselves. The mind of the suffragette appears to possess a peculiar aptitude for that absurdity which makes a man impatient and finally contemptuous of all femininity, and resolute to adhere to his own ideal. A woman may be foolish and yet be charming. She emancipates herself when she becomes an object of aversion.

Andrew MacPhail, McGill University professor, address, "The Psychology of the Suffragette,"

Toronto, 20 January 1910, The Empire Club of Canada.

The true liberation of women cannot take place without the liberation of men. Basically, the women's liberation movement is not only feminist in inspiration, it is also humanist. Let men and women look at one another honestly and try together to give a society a new set of values.

Thérèse Casgrain, feminist, quoted by Fernande Saint-Martin in *Châtelaine*, October 1960.

The evidence is, thus far, purely circumstantial, but it suggests to me that this first great wave of feminist enthusiasm was made possible by the securing of good health for women. If I am right about this conjunction of health, feminism, and modern family life, the first surge of feminism would turn out to have taken place in alliance with men rather than in the context of traditional women's culture.

Edward Shorter, historian, *A History of Women's Bodies* (1982).

Let me tell you how I became "wife of...." In Canada I was a writer. I wrote for fifteen years before I went to Washington. I was known as Sondra Gotlieb the writer, I think. When I went to Washington, I was invited to a luncheon and there were sixty ladies at that luncheon. A lot of them had jobs. We all had to stand up and we were introduced as the wife of the Attorney General; the wife of the Nuclear Regulatory Agency; the wife of the Secretary of Energy; and I, for some reason, was introduced as "wife of Canada," coming right after "wife of Peru." And then, I just found it much easier to say I was the wife of the Canadian Ambassador than having to explain, "My name is Sondra Gotlieb and I used to write books in Canada," because there are thousands of different kinds of people you have to meet. It's easier for them to identify you and identify your country with you.

Sondra Gotlieb, writer, address, "Wife of ..." Toronto, 31 October 1985, The Empire Club of Canada.

Women to one side. You're all a bunch of feminists! ... Women to one side. You are all feminists, I hate feminists.

Marc Lépine, mass murderer who shot and killed 14 women students of engineering and wounded 12 others before taking his own life, École Polytechnique, Université de Montréal, 4:30 P.M., 6 December 1989.

The Sacred One who moved a great stone from the entrance to the tomb and sent women out into the Easter dawn can yet change stony hearts into hearts of flesh. For all women, whoever and wherever we are, this long time of exile will come to an end.

Joanna Manning, feminist Catholic commentator, last line, *Is the Pope Catholic? A Woman Confronts Her Church* (1999).

May I be reborn as a woman so I may break him as he breaks me this night.

Line from the opera *The Scarlet Princess*, composed by **Alexina Louie** and **David Henry Hwang**, from the advertisement for the Canadian Opera Company's concert premiere, *The Globe and Mail*, 13 April 2002.

I am a white middle class Jewish radical lesbian feminist.

Lynne Pearlman, feminist, etc., "Through Jewish Lesbian Eyes: Rethinking Clara Brett Martin" (1992), *Canadian Journal of Women and the Law* (5, 317), in Robert Ivan Martin, *The Most Dangerous Branch: How the Supreme Court of Canada Has Undermined Our Law and Our Democracy* (2003). Martin refers to this contribution as "the strangest article ever to appear in an ostensibly scholarly publication."

If the movement is to continue to prosper, we must take issue with those who sail under its banner but do not share its humanity. There is much to lose if we do not confront the pretenders, and there is much to gain from diversity, disagreement, debate, and resolution.

Neil Boyd, criminologist, closing sentences, Simon Fraser University, *Big Sister: How Extreme Feminism Has Betrayed the Fight for Sexual Equality* (2004).

FINANCE *See also* Banks & Banking; Budgets; Business; Economics; Investment; Money; Stock Market; Taxes

You have heard of Old Mother Hubbard who went to the cupboard, to get her poor dog a bone, and when she got there the cupboard was bare, and so, very reasonably, the poor dog got none. We might say that Old Mother Hubbard went to the cupboard to get her poor dog a bone, but when she got there she found only the reserves of bones and therefore she didn't give any to the dog! That is our Canadian system.

Stephen Leacock, economist and humorist, address, "The Riddle of the Depression," Toronto, 16 February 1933, The Empire Club of Canada.

What's a million?

C.D. Howe, Liberal Cabinet minister, House of Commons, 19 November 1945. Howe was explaining the war appropriation bill that called for the expenditure of $1365 million. The following day, John G. Diefenbaker, a Conservative backbencher, rose and claimed Howe had said, "We may save a million dollars, but what of that?" Howe was outraged, but the pattern was set and thereafter the frugal and pragmatic minister was known as "What's a million?" Howe.

In my book I called Bay Street Canada's "eleventh province" and it is more powerful than all the others put together.

Peter C. Newman, journalist, referring to his book *Titans*, address, "Titans: How the New Canadian Establishment Seized Power," Toronto, 10 November 1998, The Empire Club of Canada.

The auditors are the ones who are driving the getaway car.

Al Rosen, forensic and investigative accountant, referring to the role of auditors with respect to the unsecured creditors of companies in bankruptcy, in Deirdre McMurdy, "Newsmakers," *Financial Post*, 21 January 2002.

FINDLEY, TIMOTHY

Tiff, the dead stand up and salute you.

Reaction of **Timothy Findley**'s father, a veteran of the Great War, on reading his son's novel *The Wars* (1977), as recalled by Findley, *Inside Memory: Pages from a Writer's Workbook* (1991).

All I can tell you of myself and of the time in which I lived is here. This is my mark.

Passage from **Timothy Findley**'s novel *Famous Last Words* (1981), recalled by friend and companion William Whitehead at the memorial service for Findley, Festival Theatre, Stratford, Ont., 14 July 2002, in Richard Ouzounian, "Obituary," *Toronto Star*, 15 July 2002.

Timothy Findley is a man I love, a spirit I treasure, and an absence that is cruel.

William Hutt, actor and friend of the late novelist, memorial service, Festival Theatre, Stratford, Ont., 14 July 2002, in Rebecca Caldwell, "Obituary," *The Globe and Mail*, 15 July 2002.

When a writer dies, he becomes his words.

Rosemary Sullivan, biographer, on the death of Timothy Findley, "Tribute," *Maclean's*, 15 July 2002.

Without Whitehead, there would have been no Findley.

James MacGowan, interviewer, referring to companion William Whitehead, "Letting Go of Tiff: William Whitehead Talks about Life without Findley," *Ottawa Citizen*, 16 November 2003.

FIRE

The discovery of fire, at some time deep in our prehistory, was the beginning of our conquest of night. With fire we were no longer completely blind in the darkness.

Christopher Dewdney, poet and author, *Acquainted with the Night: Excursions through the World after Dark* (2004).

FIREARMS *See also* Weapons

Your Second Amendment Protection Ends at the Border / National Rifle Association.

Message to American motorists on the billboard that overlooked the highway leading to the Canadian border crossing, Niagara Falls, N.Y., May 1999. The NRA was reminding American citizens that the Second Amendment to the U.S. Constitution guarantees them the right to bear arms—but not in Canada.

We like our guns on TV rather than in real life.

Antonia Zerbisias, columnist, addressing the stars of the U.S. television series *The Sopranos* at the Toronto launch, in Rosie DiManno, "Sopranos Visit Toronto," *Toronto Star*, 7 June 2001.

FISCAL POLICY

The $23 Billion Gap.

Policy of the Government of Ontario to draw attention to the fiscal imbalance between the contribution of Ontario's taxpayers to the federal government and what they receive back in the form of services, the sum being calculated to be a "gap" of $23 billion, a policy associated with Ontario Premier **Dalton McGuinty** and Member of Provincial Parliament **Mike Colle**, April 2005.

FISH & FISHERIES *See also* Fishing

The fisheries of Newfoundland are inexhaustible and are of more value to the Empire than all the silver mines of Peru.

Sir Francis Bacon, English essayist, "Of Plantations" (1608), *The Essayes or Counsels* (1625). The supposedly inexhaustible cod stocks of Newfoundland collapsed from overfishing in 1992.

From the earliest times the Island oysters have been famous, and prices paid for them were the highest paid for any oysters in the world. That was very good for those who had oysters to sell, but it was hard on the oysters. (Laughter.)

J.A. Matheson, P.E.I. premier, address, "The Island Province," Toronto, 30 January 1913, The Empire Club of Canada.

It took just thirty years to destroy the biomass, 1960 to 1990. The fish couldn't hide.

David Boyd, former fisherman and director of the Prime Berth Fishing Museum, Twillingate, Nfld., in Alanna Mitchell, "Canadian Cod Remains a Tragic Fish Tale," *The Globe and Mail*, 26 August 2002.

We don't want things to go the way of Canada's cod.

David Boyd, former fisherman and director of the Prime Berth Fishing Museum, Twillingate, Nfld., referring to a catchphrase heard at biodiversity conferences, in Alanna Mitchell, "Canadian Cod Remains a Tragic Fish Tale," *The Globe and Mail*, 26 August 2002.

And take care of the salmon. You have the very few natural salmon that still remain in the world.

Fidel Castro, president of Cuba, impromptu press conference, Vancouver, during a stopover between Japan and Cuba, 4 March 2003, in Jason Proctor, "Leader Muses on Baseball, Salmon, War and Health," *National Post*, 5 March 2003.

In Cod We Trusted.

Amended version of the motto "In Cod We Trust" (itself a parody of the slogan that appears on U.S. currency "In God We Trust"), as noted by Margaret Atwood, "At Home among the Bluenosers," *The New York Times Magazine: The Sophisticated Traveller*, 16 November 2003. "One of the most calamitous man-trashes-nature stories of the last twenty years is surely the collapse of the once huge cod fishery of the Northeast."

FISHING *See also* Fish & Fisheries; Ice Fishing

Trout, as everyone knows who is an angler, never rise after a rain, nor before one; it is impossible to get them to rise in the heat, and any chill in the air keeps them down.

Stephen Leacock, humorist, *Here Are My Lectures and Stories* (1937).

For fishing, as I see it, is in reality not so much an activity as a state of mind.

Stephen Leacock, humorist, *My Remarkable Uncle* (1942).

FITNESS *See also* Health

Physical fitness helps you to enjoy your vices.

Lloyd Percival, fitness specialist, quoted in *The Globe and Mail*'s *Weekend Magazine*, 8 June 1974.

In 1972 PARTICIPaction introduced the famous comparison between the 60-year-old Swede and the 30-year-old Canadian in a 15-second television commercial. The idea that a 60-year-old Swede was fitter than a 30-year-old Canadian captured the nation's imagination. In fact, only when Sweden and other countries undertake a survey as comprehensive as the Canadian Fitness Survey of 1981 can true comparisons be made.

Peggy Edwards and **Jo Hauser**, fitness specialist and physician, respectively, "Fitness," *The Canadian Encyclopedia* (2nd ed., 1988). PARTICIPaction, an independent communications company, based its "comparison" on imagination and not on research.

FLAG, NATIONAL *See* National Flag

FOLKLORE *See also* Myths & Mythology

If intelligent residents in every part of the country will only take a little time to jot down what they know about the customs and beliefs prevalent in their neighbourhoods the mass of information will be valuable.

David Boyle, archaeologist, "Canadian Folk-Lore," *The Globe*, 13 November 1897.

FOOD BANKS *See also* Charity; Poverty

There are 625 McDonald's outlets nationwide; there are over 1,100 food banks and soup kitchens.

Carolyn Jack, commentator, "Children in Poverty," *The Canadian Forum*, September 1990.

Joe Berridge, a Toronto planner, has made a computer search of subjects considered in the federal Parliament of Canada during 2001 and the first half of 2002. Foot-and-mouth disease, of which there wasn't a single case in Canada, was mentioned 172 times; homelessness was mentioned just 19 times. Agricultural subsidies came up 162 times, food banks just once.

Jane Jacobs, urban planning critic, citing Berridge's report "Homelessness, Transit Left Off Ottawa Agenda" in *Toronto Star*, 27 June 2002, *Dark Age Ahead* (2004).

FOOD & DRINK *See also* Agriculture; Alcohol; Diets; Dining; Farmers & Farming; Food Banks; Hunger; Obesity; Water; Weight; Wine

Which pears from France, or grapefruits from America, he brings her home; which brown-speckled Canada apples he chooses for her among hundreds. That demonstrates many more intimacies than the orgies of so-called love!

Peter Altenberg, Viennese wit, "Little Things" (1909), *The Vienna Coffeehouse Wits: 1890–1938* (1995), translated, edited, and with an introduction by Harold B. Segel.

Commenting on his trip to Canada in 1945, he said that he was struck most by the friendliness of everyone he met and the extraordinary size of the beefsteaks.

Views of **Sir Alexander Fleming**, British scientist who discovered penicillin, interviewed by broadcaster Bernard Braden, *These English* (1949).

We are in the business of selling wholesome food, quality food, in very, very clean surroundings, giving very, very good service, and at a very reasonable price. Those are the basics of our business. It should be extremely easy for people to imitate the basic tenets of a business like McDonald's. People have tried. Competitors will come and competitors will go and McDonald's—because we understand this business and we've grown up in it—will continue to be the largest company of its kind in the world, because the management of our company is the deepest, the broadest, and the best in the business.

George Cohon, president, McDonald's Restaurants of Canada, address, "McDonald's Worldwide," Toronto, 7 April 1983, The Empire Club of Canada.

What is the ideal restaurant for you?

I'm tempted to say the ideal setup would be a two-person restaurant—one person in front to serve people in a comfortable way and the other in the kitchen preparing the meals. The problem is that it is unfair to the many people who could be contributing to the restaurant and at the same time learning how to cook. One chef (i.e., just me) is tempting but unfair.

Chris Klugman, chef, "Honour Thy Ingredients: Cooking Philosophies of Michael Stadtlander and Chris Klugman," *Wild Culture: Specimens from* The Journal of Wild Culture (1992), edited by Whitney Smith and Christopher Lowry.

Wild foods should be a central part of Canadian cooking. First of all because we have them. Canada is unique in that we still have resources whereas so many European countries have to go elsewhere—to Canada, for instance—to find them. But the fact is we don't use them, we don't take advantage of the land—or at least we don't use it properly. Also, it's a question of priorities. The wild foods are there but to a great extent they're unknown. Instead we buy crayfish from Louisiana.

Chris Klugman, chef, "Honour Thy Ingredients: Cooking Philosophies of Michael Stadtlander and Chris Klugman," *Wild Culture: Specimens from* The Journal of Wild Culture (1992), edited by Whitney Smith and Christopher Lowry.

My philosophy has always been that food should be presented as an extension of where it's grown.

Michael Stadtlander, chef, "Honour Thy Ingredients: Cooking Philosophies of Michael Stadtlander and Chris Klugman," *Wild Culture: Specimens from* The Journal of Wild Culture (1992), edited by Whitney Smith and Christopher Lowry.

While I was there [Ontario summer camp in the 1960s], I discovered the butter tart and, much to my amazement, also discovered that it was unique to us. There's no other country in the world that has this patisserie. As the croissant is to France and as the doughnut is to America, the butter tart is to English Canada. Not only did I discover that it was ours, but that there were different varieties. There were Presbyterian ones, Catholic ones, and United Church ones. Presbyterian ones are crustier. Catholic ones are deeper. I'm told that there are even Jewish butter tarts that have little poppy seeds on them. But the fact is that it was a Proustian memory. I just decided to keep painting them.

Charles Pachter, artist, address, "A Romance with Canada," Toronto, 23 June 1994, The Empire Club of Canada.

Did you know Canadian bacon is actually ordinary ham?

Remark made by the inept Mountie Dudley Do-Right (played by **Brendan Fraser**) in the movie *Dudley Do-Right* (1999), directed by Hugh Wilson.

Food, as millions of overeaters will tell you, is our friend. It's always there; it never lets us down.

Sarah Rosenthal, health specialist, *Women of the '60s Turning 50* (2000).

Visitors to Toronto who are interested in tasting authentic Canadian cuisine may find the search like rummaging through the clothes dryer for a missing sock—you know it has to be there, but it isn't in the obvious places.

Bryan Miller, U.S. restaurant critic, "From Quail Eggs to Caribou, Toronto Serves Up Uncommon Flavours," *The New York Times*, 10 September 2000.

The best recipe in the world is to eat what we have, eat what we like, and be able to share it with our loved ones.

Pasquale Carpino, host of TV series *Today's Cooking with Chef Pasquale*, in Michele Sponagle, "TV Chef," *The Globe and Mail*, 14 October 2000.

Canadians have made great contributions to world cuisine. The two most celebrated being (this is true) baby pablum and frozen peas.

William Ferguson and **Ian Ferguson**, writers, *How to Be a Canadian (Even if You Are One)* (2001).

Eat balanced and varied meals. Stop worrying so much about your food; it's almost certainly healthier than you are.

Alan McHughen, scientist, *A Consumer's Guide to Genetically Modified Food* (2001).

You've probably heard that story about the Inuit having fifty words for snow? Well, the sign of a genuine Canadian is that he has fifty words for doughnut. When a glacial wind is howling through Moose Jaw and Medicine Hat and it has been dark for five months in Tuktoyaktuk, Canadians head for Tim Hortons, Dunkin' Donuts, Robin's Donuts, Country Style, Coffee Time, Baker's Dozen, and all the rest of them. When it comes to the perfect doughnut, Canada is the unquestioned world leader.

Paul Robinson, columnist and security studies specialist, "Land of the Free," *The Spectator*, 24 May 2003.

The best airline food is in the overhead bins.

Ken MacQueen, commentator, "Junk Fare Puts the Uck in Canuck," *Maclean's*, 1 July 2003.

Authentic New York Style Greek Cuisine.

Actual heading used in the advertorial feature "Dining Today with Brett Halliday," *National Post*, 20 May 2004. The restaurant described is Avra Estiatorio in Toronto's Greek district.

Poutine. The word sums up the place called Quebec better than just about any other—better, even, than Céline, referendum, tabernac. And authentic poutine is très difficult to find outside the province.

Matthew Hays, food writer, "La Sauce C'est Tout," *Saturday Night*, November 2004.

FOOTBALL

Argos suck!

Anti-Argo chant used by vociferous fans of the Hamilton Tiger-Cats in games played against the Toronto Argonauts football team, as noted by David Naylor, "Ticats' Owner Offers Prize in Bed to Get Fans to Drop Anti-Argo Chant," *The Globe and Mail*, 11 November 2004. Apparently it has been popular since the 1970s.

Confederation works one day a year—the afternoon of the Grey Cup.

Adapted from a remark made by author **Peter C. Newman**, *The Canadian Revolution* (1995), referring to the championship cup awarded each fall since 1909 with much festivity following the season's "final" Grey Cup football match.

Canadian sports was, for many years, marked by having two football teams with the same name. Often enough, the Grey Cup, which is like the Super Bowl minus the money and the Britney Spears commercials, featured the Roughriders vs. the Rough Riders, so no one could be disappointed.

Adam Gopnik, columnist, "There Is No End to the Kick-ass Canucks," *National Post*, 2 March 2002.

FOREIGN AFFAIRS

See also America; Canada & the World; Foreign Aid; Globalism & Globalization; International Affairs; Internationalism; North American Free Trade Agreement (NAFTA); World

One of the hardest parts of my job has been to stay in any one place long enough to get laundry done.

Maurice F. Strong, environmentalist and executive co-ordinator, United Nations Office for Emergency Operations in Africa, quoted in "Strong Redux," *The New Yorker*, 11 August 1986.

The Ministry of Foreign Affairs and International Trade comes perilously close to claiming a status for Canada as a moral superpower (or to a parody of the Indigo and Chapters bookstores' slogan "The World Needs More Canada") when it says, "A better world might look like a better Canada."

J.L. Granatstein, "The Importance of Being Less Earnest," *National Post*, 22 October 2003.

Here in the peaceable kingdom, we have a distorted view of our international standing.

Over the years, our governments have woven a series of elaborate myths that make us feel better but have little relation to reality. We like to think we're perceived as a principled middle power. In truth, we're widely seen as woolly-headed moralizers. Developing countries flatter us to obtain aid dollars, or because they think we have influence with the United States. Europeans court us to pull us toward them and away from the world's only superpower.

Norman Spector, columnist and former publisher, "Canada's Global Decline," *Ottawa Citizen*, 15 March 2003. The passage is an excerpt from Spector's book, *Chronicle of a War Foretold: How Mideast Peace Became America's Fight* (2003).

This means we now take it for granted that distinctive Canadian values do exist. More intriguingly, it means that we want our foreign policy to be principally about making the world more Canadian. This interpretation always causes an initial shock whenever I have uttered it in public forums—understandably so because it is an assertive, American-style attitude. My proposition nevertheless is that, somewhat like the Americans, we have come to adopt the missionary position in foreign affairs. We are not imperialists, of course: we lack the power to be. But we are interventionists.

Richard Gwyn, columnist and essayist, "Surviving Survivalism," *Literary Review of Canada*, December 2004.

If you want to play a role on the world stage you have to have the "three Ds" of defence, diplomacy, and development.

Doug Goold, Canadian Institute of International Affairs, in Olivia Ward, "How Canada Lost Credibility," *Toronto Star*, 29 January 2005.

Ottawa wants only a superficial re-examination of defence, aid, and foreign policy, each independent of the other. The result is a Canada more responsible than inventive on the international stage, given to a kind of lofty ad hockery, inclined to embrace the next fashionable idea, be it soft power or human security, as long as it doesn't cost too much. For all its history and geography, for all its energy and diversity, is this the best that Canada can do in the world?

Andrew Cohen, author, *While Canada Slept* (2004), in Olivia Ward, "How Canada Lost Credibility," *Toronto Star*, 29 January 2005.

There are two rules of Canadian foreign policy. The first is: Don't get too close to the United States. The second is: Don't get too far from the United States.

John Manley, deputy prime minister, interviewed by Brian Stewart, CBC-TV's *Reporter's Voice*, aired on the Documentary Channel, 14 July 2005.

FOREIGN AID

See also Canada & the World; Foreign Affairs; Globalism & Globalization; United Nations; World

We are the only nation of our size in the world that is above suspicion. Even if they could do these things in many cases their efforts would be suspect in other countries.

Robert B. McClure, medical missionary, address, "Canada's Place in the Pacific Basin," Toronto, 20 March 1947, The Empire Club of Canada.

Greatness in nations as in individuals requires greatness of purpose and direction. While self-interest alone is more than sufficient to justify our assistance to the developing peoples of the world, it is not and should not be our principal motive. The concept of giving, not just of our substance but of ourselves to others in need, is central to the Judeo-Christian system of values on which our way of life is based. Today we know of the needs—we have the capacity to meet them. Surely we cannot be true to our own ideals if we "pass by on the other side."

Maurice F. Strong, director, Foreign Aid Office, address, "International Development," Toronto, 26 January 1967, The Empire Club of Canada.

A book could be written about dysfunctional, dumbed-down, out-of-touch foreign aid.

Indeed, many books have been, some by appalled outsiders, some by rueful insiders and participants. Good intentions are not lacking; subsidiarity and fiscal accountability are.

Jane Jacobs, urban planning critic, *Dark Age Ahead* (2004).

Wouldn't it be great if Canada was next and tipped the balance? After all, Canada should have been No. 1. It is the home of the 0.7.

Jeffery Sachs, professor at Columbia University and author of a report commissioned by the United Nations on levels of foreign aid, interviewed by Marcus Gee and Estanislao Oziewicz, "Rich Countries Must Boost Aid, Report Says," *The Globe and Mail*, 18 January 2005. In this slightly revised version of his remarks, Sachs is reminding Canadians that a report endorsed by Prime Minister Lester B. Pearson in the 1960s had recommended that Canada's foreign aid commitment be pegged at 0.7 percent of its gross domestic product, a level endorsed by the UN. Current spending is 0.28 percent, with increases promised but never delivered by Prime Minister Paul Martin in 2004.

The great thing about development assistance is that the money never leaves the country.

Diane Marleau, former Liberal minister and former Canadian International Development Agency minister, speaking either cynically or sentimentally, in John Lorinc, "The Best Aid Plans," *Saturday Night*, November 2004.

You can almost do as much good for poor countries by abolishing agricultural subsidies as by doubling aid programs.

Roy Culpeper, CEO, North-South Institute, in John Lorinc, "The Best Aid Plans," *Saturday Night*, November 2004.

FOREIGN OWNERSHIP *See also* Globalism & Globalization

I don't intend to be bullied, smothered or owned by any other country. There are some in this nation who feel as I do. I call them Canadians.

In a country where 75% of the major corporations; 60% of the manufacturing industry; 60% of the mining industry; 85% of the smelting and refining; 90% petroleum; 95% automobile and automobile parts; 90% rubber, 75% chemical; 75% electrical apparatus; 90% computer; and 90% of the corporations employing more than 5,000 people are foreign-owned, is it surprising that what is best for Canada's long term future is not necessarily the prime concern of business or of government? And don't expect senior executives of the more than 8,500 American subsidiaries now operating in Canada to speak out in favour of economic independence. When they do, expect them to join the ranks of the unemployed. Our Prime Minister says, "The government has no business in the bedrooms of the nation." Peter Newman says, "The U.S.A. has no business in the boardrooms of our nation." I wish Mr. Trudeau would adjust his priorities.

J.G. (Jack) McClelland, publisher and nationalist, debate, "Canadian Independence," Toronto, 3 February 1972, The Empire Club of Canada.

No other major or middle-sized developed nation would dream of allowing the degree of foreign ownership and control that we have in Canada. Can anyone imagine for a moment the U.S. allowing its petroleum industry, its automobile industry, its computer industry, or a long list of dozens of other key industries, to be taken over by foreign owners? The possibility is laughable.

Mel Hurtig, publisher and nationalist, *The Vanishing Country: Is It Too Late to Save Canada?* (2002).

FORESTS *See also* Environmentalism; Lumber & Lumbering; Resources; Trees

"Much of my life has been spent in the woods," said he, "and one speaks so little there that one comes to forget how to do it."

Observation made by a Canadian woodsman in **Sir Arthur Conan Doyle**'s novel *The Refugees: A Tale of Two Continents* (1892).

A Kwakiutl boy raised to revere the salmon forests of the Pacific Northwest as the abode of Huxwhukw and the Crooked Beak of Heaven, cannibal spirits living at the North of the world, will be a different person than a Canadian child taught that such forests exist to be cut.

Wade Davis, explorer and author, "A Dead End for Humanity," *The Globe and Mail*, 28 December 2000.

Ontario's forests need to be conserved—but we are not yet a conserving people.

Paul L. Aird, scientist, "Cultural Attitudes to Culturing the Forest," *Regenerating the Canadian Forest: Principles and Practice for Ontario* (2001), edited by Robert G. Wagner and Stephen J. Colombo.

This forest, called the boreal ecoregion, comprises one-third of the world's total forest area. It is the earth's largest natural ecosystem, greater than the Amazon rainforest and far greater than the rainforests of Africa and Southeast Asia. It is the world's largest carbon sink, a huge breathing lung that takes in carbon dioxide and replaces it with oxygen. It is the life of our planet.

Patrick Lane, poet, "The Forest's Edge," *The Walrus*, May 2005.

FORGIVENESS

Somebody said there's no forgiveness; there's just forgetting. The secret is the ability to forget.

Leonard Cohen, poet, interviewed by Eve Rockett, "Conversations with Five Men about Women," *Homemaker's Magazine*, May 1979.

This is the ultimate secret of liberation: to forgive and to be forgiven, and thus to become free, like little children.

Jean Vanier, founder of L'Arche movement, *Becoming Human* (1998).

FOX, TERRY

Somewhere the hurting must stop.... I'm not a dreamer ... but I believe in miracles. I have to.

Terry Fox, marathon runner, amputee, letter to the head office of the Canadian Cancer Society, 15 October 1979, requesting the society's sponsorship for his "run across Canada to raise money for the fight against cancer," subsequently known as the Marathon of Hope. He jogged from St. John's, Nfld., to Thunder Bay, Ont., two-thirds of the way across the country. He died of cancer in New Westminster, B.C., on 28 June 1981.

Mile 3339 / Terry Fox's / "Marathon of Hope." / September 1, 1980.

Inscription on the simple white marker in a farmer's field in Shuniah Township, northeast of Thunder Bay, Ont. It was erected by the Ontario Ministry of Transportation but is privately maintained. It marks the point on the Trans-Canada Highway at which the one-legged marathon runner collapsed. To raise funds for research against cancer, he covered 5374 painful kilometres (3339 miles), more than half the distance from Halifax to his home in Burnaby, B.C. The official point of commemoration is the Terry Fox Scenic Outlook, some miles farther west.

Who would have thought that in the early 21st century Canadians would salute Galahad questing and dying on Lake Superior's shores?

Christopher Moore, historian, referring to runner Terry Fox whose trans-Canada run was arrested by cancer near Thunder Bay, Ont., "Old Tomorrow: Today's Man," *The Globe and Mail*, 22 June 2002.

Even though his purpose was to raise money for cancer, I was inspired by his journey, by how people viewed him, and by how his disability was secondary. When people looked at Terry, they saw ability, capacity, and potential.

Rick Hansen, marathon wheelchair athlete, Man in Motion, in Barry Shainbaum, *Hope & Heroes: Portraits of Integrity & Inspiration* (2003).

Had Terry never run those daily marathons, would he still be alive? That's a good question.

Douglas Coupland, author, *Terry* (2004). The one-legged runner covered 3339 miles

(5374 km) in 143 days before he collapsed and was claimed by cancer.

To many people, Terry never stopped running. Day or night he's still near us, passing by the outskirts of the cities we live in, with his strange hop-click-thunk step, forever fine and forever keeping the best parts of ourselves alive, too.

Douglas Coupland, author and biographer of Terry Fox, marathon runner, founder of the Marathon of Hope, quoted in "In the News," *The Globe and Mail*, 7 January 2005.

FRANCE *See also* Canada & France

It is the weakness of you French—planting a drop of your precious blood in outlandish veins, in the wilderness and fancying that that addition makes them French—that by this the wilderness is converted, civilized, a new link in the chain. Never. Great as your desire may be.

William Carlos Williams, author and poet, "The Founding of Quebec," *In the American Grain: Essays* (1925). The U.S. author has in mind the French explorer Samuel de Champlain (c. 1570–1635).

Forget your stereotypes of the French as a happy people fond of light wines and dancing. The French are a tough, hardheaded lot, who haven't changed since Caesar characterized them in his Gallic Wars as "short, stubborn with round heads." I might add that those round heads are filled with big grey brains, which they are taught to use at an early age in one of the finest and most democratic education systems in the world; and that they possess a collective will that is the positive aspect of their homogeneous society. It's that collective will that has enabled the French to pull off an industrial and economic miracle in the past twenty-five years that is breathtaking.

Adrienne Clarkson, agent general for Ontario in France, address, "Ontario and the French Connection," Toronto, 21 November 1985, The Empire Club of Canada.

First we would go to see Martha's family in Canada (who said, Canadianly, "Oh, you live in Paris. How stimulating").

Adam Gopnik, Montreal-born memoirist and sometime Paris resident, *Paris to the Moon* (2000).

It would take a diviner to predict what France will look like in 50 years, let alone a hundred. But one thing is certain: France is not what it used to be. France has never been what it used to be, and it never will. So we might as well enjoy it while it lasts.

Jean-Benoît Nadeau and **Julie Barlow**, political scientists, *Sixty Million Frenchmen Can't Be Wrong (Why We Love France, but Not the French)* (2003).

FREDERICTON

Ah, Fredericton! That spot where Time lost his way and halted and could not rouse himself to move on—that fine old man, blinking by the river, demanding his rights and then dozing off again.

Bruce Hutchison, author, *The Unknown Country: Canada and Her People* (1942).

If you don't know what the capital of New Brunswick is, give yourself 10 points.

Quiz question set by **William Ferguson** and **Ian Ferguson**, *How to Be a Canadian (Even if You Are One)* (2001).

FREE ENTERPRISE *See also* Business; Capitalism; Entrepreneurship; Socialism

Quebec is the only place in North America where one can be sure that there will never be any communists, leftists, or other radicals. Compromise would be complicity.... You may be assured of one thing, free enterprise will always be respected. State ownership, even though it may prove necessary sometimes as the lesser of two evils, is not to be recommended.

Maurice Duplessis, Quebec premier, address, Canadian Manufacturers' Association, December 1946, in Conrad Black, *Duplessis* (1977).

If you're small and don't need much help, you get none; you get to help those who are big and need a lot. It's called free-enterprise socialism.

Dalton Camp, columnist, *An Eclectic Eel* (1982).

The notion that free enterprise exists has got to be acknowledged as being a myth. If I had a choice between believing in free enterprise and Santa Claus, I'd tell you I believe in Santa Claus.

Richard Hatfield, N.B. premier, address, 2 December 1983, quoted in *The Globe and Mail*, 3 December 1983.

FREE SPEECH *See also* Censorship; Communications; Language; Rights

While we cherish and honour free speech, we also cherish and honour free enterprise and freedom of choice. Advertisers have the right to make judgments about where their advertising is placed, activists have the right to object, and all citizens have a right to informed choice.

Tim Collings, engineer and inventor of the V-chip, Simon Fraser University, "Coding," *The Globe and Mail*, 28 November 1997. The V-chip enables TV viewers to block programs based on ratings and content.

FREE TRADE *See also* Business; Canada & United States; Economics; Globalism & Globalization; International Affairs; Trade

In conclusion, I want to say that we cannot stop the tides of free trade or reject reforms like the GST, which come with exporting. Ostrich economics will bury Canada if voters opt for politicians who would rip up the free trade deal despite the reality. There is no turning back. The world hurtles toward one economy whether we like it or not. Far from unwelcome, the process which began in '44 of trade, tradeoffs and sharing the wealth offers the only hope for a planet beset by poverty and pollution. Free trade is not the issue. Free trade simply exists.

Diane Francis, columnist, address, "A Look at Canada Incorporated," Toronto, 1 November 1990, The Empire Club of Canada.

How Britain's Economic, Political and Military Weakness Forced Canada into the Arms of the United States.

Title of a series of academic lectures delivered by **J.L. Granatstein**, historian, at the height of the Free Trade debate in 1988, according to Christopher Moore, "Writers of History: The Organized Man," *The Beaver*, April–May 1991.

Part of what kept this country non-American was thinking we were not American. And this economic merging knocked one prop out from under that. It weakens the nation.

J.L. Granatstein, historian, offering one of a number of criticisms of Mulroney's Free Trade Agreement of 1988, interviewed by Christopher Moore, "Writers of History: The Organized Man," *The Beaver*, April–May 1991.

It is possible to believe in the benefits of free markets and still be a Canadian nationalist. Caring is not in conflict with great ambition.

Thomas P. d'Aquino and **David Stewart-Patterson**, president and vice president, respectively, of the Business Council on National Issues, *Northern Edge: The Will to Win* (2001).

The declaration we have just signed contains a clear, unequivocal commitment to democracy, making it an essential condition for participation in the Summit of the Americas process.

Jean Chrétien, prime minister, statement about the so-called Democracy Clause in the proposed agreement for a Free Trade Area of the Americas (FTAA), news conference, Quebec City, Summit of the Americas, 22 April 2001, in Robert Fife, *National Post*, 23 April 2001.

FREEDOM *See also* Dictatorship; Fascism; Free Speech; Freedom of Expression; Homosexuality; Rights; Security & Intelligence

We can best learn to value this heritage of freedom by reflecting on its history. We can best appreciate the present in the light of the past, and in the same light we can realize the measure of our duty and obligation towards the future.

Stephen Leacock, humorist, *Canada: The Foundations of Its Future* (1941).

Once one recognizes a genuine value, one realizes how useless pure freedom is.

L.S. Cattarini, aphorist, "Freedom Is Not Enough" (1996), *Beyond Sartre and Sterility: Surviving Existentialism* (1986, 2002).

You seldom appreciate your homeland until you lose it. And then it's too late.

Peter C. Newman, columnist and author, "Love This Land, Not the Constitution," *Defining Moments: Dispatches from an Unfinished Revolution* (1997).

Freedom is the right to be wrong, not the right to do wrong.

Attributed to former Prime Minister **John G. Diefenbaker** by Greg Knight, *Right Honourable Insights: A Stirring Collection of Insults and Invective* (2000).

Neither freedom of religion nor the guarantee against discrimination based on sexual orientation is absolute. The proper place to draw the line is generally between belief and conduct. The freedom to hold beliefs is broader than the freedom to act on them.

Judgement of the Supreme Court of Canada that refused the appeal of a B.C. teachers' association to find as discriminatory the stand of an evangelical Protestant institution that accepts public moneys to operate instructional courses, in Kirk Makin, "Supreme Court Upholds Private Schools' Right to Antigay Beliefs," *The Globe and Mail,* 18 May 2001.

Religious freedom is the first of human rights, for it is religion that grounds the dignity of the human person in his relation to an authority that transcends temporal powers.

Richard John Neuhaus, founder of First Things, born in Pembroke, Ont., Lutheran pastor who became Catholic priest, "Religious Freedom in a Time of War," *First Things: The Journal of Religion and Public Life,* January 2002.

The message of history, most spectacularly driven home in the 9/11 terror attacks, is that preserving society as a whole is much more important than preserving an illusory personal freedom.

Robert J. Sawyer, science-fiction author, "Privacy: Who Needs It?" *Maclean's,* 7 October 2002.

Canada offered me the freedom to do anything I could imagine. The negative side of this freedom was that it was a freedom which arose from ignorance and indifference.

John Metcalf, critic and author, who emigrated from England to Canada, *An Aesthetic Underground: A Literary Memoir* (2003).

I already have the three single most important things in the world: freedom, family and loyal friends. The rest is ephemeral.

William Sampson, British-born Canadian engineer, on his release after 31 months of detention and torture both mental and physical in a prison in Saudi Arabia on trumped-up charges of terrorism, "I Angrily Lunged toward My Father," *National Post,* 11 September 2003.

I know it sounds stupid, but I would like to have an ice cappuccino from Tim Hortons. That is what I would like to do.

Karla Homolka, convicted murderer implicated in the deaths of three teenage girls, interviewed in French by Joyce Napier on Radio-Canada, within hours of her release after a 12-year prison sentence, 4 July 2005, "Television Interview Transcript," *National Post,* 5 July 2005.

FREEDOM OF EXPRESSION *See also*

Anti-Semitism; Censorship; Communications; Freedom; Language; Media; Political Correctness; Rights

I'm a big fan of freedom from expression.

Henry Mintzberg, economist, referring to the ever-presence of cacophony, "Why He Hates Flying, for $24.95," *Toronto Star,* 12 April 2001.

I believe there are no things that shouldn't be thought, and few things that shouldn't be said.

Julius Grey, civil-rights lawyer, after successfully defending the right of French professor Marc Angenot to say on Radio-Canada that "Yves Michaud has the right to make anti-Semitic statements and I have the right to find them contemptible," in Sean Gordon, Montreal *Gazette,* 14 May 2002. Fifteen months earlier,

Quebec parliamentarian Yves Michaud had made a careless comment about the Jewish people that was judged "anti-Semitic"; it triggered the resignation of Lucien Bouchard as Quebec premier and Parti Québécois leader.

Confidential sources are essential to the effective functioning of the media in a free and democratic society.

Ruling of Madam Justice **Mary Lou Benotto**, Ontario Superior Court, 21 January 2004, editorial, "A Win and a Loss for Press Freedom," *The Globe and Mail*, 22 January 2004.

FRENCH CANADA *See also* Canada; French Canadians; Quebec

Notre petit peuple.

Description of the French-Canadian population as "our little people" associated with **Canon Lionel Groulx**, as noted by Max Nemni and Monique Nemni, "A Conversation with Father Georges-Henri Lévesque," *Cité libre*, fall 1999.

... Will give me an unparalleled opportunity to travel to French Canada and especially the Gaspé peninsula to trace the histories of certain family lines involved ... about Canucks living in the dense, complicated French Canadian neighbourhoods of New England milltowns, the special and complete experience of their lives in America.

Lines from a letter of application to the Guggenheim Foundation outlining "Plans for Artistic Venture" to travel, research, and write the novel "The Vanity of St. Louis" (never completed) about his background, drafted in 1951, by **Jack Kerouac**, New England novelist of French-Canadian ancestry, in Randy Boswell, "Kerouac Letter," *National Post*, 21 November 2003. Kerouac signed the application "Jean-Louis." The letters made news when they were offered in public auction.

French agents in Canada, after the defeat of their army in 1753, sent the information among the Indians that the King of France had been sleeping over the past few years, but that he had now awakened and that his first words had been: "We must immediately cast forth the English who have entered the land of my red children." The news spread over the entire continent and was one of the causes of the famous Pontiac Conspiracy.

Jorge Luis Borges, Argentine author, "The King's Awakening," *Cuentos breves y extraordinarios* (1953), written with Bioy Casares, fictitiously credited to the non-existent H. Desvignes Doolittle's *Rambling Thoughts on World History* (Niagara Falls, 1903), translated by Alberto Manguel.

We had lost that French continent, but even if we did not know its history, it remained an invisible presence to us, in the same way that what is invisible is more of a presence to us than what is visible. We may try to see the invisible and may, at moments, see it in a slouch hat with a plume or a lace fan, in a stone arrowhead, or in a beaver pelt, but it cannot be made visible, as much as we try.

David Plante, American-born novelist and memoirist of Quebec background, *American Ghosts: A Memoir* (2004), in David M. Shribman, "In Search of the Canadian Within," *The Globe and Mail*, 8 January 2005.

FRENCH CANADIANS *See also* French Canada

We must be ashamed to be Canadian, and we must keep faith with our loathing.... It is up to us to ensure that the word "Canada" (what an unsavoury collection of syllables, don't you find?) becomes synonymous in every land with complacent obtuseness.

Jean Larose, commentator, *La Petite Noirceur* (1987), in Daniel Poliquin, *In the Name of the Father* (2001). Larose even talks about "Latino-Iroquois blood."

She's French Canadian. When she's Canadian, she's really quite pleasant. But today she's definitely French.

Catty remark made by one female character about another in the action movie *Vertical Limits* (2000), written by **Robert King** and directed by Martin Campbell.

Well, who else would do such dirty work, who else but one of us French? We're not called white niggers for nothing.

Elderly woman of French-Canadian background working as a washerwoman in New England, in U.S. novelist **David Plante**'s *American Ghosts: A Memoir* (2004).

Being Canuck meant, at the deepest, being a failure.

David Plante, U.S. novelist and memoirist, reflecting on his French-Canadian background, *American Ghosts: A Memoir* (2004), as noted by Philip Marchand, "Trapped in the Parish," *Toronto Star*, 26 December 2004. Plante ponders being "secreted within the tabernacle of the church of my parish, my Canuck God, the God of that country of darkness."

Quebeckers are, at best, contingent Canadians, citizens on sufferance or for reasons of strict self-interest, which explains not just their nationalism and the desire of many to leave Canada but the hardened attitudes in the rest of Canada where the wish to accommodate Quebec has shrivelled.

Jeffrey Simpson, columnist, "They Love Us, We Love Us—What's the Problem?" *The Globe and Mail*, 1 July 2005.

FRENCH LANGUAGE *See also* Language

You in Canada stand to the world as a country with two language groups and the question of how you solve your "asymmetrical rivalries between two complementary groups, conceived as different, yet nevertheless similar," is again going to make all sorts of possible echoes around the world when we are dealing with other countries that have complexities of the same kind.

Margaret Mead, ethnologist, address, "How Fast Can Man Change," Toronto, 18 April 1957, The Empire Club of Canada.

We lack a common language that is both profound and meaningfully rich. We are living, once again, in the unfinished Tower of Babel.

Alberto Manguel, writer and reader, *Reading Pictures: A History of Love and Hate* (2000).

We don't need to speak French, we need French to speak.

André Belleau, Quebec author, in Jacques Godbout, "In Quebec Culture, a Deep Skepticism of Tradition," *The New York Times*, 16 September 2001.

We should all know three languages now if we want to conquer the world, and in the United States now, French is the third language.

Louise Beaudoin, Quebec minister of international relations, address, Beverly Hills, Cal., in Doug Saunders, "Quebec Expanding Missions in the U.S.," *The Globe and Mail*, 20 May 2002.

French is the third most spoken language in the United States after English and Spanish.

In television interviews for a special on Quebec singer Céline Dion, her family members were even subtitled (French Canadian TV never subtitles Parisians, even when they are incomprehensible).

Jean-Benoît Nadeau and **Julie Barlow**, political scientists, referring to television in France, *Sixty Million Frenchmen Can't Be Wrong (Why We Love France, but Not the French)* (2003).

The idea of protecting the language against Anglicisms actually started in Quebec. In a population of seven million now, six million can be considered native speakers of French. This is a very small French pool in a sea of three hundred million English speakers——no other linguistic group has a similar situation except, maybe, Baltic-language speakers with respect to Russian, or Hebrew speakers with respect to Arabic.

Jean-Benoît Nadeau and **Julie Barlow**, political scientists, *Sixty Million Frenchmen Can't Be Wrong (Why We Love France, but Not the French)* (2003).

Don Cherry has nothing against French immersion. He just figures they don't hold them down long enough.

Ron MacLean, hockey commentator, referring to his fellow commentator Don Cherry of CBC-TV's *Hockey Night in Canada*'s "Coach's Corner" intermission feature, remark, at the opening of the Bobby Orr Hall of Fame, Parry Sound, Ont., July 2003.

The number of people who speak English as a mother tongue is approaching four hundred million. More than one and a half billion may speak it as a foreign language, fluently or otherwise. The combined total far surpasses the number of speakers for any other language in history.

Mark Abley, author, *Spoken Here: Travels among Threatened Languages* (2003).

I am the only one besides Maurice Chevalier who ever had to practise to keep the French accent in English…

Jean Chrétien, prime minister, final speech, House of Commons, 6 November 2003.

All forms of oppression experienced by Francophones in Canada need to be addressed in order to counteract multiple facets of marginalization and their intersectionality with other social locations of disadvantage like religion, nationality, social class, ethnicity and race.

Josée Makropoulos, sociologist, "Speak White! Language and Race in the Social Construction of Frenchness in Canada," *Racism, Eh? A Critical Inter-Disciplinary Anthology of Race and Racism in Canada* (2004), edited by Camille A. Nelson and Charmaine A. Nelson.

You don't have to speak French. If it's important enough, they'll say it in English.

Peter C. Newman, journalist and memoirist, referring to politicians and bureaucrats in Ottawa, *Here Be Dragons: Telling Tales of People, Passion, and Power* (2004).

FRIENDSHIP

Never exaggerate your faults; you friends will attend to that.

Bob Edwards, publisher, *Calgary Eye Opener*, 2 November 1912.

My friends are the light in the dark of my life.

Grattan O'Leary, senator, in Christina McCall-Newman, *Saturday Night*, May 1977.

The great Martin Luther King, in describing times of trial and tribulation, once said that: "In the end, it is not the words of your enemies that you remember, it is the silence of your friends."

Jean Chrétien, prime minister, addressing Paul Cellucci, U.S. ambassador to Canada, memorial service for victims of the 11 September 2001 disaster, Parliament Hill, Ottawa, 14 September 2001.

In time, all friendships become liabilities.

Mavor Moore, theatre personality, characteristic observation, 22 December 2002.

FRONT DE LIBÉRATION DU QUÉBEC (FLQ) *See* October Crisis

FRYE, NORTHROP

He resembles nobody so much as a poetic Midas—everything he touches turns to metaphor.

John Robert Colombo, reviewer, "Polished Performance by a Canadian Essayist," *Toronto Star*, 20 May 1971.

Not long ago I was asked to speak to a group of alumni in a neighbouring city, and a reporter on a paper in that city phoned my secretary and asked if this was to be a "hot" item. My secretary explained that Professor Frye was what his late colleague Marshall McLuhan would have called a cool medium of low definition, and that he could well skip the occasion, which he did with obvious relief. The incident was trivial, but it started me thinking about the curiously topsy-turvy world of "news" as reported today.

Northrop Frye, cultural and literary critic, address, "The Authority of Learning," Toronto, 19 June 1984, The Empire Club of Canada.

Norrie is not struggling for his place in the sun. He is the sun.

Marshall McLuhan, media philosopher, paying tribute to his colleague at the University of Toronto, literary critic Northrop Frye, quoted on the jacket of the hardcover edition of John Ayre, *Northrop Frye: A Biography* (1989).

Only Ulysses can bend the bow of Ulysses.

Robertson Davies, man of letters, offering a response to the rhetorical question who would "replace" Northrop Frye, the literary critic who died on 22 January 1991, interviewed on CBC Radio, 23 January 1991.

FUTURE *See also* Destiny; Past; Science Fiction

However, I may indulge in a generality and say with conviction that Canada, being a young country, is full of possibilities that are incalculable. She has neither exhausted her material resources nor those of her mind and character. She has not yet produced in her psychology the self-toxin of fatigue that old civilisations suffer from in the shape of cynicism and spiritual insensitiveness. Her creative youth is still before her, and the faith needed for building up a new world is still fresh and strong.

Rabindranath Tagore, Bengali sage, "Farewell to Canada," 13 April 1929, *Education and Leisure: Addresses Delivered at the Fourth Triennial Conference on Education Held at Victoria and Vancouver, Canada, April 1929* (1929), edited by S.E. Lang.

In my knowledge of human nature I have learned that most men, whatever they may think of the present, have some hope for the future. It is a kind of instinctive faith, just as they have a belief in the fabled past. They dream that there was a time when mankind was prosperous, happy, and they dream, too, that that time may come again. It is one of the deep human instincts.

John W. Dafoe, publisher, address, "Roads to the Future," Toronto, 30 January 1936, The Empire Club of Canada.

As life goes on, the future becomes steadily more predictable, & the lift consequently less interesting. Children fascinate us; old men bore us because they conceal no surprises.

Northrop Frye, cultural and literary critic, aphorism, "Notebook 3" (1946–1948), *Northrop Frye Newsletter*, fall 2000.

We can imagine what we please and dub this a possible future; but this is not the future of things and the world as we know them, which is the future.

Fraser Cowley, philosopher, *A Critique of British Empiricism* (1968).

The future of the future is the present.

Marshall McLuhan, media philosopher, *Take Today: The Executive as Dropout* (1972).

The future is not what it used to be, and it is now possible to predict the past in many scientific senses. With "carbon 14" tests available, we can now predict why we shall have to re-write most of the past, simply because we can see much more of it simultaneously.

Marshall McLuhan, media philosopher, address, "The End of the Work Ethic," 16 November 1972, The Empire Club of Canada.

Some people despair because they feel the future may escape us. But I speak to those who know the future cannot be guaranteed to any person, province or country—and that the future will be what we make of it. It's up to us to know what to do with this country we love.

Pierre Elliott Trudeau, prime minister, rally, Fort Langley, B.C., 17 June 1968, in Brian Stewart, "Trudeau, the Man Who Gets to the Mob, Finally Let the People Get to Him," Montreal *Gazette*, 18 June 1968.

A long time ago, in the future.

Inuit proverbial expression as recalled by **James Houston**, quoted in the *Toronto Star*, 24 November 1985.

A wise man in China asked his gardener to plant a shrub. The gardener objected that it only flowered once in a hundred years. "In that case," said the wise man, "plant it immediately."

John C. Polanyi, chemist, address, "A Scientist and the World He Lives In," Toronto, 27 November 1986, The Empire Club of Canada.

Throughout the past, we have been fascinated with the future.

David A. Wilson, academic, opening sentence, *The History of the Future* (2000).

To embrace the Future.... Let go of the Past.

Maxim of **Peter de Jager**, professional speaker and Y2K specialist, homepage, website, 3 November 2000.

I am often struck by the thought that I have survived into the future.

Robert Hunter, activist and author, *2030: Confronting Thermageddon in Our Lifetime* (2002).

In my universe, everyone can be immortal, rich and beautiful, and the stars are their stepping-stones.

Spider Robinson, science-fiction writer, distinguishing between "magical age" fantasy fiction and "future-perfect" science fiction, "Forward—Into the Past!" *The Globe and Mail*, 1 January 2002.

g

GAMES & GAMBLING *See also* Lotteries; Luck

We need to develop a game culture of mutual benefit and personal realization through physical activity, not one of "mutually exclusive goal attainment" or "zero-sum" competition.

Varda Burstyn, cultural critic, *The Rites of Men: Manhood, Politics, and the Culture of Sport* (1999).

GARDENS & GARDENING

"For everyone a garden" was the way I phrased this goal for myself, the inspiration for a new type of urban living.

Moshe Safdie, architect, referring to his concept for Habitat '67 at Montreal's Expo 67 exhibition, *The City after the Automobile: An Architect's Vision* (1997), with Wendy Kohn. As well as the title of an earlier publication, this maxim guided Safdie in his design of Montreal's Habitat '67 with its terraces on balconies.

Perhaps no other activity has grown so exponentially in recent decades in this country as has gardening. Classified as a leisure activity (although leisure seems hardly the right adjective!), Statistics Canada puts it at the top of the list with more than 80% of adult Canadians claiming to garden to some extent. All signs indicate that this passion for gardening will only increase in the future.

Carol Martin, curator, "Cultivating Canada's Gardens," Library and Archives Canada, website, 15 June 2005.

GARRISON MENTALITY

A garrison is a closely knit and beleaguered society, and its moral and social values are unquestionable. In a perilous enterprise one does not discuss causes or motives: one is either a fighter or a deserter.

Northrop Frye, cultural and literary critic, establishing the now-standard image for Upper Canada and southwestern Ontario, "Conclusion," *Literary History of Canada* (1965), edited by Carl F. Klinck.

But garrison is too dark a word. "Garrison" suggests gnawing despair and impending attack. I prefer the term "outpost," because it includes a wider range of possibilities. Outposts are not only geographic; they can be linguistic, political, cultural—even philosophical.

Will Ferguson, travel writer, "On the Road with Will," *Maclean's*, 15 October 2004. This is a reference to Northrop Frye's well-known characterization of the society and culture of southern Ontario in terms of a "garrison."

GAYS & LESBIANS *See* Freedom; Homosexuality; Same-sex Marriage

GENETIC ENGINEERING *See also* Clones; Medicine; Research; Technology

But genetic engineering and nanotechnology will allow us to so vastly improve humanity's lot that we'd be fools to turn our backs on them—despite the risks.

Robert J. Sawyer, science-fiction author, "Is Risk Our Business?" (2000), *Relativity: Stories and Essays* (2004).

GENOCIDE *See also* Holocaust, Murder; Peacekeeping; War

"Did the Turks say they were sorry?"
"No."
"Well, why not?"

Atom Egoyan, questioned by his five-year-old son in Toronto in the late 1990s about the continued denial and refusal of the Turkish government to admit its guilt in the massacre of its Armenian population in 1915, explained, "That's the issue, that's the point behind the film," at the press conference for the premiere of *Ararat*, Toronto International Film Festival, 6 September 2002, quoted in "On the Scene," *The Globe and Mail*, 7 September 2002.

My force was standing knee-deep in mutilated bodies, surrounded by the guttural moans of dying people, looking into the eyes of children bleeding to death with their wounds burning in the sun and being invaded by maggots and flies. I found myself walking through villages where the only sign of life was a goat, or a chicken, or a songbird, as all of the people were dead, their bodies being eaten by voracious packs of wild dogs.

Roméo Dallaire, former commander, UN Assistance Mission in Rwanda, recalling the Hutu government's massacre of the country's Tutsi minority in 1994, "Bystanders to Genocide," *Atlantic*, September 2001.

The following is my story of what happened in Rwanda in 1994. It's a story of betrayal, failure, *naïveté*, indifference, hatred, genocide, war, inhumanity, and evil. Although strong relationships were built and moral, ethical, and courageous behaviour was often displayed, they were overshadowed by one of the fastest, most efficient, most evident genocides in recent history.

Roméo Dallaire, lieutenant general, with Major Brent Beardsley, *Shake Hands with the Devil: The Failure of Humanity in Rwanda* (2003). He is referring to the failure of the United Nations to act to halt the murder of more than 800 000 innocent Rwandans.

Almost fifty years to the day that my father and father-in-law helped to liberate Europe—when the extermination camps were uncovered and when, in one voice, humanity said, "Never again"—we once again sat back and permitted this unspeakable horror to occur.

Roméo Dallaire, lieutenant general, with Major Brent Beardsley, *Shake Hands with the Devil: The Failure of Humanity in Rwanda* (2003). He is referring to the genocide in Rwanda in 1994 that resulted in the deaths of more than 800 000 innocent Rwandan men, women, and children.

I am a holocaust victim. We lost over 100 million people over the last 500 years.

David Ahenakew, former chief, Assembly of First Nations, protest, Saskatoon court, 7 April 2005, in Katherine Harding, "Ahenakew: 'I am a holocaust victim,'" *The Globe and Mail*, 8 April 2005. Ahenakew is echoing his defence that by publishing his racist remarks he has been victimized.

It is the human race that is genocidal, not the Germans. Saying this is not to excuse the Germans, but to note a fact. In one vital sense we are all Jews and we are all Germans, potentially, depending on the conditions in which we find ourselves.

George Jonas, memoirist, "Provocation," *Maclean's*, 12 September 2005.

GEOGRAPHY *See also* Earth; Land; Landscape

If some countries have too much history, we have too much geography.

W.L. Mackenzie King, prime minister, House of Commons, 18 June 1936. This widely quoted observation grows less true over time.

If one studies a map of the earth with an eye to the shape and placement of the continents, one is struck by a paradox that comes to view: where every other great land mass appears to be planted block-like and unyielding in its oceans, North America—supposedly the firmest and weightiest of all—looks as though it were made of malleable or even volatile material and were pinned down only in the north while swinging free elsewhere. There is a curving sweep to eastward except at the Arctic, and the whole continent seems to trail off to the south, growing ever more attenuated, like smoke on the wind or patches of seaweed on the water.

Marjorie Spock, student of anthroposophy, "North America under a Light Sky," *The Golden Blade* (1971), edited by Arnold Freeman and Charles Waterman.

Located first of all in the Gulf of St. Lawrence, moved to the zone of the Bering Strait then unknown, and finally placed somewhere along the north-west coast of America, the Strait of Anian invented in 1500 ceased to occupy a place in geographical literature as recently as the early nineteenth century. And who knows: There might be someone who believes in the Strait of Anian even today!

Philip Ward, researcher, "Corte-Real and the Strait of Anian," A *Dictionary of Common Fallacies,* Volume II (1980, 1989).

Space, land and winter—these are the overwhelming realities of Canada.

Wade Davis, ethnobotanist and essayist, *Shadows in the Sun* (1992).

Marge: It took the children forty minutes to locate Canada on the map.
Homer: Marge, anyone could miss Canada. All tucked away down there.

Exchange between the character Marge and her husband, Homer, in episode of the U.S. TV series *The Simpsons,* aired 16 April 1995.

GEOLOGY *See also* Mining

This is perhaps the oldest country in the world. Till yesterday it seemed destined to eternal solitude.

Stephen Leacock, humorist, *Canada: The Foundations of Its Future* (1941).

Nowhere on the surface of the world will there be found more of the modified remnants of these ancient preocean rocks than in northeastern Canada around Hudson Bay.

Passage from *The Urantia Book* (1955), Paper 57 ("The Origin of Urantia"), dictated to a Chicago dentist in 1934 by "Ancients of Days," which is "a composite presentation by many beings."

GERMANY

Federal loyalty invites every partner of this Federation to work, at home and abroad, to strengthen the constitutional alliance and to promote the interests of all, not just one's own. This is a key to success at this dawn of a new century.... I also see in this principle the proof that Canada benefits from understanding Germany. Long live our two federations.

Stéphane Dion, minister of International Affairs, address, "Atlantik-Brücke," Feldafing, Germany, 28 October 2001, website, German Embassy in Ottawa.

Canada won its independence mostly by fighting against Germans.

F.R. Scott, lawyer and poet, aphorism recorded by editor John Robert Colombo in 1973.

GHOSTS *See also* Belief

The arrival of the ghosts has been somewhat delayed, but they have come. They were sure to come. Why shouldn't we have visitors of this kind in Canada as well as in countries much less favoured in every other respect? Don't we also require to be warned, to be admonished, to be scared, to be reminded of our latter end, of some other folks' latter ends? Certainly we do—hence our genuine, original and up-to-date Canadian ghosts, notwithstanding any strong family resemblance they may bear to old-fashioned European "disembodied spirits," both as to general "get up" and methods of conducting themselves, unless, indeed, we claim that our home-made ghosts possess some advantage over the old country ones in the matter of speech, for it will be observed in more than one instance following that Ontario ghosts have the power of utterance, which is much more satisfactory than just to see an "airy nothing" gliding noiselessly through chairs and tables and windows and things, without saying a single word.

David Boyle, archaeologist, "Canadian Folk-Lore," *The Globe,* 1 January 1898.

Ghosts are natural inhabitants of our nocturnal ambiguity, moving with uncertain ease through the half-dreamed shapes of ears and memory, and they have varying abilities to terrify us.

Christopher Dewdney, poet and author, *Acquainted with the Night: Excursions through the World after Dark* (2004).

GIFTS & GIVING *See also* Charity; Philanthropy

Someone once said that the greatest gift any human being can give to another is the gift of a good example.

Bill Sherk, author, address to the Leamington-Mersea Historical Society on the role of volunteers in tree-planting, Leamington, Ont., 27 April 2005.

GLOBAL VILLAGE *See also* Communications; Globalism & Globalization

The new electronic independence recreates the world in the image of a global village.

Marshall McLuhan, communications theorist, *The Gutenberg Galaxy* (1962). He had in mind turning strangers into neighbours through instant, reactive, and interactive communications, in anticipation of the World Wide Web and the internet. The notion goes back to Wyndham Lewis, *America and Cosmic Man* (1948), who wrote, "The earth has become one big village...." Anthropologist and associate Edmund Carpenter suggested that McLuhan meant "global theatre."

Global Village ... it was just an accidental phrase that popped up. What it means, literally, is that, transmitted at the speed of light, all events on this planet are simultaneous. In the electric age of information, all events are simultaneous. There is no time or space separating events.

Marshall McLuhan, media philosopher, conversation with Louis Forsdale, "McLuhan Issue," *The Antigonish Review*, summer–autumn 1988.

GLOBAL WARMING *See also* Environmentalism; Greenhouse Effect; Kyoto Accord

I've yet to hear about someone dying from global warming.

Patrick Luciani, executive director, Donner Canadian Foundation, "Environmental Crisis? What Rot!" *National Post*, 15 July 2000.

I mean, quit breathing? You know, if all of us quit breathing, can you imagine how much carbon dioxide we could avoid sending into the atmosphere?

Ralph Klein, Alberta premier and one-time provincial environment minister, remark on how breathing contributes to global warming, in Jim Mahoney, "Klein on Cutting Smog: Just 'Quit Smoking,'" *The Globe and Mail*, 27 February 2002.

Global warming is not merely an inconvenience for skiers and polar bears. If it induces wild weather swings (as it has many times naturally in the past), crops will fail worldwide and bring civilization to its knees.

Ronald Wright, essayist, "What Price Progress?" *The Globe and Mail*, 4 May 2005.

GLOBALISM & GLOBALIZATION *See also* Business; Corporations; Countries; Economics; Free Trade; Multinationalism; Nationalism

I am not one of those who blame the Americans for the growing foreign control of the Canadian economy. We have no one to blame but ourselves. For years we have taken the path of least resistance.

T.C. Douglas, NDP leader, address, "Canada: A Nation or a Satellite," Toronto, 16 April 1964, The Empire Club of Canada.

Multilateralism in a unipolar world is a contradiction in terms.... The new rule is going to be a reworked version of an old Canadian rule—multilateralism if necessary but not necessarily multilateralism.

Richard Gwyn, columnist, "The Broader Lessons of SARS," *Toronto Star*, 27 April 2003.

U.S. policy choices are unsentimental. It is multilateral when it wants to be, unilateral when it must, and it uses its power to enforce a new international division of labour in which America does the fighting; the Canadians, French, British, and Germans do the police patrols in the border zones; and the Dutch, Swiss, and Scandinavians provide the humanitarian aid.

Michael Ignatieff, commentator, "The Power and the Will to Do Good," excerpt from *Empire Lite*, *National Post*, 18 August 2003.

Thinking Globally, Acting Locally.

Byword of the globalization movement, coined by futurist **Frank Feather** in 1980, during a brainstorming meeting to develop a theme for the First Global Conference on the Future held later that year in Toronto, which Feather chaired, the largest gathering of its kind ever held. Over the years "globalists" turned the two infinitives into imperatives: "Think Globally, Act Locally." In the early 1980s, Feather invented the neologism *glocal* (combining *global* and *local*). He also developed the concept of *webolution* (to describe the Internet Revolution) and *webpreneurs* (to describe entrepreneurial use of the Web). Email from the author, 8 July 2005.

I think we must realize that no nation-state can thrive in isolation in our interdependent world. Too often this country has resisted interdependence with the rest of the world in the mistaken belief that economic nationalism will preserve our national identity. Fortunately, I now sense a feeling in many quarters in Canada that we have gone too far down the road of economic nationalism. I am convinced that our own economic interests would best be served by pursuing more open-door international policies.

Thomas J. Bata, Bata Limited, address, "Canada in a Fragile World," Toronto, 25 November 1982, The Empire Club of Canada.

When my father and uncle moved from their original garage to the corner of Yonge and Gould Streets, they would change their company's name to "Canadian Tire" because such a grand name would suggest to the world that their tiny enterprise was much grander than it actually was. Now I have no illusions that we will be changing our company name to "Global Tire," but I do know that my father and uncle's small company grew into its name.

Martha Billes, Canadian Tire, address, "The Ethics of Self-Reliance," Toronto, 8 February 2001, The Empire Club of Canada.

Globalization is many things to many people, but it is important to recognize that, above all, it is the denial of any standpoint other than profit.

Ursula Franklin, scientist and social justice activist, "Legitimate Expectations," *Canadian Perspectives*, winter 2001.

Precisely because Canada is not obligated to determine the world's economic and political future, as its southern neighbour seems to be, it is in a perfect position to ask questions about how the buzzword "global" can be attached to something deeper, more durable, than "global markets" and "global networks."

Pico Iyer, traveller and writer, "Mongrel Beauties," *Saturday Night*, 31 March 2001.

We live in a culture that looks like Disney, tastes like Coke, and smells like shit.

Jaggi Singh, activist protesting corporate globalization, in Rhéal Séguin, "'The Creation of the Media,'" *The Globe and Mail*, 5 May 2001.

I think the next stage in Canada's mental evolution is to learn how to subvert existing transnational systems to our own ends, rather than having them subvert us. It sounds simplistic, but it's something that still has to happen.

Douglas Coupland, novelist and essayist, "Strong and Free," *Maclean's*, 25 November 2002.

Canadians who imagine themselves to be not-right are regularly critical of globalization. They are happily unaware that their obsession with human rights has become a major globalizing force.

Robert Ivan Martin, law professor, *The Most Dangerous Branch: How the Supreme Court of Canada Has Undermined Our Law and Our Democracy* (2003).

Globalism and multiculturalism caught on in Canada long before they were accepted in the United States. Toronto has thought itself through.

Pico Iyer, traveller and essayist, interviewed by Tina Srebotnjak, host of CLT's *Book Television*, 7 November 2003.

Grand economic theories rarely last more than a few decades. Some, if they are particularly in tune with technological or political events, may make it to half a century. Beyond that, little short of military force can keep them in place.

John Ralston Saul, philosopher, "The Collapse of Globalism and the Rebirth of Nationalism," *Harper's*, March 2004. The opening sentence of this major essay—like its ensuing argument—occasioned much comment and criticism.

This is what happens every few decades. The world turns, shifts, takes a new tack, or retries an old one. Civilization rushes around one of those blind corners filled with uncertainties. Then, abruptly, the opportunities present themselves to those who move with skill and commitment.

John Ralston Saul, philosopher, closing statement, "The Collapse of Globalism and the Rebirth of Nationalism," *Harper's*, March 2004.

The one political cause in recent years that really mobilized young Canadians was the anti-globalization movement, which itself was a wholly globalized phenomenon.

Richard Gwyn, columnist and essayist, "Surviving Survivalism," *Literary Review of Canada*, December 2004.

GODS *See also* Belief; Monsters; Native Culture

It may be questioned whether more comfort or sorrow has come to the race since man peopled the unseen world with spirits to bless and demons to damn him.

Sir William Osler, physician, *Science and Immortality* (1905).

Things used to be left then to the individual. Very little is left now to the individual, except to violate law. (Laughter.) And in those days, I think also, a little more than is now left used to be left to God. We pay so much attention to the government that we leave God out of sight now-a-days. We have reduced Him, as it were, to the position of a governor-general of Canada under the British North America Act. He is expected to preside formally, and attend the opening and closing of Parliament; but if He were to interfere practically in any of our attempts to save our souls by our own democratic methods we should be extremely peeved. (Applause.)

B.K. Sandwell, professor of English, address, "On Being Sorry for Ourselves," Toronto, 24 January 1924, The Empire Club of Canada.

Only if we let this spirit of God come into us, change our being, break down the fears which are in each, break down the barriers that each has created in himself, then only will each one of us be able, without fear, to love his brother, be he in India, be he in the slums of Bombay, be he in China or in Czechoslovakia, be he in Holland or be he in the slums of Toronto, be he in the luxury apartments of Toronto. We will love each of our brothers and we will try to give hope to the afflicted and oppressed and we will try to help the rich and the powerful, and those who are famous, to discover that life is not possessing but life is sharing and opening oneself up.

Jean Vanier, humanitarian, address, "A World in Violence: Eruption to Hope?" Toronto, 11 February 1971, The Empire Club of Canada.

No decent historian would ask whether or not the course of human history proves there is a god. On the other hand, the question of what the ancient Israelites thought about their god is perfectly sensible.

Donald Harman Akenson, historian, *Surpassing Wonder: The Invention of the Bible and the Talmuds* (1998).

The petitioners, members of the Humanist Association of Canada and others, seek changes to the preamble to Canada's constitution and to the charter of rights. They wish to remove the reference to the supremacy of God in the preamble and to change the wording of the charter of rights to reflect the fact that Canada is a secular country which respects the deeply held views of people of many different religious faiths as well as those who have no religious beliefs.

Svend J. Robinson, Member of Parliament, presenting his petition on the Constitution, House of Commons, 8 June 1999. Outside the

House, Robinson added this explanation: "It is inappropriate to include a reference to God in the Constitution when Canada is a secular society, and includes people with no religious belief. Our Constitution should be as inclusive as possible." Noted by Bob Harvey, "Anti-God Petition Mocked in Commons: Bid to Remove Deity from Charter Fizzles," *Ottawa Citizen*, 9 June 1999.

Now that it's possible to explore the universe by rocket, it's difficult to keep believing that there's a loving God way out there somewhere.

Ken Walker, physician and medical columnist (aka Dr. Gifford-Jones), *"You're Going to Do What?": The Memoirs of Dr. W. Gifford-Jones* (2000).

If both perfection and imperfection are taken as proof of God's existence, then the whole idea of proof simply falls apart.

Robert J. Sawyer, science-fiction author, "Science and God" (2000), *Relativity: Stories and Essays* (2004).

The presence of God is the finest of rewards.

Thoughts of the narrator in **Yann Martel**'s *The Life of Pi: A Novel* (2002).

However, we all—believers in an external deity and nonbelievers—need to acknowledge the fact that the human brain is designed and prepatterned to tell us that there is an external god, whether there is one or not.

Robert Buckman, physician and humanist, *Can We Be Good without God? Biology, Behaviour and the Need to Believe* (2002).

It is the clash of two cultures, each of which believes God is on its side. And when God is on both sides at once, the devil has the entire court to himself.

Christopher Dewdney, author, "Us and Them," *Toronto Star*, 7 September 2002.

Instead of God creating our brains, our brains created God.

Michael Persinger, cognitive psychologist, interviewed by Robert Hercz, "The God Helmet," *Saturday Night*, October 2002.

After one of my many presentations following my return from Rwanda, a Canadian Forces padre asked me how, after all I had seen and experienced, I could still believe in God. I answered that I know there is a God because in Rwanda I shook hands with the devil. I have seen him, I have smelled him, and I have touched him. I know the devil exists, and therefore I know there is a God. Peux ce que veux. Allons-y.

Roméo Dallaire, lieutenant general, head of the UN Assistance Mission for Rwanda 1993–1994, reacting to the 1994 crisis, with Major Brent Beardsley, *Shake Hands with the Devil: The Failure of Humanity in Rwanda* (2003). Allan Thompson quotes Dallaire's words in 1997 as "I know that God exists because I shook hands with the devil," "Troubled Witness to Relieve Rwandan Horror," *Toronto Star*, 17 January 2004.

There is a saying that only those who do not believe in God can do God's will.

Reg Hartt, film exhibitor, email, 18 August 2003.

I don't think that if a god exists it is necessarily true that it will always elude our comprehension.

Robert J. Sawyer, science-fiction author, "Autobiography" (2004), *Relativity: Stories and Essays* (2004).

We cannot hold or grasp. Only cling to God, the eternal present, who tries every way to enter the human heart.

M. Owen Lee, priest and memorist, *A Book of Hours: Music, Literature, and Life—A Memoir* (2004).

GOLD RUSH *See* Klondike

GOLDEN AGES *See also* Myths & Mythology

No age, no age is called golden until it is long past. Any age is merely foot-slogging and twenty-four-hour days. To survive you need a good capacity to absorb disappointments.

Andrew Allan, CBC producer, in Harry J. Boyle, introduction, *Andrew Allan* (1974).

Ancient Greeks, like ancient Hebrews and groups with stories of gods as progenitors, retain wisps of ancient myths wafting ghostly regrets about vanished Golden Ages. Many an age that was Golden compared with what came after it has indeed vanished.

Jane Jacobs, urban planning critic, *Dark Age Ahead* (2004).

GOLF

It's one of those unintended consequences of the game: You go out to make pars, and you make friends.

Lorne Rubenstein, sports columnist and author, *Links* (1990).

To call them Westmount cheap would be an oxymoron.

Jean Chrétien, former prime minister, statement delivered as part of his testimony before the inquiry into corruption headed by Judge John H. Gomery, Ottawa, 8 February 2005, in Les Whittington, "Ex-P.M. Gets Out His Golf Balls … and Chips Away at Judge," *Toronto Star*, 9 February 2005. When Chrétien was interviewed a month earlier, Judge Gomery had foolishly referred to the former prime minister's monographed golf balls as an act that was "small-town cheap." As part of his statement, Chrétien produced balls with the monographs of U.S. President George W. Bush and the Montreal law firm of Ogilvy Renault.

GOOD & EVIL *See also* Crime; Cruelty; Ethics; Law; Philosophy

Philosophy since time began has concerned itself with good and evil. I don't think the natural man is either good or evil: I think he is just a little bad.

Gregory Clark, humorist, address, "Sportsmen, Indeed?" Toronto, 13 April 1950, The Empire Club of Canada.

Where there is goodness they beget wonders, and where there is evil they grow demons.

Thoughts about mankind of the scholar Hasso in "the world Sol Three that they call Earth" in **Phyllis Gotlieb**'s science-fiction novel *MindWorlds* (2002).

For evil in the open is but evil from within that has been let out. The main battlefield for good is not the open ground of the public arena but the small clearing of each heart.

Thoughts of the narrator in **Yann Martel**'s *The Life of Pi: A Novel* (2002).

There are many people who I would describe as completely evil. They have ignored the small guy, the child, and have said that money is more important.

Nancy Olivieri, medical researcher and physician, a founder of Doctors for Research Integrity, in Barry Shainbaum, *Hope & Heroes: Portraits of Integrity & Inspiration* (2003).

Keeping lesser evils from becoming greater ones is more than a matter of democratic accountability. It is also a matter of individual conscience.

Michael Ignatieff, essayist, *The Lesser Evil: Political Ethics in an Age of Terror* (2004).

GOODS & SERVICES TAX *See also* Taxes

This goods and services tax is iniquitous, because it's once again forcing us to pay this deficit off the backs of the poor.

Remi J. De Roo, bishop of Victoria, in George Mortimore, *The Canadian Forum*, May 1990.

Q. How does a Canadian child recite the alphabet?

A. A-B-C-D-E-F-G-S-T….

Urban lore collected in February 2000.

GOULD, GLENN *See also* Music

How can you explain that the best pianist in the world suddenly stops playing and starts to make strange radio shows exploring the loneliness of people living under the Arctic circle?

Denys Arcand, Quebec film director, foreword to the screenplay *Thirty-two Short Films about Glenn Gould* (1995), by François Girard and Don McKellar.

Now at that point in my life I had never heard *The Goldberg Variations.* Listening to them for the first time played live by Glenn Gould is a little bit like losing your virginity with

Marilyn Monroe: you never entirely recuperate from it.

Denys Arcand, Quebec film director, foreword to the screenplay *Thirty-two Short Films about Glenn Gould* (1995), by François Girard and Don McKellar.

A small picture of Glenn Gould scrolls centre frame, the only image of Gould in the film. It holds for a moment and fades.

This explanation appears in the screenplay *Thirty-two Short Films about Glenn Gould* (1995), by **François Girard** and **Don McKellar**. Only in the credits at the end does there appear an actual photograph of the pianist in the documentary film *Thirty-two Short Films about Glenn Gould* (A Rhombus Media Production, 1993), directed by François Girard with screenplay by Girard and Don McKellar. All other likenesses are dramatic recreations starring the actor Colm Feore.

Many of Gould's performances were right and sublime, many were wrong and both interesting and stimulating, and some were wrong and simply awful: it was probably the last two categories that gave him much of his celebrity.

Charles Rosen, pianist and essayist, "Culture on the Market," *The New York Review of Books*, 6 November 2003.

GOVERNANCE *See also* Business; Commerce; Government

The governments in which we trust to restrain, indeed, retrain us and guide us to new patterns that can make use of our astonishing technology, not for destruction, but to enable both the people and the planet to survive in harmony and comfort—these governments are caught in the old patterns of pride and place even more ruinously than the individuals they claim to govern.

Judith Merril, science-fiction personality, *Better to Have Loved: The Life of Judith Merril* (2002), with Emily Pohl-Weary. This is an excerpt from the amazing, impassioned "crone" speech, which Merril delivered on Parliament Hill, Ottawa, 21 June 1990, to accompany the exorcism of the Houses of Parliament by poet and wiccan Robin Skelton.

Year after year, throughout the 1990s, we drifted complacently, living on a sense of high moral superiority and low currency, while the institutions of our government became corroded and discredited, paralleling our military and diplomatic decline.

Michael Bliss, historian and columnist, "Sept. 11: The End of Canadian Nationalism," *National Post*, 29 September 2001.

Canada has an experience of governance of which much of the world stands in dire need.

Aga Khan, spiritual leader of the Shia Ismaili Muslims, address, Conference on Leadership and Diversity, Ottawa, 19 May 2004, printed in *The Globe and Mail*, 20 May 2004.

The secret of governing Canada is knowing what not to touch. The first (and only) irrevocable law of politics in these northern latitiudes is to make the necessary possible.

Peter C. Newman, author and biographer, *The Secret Mulroney Tapes: Unguarded Confessions of a Prime Minister* (2005).

GOVERNMENT *See also* Bureaucracy; Communism; Democracy; Dictatorship; Fascism; Federal–Provincial Relations; Governance; House of Commons; Injustice; Justice; Liberal Party; Patronage; Politics; Premiers; Prime Ministers; Public Service; Socialism; Values

The exercise of governmental authority is one of the most expensive privileges that any community can enjoy. The more you ask the government to do, the more the government will have to collect out of your pockets for doing it; and if what you want it to do is something that you can do yourselves you will find that the government will charge you ten times what it would cost you to do it yourselves.

B.K. Sandwell, professor of English, address, "On Being Sorry for Ourselves," Toronto, 24 January 1924, The Empire Club of Canada.

What I am really trying to say is that all government rests, not on codes and laws (those are for criminals), but on decency, kindly feeling and a proper idea of the merits and rights and the good sides of others.

Stephen Leacock, humorist, *Last Leaves* (1945).

The Liberal Party is the party of government.

J.W. Pickersgill, eminence grise of the Liberal Party from 1937 to 1967, characteristic remark. In a letter to John Robert Colombo, 24 November 1978, he explained: "I do not know who said the Liberals are the party of government. It is conceivable, but unlikely, I said it in jest, but knowing how dangerous it is for Canadian politicians to jest I think it improbable." It goes without saying that if the Liberal Party is the "party of government," then the Conservative Party is the "party of opposition."

In Canada we have the rather naive idea that the cabinet (that handful of men and sometimes women who meet behind closed doors in a secrecy enshrined in oaths) make all the decisions; that they're the ones who come up with brilliant ideas, schemes and policies; and that once they have decided what they are going to do they tell the civil servants in their various ministries to go and do it believing that it will be done.

Richard Rohmer, public figure, address, "The Runaway Growth of Bureaucracy," Toronto, 14 March 1974, The Empire Club of Canada.

I have to stress that I have very modest expectations of politicians. My definition of good government is that things get worse a little more slowly.

Peter C. Newman, author, address, "The Canadian Revolution," Toronto, 30 November 1995, The Empire Club of Canada.

Government is not a business: If it were, we would not need a government.

Elliott Leyton, anthropologist and criminologist, *Men of Blood: Murder in Everyday Life* (1995, 1996).

The role of government is not simply to stand still or to stand aside. Its role must in fact be to stand with those Canadians having difficulty adjusting to a turbulent world.

Paul Martin, finance minister, Budget Speech, House of Commons, 18 February 1997.

The government should be getting out of the business of being in business.

Ralph Klein, Alberta premier, interviewed on CBC Radio's *This Morning*, 23 March 1998.

Since Confederation, Canadians have repeatedly refused to elect a party running to the right of the governing party.

David Orchard, economic nationalist, "PCs Belong in the Centre," *The Globe and Mail*, 14 March 2001.

And the system truly is unresponsive. Governments continually give us what we do not want, and the opposition abandons its opposition once it becomes the government. Most Canadians, for example, clearly did not want NAFTA, post office closures, the GST, the HST, the metric system, or the loonie. We do not want municipal amalgamations, more cuts to social services, school consolidation, or the wholesale privatization of public assets. But that's what we get, no matter who's in power—and the same is true in most developed nations. Elections change the label on the container, but not the contents. M.P.s and M.L.A.s have become frightened sheep who check their consciences at the door and simply vote the party line. There is more real debate in Canada's taverns than in its Parliament. Since voting makes no difference, fewer and fewer people even bother to vote.

Silver Donald Cameron, columnist, "The Sunlight of the Solstice," *The St. John's Herald*, 12 June 2001.

I would hold that, at this point in history, Canadians are not governed but administered. We are administered on behalf of powers that do not have our standpoint, that are not in fact concerned about the well-being of Canadians. Instead of laws we find frameworks, instead of citizens we find ourselves designated stakeholders. Instead of legitimate expectations of governance we have to deal with a somewhat colonial administration.

Ursula Franklin, scientist and social justice activist, "Legitimate Expectations," *Canadian Perspectives*, winter 2001.

To be one of the best countries in the world, we need a strong national government with a clear vision of a truly great country for all of its citizens. What we don't need is the new Northern Balkan States.

Mel Hurtig, publisher and nationalist, chapter opening, *The Vanishing Country: Is It Too Late to Save Canada?* (2002).

Winston Churchill said people get the government they deserve. Canada is a most undeserving nation.

Bruce Fauman, marketing consultant, characteristic remark, 6 November 2002.

In Quebec, the provincial government is not only a government; it has long been seen as a liberator.

André Pratt, columnist, "Quebec's Quiet Counter-revolution," *The Globe and Mail*, 7 November 2002.

Many Canadians appear to believe that the sole point of constitutional government is the protection of human rights. It is conveniently forgotten that self-government is also a human right. Mesmerized by human rights rhetoric and the blandishments of lawyers and law professors, Canadians have stood by quietly and meekly while the judges hijacked their country.

Robert Ivan Martin, law professor, *The Most Dangerous Branch: How the Supreme Court of Canada Has Undermined Our Law and Our Democracy* (2003).

The member for Davenport said that one of the very important tasks of the leader of the government is to make sure that the opposition is actually well divided. I think, collectively, we have been quite successful…

Jean Chrétien, prime minister, final speech, House of Commons, 6 November 2003, "His Final Speech: 2003," *National Post*, 7 November 2003.

To me government is an organized body that is overseeing the mass destruction of human and non-human life.

Paul Watson, environmental activist, interviewed by John F. Schumaker, "Earth Warrior," *The CCPA Monitor*, December 2003–January 2004.

Underlying the democratic ideal of government by consent of the governed is a consent more profound than exercise of the right to vote and obligation to respect the result; it is the consent of the governed to behave themselves—not so much to honour a social contract with authority nor with abstract society as to honour an understood social contract of fair and just behaviour toward one another.

Jane Jacobs, urban planning critic, *Dark Age Ahead* (2004).

In politics the world over, there is a template for matters of this kind, and it runs like this: 1. Government makes a controversial decision. 2. Tragedy results. 3. Public is outraged. 4. Government backs down.

Ivor Shapiro, researcher, referring narrowly to the rationing of health-care services but applicable broadly to social policy, "Life, at What Price?" *The Walrus*, November 2004. The rural Ontario observation applies: "Disaster precedes reform."

There should be a new operating rule for federal cabinet-making.

The fisheries minister should not come from any region where fish are caught. The agricultural minister should not represent a farming area. The industry minister should not come from grant-hungry Montreal. And no immigration minister should be from Toronto.

Jeffrey Simpson, columnist, "The Slippery Slope of Immigration Politics," *The Globe and Mail*, 15 January 2005.

GOVERNOR GENERAL

When the Governor-General came to town / His lady wore a purple gown, / But when his lordship went away / Her ladyship wore a gown of gray.

Verse written by **David Boyle** in *Uncle Jim's Canadian Nursery Rhymes for Family and Kindergarten Use* (1908).

Man, according to Aristotle, is a political animal, but there is an exception in the case of a Governor General. His views on public policy can only be the views of his Ministers. If he touches on the subject he must confine himself to what may be called Governor-Generalities.

John Buchan, Lord Tweedsmuir, governor general from 1935 to his death in 1940, giving expression to a canny Scottish sense of occasion with a light, deft touch, *Canadian Occasions: Addresses* (1940).

The role of the Governor General is to show how Canadians live to other Canadians—this is what I think I'm here for.

Adrienne Clarkson, governor general, interviewed by Christopher Guly, "Class Act at Rideau Hall," *Forever Young*, July 2003.

A governor general's job is simplicity itself: to radiate the natural enthusiasm of her fellow citizens' enthusiasm for their country; to sharpen that enthusiasm and give it clear voice. It is to speak and enhance the national character, and over the course of her tenure, to defend our allegiance to, and appreciation of, a country that in an angry and frequently tormented world seems exempt from so many of the mischiefs and miseries of the world. How the choice for so plain a task could have been made controversial perplexes me.

Rex Murphy, commentator and columnist, "Shooting Ourselves in the Flag," *The Globe and Mail*, 20 August 2005.

GRATITUDE

Appreciation grows the more it is divided.

Stephen Leacock, humorist, *How to Write* (1943).

In a sense that may seem paradoxical, you outdid yourselves this time because you responded immediately, unanimously, unstintingly and with all conceivable goodness, when no real danger, but merely fear and substantial inconvenience, dogged your refugees for a few days. Our lives did not depend upon you, but you gave us everything nonetheless. We, 9,000 strong, are forever in your debt, and all humanity glows in the light of your unselfish goodness.

Stephen Jay Gould, paleontologist and author, "An Ode to Human Decency," *The Globe and Mail*, 20 September 2001. Gould and his family had their Milan–New York City flight diverted to Halifax on 11 September 2001. Here he is addressing the Haligonians who cared for the thousands of stranded passengers for a few days in the aftermath of the World Trade Center disaster.

I didn't necessarily think it was important to praise a brother. After all, we're talking about family.

George W. Bush, U.S. president, press conference, White House, following a meeting with Prime Minister Jean Chrétien, 24 September 2001, in Barrie McKenna, *The Globe and Mail*, 25 September 2001. Bush was accounting for the egregious omission of any reference to Canada in the speech he had just delivered before a joint sitting of the U.S. Congress—an oversight, claimed Paul Cellucci in his memoirs *Unquiet Diplomacy* (2005), who quoted Bush as saying, "I didn't think it was important to praise a brother; after all, we're talking about family."

How does a person say thank you to a nation? Well, that's something a president can do. And so let me say directly to the Canadian people and to all of you here today who welcomed Americans: Thank you for your kindness to America in an hour of need.

George W. Bush, U.S. president, offering belated thanks to Canadians, particularly in Atlantic Canada, for extending hospitality to stranded American airline passengers following the 9/11 attack, address, Pier 21, Halifax, 1 December 2004, in Brian Laghi and Alan Freeman, "Evoking World War II, Bush Prods Canadians," *The Globe and Mail*, 2 December 2004.

GREAT BRITAIN *See* British Empire; Canada & United Kingdom

GREAT LAKES *See also* Border, Canada–United States; Lakes; Water

As loyal Canadians we are very proud of the Great Lakes, and we think they are exactly where they ought to be. (Laughter.) But are they? Why should there be any Great Lakes as a boundary between Canada and the United States? Why do not other countries have great lakes, a string of them tied together by rivers, but which finally plunge over the Fall at Niagara and over the series of rapids in the St. Lawrence? It is an extraordinary arrangement, and there is nothing in the world to compare with it.

A.P. Coleman, geologist, address, "History of the Great Lakes," Toronto, 29 November 1923, The Empire Club of Canada.

GREATNESS *See also* Excellence; Leadership; Perfection

The search for greatness of spirit has compelled me to work harder—to strive for perfection, knowing it to be unattainable. My quest has brought me great joy while something close to my ideal has been attained. It has kept me young at heart, adventurous, forever seeking, and always aware that the heart and the mind are the true lens of the camera.

Yousuf Karsh, portrait photographer, *Karsh: A Fifty-year Retrospective* (1983).

Everywhere greatness is recognized by acclamation. In Canada it comes by appointment.

Louis Dudek, aphorist, "Can. Lit. Notes," *The Bumper Book* (1986), edited by John Metcalf.

GREED

We are also taught to deny the consequences of greed.

Paul Watson, environmental activist, interviewed by John F. Schumaker, "Earth Warrior," *The CCPA Monitor*, December 2003–January 2004.

Greed … has been severely underestimated and denigrated, unfairly so, in my opinion. It is a motive that has not failed to move me from time to time.

Conrad Black, CEO, interviewed by Peter C. Newman, *Here Be Dragons: Telling Tales of People, Passion, and Power* (2004).

Remember, greed is good for you. It's a very underrated emotion. Greed is good for us. It is the single natural dominant motive of our political, economic, and social behaviour. It is mankind's one honest impulse, and it is the root of all human interaction.

Speech written for tax lawyer Nathan Carter in **Guy Sprung**'s play *Death and Taxes*, noted by J. Kelly Nestruck, "Canada: A People's History of Moral Decay," *National Post*, 17 March 2005.

GREENHOUSE EFFECT *See also* Environmentalism; Global Warming; Kyoto Accord

Global concentrations of greenhouse gases will assuredly increase for most of the next century, no matter what we do, and they will assuredly cause warming.

Lydia Dotto, science commentator, *Storm Warning: Gambling with the Climate of Our Planet* (1999).

Golf courses in southern Ontario were open in December, but ski hills were not.

Stewart Cohen et al., "Regional Adaptation Strategies," *Hard Choices: Climate Change in Canada* (2004), edited by Harold Coward and Andrew J. Weaver.

Hunters in Iqaluit noticed that the past few years had been getting warmer and that it takes longer for the ice to form.

Stewart Cohen et al., "Regional Adaptation Strategies," *Hard Choices: Climate Change in Canada* (2004), edited by Harold Coward and Andrew J. Weaver.

GRETZKY, WAYNE *See also* Hockey

I skate to where the puck is going to be, not where it's been.

Wayne Gretzky, hockey star, quoted in *Let's Do It! A Vision of Canadian Broadcasting Proposed by the CBC to the Federal Task Force on Broadcasting Policy* (1985).

If you remember where you were the day Wayne was traded: 1 point.

Quiz question set by **William Ferguson** and **Ian Ferguson**, *How to Be a Canadian (Even if You Are One)* (2001). The authors are referring to the "day of the trade," 9 August 1988.

GROUP OF SEVEN *See also* Arts & Artists

Before I sit down I am going to give a word of admonition to our friends of the Group of Seven. They continually go further north. They have deserted the Georgian Bay, and I dare say they will emerge at the North Pole some day and give us a more simple type of landscape. They may even reproduce that solitary tree which seems to be their obsession today, but I hope that the public schools will have extended such a degree of education amongst the public in general that they will not mistake that solitary tree for the North Pole itself. (Laughter.)

Wylie Grier, critic, address, "Two Views of Canadian Art," Toronto, 26 February 1925, The Empire Club of Canada.

Now, a last word on modern Canadian art, because tomorrow we shall all be academic. When the last cow is taken from the drawing room and the walls are alive with red maple, yellow birch, blue lakes and sparkling snowscapes, I can hear the young modern painter up north say to his pal, "There's the trail that those old academic Johnnies, the Group of Seven, blazed." (Laughter and applause.)

A.Y. Jackson, artist, address, "Two Views of Canadian Art," Toronto, 26 February 1925, The Empire Club of Canada.

I suppose, when you look back, nobody—no group of painters—has ever covered the country as thoroughly as the Group did, from East to West, North to South. I often said to my old friend Jackson in later years, "Alex, you painted everything in Canada except one place, the Niagara Peninsula." He looked at me and said, "Can you imagine me painting a nice sweet thing with apple blossoms?"

A.J. Casson, painter, address, "Reminiscences of the Group of Seven," Toronto, 14 October 1982, The Empire Club of Canada.

GROWTH *See also* Business; Economics; Progress

I would suggest that we have to look at the way that economics has changed in the last few decades. We have come as a society to equate progress with economic growth. If there is no economic growth, we say that we have stagnated, that we have a crisis, we have a recession. Growth and progress have become equivalent and most of the growth we deal with is in terms of profit. So growth, progress and profit have become interchangeable terms—growth has become an end in itself. If we don't grow, we don't progress. The problem with that is that nothing in the universe continues to grow in that way indefinitely, exponentially. It's a ludicrous kind of notion. If growth becomes an end in itself, then there is no further end.

David Suzuki, scientist and broadcaster, address, "The Challenge of the 21st Century," Toronto, 8 December 1988, The Empire Club of Canada.

Canada's potential is immense. The avenues for realizing that potential are clear. The only missing ingredients are the will to win and the determination not to waste a minute more. The blade is ready. Our northern edge waits to be honed. Using it to maximum advantage is the key to the triumph of Canadians in the global economy of tomorrow.

Thomas P. d'Aquino and **David Stewart-Patterson**, president and vice president, respectively, of the Business Council on National Issues, *Northern Edge: The Will to Win* (2001).

We cannot not know what we have learned. In other words, once we have experienced growth, despite the consequences, there is no going back to how or where we were before.

Barry Shainbaum, speaker, photographer, and author, characteristic observation, 27 July 2005.

GST *See* Goods & Services Tax

GUATEMALA

A good example of what we do now is that we are being asked to work on a vision for the future of Guatemala. How can we design Guatemala over the next ten years?

Bruce Mau, designer, "Designs for Living," *The New York Times Magazine*, 26 September 2004.

GUILT *See also* Law

The real surprise—to me anyway—was not really what I did, but how I felt afterwards. Shocked, of course. But not guilty. You might say, and be right, that the very least a woman can be is shocked when she walks out on a sick and blameless husband after forty years. But to feel no guilt at all—feel nothing, in fact, but simple relief and pleasure—that did seem odd, to say the least.

Celebrated opening sentences of **Constance Beresford-Howe**'s novel *The Book of Eve* (1973).

The most important, the most frequent question I am asked, the question that comes up at my cocktail parties, is: How do we represent a guilty man? There is a simple, quick and complete answer. Our whole system of criminal justice is built on the basic premise that every man is presumed innocent until he is proven guilty beyond a reasonable doubt. His guilt must be shown by evidence produced by a prosecutor in a courtroom—not in a newspaper or broadcast. "Guilty" in this frame of reference is not a moral term. It is a legal term. No one is legally guilty until a judgment of guilt has been made by the court. The lawyer is neither expected nor qualified to make a moral judgment on the person seeking his help. Moral guilt or innocence is no more within the province of the lawyer than within the jurisdiction of the court.

Edward L. Greenspan, advocate, address, "The Role of the Defence Counsel," Toronto, 19 November 1987, The Empire Club of Canada.

GULF WAR *See also* Middle East; War

There is an enormous amount of history here and a great consciousness of history and almost more consciousness of history than there is a willingness to make history.

Joe Clark, minister of External Affairs, discussing the ancient animosities of the Middle East, news conference, Damascus, 11 March 1991, in Rod Goodman, *Toronto Star*, 24 March 1991. It seems Clark is turning Mackenzie King's remark upside down, stating that the Middle East is a region of the world with more history than geography.

GUNS *See* Firearms; Weapons

GZOWSKI, PETER

Cadham: For fifteen years, you and *Morningside* have held us together, set the example, given us a place to connect with one another. Now, what would you suggest that each of us do to make a difference?

Gzowski: I would turn off the TV, cancel the newspapers and magazines, turn off the radio and open the window. I would look out the window and I would say, "Do you realize what an incredible country this is?"

Joan Eyolfson Cadham, interviewer, and Peter Gzowski, interviewee, Peacock Auditorium, Moose Jaw, Sask., the night before the final *Morningside* broadcast on 30 May 1997, as quoted in "The Mail," *Maclean's*, 18 February 2002. The broadcaster added that an observer would see Canadians co-operating and enjoying themselves. "If we just woke up to the beauty of this country, the dignity and gentility and civility of its traditions and its people, by and large, if we just woke up to it and said, 'What the hell are we whining about?' then I think we'd move a long way forward."

If you repeated the contest today to finish the phrase "As Canadian as …" the only answer possible would be "Peter Gzowski."

Ron Karras, Montreal radio listener, in Edna Barker, *Remembering Peter Gzowski: A Book of Tributes* (2002).

If attentiveness had been an academic subject, Gzowski would have had a Ph.D.

Robert Fulford, columnist, in Edna Barker, *Remembering Peter Gzowski: A Book of Tributes* (2002).

Before Homer was a Simpson or a fan, he was a blind Greek poet. Gzowski was our Homer of Homers, a complicated man who apparently chose to be without guile.

Jay Teitel, writer, on the apparent guilelessness of radio personality Peter Gzowski, "The Importance of Being Earnest," *Saturday Night*, April 2002. Teitel explained, "Homers are loyal to the idea of loyalty."

h

HAITI

My own story begins as a young child in another country, one "draped in barbed wire from head to toe," in the powerful words of the Haitian poet-in-exile, René Depestre, who is also my uncle.

Michaëlle Jean, Haitian-born governor general, installation address, Ottawa, 27 September 2005, published in the *Toronto Star*, 28 September 2005.

HALIFAX

Halifax slumbers between wars.

Remark attributed to **Thomas Raddall**, novelist, by Silver Donald Cameron, "War in Halifax," *The Sunday Herald* (Halifax), 13 November 2002.

May it then be recorded; may it be inscribed forever in the Book of Life: Bless the good people of Halifax who did not sleep, who took strangers into their homes, who opened their hearts and shelters, who rushed in enough food and clothing to supply an army, who offered tours of their beautiful city and, above all, who listened with a simple empathy that brought this tough and fully grown man to tears, over and over again. I heard not a single harsh word, saw not the slightest gesture of frustration, and felt nothing but pure and honest welcome.

Stephen Jay Gould, paleontologist and author, "An Ode to Human Decency," *The Globe and Mail*, 20 September 2001. Gould and his family had their Milan–New York City flight diverted to Halifax on 11 September 2001, the day of the World Trade Center disaster.

HALLUCINOGENICS *See also* Drugs & Drug Trade

Huxley: He's a Canadian psychiatrist who works with mescaline.

Maria: But he may have a beard and we may not like him.

Discussion between **Aldous Huxley** and his wife, Maria, about inviting Dr. Humphry Osmond, English-born, Saskatchewan-based psychiatrist and experimenter with mescaline, to stay with them in Hollywood, recalled by Osmond in the essay "May Morning in Hollywood" (1953), *Moksha: Aldous Huxley's Classic Writings on Psychedelics and the Visionary Experience* (1977, 1999), edited by Michael Horowitz and Cynthia Palmer.

HANDICAPS *See* Disabilities

HAPPINESS

We shall never be happier than our honesty allows.

L.S. Cattarini, aphorist, "The Intimation of Destiny" (1986), *Beyond Sartre and Sterility: Surviving Existentialism* (1986, 2002).

I'm the happiest man in the world.

Choi Hong Hi, retired South Korean general, formulator of the principles of the martial art that he named Taekwon-Do in 1955, for 30 years a resident of Mississauga, Ont.; his dying words, Pyongyang, North Korea, 15 June 2002, heard at his bedside by his former student and grandmaster Jong Soo Park; quoted in his obituary by Peter Edwards, *Toronto Star*, 24 June 2002.

I have come to understand that it's only moments that make us happy. Sometimes it's the really simple joys, like going out and finding some peace on a lake or river, or watching my eighteen-month-old sleeping in my arms, or the sound of my children's voices....

Silken Laumann, champion rower, in Barry Shainbaum, *Hope & Heroes: Portraits of Integrity & Inspiration* (2003).

Science doesn't supply happiness; but neither does its lack. The same can be said of social utopias: they aren't created by science, but neither does lack of science provide them.

Jane Jacobs, urban planning critic, *Dark Age Ahead* (2004).

HATE *See also* Anti-Semitism; Holocaust; Genocide; Prejudice; Race & Racism

One of the more important instruments in any counter-terrorism policy is to combat the promotion of hatred, the demonization of the "other"—which, as we saw in Rwanda, can take us down the road to genocide. As the Supreme Court of Canada said in upholding the constitutionality of Canada's anti-hate legislation, "The Holocaust did not begin in the gas chambers, it began with words." Canada, with expertise in combating incitement to hatred, can play an important role in developing this centrepiece of a counter-terrorism law and policy.

Irwin Cotler, professor, Member of Parliament, and human-rights advocate, "Comment," *The Globe and Mail*, 23 October 2001.

The disturbing possibility is that Canada is not an asylum from hatred but an incubator of hatred.

Michael Ignatieff, commentator, "Immigration: The Hate Stops Here," *The Globe and Mail*, 25 October 2001.

That's how Hitler came in. He was going to make damn sure that the Jews didn't take over Germany and Europe. That's why he fried six million of those guys, you know. Jews would have owned the goddamned world. And look what they're doing. They're killing people in Arab countries.... How do you get rid of a disease like that, that's going to take over, that's going to dominate? ... I don't support Hitler. But he cleaned up a hell of a lot of things, didn't he? You would be owned by Jews right now the world over.... My great-grandson goes to school here in Saskatoon. These goddamned immigrants—East Indians, Pakistanis, Afghanistan, whites and so forth—call him a dirty little Indian.... That's what I'm saying. It's starting right there, at six years old.

David Ahenakew, former leader of the Assembly of First Nations, remarks made on 13 December 2002 to a reporter with the Saskatoon *StarPhoenix*, after addressing a meeting devoted to Native rights and health care sponsored by the Federation of Saskatchewan Indian Nations, Saskatoon, in Erin Anderssen, "Native Leader Applauds Hitler," *The Globe and Mail*, 16 December 2002.

HEALING *See also* Health; Medicine

For many years, accounts of cures among primitive peoples by medicine men, shamans and the like aroused little attention among psychiatrists. The development of modern psychotherapy has drawn attention to the mystery of the mechanism of psychological healing and shown how many of its details still puzzle us.

Henri F. Ellenberger, historian and psychiatrist, *The Discovery of the Unconscious* (1970).

A closed mind is locked from the inside.

Adam, a psychic healer ("the DreamHealer," whose last name is withheld), rejecting skepticism of his power to enter into "quantum holograms" to heal people, interviewed by Catharine Tarmas, "Life," *Maclean's*, 12 April 2004.

HEALTH *See also* Addiction; Disease; Doctors; Exercise; Fitness; Healing; Health Care; Hospices; Hospitalization; Medicine; Mental Illness; Pain & Suffering

The first point she would hammer home to young people is that "good health works like compound interest." Start saving early, watch the compound interest grow and you end up wealthy. Einstein called compound interest one of the seven wonders of the world.

Kenneth Walker, physician and columnist (aka Dr. Gifford-Jones), address, "The Healthy Barmaid, The New Minister of Health?" Toronto, 11 April 1996, The Empire Club of Canada.

Physicians prefer to diagnose conditions they can treat rather than those they can't.

Edward Shorter, historian, *A History of Psychiatry: From the Era of the Asylum to the Age of Prozac* (1997).

I'd like to be treated as well as the family dog.

Kenneth Walker, physician and columnist (aka Dr. Gifford-Jones), referring to the care and concern owners lavish on their pets, *"You're Going to Do What?": The Memoirs of Dr. W. Gifford-Jones* (2000).

All of us must realize that our health and wellness are not simply responsibilities of the state. Rather, medicare is a defining aspect of our citizenship.

Roy Romanow, commissioner, Royal Commission on the Future of Health Care in Canada, "Comment," *The Globe and Mail*, 29 November 2002.

Viruses don't have visas. International air travel is just a credit card and an e-ticket away. Where once we might have thought it preposterous, exotic, but extremely virulent viruses are just a few hours away from landing anywhere in Canada.

Dana Hanson, president, Canadian Medical Association, speaking in Ottawa on SARS, 25 June 2003, in Mark Kennedy, "Canada Not Ready for Another Health Crisis: CMA," *National Post*, 26 June 2003.

Zero. A low number, but still a number. It seems to suggest that we human beings are capable of comparing life to death and, sometimes, finding death preferable. It seemed to suggest that there is a place—definable in mathematical terms—where living is worse than dying. In light of the dying I had been witnessing, this possibility no longer seemed far-fetched.

Ivor Shapiro, researcher, contemplating the words "zero quality of life" with respect to the health care of the elderly, "Life, at What Price?" *The Walrus*, November 2004.

I think of my annual checkup as a pre-mortem.

Rob McKenzie, columnist, "Commentary," *National Post*, 19 August 2004.

Health, that greatest of blessings, is what I never truly enjoyed until I saw Fair Canada. The change it has wrought, I am convinced, is truly wonderful.

Horatio Nelson, future British naval hero, on his brief residency in Quebec City, winter 1781, during which period of recuperation from various ills he conducted a romance with a young woman named Mary Simpson; quoted by Bill Twaito, "Nelson's Quebec Love," *National Post*, 20 October 2005.

HEALTH CARE *See also* Health; Medicine

The Premier looked at me, and I was quite certain he was hearing what I was saying. We weren't more than a few feet apart and then he basically turned away from me, and as far as I was concerned the Premier was turning his back on public health.

Richard Schabas, Ontario's chief medical officer of Health (1987–1997), testifying in the Walkerton tainted-water inquiry, in Martin Mittelstaedt, "Walkerton Inquiry: Harris Accused of Snub to Health Watchdog," *The Globe and Mail*, 26 June 2001. As Mittelstaedt explained, "The incident took place in late March of 1997 at a meeting of the powerful policy and priorities committee to cabinet, which is chaired by Mr. Harris and sets the government's overall direction. Dr. Schabas had been sent by Jim Wilson, who was then health minister, to try to make sure the committee would decide to continue to provide almost full funding for health boards. Instead, the government shifted all the cost of public-health boards to municipalities starting in 1998, a course Dr. Schabas worried would make medical officers of health vulnerable to bullying from small-town politicians." Soon after, Dr. Schabas took a leave of absence and then resigned on principle. His testimony, given four years after the incident, effectively concluded Premier Harris's career in public life.

The longer I practise medicine the more I'm convinced there are two kinds of diseases—those we get and those we make. The secret is learning how to prevent the ones we make.

Kenneth Walker, physician and columnist (aka Dr. Gifford-Jones), address, "The Healthy Barmaid, The New Minister of Health?" Toronto, 11 April 1996, The Empire Club of Canada.

Health care in this country is a doctrine before it is a policy. It is not the third rail of Canadian politics. It is the back-up generator of Canadian self-understanding. Health care is the surrogate or default mechanism of Canadian patriotism.

Rex Murphy, broadcaster, address, "Canada after September 11," Toronto, 6 December 2001, The Empire Club of Canada.

There are more than 7,000 people in the federal department of health. The federal department of health delivers health care only to aboriginals. The provinces have the responsibility of delivering health care services to real people in real towns—hospitals, doctors, nurses ... that is our responsibility and that is where the real dollars should be.

Jim Flaherty, Ontario Conservative leadership candidate, Ottawa, 21 January 2002, in Tim Harper, "Flaherty 'Native' Remark Sparks Storm," *Toronto Star*, 22 January 2002. Flaherty's distinction between Native peoples on reserves and "real people in real towns" caused an outcry.

In fact, one of the wonders of the downsizing of hospitals is that, though patient quarters get tighter and tighter, administrative space and doctors' offices get larger and larger.

Mary V. Seeman, psychiatrist, "Schizophrenia: Two Sides of the Mirror," *Queen's Quarterly*, summer 2002.

A new Canadian Health Covenant should be established as a common declaration of Canadians' and their governments' commitment to a universally accessible, publicly funded health care system.

The first of 47 recommendations in *Building on Values: The Future of Health Care in Canada: The Final Report of the Royal Commission on the Future of Health Care in Canada* (2002), led by **Roy J. Romanow**. The conclusion reads: "Medicare is a worthy national achievement, a defining aspect of our citizenship and an expression of social cohesion. Let's unite to keep it so."

The next time an American politician touts the superiority of Canadian care, ask him whether he'd fly to Toronto to have his hip replaced.

Last paragraph of the unsigned editorial "Woe, Canada" that appeared in *The Wall Street Journal*, 3 September 2002.

Canadians view medicare as a moral enterprise, not a business venture. They want their health-care system renovated; they do not want it demolished.

Roy Romanow, commissioner, Royal Commission on the Future of Health Care in Canada, "Comment," *The Globe and Mail*, 29 November 2002.

The U.S. needs a Canadian-style national health-care system. My father had a heart attack, and to pay the bills, our family had to sell our house. Under the Canadian system, we would have inherited it.

Emo Philips, U.S. comedian, characteristic remark on his website, www.emophilips.com, November 2003.

Any rational person would prefer actual health care to a right to health care.

Robert Ivan Martin, law professor, *The Most Dangerous Branch: How the Supreme Court of Canada Has Undermined Our Law and Our Democracy* (2003).

You can buy a new car, you can buy a new house, you can buy clothes for your wife, you can buy clothes for yourself, you can do anything in the world. The only thing you can't do in this country is spend money on your own health care. I think it is wrong.

Ralph Klein, Alberta premier, interview, Council of the Federation, Niagara-on-the-Lake, Ont., 29 July 2004, in April Lindgren and Mark Kennedy, "Klein Predicts Health Meeting 'Gong Show,'" *National Post*, 30 July 2004.

A dollar for health care should be a dollar for health care, and not 90¢ for and 10¢ for someone's profit as an investor.

Lorne Calvert, Saskatchewan premier, interview, Council of the Federation, Niagara-on-the-Lake, Ont., 29 July 2004, in April Lindgren and Mark Kennedy, "Klein Predicts Health Meeting 'Gong Show,'" *National Post*, 30 July 2004.

I'd never argue that U.S. health care is better for everyone. You know the joke. In the U.S. you can get it but you can't necessarily afford it, as in Canada you can afford it, but you can't necessarily get it.

Margaret Wente, columnist, "If My Dad Were Canadian ... He'd Be Dead," *The Globe and Mail*, 30 September 2004.

All it would take to immediately abolish the long lines for cataract surgery is for the Health Minister to decriminalize privately provided medical care. We wouldn't tolerate it if private car-insurance companies had policies that car repairs could only be done at specified repair shops at which the waiting time is two years and it was illegal to get your car repaired somewhere else.

Arnie Aberman, former dean of the University of Toronto School of Medicine, in Margaret Wente, "What Causes Blindness in Ontario? Ideology," *The Globe and Mail*, 19 October 2004.

Health care in Canada is a compromise arrangement between political reality and the vision of Justice Emmett Hall's Royal Commission report in 1964. Hall had proposed comprehensive coverage for medical services, drugs, and home care, and for dental and optical services for kids. The Trudeau government sawed it off at medical services, and some (not a lot) of the rest gets covered (sort of) by some provinces. The 1984 Canada Health Act made it official: to get federal funding, provinces need only cover physicians' and hospitals' services—and only those deemed "medically necessary."

Ivor Shapiro, researcher, "Life, at What Price?" *The Walrus*, November 2004.

For every dollar in the Canadian economy, a dime is spent on health care.

Ivor Shapiro, researcher, "Life, at What Price?" *The Walrus*, November 2004.

Consider that in Quebec and other provinces there are waiting lists in specialized oncology clinics, but none at the veterinarian's office. That's because we are allowed to spend all the money we want to treat the cancer in our dogs, but we aren't allowed to subscribe to a complementary private insurance plan that allows us—that is, human patients—to improve the quality of the oncological care we receive.

Mario Dumont, leader of Action démocratique du Quêbec, address, Calgary, 1 March 2005, reprinted in part as "End the Government Health Care Monopoly," *National Post*, 14 March 2005.

Canada has become a nation in waiting—with the waiting line defining our national identity—waiting for things for which the people of an advanced, industrialized democracy ought not to have to wait.

Preston Manning, founder and leader of the Reform Party, "We Have Become a Nation in Waiting," *The Globe and Mail*, 27 April 2005.

Access to a waiting list is not access to health care.

Beverley McLachlin et al., Justices of the Supreme Court of Canada, Joint Reasons for deciding against the Quebec law that bans private medical insurance, 9 June 2005.

Canada is the only nation other than Cuba and North Korea that bans private health insurance, according to Sally Pipes, head of the Pacific Research Institute in San Francisco and author of a recent book on Canada's health care system.

Editorial, *The Wall Street Journal*, 13 June 2005.

In Canada, parents are allowed to send their children to private schools at their own expense if they choose. By so doing, these parents are paying for education more than once—they are contributing tax dollars to the public education system, thus reducing the attendance without reducing the dollars available. Parallel health care will deliver the same benefits.

Diane Francis, "Comment," *National Post*, 14 June 2005.

HEART

Canada is not a country for the cold of heart or the cold of feet.

Pierre Elliott Trudeau, prime minister, address, National Newspaper Awards Dinner, 8 April 1972. He later recalled his homily at the press conference called to announce his resignation from politics, 9 February 1984.

You've always been a sort of professor fellow. Your heart is in it, and where your heart is, your treasure will be.

Attributed to Prime Minister **W.L. Mackenzie King** to his young aide, James Gibson, former Rhodes Scholar, later president of Brock University, a member of the Department of External Affairs for eight years, as recalled for Caroline Byrne, "Rhodes Scholar Still Tops Class," *The Globe and Mail*, 5 July 2003.

The heart is not a knee, it does not bend.

Line from **Makeda Silvera**'s novel *The Heart Does Not Bend* (2002).

HEAVEN *See also* Stars

Heaven is a great land. In that land are many holes. These holes we call stars.

Elder among the Pallirmiut, in Knud Rasmussen, *Observations on the Intellectual Culture of the Caribou Eskimos* (1930), Volume 7, Number 2, "Report of the Fifth Thule Expedition, 1921–24."

Anyone who has been to Algonquin Park will be disappointed when they get to Heaven.

Ralph Bice, elderly trapper and friend of painter Tom Thomson, in Roy MacGregor, *Escape: In Search of the National Soul of Canada* (2002).

HERITAGE *See also* Architecture; Civilization; History; History: Canadian; Tradition; Past

Greece is still known to us today; her glory has not faded.... [H]er poets expressed her soul in terms so memorable that it passed on to humanity as a most glorious part of itself. Canada will really begin to exist in the eyes of the world and posterity only when she awakens to the tremendous value of art and thought as a means of bringing her own soul into existence. Then she will become a nation. And then only. Our spiritual dependence on colonialism meanwhile will remain evident to all.

Marius Barbeau, folklorist, address, "Folk Songs of French Canada," Toronto, 7 March 1929, The Empire Club of Canada.

So let me give you our definition of a heritage building. Any building that is structurally sound and for which an economically viable use can be found is a heritage building.

Pierre Berton, chair, Heritage Foundation, address, "Heritage Preservation and the Energy Crisis," Toronto, 11 February 1982, Empire Club of Canada.

Heritage helps us understand the past, gives meaning to the present, and influences the future.

Paul Bator, archivist, "Ontario Heritage Foundation Vision" (1994), *Ontario's Heritage: A Celebration of Conservation* (1997).

In a world of great social and ethical strains, and confusion about the very purpose of life, Canadians have an incomparable treasure to contribute—on condition that they preserve what is deep and good and valid in their own heritage.

John Paul II, pope, speech on arrival, Toronto, 23 July 2002, published in the *National Post*, 24 July 2002. The head of the Roman Catholic Church appeared in Toronto to celebrate "World Youth Day," a week-long festival of young Catholics from around the world. It was his third papal visit, the earlier two having been in 1984 and 1987.

HEROES & HEROISM *See also* Idealism; Leadership; Mentoring

Being bored with nihilism is the beginning of heroism.

L.S. Cattarini, aphorist, "The Intimation of Destiny" (2000), *Beyond Sartre and Sterility: Surviving Existentialism* (1986, 2002).

It is not an inferiority complex that makes us diffident towards the individual. It is quite the opposite. We look upon someone who has done something amazingly out of the ordinary and we say, you are good, but you are no better than the rest of us.

Wayne Grady, author, *Chasing the Chinook: On the Trail of Canadian Words and Culture* (1998).

We must examine all texts—novels, poems, plays, religious, journalistic, and legal materials—to begin to determine the lives of our "martyrs" in colonial, modern, and postmodern Canada, and to begin to hear their voices speaking back to us.

George Elliott Clarke, scholar, "Raising Raced and Erased Executions in African-Canadian Literature," *Racism, Eh?: A Critical Inter-Disciplinary Anthology of Race and Racism in Canada* (2004), edited by Camille A. Nelson and Charmaine A. Nelson.

HISTORY *See also* Heritage

This very novelty is an inspiration. This very lack of history is the foundation of history itself. We can begin at the beginning.

Stephen Leacock, humorist and historian, *Canada: The Foundations of Its Future* (1941).

In other words the cart doesn't go before the horse. Not at all. The horse, the mass of human intelligence, draws along the cart of history in which stands the professor, looking backward and explaining the scenery. This is not said unkindly. If he looked forward he wouldn't see any more than the horse does; and the horse sees nothing.

Stephen Leacock, humorist, *My Remarkable Uncle* (1942).

Perhaps no truly objective history of anything is ever popular.

Elwy Yost, film enthusiast, *Magic Moments at the Movies* (1979).

The great thing about professional historians is that, if the scholars are any good, the questions they ask invariably are easy ones. The impossible questions are asked by amateurs and bad scholars, for they ask things that cannot be answered.

Donald Harman Akenson, historian, *Surpassing Wonder: The Invention of the Bible and the Talmuds* (1998).

Sound history, accurate history, interesting history—local or national—cannot be reconstructed through the distorting lens of a single identity. "Identities are not like hats," Linda Colley has wisely observed. "Human beings can and do put on several at a time."

Ramsay Cook, historian, "'Identities Are Not Like Hats,'" *Canadian Historical Review*, June 2000. He is quoting Linda Colley, Princeton scholar, in Australian historian Inga Clendinnen, *Reading the Holocaust* (1999).

The amazing thing about history is not that it so often repeats itself, but that it fails to bore us.

Irena F. Karafilly, aphorist, characteristic expression, 7 November 2000.

History is fascinating. Why wouldn't it be? It's mathematically impossible to have 30 million people and not have an interesting history, if you think about it.

Mark Starowicz, TV producer, address, "The Canadian Experience," Toronto, 28 June 2001, The Empire Club of Canada.

What you learn from the study of history is that no one learned from the study of history.

James Bacque, researcher and novelist, characteristic remark, 27 May 2003.

History thickens daily existence and gives life meaning by linking us with chains of ancestors. History, if understood even a little, becomes the background against which we enact our lives.

Robert Fulford, commentator, "A Box Full of History: TV and Our Sense of the Past," *Queen's Quarterly*, spring 2005.

HISTORY: CANADIAN *See also* Heritage

Keeping the Americans out, the French in, and trying to get the Natives to somehow disappear.

Three themes in Canadian history attributed to **Will Ferguson** in *Why I Hate Canadians* (1997), according to Paul Lavoie, "How to Reinvent the Brand," *The Globe and Mail's Report on Business*, May 2001.

Really, who cares about the history of housemaid's knee in Belleville in the 1890s? And the way they write—trying to make historians sound like economists or political scientists—guarantees no one will listen to them.

J.L. Granatstein, historian, in Christopher Moore, "Jack Granatstein: The Organized Man," *The Beaver*, April–May 1991. The reference to "the history of housemaid's knee in Belleville" sounds a tocsin for the return of "old" traditional, national, non-partisan, political, and military history which, on every front, is in danger of being overtaken by "new" local, social, partisan, and micro-studies largely prompted by emphases such as feminism and multiculturalism. The "housemaid's knee" reference is now a catchphrase among historians for a concern for trivia at the expense of narrative.

So who killed Canadian history? Who are the guilty people? You and me by not paying attention to what was going on in the schools we sent our children to, by voting for school trustees and MPPs who have literally no interest in education.Who can resurrect Canadian history? Again you and me by demanding changes, by voting for those who promise to restore the past, the understanding of the past for the present, because if we can do that, then maybe we just might have a future.

J.L. Granatstein, historian, address, "Who Killed Canadian History?" Toronto, 17 September 1998, The Empire Club of Canada.

We do have a history and we do need to study it and to learn from it. Canadians have worked together to build a nation, a nation that is far stronger than the misguided fools who would try to tear it down. We made a nation by working together, by doing great deeds in the past, knowing we can do more in the future—the usual definition of a nation. We need to know this for if we kill Canadian history, we will surely destroy our present and future.

J.L. Granatstein, historian, address, "Who Killed Canadian History?" Toronto, 17 September 1998, The Empire Club of Canada.

Canadian history is neither dead nor even seriously wounded; it is alive, well, even thriving as it becomes increasingly inclusive of all its past actors.

Ramsay Cook, historian, "'Identities Are Not Like Hats,'" *Canadian Historical Review*, June 2000.

Canadian history is not boring, or marginal to the world. In fact, how we didn't become Yugoslavia or Northern Ireland is a far more intriguing historical mystery than Napoleon, and far more pertinent to the modern world. The children of the defeated and the marginalized possess one of the most relevant histories in the global era.

Mark Starowicz, TV producer, "The Death of History," *The Globe and Mail*, 20 September 2000.

The problem with Canada is that most storytellers are not very good.

Jacques Godbout, novelist and filmmaker, contrasting storytellers with historians, interviewed by Christine Pochmursky, Documentary Channel's *Masterpieces*, 13 August. 2003.

The Canada of the present has an umbilical cord linking it to the Canada of the past, with its history of violence against the First Peoples, the enslavement of people of African descent, institutional discrimination against racialized communities and political dominance and cultural hegemony by Anglophones.

Anver Saloojee, political scientist, "Social Cohesion and the Limits of Multiculturalism in Canada," in *Racism, Eh? A Critical Inter-Disciplinary Anthology of Race and Racism in Canada* (2004), edited by Camille A. Nelson and Charmaine A. Nelson.

HITLER, ADOLF *See also* Dictatorship; Fascism; World War II

Hitler … will rank some day with Joan of Arc among the deliverers of his people, & if he is only careful may yet be the deliverer of Europe.… He impressed me as a man of deep sincerity and a genuine patriot.

W.L. Mackenzie King, prime minister, impression of Adolf Hitler following their meeting in Berlin, recorded by King in his diary, 27 March 1938, and quoted by C.P. Stacey, *A Very Double Life: The Private World of Mackenzie King* (1976). King continued to rhapsodize on Hitler, as noted by Irving Abella and Harold Troper, *None Is Too Many* (1983): "very sincere man … sweet … although he was clearly a dreamer and gave the impression of having an artistic temperament." After the war King entertained second thoughts: "Hitler might come to be thought of as one of the saviours of the world. He had the chance at Nuremberg, but was looking to Force, to Might, and to Violence as means to achieving his ends, which were, I believe, at heart, the well being of his fellow-man; not all fellow-men, but those of his own race."

Can we doubt, knowing of his devotion to the Master of Bayreuth, knowing of his impressionable and highly romantic nature, that Hitler sees himself as a knight in shining armour, appearing like Lohengrin at the most critical moment of Germany's history, to rescue her, as Lohengrin rescued Elsa, from slander, torture and death? … Premonitions of his approaching death, said to be familiar to members of his entourage, and hinted at in his speech of September 1, 1939, lead one to suppose that he may regard the present holocaust in the light of a sort of *Götterdämmerung* with the whole of Europe afire as a funeral pyre for Adolf Hitler.

Sir Ernest MacMillan, musician and musicologist, address, "Hitler and Wagernism," Vancouver Institute, October 1939, *Queen's Quarterly*, summer 1941. Ezra Shabas, writing in *Sir Ernest MacMillan: The Importance of Being Canadian* (1996), finds this a prophecy "almost precisely foretelling what was to come."

In Canada, for example, there are 2.6 persons per square mile; in other countries perhaps 16, 18, 20, or 26 persons. Well, no matter how stupidly one managed one's affairs in such a country, a decent living would still be possible.

Adolf Hitler, German dictator, observation about the relationship between demographics and economics, Berlin speech, 10 December 1940, *Hitler's Words* (1944), edited by Gordon W. Prange.

They are upon us, the prophets, minor and major! / Madame Yolanda rubs the foggy crystal. / She peers, she ponders, the future does engage her; / She sees the *Fuehrer* purged by Nazi pistol.

Lines from **A.M. Klein**'s poem "Psalm XXV," *Poems* (1944). The Montreal poet thus predicted the way Adolf Hitler, leader of the Nazi party and German dictator, would end his life, 30 April 1945. Klein wrote "Psalm XXV" in 1940; it first appeared in print in the magazine *Opinion*, October 1941.

Jews are forbidden to give Hitler a posthumous victory.

Emil L. Fackenheim, rabbi and philosopher at the University of Toronto, one of the most widely quoted injunctions of the era, first uttered in 1967. Fackenheim discusses the statement in "To Mend the World," *Viewpoints: The Canadian Monthly*, October–November 1985. The Torah, the Hebrew Bible, has a total of 613 commandments; Fackenheim—or the Holocaust—added one new one.

But when EU leaders proudly proclaim that war has finally been banished from the European political arsenal, this could ironically be the grandest of Hitler's legacies.

Modris Eksteins, historian, referring to the European Union that rose from the ashes of World War II, "Humanity's Curse," *National Post*, 30 April 2005.

HOBBIES *See also* Gardens & Gardening; Leisure; Sports

But Germany did not want to let him out and the United States did not want to let him in.

Fortunately, he managed to finagle an invitation for a three-week ski vacation to Canada. He arrived to Halifax on New Year's Day 1937. All he had with him was a $200 camera and a suitcase which contained a complete magician's kit of tricks: rings, coloured handkerchiefs and the like. A puzzled customs officer asked, "Why the hell does a skier need all this?" Heinz, who then hardly spoke any English, calmly replied, "A man's got to have a hobby."

Thomas A. Ban, historian of medicine, referring to German-born refugee Heinz E. Lehmann, who joined the Verdun Protestant Hospital outside Montreal where he introduced the first therapeutically effective antipsychotic and antidepressant drugs in North America in the 1950s, recalled in "My Personal Notes on Heinz," address to 12th Annual New York State Office of Mental Health Research Conference, 7 December 1999.

HOCKEY

We endeavour to keep ourselves in good humour, health and spirits by an agreeable variety of useful occupation and amusement. Till the snow fell, the game of hockey played on ice was the morning's sport. They were invariably joined by the officers. By thus participating in their amusements, the men became more attached to us, at the same time that we contributed to their health and cheerfulness.

Sir John Franklin, Arctic explorer, 2nd Arctic Expedition, winter camp, now known as Fort Franklin, Great Bear Lake, N.W.T., letter of 1825, addressed to the British geologist Roderick Murchison, in Randy Boswell, "Franklin Missive Mentions Hockey," *Ottawa Citizen*, 3 May 2003. Various Canadian cities claim the honour of being "the birthplace of ice hockey": Kingston, Ont., in 1843; Windsor, N.S., in 1844; Montreal, Que., in 1875. Certainly the basic rules and regulations were established with a match at Montreal's Victoria Skating Rink, 3 March 1875. But perhaps pride of place should go to Fort Franklin, N.W.T.

Began to skate this year, improved quickly and had great fun at hockey on the ice.

Arthur Henry Freeling, British military engineer stationed at Kingston, U.C., January 1843, letter, in Randy Boswell, "Franklin Missive Mentions Hockey," *Ottawa Citizen*, 3 May 2003. This letter includes a very early reference to the winter sport and is the basis of Kingston's claim to be "the birthplace of ice hockey."

He shoots! He scores!

Foster Hewitt, sports broadcaster, covering overtime play in the hockey match at Toronto's Mutual Street Arena between the Maple Leafs and the Boston Bruins, 1:45 A.M., 4 April 1933. The player is the Leafs' Ken Doraty, who scored the winning goal. Rather than a shout, the four words were an exhausted murmur from a tired Hewitt. Thus was born a legend that united the worlds of hockey and broadcasting.

One of my predecessors in office expressed it very well when an American fan once asked him, "Why do you people have that silly arrangement with two intermissions? Every sensible game only has one." He said, "We have two to enable the customers to rest up."

Clarence Campbell, resident, National Hockey League, address, "Hockey as a Business and as a Career," Toronto, 21 March 1936, The Empire Club of Canada.

If you can't lick 'em in the alley, you can't beat 'em on the ice.

Conn Smythe, hockey personality, interviewed by Trent Frayne in 1952, according to Bob Pennington in *Toronto Star*, 1 October 1973. The remark seems to equate manly qualities of hockey players with violence on the ice.

And the man called Richard had something of the passionate glittering fatal alien quality of snakes.

William Faulkner, novelist, Madison Square Garden, describing the glare of hockey personality Henri (Rocket) Richard, as noted by Andy O'Brien, *Rocket Richard* (1961), and Jean-Marie Pellerin, *Maurice Richard: L'idole d'un peuple* (1976). The quotation, said to originate in *Sports Illustrated* in 1951, has not been found there.

When I scored that final goal, I finally realized what democracy was all about.

Paul Henderson, left-winger on Team Canada, scoring at the last minute the winning goal against the Soviet team, Moscow's Luzhniki Stadium, 28 September 1972. Hockey commentator Dick Beddoes attributed the words to Henderson, *Hockey Night in Minsk* (1972).

Canada 6, Russia 5.

William Hutt, actor, unofficially announcing the outcome of the Team Canada–USSR Summit Series from the stage of the Stratford Festival at a student matinee performance of *King Lear*, 28 September 1972. According to Richard Ouzounian, "Taking a Final Bow," *Toronto Star*, 10 April 2005: "Hutt sensed the audience would all rather be elsewhere, but he soldiered bravely ahead as the mad king. Just before the famous storm sequence, Hutt heard in the wings that Paul Henderson had scored the decisive goal. He played through the scene with full passion, then, at the conclusion, turned to the people and simply said, 'Canada 6, Russia 5.' The crowd went wild."

How would you like a job where, every time you make a mistake, a big red light goes on and 18,000 people boo?

Jacques Plante, goalkeeper, first professional player to don a protective face mask in 1959; remark recalled after his death in Switzerland, 26 February 1986.

The more rabid sports chauvinists conveniently ignore the fact that many hockey players, including some of the game's gods, also loved baseball. Lionel Conacher even died playing ball, but then that would only confirm nationalist suspicions about the game.

John Bell, editor, discussing prejudices against baseball's popularity, introduction, *The Grand-Slam Book of Canadian Baseball Writing* (1993).

Now that I have been away from pro hockey for six weeks, I realize that players in the NHL don't play what I call hockey. Rather, they play NHL hockey. There's a huge difference.

David Bidini, guitarist, traveller, and amateur hockey player, *Tropic of Hockey: My Search for the Game in Unlikely Places* (2000).

Hockey is one of the things we all do here—like rugby to the Welsh, cattle to the Masai, qat to the Yemenis. It just wouldn't be the same without the Habs.

Norman Webster, columnist, on the decline of the Montreal Canadiens hockey team, known as the Habs and winners of 24 Stanley Cups (and lately as the "Hab nots" and "hapless Habs," "Hockey Plight in Canada," *The Globe and Mail*, 22 December 2000.

Hockey takes more diligence, more discipline, and more true grit than any other game. Almost nothing in sport is more devastating than a perfectly legal, open-ice body check. (To experience the sensation, just close your eyes and run into a post at full speed.) It is the sport that most rewards players who simply will not give in.

Norman Webster, columnist, "Hockey Plight in Canada," *The Globe and Mail*, 22 December 2000.

Team motto: "Winning isn't everything!" The Leafs are sometimes erroneously referred to as the "Maple Laffs," but that would suggest a certain entertainment value. Famous for not quite winning.

William Ferguson and **Ian Ferguson**, writers, *How to Be a Canadian (Even if You Are One)* (2001).

The recognition factor still overwhelms. Everywhere I go in this country people know who I am, and it's for one reason: I'm on *Hockey Night in Canada*.

Dick Irvin, hockey personality and regular on CBC-TV's *Hockey Night in Canada*, in Chris Zelkovich, "50 Years of *Hockey Night in Canada*," *Toronto Star*'s *StarWeek*, 6 October 2001.

Hockey does not promote civic engagement. It destroys it.

Margaret Wente, columnist, "Counterpoint: It's Okay to Hate Hockey," *The Globe and Mail*, 10 January 2002.

If hockey players don't start out as toothless morons, they'll probably wind up that way.

Margaret Wente, columnist, "Counterpoint: It's Okay to Hate Hockey," *The Globe and Mail*, 10 January 2002.

Hockey, per se, is obviously a big part of what makes us us.

Stephen Brunt, columnist, in Margaret Wente, "Counterpoint," *The Globe and Mail*, 10 January 2002. Wente added, "As for my esteemed colleague, Mr. Brunt: Who you calling us, white man?"

These Canadians are an ambivalent lot—one minute they want to be peacekeepers, next minute they punch the hell out of each other on the ice rink.

Ken Wiwa, columnist, "Am I Canadian?" *The Globe and Mail*, 1 July 2003.

"She shoots! She scores!"

Amusing opening line of **Robert J. Sawyer**'s short story "The Stanley Cup Caper," set in Toronto in the near future, published in the *Toronto Star*, 24 August 2003.

I have no choice but to announce the formal cancellation of play for 2004–2005. This is a sad, regrettable day that all of us wish could have been avoided.

Gary Bettman, NHL commissioner, announcement, press conference, New York City, 16 February 2004, quoted in *The Globe and Mail*, 17 February 2004.

Most of the guys that wear them are Europeans or French guys, and you cannot have half the League have them and [half] not.

Don Cherry, hockey commentator, in conversation with Ron MacLean on the "Coach's Corner" segment of CBC-TV's *Hockey Night in Canada*, 24 January 2004. Cherry's implication was that NHL players who wore visors were cowards. The remark was recalled by Jeff Gray, *The Globe and Mail*, 5 February 2004, once the CBC and the Commissioner of Official Languages took exception to it as possibly "anti-French." No one seemed concerned that it might be "anti-European."

To all those people who want a more open game, but who want the rules mostly the same, I suggest we go back to an NHL where players are 5 foot 10 ¾, 175 pounds and play two-minute shifts. Because if we don't, nothing much else is going to happen.

Ken Dryden, hockey personality, "Saving the Game," *The Globe and Mail*, 27 March 2004.

Hockey has always been dead-square, mainstream Canadian. But hockey is at risk today of becoming an extreme sport, with excitement and danger, thrills and spills, but without the same emotional, in-the-bone connection. Something to watch, not something to do yourself. Something to be amazed about, not something to identify with. Something other, not something me.

Ken Dryden, hockey personality, "Saving the Game," *The Globe and Mail*, 27 March 2004.

There is only one real sport in Canada. It is called hockey. Regardless of any trivia question, the answer is "Wayne Gretzky."

Quotation from the listing of "Canuckisms" in the booklet *How to Speak Canadian, Eh?* part of "Go Canadian," a package of travel gear designed for Americans who wish to travel abroad "as Canadians," issued by the t-shirtking.com, a New Mexico–based manufacturer, on 12 November 2004, 10 days following the re-election of U.S. President George W. Bush.

It must be understood that the appeal of hockey for Canadians extends way beyond a game: it is the only sanctioned outlet for both an otherwise repressed violent streak, and a secret appreciation for grace and beauty that would be deemed an admission of sissyhood if lavished on, say, dance. In brief, hockey equals group therapy.

Bruce McCall, Canadian-born New York humorist, "O Canada! That Fractured, Frosty Land," *The New York Times*, 21 November 2004.

Owner Peter Pocklington wanted to sell the Edmonton Oilers a few years back and reporters asked him what would become of a major city without an NHL team.

"It wouldn't be so bad," he reportedly said. "We'd be Toronto."

Anecdote about **Peter Pocklington** recalled from the year of the sale, 1988, by **Linda Diebel**, "Why Do They Hate Toronto?" *Toronto Star*, 6 February 2005.

Only from ashes does a phoenix arise. Only from ashes might emerge a sport with new leadership that stops taking its audience for granted, improves the on-ice product, and creates an economic structure that works for franchises, players, and fans.

Jeffrey Simpson, columnist, finding some value in the cancelled 2004–2005 hockey season, "NHL Hockey Is Dead, Long Live Hockey," *The Globe and Mail*, 12 February 2005.

Canadians will have to decide whether hockey is a habit or a passion.

Ken Dryden, former hockey star and federal Liberal minister, referring to the long lockout that brought about the cancellation of the 2004–2005 hockey season, quoted on *CBC Radio News*, 16 February 2005.

Whenever the NHL gets back to playing hockey, the league will be smaller, poorer and less noticed. And perhaps, once again, it will be ours.

Raymond J. de Souza, columnist, "Seventeen Years Later, Hockey Comes Down to Earth," *National Post*, 23 February 2005.

When you come right down to it, this is a labour dispute between billionaires and billionaires.

Bobby Hull, hockey personality, referring to the 301-day lockout by owners of players, in Christopher Grosskurth, *CBC Radio News*, 13 July 2005.

HOLIDAYS *See also* Christmas

Holidays are the greatest learning experience unknown to man.

Frank Ogden, futurist, *obiter dictum*, fall 1983.

Canada Day

What's the difference between Dominion Day and Independence Day, between the First of July and the Glorious Fourth? ... not much—only forty-eight hours.

James Eayrs, political scientist, "Canadianism: Back and Forth on the National Swing," *Toronto Star*, 3 July 1975.

Christmas *See* Christmas

Easter

Life can begin again! That is the central message of Easter, on which all the rest is commentary. Rebirth is possible, both for the individual and for society as a whole. And this is why Easter always belongs to all people, not just to those who call themselves Christians.

Tom Harpur, author and minister, *Harpur's Heaven and Hell* (1983).

New Year's Day

Cheer up! Happy New Year! All the good people don't die young. Lots of them live to a ripe old age and die poor.

Bob Edwards, publisher, *Calgary Eye Opener*, 1 January 1910.

New Year's Eve

When I go I'm going to take New Year's with me.

Guy Lombardo and his Royal Canadians, who greeted the New Year from the main ballroom of New York's Waldorf-Astoria on radio and television from the 1930s through to the year before his death in 1977.

For most of the Western world, New Year's Eve is the only completely secular night festival besides Halloween, and it is celebrated with the same excess and revelry as was the Roman Saturnalia.

Christopher Dewdney, poet and author, *Acquainted with the Night: Excursions through the World after Dark* (2004).

I forget who quipped that an optimist stays up until midnight to see in the New Year while a pessimist stays up to make sure the Old Year leaves.

Ken Wiwa, columnist, "Will Compassion Endure When the Passion Passes?" *The Globe and Mail*, 8 January 2005.

Remembrance Day

Unlike troops returning from the First and Second World Wars, who received enthusiastic official receptions upon their arrival home, Canadian Forces on peacekeeping duty do not receive such a welcome back. It is quite a letdown for those who have been wounded to have risked their lives not to be granted some public recognition. On Remembrance Day we remember those killed in both world wars and in Korea. Why do we not also honour those killed on peacekeeping duty?

Fred Gaffen, historian, *In the Eye of the Storm: A History of Canadian Peacekeeping* (1987).

St. Jean Baptiste Day

I, myself, no longer celebrate the holiday of Saint Jean on the 24th. It is too depressing.

Hélène Jutras, commentator, *Québec Is Killing Me* (1995), translated by Jutras and Michael Gnarowski.

Thanksgiving

Forgiveness and celebration are at the heart of community. These are the two faces of love. Celebration is a communal experience of joy, a song of thanksgiving.

Jean Vanier, founder of L'Arche movement, *Community and Growth: Our Pilgrimage Together* (1979).

Victoria Day

The twenty-fourth of May / Is the Queen's Birthday; / If you don't give us a holiday, / We'll all run away.

Traditional ball-bouncing rhyme, once known to generations of Canadian children, quoted in this form by **Sara Jeannette Duncan** in her novel *The Imperialist* (1904), which is based on her contemporary society in Brantford, Ont. The date marked the anniversary of the birth of Queen Victoria with a statutory holiday on the Monday closest to 24 May. The rhyme (and the fireworks) have outlived both that monarch and the British Empire.

I have every reason for feeling very much at home in Canada. I was born in Buffalo on the 24th of May—(laughter and applause)—and whenever the day came around I always used to cross the river into Canada and let you celebrate my birthday by shooting off firecrackers for the Queen. (Laughter.)

Harry Emerson Fosdick, American preacher and author, address, "A Challenge of International Relations," Toronto, 27 April 1927, The Empire Club of Canada. Fosdick was well aware that Canadians have long celebrated the Queen's Birthday and Empire Day on 24 May.

Any nation that continues to celebrate Queen Victoria's birthday eighty-five years after the sour-duck breathed her last must hold in its psychic cupboard of toys any number of archaic baubles that can't help but render ineffective any emergent sense of a distinctly Canadian national identity.

Stephen Brook, English travel writer, *Maple Leaf Rag: Travels across Canada* (1987).

HOLLYWOOD *See also* Celebrities; Cinema

Sound by Douglas Shearer.

Line of credit on more than one hundred feature films released by MGM in Hollywood between 1925 and 1968, acknowledging the mastery of the sound-recording techniques of Douglas Shearer, brother of movie star Norma Shearer, as noted by Charles Foster, *Stardust and Shadows: Canadians in Early Hollywood* (2000). After receiving one dozen Academy Awards, he shared the 13th Oscar with MGM's entire research department.

Isn't it super cool that "America's sweetheart" was a Canadian....

Beatrice Lillie, comedienne, *Every Other Inch a Lady* (1972). She was referring to Mary Pickford with whom she attended Gladstone Avenue School in Toronto.

A tourist in Paris or Rome, roaming the streets and parks and wide piazzas, catching the slipstream of crowds, is also in those moments a citizen, a Parisian or Roman; a tourist in Hollywood is always a rank outsider. Only in the movie theatres do we become full-fledged citizens of Hollywood. In the place itself we are alienated, displaced—the only Hollywood communion is virtual. It is also one that can be savoured the world over. For it is nowhere and yet everywhere at once.

Justine Brown, academic, *Hollywood Utopia* (2002).

The late president Ronald Reagan, on a visit to Canada, told Parliament that twenty percent of the American entertainment industry was Canadian, and that number has only grown.

Murray White, correspondent, "Hollywood Canuck Pioneers," *Toronto Star*, 20 June 2004.

HOLOCAUST *See also* Anti-Semitism; Genocide; Jewish Culture

The Holocaust is the ultimate crime, the systematic elimination of a people, a negation of human conscience and dignity. Jews cannot be reproached for being traumatized. This unspeakable tragedy cannot undergo comparisons.

Lucien Bouchard, Quebec premier, resignation speech, National Assembly, Quebec City, 11 January 2001, in Sean Gordon, "A Dream Unfulfilled," Montreal *Gazette*, 12 January 2001. Bouchard was referring to "comparative quantification of the suffering of the Jewish people" with that of Quebeckers within Canada.

The Holocaust did not begin in the gas chambers; it began with words.

Irwin Cotler, Member of Parliament and activist, in Robert Fife, "UN Promotes Systematic Hatred of Jews, M.P. Says," *National Post*, 2 April 2002.

Montreal today has the world's third-largest community of Holocaust survivors.

Ingrid Peritz, journalist, "Guardian of Yiddish Culture Dies," *The Globe and Mail*, 17 December 2003. The article paid tribute to the late Dora Wasserman who established in Montreal the only resident Yiddish theatre in North America at the time.

We are the generation that saw and survived the Holocaust. We must therefore be the generation that rails most vigilantly against the intolerance that produced it.

Rosalie Abella, justice, Supreme Court of Canada, *I Am Jewish: Personal Reflections Inspired by the Last Words of Daniel Pearl* (2004), edited by Judea and Ruth Pearl.

It's like looking at headlines before you've had your first cup of coffee in the morning, then setting the paper aside. It's only when you've had a couple of cups of coffee and sit down again with the paper that the headlines begin to have meaning.

Gerald Tulchinsky, historian, reflecting on the reluctance of both Jews and Gentiles to face the enormity and the import of the Holocaust, in Michael Valpy, "Anti-Semitism," *The Globe and Mail*, 26 March 2005.

HOMELESSNESS *See also* Charity; Food Banks; Poverty

Caves and the cave man. Slums and the slum dwellers. Wherein lies the difference in their conditions of life? Hardships are the same in all ages: the passing of centuries does not make them easier to endure or man better able to endure them. The cave man of old was, if you will, a victim of circumstances struggling to better himself against conditions that were not of his making. And civilization itself is surely nothing more than a purposeful improvement of the conditions in which men live: a steady upbuilding of the health of mind and body and spirit through intelligently organized human effort.

Herbert Bruce, lieutenant-governor of Ontario, address, "Civilization and the Cave Man," Toronto, 17 March 1937, The Empire Club of Canada.

Some of the conditions in Toronto shelters are worse than in refugee camps in Rwanda, in terms of space, sanitation and preventative health care practices.

Rick Wallace, former UN aid worker and author, with health researcher Dr. Stephen Hwang, of a report on shelters for the Toronto Disaster Relief Committee, in Jane Jacobs, *Dark Age Ahead* (2004).

HOMES

In the United States, the title of Thomas Wolfe's *You Can't Go Home Again* has entered the common language. In Canada, one would be more accurate to say *You must go home again.*

George Fetherling, editor, preface, *The Vintage Book of Canadian Memoirs* (2001).

Big houses for small lives are sad things.

Kelvin Browne, museum curator, "Maintaining Design Integrity Worthwhile," *National Post*, 17 February 2005.

HOMOSEXUALITY *See also* Freedom; Same-sex Marriage; Sex

But to the Indian, a homosexual is one of the most gifted persons there is. I think all shamans are homosexual or, anyway, bisexual.

Norval Morrisseau, Native artist, "My Name Is Norval Morrisseau," *The Art of Norval Morrisseau* (1979), by Lister Sinclair and Jack Pollock.

The discriminating homosexual has far more appreciation of beautiful women than the macho moron who is constantly chinning himself on his own sexuality.

Edward O. Phillips, novelist, *Buried on Sunday* (1986).

I may have to go on calling myself a lesbian into great old age, not because it is any longer true but because it takes such a long time to make the simple point that I have the right to be.

Jane Rule, novelist and essayist, "Hindsight," *A Hot-eyed Moderate* (1986).

The homosexual man has the possibility in society to live an erotic life, period.

Scott Symons, novelist and cultural commentator, interviewed in *The Idler*, May–June 1990.

The campaign for supposed Gay rights is to a large extent a middle-class battle, one supported by money and market because money and the market believes in low taxes and low morals.

Michael Coren, author and broadcaster, "Gay Marriage," *All Things Considered: Collected Columns and Essays* (2001).

One of the more tedious aspects of life in Canada today is being subjected to relentless homosexual propaganda.... Nowadays, it seems that the love which once dared not speak its name seldom shuts up.

Robert Ivan Martin, law professor, *The Most Dangerous Branch: How the Supreme Court of Canada Has Undermined Our Law and Our Democracy* (2003).

So beautiful you'd think the architect was gay.

First line of text of a full-page advertisement for "Spire: The Condominium" placed by the builder (a group named Context: Different by Design) in *fab: The Gay Scene Magazine*, 25 March 2004.

And I have to admit that Elinor and I have a novel relationship. We have both known a number of men, although Elinor feels a little bit naughty about talking double digits.

Lines spoken by a male character in **Edward O. Phillips**'s novel *A Voyage on Sunday* (2004).

If the all-knowing, all-powerful God didn't wish to make me a lesbian, then why didn't he make someone else in my place?

Irshad Manji, television personality and proponent of the Islamic tradition of *ijtihad* (questioning), *The Trouble with Islam: A Muslim's Call for Reform in Her Faith* (2004).

HONESTY *See also* Authenticity; Integrity; Lies; Truth

The road each of us follows should be as crooked or straight as our honesty demands.

L.S. Cattarini, aphorist, "The Intimation of Destiny" (1993), *Beyond Sartre and Sterility: Surviving Existentialism* (1986, 2002).

HOPE *See also* Optimism

Hope for the best and then hustle for it.

Bob Edwards, publisher, *Calgary Eye Opener*, 9 March 1912.

The world is really not worse than it was—(hear, hear); or if it is, it is only because the individuals in it are worse, less confident, less energetic, less self-reliant, less disposed to perform their tasks as individuals in the world. Personally I believe the world just as good a place as it ever was, and that everything is in the way you look at it.

B.K. Sandwell, professor of English, address, "On Being Sorry for Ourselves," Toronto, 24 January 1924, The Empire Club of Canada.

Our hope is that our hearts of stone will be changed into hearts of flesh. Our hope is that in confrontation to violence we will find new forms of love, non-violence in the spirit of Mahatma Gandhi, who himself lived in the spirit of the Beatitudes. Unless we adopt these new forms of action, unless we share radically and do not let our bank balances mount up, mount up, mount up, unless we share, unless we become as creative in the political life and as creative in the social domain and as creative in the domain of creating homes for the handicapped, creative in the ways we can help other countries, creative in our social problems and in finding work for those who have no work, unless we have the same creativity which we use in industry and in publicity, we will continue on the downhill road which will lead to greater violence and greater despair.

Jean Vanier, humanitarian, address, "A World in Violence: Eruption to Hope?" Toronto, 11 February 1971, The Empire Club of Canada.

It is time to make this nation a place of great hopes once again.

Paul Martin, finance minister, Budget Speech, House of Commons, 18 February 1997.

We cry out only when there is hope that someone may hear us.

Jean Vanier, founder of L'Arche movement, *Becoming Human* (1998).

We will starve cynicism and we will feed hope.

Dalton McGuinty, Ontario premier, inaugural address, Queen's Park, Toronto, 23 October 2003, broadcast on CBC Radio later that day.

HOSPICES *See also* Health

In medieval times, a hospice was a place of shelter or sanctuary for travelers, pilgrims and others. No journey in life is more difficult than the path followed by those suffering a life-threatening illness, so "hospice" has now become a philosophy of care built around the quality of life for the dying and those that care for them.

Hospice Association of Ontario, FAQ, website, 15 June 2005.

HOSPITALITY

The hospitality of Canada has been such that I am tempted to remember the story that was told to me yesterday of a farmer who had been chased by his bull and after he had been around the field three times with his knees almost on his chin, he turned around to the bull and said, "Well, you can please yourself but this is my last time around."

Sir Cedric Hardwicke, touring British actor, address, "The Theatre as a Desirable Cultural Force," 24 February 1937, The Empire Club of Canada.

HOSPITALIZATION *See also* Health; Hospices

A total institution may be defined as a place of residence and work where a large number of like-situated individuals, cut off from the wider society for an appreciable period of time, together lead an enclosed, formally administered round of life. Prisons serve as a clear example, providing we appreciate that what is prison-like about prisons is found in institutions whose members have broken no laws. This volume deals with total institutions in general and one example, mental hospitals, in particular.

Erving Goffman, sociologist who developed the concept of the "total institution," *Asylums: Essays on the Social Situation of Mental Patients and Other Inmates* (1961).

HOTELS

There is no railway that is not bankrupt and the Royal York, the hotel we stayed at in Toronto, and one of the best in America, was bankrupt too. Orchestras play Scarlatti, magnificent dinners are served, the uniforms of the commissioners are of guards standards, but it is bankrupt.

Wyndham Lewis, English author, one-time Toronto resident, *America, I Presume* (1940).

HOUSE OF COMMONS *See also* Government; Parliament; Senate

They do one of two things—they grow, or they swell.

John G. Diefenbaker, former prime minister, referring to newly elected Parliamentarians, in Scott Young, *The Globe and Mail*, 7 November 1974.

Trained seals ... loose fish.

Pejorative portrayals of subservient or maverick Members of Parliament. "Trained seals" is associated with George Drew, former Ontario premier and later federal Conservative leader from 1948 to 1956; "loose fish" with Pierre Elliott Trudeau in 1977. The expression "loose fish" dates back to Sir John A. Macdonald in the 1890s.

HOUSING *See also* Cities & Towns

Housing is an important aspect of livability, and here again, there's no comparison. In Canada, unless you live in an igloo or at the Salvation Army, you have two or three stories with so many rooms that a family never sees one another except at weddings. Like, who needs a living room and a den and an office and a work room and a guest room and a spare room, not to mention a spacious attic and a fully furnished basement, two-car garage, driveway, front lawn and backyard, and obligatory built-in skating rink? That's for your basic Canadian three-person family, and does not include the summer cottage. For a basic, average Israeli family of six (not including the relatives and neighbours who come and go), a living room is all we need, and who doesn't have one?

Sam Orbaum, Montreal-born columnist, "I'd Rather Live in Israel," *The Jerusalem Post Magazine*, 13 July 2001.

HUDSON BAY

Rich as the trade to these parts has been or may be, the way of living is such that we can not reckon any man happy whose lot is cast upon this Bay.... For that country is so prodigiously cold that nature is never impregnated by the sun; or, rather, her barren womb produces nothing for the subsistence of man.

John Oldmixon, antiquary, *The British Empire in America* (1708), as quoted by Peter C. Newman, *Empire of the Bay: An Illustrated History of the Hudson's Bay Company* (1989).

It has been said that the Prairie Provinces of Canada are equivalent to the whole of Russia; well, I believe that the Hudson's Bay region is equivalent to the whole of Scandinavia and Finland—a country capable of considerable development and of sustaining a hardy, energetic and prosperous race of people.

L.S. Amery, colonial editor, *The London Times*, address, "Hudson's Bay: Its Conditions and Problems," Toronto, 22 September 1910, The Empire Club of Canada.

Half a million more mobile homes had set down on the shores of Hudson Bay than had migrated by the same date last year.

Description of population growth in **Robert A. Heinlein**'s novel set in the future *Stranger in a Strange Land* (1961).

If Joseph Conrad had been Canadian, he would have set *Heart of Darkness* on Hudson Bay.

Will Ferguson, author, *Beauty Tips from Moose Jaw: Travels in Search of Canada* (2004).

HUDSON'S BAY COMPANY

We were Caesars, being nobody to contradict us.

Pierre-Esprit Radisson, French explorer and fur trader, journal entry of 1661, *The Explorations of Pierre-Esprit Radisson* (1961), edited by Arthur T. Adams.

At the peak of its expansion it controlled nearly three million square miles of territory—nearly a twelfth of the earth's land surface and an area ten times that of the Holy Roman Empire at its height.

Peter C. Newman, author, *Empire of the Bay: An Illustrated History of the Hudson's Bay Company* (1989).

In 1821 the Hudson's Bay Company and the Northwest Company merged, forming the largest corporate landlord in the world—more than 3 million square miles, from the American border to the Arctic Circle. Its Scottish president, George Simpson, governed ten times more territory than had the Roman emperors.

Arthur Herman, historian, *How the Scots Invented the Modern World* (2001). The Hudson's Bay Company, founded in 1670, at one time traded over an immense area—from the shores of the Arctic Ocean to San Francisco, from the Labrador coast to Hawaii.

I don't think he's buying the company to operate in the normal course because the normal course in the past hasn't been very successful. So obviously there's got to be some radical changes coming.

John Williams, retail analyst, quoted by CTV News, "U.S. Investor Makes Bid for Hudson's Bay Co.," CTV.ca News staff, 28 October 2005. He is referring to the planned acquisition of the Bay by South Carolina investor Jerry Zucker of Maple Leaf Heritage Investments. "Some real estate will move around but for the most part we expect this business to continue as is," Zucker spokesperson Robert Johnston was quoted as saying, adding there are no plans for a major restructuring, downsizing or "any major shakeup at this point."

HUMAN RIGHTS *See also* Canada & the World; Censorship; Government; Rights

An essential element of the orthodoxy is the belief that human rights will be better protected by the judges than by wicked "politicians."

Robert Ivan Martin, law professor, *The Most Dangerous Branch: How the Supreme Court of Canada Has Undermined Our Law and Our Democracy* (2003).

Human rights has become the twenty-first century equivalent of the nineteenth century "civilizing mission."

Robert Ivan Martin, law professor, *The Most Dangerous Branch: How the Supreme Court of Canada Has Undermined Our Law and Our Democracy* (2003).

Once you admit that human rights can be suspended in times of emergency, you are accepting that human rights are not a system of indivisible absolutes; their application requires balancing liberty and necessity, pure principle and prudence.

Michael Ignatieff, essayist, *The Lesser Evil: Political Ethics in an Age of Terror* (2004).

HUMANISM

Canadians are heirs to an extraordinarily rich humanism, enriched even more by the blend of so many different elements.

John Paul II, pope, speech on arrival, Toronto, 23 July 2002, published in the *National Post*, 24 July 2002.

HUMANITY *See also* Discovery; Future; Life; Philosophy

Presently, however, as war dies, and poverty vanishes, humanity will begin to be aware that a queer sort of uniformity, something like a great stillness, is coming over the world.

Stephen Leacock, humorist, *Back to Prosperity: The Great Opportunity of the Empire Conference* (1932).

We, today, are entering a new era in the history of humanity. Today we have discovered such fantastic power and we have made such fantastic discoveries that humanity is evolving from an age of childhood to an age of adulthood in the world of technique. Today is the age of moon exploration, of nuclear energy, of television, of electronics, and all the fantastic discoveries that science puts at our disposal.

Jean Vanier, humanitarian, address, "A World in Violence: Eruption to Hope?" Toronto, 11 February 1971, The Empire Club of Canada.

You know and I know that you should take the pulse of our society and turn your head away from the publicity and other things that are trying to fool you and you will delve into the reality of our universe and the deep tidal wave that is moving humanity towards its destiny. You want to look at the movements which may be small today but will be important and vast tomorrow; you want to see what is happening in the course of our humanity so that you will realize that mankind must take stock of this situation today and look at what is happening, look and speak to the numbers of the despised, distressed, rejected.

Jean Vanier, humanitarian, address, "A World in Violence: Eruption to Hope?" Toronto, 11 February 1971, The Empire Club of Canada.

Captain Kirk said, "Risk is our business." I don't think so; I think improving the human condition is our business.

Robert J. Sawyer, science-fiction author, "The Age of Miracle and Wonder" (1999), *Relativity: Stories and Essays* (2004).

I believe that what separates humanity from everything else in this world—spaghetti, binder paper, deep-sea creatures, edelweiss and Mount McKinley—is that humanity alone has the capacity at any given moment to commit all possible sins.

Thoughts of the student character, Cheryl Anway, and the opening sentence of **Douglas Coupland**'s novel *Hey Nostradamus!* (2003).

To stay human is to break a limitation.

Thought of a character in **Margaret Atwood**'s novel *Oryx and Crake* (2003).

HUMOUR *See also* Jokes; Laughter; Malapropisms; Newfie Jokes; Wit

The basis of the humorous, the amusing, the ludicrous, lies in the incongruity, the unfittingness, the want of harmony among things.

Stephen Leacock, humorist, *Essays and Literary Studies* (1916).

Seriousness, true seriousness, and true humour always go together. They are sprung from the same root.

Stephen Leacock, humorist, interviewed by R.E. Knowles, "Leacock Says Sir A. Currie Most Distinguished Pupil," *Toronto Daily Star*, 16 February 1933.

Take puns. They have pretty well died out now. The last of the punsters is probably dead, or in hiding. But many of us can still remember the social nuisance of the inveterate punster. This man followed conversation as a shark follows a ship.

Stephen Leacock, humorist, *Last Leaves* (1945).

From time to time, I have been asked whether, in fact, I was born balmy.

Beatrice Lillie, Toronto-born comedienne, *Every Other Inch a Lady* (1972).

Jokes are mostly concerned with grievances, and when new kinds of jokes appear, you can depend upon it, there is some sort of uncomfortable abrasive area of tension developing in the community.

Marshall McLuhan, media philosopher, address, "The End of the Work Ethic," 16 November 1972, The Empire Club of Canada.

The basis of our humour is Canadian. We find that the thing that unites Canadians everywhere is that they all detest Toronto!

Frank Shuster, comedian, in Ed Gould, *Entertaining Canadians: Canada's International Stars, 1900–1988* (1988).

I shall have to define humour, and I rather look forward to that, and shall do so in Jungian terms—that humour is implicit in the tendency of all things to run into their opposites if pushed unreasonably.

Robertson Davies, man of letters, letter, 8 February 1991, *For Your Eye Alone: Letters, 1976–1995* (1999).

The underground tradition of taboo jokes, naughty limericks, off-colour anecdotes, and *risqué* ripostes flourishes through oral passing-on.

Bill Casselman, anthologist, *Canadian Sayings: 1,200 Folk Sayings Used by Canadians* (1999).

If you think Jim Carrey is funnier than Mike Myers: 1 point. But both of them are funnier than Tom Green: 2 points. If you have no idea who Tom Green is: deduct 3 points, and congratulations on your new position as head of talent development at the CBC.

Series of quiz questions set by **William Ferguson** and **Ian Ferguson**, *How to Be a Canadian (Even if You Are One)* (2001).

Canada has two things going for it: a fierce independence and a wacko sense of humour. And God bless Canada for that irreverent sense of humour.

Leslie Nielsen, actor, on his native country's assets, in Brian Gorman, *Winnipeg Free Press*'s supplement *TV Plus*, 14 April 2001.

I believe in positioning. There aren't many products that are funny on their own. In my search to position Red Green, I decided he was the human form of duct tape.

Steve Smith, comedian known as Red Green on CBC-TV's *The Red Green Show*, star of the movie *Red Green's Duct Tape Forever*, directed by Eric Till, in Brian D. Johnson, "Will Red Green Fly on the Big Screen?" *Maclean's*, 15 April 2002.

Don't make me come back and smite you, for I am Marg—Princess Warrior.

Mary Walsh, comedian, as "Marg Delahunty, Princess Warrior," the female Roman centurion created for CBC Radio's *This Hour Has 22 Minutes*, as noted by Joan Green, Lynda Palazzi, and Marguerite Senecal, *Northern Lights: Outstanding Canadian Women* (2004).

Eighty-five per cent of Canadians think that there is an absolutely identifiable *Canadian* sense of humour.

Roy MacGregor, columnist, "This Country," *The Globe and Mail*, 18 April 2005. He is quoting the report *What Canadians Think* (2005), by Darrell Bricker and John Wright based on an Ipsos Reid opinion poll.

HUNGARIANS

Hungarians—and this is the first thing to understand about them—love a loser.

Stephen Vizinczey, Hungarian-born author, "Commentary on a Poem" (1976), *Truth and Lies in Literature: Essays and Reviews* (1986).

HUNGER *See also* Food & Drink; Poverty

The Old Life was a long walk on an empty stomach.

Inuit proverbial expression in Robin Gedalof, *Paper Stays Put: A Collection of Inuit Writing* (1980).

As the Honourable Paul Martin, minister of External Affairs, said recently: "No world can be truly at peace when half its people go to bed hungry each night, when medical relief has yet to be brought to millions, when economic opportunity for so many of our fellow men is restricted to a daily struggle with infertile land or the back-breaking labour of primitive industrial tasks. We would not tolerate these conditions in our own land, not only because they are an affront to human dignity but because they would constitute a choking rein on our progress as a nation. And what cannot be accepted in a single country cannot be allowed to exist in the world of today, where self-containment is nothing more than dangerous delusion."

Maurice F. Strong, address, "International Development," quoting Paul Martin Sr., minister of External Affairs, Toronto, 26 January 1967, The Empire Club of Canada.

Old Mother Hubbard's cupboard was bare; it's obvious she was a widow.

Betty Jane Wylie, author, *Beginnings: A Book for Widows* (1977).

HUNTING *See also* Seal Hunt; Wildlife

Maybe the hunters are, in fact, more honest than I am, but I still hate the sight of them around here. I want the wildlife in my neighbourhood to be safe. I don't want to wake up to the sound of guns, or spend my autumn evenings watching Canada geese fall like unanswered prayers.

Christina Friedrichsen, columnist, resident of rural Ontario, "Facts and Arguments," *The Globe and Mail*, 18 September 2002.

HYDRO *See* Electrical Power

i

ICE & ICEBERGS *See also* Snow

Ice is to Canadians what sand is to Saharans, almost what air is to birds.

Wayne Grady, author, *Chasing the Chinook: On the Trail of Canadian Words and Culture* (1998).

Icebergs are pure as fresh snow and tiny as diamonds. They can be as small as a tree-house or as big as a skyscraper, towering over the sea. They are the grandest things many people ever see.

Lawrence Jackson, author, *Castles in the Sea: All about Icebergs* (2000).

ICE FISHING *See also* Fishing

I gather the idea of ice-fishing is a very important element in the Canadian psyche; even those who don't go ice-fishing do think about it. I regard this as a cultural experience, not a fishing trip. I think it's an opportunity to commune with nature, very specifically to commune with ice.

Alexander McCall Smith, English mystery writer with relatives in Vancouver, interviewed by Marian Botsford Fraser, "Seven Questions," *The Globe and Mail*, 4 February 2005.

IDEALISM *See also* Heroes & Heroism; Ideas; Principles

We in the older world are facing a grave break-down in the ancient props of our civilization. From the heart of humanity rises a cry which is often a cry of despair. Knights errant of idealism are needed to take up forlorn hopes. I believe that such knights errant will be found in this nation which has not become either sophisticated or cynical, but has continued to retain the freshness of its youthful spirit.

Rabindranath Tagore, Bengali sage, farewell message delivered to the Southam newspaper chain, Fourth Triennial Conference of the National Council of Education, Vancouver, 8–13 April 1929, quoted in "Tagore," *The Canadian Theosophist*, May 1929.

I would renounce, therefore, the attempt to create heaven on earth, and focus instead on reducing the hell.

A. Alan Borovoy, general counsel, Canadian Civil Liberties Association, *When Freedoms Collide: The Case for Our Civil Liberties* (1988).

IDEAS *See also* Canadian Identity; Creativity; Critics & Criticism; Design; Education; Existence; Idealism; Ideologies; Imagination; Innovation; Intelligence; Perception; Philosophy

One of the great vanities of human beings is that they have ideas. Little ideas maybe, but when it comes to big ideas, it is the ideas that have people.

Donald Harman Akenson, historian, *Surpassing Wonder: The Invention of the Bible and the Talmuds* (1998).

Most forward-looking people have their heads turned sideways.

Harold Adams Innis, politicial scientist, in James Carey, *The Innis Research Bulletin*, Number 3, December 1995, as noted by philosopher John Ralston Saul, *On Equilibrium* (2001).

All ideas are unborn.

Northrop Frye, cultural critic, aphorism, "Notebook 3" (1946–1948), *Northrop Frye Newsletter*, fall 2000.

I believe we must reposition ourselves not as a land of stuff, but a land of ideas. It's not what we have. It's what we do with it that counts.

Paul Lavoie, president, TAXI Advertising & Design, "How to Reinvent the Brand," *The Globe and Mail*'s *Report on Business*, May 2001.

The idea and the icon come together in the ideal.

Daniel Libeskind, architect, address, IdeaCity conference, Toronto, 21 June 2002.

And we also recalled what our parents taught us: Even if millions of people seemed to believe in an idea, it can still be a very dumb idea. For many people can be fooled some of the time, and others—some tenured academics in particular—all the time.

Reuven Brenner, Faculty of Management, McGill University, "The Children of Hope Gather to Remember," *National Post*, 26 July 2003. He recalls the warning of his parents, Hungarian-speaking Romanian Jews living in Szatmár (now Satu Mare, Romania), who had suffered under the Nazis and then the Communists.

It was a highly original idea, and thousands hated it.

Ivor Shapiro, researcher, referring to the decision of the State of Oregon to ration coverage for health care services by prioritizing all known health treatments, but applicable to original ideas generally, "Life, at What Price?" *The Walrus*, November 2004.

IDENTITIES *See also* Canadian Identity; Culture: Canadian

Limited identities.

A concept introduced by Ramsay Cook, historian, "Canadian Centennial Celebrations," *International Journal*, Volume 22 (1967). In "'Identities Are Not Like Hats,'" *Canadian Historical Review*, June 2000, Cook explained: "I suggested that although Canadians might lack a single national identity, serious investigation might demonstrate their satisfaction with such 'limited identities' as class, region, and ethnicity. (I confess to having ignored 'gender' …)". In the intervening years Cook observed that "the 'identity' industry has burgeoned … (where once it was tied to the protective tariff, more recently it has been associated with the social safety net), and even a multiplicity of 'nations' with or without inherent identities." J.M.S. Careless defended the idea in "'Limited Identities' in Canada," *Canadian Historical Review*, Volume 50, Number I, 1969. Cook went on to suggest that "limited identities" are in no way inferior to "unlimited identities," among which is "national identity." He concluded, "The phrase I had coined to challenge a musty orthodoxy threatened to become another received truth, a cliché."

If the world really does outgrow its vast jungle cities, its strangling international cartels, and the deadlocked hostility of its superpowers, it may break up into smaller units in which the individual can find once more an identity and a function.

Northrop Frye, literary and cultural critic, address, "The Authority of Learning," Toronto, 19 June 1984, The Empire Club of Canada.

Not that I'm anyone, really. Myself, that's all. In the end, that's what all of us learn to accept: ourselves and the road we've travelled.

Ellen Stafford, memoirist, *Always & After: A Memoir* (1999).

In short, identities are not essential but contingent, constructed and deconstructed by changing historical circumstances. They are relational, not autonomous.

Ramsay Cook, historian, "'Identities Are Not Like Hats,'" *Canadian Historical Review*, June 2000.

That night I had a disturbing dream. I dreamed I arrived at the gates of Heaven, where I was confronted by the image of St. Peter on a computer screen. He asked me for my PIN and my mother's maiden name, but somehow I couldn't quite recall them. As the trap door opened up beneath me, I knew I'd be sorry.

Margaret Wente, columnist, conclusion of an amusing column devoted to declining memory and identity issues, "Forgot Your #%&!£@ Password? Join the Club," *The Globe and Mail*, 18 June 2005.

IDEOLOGIES *See also* Ideas; Philosophy; Principles; Values

"Find-a-way-ism," I believe, is Canada's one true ideology. Not liberalism, conservatism, socialism, or any other. In this country, we don't have the luxury of binding ourselves to rigid ideology. We need to use whatever tool we can find.

Ken Dryden, hockey personality, lawyer, author, address, Charles R. Bronfman Lecture in Canadian Studies, November, University of Ottawa, "The Canadian Way," *Maclean's*, 13 November 2000.

The middle of the road is for dead skunks and yellow lines.

Tom Long, Ontario Conservative campaign organizer, in Ian Urquhart, "Harrisites Working on Campaign for Eves," *Toronto Star*, 10 February 2003.

Rémy: But we were everything! It's incredible! Separatists, indépendantistes, souverainistes, souverainistes–associationistes….
Others: Existentialists, anti-colonialists, Marxists, Marxist–Leninists, Maoists, Trotskyists, structuralists, situationists, deconstructionists, feminists.
Rémy: Is there an ism that we haven't adored?
Others: Crétinism!

Rough approximation of a translation of the dialogue from **Denys Arcand**'s film *Les Invasions barbares* (2003), as noted by Graham Fraser, "Arcand Film an Attack on His Generation," *Toronto Star*, 11 May 2003. It scoffs at the ideologies of the 1960s generation of Quebeckers. Rémy appears also in the earlier film *Le Déclin de l'Empire Américain*. The last word is a pun on the name of Prime Minister Jean Chrétien.

The day ideology died in Canada was September 29, 2003, when the NDP issued a press release announcing that its commissioned focus groups had opted overwhelmingly that Jack Layton keep his moustache. When the only political party that could claim a vestige of underlying philosophy felt it was necessary to test public opinion before deciding whether its new leader should shave his upper lip, it was time the razor was applied elsewhere.

Peter C. Newman, journalist and memoirist, *Here Be Dragons: Telling Tales of People, Passion, and Power* (2004).

Virtually all ideologues, of any variety, are fearful and insecure, which is why they are drawn to ideologies that promise prefabricated answers for all circumstances. Every society contains such people.

Jane Jacobs, urban planning critic, *Dark Age Ahead* (2004).

Ideology, like theatre, is dependent on the willing suspension of disbelief. At the core of every ideology lies the worship of a bright new future, with only failure in the immediate past. For once the suspension goes, willingness converts into suspicion—the suspicion of the betrayed. Our brilliant leaders abruptly appear naive, even ridiculous.

John Ralston Saul, philosopher, "The Collapse of Globalism and the Rebirth of Nationalism," *Harper's*, March 2004.

Saskatchewan is where most Canadian political ideas of the left came from; Alberta is where most political ideas of the right come from.

Roy MacGregor, columnist, "This Country," *The Globe and Mail*, 17 May 2005.

IDLENESS

The history of invention is the history of applied idleness. To shirk work is to abbreviate labour. To shirk argument is to settle controversy. To shirk war is to cherish peace.

Stephen Leacock, humorist, *Essays and Literary Studies* (1916).

IGNORANCE

The greatest ignorance—the ignorance which is the conceit that a man knows what he does not know.

Sir William Osler, physician, "Chauvinism in Medicine," *Aequanimitas* (1932).

The ignorance of how to use new knowledge stockpiles exponentially.

Marshall McLuhan, communications theorist, *Take Today: The Executive as Dropout* (1972). Another observation attributed to McLuhan is "Ignorance is learned."

IMAGINATION *See also* Ideas

We are moved and stimulated to understanding far more by our imagination than by our intellect: more even than by our self-interest.

Stephen Leacock, humorist, *Hellements of Hickonomics: In Hiccoughs of Verse Done in Our Social Planning Mill* (1936).

I do not think that Canadians lack imagination, though some Canadians do.

Robertson Davies, man of letters, letter, 31 January 1977, *For Your Eye Alone: Letters, 1976–1995* (1999).

Canada existed nowhere in my imagination before I got there.

Alberto Manguel, Canadian author, born in Argentina, "Destination Ithaka," *Passages: Welcome Home to Canada* (2002), with a preface by Rudyard Griffiths.

We would contemplate the night, we would map out possible journeys into the galaxies. All it takes is imagination.

Last line of **Louise Dupré**'s novel *The Milky Way* (2002), translated from the French by Liedewy Hawke.

I am disturbed by the growing realizaton that today's bright teenagers—always science-fiction's bread and butter—no longer want to know what the future is going to be like, that they are willing to imagine no more, no better, no further, than their great-grandparents did.

Spider Robinson, science-fiction writer, worrying about the popularity of backward-looking fantasy fiction (notably *Harry Potter* and *The Lord of the Rings*) and the lack of popularity of "future-perfect" science fiction, "Forward—Into the Past!" *The Globe and Mail*, 1 January 2002.

Our task is to bring about a profound and dramatic paradigm shift, in which the imagination embraces, at last, the idea of human family.

Gary Geddes, author and poet, referring to creative thinkers, in Robert J. Wiersema, "His 30-Year Obsession with a Monk," *The Globe and Mail*, 22 February 2005.

IMMIGRATION *See also* Emigration; Exile

"Miss B. going to Canada? Why, she'll be eaten up by the tigers!" Such was the exclamation of the old family coachman on hearing of my intended marriage and emigration.

Passage from the anonymously written article "A Lady's Reflections on Canada," *Chambers's Journal of Popular Literature, Science and Art* (1873).

'E said he was born at the back o' Vancouver Island, and all the time the beggar was a balmy Barnardo Orphan.

Line of narration about the character Boy Niven in **Rudyard Kipling**'s story "Mrs. Bathurst" (1904), *Traffics and Discoveries* (1904).

Canada will, in the long run, begin to consist largely of the people who are not eligible for the United States. (Laughter.) By that time I have no doubt there will be a fairly complete barrier set up against our getting into the United States for any purposes except that of transit. It will be highly desirable, therefore, that we shall have some place under the control of the Dominion Government, if possible, on the southern side of the United States, for purposes of hibernation. This is merely a suggestion, not for immediate consideration, but for bearing in mind for the next twenty-five or fifty years that our Dominion needs to be rounded out. It is not yet a complete unit, geographically, of the kind that it ought to be, and the West Indies will help us.

B.K. Sandwell, author, address, "Democracy on Wheels," Toronto, 3 December 1925, The Empire Club of Canada.

Yesterday he sailed, under another name, for Canada, and he won't come back for a long, long time.

Statement made by Sandy Arbuthnot in Scotland about the whereabouts of the criminal menace known as Master Varrinder in **John Buchan**'s novel *The Island of Sheep* (1936).

If peasants in the Balkans can raise a family on five acres of land, why cannot Canada, by comparable concentration, add several millions to its population?

H. Watson Kirkconnell, professor, address, "Canada and Immigration," Toronto, 23 March 1944, The Empire Club of Canada.

My luck had run out; I knew that it had to. I didn't feel I could stay in that country. I felt the place was a hoax. They thought they were part of the West, but really they had become like the rest of us who had run to them for safety. They were like people far away, living on other people's land and off other people's brains, and that was all they thought they should do. That was why they were so bored and dull. I thought I would die if I stayed among them.

Thoughts of a would-be immigrant from Trinidad to Canada, in **V.S. Naipaul**'s novel *A Bend in the River* (1979). The immigrant found life in England difficult: "But after Canada I had lost my nerve. I thought I would play safe."

So if you can tolerate aliens, whether they are Mexicans or viruses, you end up with a totally different endosymbiotic relationship. You end up with a situation that is much healthier.

William Irwin Thompson, theorist, "Mind Jazz," *Wild Culture: Specimens from* The Journal of Wild Culture (1992), edited by Whitney Smith and Christopher Lowry. Thompson is discussing change in context (though it applies on all levels from organisms to political entities). His definition: "Endosymbiont is another word for a good neighbour within a cell."

The emerging consensus will require that immigrants generally adhere to an official culture, English or French, and not be publicly assisted to avoid doing so and that they be admitted to this country on a basis that does not constitute systematic importation of racial frictions that Canada has long congratulated itself on having avoided. This insistence does not mean disrespect for any group, only a determination to avoid social decomposition.

Conrad Black, newspaper magnate, address, "Post-election Prospects in Canada," Toronto, 2 November 1993, The Empire Club of Canada.

Being Canadian is a very, very precious commodity. You have to wonder what it is that people around the earth know that we don't know. Why is everyone trying to come here to a country that we take for granted? That's the only advantage that we immigrants have. We never take Canada for granted because we know what a precious place it is. I believe it is time we began to sing some songs in praise of ourselves.

Peter C. Newman, author, address, "The Canadian Revolution," Toronto, 30 November 1995, The Empire Club of Canada.

From the abandoned *filles du Roy*, the young women sent from Paris to New France, to the last jetliner to land at Toronto's Pearson International Airport, we are all boat people. We just got here at different times.

Mark Starowicz, TV producer, "The Death of History," *The Globe and Mail*, 20 September 2000.

This is a country that welcomes people, and does not demand that they come as winners or become winners. Instead, it offers something more subtle, and to me, profound: acceptance and forgiveness.

Adrienne Clarkson, governor general, interviewed by Richard Addis, "Year 1: 'I Met Canadians,'" *The Globe and Mail*, 19 October 2000.

From Poland, Canada seemed like a vast, blank sheet of prosperity. Only with its writers did the whiteness take on the first shades of colour.

Thoughts of the narrator Anna Nowicka Herzman in **Eva Stachniak**'s novel *Necessary Lies* (2000).

You will have to leave your murderous fantasies of revenge behind.

Michael Ignatieff, commentator, "Immigration: The Hate Stops Here," *The Globe and Mail*, 25 October 2001.

The problem doesn't arise when people come to Canada from the Levant; the problem arises when people come to recreate the Levant in Canada.

George Jonas, columnist, discussing the importation of divisive ethnic values,

"Multiculturalism's Volatile Mix," *National Post*, 21 June 2002.

Immigration is to natural population growth as wine is to food: enriching as a supplement; dangerous as a substitute.

David Frum, columnist, "Unto Canada, Too Few Children Are Born," *National Post*, 22 December 2004.

One in every six people in Canada immigrated, giving it the world's second-highest proportion of immigrants. Only Australia's is higher.

Clifford Krauss, journalist, "Some Skilled Foreigners Find Jobs Scarce in Canada," *The New York Times*, 5 June 2005. Annual rate of influx fluctuates between 200 000 and 250 000 immigrants.

IMMORTALITY

On the question of immortality the only enduring enlightenment is through faith.

Sir William Osler, physician, *Science and Immortality* (1905).

Yet I believe there's one chance in ten trillion that I'll go on to experience an afterlife.

Ken Walker, physician and medical columnist (aka Dr. Gifford-Jones), *"You're Going to Do What?": The Memoirs of Dr. W. Gifford-Jones* (2000).

Certainly by the end of the next century, we will be able to dispense with these fallible sacks of flesh. We will have the technology to scan our brains and upload our consciousnesses into computers, living entirely in a virtual realm. At that point, we will be truly immortal.

Robert J. Sawyer, science-fiction author, "The Age of Miracle and Wonder" (1999), *Relativity: Stories and Essays* (2004).

IMPERIALISM *See also* Colonialism

Whereas the early democracy was necessarily separative, destructive, revolutionary, iconoclastic, negative, bitter, alienating, breaking down, despairing, so the newer democracy, or Imperialism, is saner, wiser, calmer, tolerant, constructive, unifying, peaceful, practical and hopeful. It is the great principle of peace and progress today over the world, and it is this principle of sane Imperialism which should be the chief platform of all progressive parties today.

W. Wilfred Campbell, poet and imperialist, address, "Imperialism in Canada," 23 November 1904, The Empire Club of Canada.

When I hear of Australia clamouring for a navy of her own, and Canada asking for the treaty-making power, I am honestly delighted. They may be asking for the wrong things, but the fact that they should want them is right—right—right. I want to see every one of our daughter-peoples grow into triumphant and self-conscious nationhood, for it is all contributory to the well-being of the Empire.

Thoughts of Lord Launceton, "an Ex-Viceroy," in **John Buchan**'s novel *A Lodge in the Wilderness* (1906).

History has repeatedly demonstrated that empires seldom seem to retain sufficient cultural self-awareness to prevent them from overreaching and overgrasping. They have neglected to recognize that the true power of a successful culture resides in its example. This is a patient and grown-up attitude to take. To take it successfully, a society must be self-aware.

Jane Jacobs, urban planning critic, *Dark Age Ahead* (2004).

IMPRESSIONS

You always get a second chance to make a bad impression.

Chris Gudgeon, author, *You're Not as Good as You Think You Are: A Demotivational Guide* (1997).

There's something interesting about everyone for five minutes.

Martin Short, comedian, "Who's Asking?" *The New York Times Magazine*, 24 June 2001.

IMPROVEMENT *See also* Progress

You have to be stupid not to get better.

Peter Urs Bender, motivational speaker, characteristic remark, 11 May 2000.

INDEPENDENCE *See also* Freedom; Nationhood; Referenda on Quebec Sovereignty; Separatism; Sovereignty-Association

It is no coincidence (and no cause for embarrassment) that Canada was, by more than half a century, the last major country in the Western Hemisphere to achieve independence. It would probably not have escaped absorption by the United States if it had become independent sooner.

Gwynne Dyer and **Tina Viljoen**, commentator and TV producer, *The Defence of Canada: In the Arms of the Empire* (1990).

Independence is in the refrigerator but not in the freezer.

Attributed to **René Lévésque**, Quebec leader, by E.W. Bopp, correspondent, Letters, *The Globe and Mail*, 2 June 2005.

Yes, independence is not something that is given—it is something that is taken.

Michaëlle Jean, broadcaster and governor general designate, toasting the spirit of independence with a group of Quebec separatists, in the 1991 documentary film *La Manière negre* (*The Negro Way*), the script of which appeared under that title two years later, directed by her husband Jean-Daniel LaFond, in Jack Aubry, "Film Captures G-G-to-be Toasting with Separatists," *National Post*, 16 August 2005.

INDIA

How great is the interval that lies between the dawns which have arisen and those which are yet to rise?

Obscure passage from the verses "Origin of the Chants" in the *Rig-Veda*, the sacred cycle of poems preserved in ancient Sanskrit for some 3000 years and chanted to this day on the subcontinent. The passage refers to the Arctic cycle of day and night, according to Hindu scholar B.G. Tilak, *The Arctic Home in the Vedas* (1903, 1925, 1971). He argued that the ancient Aryan people had an intimate knowledge of the geography of the northern regions of North America, including the region of the Great Lakes.

"My name is Mohandas Karamchad Gandhi—and yours?"
"Gordon Allan Sinclair, Canadian."

Simple-minded introductions of the statesman **Mahatma Gandhi** and the brash young correspondent **Gordon Sinclair** who conducted an interview in Poona, India, about 1930, as noted by Sinclair, *Foot-loose in India* (1932). "You, on your incredible continent, judge a man's progress by the number of bath-tubs in his home—is that one true?" asked Gandhi. Sinclair admitted its truth. Gandhi concluded the interview by saying, "My son. These things are too deep for you. Why don't you run along to play golf and drink beer and bathe in your many, many bathtubs?"

I think we can be, Canada and India, as someone has said, good companions in this great task of making a better world.

Indira Gandhi, prime minister of India, address, "Democracy in India," Toronto, 20 June 1973, The Empire Club of Canada.

Is polo popular in your country?

Bhawani Singh, Maharajah of Jaipur, addressing visitor John Robert Colombo, Jaipur, India, 27 December 2002. Singh, a great fan of the game, once visited Calgary, a city "twinned" with Jaipur. Winnipeg boasts a Polo Park.

INDIVIDUALISM *See also* Freedom

The plain assertion that every man looks out for himself (or at best for himself and his immediate family) touches the tender conscience of humanity. It is an unpalatable truth. None the less it is the most nearly true of all the broad generalizations that can be attempted in regard to mankind.

Stephen Leacock, humorist, *The Unsolved Riddle of Social Justice* (1920).

The way to make this society constructively distinct from and truly competitive with the United States was never fabricated righteous collectivism, but civilized individualism.

Conrad Black, Lord Black of Crossharbour, address, Fraser Institute, Vancouver, 15 November 2001, published in the *National Post*, 16 November 2001.

I am not so presumptuous to speak for all individual people, but I think I am so presumptuous as to speak for 99.99999 per cent of all individual people.

Frank Stronach, auto-parts magnate, Magna International, and self-made millionaire, in Roy MacGregor, "Canada Waits to Hear from the New 'It Girl' of the Political Right," *The Globe and Mail*, 17 January 2004.

Every growth, every useful mechanical action, every aesthetic joy, derives in some measure from a misfit. Human life begins when the child no longer fits the womb. A misfit is constantly reborn.

Leslie Millin, writer and consultant, "Idols of the Cave—My Career as a Misfit," *Queen's Quarterly*, spring 2005.

INDUSTRY *See also* Business; Environmentalism; Farmers & Farming; Manufacturing

Industry is the means by which the material resources of the world are transformed, through human intelligence and human energy, with the aid of natural powers, tools, and machines, into commodities and services available for human use. It is a vast process of transformation, itself a series of transforming processes so inter-related and numerous as to unite mankind, in this age of world-wide industrial expansion, in an enterprise that encompasses the globe.

W.L. Mackenzie King, prime minister, address, "The Four Parties to Industry," Toronto, 13 March 1919, The Empire Club of Canada.

I say to you in all earnestness that those who try to block the march toward better labour–management relations are saboteurs of Canadian industry.

Claude Jodoin, president, Canadian Labour Congress, address, "The Challenge of 1963," Toronto, 17 January 1963, The Empire Club of Canada.

Subsidized, industrial farming has decimated family farms and rural communities. Subsidized, industrial fishing has closed down entire fishing communities and brought many fish stocks to the brink of extinction. Subsidized, industrial forestry has ruined many small logging communities. And these three industrial "Fs" have devastated wild nature at every turn.

Robert Bateman, artist and naturalist, "I Am a Conservative, I Conserve," *The Globe and Mail*, 13 December 2003.

INFERIORITY COMPLEX *See also* Egotism

Perhaps because I had points of comparison—unlike many native-born Canadians—I have always believed that this is the greatest country in the world. I believe that the inferiority complex that infects Canadians is the single largest factor that holds us back and prevents us from achieving our full potential as a country.

Robert J. Lantos, Hungarian-born CEO of Alliance Communications, address, "Beyond Cultural Imperialism," Toronto, 16 February 1998, The Empire Club of Canada.

INFLATION *See also* Economics; Money

The fastest way to slow down inflation is to send it through the mails.

Dave Broadfoot, comedian, comedy routine, 27 January 1976.

INFORMATION *See also* Knowledge; Privacy; Security & Intelligence

There are only two things in ordinary conversation which ordinary people dislike—information and wit.

Stephen Leacock, humorist, *The Boy I Left Behind Me* (1947).

There must also be a change in the surrounding culture. As it stands now he says, "The attitude has truly become, 'Why write it when you can speak it? Why speak it when you can nod? Why nod when you can wink?'"

John Reid, information commissioner, referring to the need to extend the jurisdiction of the Access to Information Act, in David Berlin, "A Love Affair with Secrecy," *The Walrus*, November 2004.

INFORMATION TECHNOLOGY *See also* Computers

If I had to invent a catch phrase, it might be think yesterday, re-think tomorrow. Rather than rely on a slogan, though, it might be more useful to give you a few examples of why I believe it's so imperative that we indeed should re-think our attitudes towards best ways of benefitting from information technology and the skills of those who practise it.

Sheelagh Whittaker, CEO, EDS Systemhouse, address, "Re-Thinking the IT Model," Toronto, 4 November 1999, The Empire Club of Canada.

INJUSTICE *See also* Government; Justice; Law; Liberal Party

We have no business figuring out the cost of justice until we can figure out the cost of injustice.

Attributed to Madam Justice **Rosalie Abella** by Claire L'Heureux-Dubé in the speech "Are We There Yet? Gender Equality in the Law of Canada" (1998), in Robert Ivan Martin, *The Most Dangerous Branch: How the Supreme Court of Canada Has Undermined Our Law and Our Democracy* (2003).

Liberals don't think a government program is the solution to every injustice in our society. Injustice can only be remedied when individuals take responsibility for themselves. Individuals need programs that help them bear the burden of losing a job, losing their health, losing their way. We believe in a market economy, not the law of the jungle.

Michael Ignatieff, commentator, address, biennial policy conference of the Liberal Party, Ottawa, 3 March 2005, excerpted as "A Generous Helping of Liberal Brains," *The Globe and Mail*, 4 March 2005.

INNOCENCE

One always learns one's mystery at the price of one's innocence....

Observation made by the magician Magnus Eisengrim, born Paul Dempster, to Boy Staunton in **Robertson Davies**'s novel *Fifth Business* (1970).

We have to escape the long illusion that those of us who are ordinary are innocent.

Ted Honderich, philosopher, referring to Western economic imperialism, *After the Terror* (2002).

INNOVATION *See also* Creativity; Ideas; Planning

Let us do what is necessary to ensure that Canada not only meets the standards of innovation that the world has set for today, but that we set the standards that others must meet tomorrow.

Paul Martin, finance minister, Budget Speech, House of Commons, 18 February 1997.

Take something old and apply it in a new way.

Fred Jaekel, technical innovator, in Sarah Scott, "Shock of the New," *Globe and Mail's Report on Business*, August 2002.

Death to innovation is death to economic and social development.

Jane Jacobs, urban planning critic, *Dark Age Ahead* (2004).

INSPIRATION

There's nothing like a little fear or hunger to motivate one's inspiration, and to take that away from a young artist can offer quite a disservice.

Ken Danby, artist, characteristic observation, 6 July 2005.

INSTITUTIONS

I look at the great trees of the West Coast, tremendous trees, a thousand years old, eight hundred years old. You don't have to cut them down to destroy them, just remove the bark continuously and ultimately the tree will die and that is what is happening. Institutions in our country are being surreptitiously undermined and weakened by erosion. The subtle means is much more effective than a direct one but the result will be the same.

John G. Diefenbaker, former prime minister, address, "The Things We Treasure," Toronto, 9 March 1972, The Empire Club of Canada.

INSURANCE

People have come to the conclusion that there are two rules of insurance: Always pay your premiums on time and never make a claim.

Darrell Dexter, Nova Scotia NDP leader, in Sinclair Stewart and Paul Waldie, "Insurers' Profits Fuel Wave of Outrage," *The Globe and Mail*, 19 February 2005.

I allow myself to do cocaine every other Saturday night to feel what Freud felt. I never drink liquor because it dulls the senses. If I wanted my senses dulled, I would have gone into insurance.

Boast or admission made by a researcher of Sigmund Freud's life and theories in **Catherine Gildiner**'s novel *Seduction* (2005).

INTEGRITY *See also* Authenticity; Honesty; Truth

Integrity is the dovetailing of life with the spirit of truth.

Graham Kerr, chef, "The Galloping Gourmet," in Barry Shainbaum, *Hope & Heroes: Portraits of Integrity & Inspiration* (2003).

Integrity is congruence between what we know, what we profess, and what we do. When you see a lack of congruence, you're suspicious and distrustful. You know something doesn't fit and you think, "He doesn't walk his talk."

Nathaniel Branden, Toronto-born motivational speaker and follower of Ayn Rand, in Barry Shainbaum, *Hope & Heroes: Portraits of Integrity & Inspiration* (2003).

INTELLECTUAL PROPERTY *See also* Free Trade; Information Technology

Of all nations active in nanotech, the Canadian initiative could pack the biggest impact for the USA. Under the North American Free Trade Agreement, Canada and its powerful southern neighbour have established a seamlessly integrated high-tech economy. Disputes arise in old-economy goods like wood and steel, but rarely in advanced technology. Every BlackBerry pager comes from Canada. So does half the transmission hardware in many North American telephone companies. There also exists the possibility of international cooperation, which would allow Canada and other smaller nations to pool facilities, personnel, and IP in virtual mega-institutes.

William Illsey Atkinson, science writer, *Nanocosm: Nanotechnology and the Big Changes Coming from the Inconceivably Small* (2003).

INTELLECTUALS

Canada and Mexico have produced North American intellectuals a generation ahead of the United States.

Richard Rodriguez, American commentator of Mexican background, referring to Marshall McLuhan and Octavio Paz, *Brown: The Last Discovery of America* (2002).

INTELLIGENCE *See also* Ideas

It takes a rare, dispassionate intelligence to see the self from outside, a rare, compassionate intelligence to see others from inside.

Jane Rule, author and essayist, "Notes on Autobiography," *A Hot-Eyed Moderate* (1986).

I moved here from Canada, and they think I am a little slow, eh?

Remark made by the slow-witted character Gordy in the episode "You Only Move Twice" of the U.S. TV series *The Simpsons*, aired 2 November 1996.

There are two facets to emotional intelligence: One is using your emotions intelligently, instead of the usual case of your emotions using you. And the other is evoking intelligent emotions. The most intelligent emotional states are wisdom, compassion, and joy.

Daniel Star, speaker on Emotional Intelligence, "Emotional Intelliegence at Work," *Contact Point Magazine*, fall 2000.

INTENTION

People can easily confuse intention with ambition or goals. In fact, intention is much larger and more important than those aims....

For people with intention are the most fortunate of human beings: They know that what they have to do is the same as what they most want to do. When that kind of identification happens, every person watching understands its profound impact. Impact not only on the intentional person herself, but also on her family, her country and the world in which she has influence.

Adrienne Clarkson, governor general, eulogy for Queen Elizabeth the Queen Mother, delivered in Ottawa, 8 April 2002, excerpted in the *National Post*, 9 April 2002.

INTERNATIONAL AFFAIRS *See also* Canada & the World; Globalism & Globalization; World

The Responsibility to Protect: Core Principles

Basic Principles / State sovereignty implies responsibility, and the primary responsibility for the protection of its people lies with the state itself. / Where a population is suffering serious harm, as a result of internal war, insurgency, repression or state failure, and the state in question is unwilling or unable to halt or avert it, the principle of non-intervention yields to the international responsibility to protect.

Elements / The responsibility to protect embraces three specific responsibilities: *The responsibility to prevent:* to address both the root causes and direct causes of internal conflict and other man-made crises putting populations at risk. *The responsibility to react:* to respond to situations of compelling human need with appropriate measures, which may include coercive measures like sanctions and international prosecution, and in extreme cases military intervention. *The responsibility to rebuild:* to provide, particularly after a military intervention, full assistance with recovery, reconstruction and reconciliation, addressing the causes of the harm the intervention was designed to halt or avert.

Some key concepts of the Report of the Right to Protect, a document released in December 2001. An initiative of the Government of Canada, supported by international foundations, it was prepared by the International Commission on Intervention and State Sovereignty (ICISS) and submitted for approval to the United Nations. R2P, as it is called, envisages "sovereignty-as-responsibility" and seeks to reconcile intervention for human protection purposes with a respect for the rights of sovereign nations.

Recently, from stage left, we've seen the entrance of the Canadian Responsibility to Protect (R2P) initiative. For all intents and purposes, this initiative, recommended by a committee of eminent international statesmen reporting to the UN Secretary-General, has been accepted by the UN and will be formally adopted in September. R2P addresses the long-standing conflict between two principles: respect for a nation's sovereignty and the need to act when that nation's government is not prepared or is unwilling to protect its own citizens. After other options have been exhausted, R2P not only authorized intervention over sovereign borders, it encourages such action to protect the innocents.

Lewis MacKenzie, retired general, former peacekeeper, and columnist, "Roméo, Roméo, Wherefore Art Thou Partisan?" *The Globe and Mail*, 19 May 2005.

INTERNATIONALISM *See also* Globalism & Globalization; Isolationism

And I would venture to say this: it seems a long way from Toronto to Cairo, but Canada has an interest as a partner in the Empire in the decision of these great matters. Anything that happens injuriously to the interests of Australia and New Zealand must affect Canadian interests and Canadian sentiment. (Hear, hear.) Anything that affects the welfare of the whole affects the welfare of every part. Canada should have her opinion upon this subject of Egypt too. (Applause.)

Winston Churchill, statesman, address, "British Imperial Interests," Toronto, 13 August 1929, The Empire Club of Canada.

We have love for our neighbour of whatever creed or colour; / We have love for our cities and our valleys and our plains; / We have a voice that is calling, telling all the world we're willing / To welcome them to this great land for that's what Canada is....

Verse of the song "Canada Is," an unabashed paean of praise composed and sung in the 1990s by the U.S. singer-songwriter **Roger Whittaker**.

The world needs more Canada.

Catchphrase coined by someone in the Indigo book chain, according to columnist Richard Gwyn, "Surviving Survivalism," *Literary Review of Canada,* December 2004. The phrase, which seems to date from the early 1990s and to the pre–Indigo Chapters book chain, was used to good effect by the lead singer of U2, Bono, who identified it with Prime Minister Paul Martin's initiative for international humanitarian aid during the general election of 2004.

It is because young Canadians feel so confident about being Canadian that they now feel able to reach out beyond Canada. It is the world, rather than Canada, that excites them these days, although they are turned on also by and fully at ease with the dazzling variety of our multiculturalism, itself a miniature of the wide world.

Richard Gwyn, columnist and essayist, "Surviving Survivalism," *Literary Review of Canada,* December 2004.

The Universe Needs More Canada.

The editors of the *National Post* on 30 June 2005 took one giant leap with the proposition above, the title of an article by Siri Agrell about the Russian-born, Toronto-raised model Natalie Glebova who was crowned Miss Universe 2005 in Bangkok in June.

INTERNET *See also* Communications; Computers

It took 30 years for radio to reach an audience of 60 million people and 15 years for television to accomplish the same thing. It has taken but the last three years for 100 million new people to join the Internet.

Jim Carroll and **Rick Broadhead**, computer specialists, *Canadian Internet Handbook 2000: Lightbulbs to Yottabits* (1999).

For Canada, with its vast size and cold climate, the Internet will play a significant role in making our lives easier. Keeping in touch with Aunt Sophie in Burnaby, B.C., will be as easy as keeping in touch with the Joneses next door.

Jeff Skoll, co-founder of eBay, foreword, *Canadian Internet Handbook 2000: Lightbulbs to Yottabits* (1999), by Jim Carroll and Rick Broadhead.

Like no other medium before it, the Internet allows society's marginal elements to find each other, the combined weight of their numbers revealing they're not so marginal after all.

Gabrielle Bauer, "'Un' Is In," *Saturday Night,* February 2005.

INTERVIEWS *See also* Communications; News; Questions

The task of the interviewer remains the same: to guide rather than to motivate. The subject paddles, the interviewer steers.

Peter Gzowski, host of CBC Radio's *Morningside,* in *The Private Voice: A Journal of Reflections* (1988).

I have no opinion but I agree with you.

Shelagh Rogers, host of CBC Radio's *This Morning,* 5 February 2002. She genially agreed with a guest, who made a straightforward point about the lack of Olympic sportsmanship, while maintaining professional objectivity.

In her 1995 biography of my mother, my sister Linda Frum tells the story of how my mother once asked Linda, "Would you like to know the secret of interviewing?"

"Sure," Linda answered.

"Ask short questions."

David Frum, columnist, referring to **Barbara Frum**, "Preserving the Legacy of a Radio Legend," *National Post,* 15 February 2005.

The guest plays the same role in the interview as a frog does in a classroom lecture on dissection: No frog, no lecture. Yet in the end, the frog's role is essentially secondary.

David Frum, columnist, "Preserving the Legacy of a Radio Legend," *National Post,* 15 February 2005.

INUIT *See also* Aboriginal Rights; Native Peoples

It is a matter of fact that that country is inhabited by about two thousand Eskimo. These Eskimo are a resource to the country because they are the only people who can ever make that country of any value so far as we can see, unless minerals are discovered there, which I hope may not be the case, for the sake of the Eskimo. (Laughter.)

Vilhjalmur Stefansson, Arctic explorer, address, "Our Northland, Its People and Resources," Toronto, 6 February 1913, The Empire Club of Canada.

The Andonites were still scattered over the Arctic and central Asian regions.

Passage from *The Urantia Book* (1955), Paper 78 ("The Violet Race after the Days of Adam"), dictated to a Chicago dentist in 1934 by "Ancients of Days," which is "a composite presentation by many beings." According to Urantians, the Andonites are the predecessors of today's Eskimos.

The human race has no surviving ancestry between the frog and the Eskimo.

Passage from *The Urantia Book* (1955), Paper 65 ("The Overcontrol of Evolution"), dictated to a Chicago dentist in 1934 by "Ancients of Days," "a composite presentation by many beings."

Doris had dark, black bobbed hair, a large mouth and dark pig's eyes. There was something of the Eskimo about her head, but her colouring was ruddy and her manner more vivacious than is common among that respectable race.

Description of the character Doris in **Evelyn Waugh**'s novel *Put Out More Flags* (1942).

There was another Dayout at an Eskimo settlement on Victoria Island, north of Canada. The inhabitants are cagey about what happened there, but it is believed that they were so outraged, or perhaps alarmed, at the arrival of babies so unlike their own that they exposed them almost at once. At any rate, none survived.

Explanation offered by the War Office's spokesman Bernard to the scientist Zellaby for the birth of alien infants in **John Wyndham**'s science-fiction novel *The Midwich Cuckoos* (1957). In addition to the "Dayouts" in the Arctic and in the English village of Midwich, there were confirmed "Dayouts" in Australia's Northern Territory, "behind the Curtain" (the first in the Irkutsk region near the border of Outer Mongolia, the second to the east at a place called Gizhinsk, northeast of Okhotsk), and presumably others. During a brief "Dayout," women of child-bearing years in a well-defined area become simultaneously pregnant by some strange force connected with UFOs and nine months later deliver infants that develop into mutants or hybrids with telepathic and psychokinetic powers. The Arctic reference is preserved in the film version, *Village of the Damned* (1960).

I retain the word "Eskimo." It's a good word, probably Montagnais, used since the 16th century, in no way derogatory. Preference is sometimes given to *Yup'ik* (Bering Strait), *Inupiat* (North Slope), *Inuvaluit* (Mackenzie Delta), *Kaladit* (Greenland), *Inguhuit* (Polar Eskimo), *Inuit* (Eastern Canada), etc. The Eskimos of Comock's days weren't the *Inuit* of modern Canada. This story belongs, like the people themselves, to an earlier time.

Edmund Carpenter, anthropologist, editorial note to his edition of Robert Flaherty, *Comock: The True Story of an Eskimo Hunter* ... (The Rock Foundation, 2003). The Eskimo hunter Comock and his family survived for a decade on an otherwise deserted island in Hudson Bay during the 1910s and 1920s.

May you have warmth in your igloo, oil in your lamps, and peace in your heart.

Eskimo blessing bestowed on **John Buchan**, Governor General Lord Tweedsmuir, crossing the Arctic Circle, July 1937, as noted by Andrew Lownie, *John Buchan: The Presbyterian Cavalier* (1995).

Inuit are more than First Canadians, Inuit are Canadians first.

Motto of the Inuit Tapiriit Kanatami (National Inuit Association), adopted by its president, Jose

Kusugak, in Stephen Hendrie, letter, *National Post,* 27 April 2005. Its logo consists of an aerial view of a circle formed by four Inuit holding hands to enclose the outline of a "white" maple leaf. It represents four land-claim regions: Inuvialuit, Nunavut, Nunavik, Nunatsiavut.

INVENTION

Invention is the mother of necessity.

Marshall McLuhan, communications theorist, *Culture Is Our Business* (1970).

If it were only true that necessity is the mother of invention, we would have here a political invention on the verge of happening, but since opportunity is actually the mother of invention, this needed political invention hasn't materialized.

Jane Jacobs, urban planning critic, on "the disconnection between public treasuries and local domestic needs," *Dark Age Ahead* (2004).

INVESTMENT *See also* Finance

A salesman was recently trying to sell a young housewife a freezer. Meeting some sales resistance, he told her that she could save the price of the freezer out of what she would save on her food bills. The woman replied, "That is just the trouble. We are already paying for our house out of the money we save on rent. We are paying for our car out of what we save on car fare. We are paying for the washing machine out of what we save on our laundry bills. And for the present, the simple fact is that we just can't afford to save any more money."

Frederick Gardiner, chairman, Municipality of Metropolitan Toronto, address, "Metro—Past, Present, and Future," Toronto, 12 October 1961, The Empire Club of Canada.

"Bulls make money, bears make money, pigs get slaughtered." This phrase is used in the investment industry as a warning of the perils of acting in an overly greedy manner in the markets.

David Cork, investment counsellor, *Bulls, Bears, and Pigs: How to Find Balance in Your Financial Life* (2005).

IRAN

Our proposal is that you give a piece of your land in Europe, the U.S., Canada or Alaska. If you do that, the Iranian people will no longer protest against you.

Mahmoud Ahmadinejad, Iranian president, speech in Sistan-Baluchestan, proposing that Israel be "moved" from the Middle East, 15 December 2005, in Marc Wolfensberger, "Holocaust Is a Myth, Iran's President Says," *National Post,* 15 December 2005.

IRAQ WAR *See also* America; Canada & United States; Defence; War

So we are stuck this week between the European underestimation of tyranny, and the American overestimation of it—an overestimation that is itself viewed as a form of tyranny by many Europeans and Canadians. The hand of ignorance washes that of indifference.

Doug Saunders, columnists, "Reckoning," *The Globe and Mail,* 22 March 2003.

There is no security threat to Canada that the United States would not be ready, willing, and able to help with. There would be no debate. There would be no hesitation. We would be there for Canada, part of our family. That is why so many in the United States are disappointed and upset that Canada is not fully supporting us now. For Canada the priority is trade, for us the priority is security. Security trumps trade.

Paul Cellucci, U.S. ambassador to Canada, address, Economic Club of Toronto, 25 March 2003, in Joseph Brean and Sheldon Alberts, "U.S. Loses Faith in Canada," *National Post,* 26 March 2003.

I marvel at the faith of those who believe in Weapons of Mass Destruction.

Robert Priest, poet and columnist, "God in a Warhead," *Now,* 1 May 2003.

The United States needs to lose the war in Iraq as soon as possible. Even more urgently, the whole world needs the United States to lose the war in Iraq. It would be nice if Iraq doesn't lose too, but that is a lesser consideration. What is at stake now is the way we run the world for the next generation or more, and really bad things will happen if we get it wrong.

Gwynne Dyer, political commentator, *Future: Tense—The Coming World Order* (2004).

Would you like me to raise my child in Canada and by the time he's twelve or thirteen be on drugs or having some homosexual relations or this and that?

Maha Elsamnah, Iraqi-born Canadian citizen, in Michelle Shephard, "Khadr Family Return Deeply Divisive," *Toronto Star*, 13 April 2004. Elsamnah is referring to her fourteen-year-old son Karim, shot in the spine and paralyzed after fighting on the side of the al-Qaeda in Pakistan in October 2003. At first the mother said she did not want to return to Canada for the above reasons; thereafter she changed her mind. Family members were close to the family of Osama bin Laden. Her husband, Ahmed Said Khadr, raised money in Canada for and was a founder of al-Qaeda; he was killed while fighting in Pakistan in 2003. Two other sons, Omar and Abdurahman, were captured by American troops and detained at Guantanamo Bay, Cuba. The third son Abdullah was said to be hiding in Pakistan. In Canada, the daughter Zaynab expressed views on the Americans and 9/11: "They deserve it. They've been doing it for such a long time, why shouldn't they feel it once in a while?" The editorial in the *Toronto Star* began, "Many Canadians are outraged that Maha Elsamnah and her son Karim Khadr—members of the Khadr clan who befriended Osama bin Laden—are back 'home' after spending years abroad living with terrorists." Elsamnah, subsequently interviewed by Colin Freeze in "Khadrs' Citizenship Fuels Public Outcry," *The Globe and Mail*, 17 April 2004, retorted, "I'm Canadian, and I'm not begging for my rights; I'm demanding my rights."

Make sure people understand, we are not joining the coalition of the willing.... We have a coalition of the willing in Iraq ... I think we need to be the coalition of the wise.

Carolyn Parrish, maverick Liberal Member of Parliament, remarks made on Parliament Hill following a meeting of the Liberal caucus at which the U.S. missile-defence initiative was discussed, addressed first to supporters and then to reporters, 25 August 2004, in Bill Curry, "Liberal M.P. Insults U.S. Again," *National Post*, 26 August 2004.

IRELAND

There may be some odd fighting along the Ulster border, or a little civil war with perhaps a little revolution every now and then, but as a question the thing is finished.

Stephen Leacock, humorist, *My Discovery of England* (1922).

In Canada the Creator had space and took advantage of the distances to work with the strong strokes of a large brush. In the limited space of Ireland He had to work with the skill of the miniature artist and every honest tourist will admit His success.

Marcus Long, philosopher, address, "A Tourist's View of Ireland," Toronto, 15 March 1956, The Empire Club of Canada.

Our Irish ancestors put it in another way: "May the road rise up to meet you, may the wind always be at your back, may the rain fall soft upon your fields and the sun shine warm upon your face, and, until we meet again, may the Lord hold you in the palm of His hand."

Traditional Irish blessing offered by **Ronald Reagan**, U.S. president, address, "Relationships," Toronto, 21 June 1988, The Empire Club of Canada.

The distance between Toronto and Vancouver is greater than the distance between Toronto and Dublin.

Roddy Doyle, Irish novelist, interviewed in Winnipeg, "Doyle's Wry Words on Canada," *Toronto Star*, 2 October 2004.

ISLAM *See also* Muslims

If there's one thing the West has indeed learned about Islam, it's that the sacred and the secular are inseparable in Islamic terms. It is this sense of a coherent spiritual identity that is baffling to the West, which has come to regard culture and religious pluralism as divine doctrine, and committed itself to strict separation between church and state.

Jack Kapica, columnist, *The Globe and Mail*, 10 April 1991.

By opening ourselves to Transcendence, we sacralize ourselves and, by so doing, we sacralize the world. Reductionism is the denial of Transcendence.

M. Ali Lakhani, editor, "Reclaiming the Centre," *Sacred Web: A Journal of Tradition and Modernity*, Number 8, December 2001.

Few Canadians had the courage to speak the truth: that what Islam calls blasphemy, the West calls Voltaire.

Robert Fulford, columnist, referring to the controversy following the banning in Islamic countries of Salman Rushdie's novel *The Satanic Verses*, "From Delusions to Destruction," *National Post*, 6 October 2001.

I hereby cease to be a refusenik. Sign me up for Operation Ijtihad.

Irshad Manji, broadcaster and writer of Ugandan Asian background, *The Trouble with Islam: A Wake-up Call for Honesty and Change* (2003). In Arabic, *jihad* is "holy war"; *ijtihad* is "questioning."

Effective immediately, CP style for the founder of Islam is Muhammad, not Mohammed, to reflect the most common usage in Canada. The "u" spelling is closer to Arabic pronunciation. Use other spellings only if preferred by a specific person for his own name or in a title or the name of an organization.

"Style Update," *Copy Talk* (The Canadian Press), April 2003.

Through our screaming self-pity and our conspicuous silences, we Muslims are conspiring against ourselves. We're in crisis, and we're dragging the rest of the world with us. If ever there was a moment for an Islamic reformation, it's now. For the love of God, what are we doing about it?

Irshad Manji, television personality and proponent of the Islamic tradition of *ijtihad* (questioning), *The Trouble with Islam: A Muslim's Call for Reform in Her Faith* (2004).

Many will insist that I'm undermining the dignity of Muslims by challenging a pillar of their identity. By urging my fellow Muslims to consider these questions, I'm showing faith in their capacity to be thoughtful and humane. I'm appealing to their heads rather than only their hearts. Ultimately I'm fighting not Islam but the routinely low expectations of those who practise it.

Irshad Manji, broadcaster and author, referring to idolizing the Koran, "Riots and Rage Won't Salvage Islam's Honour," *Toronto Star*, 19 May 2005. "She is Osama bin Laden's worst nightmare," wrote Clifford Krauss in his profile of Manji in *The New York Times*, as noted by Robert Fulford, "Talking to Americans," *Toronto Life*, June 2005.

ISOLATIONISM *See also* Internationalism

We live in a fire-proof house, far from inflammable materials.

Raoul Dandurand, Canadian delegate, address, League of Nations Assembly, The Hague, 2 October 1924. The full text of this classic description of the country's spirit of isolationism appears in *Documents on Canadian Foreign Policy: 1917–1939* (1962), edited by Walter A. Riddell.

ISRAEL *See also* Jewish Culture; Middle East

What's going on in Israel is tragic; what's happening in Canada is a farce.

Mordecai Richler, novelist and critic of Quebec's sovereignty movement, refusing to equate Palestinian terrorists with Quebec separatists, interviewed by Sam Orbaum, "Make 'Em Mad, Mordecai Richler!" *The Jerusalem Post Magazine*, 6 November 1992.

History will ask only one question of this Jewish generation: "Will you or will you not secure the State of Israel?"

Two times before, the Jewish people lost sovereignty: to the Babylonians in 586 B.C.E. and to the Romans in 70 C.E. Three strikes—

you're out. If the first two times fail, the third is decisive.

Ruth Wisse, Montreal-born professor of Near Eastern languages, Harvard University, address, Toronto, 12 December 2000, in Rick Kardonne, "Jews Must Secure Israel," *The Jewish Tribune*, 10 January 2002.

Palestinian Arab nationalism consists purely of opposition to the Jews.

Ruth Wisse, Montreal-born professor of Near Eastern languages, Harvard University, address, Toronto, 12 December 2000, in Rick Kardonne, "Jews Must Secure Israel," *The Jewish Tribune*, 10 January 2002.

Canada's entire population lives along one road, the Trans-Canada Highway which, unlike the Trans-Israel Highway, no one objects to because who gets excited about paving over holy Canadian land? Here every grain is holy, every rock is worth a debate in the United Nations.

Sam Orbaum, Montreal-born columnist, "I'd Rather Live in Israel," *The Jerusalem Post Magazine*, 13 July 2001.

In Canada, wherever you go, you have to detour around huge lakes and seas, so it takes much longer to get places. In Israel, we have one little lake far away, and our seas are conveniently placed along the sides.

Sam Orbaum, Montreal-born columnist, "I'd Rather Live in Israel," *The Jerusalem Post Magazine*, 13 July 2001.

Securing Israel is inseparable from securing democracy.

Ruth Wisse, Montreal-born professor of Near Eastern Languages, Harvard University, address, Toronto, 12 December 2000, in Rick Kardonne, "Jews Must Secure Israel," *The Jewish Tribune*, 10 January 2002.

Israel has, in effect, become the new Jew.

Brian Mulroney, former prime minister, observation, conference, Anti-Semitism: The Politicization of Prejudice in the Contemporary World, University of Toronto, in Michael Friscolani, *National Post*, 10 February 2003.

The totally innocent people [are] obviously the children, but they are not innocent if they are part of a population which is the total population of Israel [which] is part of the army.... They are part of the army ... even if they have civilian clothes. The same, if they are women in the army ... anybody above eighteen is a part of the Israeli popular army.

Mohamed Elmasry, president, Canadian Islamic Congress, offering a justification for terrorist attacks in the name of Islam against Israeli civilians, on a panel discussion devoted to terrorism led by writer and broadcaster Michael Coren on *The Michael Coren Show*, a specialty-channel TV discussion program, Toronto, 19 October 2004, as in Chris Wattie, "Ottawa Reviews Anti-Israeli Remarks," *National Post*, 23 October 2004. Elmasry, an engineer by profession, alluded to compulsory military service in Israel and blurred the line between combatant and civilian, as noted by Christie Blatchford, "The Real Mohamed Elmasry," *National Post*, 30 October 2004.

ITALIAN CULTURE

Let's call this common desire to have a thriving world-Italian culture, free of nationalism, one that will not segregate but connect our different communities: the Italic experience.

Antonio D'Alfonso, poet and essayist, "Unmeltable Ethnics," *In Italics: In Defense of Ethnicity* (1996).

Not bad for a mangia cake!

Paul Martin, Liberal minister, 1990 leadership campaign, addressing 1000 Canadian Italians in Toronto, in Jane Taber, "The Day a Close Friend Walked Out on the P.M.," *The Globe and Mail*, 20 December 2003. "Mangia cake" is Italian slang for a non-Italian, i.e., a Canadian. It drew "a big laugh from the Italian Canadian audience."

ITALY

Signor Mussolini yesterday paid a flying visit to Ottawa with a view to seeing how much of the government would need to be abolished at once and how much of it might be left over till next year.

Stephen Leacock, humorist, *Short Circuits* (1928).

Italy became my adopted home. I fell hopelessly in love with my curve of the Tiber. The best of old Rome was at my feet and there I am still planted—maple trees from Muskoka and all.

Roloff Beny, Medicine Hat–born Rome-based photographer, address, "What Is Wrong with Loving Canada?" Toronto, 27 October 1983, The Empire Club of Canada.

Of course, there are true boundaries in the same sense that the statement "Ontario is older than Italy" is true. It is true, factually and absolutely—though the truth of the statement is trivial and irrelevant.

John Bentley Mays, author, *Arrivals: Stories form the History of Ontario* (2002).

Sam Orbaum, Montreal-born columnist, "I'd Rather Live in Israel," *The Jerusalem Post Magazine*, 13 July 2001.

JAPAN

Some of the English signs in Tokyo are rather amusing. For instance, a city transfer was described on one sign as "An internal railway, baggage sent in all directions." The influx of the English language is bringing the people of that country close to ourselves. With the language come English ideas and so we draw nearer and nearer together.

Egerton Ryerson, Methodist missionary, address, "Occidental, Japan," Toronto, 13 April 1905, The Empire Club of Canada.

JEWISH CULTURE *See also* Israel; Judaism

I've always thought they were an extraordinary people. I always admired the Jews—their ability to get out of terrible situations, individually and collectively, to surpass a lot of people in the world of the arts, sciences, and business. I admire them and at the same time I pity them.... I lived with them, I shared with them, the indignity that weighs on all of us like a lead coat on us, the human species, that there was such a crime committed against the Jews.

Lucien Bouchard, Quebec premier, repudiating the ethnic views of Yves Michaud and denying him Parti Québécois candidacy, National Assembly, 20 December 2000, in Rhéal Séguin, "End Intolerance, Bouchard Urges," *The Globe and Mail*, 21 December 2000.

Jewish life in Canada is as good as it has been anywhere since the Golden Age of Spain.

Morton Weinfeld, academic, *Like Everyone Else ... but Different* (2001).

Canada has more goyim per capita than Israel, so the Jews have to behave, while here, we're free to behave like shkotzim if we want, which many do.

Sam Orbaum, Montreal-born columnist, "I'd Rather Live in Israel," *The Jerusalem Post Magazine*, 13 July 2001.

People say that Jews in Montreal are the third solitude. They were able to find their own space between the English and French, and there wasn't a clear-cut need to assimilate as much as in Toronto.

Morton Weinfeld, chair, Canadian Ethnic Studies, McGill University, in Ingrid Peritz, "Guardian of Yiddish Culture Dies," *The Globe and Mail*, 17 December 2003.

The Jew is the memory of history.

Attributed to **Roy Faibish**, Ottawa public servant, by Peter C. Newman, *Here Be Dragons: Telling Tales of People, Passion, and Power* (2004).

By asserting my Jewishness I am keeping faith with my ancestors, and thus I am being true to myself.

Edgar M. Bronfman, president, World Jewish Congress, *I Am Jewish: Personal Reflections Inspired by the Last Words of Daniel Pearl* (2004), edited by Judea and Ruth Pearl.

For me, being Jewish means keeping the vision of justice alive in tribute to the memory of those who were denied it.

Rosalie Abella, justice, Supreme Court of Canada, *I Am Jewish: Personal Reflections Inspired by the Last Words of Daniel Pearl* (2004), edited by Judea and Ruth Pearl.

JOKES *See also* Humour

We have to be funny because we don't have guns. If I had a gun, I might not feel the need to make jokes.

Robin Duke, SCTV writer, born in Scarborough, Ont., relating Canada's gun laws to its U.S.-based comedy writers, Toronto benefit, Humber College's Comedy Workshop, 1 April 2001, in Martin Knelman, "Comics Get Serious on Subject of Funny," *Toronto Star*, 2 April 2001.

It's easy to fall into the trap of making the same jokes about Canada.... The way that we've executed the jokes are more about making fun of Americans and their ignorance, than of Canada.

Tim Long, a television writer originally from Exeter, Ont., on writing an episode of the U.S. animated TV series *The Simpsons*, in which the title family takes a trip to Toronto, in Greg David, *TV Guide*, 16 February 2002.

JOURNALISM *See also* News

You needn't tell me anything about the enterprise of *The Toronto Daily Star*. I have long known that your paper has a perfect genius for features—for what is of interest to the people at large. That is a great gift, in a reporter or in a newspaper: a sense of discernment as to what is of real interest and what is not.

Stephen Leacock, humorist, page-one interview by R.E. Knowles, "Leacock Says Sir A. Currie Most Distinguished Pupil," *Toronto Daily Star*, 16 February 1933.

You will never be worth more than $25 a week to the *Winnipeg Free Press*.

Attributed to **George Ferguson**, managing editor of the *Winnipeg Free Press*, rejecting cub reporter **Scott Young**'s request for a raise in 1941, quoted in the latter's obituary, "A Multi-faceted Writing Career," *National Post*, 15 June 2005. Young quit, moved to Toronto, and became a successful writer and columnist.

I have always had a feeling that the whole foundation of the newspaper business might just rest there on curiosity.

J. Douglas MacFarlane, newspaperman, address, School of Journalism, University of Western Ontario, 1 December 1955, reproduced by Richard MacFarlane, *Canada's Newspaper Legend: The Story of J. Douglas MacFarlane* (2000).

Helicopter crash, $22.

Fabled item in an expense account submitted to the *Toronto Daily Star* in the 1960s by **William Stevenson**, foreign correspondent, as noted by Douglas Fetherling, *The Broadview Book of Canadian Anecdotes* (1988).

Journalism has become trendy, it has become fashionable. All it takes to become a journalist is the nerve and the opportunity. That's how I got into it! But we have no particular skills. Most of us type with two fingers; we can't take shorthand. The greenest stenographer entering the job market has more mechanical skills than the most exalted journalist at the end of his career.

Peter Worthington, editor, *Toronto Sun*, address, "Blame the Media," Toronto, 8 March 1979, The Empire Club of Canada.

The English poet Matthew Arnold once wrote that "Journalism is literature in a hurry." I'm not at all sure about it being literature, but, these days, it's certainly accurate to say in a paraphrase that journalism is history on the run.

Knowlton Nash, journalist and broadcaster, address, "Television News: History on the Run," Toronto, 26 June 1986, The Empire Club of Canada.

It is one of the great myths of the industry that you need journalists to produce a newspaper.

Attributed to **Conrad Black**, press baron, at the time of the 1992 strike at Quebec City's *Le Soleil*, by Peter C. Newman, *Here Be Dragons: Telling Tales of People, Passion, and Power* (2004). At the time, Newman notes, "Black had been the proud proprietor of the world's third-largest publishing empire, with five hundred newspapers and magazines spreading his word to nearly six million daily and weekly readers."

As for journalism as a profession—well, that is for journalists to decide. Organizations like the Law Society of Upper Canada, the College of Physicians and Surgeons, the accounting institutes and others set standards for themselves, however imperfectly. Only journalists can decide whether they wish to set standards of practice for their own profession—without question a difficult task indeed.

William G. Davis, former Ontario premier, address, "The Media's Role in Society," Toronto, 7 April 1994, The Empire Club of Canada.

Generally, the media is too lazy to start trouble, but—boy!—we sure know how to fan the flames.

John Fraser, journalist, address, "Personal Responsibility and the Media," Toronto, 1 December 1994, The Empire Club of Canada.

If journalists began to cover news and write features not just for their 500,000 "demographically defined consumers" or their 3.2-million mass audience, or however many readers, but instead specifically wrote their stories for their fathers and mothers, for their spouses, for their children, for their friends and close colleagues, then they might well start something very close to a revolution.

John Fraser, journalist, address, "Personal Responsibility and the Media," Toronto, 1 December 1994, The Empire Club of Canada.

You will be a journalist when you stop asking, "Is this bastard lying to me?" and start asking, "Why is this bastard lying to me?" Because that's the story.

Gwynne Dyer, journalist, in Tatjana Sulker, "Nature or Nurture in News," *Convergence Magazine* (Humber College, School of Media Studies), fall 2000.

Journalism's authority and influence is in direct proportion to the size of the matter at issue; then again, the more politicized the subject, the less reliable the coverage and the more likely readers will find shadings of editorial bias and self-interest.

Dalton Camp, columnist, "Opinion," *Toronto Star*, 3 June 2001.

"You cannot hope / To bribe or twist / Thank God! The / Canadian Journalist. / But, seeing what / The man will do / Unbribed, there's / No occasion to."

Verse attributed to **Humbert Wolfe** in "The Celestial City," as quoted by John Koopman introducing the speaker, Toronto, 15 November 2001, The Empire Club of Canada.

My experience with journalists authorized me to record that a very large number of them are ignorant, lazy, opinionated, intellectually dishonest and inadequately supervised.

Conrad Black, publisher, then aged 25 years, testimony, committee of the Canadian Senate, noted by essayist Calvin Trillin, "Paper Baron," *The New Yorker*, 17 December 2001.

I refused. I said that I had not spent thirty years in journalism attempting to pursue the truth in order to leave on a lie. If I was being fired, I wanted to be able to say so.

Russell Mills, veteran newspaperman and publisher of the *Ottawa Citizen*, referring to the financial settlement that was available if he were willing to portray his departure as a retirement and sign an agreement not to discuss the offer and conditions, "Editorial Freedom: Under the Asper Thumb," *The Globe and Mail*, 19 June 2002. David Asper of CanWest Global Communications Corp. dismissed Mills on 16 June 2002, for publishing an editorial that called for the resignation of Prime Minister Jean Chrétien.

A newsroom is a place where people are unhappy all the time.

Lise Bissonnette, author and former publisher of *Le Devoir*, interviewed by Tina Srebotnjak, host of CLT's *Book Television*, 3 November 2003.

Journalism exists to serve the public and its right to know. It has other goals too, but that is the most important one.

William Kaplan, advocate and author, *A Secret Trial: Brian Mulroney, Stevie Cameron, and the Public Trust* (2004).

If I write about rubber boots in puddles, oversized pepper shakers, kids' homework or the difference between those who drink Starbucks and those who drink Tim Hortons, my e-mail overflows. I'll get hundreds, and they will continue on for months. If I write about the plight of the cities, the situation in Ottawa, or a riding profile, I'll get, maybe, one e-mail. And yet I fear being dismissed as a "lightweight" if I do too many of the seemingly "easy" ones—even as I'm fully aware they are touching people where they live.

Roy MacGregor, columnist for *The Globe and Mail*, personal communication, 10 April 2004.

Approach each story as if you just arrived in town that morning, and write each story as if you're leaving town that night.

Walter Stewart, journalist, in Roy MacGregor, "This Country," *The Globe and Mail*, 17 September 2004.

I feel like the neighbour who interrupts a great party to say, Um, some of the cars parked outside are being tagged and towed.

Rick Salutin, columnist, referring to his role as a social critic (or village scold), "Democracy if Necessary, but Not … ," *The Globe and Mail*, 4 March 2005.

That's the dreadful suspicion: That we dip into the surface of deep events, paddle with our feet, guard our comforts, patronize our contacts, exploit great tragedies for the good of our careers, and *get the story wrong*.

Bill Cameron, journalist and broadcaster, expressing concern about the journalist's public image in 1990, in Antonia Zerbisias, "Obituary," *Toronto Star*, 13 March 2005.

JOURNEY *See also* Travel

Something in the very roundness of the world suggests that every journey is always to be continued.

Alberto Manguel, Canadian author, born in Argentina, "Destination Ithaka," *Passages: Welcome Home to Canada* (2002), with a preface by Rudyard Griffiths.

JOY

Joy is greatly underrated as an aspect of human life. We are supposed to be serious to the exclusion of joy. Yet joy is possible to all of us if we understand what is genuine and what is false, what is true and what is delusion. What is human and what denies humanity.

Adrienne Clarkson, governor general, address, University of Toronto, 19 June 2001, "Worth Repeating," *Toronto Star*, 20 June 2001.

The way that we bring joy into our lives is by bringing joy into the lives of others.

Craig Kielburger, youthful founder of Kids Can Free the Children, in 1996 at the age of twelve, in Barry Shainbaum, *Hope & Heroes: Portraits of Integrity & Inspiration* (2003).

JUDAISM *See also* Anti-Semitism; Holocaust; Israel; Jewish Culture; Middle East

The religion called Judaism I find quite fascinating. Although I have some quarrels with the strict interpretations of the Orthodox and even more so with the Ultra-Orthodox, I am very happy with the essentials of my religion. I like the fact that we each are directly responsible and responsive to the Almighty.

Edgar M. Bronfman, Canadian-born president, World Jewish Congress, *I Am Jewish: Personal Reflections Inspired by the Last Words of Daniel Pearl* (2004), edited by Judea and Ruth Pearl.

I had decided to stop being not-a-Christian and to become not-a-Jew. I am a Jewish nonbeliever. I do not believe in God. It is the same conversion as Ruth's in the Bible: "Your people shall be my people." I have a tremendous respect for the culture and the ethic, the Jewish emphasis on this world, the idea that God is unknowable.

Robert Adams, lecturer, explaining his conversion from Calvinism to Judaism, in Cecily Ross, "Robert Adams Says Goodbye," *The Globe and Mail*, 23 May 2005.

JUDGES *See also* Law

Of a frontier judge on a day now happily past, it is related that he came into Court one morning and said, "Yesterday I received a letter in the mail from the plaintiff containing a cheque for $1,000. This morning I received a letter in the mail from the defendant containing a cheque for $1,500. I propose to return $500 to the defendant in order that I should be able to try this case on its merits."

Samuel Freedman, judge, address, "Some Aspects of My Profession," Toronto, 5 January 1961, The Empire Club of Canada.

After the Russian Revolution of October 1917, an important slogan used by the Bolsheviks was, "All power to the Soviets." The slogan of Canada's ruling clique today appears to be, "All power to the judges."

Robert Ivan Martin, law professor, *The Most Dangerous Branch: How the Supreme Court of Canada Has Undermined Our Law and Our Democracy* (2003).

I guess the thing to remember as a judge is that you have an important role to play, but you are not an important person.

Patrick LeSage, judge, Superior Court of Justice, Ontario, interviewed on his retirement by Tracy Tyler, "LeSage: Beyond the Bench," *Toronto Star*, 13 April 2004.

JUSTICE *See also* Injustice; Law

There are many in this old world of ours who hold that things break even for all of us. I have observed, for example, that we all get the same amount of ice. The rich get it in the summertime, and the poor get it in the winter.

Bat (William Barclay) Masterson (1853–1921), Canadian-born American outlaw-turned-sheriff, characteristic remark, quoted in *The Toastmaster's Treasure Chest* (1979), edited by Herbert V. Prochnow and Herbert V. Prochnow Jr.

A just society.

Phrase from an essay written by **F.R. Scott** and published in 1939 that inspired the electoral slogan "The Just Society," adopted in 1968 by the Liberals under Pierre Elliott Trudeau, according to Graham Fraser, "The Fight for Canada's Rights," *Toronto Star*, 13 April 2002.

For justice is only a response to evil after evil is done. A necessary but never fulfilling recompense.

Erna Paris, author, *Long Shadows: Truth, Lies and History* (2000).

Justice alone will never bring peace to our planet.

Louise Arbour, Canadian jurist and head of the world's first international court, interviewed by Erna Paris, *Long Shadows: Truth, Lies and History* (2000).

Martin: What do you do with a guy who has all kinds of ideas about human rights in terms of justice?
Cotler: Well, I always thought human rights meant justice.
Martin: Congratulations, Minister of Justice.

Telephone conversation between newly elected Prime Minister **Paul Martin** and **Irwin Cotler**, activist, academic, and human-rights lawyer, 11 December 2003, appointed minister of Justice on 12 December 2003. Recalled by Cotler in Tonda MacCharles, "Cotler Not Afraid to Speak His Mind," *Toronto Star*, 13 December 2003.

Indifference is injustice's incubator. It is not just what you stand for, it is what you stand up for.

Rosalie Abella, justice, Supreme Court of Canada, *I Am Jewish: Personal Reflections Inspired by the Last Words of Daniel Pearl* (2004), edited by Judea and Ruth Pearl.

There's no real innocence, just unproven guilt.

James LeCraw, victim of unproven charges that were later dropped, who subsequently committed suicide, quoted in the editorial "The Dark Consequences of Naming and Shaming," *The Globe and Mail*, 29 November 2004.

k

KIDNAPPING *See also* Law

Your shift is over, you can go home now.

Norbert Reinhart, owner of the Canadian-based geological exploration company Terramundo Drilling, who volunteered to be held hostage by the Revolutionary Armed Forces of Columbia (FARC) in exchange for the freedom of his foreman, Edward Leonard. With these words, Reinhart addressed Leonard, who had been kidnapped in June 1998, near Bucaramanga, Colombia. In September, Reinhart changed places with him and thereafter secured his own release by paying a ransom to his guerilla captors. In Barry Shainbaum, *Hope & Heroes: Portraits of Integrity & Inspiration* (2003).

KILLING *See* Murder

KING, W.L. MACKENZIE

Now, there has been a great deal said about national unity. I am just going to make this one observation with regard to my friend, William Lyon Mackenzie King, and I want it made very clear here that when I drank the Toast to the King, a few moments ago, it was to Our Majesty, the King. They said all around me, "The King." I wanted to make myself clear on that point. This gentleman at this moment is charging me with entering into a conspiracy to destroy Confederation. Now, I deny the allegation most emphatically. There isn't a more loyal Canadian in this great gathering than myself.

Mitch Hepburn, Ontario premier, address, "Present Day Problems," Toronto, 15 December 1938, The Empire Club of Canada.

He skillfully avoided what was wrong / Without saying what was right, / And he never let his on the one hand / Know what his on the other hand was doing.

Oft-quoted lines from **F.R. Scott**'s satiric poem "W.L.M.K." (1957), *Selected Poems* (1966).

KISSES *See also* Love

A smile is an open window, a kiss is an open door.

Arnold Haultain, aphorist, *Hints for Lovers* (1909).

He kisses her on the nose. On the nose it's treason, on the forehead it's tenderness, on the cheek it's friendship, on the mouth it's love, on the neck it's passion.

Thoughts of a character in **Jacques Poulin**'s novel *Jimmy* (1969).

KLONDIKE

It is doubtful if the Dominion, as we now understand it, would have come into being, with British Columbia as the Western side, but for the finding of gold. No one would have thought of building a railway through that wilderness if there had not been a powerful magnet at the end. You are all young enough to know exactly what happened in the Klondike, and I need not refer to the part that gold played there. The Klondike would have been the Arctic region which it is generally supposed to be (although in reality it has a delightful summer) if it had not been for the discovery of gold. Perhaps worth mentioning is the fact that the richest creek ever known in the world was Eldorado Creek in the Klondike. $20,000,000 worth of gold was taken out of it. So much for our part of the Empire.

A.P. Coleman, geologist, address, "Gold and the Empire," Toronto, 28 March 1907, The Empire Club of Canada.

Like my conception of the Klondyke, full of gold-rush, built on sands in every sense....

Isaiah Berlin, British philosopher, letter addressed to Felix and Marion Frankfurter during a visit to Palestine in 1934, comparing the city of Tel Aviv to the Klondike, in Berlin's

Letters: 1928–1946 (2004), edited by Henry Hardy, as noted by Nicholas Fraser, "Lucky Berlin," *Harper's*, January 2005.

This is the Cariboo Trail, mister: a broken heart for every rock, a dead man for every tree.

Line spoken by the character played by actor **George "Gabby" Hayes** in the movie *The Cariboo Trail* (1950), starring Randolph Scott … and Gabby Hayes.

There can never be another Klondike-style stampede. Today the Chilkoot Pass is for sightseers who go on to Dawson by bus or automobile. The thrill of discovery that once lured explorers has been replaced by the thrill of stranger discoveries in outer space.

Pierre Berton, author, *Captives of the North* (2004).

Dawson City in those days was a unique community, a cosmopolitan village where everybody knew everybody else, full of adventurous spirits who had come from every corner of the globe to profit from the great stampede of 1898.

Pierre Berton, author, *Captives of the North* (2004).

KNOWLEDGE *See also* Ideas; Wisdom

The seeing or observing is not part of the experimental finding: only what is seen and observed is that. The seeing or observing are subjective: what is seen or observed is objective. But without seeing, nothing would be seen, no observation would be made, and no hypothesis tested.

Fraser Cowley, philosopher, *A Critique of British Empiricism* (1968).

As long as we have to rely on the brain, we are simply not capable of knowing whether what we think we are seeing, smelling, hearing or remembering is real, close to reality or some hastily made up re-creation of reality. But what else can we rely on?

Jay Ingram, broadcaster, *The Burning House: Unlocking the Mysteries of the Brain* (1994).

The pursuit of knowledge, then, is the pursuit of an unknown, and the possibility of that pursuit is the existence of an ideal.

Bernard Lonergan, theologian, *Insight: A Study of Human Understanding* (1953), in *The Lonergan Reader* (1997), edited by Mark D. Morelli and Elizabeth A. Morelli.

Knowledge begins in an observing person and ends by changing the person.

George Whalley, scholar, commencement address, Rothesay College School, N.B., 1959, *George Whalley: Remembrances* (1989), edited by Michael D. Moore.

The knowledge that you can have is inexhaustible, and what is inexhaustible is benevolent. The knowledge that you cannot have is of the riddles of birth and death, of our future destiny and the purposes of God. Here there is no knowledge, but illusions that restrict freedom and limit hope. Accept the mystery behind knowledge: It is not darkness but shadow.

Northrop Frye, literary theorist, cultural critic and ordained Anglican minister, address, Metropolitan United Church, Toronto, 10 April 1988, *Northrop Frye on Religion* (2000), Volume 4, *Collected Works*, edited by Alvin A. Lee and Jean O'Grady.

KOREA

The Cunning Man is going well, and in funny places: I signed a contract for publication in Korea last week. Now what do Koreans want with a book like that?

Robertson Davies, man of letters, referring to the translation of the novel by that name into Korean, letter, 22 July 1995, *For Your Eye Alone: Letters, 1976–1995* (1999).

KYOTO ACCORD *See also* Global Warming

Canada will not meet the Kyoto targets for reduction in its carbon dioxide emissions and remains at the top of the list of the world's largest per-capita contributors to the build-up of greenhouse gases in the atmosphere. And we have no viable plan to meet these targets. We should take no comfort from the fact that measures to do so may be temporarily relieved by the impasse in the climate change negotiations. Delay will only increase the costs and the risks of dealing with this issue, which is of decisive importance to the human future. The irony is that this weakening of the will to deal with climate change comes just as the scientific evidence of the effects we are having on climate and its consequences for our future has become more compelling.

Maurice F. Strong, UN adviser, address, "Does the Environment Matter to Canada?" Toronto, 3 April 2001, The Empire Club of Canada.

But it is just a matter of time before the Alps are snowless, the Arctic Ocean ice-free, the Amazon rainforests and the boreal canopy of the Canadian Shield burned, the salmon vanished, the coral reefs bleached away, the Everglades inundated by salt water, the Gulf Stream itself thrown out of whack. How long before the seasons as we know them have disappeared under a chemical shroud?

Robert Hunter, activist and author, *2030: Confronting Thermageddon in Our Lifetime* (2002).

In every discussion we've had, provinces differ with provinces quite bitterly over different issues. The fact is we have a compromise, and that compromise is an effort to deal with all the provincial issues that have been raised, but we know that some will find their concerns have not been accommodated enough.

David Anderson, minister of the Environment, reacting to differing provincial concerns over the federal government's plan to implement the 12 Kyoto accords on greenhouse-gas reduction strategy, as quoted in "Provinces Unanimous on 12 Kyoto Principles," Montreal *Gazette*, 29 October 2002.

We have to realize it's a long-term problem. Kyoto is not and should not be the objective—it's a stepping stone.

Joseph Doucet, academic, University of Alberta, in Geoff McMaster, "The Kyoto Accord," ExpressNews, website, 28 December 2005.

L

LABOUR *See also* Employment; Unemployment; Unions; Welfare

Grass will grow, the river will reach the sea, the boy will become a man, and labour will come into its own.

F.J. (Fred) Dixon, union leader charged with seditious conspiracy following the Winnipeg General Strike, address to the jury, Winnipeg, 13–14 February 1920.

We are thankful for these and all the good things of life. We recognize that they are part of our common heritage and come to us through the efforts of our brothers and sisters the world over. What we desire for ourselves we wish for all. To this end may we take our share in the world's work and the world's struggles.

J.S. Woodsworth, socialist and a founder of the Labour Church, the prayer "Grace before Meat" he said at dinner in the 1920s, in Kenneth J. McNaught, *A Prophet in Politics* (1959).

In my official capacity I have travelled the middle of the road, but now that you have put the extreme alternative to me, my place is marching with the workers rather than riding with General Motors. At this late date I cannot oppose unionism and the workers and labour as a whole.

David A. Croll, Ontario minister of Public Welfare, Labour, and Municipal Affairs, letter of resignation to Premier Mitchell Hepburn, 14 April 1937. The text of the letter appeared on 15 April 1937 in the *Toronto Daily Star.*

The most mobile workers in the world come to Canada and find themselves immobilized.

Faviola Fernandez, teacher from Singapore, unable to teach in Canada, in Clifford Krauss, "Some Skilled Foreigners Find Jobs Scarce in Canada," *The New York Times*, 5 June 2005.

LABRADOR *See also* Newfoundland & Labrador

A few minutes ago, in order to satisfy my own curiosity, I asked Dr. Grenfell why it was that Labrador was usually called "the Labrador," and he said he thought it was the result of the old sailing days, when the old sailor himself shortened the term "the Labrador Coast" to "the Labrador"; and so, in speaking of it as "the Labrador," I want to introduce to you "the Grenfell." (Applause.)

C.H. Mitchell, president, Empire Club, introducing Sir William T. Grenfell, medical doctor and missionary to Labrador, address, Toronto, 17 November 1921, The Empire Club of Canada.

For one thing, there is the question of the boundaries of Quebec. I don't think there is any doubt that the Parti Québécois would want to seize, by some means or other, Labrador. I am a fifth-generation Newfoundlander, and I have said more than once, publicly and privately, that if there is any question of trying to seize Labrador every Newfoundlander in the world would rise to the defence of that boundary, and all the dead ones would rise from their graves and join us.

Eugene Forsey, constitutional specialist, address, "Canada, Quebec, and the Constitution," Toronto, 28 April 1977, The Empire Club of Canada.

LAKES *See also* Great Lakes; Water

I have seen one of the most beautiful lakes in the North, Kluane Lake, where there are measurably nine different shades of green and purple from the margin to the centre.

Pierre Berton, author, address, "The Future of the North," Toronto, 11 October 1973, The Empire Club of Canada.

LAND *See also* Arts & Artists; Countries; Geography; Land Claims; Nationalism; Property

The time I have spent in Canada has been all too short, and I greatly wish I might have been able to stay longer to see your beautiful country, especially in its grand mountain ranges and where its lakes empty their waters into the mighty river St. Lawrence in your eastern provinces.

Rabindranath Tagore, Bengali sage, farewell message delivered to the Southam newspaper chain, Fourth Triennial Conference of the National Council of Education, Vancouver, 8–13 April 1929, quoted in "Tagore," *The Canadian Theosophist*, May 1929.

A man without land is nobody. Remember that, Duddel.

Grandfather's advice to young Duddel, or Duddy, in **Mordecai Richler**'s novel *The Apprenticeship of Duddy Kravitz* (1959) and the movie based on it, directed by Ted Kotcheff in 1974.

Who am I then to take such expanses of space, to comprehend a hundred thousand lakes, seventy-five rivers, ten chains of mountains, three oceans, the North Pole and the sun that never sets on my country?

Lines from **Jean-Guy Pilon**'s prose poem "The Needs of the Land!" *Recours au pays* (1961), translated by Louis Dudek, *Poetry of Our Time* (1965), edited by Louis Dudek.

Since we can't export the scenery / We shall have to import the tourists.

Sir William C. Van Horne, builder of the Canadian Pacific Railway, inscription on the base of the statue erected in his honour on the grounds of the Banff Springs Hotel, Banff, Alta., unveiled 11 January 1991.

Even though most Canadians think the pre-Cambrian Shield is a birth control device, territorial integrity is what gives us our turf and our integrity. Our men and women are sons and daughters of their landscapes, but nowhere is this more true than in Canada where the dominant gene of nationhood has been possession of the land itself. We laid claim to this large land by planting settlements in the shoulders of our shores, the elbows of our rivers, and the laps of our mountains, always testing nature rather than trying to conquer it.

Peter C. Newman, author, address, "The Canadian Revolution," Toronto, 30 November 1995, The Empire Club of Canada.

LAND CLAIMS *See also* Aboriginal Rights; Land

In December 1995, the Fraser Institute, an influential right-wing think-tank in Vancouver, reported on what it thought about Native land claims in British Columbia. Given, the report stated, that there were forty-eight tribal groups representing 86,978 Native people claiming 1,048,744 square kilometres of British Columbia (111 percent of the total land mass of the province), the only sensible thing the B.C. government could do was divide the province into small parcels and give one parcel to each resident of British Columbia, just as the federal government had done in the 1860s.

Wayne Grady, author, *Chasing the Chinook: On the Trail of Canadian Words and Culture* (1998).

The Royal Assent of our treaty signifies the end of the colonial era for the Nisga'a people. It is a great and historic day for all Canadians, and this achievement is a beacon of hope for colonized people in our own country and throughout the world.

Joseph Gosnell, elected chief of the Nisga'a, address, 13 April 2000, on the passing into Canadian law of the Nisga'a Treaty, which recognizes the legal principle of the inherent right of aboriginal self-government.

LAND MINES *See also* War

The Ottawa Convention, the way we dealt with the landmine issue, changed thinking about how we could deal with humanitarian crises. It was a novel, people-based approach to disarmament that took aim directly at weapons that cause the most damage to individuals. The Ottawa Process is only one example of the human security agenda at work.

Lloyd Axworthy, minister of Foreign Affairs, referring to the Ottawa Convention against land mines, address, "Canada's Actions against Land Mines," Toronto, 28 June 1999, The Empire Club of Canada. The treaty banning land mines was signed in Ottawa on 3 December 1997.

LANDRY, BERNARD *See also* Separatism

And Mr. Landry is simply the latest in a long line of embarrassments who deserves a one-way ticket to political oblivion but will continue to torment us all. Because we let him.

Diane Francis, columnist, "How Landry Gets Away Scot-free," *Financial Post*, 1 December 2001. Mordecai Richler always referred to him as "Dirty Laundry."

Don't talk to me about women's groups. I would rather meet the president of Sun Life.

Bernard Landry, Quebec premier, candid remark made during a debate on a resolution calling for equal numbers of men and women candidates for the Parti Québécois, convention, 9 March 2003, in Graham Fraser, "Women's Groups Blast Comments by Landry," *Toronto Star*, 11 March 2003. Landry thought he was distancing himself from social activists. Sun Life remains a sore point with separatists; when the Parti Québécois came to power, its executives moved the corporation's head office from Montreal to Toronto. Landry himself was sore because he had met with hostility for his "bird brain" remark that poor women should be bright enough to feed their children.

The future is either Catalan or Taliban.

Bernard Landry, Quebec premier, remark made in a speech in the aftermath of September 11, 2001, suggesting that the world faces the alternatives of separation or terrorism, recalled by Paul Wells, "Commentary," *National Post*, 12 March 2003.

À la prochain.

Bernard Landry, Quebec premier, conceding defeat, provincial election, Théâtre du Capitole, Quebec City, 14 April 2003. The French words mean "until next time" and recall René Lévesque's "*À la prochaine fois*" in announcing the close results of the first sovereignty referendum on 20 May 1980.

The people are never wrong. They put us where we belong. They put us in government, they put us in opposition. We must welcome these two events in the spirit of public service and do our work with ardour.

Bernard Landry, Quebec premier, resignation speech, Quebec City, 29 April 2003, in Graeme Hamilton, "Biggest Change Since Quiet Revolution: Charest," *National Post*, 30 April 2003.

Quebec's population had endured a cataclysm comparable to the Chernobyl nuclear catastrophe.

Bernard Landry, Quebec premier, interview with *L'Express* in 1994, quoted by Peter C. Newman, *Here Be Dragons: Telling Tales of People, Passion, and Power* (2004).

LANDSCAPE *See also* Arts & Artists; Geography; Land

He was not in the frame of mind to get much comfort out of the Canadian wilds, for he was always sore with longing for a different kind of landscape.

Line about the English remittance man Jim Hallward in **John Buchan**'s story "Ship to Tarshish," *The Runagates Club* (1928).

A virile Canadianism grows out of the power and ruggedness of these vast spaces—from contact with the endless forests and lakes and mountains of the land, and the primeval spirit which flows—it should spring too from a new social consciousness—not the elevation of Canada in any one pursuit—but in all pursuits and above all from a deep sense of community and the creative consciousness that we can make a nobler quality of national life.

Lawren Harris, artist, musings of the early 1940s, in Lisa Christensen, *A Hiker's Guide to the Rocky Mountain Art of Lawren Harris* (2000).

Not to lose the feel of the mountains / while still retaining the prairies / is a difficult thing.

Lines from **John Newlove**'s poem "The Double-Headed Snake," *Black Night Window* (1968).

It's true. I am obsessed with this country. I am obsessed with its beauty, with its size, with the grandeur of it, with the complexity of it, with its past, with its present and with its future.

Charles Pachter, artist, address, "A Romance with Canada," Toronto, 23 June 1994, The Empire Club of Canada.

We are in the country, and it is very beautiful. I sometimes wonder if Canada is not the most beautiful country in the world, when you get outside the towns.

Robertson Davies, man of letters, letter written from his estate "Windhover," Caledon East, Ont., 27 December 1992, *For Your Eye Alone: Letters, 1976–1995* (1999).

LANGUAGE *See also* Accent; Aphorisms; Authors; Canadian English; Critics & Criticism; Free Speech; French Language; Literature; Malaproprisms; Native Languages; Science Fiction; Signs; Speech; Translation; Words; Writers & Writing

I sometimes wonder what you are going to do when ... all Canadians speak several languages.... Twenty-five years from now we ought to be able to teach any school child to learn any language in six weeks. Then we are going to have Chinese-speaking, Urdu-speaking, German-speaking, English-speaking Canadians.... The terms "English-speaking" and "French-speaking" have become part of the protocol of intercultural relations within Canada. When you add five other kinds of speaking [and] ... If you can keep it that way ... it will make other countries conscious of just where their particular problems fit in with Canada's particular problem.

Margaret Mead, ethnologist, address, "How Fast Can Man Change," Toronto, 18 April 1957, The Empire Club of Canada.

If the function of the English language to act as a cohesive element among the free peoples of the world is not to be similarly dissolved, it is not sufficient that it should be spoken. It must also be written and read by mass populations, not just by a small elite. This reinforces the need for highly-developed media of mass communication, as a major factor in promoting a high level of literacy.

Roy Thomson, chairman, Thomson Newspapers Limited, address, "The Winds of Change in the New Nations," Toronto, 7 January 1963, The Empire Club of Canada.

If we read Hansard we might have to go all the way back to Arthur Meighen to find a political leader who habitually used the language with skill and precision, and the correlation of his ability to speak with his success at the polls seems to me significant.... There is a story ... of a late colleague of mine, a professor of English who was private secretary to Prime Minister Mackenzie King during the war. In working on King's speeches, he inserted various quotations from Canadian poets, English and French, touched up clichés with a few metaphors, rounded out stock formulas with more concrete and lively language. These were ... routinely struck out. Eventually, the Prime Minister said: "Professor, the public memory for a picturesque phrase is very retentive."

Northrop Frye, literary and cultural critic, address, "The Authority of Learning," Toronto, 19 June 1984, The Empire Club of Canada.

Language is a voice that answers your questions, that questions your answers.

Line from **Antonio D'Alfonso**'s prose poem "You Refuse to Write," *The Other Shore* (1988).

The workings of language are as far from our awareness as the rationale for egg-laying is from the fly's. Our thoughts come out of our mouths so effortlessly that they often embarrass us, having eluded our mental censors. When we are comprehending sentences, the stream of words is transparent; we see through to the meaning so automatically that we can forget that a movie is in a foreign language and subtitled.

Stephen Pinker, Canadian-born evolutionary psychologist, Masschusetts Institute of Technology, *The Language of Instinct* (1994).

I just take the view that strong language is a spice. If you use too much, you can't taste the food; too little, and you're at the Olive Garden.

Mark Breslin, founder of Yuk Yuk's comedy clubs, "Cruel to Be Funny," *Toronto Star*, 21 May 2000.

A language, of course, is not simply vocabulary and grammar; it's a flash of the human spirit, the vehicle by which the soul of a culture comes into the material realm. Each language represents a unique intellectual and spiritual achievement.

Wade Davis, explorer and author, "A Dead End for Humanity," *The Globe and Mail*, 28 December 2000.

The language most often heard in my Toronto neighbourhood is Portuguese. But one can live and die in Ontario speaking only Italian or Chinese or Tibetan or French or Cree. It's always been like that here, from the beginning.

John Bentley Mays, author, *Arrivals: Stories form the History of Ontario* (2002).

Within our children's lifetimes, thousands of human languages seem fated to dwindle away.

Mark Abley, author, *Spoken Here: Travels among Threatened Languages* (2003).

If writing is a lonely profession, the Yiddish writer's loneliness has an additional dimension. Her readership has perished. Her language has gone up with the smoke of the crematoria. She creates in a vacuum, almost without a readership, out of fidelity to a vanished language, as if to prove that Nazism did not succeed in extinguishing that language's last breath, that it is still alive.

Chava Rosenfarb, poet and novelist, in Mark Abley, *Spoken Here: Travels among Threatened Languages* (2003).

No language is neutral.

Dionne Brand, poet, thesis and title of her sixth collection of poems *No Language Is Neutral* (1998). "Brand's narrative, documentary, autobiographical writing addresses her cultural roots in Trinidad, the lives of her mother and grandmother, her experiences as an immigrant in Toronto, and the affirmation of her lesbian sexuality." So explains historian Lynda Hall, "Each Sentence Jumps ...," *Racism, Eh? A Critical Inter-Disciplinary Anthology of Race and Racism in Canada* (2004), edited by Camille A. Nelson and Charmaine A. Nelson.

When I go to English Canada, I sacrifice half of myself. When I'm in France, I sacrifice the other side. But here ... I feel complete.

Nancy Huston, bilingual author born in Alberta and resident of France, visiting Quebec, in J. Kelly Nestruck, "A Writer's Voice *en français*," *National Post*, 20 April 2005.

LAUGHTER *See also* Humour

Like song that sweetens toil, laughter brightens the road of life, and to be born with a sense of the comic is a precious heritage.

Sir William Osler, physician, "Two Frenchmen on Laughter," *Men and Books* (1987).

Laughter is the last refuge of sorrow or oppression.

Stephen Leacock, humorist, *My Remarkable Uncle* (1942).

Heaven echoed with the laughter of the gods. It must have been a hell of a heaven.

Stephen Leacock, humorist, *How to Write* (1943).

Laughter would seem a pleasant way to begin a man–woman relationship; a good way to maintain it; and the only way to conclude it.

Richard J. Needham, columnist, "Needham," *The Globe and Mail*, 17 November 1980.

LAW *See also* Ethics; Injustice; Judges; Justice; Lawyers; Order; Police; Regulations; Supreme Court of Canada

If then, in the course of my remarks, I should refer to the law's shortcomings, I do so in the spirit of Mr. Justice Holmes who said that "One may criticize even what one reveres."

Samuel Freedman, judge, address, "Some Aspects of My Profession," Toronto, 5 January 1961, The Empire Club of Canada.

No law is natural, no nature is law.

Line from the prose poem "The Machine" from **Antonio D'Alfonso**'s *The Other Shore* (1988).

Ignoring the law can be wiser than enforcing, interpreting, or revising it. The same principle applies to many other aspects of life.

William Thorsell, columnist, "The Importance of Being Earnest and Doing Nothing," *The Globe and Mail*, 22 April 2002.

Canada has reached the same point as noted by de Tocqueville in *Democracy in America*, where all social issues eventually become legal issues. We also appear to have arrived at a point where the social, intellectual, and moral agendas are set by lawyers.

Robert Ivan Martin, law professor, *The Most Dangerous Branch: How the Supreme Court of Canada Has Undermined Our Law and Our Democracy* (2003).

Law is in large part the interpretation and application of language to factual situations. The reason for legalese is solely to ensure that we have, as a society, a language to form relationships with some certainty in their intention.

David A. Fram, solicitor, email to consulting lexicographer, 14 May 2003.

I urge you not to allow the world of practice to crush the optimism and the idealism present in the air today. The law is well suited to translate moral courage into righteous conduct.

Morris Fish, justice, Supreme Court of Canada, address to new law graduates, in Harold Levy, "A Judge Who Has Always Made a Difference," *Toronto Star*, 10 August 2003.

Never underestimate litigation as a form of human discourse.

Douglas M. Cunningham, barrister and solicitor, characteristic observation, 17 May 2004.

LAWYERS *See also* Law

If any young man should ask me whether I would recommend law as a profession, I would tell him that if he sought rewards of great wealth, the law was not its best source; that if he expected an easy life, unmarked by study and toil, the law was not for him; that if he expected complete mastery of his field, it could not be accomplished in law for there, perhaps more than anywhere else, what one knows is always so measurably less than what needs to be known, performance lags behind aspiration, and man's portion is the road and not the goal.

Samuel Freedman, judge, address, "Some Aspects of My Profession," Toronto, 5 January 1961, The Empire Club of Canada.

Admittedly, the lawyer is not always a popular figure. I recall the statement of the lady who said, "Lawyers! Don't talk to me about lawyers. I have had so much trouble with my husband's estate that sometimes I wish he hadn't died."

Samuel Freedman, judge, address, "Some Aspects of My Profession," Toronto, 5 January 1961, The Empire Club of Canada.

The movement toward a government of lawyers, by lawyers, for lawyers is not uniquely Canadian; it is also an international phenomenon.

Robert Ivan Martin, law professor, *The Most Dangerous Branch: How the Supreme Court of Canada Has Undermined Our Law and Our Democracy* (2003). Martin is referring specifically to the establishment of quasi-legal institutions that supplant national sovereignty, such as the International War Crimes Tribunal.

LEACOCK, STEPHEN *See also* Humour; Life

Cracks in the ice near Orillia are being attributed to the heavings of a sea-serpent. But as Steve Leacock has a house thereabouts, they are more likely to be wisecracks.

Anonymous item, *The Globe*, 22 January 1930.

"Mr. Leacock," I began, "is it pronounced 'Leecock' or 'Laycock'?"

"'Laycock,'" settled he.

Stephen Leacock, humorist, in conversation with R.E. Knowles, "Leacock Says Sir A. Currie Most Distinguished Pupil," *Toronto Daily Star*, 16 February 1933.

I can write up anything now at a hundred yards.

Stephen Leacock, humorist, *How to Write* (1943).

Never be as funny as you can.

Said to be **Stephen Leacock**'s advice to humorists, according to Robertson Davies, letter, 2 May 1995, *For Your Eye Alone: Letters, 1976–1995* (1999).

For this reason alone Leacock should continue to be invaluable to us all, Canadians and the less fortunate equally. He is a safeguard against the hypocrisy of others and ourselves; or, if that sounds too harsh for Leacock, he is a reminder of our tendency individually and en masse towards damn foolishness (he kept a file folder labelled "Letters from damn fools").

Gerald Lynch, academic, introduction, *Leacock on Life* (2002).

LEADERSHIP *See also* Heroes & Heroism

Leadership—that indeed is the question today. If we are led by people who accept sacrifice themselves before inflicting hardship on others; who practise the virtues of thrift, compassion and humility before exacting them from us; who respect Parliament and its institutions before castigating those who have walked the slippery road of defiance; who tell us the truth even when they think we don't want to hear it—if we have that kind of leadership, and have it we must, Canada may yet fulfill that most splendid promise of her youth.

Brian Mulroney, labour lawyer and later prime minister, address, "Law and Order in the Labour Movement," Toronto, 15 October 1975, The Empire Club of Canada.

Five manitous from another world came to them by sea and showed them how to develop their human talent and labour to provide for five basic necessities of survival: life, guardianship, healing, leading, and teaching.

Basil Johnston, elder, *The Manitous: The Spiritual World of the Ojibway* (1995).

Powerful leadership comes from knowing yourself. Power presentations come from expressing yourself effectively.

Peter Urs Bender, motivational speaker, *Leadership from Within* (1997), with Eric Hellman.

There are two different kinds of leaders. One kind has the dramatic "burning bush" experience, like Moses. The other kind has what I call the "burning heart" experience. I am the second kind. I have a burning heart for my people.

Matthew Coon Come, Cree, grand chief of the Mistissini First Nation, interviewed by Allen Abel, "Chief of First Nations Straddles Two Galaxies," *National Post*, 19 July 2000.

For me, a criminal lawyer who refuses to act for an alleged "organized" criminal, a corporate accused, a businessman (and there are such lawyers), a Nazi, or for someone accused of crimes against women, children or the environment is like a medical doctor who refuses as a matter of principle to treat someone suffering from syphilis or AIDS.

Edward L. Greenspan, advocate, address, "The Role of the Defence Counsel," Toronto, 19 November 1987, The Empire Club of Canada.

Of course, the lead dog is the only dog that gets a change of view.

Northern expression used by **Eric Nielsen**, Yukon-born Member of Parliament, interviewed by Peter Gzowski on CBC Radio's *Morningside*, as noted by Jay Teitel, "The Importance of Being Earnest," *Saturday Night*, April 2002.

At times of crisis political leadership should not qualify as an oxymoron.

Lewis MacKenzie, retired major general, "Chrétien's Cavalier Performance," *National Post*, 20 March 2003.

You know you must be a leader when you get kicked in the rear a lot.

Belinda Stronach, Conservative Party leadership contender, subsequent Liberal Cabinet minister, and former head of Magna International, in Gloria Galloway, "The Knives

Come Out for Stronach," *The Globe and Mail*, 19 January 2004.

You have to understand people. You have to like people. You would fail as a leader if you allowed vindictiveness or mean-spiritedness to enter your judgment or your personality. This is for the book, right?

Brian Mulroney, prime minister, interviewed for a biography by Peter C. Newman, *The Secret Mulroney Tapes: Unguarded Confessions of a Prime Minister* (2005).

LEARNING *See also* Education; Universities & Colleges

During 1942 the three large English-speaking powers moved to mingle their military personnel for training on complex equipment such as anti-aircraft gunnery predictors or submarine detectors. While standardized intelligence tests showed there was little or no difference in average intelligence among the three groups, the Americans taken as a whole learned a bit more quickly than the Canadians, and the Canadians more quickly than the British. This puzzled and bothered a few social scientists enough that they tried to figure out why it was so.... Finally they discovered an almost uncanny correlation between the levels of training performance of the three groups and the percentage of the population in each country who before the war had taken out drivers' licences.

E.F. Schumacher, economist, *Good Work* (1979).

Once we think of learning as a disentangling & relaxing process, we think of ideas tending toward wisdom, or the growth of a free spirit, instead of to more & more learning.

Northrop Frye, literary and cultural critic, aphorism, "Notebook 3" (1946–1948), *Northrop Frye Newsletter*, fall 2000.

The simple ability to read, write, and count is essentially a passive acquirement, a means of social adjustment. All genuine teaching starts with this passive literacy and then tries to transform it into an activity, reading with discrimination and writing with articulateness. Without this background, one may be able to read and write and still be functionally illiterate. It is discouraging for a student to find that he has reached university and is still totally unable to say what he thinks.

Northrop Frye, literary and cultural critic, address, "The Authority of Learning," Toronto, 19 June 1984, The Empire Club of Canada.

LEBANON *See also* Middle East

It is clear if the Syrians are in Lebanon, it's because one must maintain the peace.

Paul Martin, prime minister, addressing reporters, Parliament Hill, 17 February 2005, in Aileen McCabe and Sheldon Alberts, "Martin 'Ironically' Calls Syrians Peacekeepers," *National Post*, 18 February 2005. Later that day the prime minister rose in the House of Commons to say, "I have said clearly that we support the UN resolutions and that the Syrians must withdraw from Lebanon." He explained he was speaking "ironically." At the time the Syrian army was occupying Lebanon.

LEGEND *See also* Myths & Mythology

It is on the achievements of such men that a culture of a country rests. To say that they teach us is a poor description of what they do, for in reality they reveal to us things that we are eager to know but which we cannot understand unaided. Their work is not education, but revelation, and there is always about it something of prophetic splendour. Sometimes, before they die, they become heroes of legend, and when they die we are aware, not of loss, but only a growing splendour in the legend.

Robertson Davies, author, tribute to the late Sir Ernest MacMillan and to other cultural contributors, "A Leader of Us Who Faced the Music," *The Canadian Composer*, July 1973, in Ezra Shabas, *Sir Ernest MacMillan: The Importance of Being Canadian* (1996).

LEISURE *See also* Hobbies

An extension of leisure time and a longer span of life could be tremendously beneficial. We go to great lengths to educate ourselves for our working years. Isn't it now time to think of educating ourselves for the increased leisure and the longer years which the future promises?

Thomas B. Costain, novelist, address, "A Glance at the Future," 8 May 1951, The Empire Club of Canada.

LÉVESQUE, RENÉ *See also* Separatism; Parti Québécois

They were the two poles of Quebec politics. Lévesque is what we are; Trudeau is what we would like to be.

Claude Charron, former Quebec Cabinet minister, noting that Quebeckers were voting for separatist René Lévesque provincially and for federalist Pierre Elliott Trudeau nationally, noted by Donald Brittain in the National Film Board production *The Champions*, CBC-TV, 14–16 September 1986.

If the Quebec separatist movement did nothing but produce Lévesque, it would have been worth it. He realized that politics is not a science decided by the elegant droppings of computers, but an exercise in sorcery filled with illusions and enchantments.

Peter C. Newman, columnist, "Adieu to Separatism?" *Maclean's*, 12 May 2003.

LIBERAL PARTY *See also* Liberalism; Political Parties

I am a Liberal. I am one of those who think that everywhere, in human things, there are abuses to be reformed, new horizons to be opened up, and new forces to be developed.

Attributed to **Sir Wilfrid Laurier**, turn-of-the-20th-century Liberal prime minister (1896–1911), by John Duffy, "The Curse of the New Leader," *The Globe and Mail*, 31 March 2004.

The Liberals are the party of government; the Conservatives are like the mumps, you get them once in your life.

Attributed to **Jack Pickersgill**, Liberal adviser, in 1961 by Conrad Black, *A Life in Progress* (1993).

Not too many Americans have the vaguest idea of what a Grit is or where the name came from. Most Americans think it is a new breakfast food, possibly a welcome substitute for oat bran.

Jack Valenti, CEO, Motion Picture Association of America, address, "The Cinema Future," Toronto, 19 October 1989, The Empire Club of Canada.

The federal Liberals governed this country for most of the past century because they understood that about us. As the other parties clung righteously to ideology, the Liberals used conservative or socialist tools—whatever a situation called for. The federal Liberals are a "find a way" party.

Ken Dryden, hockey personality, lawyer, and author, address, Charles R. Bronfman Lecture in Canadian Studies, November, University of Ottawa, "The Canadian Way," *Maclean's*, 13 November 2000.

It would be nice to know we could one day heave out the Liberals, not to change anything but to humble them.

Richard Gwyn, columnist, "Home and Away," *Toronto Star*, 21 June 2001.

Gritlock.

The word was popularized by authors **Peter G. White** and **Adam Daifallah** in their tract *Gritlock: Are the Liberals in Forever?* (2002). The word combines *grit*, the popular term for the Liberal Party, with *lock*, as in *gridlock*, the term used to describe a bottleneck or deadlock in football coverage and traffic reports. The book argues that "until the Progressive Conservatives and the Canadian Alliance can form of single conservative alternative, the nation will be governed by Liberals indefinitely—it's perpetual *gritlock*." The authors attribute the neologism to editorial consultant Frances Hannah.

The Liberal Party has been like a family to me.

Jean Chrétien, prime minister, retirement address, Air Canada Centre, Toronto, 13 November 2003, in Andrew Ryan, "Liberal Convention," *The Globe and Mail*, 14 November 2003.

Watching the Liberals in action for nearly half a century, I concluded that their philosophy was simplicity itself: to govern Canada by striking the most marketable balance between elitism and egalitarianism—a sedate form of populism with an extended shelf life.

Peter C. Newman, journalist and memoirist, *Here Be Dragons: Telling Tales of People, Passion, and Power* (2004).

There's something wrong with a country that allows one party political hegemony.

Michael Bliss, historian, interviewed by Michael Enright, CBC Radio's *Sunday Morning*, 4 January 2004.

I remember that former NDP leader Tommy Douglas once said the Liberals will give you stable government, if you can stand the smell of the stable.

Kenneth Whyte, publisher, *Maclean's*, referring to T.C. Douglas, former premier of Saskatchewan, "Interview with Ed Broadbent," *Maclean's*, 28 December 2005.

LIBERALISM *See also* Injustice; Liberal Party

My favourite word is balance. I guess that's why I am a Liberal.

Barney Danson, former Liberal Member of Parliament, characteristic remark, personal communication, 20 July 2003.

There is one liberal value we must not forget. When my mother passed the pie over the table, she told us to have a "liberal" helping. Liberal meant generous. Generosity means trusting each other, helping without counting the cost, taking risks together. Generosity, unity, sovereignty, justice. These are the beacons of liberal politics.

Michael Ignatieff, commentator, address, biennial policy conference of the Liberal Party, Ottawa, 3 March 2005, excerpted as "A Generous Helping of Liberal Brains," *The Globe and Mail*, 4 March 2005.

LIBERTY & LIBERTIES *See* Freedom; Rights

LIBRARIES *See also* Books

Tous ces livres sont à toi!

Aegidius Fauteux, Quebec printer and publisher, statement from the essay "Les Bibliothèques" (1901), "All these books are for you!" recalled by art director Michel-Marc Bouchard at the official opening of Le Grande Bibliothèque de la Bibliothèque nationale du Québec, Montreal, 29 April 2005.

But a big library really has the gift of tongues & vast potencies of telepathic communication.

Northrop Frye, cultural critic, aphorism, "Notebook 3" (1946–1948), *Northrop Frye Newsletter*, fall 2000.

I love libraries, but I will be damned if I will ever walk into a "Resource Centre."

Richard Needham, columnist, *The Wit and Wisdom of Richard Needham* (1977).

I arrive at the Reference Section with no sign of alien activity. Perhaps invaders from another solar system hesitate to interfere with the operation of the Toronto Public Library system.

Thoughts of the narrator about a man who lives in Toronto and believes he is being repeatedly abducted by alien beings in **Hugh A.D. Spencer**'s story "Why I Hunt Flying Saucers," *On Spec: The First Five Years* (1995), edited by the On Spec Editorial Collective.

The world encyclopedia, the universal library, already exists and is the world itself.

Alberto Manguel, author and reader, "The Pursuit of Knowledge, from Genesis to Google," *The New York Times*, 19 December 2004.

All who work for the good of public libraries know that we will need some careful navigation to get them to a safer harbour. But this we must do. Our links to the past, our bonds with the present, our path to a civilized tomorrow are all maintained by libraries. They are agencies of the public good. They allow all of us to be, as the Hebrew saying goes, pilgrims at the gate of a new city.

Adrienne Clarkson, governor general, address, Regina Public Library, 16 May 2005.

LIBYA

To use Paul Martin's latest travel destination as an example, while Tripoli is no closer to Ottawa than it was in 1950, Ottawa is getting closer to Tripoli.

George Jonas, columnist, "Exporting Freedom, Importing Intolerance," *National Post*, 27 December 2004. This is a reference to the prime minister's trade visit to meet Mu'ammer Qaddafi, the Libyan colonel who has wielded dictatorial power since 1969.

LIES *See also* Truth

In Toronto the custom for the boy asseverating is to wet the point of one finger on his tongue then to draw the wet finger down the breast of his coat, saying meanwhile, "Now it's wet, and now it's dry, may God cut my throat if I tell a lie." Have Hamilton, London, Ottawa, Kingston and our other cities and towns anything different in this line? It is to be hoped they have something better, something less incongruous—less profane.

David Boyle, archaeologist, "Canadian Folk-Lore," *The Globe*, 13 November 1897.

Tell a lie today so that it may become true tomorrow.

Attributed to **John Grierson**, National Film Board commissioner, by film producer Tom Daly in the 1940s and quoted by D.B. Jones, *The Best Butler in the Business: Tom Daly of the National Film Board of Canada* (1996).

"*Lebenslüge*.... This is what you get here, in this country. A lie you live with for so long that it transforms your life. But also," she added after a moment, "a lie that enables you to live."

Thoughts about Poland and lies entertained by the narrator Anna Nowicka Herzman in **Eva Stachniak**'s novel *Necessary Lies* (2000).

In the twenty-first century, the most important ethical imperative for politicians, business people, and the media to rediscover and reassert will be that of "telling the truth."

Preston Manning, politician, leader of Reform Party and later the Canadian Alliance, describing Question Period in the House of Commons, *Think Big: Adventures in Life and Democracy* (2002).

People don't lie when they're asleep.

Observation made by the narrator of **Louise Dupré**'s novel *The Milky Way* (2002), translated from the French by Liedewy Hawke.

In any situation where estimates are used (casualties, crowds, etc.) the largest estimate is the most accurate.

Peter C. Newman, journalist and memoirist, *Here Be Dragons: Telling Tales of People, Passion, and Power* (2004).

LIFE *See also* Existence; Humanity; Philosophy

A little while and I will be gone from among you, whither I cannot tell. From nowhere we came, into nowhere we go. What is life? It is a flash of a firefly in the night. It is a breath of a buffalo in the winter time. It is as the little shadow that runs across the grass and loses itself in the sunset.

Dying words of **Crowfoot**, the Blackfoot chief, Bow River, 25 April 1890, according to John Peter Turner, *The North-West Mounted Police: 1873–1893* (1950). Alas, historian Robert S. Carlisle establishes the source of these moving words in the pages of Sir H. Rider Haggard's famous adventure novel *King Solomon's Mines* (1885).

We shall have missed the fullness of life unless we develop a power to respond like a harp to every breath of life that blows, and grows eyes that can catch the romance, the high significance, the interestingness of every single thing in the world.

Ernest Raymond, conference attendee, Conference Sermon at Christ Church Cathedral, Victoria, B.C., 7 April 1929, *Education and Leisure: Addresses Delivered at the Fourth Triennial Conference on Education Held at Victoria and Vancouver, Canada, April 1929* (1929), edited by S.E. Lang.

Life has all too little evening. It has all run in arrears and never catches up.

Stephen Leacock, humorist, *Too Much College, or Education Eating Up Life: With Kindred Essays in Education and Humour* (1939).

For the reality of life, we learn too late, is in the living tissue of it from day to day, not in the expectation of better, nor in the fear of worse. Those two things, to be always looking ahead and to worry over things that haven't yet happened and very likely won't happen—those take the very essence out of life.

Stephen Leacock, humorist, *My Remarkable Uncle* (1942).

The way of life that I preach is a habit to be acquired gradually by long and steady repetition. It is the practice of living for the day only, and for the day's work. Life in day-tight compartments.

Sir William Osler, physician, "A Way of Life," *A Way of Life and Selected Writings* (1951).

If you go through life treating everyone a little better than they treat you, your life will not have been in vain.

Ned Sparks, Hollywood actor and the original "deadpan" comedian, born in Guelph, Ont., in 1883, characteristic remark, recalled following his death in 1957 in Victoriaville, San Bernardino, Cal., by friend and crooner Bing Crosby, as noted by Charles Foster, *Once Upon a Time in Paradise: Canadians in the Golden Age of Hollywood* (2003). Crosby added, "Ned Sparks's life was not in vain. He was loved by more people than he ever realized."

One of the few rules I have for living is, Be pleased with what is intended to please.

Beatrice Lillie, comedienne, *Every Other Inch a Lady* (1972).

Most of life is not definable, and yet for a long time our education was almost totally involved only with what the mind could do.

Tom Daly, producer and director, "Running Past Our Habit Patterns," *Pot-Pourri* (National Film Board), September 1973.

To watch a dandelion head open and turn to the sun, or a pigeon pecking at grass seeds, in a park, is to experience one minute in the history of life on this planet.

Wayne Grady, writer and naturalist, *Toronto the Wild: Field Notes of an Urban Naturalist* (1995).

Life is a challenge—meet it. / Life is a gift—appreciate it. / Life is a duty—perform it. / Life is a game—play it. / Life is a song—sing it. / Life is an opportunity—take it. / Life is a struggle—grow from it. / Life is a goal—achieve it. / Life is a journey—complete it.

Marvelle Koffler, philanthropist, excerpt from a convocation address, 1996, wording on plaque, Koffler Student Centre, University of Toronto.

It is the ultimate conundrum. In order to be somebody I have to be somebody else. I am the way I play these roles.

Wilson Duff, anthropologist, random observation, in *Bird of Paradox: The Unpublished Writings of Wilson Duff* (1996), edited by E.N. Anderson.

I was in New Brunswick once covering a by-election. When a reporter goes into a place he has never been he tries to find someone who looks as though he has been around for a while. I saw a fisherman puffing his pipe at a wharf and I went up to him to start a conversation. I said, "Have you lived here all your life?"

And his answer reflected the quiet optimism I feel about Canada. He said, "No, not yet."

Peter C. Newman, journalist, address, "Titans: How the New Canadian Establishment Seized Power," Toronto, 10 November 1998, The Empire Club of Canada.

Our lives are a mystery of growth from weakness to weakness, from the weakness of the little baby to the weakness of the aged.

Jean Vanier, founder of L'Arche movement, *Becoming Human* (1998).

Dickens wrote that what is meant by knowledge of the world is simply an acquaintance with the infirmities of man. In other words, to be truly knowledgeable, we must recognize human frailty. And that's how I see my work, as the art and craft of telling stories of the human condition. That's my mission; that's my life's work. Now do you see why I love it?

Pamela Wallin, broadcaster, *Since You Asked* (1998).

Life is not always beautiful, but the struggle to make it so is nothing short of sublime.

Irena F. Karafilly, memoirist, *The Stranger in the Plumed Hat: A Memoir* (2000).

Life: a safe with the combination locked inside.

Hugh Arscott, aphorist, *Hugh's Views: Volume 5* (2001).

Life Internal Forever Eternal.

Something of a motto of **Reg Hartt**, cinéaste, first noted in private conversation, August 2001.

Nothing you will ever do is as important as discovering the meaning of your life!

Ian Percy, motivational speaker, *The Seven Secrets to a Life of Meaning* (2001).

There is an eternal, ever-present One Life beyond the myriad forms of life that are subject to birth and death. Many people use the word God to describe it; I often call it Being. The word Being explains nothing, but nor does God. Being, however, has the advantage that it is an open concept.

Eckhart Tolle, motivational speaker, *Practising the Power of Now* (2001).

If you can't live dangerously, live joyously.

C.C. (Kelly) Gotlieb, computer scientist, characteristic remark first made in the 1970s, recorded in private conversation, 7 November 2001.

Life is like the universe, absolutely limitless, to be experienced and savoured.

Barney Danson, politician, *Not Bad for a Sergeant: The Memoirs of Barney Danson* (2002).

Redundancy is expensive but indispensable. Perhaps this is merely to point out that life is expensive. Just to keep itself going, life makes demands on energy, supplied from inside and outside a living being, that are voracious compared with the undemanding thriftiness of death and decay. A culture, just to keep itself going, makes voracious demands on the energies of many people for hands-on mentoring.

Jane Jacobs, urban planning critic, *Dark Age Ahead* (2004).

I sometimes find the mysteries of life as impenetrable as a *Globe and Mail* editorial.

Peter C. Newman, journalist and memoirist, *Here Be Dragons: Telling Tales of People, Passion, and Power* (2004).

When they say "Life begins at forty," maybe what they mean is that being forty forces you to accept your limits.

Rob McKenzie, columnist, "Commentary," *National Post*, 19 August 2004.

Any place where people are not in control of their lives is an institution.

Patrick Worth, proponent of self-advocacy for the developmentally delayed and champion of inclusion advocacy groups, in Catherine Dunphy, "Talented Speaker Gave Others Voice," *Toronto Star*, 13 December 2004.

At a certain point I think it's really important to just accept everything you are, everything you've been, bless your experience and realize that maybe everything had to be just exactly the way it was.

Jennifer Dale, actress, interviewed by Brent Turnbull, *The Village Post*'s *City Magazine*, December 2004.

It's up to all of us to create a world in which the admired life combines material sufficiency with more noble aims, with a deeper consciousness.

Raffi (born Raffi Cavoukian), children's performer, in Gary Stephen Ross, "Raffi Grows Up," *Saturday Night*, March 2005.

We are the combination of our thoughts and our emotions. Everything we have ever thought and felt becomes part of us, and influences our decisions in the future.

Barry Shainbaum, speaker, photographer, and author, characteristic observation, 27 July 2005.

LIFESTYLE

All too often I hear grieving relatives who have lost a loved one say: "Why did he or she have to die so young?" Sometimes you feel like saying: "It happened because your loved one was a damn fool." He or she was grossly overweight, smoked two packs of cigarettes a day, watched TV for hours on end every week while munching potato chips, and drove the car to the corner store. A small hole will sink a big ship and small faulty lifestyle habits add up to sink humans.

Kenneth Walker, physician and columnist (aka Dr. Gifford-Jones), address, "The Healthy Barmaid, The New Minister of Health?" Toronto, 11 April 1996, The Empire Club of Canada.

Being a vegetarian, a lesbian, and a Buddhist, I am the alternative to the mainstream of North America.

k.d. lang, singer-songwriter, interviewed by Evan Solomon, CBC-TV's *Sunday Morning*, 6 November 2005.

LIGHT *See also* Stars

Many Hindus are convinced that only in the pitch black of a moonless night can the inner light of universal wisdom reveal itself. Out of the darkness, they insist, comes true light.

Christopher Dewdney, poet and author, *Acquainted with the Night: Excursions through the World after Dark* (2004).

The night sky is a mosaic of fossil light—light from the Roman era, light from the age of dinosaurs, light from before our solar system existed. Perhaps light from suns that shone on fantastic civilizations that have been extinct for millions of years.

Christopher Dewdney, poet and author, *Acquainted with the Night: Excursions through the World after Dark* (2004).

LITERACY *See also* Language

The high school graduate who has taken French enjoys the advantage of being illiterate in two languages.

Richard Needham, columnist, *The Wit and Wisdom of Richard Needham* (1977).

A recent investigation reveals that five million Canadian adults are "functionally illiterate." But why, one wonders, do so many of these seek, and achieve, election?

Robertson Davies, man of letters, "The Canadian Imagination," *The Globe and Mail*, 17 December 1977.

LITERATURE *See also* Authors; Books; Canadian Literature; Language; Libraries; Poetry

You cannot, of course, hope to produce a great Canadian novel overnight. Our cousins across the line, with their population of one hundred million, are still forlornly looking for the great American novel, and remembering the age and character of this Dominion I very much doubt if you will ever have the great Canadian novel, for the author of any such master-piece would have to have the geographical restlessness of a Casey Jones and the lyric fervour of an Archibald Lampman and the diligence of an Arnold Bennett and the humour of a Cervantes and the realism of a Zola and the fantasticism of a Wilson MacDonald and the scholarship of a Charles G.D. Roberts. But if and when that great Canadian novel comes along, I hope you will remember the trail blazers and the sod breakers, the men who preceded the masters, for they are the pioneers, the pioneers of the pen, just as there have been pioneers of the plough, and it takes courage and insight and power to blaze a literary trail throughout a new country. It is easy to follow in the footsteps of others.

Arthur Stringer, novelist, address, "The Interpreters of Canada," Toronto, 7 April 1932, The Empire Club of Canada.

And now I will say one further thing about the classics. There are not going to be any more. We have them all now, all that there are ever going to be.

Stephen Leacock, humorist, *My Remarkable Uncle* (1942).

It has taken me a long time to realize that literature is an autonomous verbal organization, & that one should not copy life but other books.

Northrop Frye, literary and cultural critic, aphorism, "Notebook 3" (1946–1948), *Northrop Frye Newsletter*, fall 2000.

I still prefer the fine stories of earlier days to symbolic writing and the stream of consciousness novel; which is often a very muddy stream indeed. I feel a happy expansion of spirit when I look at a Rembrandt or any great canvas of the past but I come away from an exhibition of modern painting in a puzzled and somewhat depressed state of mind. I delight in the melodious music of the past but find dissonance hard on my ears. In other words, I am very old fashioned indeed.

Thomas B. Costain, novelist, address, "A Glance at the Future," Toronto, 8 May 1951, The Empire Club of Canada.

Boy Meets Girl in Winnipeg and Who Cares?

Title of a magazine article by **Hugh MacLennan**, essayist and novelist, about the fact that Canadian editors, publishers, and readers prefer their romances and dramas set in foreign locations rather than in presumably non-romantic and non-dramatic places like Winnipeg. The article appears in MacLennan's *Scotchman's Return and Other Essays* (1960).

So far as I am concerned a Canadian novel is so because it is written by a Canadian. I cannot think of any other definition that has any value.

Robertson Davies, man of letters, letter, 31 January 1977, *For Your Eye Alone: Letters, 1976–1995* (1999).

Literature, then, is not a collection of allegedly "beautiful" utterances, but the only record we have of the "feel" of things, past, present, and future; things as grasped by exceptional persons gifted in language, richly endowed in experience.

George Whalley, scholar, commencement address, Rothesay College School, N.B., 1959, *George Whalley: Remembrances* (1989), edited by Michael D. Moore.

Literature is conscious mythology: as society develops, its mythical stories become structural principles of story-telling, its mythical concepts, sun-gods and the like, become habits of metaphoric thought. In a fully mature literary creation the writer enters into a structure of traditional stories and images.

Northrop Frye, literary theorist and cultural critic, "Conclusion to a *Literary History of Canada*" (1965), *The Bush Garden* (1971).

The novels of a Magali have never been mistaken for the works of a Michaux. It is common knowledge that for the last hundred years there has existed a profitable market in popular literature, and an unprofitable one in highly personal, often avant-garde, works. These may become tomorrow's bestsellers but for the moment they lose more money than they can earn. Publishers therefore make a living by selling paperbacks to read in the train, school books or famous works in limited editions.

Jacques Godbout, filmmaker, "A Trap: The Script," *How to Make or Not Make a Canadian Film* (1968), edited by André Pâquet.

A nation without a literature is not a nation, and the quality of its literature is one of the standards by which a nation is judged now and will be judged in the future.

Robertson Davies, author, address, "How the Author Reaches His Public," Toronto, 2 March 1972, The Empire Club of Canada.

I have a lot of respect for William Butler Yeats, but I've got to tell you his famous poem "Leda and the Swan" isn't accurate. The alleged rape of Leda didn't happen the way he described it. It was a very different kind of event. Swans do not rape. They don't have to. And only those who have gazed into the eyes of a swan will truly understand why.

Brian Fawcett, poet, "The Swan and Leda," *Wild Culture: Specimens from* The Journal of Wild Culture (1992), edited by Whitney Smith and Christopher Lowry.

Given a choice between a morning spent in the doughnut shop and a little cannibalism, which would you take—to read about, that is?

Margaret Atwood, author, introduction, *Strange Things: The Malevolent North in Canadian Literature* (1995).

The texts these three faiths created—the Tanakh, the "New Testament," and, among the Rabbinic documents, the Babylonian Talmud—are probably the strongest literary texts ever invented. What the secret of that power is can be indirectly analysed but never really explained.

Donald Harman Akenson, historian, *Surpassing Wonder: The Invention of the Bible and the Talmuds* (1998). The Tanakh: Hebrew scriptures commencing with the Torah or Pentateuch. "New Testament": Christian scriptures commencing with the Gospels. Babylonian Talmud: Rabbinical commentary on authoritative texts. Akenson sees these as the productions of wondrous "author-editors."

I do believe you could write a novel about every person.

Carol Shields, novelist, in Noah Richler, "Every Person Is a Novel," *National Post*, 2 November 2002.

All literature is regional. The Bible is regional in that it deals with sheep and goats and the Sea of Galilee. All literature comes from someplace, and people will understand that.

Alistair MacLeod, fiction writer and chronicler of the lives of Cape Bretoners, "Q&A," *Maclean's*, 24 March 2003.

The *sine qua non* of literature is individuals who have consciousness. From that point on, you can go wherever you want.

Robert J. Sawyer, author, "Science Fiction and Social Change" (2004), *Relativity: Stories and Essays* (2004).

LONDON, ENGLAND

Oh London, you are the greatest city of the world, but the saddest, so full of sin and degradation.

Margaret Addison, traveller, dean of women, diary entry, 29 October 1900, *Diary of a European Tour: 1900* (1999), edited by Jean O'Grady.

LONELINESS

But O the slowness, / the dead slowness / of the time passing; / and the aloneness.

Final verse of **George Whalley**'s poem "By the River" (1948), *The Collected Poems of George Whalley* (1986), edited by George Johnston.

Everyone is so / lonely in this / country that / it's necessary / to be fantastic.

Lines from **John Newlove**'s poem "Everyone," *Black Night Window* (1968).

Loneliness is a feeling of being guilty. Of what? Of existing? Of being judged? By whom? We do not know. Loneliness is a taste of death.

Jean Vanier, founder of L'Arche movement, *Becoming Human* (1998).

A / LAKE / A / LANE / A / LINE / A / LONE.

Words from a "concrete poem" by **bpNichol** cut into the concrete on the lane outside Coach House Press, Toronto, as noted by Sheila Heti, "The Actual Space," *The Writers' Trust of Canada: Canada Book Week*, Issue 2, "Literary Landscapes," 21–27 April 2003.

The only cure for homesickness is going home. I think loneliness is when you feel homesick, but there's no home to go to. Even if your parents are both alive and living in the same house and you go back and sleep in the den or see your old school friends, there's no past to go back to. It's mourning for something that doesn't exist.

Douglas Coupland, author and artist, interviewed by Alexandra Gill, "Mirror, Mirror on the Page," *The Globe and Mail*, 30 December 2004.

LOONIE *See* Currency; Money

LOTTERIES *See also* Games & Gambling

Statistically speaking, a Canadian is twice as likely to be *murdered* during 1977 as he is to win even one of those $10,000 Loto Canada consolation prizes.

Alan Edmonds, journalist, *The Canadian*, 12 February 1977.

The lottery is the only reliable miracle left in this age of reason. No matter what else happens this week, you can be sure that someone, somewhere, will win it big.

Chris Gudgeon and **Barbara Stewart**, authors, *The Luck of the Draw: True Life Tales of Lottery Winners and Losers* (2001).

LOSING *See* Winning & Losing

LOUISIANA

If Quebec had been an American state, it would have gone the way of Louisiana.

Mordecai Richler, novelist and critic of Quebec society, inteviewed by Sam Orbaum, "Make 'em Mad, Mordecai Richler!" *The Jerusalem Post Magazine*, 6 November 1992.

LOVE *See also* Affection; Friendship; Kisses; Lust; Marriage; Men & Women; Passion; Sex

You cannot tell a love story just as it is—because it isn't. There is something else there, something higher than our common selves and perhaps truer. When a young man sees in his girl an angel, and a young girl sees in her lover a hero, perhaps they are seeing what is really there—the self we each might have but which we grasp only in our higher moments and too late.

Stephen Leacock, humorist, *How to Write* (1943).

I could write till the end of time / and never tell exactly / the colour of your eyes / or the sweet curve of your lips.

Final verse of **George Whalley**'s poem "Seeing Ducks Asleep" (1948), *The Collected Poems of George Whalley* (1986), edited by George Johnston.

I tell you what you do, boy. Or girl. Go and look at the western sky where the noon moon, the silver shaving of the moon, hangs. Look at it over your *left* shoulder, and wish. Wish that your first love shall be your last love. And if your wish is granted, you will have put on the whole armour of life.

Greg Clark, newspaperman and humorist, *May Your First Love Be Your Last* (1969).

I have an abyss within me, and I cannot decide which bridge to place over the abyss in you.

Line from an untitled prose poem in **Antonio D'Alfonso**'s *Panick Love* (1992).

All of us are better when we're loved.

Last line of **Alistair MacLeod**'s novel *No Great Mischief* (1999).

Love is a key you find long before you've got a door.

Irena F. Karafilly, aphorist, characteristic observation, 7 November 2000.

I like to talk and I like to learn, which is why I always loved women older than myself.

Stephen Vizinczey, novelist and essayist, "In Praise of Intelligence," *National Post*, 10 February 2001.

Love never happens at the right moment.

Observation made by the narrator of **Louise Dupré**'s novel *The Milky Way* (2002), translated from the French by Liedewy Hawke.

I've learned something I never suspected when I was young. I've learned that human beings never outgrow their capacity for tenderness and passion, and that love among the ruins is the most satisfying love of all.

Margaret Wente, columnist, referring to returning to early romances in later years, "Love among the Ruins," *The Globe and Mail*, 12 February 2005.

LOYALISTS

To Hell or Halifax.

Identified as a "Loyalist aphorism" by Reginald C. Stuart, *United States Expansionism and British North America, 1775–1871* (1988).

The U.E. Loyalists have been as a barrier of rock against which the waves of Republicanism have dashed in vain.

William Canniff, historian, on the influence of the United Empire Loyalists in British North America, *History of the Settlement of Upper Canada* (1869).

LOYALTY

Every man who accepts the idea of an organized society owes loyalties—to himself, to his family, his community, his province, his nation; and now at last to something approaching a world federation. All these loyalties are independent.

Roderick Haig-Brown, naturalist and author, "An Outsider Looks at Education" (1950), *Writings and Reflections* (1982), edited by Valerie Haig-Brown.

LUCK

Notwithstanding the teachings of all the churches, there is no more popular belief than in good and ill luck.

David Boyle, archaeologist, "Canadian Folk-Lore," *The Globe*, 13 November 1897.

I am a great believer in luck, and I find the harder I work the more I have of it.

Stephen Leacock, humorist, undated observation, *The Stephen Leacock Quote Book* (2004), compiled by John Robert Colombo.

I like luck. Luck is good too.

Chris Hadfield, astronaut, after a discussion of education and training, in conversation with Jay Ingram, CBC Radio's *Quirks & Quarks*, 14 April 2001.

You've got to be good to be lucky.

Bob Cole, hockey broadcaster, in Murray Campbell, "Queen's Park," *The Globe and Mail*, 7 November 2002.

LUMBER & LUMBERING *See also* Environmentalism; Forests; Resources; Trees

We are recklessly destroying the timber of Canada and there is scarcely the possibility of replacing it.

Sir John A. Macdonald, prime minister, letter to Ontario Premier John Sandfield Macdonald, 1871, in Paul L. Aird, "Cultural Attitudes to Culturing the Forest," *Regenerating the Canadian Forest: Principles and Practice for Ontario* (2001), edited by Robert G. Wagner and Stephen J. Colombo.

Today the land is flat, a checkerboard of fertile cornfields and grain silos. Then it was almost entirely forest, which the hardy Highlanders cut down and shipped to Quebec. Many stayed with the lumber business and followed it into northern Ontario, down to Michigan and Minnesota, and across to British Columbia. They became the Glengarry "shantymen," the most skilled lumberjacks in North America, artists with the ax and saw.

Arthur Herman, historian, *How the Scots Invented the Modern World* (2001).

Another thing. I'd like to apologize for Canada's trees. You know, this is a big country and the darn pines and other softwoods keep popping up everywhere. We cut them down and we saw them into lumber and we send them down to your country so you can build good, cheap housing, but we just can't get rid of them all.

Colin Mochrie, actor-comedian, "A Canadian Apologizes," routine posted on a website, 8 June 2002. Mochrie's routine takes the form of a mock letter addressed to U.S. President George W. Bush.

LUST *See also* Love; Sex

The difference between love & lust is, of course, that the former is personal & particular, & the latter impersonal & general.

Northrop Frye, cultural and literary critic, aphorism, "Notebook 3" (1946–1948), *Northrop Frye Newsletter*, fall 2000.

I have always been cursed with absolutely age-appropriate lust.

Christie Blatchford, columnist, "An Attack of Age-Appropriate Lust," *National Post*, 1 June 2002.

MACDONALD, SIR JOHN A.

Any student of Canada knows that Canadians have a peculiar gift for cautious mediocrity, and a special esteem for it in those to whom we entrust leadership in our affairs. But it was not a cautious mediocrity that produced Confederation, nor was it prudence and precaution that characterized Macdonald. The Confederation of the British North American colonies was one of the great events of the nineteenth century, as its revision and renewal will be one of the important events of the twentieth. Macdonald was always at the centre of the Confederation of a century ago; he was its informing mind, and I am sure that the recreation of Confederation must be infused with the same spirit and the same heart as Macdonald brought to the work a century ago.

W.L. Morton, historian, address, "Macdonald's Greatness in His Times," Toronto, 28 January 1965, The Empire Club of Canada.

Macdonald was, odd as it may seem, a man who might well have been as great in a larger role as he was in the actual one he played.

W.L. Morton, historian, address, "Macdonald's Greatness in His Times," Toronto, 28 January 1965, The Empire Club of Canada.

Children, five to nine years old, have a 98 per cent awareness level of both Santa Claus and Ronald McDonald. In response to the question "Who is Sir John A. Macdonald?" 70 per cent of the children said that he owned a restaurant chain. I guess that's not too good for Canadian history, but it is funny to laugh about. When the paper asked me for a quote, I said, "That means we only have 30 per cent to get."

George Cohon, president, McDonald's Restaurants of Canada Ltd., referring to the Ronald McDonald clown, address, "McDonald's Worldwide," Toronto, 7 April 1983, The Empire Club of Canada.

At bottom, a vote for John A. is a vote for Canada, a vote for love-this-country patriotic emotion (an emotion more prevalent than most Canadians admit). The flag he wrapped himself in wasn't the Maple Leaf, but as Canada Day approaches, we imagine it was.

Christopher Moore, historian, "Old Tomorrow: Today's Man," *The Globe and Mail*, 22 June 2002.

MACKENZIE RIVER *See also* Rivers

I have had the same feeling of malevolence in a place like the delta of the Mackenzie, where the river pours its billions of tons of foul water through bottomless mires scummed with coarse vegetation; or on a mountain range like the Alaskan, which is not passive like the Alps under man's efforts but seems to react savagely against him.

John Buchan, Governor General Lord Tweedsmuir, *Memory Hold-the-Door* (1940). Informing this passage are the notions of William Wordsworth's *Natura Benigna* and Aldous Huxley's *Natura Maligna.*

MCLUHAN, MARSHALL *See also* Communications; Global Village

The medium is the message.

Marshall McLuhan, communications theorist, assertion first made in the Vancouver home of educator Alan Thomas, following a symposium at the University of British Columbia on the subject of music and mass media, 30 July 1959. The celebrated aphorism, the most famous and familiar of Canadian quotations of all time, first appeared in print in McLuhan's *Understanding Media* (1964). Rivalling it is his description of the world as "a global village," the term "the media" (to replace "mass media"), and even the label "word processing." Media personality Tom Wolfe Jr. asked the astonishing question: "Suppose he is what he sounds like, the most important thinker since Newton, Darwin, Freud, Einstein, and Pavlov—what if he is right?" Variations on these McLuhanisms appear in *Colombo's All-Time Great Canadian Quotations* (1994).

The media extend our senses.

Attributed to media philosopher **Marshall McLuhan** by Dan Donovan, student in the 1950s, in Nicholas Kohler, "Papal Thoughts Delivered to the Palm of Your Hand," *The Globe and Mail*, 30 December 2003.

I don't want them to believe me. I just want them to think.

Marshall McLuhan, communications theorist, referring to people critical of his probes, quoted in Wallace Turner, "Understand McLuhan by Him," *The New York Times*, 22 November 1966.

It's not that seagulls are stupid, they are very wild and very emotional. They just can't be trained like eagles, hawks and ravens.

Marshall McLuhan, media philosopher, opening sentence of address, which no doubt astonished his audience of businessmen, "The End of the Work Ethic," Toronto, 16 November 1972, The Empire Club of Canada.

Personally speaking, my own approach to media study has always been to report the subliminal effects of our own technologies upon our psyches, to report not the program, but the impact of the medium upon the human user. Surprisingly, this kind of reporting of the hidden effects of media creates much indignation. Many people would rather die than defend themselves against these effects.

Marshall McLuhan, media philosopher, address, "The End of the Work Ethic," Toronto, 16 November 1972, The Empire Club of Canada.

Marshall McLuhan observed the moment America's culture becomes the culture of the world it is no longer American culture.

Richard Rodriguez, American commentator, *Brown: The Last Discovery of America* (2002).

Dear God—if only Marshall had been alive during the 1990s! What heaven those ten years would have been for him! How he would have loved the Web! What a shimmering Oz he would have turned his global village into! The fulfillment of prophecies made thirty years before!

Tom Wolfe, author, foreword, *Understanding Me* (2003), a collection of McLuhan lectures and interviews edited by Stephanie McLuhan and David Staines.

MADNESS *See also* Psychiatry

Crazy people are good news. Why people go crazy isn't.

Brian Fawcett, poet, "The Swan and Leda," *Wild Culture: Specimens from* The Journal of Wild Culture (1992), edited by Whitney Smith and Christopher Lowry.

MAGIC

Make way for magic! Make way for objective mystery! Make way for love! Make way for what is needed!

Paul-Émile Borduas, artist and principal writer of the artistic manifesto *Refus global* (Global refusal), which called for artistic and imaginative freedom, 400 mimeographed copies of which were released and distributed from Mont-Saint-Hilaire, Quebec, 9 August 1948; *Refus global et ses environs* (1988), edited by André-G. Bourassa and Gilles Lapointe.

God is alive. Magic is afoot. God is alive. Magic is afoot. God is afoot. Magic is alive. Alive is afoot. Magic never died.

Mantra-like passage attesting to the power of magic and miracle from **Leonard Cohen**'s poetic novel *Beautiful Losers* (1966).

Agatha Christie doesn't have to murder someone to write her mysteries.

Stewart James, master puzzle-maker, in Sylvia Fraser, "The Mogul and the Magician," *Toronto Life*, April 2001. James, who worked as postman at Courtright, Ont., created illusions and published them instead of performing them.

As Canadians, we have an observational nature, and that ability to see all aspects of a problem, along with attention to detail, is integral to being a great magician. These are also the same qualities that make Canadians outstanding comedians.

David Ben, magician, in Sylvia Fraser, "The Mogul and the Magician," *Toronto Life*, April 2001. Among Canadian-born magicians with global reputations are Stewart James, James Randi, Doug Henning, and Dai Vernon. Outstanding Canadian comedians are legion.

For me, the thrill of magic is in the elegance of its execution, like watching a performance by Mikhail Baryshnikov.

Patrick Watson, broadcaster and lover of magical effects, in Sylvia Fraser, "The Mogul and the Magician," *Toronto Life*, April 2001.

Possessing neither skill nor patience, I did not become a conjuror, though I did retain a lifetime interest in that twilight zone where magic shades into mystery—that outer edge of creativity and invention in which peculiar things seem to happen, sometimes appearing to defy the so-called laws of nature.

Sylvia Fraser, author, discussing the roles of illusion and mystery in her life, "The Mogul and the Magician," *Toronto Life*, April 2001.

Think of a card.

Attributed to conjurer **Dai Vernon** by Paul Quarrington, "Do You Believe in Magic?" *The Globe and Mail*, 28 September 2002. Known as "The Professor" and also as "The Man Who Fooled Houdini," Vernon was the Canadian-born specialist in close-up magic. He introduced the mental variation above on the physical routine that begins "Pick a card, any card."

We are moving from the awareness and reality of Moore's law to the awe and wonder of Clarke's Third Law, where pure magic reigns.

Frank Ogden, futurist, characteristic observation, 1 June 2003. Moore's law: "Computer-chip capacity doubles every seven years." Clarke's law: "Any sufficiently advanced technology is indistinguishable from magic."

Some thoughtful people complain that science has erased enchantment from the world. They have a point. Miracles, magic, and other fascinating impossibilities are no longer much encountered except in the movies. But in the light shed by the best science and scientists, everything is fascinating, and the more so the more that is known of its reality.

Jane Jacobs, urban planning critic, *Dark Age Ahead* (2004).

MALAPROPISMS *See also* Humour; Language; Words

He never forgave Mackenzie King for warning the Canadian public in 1940 that the prospect of German victory "towers above us like an avalanche" and remonstrated fiercely with Jack Pickersgill on the issue. (Jack, who was King's private secretary and speech-writer, strenuously professed agreement and innocence.)

Attributed to Prime Minister **Mackenzie King** by George Montegu Black, father of Conrad Black, who notes it in *A Life in Progress* (1993).

You have been listening to a message by our honourable Minister of Wealth and Hellfire.

Attributed to an unidentified Canadian radio announcer by Leo Rosten in *Carnival of Wit* (1994). In the same league is the unidentified news announcer who concluded a report with the words "This has been the news from the Canadian Broadcorping Castration."

You took the water right out of my mouth. / You can count them on the back of your hand. / This type of injury is very painful, especially when it hurts. / Never throw in the towel before killing it. / We're finally starting to see the train at the end of the tunnel. / It's the cherry that topples the sundae! / It's time the players rolled up their elbows. / Since then a lot of ink has flowed under the bridge. / There are no rumours without fire! / Such mistakes are small but monumental. / It's the tip of the asparagus. / As for Pat Burns, his toast is cooked. / Ron Hextall has a single weakness, and it's between his legs. / John Kordic is living proof that steroids kill.

Slips of the tongue attributed to **Jean Perron**, hockey coach (1985–1989) who turned sports commentator. Some of them come from the page of "Perronismes" on the www.hockeyzoneplus.com website; others are included in the collection *Les Perronismes* (2001), edited by Michel Morin and Yvon Landry (which Perron himself repudiated).

I went through Hansard and these were some of the things that our politicians have said. It shows that they may not be very good at governing but they're wonderful at torturing the English language. This was a Tory from New Brunswick and what he said was: "To shoot off your face is one thing, but to put your shoulder to the wheel, that's a horse of a different colour." And a Liberal got himself all wound up in his own rhetoric and said: "I see before me the footsteps of the hand of destiny." There was an interjection: "My conscience is clear. I never use it." But my favourite is an NDPer who was urging the government to action and he said: "It's time to grab the bull by the tail and look the situation straight in the face."

Peter C. Newman, author, address, "The Canadian Revolution," Toronto, 30 November 1995, The Empire Club of Canada.

We'll get the bugs ironed out. / Don't put all your bread in one basket. / If opportunity comes knocking we'll build you a door.

Characteristic malapropisms of former Ontario Cabinet minister **Al Palladini**, recalled by Mike Harris, Ontario premier, in Robert Benzie, "Al Palladini Funeral," *National Post*, 13 March 2001. Harris called the deceased "a palladini of mine."

People should just fish and cut bait.

Malapropism attributed to **Chuck Strahl**, Canadian Alliance House leader, as he considered calling for the resignation of party leader Stockwell Day, caucus meeting, Ottawa, 9 May 2001. However, according to Brian Hutchinson, "Cue for Treason," *Saturday Night*, 7 July 2001, he said, "People should just fish or cut bait."

Sixty years ago, Canadians were working alongside their British and American allies planning for the invasion of Norway and the liberation of Europe.... Today, it is every bit as important that Canada step forward—just as we did during the invasion of Norway.

Paul Martin, prime minister, slip of the tongue, speech, 14 April 2004, CFB Gagetown, N.B., in Colby Cosh, "'Norway' Is a Symptom of a Liberal Disease," *National Post*, 16 April 2004. The Normandy invasion took place on 6 June 1944.

When your roof is leaking you still have to call the plumber.

Jean Chrétien, former prime minister, testimony before the inquiry into corruption headed by Judge John H. Gomery, Ottawa, 8 February 2005, in Susan Delacourt and Les Whittington, "Defiant Chrétien Scolds His Critics," *Toronto Star*, 9 February 2005.

MANAGEMENT *See also* Bureaucracy; Business; Governance; Meetings

Management is a curious phenomenon. It is generously paid, enormously influential, and significantly devoid of common sense.

Henry Mintzberg, professor of management, McGill University, "Musings on Management," *Harvard Business Review*, July–August 1996.

Anyone can manage when things go right. It takes a leader to take charge when things go wrong.

George Torok, motivational speaker, characteristic remark, Canadian Management Centre, Toronto, 11 May 2000.

A product manager has all the responsibility without any authority. I have never seen a Product Manager fire a Salesperson!

R. Stephen Rayfield, marketing mentor, address, product management group, Washington, D.C., 27 March 2005.

MANITOBA

My native province has always seemed to me an unusual and fascinating place, possessed both of a sense of great interest and of a deep sense of history.

W.L. Morton, historian, *Manitoba: A History* (1957).

In North America's only socialist province, the sky belongs to the people. The rest, mostly to members of the Manitoba Club.

Mordecai Richler, novelist, "Pages from a Western Journal" (1970), *Home Sweet Home: My Canadian Album* (1984).

I really believe our province is the key position of North America and truly is the heart of the continent.

Ed Russenholt, CBC-TV weatherman (1954–1962), quoted in his obituary by the Winnipeg columnist Gordon Sinclair, *Winnipeg Free Press*, 5 February 1991.

Today the Red River Valley is no longer "the West"; it is the geographical heart of Canada. It may also be the ethnic and social heart as well.

Hugh MacLennan, novelist, *Rivers of Canada* (1974).

She thought of her now, living with her jobless, worthless husband in a trailer somewhere in Manitoba with a string of children.

Thoughts of a character in India about her sister in Canada in **Anita Desai**'s story "Winterscape," *Diamond Dust and Other Stories* (2000).

MANKIND *See also* Humanity; Life; Men & Women; Women

From great-grandparents to great-grandchildren we are only knots in a string.

Naskapi Indian proverbial expression, in Frank G. Speck, *Naskapi: The Savage Hunters of the Labrador Peninsula* (1935).

Man, n. An animal so lost in rapturous contemplation of what he thinks he is as to overlook what he indubitably ought to be. His chief occupation is extermination of other animals and his own species, which, however, multiplies with such insistent rapidity as to infest the whole habitable earth and Canada.

Ambrose Bierce, American author, *The Enlarged Devil's Dictionary* (1906, 1967), edited by Ernest Jerome Hopkins.

For it is the paradox of man that what he is by nature is so much less than what he can become; and it is the tragedy of man that the truth, which portrays him as actually he is, can descend like an iron curtain to frustrate what he would and might be.

Bernard Lonergan, theologian, "The Original Preface to *Insight*" (c. 1949), *The Lonergan Reader* (1997), edited by Mark D. Morelli and Elizabeth A. Morelli.

The most amazing thing ever manufactured was the human being.

Monty Hall, game-show host, in Barry Shainbaum, *Hope & Heroes: Portraits of Integrity & Inspiration* (2003).

The proper study of Mankind is Everything.

Thought of a character in **Margaret Atwood**'s novel *Oryx and Crake* (2003).

MANNING, PRESTON

Manning painted himself as being different from the rest of us lowlifes—he was like the Blessed Virgin Mary and the rest of us were a bunch of pretty bad actors.

Brian Mulroney, prime minister, in Peter C. Newman, *The Secret Mulroney Tapes: Unguarded Confessions of a Prime Minister* (2005).

Those of us who are inspired by a democratic passion must scout the heartland and frontiers of democracy to discover the causes of its decline and ways to improve and secure its vitality.

Preston Manning, co-founder of the Reform Party and the Canadian Alliance, "Scouting 21st Century Frontiers," website, 27 November 2005.

MANUFACTURING *See also* Business; Industry

Fortunately, I landed in Canada as an apprentice to a group of English (Lancashire) and German cotton mill machine fitters. Here I learned to assemble and erect cotton mill machinery. I finally mastered on my own the assemblage and installation of each and every type of cotton manufacturing machine. The installation included running of the pully-shafting throughout the buildings and its over-all alignment from the power house take-off through to each belted-in and aligned production machine. I stayed on to help put the mill into operation.

R. Buckminster Fuller, U.S. designer and developer of the geodesic dome, *Ideas and Integrities: A Spontaneous Autobiographical Disclosure* (1963), edited by Robert W. Marks. Fuller is recalling his first experiences with mechanized work at a cotton mill at Sherbrooke, Que., in 1913–1914. Here he explored the "addition of value (or wealth) by manufacture."

A product is made in a factory. A service is made in front of the user. A brand is made in the mind.

R. Stephen Rayfield, marketing mentor, address, Management Group, DME Corporation, Orlando, Florida, 28 June 2005.

MAPLE LEAF *See also* National Emblems; National Flag; Symbols

Prairie children will know only the Manitoba maple with its yellow autumn leaves. The teacher should describe to them the hard maple with its fine, clean trunk, graceful shape, and glorious autumn scarlet. Pictures of the maple tree and its scarlet leaves are common enough and will help the imagination of the pupils. Help them to see in it the fit emblem of our young red-blooded nation.

Instructions to teachers on the Prairies of a poem about the maple leaf, appendix, *The Canadian Poetry Book: A Book of Modern Verse* (1922), edited by D.J. Dickie.

The first thing a Canadian does when setting off for overseas is to place a maple leaf pin in his lapel—and the maple leaf, the world over, is one of the most recognizable of global symbols of democratic values.

Charles, Prince of Wales, "A Prince's Unsung Heroes," *The Globe and Mail*, 24 April 2001.

MAPS

'Tis truth that surely maps the way, / Geographers will find; / And not through paper all cartouched, / Or hued and rhumbéd lined.

Joe C.W. Armstrong, historian and author, *From Sea Unto Sea: Art & Discovery Maps of Canada* (1982).

MARIJUANA *See also* Drugs & Drug Trade

In a new poll, 54% of Canadian teenagers say they use marijuana. The other 46% say they grow marijuana!

Conan O'Brien, TV host, *Late Night with Conan O'Brien Show*, Elgin Theatre, Toronto, 10 February 2004, in Jason Chow, "Everything but the Beaver," *National Post*, 11 February 2004.

MARITIME PROVINCES *See* New Brunswick; Newfoundland & Labrador; Nova Scotia; Prince Edward Island

MARKETS & MARKETING *See also* Advertising; Consumerism; Merchandising; Salesmanship; Shopping

Marketing is the management and development of a business through analysis, making decisions, and executing programs to satisfy the company needs, while generating profitable revenues, within corporate guidelines.

R. Stephen Rayfield, marketing specialist, *Why My Company Needs Integrated Marketing Now!* (1999).

Selling is immediate. It is short term. Marketing is everything else you do that makes it easier to sell. Marketing is long term.

George Torok, motivational speaker, address, Ontario Junior Achievement, conference, Hamilton, Ont., 5 February 2000, quoted in *The Hamilton Spectator*, 14 February 2000.

We need to be more focused and more confident about what it is to be Canadian and celebrate these values in everything we do. Designing these qualities into our products would be a very tangible start.

Paul Lavoie, president, TAXI Advertising & Design, "How to Reinvent the Brand," *The Globe and Mail's Report on Business*, May 2001.

Hi, I'm James Gosling, and this is my home page. I'm a guy that works at JavaSoft, a division of Sun Microsystems, where I do odd jobs like helping out with the system architecture and wandering around the country giving talks like why Java is the greatest thing since sliced bread.

James Gosling, creator of the computer program Java, principal in Sun Microsystems, website, in Leonard Brody et al., *Innovation Nation: Canadian Leadership from Java to Jurassic Park* (2002).

Blind faith in markets is just as dangerous as blind faith in central planning.

Mark Jaccard, economist, former chief of the B.C. Utilities Commission, writing in a publication of the C.D. Howe Institute, in Thomas Walkom, "Confusion Reigns over Electricity," *Toronto Star*, 24 February 2002.

But what's missing in Rothesay, and all of the bedroom communities like it throughout the Maritimes, are the entrepreneurs, the visionaries, who are willing to take a chance on the region's future. But, I'd wager they would if they had unrestricted access—both physically and politically—to one of the world's biggest consumer markets. Then every fish in Canada, be they small or large, might find a new pond in which to flourish.

Derek Oland, Moosehead Breweries, address, "Can Canada's Regional Companies Succeed in the Global Economy?" Toronto, 9 April 2002, The Empire Club of Canada.

Canada as a brand is still invisible. But we have some incredible stories to tell the world.

Paul Lavoie, president, TAXI Advertising & Design, upon being inducted into the Marketing Hall of Legends, in Tony Wong, "Drive and Charisma Define First Inductees," *Toronto Star*, 28 January 2005.

I do not know what marketing does. Marketers don't make anything. They don't sell anything. And they spend a lot of money.

R. Stephen Rayfield, marketing mentor, address, Management Group, Canadian Management Centre, 19 July 2005.

MARRIAGE *See also* Divorce; Love; Same-sex Marriage

People who have never married have not really lived.

Stephen Leacock, humorist, *Last Leaves* (1945).

Marriage should be the cemetery of love: I don't mean a place where it doesn't have to be an issue; a place where one's love is affirmed automatically by the situation, and one can be something other than a lover.

Leonard Cohen, poet, interviewed by Eve Rockett, "Conversations with Five Men about Women," *Homemaker's Magazine*, May 1979.

You'd have to be a fool to think you can step into that cage called marriage with another human being and not be frightened. It's fearful, it's huge.

Leonard Cohen, poet, interviewed by Eve Rockett, "Conversations with Five Men about Women," *Homemaker's Magazine*, May 1979.

The courts are taking the lead in changing society's attitudes to same-sex partnerships.

Claire L'Heureux-Dubé, justice, Supreme Court of Canada, address, "Opening Remarks to the Panel Discussion: Same-Sex Partnerships in Canada" (1999), in Robert Ivan Martin, *The Most Dangerous Branch: How the Supreme Court of Canada Has Undermined Our Law and Our Democracy* (2003). Martin notes, "In a democracy, judges should not 'take the lead' in changing society's attitudes."

A short story is to a novel what a love affair is to marriage.

Irena F. Karafilly, aphorist, in private conversation, 7 November 2000.

Four words that can save a marriage: I love you anyway.

James Bacque, researcher and novelist, characteristic remark, 27 May 2003.

Marriage is for religions to use. It's like the words Kleenex and tissue. They're interchangeable. "Do you have a Kleenex?" "No, I have a tissue." "Are you getting married?" "No, I'm having a civil union."

Marriage is universal, but in law, in legislation, when you're creating definitions, why not use a term that everybody can live with?

Stan Keyes, chair, Liberal caucus, in Bill Curry, "Alliance to Force Same-sex Marriage Vote," *National Post*, 12 August 2003. Note:

Kleenex is a registered trademark and not a generic term like tissue.

Whether entered into for love, status, money, security or family alliance, monogamous marriage between one man and one woman has proved the best institution humans have devised for furthering the human race, while advancing social stability, dignity for women and the protection of children. Its proven legitimacy arises from its enduring public achievements, not the motives people have for entering in to it.

Barbara Kay, columnist, "The Broken Windows Theory of Marriage," *National Post*, 26 January 2005.

MARTIAL ARTS

Taekwon-Do means three things. *Tae* means kicking, jumping, smashing with the feet; *kwon* means hand, strike, punch; *Do* means art.

Choi Hong Hi, retired South Korean general and formulator of the principles of the martial art that he named Taekwon-Do in 1955, for 30 years a resident of Mississauga, Ont.; quoted in his obituary by Peter Edwards, *Toronto Star*, 24 June 2002.

MARTIN, PAUL

No duo of politicians possesses greater potential for healing national rifts than Paul Martin and Jean Charest. (And, hey, Jean is twenty years younger than Paul. Guess who'll have the best shot at succeeding the man most likely to be the next prime minister of Canada.)

Peter C. Newman, columnist, referring to Quebec Premier Jean Charest and Paul Martin, contender for the Liberal leadership and prime ministership of Canada, "Adieu to Separatism?" *Maclean's*, 12 May 2003.

But we know at least one thing for sure about the prime-minister-to-be: He's totally, unquestionably a Liberal, in every sense of the word. He's the embodiment, the *beau idéal* and the very quintessence of Canadian Liberalism. If entered in an Extreme Liberal competition, he would win the gold.

Robert Fulford, columnist, "He Is the Very Model of a Modern Canadian Liberal," *National Post*, 15 November 2003.

Under Paul Martin, Canada has a new national bird: the chicken coming home to roost.

Paul Wells, columnist, "The Back Page," *Maclean's*, 5 April 2004.

Very, very important.

Paul Martin, prime minister, characteristic response to most issues and concerns, campaigning before the 28 June 2004 election and after assuming office, as noted by George Koch and John Weissenberger, "You Can Win without Quebec," *National Post*, 25 May 2004. Indeed, one journalist noted that Martin is a man of a thousand priorities.

Look, you can have a country like Canada. You can have a country like the U.S. But you can't have a country like Canada with the taxation levels of the U.S.

Attributed to Prime Minister **Paul Martin**, while electioneering, Halifax, 26 May 2004, in Brian Laghi, "Get Digs against America out of the Campaign, Harper Tells Liberals," *The Globe and Mail*, 27 May 2004.

He acts too much like a puppet, fast on both feet, trying to jump out of the way of the next crisis before it overwhelms him, by giving the store away. That's no way to lead a country. There are days when he makes Jean Chrétien look good, and that is a terrible condemnation. Chrétien may have been a thug, but at least we knew who was running the country.

Peter C. Newman, journalist and author, "Going Strong," *Maclean's*, 8 November 2004.

Paul Martin may or may not turn out to be an effective prime minister. So far, the omens are decidedly mixed. He almost lost an election he ought to have won easily. His "asymmetric federalism" sounds suspiciously like Joe Clark's "community of communities," with no one left to speak for Canada amid the cacophony of provinces all with their special deals. He has so many "priorities" he effectively has none.

Richard Gwyn, columnist and essayist, "Surviving Survivalism," *Literary Review of Canada*, December 2004.

You may be the head of the most powerful country in the world. But I'm the head of tomorrow's country.

Paul Martin, prime minister, referring to U.S. President George W. Bush, speaking before a business audience in Ottawa following Bush's address in Halifax, 1 December 2004, in Brian Laghi and Alan Freeman, "Evoking World War II, Bush Prods Canadians," *The Globe and Mail*, 2 December 2004.

Mr. Martin, a successful finance minister for almost a decade until 2002, cannot quite shake off the impression that Canada's top job is too big for him.... His faltering leadership has earned him the sobriquet of "Mr. Dithers."

Editors of *The Economist,* article posted on website on Thursday, 17 February 2005, slated to appear in the following Monday's issue, as noted by Canadian Press, "Magazine Dubs Prime Minister 'Mr. Dithers,'" *Toronto Star*, 18 February 2005. J.C. Dithers, Dagwood Bumstead's dithering boss in Chic Young's *Blondie* comic strip, was portrayed in the "Blondie" movies of the 1930s, 1940s, and 1950s by Jonathan Hale, a Hollywood character actor who is described in film literature as "Ontario-born." The response to the sobriquet was immediate. "How bad is that? But, sometimes, this Prime Minister is damned if he dithers and damned if he doesn't," wrote columnist Lawrence Martin, "It's Time for Our Very Own Manifest Destiny," *The Globe and Mail*, 17 February 2005.

"The second most powerful person in Paul Martin's government is Jean Charest," a member of Martin's government told me the other day, "because this government's worst nightmare is that we might provoke a unanimous resolution against us in Quebec's National Assembly." The current regime deems confrontation too horribly confrontational to contemplate.

Paul Wells, columnist, "Have You Heard This One?" *Maclean's*, 21 February 2005.

MATHEMATICS

The Fields medal is now indisputably the best known and most influential award in mathematics. Sometimes it is compared with the Nobel Prize, since there is no Nobel Prize for mathematics. Publishers and journalists especially like this comparison.

Michael Monastyrsky, mathematician, "Some Trends in Modern Mathematics and the Fields Medal," address at the symposium "The Legacy of John Charles Fields," 7–9 June 2000. The author points out that the Fields medal is awarded every four years to a mathematician under the age of 40. He added that "the results honoured by the Fields medals substantially determined the development of mathematics in our time."

No math is worth doing, unless it is beautiful.

H.S.M. Coxeter, geometer and retired professor of mathematics, characteristic remark, in Siobhan Roberts, "I've Been Coxetering Today," *National Post*, 1 September 2001.

I'm Coxetering today.

M.C. Escher, Dutch surrealist artist, referring to Toronto mathematician H.S.M. (Donald) Coxeter while working on his "Circle Limit III" series of drawings and prints, in Siobhan Roberts, "Donald Coxeter, 1907–2003," *The Globe and Mail*, 12 April 2003. The artist and the geometer met at the International Mathematical Congress held in Amsterdam in 1954 and maintained a friendship based on influence and admiration.

MATURITY *See also* Adolescence; Age; Youth

Perhaps one of the surest signs of middle age is to realize you are far less interested in tailoring yourself to other people's expectations than in trying to live up to those you have set for yourself.

Lines from **Edward O. Phillips**'s novel *Sunday Best* (1990).

MEDIA *See also* Communications

I can tell you all the attention has somewhat embarrassed me. I'm supposed to be in the business of reporting news, not making it.

And, believe me, I certainly prefer it that way. A lot has been said about my rather simple decision to stay with the CBC and in Canada, and a lot of what's been said has blown things somewhat out of proportion. It's been said that I wear special Maple Leaf underpants and that at night before I climb into bed I wrap myself in the flag for comfort. Let me assure you neither is true.

Peter Mansbridge, anchor, CBC TV's *The National*, address, "The Journalist as Celebrity," Toronto, 30 June 1988, The Empire Club of Canada.

It continues to amaze me when people refer to film, radio, theatre and television as "art forms." They are not. They are media through which art can be purveyed, and the only challenges they offer are in techniques.

Bernard Braden, Vancouver-born light-comedy actor, long-time resident in England, *The Kindness of Strangers* (1990).

All media translate experience into other modes of perception. Today, we are living stressfully between the virtual and the real, the simple and the complex. Simple truths now seem to us as complex as the archetypes that haunt our dreams.

Frank Zingrone, theorist, *The Media Symplex: At the Edge of Meaning in the Age of Chaos* (2001).

All these ingenious ways of sending messages have no importance in themselves. The "medium is the message" is one of the world's silliest remarks. The message is the messenger, and it doesn't matter whether you send it by e-mail, a note in a bottle, or on a picture postcard.

John Mortimer, English writer, tilting at Marshall McLuhan's adage "The medium is the message," *Where There's a Will* (2003).

The media are allergic to good news, and run from it as from holy water.

David Warren, columnist, "A Free Palestinian State Is Back on the Table," *National Post*, 18 December 2004.

MEDICAL CARE *See* Medicare

MEDICAL RESEARCH *See also* Medicine

Diabetus. Ligate pancreatic ducts of dogs. Keep dogs alive till acini degenerate leaving Islets. Try to isolate the internal secretion of these to relieve glyosuria.

Frederick G. Banting, physician and medical researcher, notation in his notebook, 2:00 A.M., 31 October 1920. These 25 words led to the isolation of insulin for the treatment of diabetes, as documented by Michael Bliss, *The Discovery of Insulin* (1982).

Our views alter rapidly in these days. In the last twenty years, for instance, I have seen the rise of antibiotics, whose use has now become a commonplace. Yet I can well recall being taught that such an idea was fallacious on the face of it, for what agent could harm a bacterium that would not be equally harmful to its host?

Evan Shute, physician and theorist, *Flaws in the Theory of Evolution* (1961).

Evidence-based medicine is a way of practising and teaching clinical medicine whereby external evidence is explicitly integrated with clinical expertise and patient preferences to improve clinical decision-making.

David Guyatt, professor of medicine and clinical epidemiology and biostatistics, McMaster University, Hamilton, Ont. Dr. Guyatt, who coined this important and influential term in fall 1990, explained, "The term and the approach are widely used in medical education and clinical practice. The term evidence-based medicine (EBM) first appeared in print in Autumn 1990 in an informational document intended for residents entering or considering application to McMaster's residency program. The term subsequently appeared in print in the *ACP Journal Club* (1991; 114: A-16)." In an email dated 20 December 2001 Dr. Guyatt offered three definitions of EBM: (1) "Evidence-based medicine is a way of practising and teaching clinical medicine whereby external evidence is explicitly integrated with clinical expertise and patient preferences to improve clinical decision-making." (2) "Evidence-based medicine involves an awareness of the strength of evidence that forms the basis of one's clinical decisions, and an integration of that evidence with patient values and preferences in making recommendations to patients." (3) "Evidence-based health care is the conscientious and judicious use of current best evidence from clinical care research in making health care decisions." EBM is one of the most significant and influential terms of Canadian origin of our time.

The E.B.M. movement began when six doctors in Canada came up with the idea of skimming the most dependable studies and crunching the results into an accessible, reliable data base.

Jack Hitt, journalist, "Evidence-Based Medicine," *The New York Times Magazine*, 9 December 2001. As an aside: Its use permits a ready distinction between "mainstream" medicine and other modes of treatment, including alternative, complementary, and traditional therapies, as well as household nostrums, and folk remedies.

The metaphor is apt, for evidence-based medicine is rapidly becoming gospel for modern clinical practice. The idea is to give doctors at-their-fingertips data on how treatments actually work (as opposed, for example, to the promotional data that comes with new drugs), to help doctors know which colour pill actually makes patients feel better, and for a longer time, than the others.

Ivor Shapiro, researcher, "Life, at What Price?" *The Walrus*, November 2004.

MEDICARE *See also* Health; Medicine; Socialism

Let us speak loudly and clearly to those who believe that we cannot afford medicare anymore. Let us say that if there was ever a time in our history when we cannot afford not to have medicare, it is now—and let us go on to strengthen it, for all time.

Paul Martin, finance minister, Budget Speech, House of Commons, 18 February 1997.

Not one Canadian in fifty would trade socialized medicine for an American-style health care system. Canadians are healthier, live longer and are not financially wiped out by catastrophic illness. Moreover, they have all of this at a cost of only 9 per cent of GDP, while the USA devotes 14 per cent to health care with only three-quarters of its population covered. Institutions such as socialized medicine have improved the quality of life enormously, and these piecemeal socialist achievements should be trumpeted, not dismissed.

James Robert Brown, philosopher, University of Toronto, "As Real as Rocks," a review of Steven Weinberg's *Facing Up*, *The Times Literary Supplement*, 11 January 2002.

Canadians remain deeply attached to the core values at the heart of medicare and the system has served them well. While medicare is as sustainable as Canadians want it to be, we now need to transform it into a truly national, responsive and accountable health-care system. Making Canadians the healthiest people in the world must become the system's overriding objective.

Roy Romanow, commissioner, Royal Commission on the Future of Health Care in Canada, "Comment," *The Globe and Mail*, 29 November 2002.

Saskatchewan is where medicare came from; Alberta may be where it is going.

Roy MacGregor, columnist, "This Country," *The Globe and Mail*, 17 May 2005.

MEDICINE *See also* Activism; Chiropractic; Depression; Doctors; Drugs & Drug Trade; Medical Research; Medicare; Mental Illness; Pain & Suffering; Pharmacology; Psychiatry; Psychology; Research; Science; Therapy

Live in the ward. Do not waste the hours of daylight in listening to that which you may read by night. But when you have seen, read. And when you can, read the original descriptions of the masters who, with crude methods of study, saw so clearly.

Sir William Osler, physician, in W.S. Thayer, "Osler the Teacher," *Osler and Other Papers* (1931).

Medicine is a science of uncertainty and an art of probability.

Sir William Osler, physician, *Aphorisms from his Bedside Teachings and Writings* (1968), edited by W.B. Bean.

For better or worse, women in the 1930s started placing responsibility for their medical fate in the hands of doctors and abandoning self-help.

Edward Shorter, historian, *A History of Women's Bodies* (1982).

Many clients I see in my private practice are leery about taking prescription drugs and would rather first try an herbal remedy. They feel it's safer and more natural.

Leslie Beck, nutrition consultant, *Leslie Beck's Nutrition Encyclopedia* (2001).

Although the skills of the psychologist and social worker are not to be denigrated, the history of medicine suggests that patients derive some kind of bonus from the knowledge that they are dealing with a physician. It seems to be true that the kind of catharsis achieved from telling one's story to a figure of respect is heightened when that figure is not merely a friend or confidant, but a doctor.

Edward Shorter, historian, *A History of Psychiatry: From the Era of the Asylum to the Age of Prozac* (1997).

MEDIOCRITY *See also* Excellence

In the search for mediocrity / We are the second best. / We much prefer to stay behind / And follow with the rest.

Joe C. W. Armstrong, historian, *Farewell the Peaceful Kingdom: The Seduction and Rape of Canada, 1963 to 1994* (1995).

The enemy of excellence is mediocrity. And it is mediocrity which is the greatest enemy to the good and true life.... Mediocrity is safe, very easy—and therefore to be avoided at all costs! The purpose of life, it seems to me, is to leave no one and nothing indifferent. It means taking risks, going down paths that are not approved. It means the possibility of loneliness and isolation. It means, in sum, all that is opposite to mediocrity.

Adrienne Clarkson, governor general, address, University of Toronto, 19 June 2001, "Worth Repeating," *Toronto Star*, 20 June 2001.

MEECH LAKE ACCORD *See* Distinct Society

MEETINGS *See also* Management

If I were King of the World, there would be fewer meetings, and every meeting would be shorter. There are three types of meetings—boring, complete waste of time, and postponed.

George Torok, motivational speaker, Canadian Management Centre, 11 May 2000.

MEMBERS OF PARLIAMENT *See* Parliament

MEMORY

Flashbulb memories are those incredibly vivid mental pictures you have of events like the Challenger disaster or the Kennedy assassination. Canadians would probably add Paul Henderson's series-winning goal in the 1972 Canada–Soviet Union hockey series.

Jay Ingram, broadcaster, *The Burning House: Unlocking the Mysteries of the Brain* (1994). The memorable day for Canadians (less so for Soviets) was Thursday, 28 September 1972.

Memories are a mirage. There are some places that I would swear looked a certain way, but I go back to visit them, and I was wrong. I look at my notes and say, "How could I have written that?" Perhaps what is most important is simply what remains vivid.

Leon Edel, literary critic, in Stephen Godfrey, *The Globe and Mail*, 11 May 1989.

And as the novelists always implied when desire goes, memory comes.

Observation of the narrator of **Lisa Appignanesi**'s novel *The Memory Man* (2004).

But memories reside in consciousness, and in time the dead are conveyed gradually to its furthest reaches, returning only when summoned by keepsake or song, on anniversary dates, in dreams.

Thoughts of literary book editor Daniel Fielding, in **Richard Wright**'s novel *Adultery* (2004).

I don't remember anything specific about anything in general.

Attributed to **Vince Nigro**, former aide to Toronto mayor Mel Lastman, during his testimony in an influence-peddling inquiry, November 2003, recalled in "Inside City Hall," *The Globe and Mail*, 2 January 2004.

There are times when memory lets us down. And perhaps it's just as well.

Concluding lines spoken by the narrator of **Edward O. Phillips**'s novel *Voyage on Sunday* (2004).

MEN & WOMEN *See also* Humanity; Love; Mankind

Canadian men are much like those in the U.S., only more modest and a *leetle* more tranquillity.

Lily Pons, singer, unidiomatically expressed observation to an interviewer, *Winnipeg Free Press*, quoted in "Cross-Canada 'Chit-Chat,'" *Liberty*, December 1954.

We need each other, but we can't even express our need until we're together. Only when we're together do we find out what we need from one another.

Leonard Cohen, poet, interviewed by Eve Rockett, "Conversations with Five Men about Women," *Homemaker's Magazine*, May 1979.

We approach each other with fear and trembling, as we would approach gods. This is deep within our nature, because we're approaching the unknown. We are each other's mystery, and there's no resolution or solving of it. It's not meant to be solved. Men and women are merely meant to be together, to celebrate it.

Leonard Cohen, poet, interviewed by Eve Rockett, "Conversations with Five Men about Women," *Homemaker's Magazine*, May 1979.

A woman is never as irresistible to a man as when another finds her so.

Irena F. Karafilly, aphorist, characteristic observation, 7 November 2000.

Our society has long moved from the notion that males and females have no differences. Today's real cutting-edge philosophy is that men and women are the same if being the same is an advantage to women, and they are different if being different is an advantage to women. This is a simple and eloquent proposition easily recognized and applied by a number of people in our judiciary and academy....

Barbara Amiel, columnist, "Amy Gehring's Legacy," *Maclean's*, 4 March 2002.

Women have proved to be more honest, courageous, and hard-working, but this is no reason not to have more of them in government.

Eric Nicol, humorist, *Canadian Politics Unplugged* (2003), with Peter Whalley.

If women don't find you handsome, they should at least find you handy.

Red Green, persona of comic actor Steve Smith, *The Red Green Show*, about a handyman mad about duct tape, in Jim Coyle, "A Little Duct Tape for the Canadian Soul," *Toronto Star*, 1 September 2005.

MENOPAUSE *See also* Health

Considering the number of women who are just beginning to really live at fifty, it seems absurd to read about menopause, doesn't it?

Sarah Rosenthal, health specialist, *Women of the '60s Turning 50* (2000).

Women just do not have time for menopause. But while they don't even have time for marking the start of the process, pharmaceutical companies, government planning sectors, and non-government organizations with health initiatives can't wait for it to begin.

Jean Marmoreo, physician and columnist, *The New Middle Ages: Women in Midlife* (2002).

MENTAL ILLNESS *See also* Addiction; Depression; Health; Madness; Medicine; Pharmacology; Psychiatry

Mental illness is the same everywhere in the world. There is just no good reason to teach a different psychiatry in Budapest, Montreal and Nashville and, if businessmen can form multinational pharmaceutical corporations which develop and market psychotropic drugs across countries, psychiatrists should be able to form multinational educational corporations which develop and disseminate educational material on how to use these drugs optimally in mental illness around the world.

Thomas A. Ban, psychiatrist and medical historian, interviewed by David Healy, "They Used to Call It Psychiatry," *The Psychopharmacologists* (1996).

Psychiatric illness: Was it a psychogenic disorder of mind, arising from unconscious conflicts of a sexual nature? Or was it a neurogenic disorder of brain, arising from "chemical imbalances"? The great wheel of fashion in psychiatry, arrested for years at psychoanalysis and depth psychiatry, began to turn slowly on, toward brain biological theories for which pharmaceutical strategies were indicated.

Edward Shorter, medical historian, introduction, *A Dictionary of Psychiatry* (2005).

The "couch," for example, began disappearing from psychiatrists' offices, and the "*PDR*," the *Physician's Desk Reference* for use of American doctors in prescribing, became instead a steady companion.

Edward Shorter, medical historian, introduction, *A Dictionary of Psychiatry* (2005). The ascent of psychopharmacology coincided with the descent of psychoanalysis.

MENTORING *See also* Coaching; Heroes & Heroism; Leadership

Even a poor society can afford a redundancy of mentors and examples, because people in their communities fill those roles by the way, while enjoying themselves or earning their livings by other means: storytellers, skilled tradespeople and craftspeople, musicians, bird-watchers and other nature hobbyists, artists, adventurers, feminists, cosmopolitans, poets, volunteers and activists, chess players, domino players, moralists, life-taught and book-taught philosophers—visible in a community, but invisible to the young when community becomes invisible.

Jane Jacobs, urban planning critic, *Dark Age Ahead* (2004).

MERCHANDISING *See also* Advertising; Consumerism; Markets & Marketing; Salesmanship; Shopping

Goods Satisfactory or Money Refunded.

Famous guarantee identified with The T. Eaton Co., founded by merchant **Timothy Eaton** in Toronto in 1869, associated specifically with the *Eaton's Catalogue*, a mail-order "dream book" issued annually from 1884 to 1976. The wording above dates from 1913. Competitor **C.L. Burton** of The Robert Simpson Co. Ltd. exceeded Eaton's promise in 1928 by guaranteeing not just goods but also a psychological state: "Satisfaction Guaranteed."

We are all products. Some people recognize this more clearly than others and some are more creative and take more risks in packaging themselves.

Leslie Bendaly, motivational speaker, *Winner Instinct: The 6 New Laws of Success* (1999).

METAPHORS *See also* Ideas; Language

The basis of my approach as a teacher has always been that we participate in society by means of our imagination or the quality of our social vision. Our visions of what our society is, what it could be, and what it should be, are all structures of metaphor, because the metaphor is the unit of all imagination. Logical thinking in this field seldom does more than rationalize these metaphorical visions.

Northrop Frye, literary and cultural critic, address, "The Authority of Learning," Toronto, 19 June 1984, The Empire Club of Canada.

Metaphors influence the mind in many unnoticed ways. The willingness to describe fierce disagreement in terms of metaphors of war makes the very existence of real wars seem more natural, more inevitable, more a part of the human condition.

Ian Hacking, philosopher, *The Social Construction of What?* (1999).

METAPHYSICS

Just as the notion of being underlies and penetrates and goes beyond all other notions, so also metaphysics is the department of human knowledge that underlies, penetrates, transforms, and unifies all other departments.

Bernard Lonergan, theologian, *Insight: A Study of Human Understanding* (1953) in *The Lonergan Reader* (1997), edited by Mark D. Morelli and Elizabeth A. Morelli.

Metaphysics, then, is the whole in knowledge but not the whole of knowledge. A whole is not without its parts, nor independent of them, nor identical with them.

Bernard Lonergan, theologian, *Insight: A Study of Human Understanding* (1953) in *The Lonergan Reader* (1997), edited by Mark D. Morelli and Elizabeth A. Morelli.

MÉTIS *See also* Native Peoples; Nationhood

A standard version of the Métis answer to those curious as to when the Métis originated has been: "Nine months after the first white man set foot in Canada."

D. Bruce Sealey and **Antoine S. Lussier**, historians, *The Métis: Canada's Forgotten People* (1975).

MEXICO *See also* America

Trudeau: You must live in San Miguel because of the quality of the light.
Brooks: No, Mr. Prime Minister, I'm here because of the quality of the life.

Exchange between Prime Minister **Pierre Elliott Trudeau**, visiting Mexico on a state visit, and **Reva Brooks**, Toronto-born photographer, wife of painter Leonard Brooks, and permanent resident of the artists' colony at San Miguel de Allende, Mexico, as recalled by Allison Lawlor, "Obituary," *The Globe and Mail*, 6 February 2004.

When Canada, Mexico, and the United States signed the North American Free Trade Agreement, the Canadian and the American politely acknowledged each other, as rumours sometimes do upon meeting. *Haut* shook hands with *Sur*. A vertical alignment, yet, but Nafta signified more than a meeting of basement and balcony.

Richard Rodriguez, American commentator, *Brown: The Last Discovery of America* (2002).

MIDDLE CLASS

Anything that isn't middle class is still in the trees.

Attributed to **Northrop Frye**, literary critic, by Wayne Grady, *Toronto the Wild: Field Notes of an Urban Naturalist* (1995).

MIDDLE EAST *See also* Islam; Israel; Judaism

Specifically, I would say, let us be aware that the Middle Eastern situation is essentially a new one on the world stage, and let us, above all, avoid resented interventions and galling interferences and cling instead to what I believe to be the policy of true wisdom—that of (in two words) benevolent non-involvement.

Stephen Longrigg, brigadier, address, "Oil, Power Politics and the Arab Awakening," Toronto, 30 April 1959, The Empire Club of Canada.

Madame Chancellor, Ladies and Gentlemen, *The Canadian Encyclopedia* considers the Indian-derived name of Toronto to mean: "Place of Meeting." My country, Jordan, has been for millennia a place of meeting not only of peoples but also of the three great monotheistic religions. In your modern city of Toronto things have somewhat changed since the times of Étienne Brûlé and the fur traders! Indeed, trails and canoes have given place to your "little bang" and the $1 trillion money market of today! Our region of the Middle East has also been progressive into modernity. But although our "bangs" have regrettably tended to be of a different sort, hopes are high that the nineties will finally witness the resolution of the Arab–Israeli conflict which has been tearing our region apart for most of this century.

King Hussein of Jordan, address, "Canada and Jordan," Toronto, 12 October 1989, The Empire Club of Canada.

It's easier to keep your hands clean eating falafel than dealing with Middle East politics.

Irena F. Karafilly, aphorist, characteristic observation, 7 November 2000.

As you know this party controls ninety percent of the Canadian Media. [Referring to an otherwise identified group he calls "the Zionist party,"] / I am afraid that Canadians would have the urgency to wear a non-Canadian T-shirt in Lebanon and the Arabic world. / Canadian police always suspect every man with a beard and every woman with a veil.

Raymond Baaklini, Lebanon's ambassador to Canada, quoted in the Arabic-language Lebanese newspaper *Sada al Machric*, 31 December 2002, as reported by Stewart Bell, "Envoy Says Zionists Run Media," *National Post*, 10 January 2003. Interviewed by Bell, the outspoken ambassador went further: "I wanted to say exactly that ninety percent of the mass media in Canada is controlled by Jews or Zionists, and those Jews and Zionists, they are also supported by other organizations in the States."

Jews were for sale, and I was buying them.

Judy Feld Carr, human-rights activist, describing her efforts running a network that rescued more than 3000 Jews from oppression in Syria by bribing state officials with ransom money, on being honoured in Toronto by the Friends of Simon Wiesenthal, in Sharon Dunn, "Society," *National Post*, 10 June 2002.

In order to retain a neutral status in the Middle East Peace Process, Canada must strengthen bilateral relations and downplay its increasing continental relationship with the United States. Due to an increasingly prevalent anti-American sentiment in the Middle East, Canada must distinguish itself by collaborating directly, not only with Middle East states, but with a variety of civil society groups, social movements, and communities. These actors will hold a more significant political role if and when conflict in the region is resolved and democracy is established. This civilian component of conflict resolution in the Middle East can be picked up by the Canadian private sector as a source of employment and opportunity.

Tami Jacoby, analyst, Centre for Defence and Security Studies, University of Manitoba, Winnipeg, Canadian Security and Defence Policy regarding the Middle East, CDS webpage, 19 June 2005.

MILITARY *See* Canadian Armed Forces

MILLENNIUM *See also* Twenty-first Century; Y2K

Every thousand years, a new millennium approaches—relentless like a glacier, invisible like some shifting temporal tectonic plate. Every thousand years, the question must be confronted: What is to be done?

John Ferguson, architect, "Northern Lights," *Wild Culture: Specimens from* The Journal of Wild Culture (1992), edited by Whitney Smith and Christopher Lowry.

The information systems community is heading toward an event more devastating than a car crash. We are heading toward the year 2000. We are heading toward a failure of our standard date format: MM/DD/YY.... There is no way to avoid the fact that our information systems are based on a faulty standard that will cost the worldwide computer community billions of dollars in programming effort.

Peter de Jager, information specialist, "Doomsday 2000," *Computerworld*, 6 September 1993. This popular article, suitably alarmist in tone, alerted the computer and business communities to the consequences of the breakdown of the programmers' two-digit date system and the fact that it would cost $50 billion in repair costs on 1 January 2000. In 1999, de Jager published a follow-up article titled "Doomsday Avoided."

MILLIONAIRES *See also* Finance; Money

To be a millionaire today is to be a nobody. There are more than 7 million of them around the world. Only multiple-millions (there are now 425 billionaires) can confer distinction, and command attention.

Richard Gwyn, columnist, "Home and Away," *Toronto Star*, 20 June 2001.

MINING *See also* Geology; Resources; Stock Market

Minerals—Mines are numerous and all are profitable. Those which do not yield minerals yield large blocks of beautifully graven sheets of paper printed in London and New York, which are sold in fabulous amounts and for fancy sums to the genus "Sucker."

Eugene C. Allen, editor of *The Yukon Nugget*, 3 May 1899, in Russell A. Bankson, *The Klondike Nugget* (1935).

But fortunately this vast tract now appears to be rich in minerals; nickel and copper mines of world wide fame of an immense value are now coming into play. For the rest there is nothing that could live here but the roving Indian or wild animal.

Winston Churchill, British statesman, writing about the country north of Lake Superior to his wife, 22 August 1929, in David Dilks, *"The Great Dominion": Winston Churchill in Canada 1900–1954* (2005).

The towering skyline of Toronto in the 1930s depends on the mines in the northern ranges of Ontario. The height of the one is in balance with the depth of the other.

Adapted from a remark by **John W. Dafoe**, publisher, as noted by E.K. Brown, "Now, Take Ontario" (1947), *Responses and Evaluations: Essays on Canada* (1977), edited by David Staines.

There is only one sure way to stop losing, and that is not to buy mining stocks at all. That's it.

Ivan Shaffer, writer, *The Stock Promotion Business* (1967).

Mining is a business, but exploration's an adventure.

Frank Joubin, uranium prospector, interviewed by John Picton, *Toronto Star*, 9 May 1982.

MINORITIES *See also* Diversity; Ethnicity; Multiculturalism; Prejudice

The United States of America solves its minority problems, more or less, by trying to make every citizen a 100 per cent American. They make everyone conform to a certain type. Other countries, with a longer and more complicated past, are not so favourably situated. Even Canada has its strong race-, religion-, and language-conscious French group. In Europe, the barriers are higher and deeper.

Jawaharlal Nehru, prime minister of India, *The Discovery of India* (1946, 1960).

I am oppressed by the amount of crap that comes over my desk about how tough it is to be a woman, or gay, or a lesbian or a Red Indian, and that every peewee minority has a "right" to a literature of its own.

Robertson Davies, man of letters, letter, 8 February 1991, *For Your Eye Alone: Letters, 1976–1995* (1999).

MIRACLES *See also* Wonders

Miracles This Way.

Sign in a parking lot pointing to a former Safeway store used for evangelical services, described in **Gail Anderson-Dargatz**'s novel *A Rhinestone Button* (2002).

MODERATION *See also* Extremism

Beyond a certain point, moderation is not only a virtue but an evolutionary necessity.

John A. Livingston, naturalist, *One Cosmic Instant: A Natural History of Human Arrogance* (1973).

MODERNITY *See also* Post-modernism

As Pascal said about human beings, modernity is characterized by grandeur as well as by *misère*. Only a view that embraces both can give us the undistorted insight into our era that we need to rise to its greatest challenge.

Charles Taylor, philosopher, concluding sentences of his Massey Lectures, *The Malaise of Modernity* (1991).

MODESTY *See also* Canadian Identity; Egotism

This is a problem that we face very often in dealing with Canadians' statements about themselves because they deal with their vastness in such a quiet tone of voice. The combination of the recognition of the size and importance and future of the country with appropriate modesty which will demonstrate that under no circumstances would a Canadian boast in the way that an American does—it seems difficult to define, especially under the present conditions of enormous progress in Canada. To treat the present Canadian progress in an appropriately dignified and modest and slightly pessimistic and a little skeptical tone of voice requires a great deal of skill which no one would say you don't have. But it is a little puzzling in the whole picture.

Margaret Mead, ethnologist, address, "How Fast Can Man Change," Toronto, 18 April 1957, The Empire Club of Canada.

MONARCHY *See* British Monarchy

MONEY *See also* Currency; Finance; Wealth

Will Pay to the Bearer on Demand.

Familiar wording on bank notes issued by the Government of Canada from the First Issue in 1935 through the Third Issue in 1954, including the $1 Centennial Commemorative of 1967. With the multicoloured Fourth Issue of 1969, the forthright line is conspicuous by its absence, replaced by the tautologous sentence "This Note Is Legal Tender."

And the times when you can mention dollars—dollars are very bad when they are American—they are symbols of materialism, but a Canadian dollar isn't a symbol of materialism. It has more dignity, more decorum. There is a suggestion that the ethics connected with its acquisition are higher. So when it becomes valuable to talk about dollars, very often Canadian dollars are more appropriate and fortunately, we use the same word.

Margaret Mead, ethnologist, address, "How Fast Can Man Change," Toronto, 18 April 1957, The Empire Club of Canada.

To turn $100 into $110 is work. But to turn $100 million into $110 million is inevitable.

Samuel Bronfman, executive, in Peter C. Newman, *The Bronfman Dynasty: The Rothschilds of the New World* (1978).

A one-way trip across the Styx is free: / the meters saying, "No Canadian dimes, / no tokens" are left standing, as you see / but only to remind us of old times.

Lines from Polish poet **Wisława Szymborska**'s poem "On the Banks of the Styx," *View with a Grain of Sand* (1993), translated by Stanisław Barańczak and Clare Cavanagh.

Canadians don't talk about money, especially when they're doing well. They think it's in bad taste.

Sylvia Tyson, singer, foreword in Chris Gudgeon, *An Unfinished Conversation: The Life and Music of Stan Rogers* (1993).

Money is like a *soufflé* because it has to be consumed at its peak desirability. And that's when you get the maximum enjoyment of it. It cooks—like incubating money—and bakes and rises and after 23 minutes it's turned into great mound of treat. But if you wait and try to put it away and hide it under a bed, it's dreadful.

James Barber, chef known as the Urban Peasant, in Jason Crow, "This Peasant Has No Patience with Money," *National Post*, 10 March 2001.

I predict that the purchasing power of the dollar will be 10 per cent of what it is now in five years' time. I may be wrong by a few years, but I won't be wrong by much.

Christopher Ondaatje, financier and philanthropist, in Sharon Dunn, "Where Indiana Jones Retired," *National Post*, 12 August 2002.

MONSTERS *See also* Native Culture; Sasquatch; Wendigo

I'm looking for the Ogopogo, / The bunny-hugging Ogopogo. / His mother was a mutton, his father was a whale. / I'm going to put a little bit of salt on his tail. / I'm looking for the Ogopogo.

Local version of the English music-hall number written by **Ralph Butler**, adapted by H.F. Beattie of the Okanagan Valley, 23 August 1926. "Bunny-hugging" refers to the 1920s dance and "his mother was a mutton" alludes to the eyewitness's description of the lake monster as having a ship's head. Noted by Mary Moon, *Ogopogo: The Okanagan Mystery* (1977).

Any fool can disbelieve a sea serpent.

Characteristic remark of **Archie Willis**, editor of *The Victoria Daily Times* in the 1930s, who gave the name "Caddy" for "Cadborosaurus" to the sea serpent believed to inhabit the waters of Cadboro Bay, Victoria, B.C.

I hope to lead the reader to the conclusion that there is a serious side to this nonsense and that there is in reality a small population of aquatic fish-eating animals rising in Lake Okanagan and perhaps a few other Canadian lakes. And I will suggest what these creatures most probably are.

Roy P. Mackal, scientist, *Searching for Hidden Animals* (1980).

Cryptid.

Neologism coined by **John E. Wall**, researcher, Altona, Man. "'Cryptid' is a relatively new word used among professionals and laypeople to denote an animal of interest to cryptozoology. John E. Wall of Manitoba coined it in a letter published in the summer 1983 issue of the *ISC Newsletter* (Volume 2, Number 2, p. 10), published by the International Society of Cryptozoology. Recently 'cryptid' was recognized by the lexicographers at Merriam-Webster as a word of legitimate coinage, though it has yet to appear in their dictionary"; in Loren Coleman and Jerome Clark, *Cryptozoology A to Z* (1999).

What with whales at Edmonton, sharks at Calgary, lobsters at Okotoks and suckers everywhere, Alberta bids fair to become an interesting aquarium of marine curiosities.

Bob Edwards, publisher, *Calgary Eye Opener*, in Grant MacEwan, "Marine Monsters Great Boon for Tourism," *Calgary Herald*, 15 December 1984.

I think all of us sort of like to believe that, in the depths of the ocean, or the depths of the sea—kind of like our own subconscious—there's something lurking there. We always like to believe and hope that we haven't found and discovered everything in this world.

Elizabeth Nicholls, scientist and specialist in ancient marine reptiles, Royal Tyrrell Museum, Drumheller, Alta., in Nicholaas Van Rijn, "With Nessie, Seeing Isn't Believing," *Toronto Star*, 29 July 2003.

MONTREAL

We call this mountain "le Mont Royal."

Jacques Cartier, French navigator, exploring the site of present-day Montreal, 1535, *Jacques Cartier and His Four Voyages to Canada* (1890), edited by Hiram B. Stephens.

You are a grain of mustard seed that shall rise and grow until its branches overshadow the earth. You are few, but your work is the work of God. His smile is on you, and your children shall fill the land.

Sieur de Maisonneuve, French colonist, sermon delivered on the founding of the colony of Ville-Marie, today's Montreal, 18 May 1642, in Francis Parkman, *The Jesuits in North America in the Seventeenth Century* (1867).

This is the first time I was ever in a city where you couldn't throw a brick without breaking a church window.

Mark Twain, American humorist, address, Windsor Hotel, Montreal, 7 December 1881, in Stephen Leacock, *Queen's Quarterly*, summer 1935.

Am in Montreal. Where am I supposed to be?

Attributed to **G.K. Chesterton**, man of letters, "who was wont to wire his wife," according to Cameron Hollyer, "The Curator's Egg," *Lasting Impressions: The 25th Anniversary of The Bootmakers of Toronto, The Sherlock Holmes Society of Canada* (1997), edited by George A. Vanderburgh.

This is a city of hatreds. I can smell them.

Brendan Behan, Irish playwright, on Montreal's St. Laurent Blvd. in December

1960, as observed by Tony Aspler, *Travels with My Corkscrew: Memoirs of a Wine Lover* (1997).

We lived in Montreal, a city that is a hyphen between the English and French worlds.

Jean-Benoît Nadeau and **Julie Barlow**, political scientists, *Sixty Million Frenchmen Can't Be Wrong (Why We Love France, but Not the French)* (2003).

Montreal has been spared the affliction of SARS suffered by Toronto, 200 miles away, and has no reported cases.

Clifford Krauss, newspaperman, "What's Doing in Montreal," *The New York Times*, 25 May 2003. Krauss, the *New York Times*'s Canadian bureau chief, underestimated by one-third the distance between the two cities. The official distance between Montreal and Toronto is 539 km, or 335 miles.

Favourite city: Montreal. I was born in the United States. And I've always felt like more of an American than a Canadian, even though I was brought up in Canada. But above being an American, I feel like a Montrealer. It's a very cosmopolitan, beautiful city. There's something about French Canadians; they're kind of like aliens.

Rufus Wainwright, singer-songwriter, raised in Montreal, "Domains," *The New York Times Magazine*, 14 March 2004.

MOON

When the Apollo astronauts visited its rock-strewn surface, the moon revealed a handful of secrets more subtle than any we had ever dreamed of.

Christopher Dewdney, poet and author, *Acquainted with the Night: Excursions through the World after Dark* (2004).

There's a tombstone somewhere for manned lunar exploration with the dates 1969–1972 carved into it.

Robert J. Sawyer, science-fiction author, referring to the period of the Apollo moon landings, "Science Fiction and Social Change" (2004), *Relativity: Stories and Essays* (2004). The SF writer added: "Since then, no human being has gone more than five hundred miles from Earth—five hundred miles in the last thirty-two years! Not a single science-fiction writer predicted that sort of failed dream."

MOOSE *See also* Animals

Save the Moose / Today Moosehead is calling on all Canadians to help bring back the moose. We want Canadians to send a message to Ottawa that they can't ignore one of the country's biggest assets. People around the world know that when they see a moose it's like seeing a maple leaf—it's Canada.

Public relations campaign launched by Moosehead Breweries of Saint John, N.B. The petition on the company's website, May 2005, runs: "Whereas the Canadian Tourism Commission (CTC) has decided to remove 'mountains, moose and the Mounties' from Canadian travel materials; and whereas the CTC states that the French are known for cuisine, the Swiss for precision, and the Italians for fine clothing, and believes these are 'good' clichés; we believe the CTC should continue to tell Canadians and people around the world about the contribution of the Royal Canadian Mounted Police, [about] the sheer natural beauty of the majestic Canadian Rockies, and about the king of the Canadian forest–the moose. If you agree, please add your name and address to our petition to receive a Moosehead lapel pin while supply lasts."

MOSAIC *See* Cultural Mosaic

MOSQUITOES

I am too great / to be bitten / by those little mosquitoes / that are flying about.

Kwakiutl song, "Boastful Chief," *Songs of the Great Land* (1989, 2004), edited by John Robert Colombo.

Everybody knows mosquitoes are dunning, malicious darts of the devil, devised for human torture. Let one bite you and it will breed a million more.

Tim Ward, traveller and writer, *What the Buddha Never Taught* (1998).

MOTHERHOOD *See also* Family

Pearl: Don't ever forget the idea that you're too big to say hello to your mother.
Allen: Hello, mom.

Exchange between bandleader **Bert Pearl** and comedian **Eddie Allen** of The Happy Gang radio troop, adapted by James McCready, "Eddie Allen, 1920–2003," *The Globe and Mail,* 12 July 2003. Allen made this his signature greeting during wartime broadcasts.

But if pregnancy and child care became one of life's executive positions; if we educated the young in the power of female fertility as well as the perils of sexuality; if nursing mothers were paid $42,000 a year ... well, dream on. Until that happens, we blame hormones, not history.

Marni Jackson, journalist, "Hormones or History?" *Wild Culture: Specimens from* The Journal of Wild Culture (1992), edited by Whitney Smith and Christopher Lowry.

Many women decide to be mothers not really understanding the job description, and are imprisoned for years in domestic drudgery without time off for good behaviour. The harder you work at it, the worse it gets. The more responsibility the mother takes, the less responsibility the child takes.

Remarks made by the character Kate Fitzgerald, in **Catherine Gildiner**'s novel *Seduction* (2005).

MOTHS

The night is full of hidden wonders, but the giant saturniid moths that flutter around lights on early summer evenings are the most ravishing incarnation of night. They are like emblematic talismans, all the more mysterious because they themselves are unaware that they depict the essence of darkness.

Christopher Dewdney, poet and author, *Acquainted with the Night: Excursions through the World after Dark* (2004).

MOTION PICTURES *See* Cinema

MOTIVATION *See also* Ambition; Philosophy

There are only two types of motivation: fear and desire. Your greatest fear or desire always wins.

George Torok, motivational speaker, Canadian Management Centre, 11 May 2000.

MOTTO *See also* National Anthem; National Flag; Symbols

Canada, Land of the Understatement. I once proposed their national motto should be: "Now, Let's Not Get Excited." Not that I would ever generalize. I attribute their commendable phlegm to being too cold to waste much energy, and also to a regular ingestion of oatmeal.

Molly Ivens, U.S. commentator, "Tough Sledding in the North," *The CCPA Monitor,* October 2004.

The display of national confidence makes Canadians cringe. If we had to come up with a new motto, it would probably be "Canada. Not bad! / Le Canada. Pas mal!"

Margaret Wente, columnist, *An Accidental Canadian: Reflections on My Home and (Not) Native Land* (2004).

MOUNTAINS

We gazed at the venerable Laurentian Mountains, said to be the oldest geological formation in the world. This claim has also seemed to me a true one, though I know less than nothing of the science of geology, as there is something so exquisitely timeless in their aspect, and the outlines have the precision and charm of a cameo.

Susan Buchan, compiler of *John Buchan by His Wife and Friends* (1947), describing the approach to Quebec City by sea of herself and her husband, the future Governor General Lord Tweedsmuir, October 1935.

The point I want to finish on is that I think very few of us in life are ever lucky enough to get a glimpse of what we are actually capable of doing and I think in a sense we're all climbers in a way.

Laurie Skreslet, mountain climber, address, "To Reach the Highest Mountain," Toronto, 25 January 1990, The Empire Club of Canada.

As soon as I learned to walk, I learned to walk away. Not from responsibilities, but rather, away from mediocrity.

Stephen Canning, mountaineer, environmentalist, defining himself on a Grade XII scholarship application, recalled by Shandell Susin, "Lives Lived," *The Globe and Mail*, 26 August 2004. He died from a fall on Mount Logan, Y.T., at the age of 22.

MOVEMENT *See also* Action

Everyone and everything on this planet moves—the earth and all that exists above, upon, and beneath it. Some things move faster than the human eye can register; others move so slowly that a lifetime passes before a shift occurs. This is the dance that all people share.

Janice Pomer, instructor of movement and dance, *Perpetual Motion: Creative Movement Exercises for Dance and Dramatic Arts* (2001).

Freedom of movement leads to freedom from pain.

Line Troster, physiotherapist and rehabilitation specialist, goal, introductory pamphlet, April 2005.

MOVIES *See* Actors & Acting; Celebrities; Cinema; Fame; Hollywood

MULRONEY, BRIAN

We thought Mulroney was going to be a one-term blip. Now he's a two-term disaster.

J.L. Granatstein, historian, *Sacred Trust? Brian Mulroney and the Conservative Party in Power* (1986), with David Bercuson and William Young.

Mulroney will have had more influence than any other prime minister for a very long time—including Trudeau.

J.L. Granatstein, historian, amending his previous view that Brian Mulroney was "another one-term Tory leader, a blip in history," in the words of interviewer Christopher Moore, "Writers of History: The Organized Man," *The Beaver*, April–May 1991.

Democratic countries normally get the governments they deserve, but I am not convinced that such an envious, whingeing people as Canada had become in the mid-eighties really deserved so fundamentally well-intentioned a political chameleon as Brian Mulroney.

Conrad Black, publisher and historian, *A Life in Progress* (1993).

The legacy of the Mulroney years is that Canadians have lost their faith in government, and they've lost their trust in politicians. Politicians everywhere are paying for what those bozos did.

Stevie Cameron, investigative journalist and author, address, "Corruption in Government," Toronto, 17 November 1994, The Empire Club of Canada.

Thank you. Thank you very much.

Brian Mulroney, former prime minister, accepting "the large envelope containing $100,000 in cash" from Karlheinz Schreiber, arms dealer and principal in the Airbus scandal, Montreal, first of payments totalling $300 000 made from June 1993 through December 1994, in William Kaplan, *A Secret Trial: Brian Mulroney, Stevie Cameron, and the Public Trust* (2004). Kaplan: "Ordinary Canadians would not begin to understand the payment of $300,000 in cash—payments made in hotels and for services that have never been adequately explained."

Based on the evidence received to date, the RCMP acknowledges that any conclusions of wrongdoing by the former prime minister were—and are—unjustified. The government of Canada and the RCMP regret any damage suffered by Mr. Mulroney and his family and fully apologize to them.

Apology from the RCMP and the Department of Justice in the $50-million defamation action launched by Brian Mulroney in the aftermath of the Airbus scandal, January 1997, as in William Kaplan, *A Secret Trial: Brian Mulroney, Stevie Cameron, and the Public Trust* (2004).

Mr. Mulroney's admission that, after leaving office as prime minister in 1993, he received $300,000 in cash from Mr. Schreiber was the real story in their recent series. I was the sideshow.

Stevie Cameron, investigative journalist and author, "Mulroney Was the Real Story," *The Globe and Mail*, 22 November 2003, in William Kaplan, *A Secret Trial: Brian Mulroney, Stevie Cameron, and the Public Trust* (2004).

I think that Brian Mulroney made one fatal mistake. He wanted so badly to be loved. He didn't want to make enemies. He didn't understand that prime ministers don't need to be loved. They need to be respected. Trudeau, as much as we hated him, was always respected and Mulroney tried so hard to be loved that it didn't work.

Peter C. Newman, author, address, "The Canadian Revolution," Toronto, 30 November 1995, The Empire Club of Canada.

Brian has great contacts. He knows every dictator in the world on a first-name basis.

Peter Munk, financier and friend of former prime minister Brian Mulroney, in Peter C. Newman, "Back in the Limelight," *National Post*, 11 May 2002.

Martin Brian Mulroney, eighteenth prime minister of Canada (1984–93), retired from office the most hated politician in Canada—possibly the most hated prime minister in Canadian history.

William Kaplan, advocate and author, *A Secret Trial: Brian Mulroney, Stevie Cameron, and the Public Trust* (2004).

I could sum up his legacy in one sentence: The 20th century never did belong to Canada, but Mulroney made sure Canada could belong to the 21st century.

Peter C. Newman, biographer, interviewed about *The Secret Mulroney Tapes* (2005), in John Ivison, "Mulroney Ruled by Insecurities," *National Post*, 13 September 2005.

I think he was a very special kind of liar, who believed his own lies.

Peter C. Newman, interviewed about *The Secret Mulroney Tapes* (2005), in Susan Delacourt, "Mulroney Regrets 'Reckless' Comments," *Toronto Star*, 13 September 2005. In the book Newman quotes former Ontario premier David Peterson: "He is a pathological liar. In fairness, I don't believe he knows he's lying.... Oh, God, you couldn't take anything he said at face value. His essential Achilles heel is his baloney."

And yet, he bugs us still....

Peter C. Newman, biographer, referring to former Prime Minister Brian Mulroney and echoing the "haunts us still" line about Trudeau, *The Secret Mulroney Tapes: Unguarded Confessions of a Prime Minister* (2005), as quoted in *Maclean's*, 19 September 2005.

He believes he will go down in Canadian history as the best prime minister since Sir John A. Macdonald. He most certainly will go down as the most profane.

Roy MacGregor, columnist, referring to Newman's *The Secret Mulroney Tapes* (2005), *The Globe and Mail*, 12 September 2005.

Similarly, Brian Mulroney would probably have done a good job as public works minister in the Sir John A. Government. Well, perhaps not.... Brian Mulroney would have had a more secure place in history, and more respect from his constituents, if he had been mayor of Boston in the 1940s.

Michael Bliss, historian, "Mulroney's Place in History," *National Post*, 15 September 2005.

Your Excellencies, Prime Minister, Heads of the Opposition Parties, Justices of the Supreme Court of Canada, Senators and Senatoresses, Members of the Cabinet, distinguished Members of the Press Gallery, Madames et Messieurs, good evening. Peter Newman, go fuck yourself. (Uproarious laughter and spontaneous applause.) Thank you very much, ladies and gentlemen, and good night. (Loud applause.)

Brian Mulroney, former prime minister, videotaped presentation, Annual Press Gallery Dinner, Ottawa, 22 October 2005. The calculated insult was later broadcast by CBC Radio and CBC-TV with the twelfth-last word bleeped out.

MULTICULTURALISM *See also* Canadian Identity; Cultural Mosaic; Diversity; Ethnicity; Values

I'm not saying that you should forget where you've come from or who you are. But you should be careful that your own personality is not frozen by the little group into which you've inserted yourself because it's so comfortable. Part of immigration is uncomfortable, and I suppose it is only human to flee from that. But dealing with the discomfort can help you to achieve what you dreamt of achieving when you first immigrated. This new society holds the promises that you came for in the first place.

Neil Bissoondath, novelist, interviewed by Aja Norgaard, "Aurora Online," website, fall 1989.

I believe we must also put an end to our government-sponsored policy of multiculturalism. It has fragmented our society and divided us. I came to this country because I heard a lot of great things about Canada. I think it's time that we begin to re-affirm our Canadian values of law and order, hard work and individual initiative. Because of government-fostered multicultural policies, we have strayed from the core values that made this country one of the greatest in the world.

Frank Stronach, manufacturer, Magna International, address, "Operating within a Global Economy," Toronto, 10 February 1994, The Empire Club of Canada.

I am, however, confident that a new spirit will rise from this country, and it will influence the whole world. This new spirit is called pluricultural federalism.

Antonio D'Alfonso, poet and essayist, "To Break the Code of Silence," *In Italics: In Defense of Ethnicity* (1996).

I wish we were a little more Anglo; I weary of turbaned taxi-drivers who don't know where anything is.

Robertson Davies, man of letters, letter, 1 August 1994, *For Your Eye Alone: Letters, 1976–1995* (1999).

And insofar as international beings—or "global souls," as I have called them—are more and more urgently discussing new notions of identity and belonging, more and more of us are honorary Canadians, worrying at the very issues of globalism and multiculturalism that Canada was addressing before the rest of us knew they existed.

Pico Iyer, traveller and writer, "Mongrel Beauties," *Saturday Night*, 31 March 2001.

A multicultural Canada is a great idea in principle, but in reality it is more like a tacit contract of mutual indifference.

Michael Ignatieff, commentator, "Immigration: The Hate Stops Here," *The Globe and Mail*, 25 October 2001.

Canadian multiculturalism, in other words, is not "multi" at all, but culturally biased to the degree that it expresses a Canadian respect for individualism not shared by most countries in the world.

Richard Rodriguez, American commentator, *Brown: The Last Discovery of America* (2002).

Canada is today the most successful pluralist society on the face of the globe, without any doubt in my mind.... That is something unique to Canada. It is an amazing global asset.

Aga Khan IV, spiritual leader of the Ismaili Muslims, interviewed in Ottawa by John Stackhouse and Patrick Martin, "Interview with the Aga Khan," *The Globe and Mail*, 2 February 2002.

People from every corner of the world are coming to Canada, on arrival, looking around to see that they are surrounded by people from the other three corners.

Pico Iyer, traveller and essayist, "The Last Refuge," *Harper's*, June 2002.

Canada is more than a peaceful microcosm of Europe; it is increasingly a peaceful microcosm of the entire world whose many interests and interdependencies are multipolar. Canada is becoming the home of a unique postmodern, postmaterial multiculturalism, generating hardy strains of new hybrids that will enrich this country and many others in the world.

Michael Adams, consultant, *Fire and Ice: The United States, Canada and the Myth of Converging Values* (2003), with Amy Langstaff and David Jamieson.

Fiercely Canadian, Proud of Heritage.

Inscription on the statue raised in honour of **Johnny Lombardi**, Italian broadcaster, Little Italy neighbourhood of Toronto, unveiled 17 June 2004. Veronica De Nogales and Edwin Dam created the statue.

First Nations communities and other historically marginalized communities are asserting their rights and challenging the limits of multiculturalism. Multiculturalism contains within it the seeds of its own transformation. It must identify prejudice and discrimination and "Othering" as important sources of exclusion; it must assert that the Canada of the past should not be reclaimed, as it was built on violence and systematic exclusion; and it must affirm and value differences as central to a redefined social cohesion.

Anver Saloojee, political scientist, "Social Cohesion and the Limits of Multiculturalism in Canada," in *Racism, Eh? A Critical Inter-Disciplinary Anthology of Race and Racism in Canada* (2004), edited by Camille A. Nelson and Charmaine A. Nelson.

The "pretend pluralism" of a monocultural multiculturalism is subliminally racist because such cultural neutrality denies and excludes those who want their cultural differences recognized in living together differently.... official multiculturalism is essentially a Canada-building exercise that seeks to depoliticize differences through institutional inclusion and removal of discriminatory barriers both social and cultural.

Augie Fleras, sociologist, "Racializing Culture / Culturalizing Race," in *Racism, Eh? A Critical Inter-Disciplinary Anthology of Race and Racism in Canada* (2004), edited by Camille A. Nelson and Charmaine A. Nelson.

Multiculturalism in Canada is predicated on the principle that people from many cultures can live together differently as long as these cultural differences aren't taken seriously.

Augie Fleras, sociologist, "Racializing Culture / Culturalizing Race," in *Racism, Eh? A Critical Inter-Disciplinary Anthology of Race and Racism in Canada* (2004), edited by Camille A. Nelson and Charmaine A. Nelson.

Canada has successfully constructed a public sphere predicated on the ethic of respect for human dignity. It recognizes and builds on difference, enables a spirit of compromise and consensus in public and legislative policies, and marks out a healthy space for the role of civil society as a sound (indeed, essential) bulwark for democratic processes.

Aga Khan, spiritual leader of the Shia Ismaili Muslims, address, Conference on Leadership and Diversity, Ottawa, 19 May 2004, published in *The Globe and Mail*, 20 May 2004.

Seen from afar, Canada is a noble experiment: whether peoples speaking different languages, divided into five regions, can survive and prosper as a united country. If we fail, the future of the multilingual, multicultural state in the modern world will be grim indeed.

Michael Ignatieff, commentator, address, biennial policy conference of the Liberal Party, Ottawa, 3 March 2005, excerpted as "A Generous Helping of Liberal Brains," *The Globe and Mail*, 4 March 2005.

I am Russian by name, I am Portuguese by surname, I am Indian by origin, Ugandan by birth, English by education, Canadian by residence, and I am Scotch by consumption.

Ivan John Anthony Fernandes, Crown attorney, quoted by John W. Morden, "Lives Lived," *Globe and Mail*, 15 November 2005.

MULTINATIONALISM *See also* Corporations; Globalism & Globalization

The multinational firm ... avoids the suggestion of an American monopoly of this development.

Howe Martyn, Canadian-born political scientist teaching in the United States, introduced this widely used term in 1959, as noted in "Origins of the Multinational Firm," *The Multinational Corporation in World Politics* (1973), edited by Abdul Said.

MURDER *See also* Crime; Euthanasia; Genocide; Violence

You have to kill, to secure the continuity of the universe of which you are the centre.

Wilson Duff, anthropologist, random observation, quoted in *Bird of Paradox: The Unpublished Writings of Wilson Duff* (1996), edited by E.N. Anderson.

If God told me to kill, I would do it in His name. Yes or No.

Line on a questionnaire of the Personal Philosophy Inventory developed in the 1980s by **Michael Persinger**, psychologist, as noted by Dr. Robert Buckman, *Can We Be Good without God?* (2002). Yes or no answers were correlated with the respondents' electric fragility of the temporal lobes. Persinger found that 7 percent of the people tested said, "Yes, I would kill in God's name." Briefly, "yes" was the response of 10 percent of males, 5 percent of females; among churchgoers, the percentages were 25 percent and 9 percent. Among male respondents who reported religious experiences, the figure rose to 35 percent, and among that group with high scores on temporal-lobe questions, the proportion rose to 50 percent of men, 15 percent of women. Persinger found a convincing correlation of belief in God, murderous behaviour, and temporal-lobe lability.

It's really embarrassing to admit, but I forget why I killed my husband.

Opening sentence and startling admission of protagonist Kate Fitzgerald in **Catherine Gildiner**'s novel *Seduction* (2005).

MUSEUMS & COLLECTIONS *See also* Civilization; Culture

Where are the museums for forgotten sounds?

R. Murray Schafer, composer and theorist, *The Tuning of the World* (1977).

The Museum of Civilization is the only museum in the world that is more interesting on the outside than it is on the inside.

Roy MacGregor, columnist, "This Country," *The Globe and Mail*, 24 September 2002.

Museum collections are subjective interpretations of cultural beliefs and values. Moreover, the fact that an exhibition is a construction from a particular point of view is subverted by its design, which seduces the viewer into believing that the objects have either effortlessly come together on their own, or that they represent some kind of accurate whole. The silences, those objects that do not fit into this structure, are rendered invisible within the exhibition.

Johanna K. Mizgala, art curator, "Lance Belanger's Tango Lessons," *Racism, Eh? A Critical Inter-Disciplinary Anthology of Race and Racism in Canada* (2004), edited by Camille A. Nelson and Charmaine A. Nelson.

MUSIC *See also* Arts & Artists; Ballet; Composers; Dance; Opera; Singers & Songs

The true recording artist, who really understands the values and implications of recording, is someone who is looking at the totality—sees it so clearly that it doesn't matter if you start with the middle note in the middle movement and work in either direction like a crab going back and forth. The mark of a true recording artist is an ability to be able to cut in at any moment in any work and say, "This works in a way that's only appropriate for this recording."

Glenn Gould, pianist, interviewed by Ulla Colgrass, *For the Love of Music* (1988).

Classical Music

Canada's composers are skilled, productive, and as varied in outlook as those of any other nation today; perhaps soon it will no longer be necessary to ask the reader to take such a statement largely on faith.

John Beckwith, composer and teacher, "Music," *The Culture of Contemporary Canada* (1957), edited by Julian Park.

There isn't and there oughtn't.

R. Murray Schafer, composer, asked in the 1960s whether there is or ought to be a distinctively Canadian music, in William Littler, *The New York Times*, 3 June 1984.

I have met Canadians in many parts of the world but I have never met any who bragged about their music education, chamber music or anything else about musical achievements.

Yehudi Menuhin, violinist, addressing the World Music Week Conference, Montreal, October 1975, quoted in *Closed Circuit*, 15 October 1975.

Read a book on Canada and you will find little in it about music. Read a book on music and you will find even less in it about Canada. A Canadian composer, not wishing to be a human contradiction in terms, tries to locate the ways in which the two concepts "Canada" and "music" have evidently influenced his peculiar identity.

John Beckwith, composer and teacher, 1977 essay, *Music Papers: Articles and Talks by a Canadian Composer, 1961–1994* (1997).

If God had intended Canada to have a music, Mozart would have been born in Regina.

R. Murray Schafer, composer, *On Canadian Music* (1984). Schafer is responding to the following passage in the *Report of the Federal Cultural Policy Review Committee* (1982): "We yearn for our Mozarts, our Shakespeares and our Picassos. Nation-building is a matter of establishing links; and to the extent that the Great Artist is lacking, Canadians face the problem of a missing link."

Composing is a lonely occupation, but I don't feel alone when my mind is immersed in the creation of a piece. The feeling of isolation is due to the situation in Canada, where serious music doesn't have a very high rating. Composers don't die of starvation here. They die of frustration.

John Weinzweig, composer and teacher, in Pearl Sheffy Gefen, *The Globe and Mail*, 24 November 1989.

I won't linger longer.

Ben Heppner, heroic tenor, addressing the audience, experiencing voice difficulties singing the fifth of nine songs by Paolo Tosti at Roy Thomson Hall, Toronto, 27 November 2003, in Robert Everett-Green, "Classical Music," *The Globe and Mail*, 29 November 2003. He experienced similar difficulties singing the lead in Berlioz's *Les Troyens* at the Metropolitan Opera in New York City, 17 January 2002, but subsequently overcame the trouble.

Popular Music

Come give us a listen, and if you ever bump into me somewhere, give me a smile and let me buy you a beer, because all of this music is for you, you know.

Stan Rogers, singer-composer, press kit of 1974, in Chris Gudgeon, *An Unfinished Conversation: The Life and Music of Stan Rogers* (1993).

I'm a legend in my own mind.

Rompin' **Ronnie Hawkins**, rock 'n' roll singer, characteristic remark first recorded in 1985.

Muzak goes in one ear and out some other opening.

Anton Kuerti, pianist, interviewed by Ulla Colgrass, *For the Love of Music* (1988).

I'm also alternative because of Canada—there's something romantic about being Canadian. We're a relatively unpopulated, somewhat civilized, and clean and resourceful country. I always push the fact that I'm Canadian.

k.d. lang, singer-songwriter, *k.d. lang: in her own words* (1995).

Eileen "Shania" Twain, the million-CD-selling country-and-western singer-composer, grew up in Timmins as Eileen Twain and got her start singing at Ontario's Deerhurst Inn. She won several awards for her work at the

1996 Grammys. Shania was the name of a girl she worked with at the Deerhurst Inn, and, when it came time to confect a show-biz name, she chose Shania (pronounced sha-NYE-a), which is Ojibwa for "on my way."

Bill Casselman, writer and broadcaster, *Casselmania: More Wacky Canadian Words & Sayings* (1996).

I don't think that constant movement is good for a person. I need to be home for a little while. This has been ten years of non-stop work. Maybe René [Angelil, Céline Dion's husband] has some sperm left over and I can have a short baby with a beard.

Jann Arden, Alberta-based pop singer, on a reprieve from her touring, in Bartley Kives, *Winnipeg Free Press*, 30 October 2001.

The perception [is] that pop music—especially rock and roll—has produced some of the best works of musical art of the modern world. In my view, pop music is fun art, not profound art. How can anyone even think of comparing jazz, rock, and rap pieces to the works of a Mozart or a Beethoven, as many music critics now do on a regular basis? There is absolutely nothing in the pop-music repertoire that comes close to the profundity of Mozart's Requiem Mass or Beethoven's Ninth Symphony.

Marcel Danesi, semiotician, *Forever Young: The "Teen-Aging" of Modern Culture* (2003).

Now I don't want you behaving like normally restrained Canadians.

Mick Jagger, rock performer, addressing a crowd of 59 000 fans at Toronto's SkyDome, "Steel Wheels" show, December 1989, in Mariella Frostrup, "Why Jagger Is Still at It as He Turns Sixty," *Toronto Star*, 19 July 2003.

I hope to see you somewhere down the path.

Gordon Lightfoot, composer-singer, closing words on his induction into the Canadian Songwriters Hall of Fame during the inaugural ceremony, Toronto, 3 December 2003, in Greg Quill, "'I'll Be Back,'" *Toronto Star*, 4 December 2003.

Traditional Music

If you hear a group of youngsters chanting some verses that sound as though they had been made up on the spot, the chances are that they can be matched by similar ones dating back several generations—or several centuries.

Edith Fowke, folklorist, *Sally Go Round the Sun: Three Hundred Children's Songs, Rhymes and Games* (1969).

It has been said that French Canada helped France to rediscover its own folk music.

Ezra Shabas, biographer, referring to the groundbreaking work of Marius Barbeau, Edward Sapir, and Ernest MacMillan in preserving the traditional songs of French-Canada that were French in origin, *Sir Ernest MacMillan: The Importance of Being Canadian* (1996).

MUSLIMS *See also* Islam

This could not have happened in some lands.... It is significant that people of many faiths are sitting friendly together.

John Fry, Edmonton mayor, observation made at the dedication of the Al Rashid Mosque, Edmonton, 12 December 1938. The building was erected by the children of Muslim farmers and fur traders and its Ukrainian contractor gave it two onion-shaped domes. It has since been moved to Fort Edmonton Park, replaced by an immense mosque and cultural centre. Al Rashid Mosque has the distinction of being the first mosque erected in Canada and the United States.

Muslims participated in almost every major event in the economic history of Canada. They hewed rocks, laid tracks and struck nails to build the Canadian Pacific Railway in the late 19th century, an event dubbed the "national dream" because of its importance. Muslim farmers were among the pioneers who opened up Alberta and Saskatchewan for cultivation and settlement in the beginning of the 20th century. Skilled and professional Muslim immigrants kept up the tempo of economic growth in the 1960s and 1970s. Muslim educators responded to the need for teachers and professors as the baby boom of the post–Second World War period rolled into grade schools and then graduate schools, thus strengthening the foundation for a secure and prosperous economic future for the country.

Daood Hassan Hamdani, spokesperson, "An Unnoticed Part of Our History: An Address on the Occasion of Eid-al-Adha," Parliament Buildings, Ottawa, 2 May 1996, published in *Hamdard Islamicus*, September 1997.

This is a watershed moment for Canadian Muslims. Will we remain spiritually infantile, shackled by cultural expectations to clam up and conform, or will we mature into citizens, defending the very pluralism of interpretations and values that makes it possible for us to be here in the first place?

Irshad Manji, television personality, referring to September 11, 2001, "A Muslim Plea for Introspection," *The Globe and Mail*, 8 November 2001.

I owe the West my willingness to help reform Islam. In all honesty, my fellow Muslims, you do too.

Irshad Manji, broadcaster and writer of Ugandan Asian background, *The Trouble with Islam: A Wake-up Call for Honesty and Change* (2003).

MYSTERIES *See also* Myths & Mythology; Puzzles; Secrets

Myth and mystery appeal to our nature, and too often we refuse to apply to matters of this kind the reason and judgment by means of which we estimate statements and conditions pertaining to almost anything else.

David Boyle, archaeologist, "Canadian Folk-Lore," *The Globe*, 13 November 1897.

And of the northern mysteries / What memories remain?

Lines from **Stan Rogers**'s song "Pocketful of Gold" (1972) in Chris Gudgeon, *An Unfinished Conversation: The Life and Music of Stan Rogers* (1993).

Why the inhabitants of Easter Island put up those immense statues is a profound & inscrutable mystery. Almost as profound and inscrutable as why anybody would carve a gigantic head of Theodore Roosevelt on a mountain in South Dakota.

Northrop Frye, cultural critic, Northrop Frye's *Late Notebooks, 1985–1990* (2000), edited by Robert Denham.

Canada, our neighbour to the north and the world's second largest country, holds riddles which have never received the exposure they deserve.

Scott Corrales, U.S. researcher, "High Strangeness in the High Arctic," *Fate*, January 2003.

MYSTICISM *See also* Spiritualism

Canadians have a greater sense of mysticism than Americans. It could be all that Scottish-Irish background. The Irish and Scotch are always talking about little fairies and trolls and invisible people.

Shirley MacLaine, performer and champion of the New Age, interviewed by Linda Frum, *National Post*, 20 May 2000. MacLaine's mother was born in the Maritimes.

MYTHS & MYTHOLOGY *See also* Belief; Folklore; Ghosts; Monsters; Mysteries

Not all of Saturday's *Globe* would be sufficient to contain the stories connected with this Algonkin myth-being. Even his names form a long list, of which one is Hiawatha.

David Boyle, archaeologist, "Canadian Folk-Lore," *The Globe*, 5 February 1898. Boyle is referring to the Algonkian culture hero variously known as Nanabozhoo, Nanabush, etc.: "He was a sort of nondescript being—more than a man, less than a Manitou, and an extremely gullible old fool."

A myth is a story, and it is a story that insistently recurs: a piece of timelessness caught like an eddy in narrative form.

Robert Bringhurst, scholar and poet, *A Story as Sharp as a Knife: The Classical Haida Mythtellers and Their World* (1999).

The myths exist, most mythtellers say, independently of any human culture.

Robert Bringhurst, scholar and poet, *A Story as Sharp as a Knife: The Classical Haida Mythtellers and Their World* (1999).

The myth that Canadians were not interested in their history died that night—October 22, 2000. What emerged instead was that we had starved Canadians of their history. We had so deprived them of their stories and their experiences, and substituted an imported system of American mythology, that we had deluded our own people, through omission, into believing they didn't have one. That is the single staggering lesson to be taken from this project.

Mark Starowicz, TV producer, address, "The Canadian Experience," Toronto, 28 June 2001, The Empire Club of Canada. The night saw the launch on CBC-TV of the series *Canada: A People's History.*

We can't as an act of will decide on our myths. The culture and the unconscious have minds of their own; they pick our myths for us. I used to think we were entitled to live by any myths we wished, but I'm not so broad-minded anymore. Now, I stick with stories that have withstood the test of time.

Gordon Warme, psychiatrist, *A Psychiatrist's Cautionary Tale* (2003).

The way myth embodies a culture isn't always pretty. A myth can be the distillation of a sacred truth or simply a lie repeated often enough. Hockey is a bit of both.

Don Gillmor, journalist, "Hockey: The Great Literary Shutout," *The Walrus*, February 2005.

n

NAFTA *See* North American Free Trade Agreement

NAMES *See also* Language; Place Names; Words

His Name is His Fortune. / The Kwakiutl Indians of British Columbia pawn their names if they need money! Until the loan is repaid the borrower is nameless.

> **Robert L. Ripley**, cartoonist, *Ripley's New Believe It or Not!* (1950).

The only male French names that seem to have been adopted in recent times by English-speaking Canadians are *Michel* and *Pierre*. It will be interesting to see whether use of these names spreads to other English-speaking countries.

> **Leslie Alan Dunkling**, English linguist, *First Names First* (1977). Dunkling claimed the most distinctive Canadian first name was *Murray*. The most popular first names in English Canada in 1970 were, for women, *Jennifer, Sarah, Tania*, and, for men, *Michael, Scott, Christopher*.

On reading the previous day's Hansard during Question Period, I noted I was mentioned as "Barley" Danson. I immediately rose on a Point of Privilege and drew Mr. Speaker's attention to this error and said, "Mr. Speaker, I ask that this grievous error be corrected as my name is Barney and barley goes against the grain."

> **Barney Danson**, former minister of Defence, referring to the official record of proceedings of the House of Commons, recalled in personal communication, 20 July 2003.

NATION *See also* Nationhood

Most nations have been formed, not by people who desired intensely to live together, but rather by people who could not live apart.

> **Jean-Charles Bonenfant**, sociologist, *"L'Esprit de 1867"* (1963), in Ramsay Cook, *Canada and the French-Canadian Question* (1966).

A nation is a body of people who have done great things together in the past and who hope to do great things together in the future.

> **F.H. Underhill**, historian, *The Image of Confederation* (1964). This definition has also been attributed to the French philosopher Ernest Renan.

A nation struggling within the confines of provincehood.

> Description of Quebec offered by "a cabinet minister with impeccable federalist credentials in Jean Charest's government," as noted by columnist John Ibbitson, "Michaëlle Jean Is Our Postnationalist Future," *The Globe and Mail*, 17 August 2005.

NATIONAL ANTHEM *See also* National Emblems

Today, across the country, the playing of the anthem is limited to opening nights with the Lieutenant-Governor in attendance, in which case the orchestra provides the front half of "The Queen" followed by the back half of "O Canada," which is all anyone can remember. It establishes the mood.

> **Mavor Moore**, theatre personality, "Now Let's Hear It for the Audience," *The Globe and Mail*, 28 November 1983.

National anthems, like gift horses, should not be looked in the mouth, and Canada's does have a pretty good tune, sharing some bars with "The March of the Priests" from Mozart's *Magic Flute*.

> **Peter Brimelow**, journalist, *The Patriot Game: National Dreams and Political Realities* (1986).

If you don't want to see me go to water, don't perform in my vicinity "Amazing Grace"—the slow bagpipe version is the most potent—Taps, or, for some reason, "O Canada," although I can listen quite unmoved to "The Star-Spangled Banner." Is this vulnerability to sentimental emotion the result of simply aging, with attendant self-pity, or has it something to do with the war?

Paul Fussell, literary critic and U.S. Army veteran, *Doing Battle: The Making of a Skeptic* (1996).

I know this place is where I am; / No other place is better than. / No matter where I go I am / Proud to be Ca-na-di-an.

Refrain of the 90-second nationalistic commercial "Anthem," sponsored by Molson's Canadian lager beer, premiered on television, 13 June 2001, in James Deacon, "The Patriot Game," *Maclean's*, 18 June 2001. Composed by **Robert Armes**, it was created by **Glen Hunt** of Bensimon–Byrne D'Arcy advertising agency.

If you know almost all the words to "Barrett's Privateers" but you don't know the words to the national anthem: 10 points.

Quiz question set by **William Ferguson** and **Ian Ferguson**, *How to Be a Canadian (Even if You Are One)* (2001). The reference is to the powerful song by Stan Rogers (as well as to the national anthem "O Canada").

NATIONAL EMBLEMS *See also* National Anthem; National Flag; Symbols

Canada's national symbol, I have often thought, should not be the beaver, but the carp.

Mavor Moore, theatre personality, *Reinventing Myself: Memoirs* (1994).

Canada's national emblem is a fallen leaf.

William Ferguson and **Ian Ferguson**, writers, *How to Be a Canadian (Even if You Are One)* (2001).

NATIONAL FILM BOARD OF CANADA *See* Cinema

NATIONAL FLAG

Today, while Europe tilted, drying the Baltic, / I read of a battle between brothers in anguish. / A flag moved a mile.

Lines from **F.R. Scott**'s poem "A Grain of Rice" (1952), *The Selected Poems of F.R. Scott* (1981).

The most surprising thing about Mr. Pearson's new flag is something that no one seems to have noticed. The Government is firmly committed to "the basically bicultural character of our country," yet it proposes a flag which contains not the slightest reference to any culture whatever, even agriculture. (The maple tree grows wild.) ... Voltaire is said to have described Canada as "some acres of snow." Mr. Pearson's flag may be an adequate symbol of that conception of Canada.... We have been promised a flag. Are we to be fobbed off with a dish towel from Woolworth's?

Eugene Forsey, constitutional specialist, *The Ottawa Journal*, 13 June 1964, in J.E. Hodgetts, *The Sound of One Voice: Eugene Forsey and His Letters to the Press* (2000).

Even Leonard Cohen got into the act, suggesting that Canada adopt *four* Maple Leaf designs, one for each season—a small green leaf for spring, a larger green leaf for summer, a red leaf for autumn, and a "white outline" of a leaf against a white background, for winter.

Peter C. Newman, journalist and memoirist, *Here Be Dragons: Telling Tales of People, Passion, and Power* (2004). Newman recalls that celebrities and children and members of the general public were asked for their design suggestions for the Maple Leaf flag that replaced the Union Jack as the national flag on 15 February 1965.

The flag. It became my obsession for quite a long time. I watched it floating in the breeze and began to realize how beautiful it was as an abstract shape, when influenced by the elements.

Charles Pachter, artist, address, "A Romance with Canada," Toronto, 23 June 1994, The Empire Club of Canada.

Quebec will not prostitute itself for bits of red flag or for anything else.

Bernard Landry, Quebec deputy premier, news conference, Lac-Beauport, Que., 23 January 2001, in Robert McKenzie, "Landry Savages Canada," *Toronto Star*, 24 January 2001. Graeme Hamilton, in the *National Post*, translated the offensive words as "bits of red rag." After the speech, Landry explained that he had employed the French term *chiffon rouge*, which means "red rag" (to refer to the cape the matador waves before the bull in the ring). "The 'red-flag reference' was an allusion to bull-fighting," he added. "Bilingualism is provocation—hence the red cloth in front of the bull." The "provocation" was the rejection of the federal government's offer of $16 million for a zoo in Quebec City that stipulated that a Canadian flag be flown on the site for a period of 40 years. Landry found this requirement unacceptable; as well, he had previously announced his candidacy for the Parti Québécois leadership and the Quebec premiership.

Canada is the wind that wants a flag.

Attributed to **Keith Spicer**, chair of the Citizens' Forum on Canada's Future, 1990–1991, by Roy MacGregor, "This Country," *The Globe and Mail*, 15 April 2003.

Unlike the Americans, we do not salute our flag. In fact, we got along for a century without one.

Mitchell Sharp, former Cabinet minister, in Peter C. Newman, *Here Be Dragons: Telling Tales of People, Passion, and Power* (2004).

One wind moves many flags.

Robert Priest, poet and columnist, "Aussie Oddity," *Now*, 30 September 2004.

NATIONAL INTERESTS *See also* Canadian Identity; Nationalism; Sovereignty

It is urgent that Canada define a national interest to reflect the needs and values of the majority of the country so we speak with one voice and are clearly understood.

Diane Francis, columnist, "A Wake Up Call for Canada–U.S. Relations," *National Post*, 12 April 2003.

National interests are not difficult to detail for most nations, and Canada's, in fact, are very clear:

1. Canada must protect its territory, the security of its people, and its unity.

2. It must strive to protect and enhance its independence.

3. It must promote the economic growth of the nation to support the prosperity and welfare of its people.

4. It must work with like-minded states, in and outside international forums, for the protection and enhancement of democracy and freedom.

J.L. Granatstein, "The Importance of Being Less Earnest," *National Post*, 22 October 2003.

Canada is a nation that rarely discusses its national interests.... The idea of national interests seems to have drifted away almost totally, while the nation endlessly prattles about superior values.

J.L. Granatstein, "The Importance of Being Less Earnest," *National Post*, 22 October 2003.

NATIONAL UNITY *See also* Independence; Negotiation

If we are true to ourselves, Canadian unity may well serve as a model for the wider unity of humanity. In the unity of mankind lies the one sure foundation of enduring peace.

W.L. Mackenzie King, prime minister, inaugural broadcast, CBC Radio's International Service, 25 February 1945, in James L. Hall, *Radio Canada International: Voice of a Middle Power* (1997).

The important thing is that we talk and keep talking whatever the difficulties. This is probably the most difficult solution in the long run, but it is the only solution that can keep us together.

Pierre Elliott Trudeau, prime minister, rally, Fort Langley, B.C., 17 June 1968, in Brian Stewart, "Trudeau, the Man Who Gets to the Mob, Finally Let the People Get to Him," Montreal *Gazette*, 18 June 1968.

I would have seen the janitor if it would have helped the cause of Canadian unity.

Jean Pelletier, former PMO chief of staff and former chairman of VIA Rail, statement before the Parliamentary inquiry on the Sponsorship Scandal, 6 April 2004, in Daniel LeBlanc, "Pelletier's Denial Spurs Martin to Soften Attack," *The Globe and Mail*, 7 April 2004.

The specific reference is to whether he met with and was influenced by senior bureaucrats and Liberal politicians in the Advertising and Sponsorship Scandal.

NATIONALISM *See also* Canadian Identity; Colonialism; Countries; Globalism & Globalization; Land; Nationhood; Sovereignty

What we need to do, therefore, in Canada for our salvation is, first of all, to renew a right heart and spirit within us. We need first of all an ardent purpose to make things better.

Stephen Leacock, humorist, *My Discovery of the West: A Discussion of East and West in Canada* (1937).

Canadian nationalism was systematically encouraged and exploited by American capital. Canada moved from colony to nation to colony.

Harold Adams Innis, economist and historian, "Great Britain, the United States and Canada" (1948), *Essays in Canadian Economic History* (1956), edited by Mary Quayle Innis.

Anyway, at one point, Diefenbaker was talking in his inimitable way about Canada, the dream of a greater and better Canada. I told him: "Well, let's leave it at this. One Canada where everybody will live together in harmony." I remember the word "harmony." My God, it was as if I had put a bomb under his seat. He got up and said, "That's it! Yes. One Canada." Then, he stared right there in front of us all and he said, "One Canada! What we can build around that slogan!"

Pierre Sévigny, future Conservative Cabinet minister, prior to the election of 1957, in Peter Stursberg, *Diefenbaker: Leadership Gained, 1956–1962* (1975).

In this "branch factory" land nothing much of distinctively Canadian importance is done by private enterprise. Which is not to say it can't happen. Will Canadian business men tire of their emasculation and decide to become their own man?

Allan King, filmmaker, "Canadian—Cinema—Vancouver," distinguishing between American-style and Canadian-made movies, *How to Make or Not Make a Canadian Film* (1968), edited by André Pâquet.

I hope the poet is not the last nationalist.

F.R. Scott, poet and constitutional law specialist, addressing a session of the Expo World Poetry Conference 1967, in John Robert Colombo, "Poetry at Expo," *The Canadian Forum*, October 1967.

Nationalism without Borders.

This notion is attributed to **Paul Martin**, minister of Finance and future prime minister, by Richard Gwyn, who used it as the title of his book, *Nationalism without Borders: The Unbearable Lightness of Being Canadian* (1995).

There is still a passion for Canada out there, but as the years go by, that passion sometimes seems more romantic than realistic.

Angus Reid, pollster, in Steven Pearlstein, "O Canada! A National Swan Song?" *The Washington Post*, 5 September 2000.

The two [Quebec nationalism and English Canadian nationalism] come together in the sense that both are built on a culture of dominated peoples, Quebeckers being losers and Canadians being underdogs.

Alain Dubuc, editorialist for *La Presse*, LaFontaine-Baldwin Lecture, published in *The Globe and Mail*, 10 March 2001.

Canadian nationalism is an oxymoron. Canada has never been a religious entity or romantic creation. Its schoolchildren barely know the lyrics, in either official language, of its national anthem. More significantly, the words keep changing, in accordance with the politically correct language of the day.

Diane Francis, columnist, "A Wake Up Call for Canada–U.S. Relations," *National Post*, 12 April 2003. Francis's first sentence evoked the following rejoinder from a former columnist, **Patricia Pearson**, "Comment," *The Globe and Mail*, 19 April 2003: "Really, Ms. Francis? Well, call me a freak of nature, but I am an ardent Canadian nationalist. I love my country, and I am fiercely proud of it. I cannot sit back and watch this nation attacked, relentlessly and viciously, by a newspaper that would trash so much of what we believe in, from tolerant social values to international law, belittling us for having our beliefs, while turning around and saying that what makes America great is Americans' ardour in defending their beliefs."

The return of the idea of national power has also meant the return of the idea of choice—choice for citizens and choice for countries. But with choice comes uncertainty, which provokes fear. The moment we entered the post-Globalization vacuum, you could feel that fear begin to rise.

John Ralston Saul, philosopher, "The Collapse of Globalism and the Rebirth of Nationalism," *Harper's*, March 2004.

I don't think about Quebec versus Canada.... Canada isn't just a country. It's my team.

Chantal Petitclerc, Quebec athlete and wheelchair racer, Paralympic Games champion at Athens, in Jan Wong, "Chantal Petitclerc: Nation Builder of 2004," *The Globe and Mail*, 11 December 2004.

NATIONHOOD *See also* America; British Empire; Colonialism; Emigration; Immigration

It should be easy now to define the essential characteristic of nationhood. Nationhood must depend on a new or distinctive shade in the generally tragic reaction of the human soul to the fundamental conditions of man's life on earth.

Frederick Philip Grove, author, address, "Nation within the Empire," Toronto, 28 February 1929, The Empire Club of Canada.

Canada wants to be a country but it acts like a nation. As long as it acts like a nation we know toward which terrible end we are heading.

Antonio D'Alfonso, poet and essayist, "Cultural Trends in Quebec," *In Italics: In Defense of Ethnicity* (1996).

A Continent of Nations.

Theme of CBC-TV's *Canada: A People's History*, a 16-episode, 30-hour documentary series, executive producer **Mark Starowicz**, premiered 22 October 2000. It had in mind the so-called Indian nations before their contact with Europeans.

There are only 191 members of the United Nations, but our political class pretends Canada consists of 633 First Nations, plus the Métis Nation, plus (for many) the Québécois Nation, plus the Inuit (who haven't settled on a term yet).

Tom Flanagan, historian, "One Nation, Deux Nations, 633 First Nations," *National Post*, 4 April 2001.

NATIVE CULTURE *See also* Monsters; Native Peoples; Wendigo

No new stories about him have been made up for generations, and the old ones have been all but forgotten. Because of the present generation's indifference to its language, traditions, and heritage, the spirit of Nana'b'oozoo is unlikely to return to inspire storytellers to add to the national Anishinaubae legacy, enriching the meaning and the value of the bequest as it is meant to be enriched. And there are few who mourn the loss to the Anishinaubae nation.

Basil Johnston, elder, *The Manitous: The Spiritual World of the Ojibway* (1995). Nana'b'oozoo is a manitou or the archetypal human being with all strengths and weaknesses of mankind. The Anishinaubae (plural "Anishinaubaek") are human beings, specifically good human beings; it is the traditional term for the Ojibway.

Poor Haidas! They had an impossibly perfect model held up to them and tried desperately to emulate its perfection. They painted themselves into a corner.

Wilson Duff, anthropologist, specialist in Haida art, random observation, quoted in *Bird of Paradox: The Unpublished Writings of Wilson Duff* (1996), edited by E.N. Anderson.

NATIVE LANGUAGES *See also* Language

I envision language as a 1-800 number to my ancestors.

Tiorahkwáthe, the councillor at Kahnawake responsible for the status of the Mohawk language, in Mark Abley, *Spoken Here: Travels among Threatened Languages* (2003). Abley explains, "His choice of metaphor is revealing: not a trail, a canoe route, or a smoke signal, but a toll-free line. Even when minority languages maintain a priceless link with history, they don't have to be mired in the past."

Without the language, our ceremonies, songs and dances will cease.... The Confederacy will cease to function.... The names themselves will lose their meaning. Without the language, we will lose our traditional way of thinking and our distinctive view of the world.

Brian Maracle, spokesperson, in Mark Abley, *Spoken Here: Travels among Threatened Languages* (2003).

Inuktitut has been written in a Roman alphabet with Danish influence (in Greenland), a Roman alphabet with Moravian German influence (in Labrador), a Roman alphabet with French influence (in Quebec), a Roman alphabet with American and British influence (in Alaska and much of northern Canada), a syllabic alphabet (in other parts of northern Canada), and a Cyrillic alphabet with Russian influence (in Siberia). One consequence is that no two English–Inuktitut dictionaries agree on very much.

Mark Abley, author, *Spoken Here: Travels among Threatened Languages* (2003).

NATIVE PEOPLES *See also* Aboriginal Rights; Inuit; Land Claims; Métis; Native Culture

When they will not give a doit to relieve a lame beggar, they will lay out ten to see a dead Indian.

Line spoken by Trinculo to Caliban in **William Shakespeare**'s play *The Tempest*, Act II, Scene ii (*c.* 1610). The reference is to the English who will pay to satisfy their curiosity about the Native people of North America. Thereafter Stephano says to Caliban, "What's the matter? Have we devils here? Do you put tricks upon us with savages and men of Ind? Ha?"

And they come and ask me to whip myself of my own free will, which I'd as soon do as turn Red Indian.

Speech of the squire Sancho Panza character about self-flagellation, Book Two, of **Miguel de Cervantes**'s *The Adventures of Don Quixote* (1604, 1614), translated by J.M. Cohen in 1950.

There is, on the American side of the line, the saying that the only good Indian is a dead Indian; that was so because the Indian, as well as the buffalo, encumbered the farmer's land. But in the north the only good Indian is a live Indian, because he secures furs. That is one of the reasons why the Hudson's Bay Company had a policy so diametrically opposed to the policy of the American Government. That is one of the reasons that has kept the Indian in the northern part of this country. If it be true of the Indian in the Hudson Bay and Mackenzie River Districts that the only good Indian is a live Indian, it is more true of the Eskimo, because he inhabits the fringe of your country, which cannot be used by anybody so well as by him.

Vilhjalmur Stefansson, Arctic explorer, address, "Our Northland, Its People and Resources," Toronto, 6 February 1913, The Empire Club of Canada.

When the civilized people of Europe came amongst the Red Indians of America and showed them how they expressed their thoughts on paper, the Red Indians were quite alarmed and thought it was the work of the devil. They were terrified of the little demons who were lurking behind the written letters. They immediately concluded that the Europeans dealt in black magic, for people have a habit of attributing to black magic whatever they cannot understand.

Rudolf Steiner, philosopher, *The Roots of Education* (1968), translated from the 1924 German edition by Helen Fox; in *The Essential Steiner: Basic Writings of Rudolf Steiner* (1984), edited by Robert A. McDermott. The philosopher was born of Austrian parents in an area of Hungary that later became part of Yugoslavia. No references to Canada are known in his writings and addresses, but his references to "America" abound, specifically to the Native peoples.

A deeper interest in the real Indian—in his ways of thinking and feeling, rather than his outward circumstances—would no doubt bring revelations.

Sir Ernest MacMillan, musician and musicologist, reviewing Marius Barbeau and Edward Sapir's *Folk Songs of French Canada, The Canadian Forum,* December 1925, as noted by Ezra Shabas, *Sir Ernest MacMillan: The Importance of Being Canadian* (1996).

Do you realize that there is only one-quarter of Canada in the hands of civilization? The other three-quarters are in the hands of the Indians, for all anybody dare tell them it isn't. That is the richest part of Canada.

Grey Owl, author and conservationist, address, "A Plea for the Canadian Northland," Toronto, 12 November 1936, The Empire Club of Canada.

The Indians we had seen in their Reservations are often dressed, the men in shabby shirts and dirty flannel trousers, the women in declining woollen jumpers and old skirts. Their Reservations are apt to look like Heath Robinson drawings, as everything is off the straight and the doors hang crazily on one hinge.

Susan Buchan, compiler of *John Buchan by His Wife and Friends* (1947), describing conditions in the province of Alberta in the late 1930s in terms of Heath Robinson's cartoon art.

Kemo Sabe.

Jay Silverheels, Indian athlete and actor, born Harry Smith on the Six Nations Reserve, near Brantford, Ont., who played in countless radio, movie, and television productions between 1949 and 1958 as the "faithful Indian companion Tonto" to the Lone Ranger. He kept agreeing: "Yes, *Kemo Sabe.*" Dick Brown, writing in *The Canadian,* 9 August 1975, quoted Silverheels: "*Kemo Sabe.* Good friend.... Actually, I never did find out what it really means." Explanations and anecdotes abound in *Colombo's All-Time Great Canadian Quotations* (1994). It was not until the politically correct decade of the 1990s that words were seen as capable of belittling members of minority groups.

Of these four contemporary initiated beings, one comes from amongst those who are called "redskins" who dwell on the continent America; another, from among the beings dwelling on what are called the Philippine Islands; the third, from the beings of the continent Asia, from the country called "The-Source-of-the-River-Pianje"; and the fourth and last, from amongst those who are called "Eskimos."

G.I. Gurdjieff, philosopher, *All and Everything: Ten Books, in Three Series, of Which This Is the First Series* (1950).

I hope natives outlast missionaries.

Richard Harrington, photographer, *Padlei Diary, 1950: An Account of the Padleimiut Eskimo in the Keewatin District west of Hudson Bay during the Early Months of 1950* (2000), edited by Edmund Carpenter.

Permit me to repeat this description of the Church in some of your own languages; this will be a way to come closer to you and to express to you my fraternal affection.

The Church is ASADJIGAN of God for you (Algonquin).

The Church is SHESHEPETAN of God for you (Montagnais).

The Church is SHISHITITAGN of God for you (Cree).

The Church is TESHITATGAN of God for you (Atikamek).

The Church is IA-IEN-TA-IEN-TA-KWA of God for you (Mohawk).

The Church is APATAGAT of God for you (Micmac).

Now we must say goodbye. In the language of our Inuit brothers and sisters, I would like to [assure] you that you are my friends, all of you are loved by God! ILANNAARIVAPSI TAMAPSI NAGLIJAUVUSI JISUSINUT.

John Paul II, pope, address, "To the Native Peoples, Ste-Anne-de-Beaupré," Que., 10 September 1984, *The Canadian Catholic Review: The Papal Visit, Oct. 1984.*

Thus the one faith is expressed in different ways. There can be no question of adulterating the word of God or of emptying the Cross of its power, but rather of Christ animating the very centre of all culture. Thus, not only is Christianity relevant to the Indian peoples, but Christ, in the members of his Body, is himself Indian.

John Paul II, pope, address, Celebration of the Word, Martyrs' Shine, 15 September 1984, *The Canadian Catholic Review: The Papal Visit, Oct. 1984.* Roman Catholic theologians regard this expression of the faith as of singular interest and significance.

I realize that many of you have made this pilgrimage from all parts of Canada—from the frozen Arctic and the prairie plains, from the forests and the lakehead regions, from East and West, North and South. I am very pleased that nothing has deterred you from coming to this meeting.

John Paul II, pope, address to the Native peoples, Fort Simpson, N.W.T., 18 September 1984, *The Canadian Catholic Review: The Papal Visit, Oct. 1984.* Alas, on this occasion the Pope was unable to make this visit or deliver this pre-scripted address, the airport being fogged in. (Two years later he was able to fly to Fort Simpson as an extension of his U.S. tour.)

I don't need to be Native; I have my own tribe. I am a Celt. But I am grateful for the example of First Nations people as I slowly learn to value my own identity, my own love for the earth, that came from my own ancestors.

Donna Sinclair, author, *Jacob's Blessing: Dreams, Hopes, & Visions for the Church* (2000), with Christopher White.

I am not a Canadian.

Matthew Coon Come, national chief of the Assembly of First Nations, defining himself as the member of a First Nation, declining the opportunity to vote in a federal election, in Tom Flanagan, "Are Aboriginals Canadian?" *Cité libre*, fall 2000.

Each of the 633 Indian bands in Canada is now referred to as a First Nation. Both federal and provincial governments quickly adopted the usage, so that the phrase "First Nations" is now almost de rigueur in public life. The word "Indian," even though it appeared in the constitutional amendments of 1982, is now politically incorrect and avoided by most people when they speak in public. It is close to becoming a racial epithet like "nigger."

Tom Flanagan, political scientist, "Are Aboriginals Canadian?" *Cité libre*, fall 2000.

Aboriginal peoples as collectivities can control enormous amounts of land and natural resources and yet their people will remain poor as individuals unless they acquire skills that can be sold in the marketplace.

Tom Flanagan, political scientist, "Are Aboriginals Canadian?" *Cité libre*, fall 2000.

All of Canada still belongs to the First Nations.

Attributed to **Matthew Coon Come**, national chief of the Assembly of First Nations, according to Tom Flanagan, "Are Aboriginals Canadian?" *Cité libre*, fall 2000.

Let's face it, we are all here to stay.

Antonio Lamer, chief justice, Supreme Court of Canada, Ottawa, remark made while delivering judgement in the case of Delagmuukw v. the B.C. Government, 11 December 1997. Delgamuukw, otherwise known as Earl Muldoe, led a group of British Columbia's hereditary chiefs to press for recognition of aboriginal land title and the acceptance of oral evidence, as noted by Michael Ignatieff, *The Rights Revolution* (2000).

I think it's important to know where you come from. I feel comfortable in both worlds. I have no identity problem—I know who I am. To myself, I am Innu. To the anthropologists, I am a Cree. I am a Christian. I am a leader.

Matthew Coon Come, Cree, grand chief of the Mistissini First Nation, interviewed by Allen Abel, "Chief of First Nations Straddles Two Galaxies," *National Post*, 19 July 2000.

We need education all right, but we'll have to teach ourselves a few things about prejudice and discrimination first. We'll also have to teach the Indians to want our kind of education. We'll have to do what amounts to coaxing him into our world bit by bit, for unlike the American Negro and the black African, the Canadian Indian really does have something to preserve that total integration would take away: the bare but guaranteed subsistence of the reserves.

Peter Gzowski, journalist and broadcaster, "Last Chance to Head off a Showdown with the Canadian Indian," *Canadian Living*, August 2000.

NATURE *See also* Animals; Environmentalism; Trees; Wildlife

Everybody needs beauty as well as bread, places to lay in and pray in, where nature may heal and give strength to body and soul alike.

John Muir, environmentalist, words written in 1912, in Cameron Smith, "Muir's Long Cabin the Bush," *Toronto Star*, 11 October 2003. For two years (1865–1866), Muir lived in a log cabin (since demolished) on the bank of the Bighead River near Meaford, Ont. In 1892 he established the Sierra Club to protect the environment.

I feel the same way about bald eagles. In fact, if we were only sensitive enough and tuned in enough to the world of nature, it may be that everything is very particular and very individual and very specific. Maybe every cricket has a different face, just as different as lions or people. We're just not tuned in.

Robert Bateman, artist, address, "My Art and My Life," Toronto, 13 November 1986, The Empire Club of Canada.

I think art begins where nature ends and I totally reconstruct whatever I see to suit artistic purposes.

Robert Bateman, artist, address, "My Art and My Life," Toronto, 13 November 1986, The Empire Club of Canada.

We have long suspected that the total destruction of nature would be the logical consequence of modern technological progress.

Steven Klein, communications specialist, "The Greening of Madison Avenue," *Wild Culture: Specimens from* The Journal of Wild Culture (1992), edited by Whitney Smith and Christopher Lowry.

But there is no such thing as that nature; that's fiction! Nature is the horizon of culture. Every time you change cultures, you change the horizons.... Whatever state you are in, and whatever human activity, you will always have a horizon.

William Irwin Thompson, theorist, "Mind Jazz," *Wild Culture: Specimens from* The Journal of Wild Culture (1992), edited by Whitney Smith and Christopher Lowry.

I rather like the idea that if I stand in one place long enough, I will eventually be in a different place. Nature loves change, which is why it abhors a vacuum.

Wayne Grady, writer and naturalist, *Toronto the Wild: Field Notes of an Urban Naturalist* (1995).

Two forces shape the world—nature and human nature.

Paul L. Aird, scientist, "Cultural Attitudes to Culturing the Forest," *Regenerating the Canadian Forest: Principles and Practice for Ontario* (2001), edited by Robert G. Wagner and Stephen J. Colombo.

The love we feel for concrete particulars—a stand of birch, a stretch of river, no less than other human beings—is as biologically basic as our sexual mode of reproduction. We must love what dies and we must love because we die.

Jan Zwicky, poet, introduction, *Hard Choices: Climate Change in Canada* (2004), edited by Harold Coward and Andrew J. Weaver.

As Canadians know—in the depths of February, at least—nature is actively trying to kill us.

Brian Bethune, journalist, "Novel Notions," *Maclean's Special Commemorative Issue 100*, October 2004.

NAVY *See* Canadian Armed Forces

NEGOTIATION *See also* Diplomacy; Governance; Government; National Unity

I am more interested in proposition than in opposition.

Jack Layton, Toronto city councillor and later New Democratic Party leader, in Jack Lakey, "The Mellowing of Jack Layton," *Toronto Star*, 4 January 1999.

You Canadians! Every time you see a difference, you want to negotiate with it.

Impatient outburst of an American conservative academic recalled by the philosopher **Charles Taylor**, in Charlie Gillis, "For the Common Good," *Maclean's* Special Commemorative Issue 100, October 2004.

NEPOTISM *See also* Corruption; Government; Patronage; Politics

You can't do anything about it; it's what they say after "Daddy's little girl" that I'm interested in.

Belinda Stronach, corporate executive, erstwhile Conservative leadership candidate, Liberal Cabinet minister, daughter of auto-parts magnate Frank Stronach of Magna International, in Roy MacGregor, "Canada Waits to Hear from the New 'It Girl' of the Political Right," *The Globe and Mail*, 17 January 2004.

NEUTRALITY

"May your enemies always underestimate you" is useful advice when fighting is inevitable. But when the aim is to avoid fighting, "May your enemies always overestimate you" is by far the wiser counsel.

George Jonas, columnist, "A Lesson from the Swiss," *National Post*, 2 May 2005.

NEW BRUNSWICK

The map of New Brunswick, Canada's "Picture Province," when viewed upside down forms a likeness of Jacques Cartier—discoverer of the St. Lawrence River.

Robert L. Ripley, cartoonist, *Ripley's Believe It or Not! Seventh Series* (1971).

Once you've been Premier of New Brunswick, why would you want to be Prime Minister of Canada?

Frank McKenna, New Brunswick premier, announcing his retirement, Fredericton, 8 October 1997, in Kevin Cox, *The Globe and Mail*, 9 October 1997.

I write this from New Brunswick, widely known as "Canada's picture province"—a slogan I invented and which has survived despite frenzied attempts by the former McKenna Liberal government to expunge it from all memory.

Dalton Camp, columnist, "Trust Me, I Discovered a Lot of Things," *Toronto Star*, 11 October 2000.

Premium / Is the word for the people....

Lines from an untitled and previously unpublished free-verse poem found on the hard drive of the computer **Richard Hatfield** used at the time the former New Brunswick premier died in 1991; first made public by Shawna Richler, "A Million Stories and a Single Poem," *The Globe and Mail*, 4 September 2004.

There's only one Lord who can come back from the dead.

Remark made about **Bernard Lord**, premier of New Brunswick, that recalls the ups-and-downs of his political career and puns on his surname, as noted by John Ivison, "The Tories with Buzz," *National Post*, 17 March 2006.

NEW DEMOCRATIC PARTY *See also* Co-operative Movement; Political Parties; Socialism

We have a large party gathering now. I don't want to talk politics and I mustn't name them, because I never can quite remember their name. (Laughter.) It is called the Co-Operative—something, and if there are any members here remember that it is not your particular co-operative, but all co-operatives, and as I understand that new movement, all kinds of people—farmers, householders, lawyers, clerks and intellectuals—are all coming into it, but each one has the idea that he is going to socialize the other—not himself!

Stephen Leacock, economist and humorist, referring to the Canadian Co-operative Confederation (CCF), forerunner of the New Democratic Party (NDP), address, "The Riddle of the Depression," Toronto, 16 February 1933, The Empire Club of Canada.

The NDP is the United Church at work.

Lorne Calvert, United Church minister, provincial NDP leader-elect, future Saskatchewan premier, quoted by Norman Spector, *The Globe and Mail*, 30 January 2001.

I'm not here to offer bones to anybody or bonuses, either.... I'm giving leadership on the issues that I believe passionately in.

Alexa McDonough, NDP leader, Winnipeg convention at which she competed for the leadership, 24 November 2001, in Valerie Lawton, "NDP Rejects Demands for New Left-wing Party," *Toronto Star*, 25 November 2001.

Once upon a time we had Stockwell Day; today it's Jack Layton. The two share little except an unshakable fondness for whatever pops into their heads.

Paul Wells, columnist, "Quick—Make a Decision," *Maclean's*, 31 January 2005.

NEWFIE

The first recorded use of the N-word was by Joe Smallwood, a future premier and the person who sold the island on the idea of Confederation. Smallwood was a popular radio personality before becoming a politician. One of his on-air skits from the late 1930s featured a New Yorker deriding a Newfoundlander—and calling him a Newfie.

Joe O'Connor, columnist, discussing the possible origin of the so-called N-word, Newfie, "Just How Wily Are Coyotes?" *Saturday Night*, March 2005.

NEWFIE JOKES *See also* Humour; Laughter; Wit

The Newfie jokes represent a certain amount of mild irritation relating to group maladjustment.

Marshall McLuhan, media philosopher, address, "The End of the Work Ethic," Toronto, 16 November 1972, The Empire Club of Canada.

The last refuge of the bore is the Newfie joke.

Tim Burke, columnist, Montreal *Gazette*, 12 January 1983.

NEWFOUNDLAND & LABRADOR *See also* Labrador

I have been in Newfoundland, a country of no amusements, but there I was happy: at Halifax, a very gay and lively place full of women and those of the most obliging kind, I wished myself back to the inhospitable shores, foggy atmosphere and rugged, barren cliffs of Newfoundland.

Prince William, later King William IV, letter written from Halifax, 1 December 1786, addressed to his brother George, the Prince of Wales, while serving as an officer in the Royal Navy from Halifax, as noted by Tom Pocok, *Sailor King: The Life of King William IV* (1903).

I have a vision in my mind, and have always had—and I have been thirty years on the Coast—that some day you will be a great deal prouder of Labrador and the surroundings than perhaps we are today.

Sir Wilfred Grenfell, medical doctor, address, "Story of Labrador Medical Mission," Toronto, 17 November 1921, The Empire Club of Canada.

An ancient land, a proud people, Islanders, insular, cut off from the rest of the world, developing their own culture, their own way of life, their own viewpoint, their own outlook on life before Canada was ever even dreamed of, before New York was heard of, that old but ancient land, Newfoundland, and I assure you that it was no easy task for the people of Newfoundland to decide to abandon their ancient and honourable independence and identify themselves, become identified with this great land of Canada.

J.R. (Joey) Smallwood, premier of Newfoundland, address, "Newfoundland," Toronto

19 November 1959, The Empire Club of Canada.

The Vikings came to Newfoundland and they left because it was too tough for them. That's our history.

Rick Mercer, television comedian, "The Rock Is a Hard Place," *Maclean's*, 23 August 1993.

Newfoundland is like a mighty granite stopper stuffed into the mouth of the Gulf of St. Lawrence.

Farley Mowat, author, *The Farfarers: Before the Norse* (1998).

Newfoundland and Labrador is the only province of Canada ever to have been an independent country.

Michael Bliss, historian and columnist, referring to the status of the Dominion of Newfoundland between the 1920s and 1933, "A Country of Their Own," *National Post*, 8 January 2005.

We're not a "have-not" province. We're a "keep-not" province.

Danny Williams, Newfoundland premier, in Roy MacGregor, "'Keep-not' Province Ready to Go to the Wall," *The Globe and Mail*, 17 January 2005. Williams had in mind the past—the unbalanced Churchill Falls power-sharing arrangement with Quebec—and the present—Ottawa's preemption of offshore oil-and-gas revenues. Williams spoke of the Great Island's "last great chance" at recouping its fortunes following the collapse of the fisheries.

All I really know about Newfoundland is that it's always raining, they eat fried food every day of their lives, and they drive on the left-hand side of the road. Or maybe I'm thinking of Ireland.

Will Ferguson, author, *Beauty Tips from Moose Jaw: Travels in Search of Canada* (2004).

NEW FRANCE *See also* French Canada; Quebec

Are the streets being paved with gold over there? I fully expect to awake one morning in Versailles to see the walls of the fortress rising above the horizon.

Louis XV, king of France, remark attributed to him in the 1740s, when his military architect, Sébastien de Vauban, requested further funds to complete the construction of the fortress at Louisbourg, N.S. The sight of Louisbourg rising over the curve of the Atlantic and visible to the courtiers at Versailles is a vision worthy of the Belgian surrealist painter René Magritte.

NEWMAN, PETER C.

I remember my favourite review of my book by *Time* magazine. It praised my information and the last paragraph said: "Newman's book reads as if he was invited to the establishment homes once." It's my perfect epitaph.

Peter C. Newman, journalist, address, "Titans: How the New Canadian Establishment Seized Power," Toronto, 10 November 1998, The Empire Club of Canada.

NEWS *See also* Canadian Broadcasting Corporation; Communications; Interviews; Journalism; Media; Newspapers; Newspaper Headlines; Radio; Television

I'll be glad when this war's over so we can publish some real news.

Harry C. Hindmarsh, publisher of the *Toronto Daily Star*, remark made in 1944 to suburban editor Jack Birt. "Since he had always been keenest about local news coverage, it troubled him that the *Star* was now crowded with stories from Europe, North Africa, and other parts, leaving too little room for the latest bank robber or beauty pageant in Mimico or Long Branch," notes writer **David MacDonald** in an unpublished history of the newspaper.

News knows no schedule.... You know, there's very little that's new in the news from day to day.

J. Douglas MacFarlane, newspaperman, address, School of Journalism, University of Western Ontario, 1 December 1955, reproduced by Richard MacFarlane, *Canada's Newspaper Legend: The Story of J. Douglas MacFarlane* (2000).

And so we return to the question: Is the Press Too Sensational? and my answer: I only wish it were. News, surely by definition, is that part of life around us that is sensational. The sensational findings of the archaeologists, for instance, have always been news. What I think the public objects to, in newspapers, is the attempt to make a sensation out of something that really is not very interesting, or very important, that is not, in fact, sensational at all.

Pierre Berton, journalist, address, "Is the Press Too Sensational?" Toronto, 21 January 1960, The Empire Club of Canada.

There are reports from New York tonight that Malcolm the Tenth is dead.

Gaffe committed by **Leon Mangoff**, sportscaster, on CHCH-TV in Hamilton, Ont., 21 February 1965, later CBC-TV announcer, quoted in his obituary, *National Post*, 13 June 2000.

The future of news is old hat.

Attributed to **Marshall McLuhan**, media philosopher, by Knowlton Nash, *Trivia Pursuit: How Showbiz Values Are Corrupting the News* (1998), who added, "and while I'm not exactly sure what he meant, I've taken his words to be a comment on the speed of change in the electronic world, where yesterday's future is today's past."

What I'd like to do is to make two or three flat, and probably provocative, statements about the news business, about journalism, about our efforts to write "history on the run."

Knowlton Nash, journalist and broadcaster, address, "Television News," Toronto, 26 June 1986, The Empire Club of Canada.

The National is only 22 minutes long, the same length as all network TV newscasts on this continent. Twenty-two minutes is not very long. Pick up *The Globe and Mail* or any major newspaper and just read the front page. Read every word on the front page and it may take you 22 minutes.

Peter Mansbridge, news anchor, speech, "The Journalist as Celebrity," Toronto, 30 June 1988, The Empire Club of Canada.

What the public really wants in the news is a confirmation of their own biases.

Attributed to **Norman DePoe**, newspaperman and broadcaster, by Knowlton Nash, *Trivia Pursuit: How Showbiz Values Are Corrupting the News* (1998).

Reporting the news fairly and fearlessly is critical for a democratic society and fulfilling for the journalist.

Knowlton Nash, journalist, *Trivia Pursuit: How Showbiz Values Are Corrupting the News* (1998).

The Canadian Press / The Last Word. First.

Slogan of The Canadian Press, known as CP, the national news service, observed in 2003.

News is what I say it is!

Thomas "Tommy" Garland Lytle, newspaperman and gruff-spoken sometime news editor of the *Toronto Daily Star* (1935–1973), characteristic remark, recalled in his obituary by Philip Mascoll, *Toronto Star*, 31 January 2003.

NEWSPAPERS *See also* News; Newspaper Headlines

It's a fine thing … to find a newspaper recognizing that "newspapering" isn't the whole duty of a newspaper—it's not everything to record what happened yesterday or this morning—it's not all of a daily paper's glory to keep its readers up on the rise or fall of stocks. It's the over and above that I have always admired in *The Daily Star*. In this day, the world lives largely in its newspapers—and the true newspaper feels it fitting to enrich readers' minds with all … that appeals to their finest instincts.

Stephen Leacock, humorist, page-one interview by R.E. Knowles, "Leacock Says Sir A. Currie Most Distinguished Pupil," *Toronto Daily Star*, 16 February 1933.

There are not many newspaper offices where type can be set 24 hours each day without the aid of artificial light. That condition, however, now exists in the office of *The Klondike Nugget.* It is not the result of any special brilliancy on the part of the staff, but must rather be attributed to the kindliness of Old Sol. The sun follows the established order of things in this region and does nothing by halves.

Eugene C. Allen, editor of *The Yukon Nugget,* editorial, premier issue, 16 June 1898, in Russell A. Bankson, *The Klondike Nugget* (1935).

Believe nothing that you see in the newspapers—they have done more to create dissatisfaction than all other agencies. If you see anything in them that you know is true, begin to doubt it at once.

Sir William Osler, physician, *Aphorisms from His Bedside Teachings and Writings* (1968), edited by W.B. Bean.

Yes, I don't know if it was in the Canadian papers—if so, I missed it. I had quite enough to read with all the reports we had to deal with; I didn't bother much about the newspapers; and in any case the Canadians are so well off for newsprint that to try to read their papers is a little like starting to read the *Encyclopaedia Britannica*—you know, interesting but miscellaneous.

Remarks about newspapers made by a character in **Manning Coles**'s detective story "The Blue Envelope," *Nothing to Declare* (1960).

People don't actually read newspapers. They get into them every morning, like a hot bath.

Attributed to **Marshall McLuhan**, communications theorist, in 1965 by Elizabeth Knowles, editor of *The Oxford Dictionary of Twentieth Century Quotations* (1998).

That great Canadian wit, pillar of the York Club, and dear friend, Leonard Brockington once wrote, "According to the latest figures issued by the Dominion Bureau of Statistics, over 90% of the world's newsprint is made in Canada. May God forgive us!"

Sir Edwin Leather, governor of Bermuda, address, "Bermuda Calling," Toronto, 12 December 1974, The Empire Club of Canada.

Changing one's philosophy from broadsheet to tabloid is like changing one's eating habits. It takes a little time (like divorcing one woman and living with another). But in my own mind, tabloid is the format of the future. Offering, in one corner, a choice between a broadsheet paper established for years, sure of themselves and a tiny bit conservative, and in the other corner, a jazzy tabloid with short stories from makeup and plenty of colour.

Pierre Péladeau, publisher, address, "The Quebecor Success Story," Toronto, 25 February 1988, The Empire Club of Canada.

The one thing that is known is that any Toronto businessman who tries to read both papers will not get to work until 11:00 A.M.

Allan Fotheringham, columnist, referring to the four Toronto daily newspapers, focusing on *The Globe and Mail* and the *National Post,* "Which One Will Survive?" *Maclean's,* 18 December 2000.

Our motto used to be: "There are more masses than there are bosses."

Joe Azaria, publisher of Montreal tabloids in the 1950s, including *Midnight, Midnight Globe,* and *Globe,* defining his readership, noted in his obituary by Tu Thanh Ha, *The Globe and Mail,* 4 April 2001.

I have always thought of the *National Post* as a 250,000-word editorial wrapped around a newspaper.

Dalton Camp, columnist, "You Can't Fool the People on Capitalism," *Toronto Star,* 20 June 2001.

Newspapers are about what went wrong in the world yesterday.

William Thorsell, editor-in-chief of *The Globe and Mail,* recalled by Robert Fulford, "These Days, No News Can Ever Be Good News," *National Post,* 27 September 2003.

If I have learned one thing in half a lifetime of reading the papers, it is that you should not waste your time reading the papers. There's nothing in them most days, and what there is is always the same.

Andrew Coyne, columnist, "The Speech Martin Never Gave," *National Post*, 14 April 2004.

Some are saying that the day will eventually come when there will be only free newspapers, which is at least an improvement over all those who said the day was coming when there would be no newspapers at all.

Roy MacGregor, columnist, "This Country," *The Globe and Mail*, 17 March 2005.

NEWSPAPER HEADLINES *See also* News

KING OR CHAOS.

This amazing headline was spread across two pages of *Maclean's*, 15 October 1935, before the general election of that year, in which W.L. Mackenzie King defeated Prime Minister R.B. Bennett. It led wits to conclude that Canada had got both King and chaos. The story behind the headline is discussed by Floyd C. Chalmers, *A Gentleman of the Press* (1969).

KEEP CANADA BRITISH.
DESTROY DREW'S HOUDE.
GOD SAVE THE KING.

Three-level headline over a full-page story about the forthcoming federal election, *Toronto Daily Star*, 25 June 1949. In an unpublished history of the newspaper **David MacDonald** refers to this as "the most infamous front page in *Star* history. Save for the weather forecast—hot and humid—every line was about Monday's election." The headline writer was the newspaper's managing editor, **Harry C. Hindmarsh**, who favoured the Liberal leader Louis St. Laurent. George Drew, the Conservative leader, had forged an alliance with the Montrealer Camillien Houde who is described as "isolationist, ex-internee, foe of Britain." For a later edition, publisher **Joseph S. Atkinson** replaced the third line with "VOTE ST. LAURENT."

NIAGARA FALLS

... An ocean tumbling down out of the sky.

Nathaniel Hawthorne, American novelist, *My Visit to Niagara* (1835).

Who can behold the mighty Niagara and say "there is no God," or forget Him...?

Major Samuel Strickland, pioneer settler and brother of Susanna Moodie and Catharine Parr Traill, *Twenty-Seven Years in Canada West* (1853).

Heaven had considered this vast natural phenomenon too great for one nation.

John Quincy Adams, U.S. president, in George Menzies, *Album of the Table Rock, 1846: A Souvenir of Niagara Falls* (1864).

Every American bride is taken there, and the sight of the stupendous waterfall must be one of the earliest, if not the keenest, disappointments in American married life.

Oscar Wilde, Anglo-Irish wit, opinion offered the British press after his return from a visit to Niagara Falls in 1882, in Lloyd Lewis and Henry Justin Smith, *Oscar Wilde Discovers America* (1936). The remark is usually sharpened to "Niagara Falls is the second greatest disappointment of American married life" as in Karen Dubinsky's *The Second Greatest Disappointment: Honeymooning and Tourism at Niagara Falls* (1999).

I should have killed Holmes over there, not the Swiss Alps.

Attributed to **Sir Arthur Conan Doyle** on his visit to Niagara Falls in 1922, referring to the cataract rather than to Reichenbach Falls in the Swiss Alps, as noted by Christopher Redmond, *Welcome to America, Mr. Sherlock Holmes* (1987). Redmond notes, "The authority for the remark is bookseller Borden Clark."

Summer journeys to Nia'gra / And to other places aggra- / Vate all our cares. / We'll save our fares!

Opening verse of the lyrics of "Manhattan," composed by **Richard Rogers** and **Lorenz Hart** and sung by June Cochrane and Sterling Holloway in the revue *Garrick Gaieties* in 1925. Mickey Rooney and others revived it for the movie *Words and Music* in 1948, and Vera Miles and Bob Hope did so again in *Beau James* in 1957. Later, the Supremes recorded it as "We'll Have Manhattan" (but without the reference to "Nia'gra"). The "hit" version above was popularly sung by Ella Fitzgerald.

Thank you for that weekend at Niagara / When we hardly saw the Falls....

Two lines from a version of the popular song "Thanks for the Memory" (1938), words and music by **Leo Robin** and **Ralph Rainger**, introduced by Bob Hope and Shirley Ross in *The Big Broadcast of 1938* and winner of that year's Academy Award. The Niagara reference does not appear in Ronny S. Schiff's collection *Paramount on Parade: Famous Music from Paramount Films* (1966).

MacMurray: It was all settled.
Stanwyck: That was Niagara Falls. People aren't responsible for what they say in Niagara Falls.

Dialogue between flirtatious Fred MacMurray who declares his love for Barbara Stanwyck, who plays a loose woman, as they pass through Niagara on their way to New York, in the movie *Remember the Night* (1940), written by **Preston Sturges** and directed by Mitchell Leisen.

Marilyn Monroe and "Niagara"—a raging torrent of emotion that even nature can't control!

Advertising copy on the poster promoting the movie *Niagara* (1953), starring Marilyn Monroe and Joseph Cotten. Writer Jeremy Ferguson, "Hollywood's Not-So-True North," *The Globe and Mail*, 14 September 2005, says this campaign "almost succeeds in transforming Niagara into Viagra."

The roar of Niagara is the Delphian voice of the great spaces of North America.

Sir Osbert Sitwell, English author, *The Four Continents* (1954).

What you need is ten minutes with a good man at Niagara Falls.

Line spoken to Grace Kelly by Cary Grant in the movie *To Catch a Thief* (1955), directed by Alfred Hitchcock, with screenplay by **John Michael Hayes** and based on a novel by David Dodge.

Niagara is pure Walt. It is impossible to believe that the little man didn't have a hand in it. All around you are the towers and the waxworks, the adventure rides across the whirlpool and to the bottom of the falls; and best of all, you put on black mackintoshes and wellington boots and waterproof bonnets over paper caps and you are away down the shaft to the tunnel right under the torrent.

Robert Morley, British actor in Toronto on tour, "Confessions from a Hospitable City," *The London Observer*, 24 December 1972. He had in mind Walt Disney, not Walt Whitman.

If Canada was a "gigantic department store" of travel, Niagara was the bargain basement: cheap and widely accessible, a little bit tawdry, and a lot of fun.

Karen Dubinsky, historian, *The Second Greatest Disappointment: Honeymooning and Tourism at Niagara Falls* (1999).

NIGHT

Night is profoundly in our souls and minds, our hearts and bodies. It is woven into our language. / Night gives us permission to hope, to wish, to dream, to be whomever we wish.

Christopher Dewdney, poet and author, *Acquainted with the Night: Excursions through the World after Dark* (2004).

NINE/ELEVEN (9/11) *See* Terrorism

NOBEL PRIZE *See also* Awards & Honours; Research; Science

It must be evident that I owe the Canadian taxpayer and the departments of Government that administer scientific funding a substantial debt of gratitude. I have indeed been fortunate, and I am very grateful. To this I would add that the overwhelming generosity of Canadians—from First Ministers to janitors—has had the result that there could not possibly be a more satisfying experience than to win this particular prize in this country.

John C. Polanyi, chemist, referring to support of the University of Toronto and various grant-giving bodies that led to his being awarded the Nobel Prize in 1986, address, "A Scientist and the World He Lives In," Toronto, 27 November 1986, The Empire Club of Canada.

I guess I stood an inch taller. It's great to win the prize but the ultimate, I think, is just in being able to solve the problems and seeing your work used.

Rudolph Marcus, Montreal-born chemist based at the California Institute of Technology, on being informed at a conference of the Electrochemical Society in Toronto on 14 October 1992 that he was the 1992 Nobel laureate in Chemistry, in Reuters-CP in the *Winnipeg Free Press*, 15 October 1992. He is quoted by Sarah Binder and Stephen Ewart in the same paper as saying, "I really wish Canada would give me my Canadian citizenship back."

There's a little bit of a tendency to feel that we cannot do first rate things in Canada because we're too small. This award says the science done here is as good as the science done anywhere, and you can do science in B.C. as well as anywhere in the world.

Michael Smith, biochemist at the University of British Columbia, co-winner of the 1993 Nobel Prize for Chemistry, in Robert Matas, *The Globe and Mail*, 14 October 1993.

So you can take your pick as to which Mundell you prefer; but the Nobel committee basically honoured Mundell the younger, the economist who was iconoclastic enough to imagine that Canada, of all places, was the economy of the future—and was right.

Paul Krugman, U.S. economist, "O Canada: A Neglected Nation Gets Its Nobel" (1999), *The Great Unraveling: Losing Our Way in the New Century* (2003). Krugman is writing about the economist Robert Mundell, recipient of the Nobel Prize for analyses done in the 1960s based on Canadian monetary policies and practices.

NORTH *See also* North Pole

In civilization there is no peace. Here, in the North, in my country, there is peace. No past, no future, no regret, no anticipation: just doing. That is peace.

John Hornby, adventurer in the Barrens of the Eastern Arctic, remarks made to his Native guide Denny LaNauze, as noted by Pierre Berton, *Captives of the North* (2004).

We have not as yet had the good fortune of developing in southern Canada any religious sect or other group so unpopular that they have been driven north to help dispel the Arctic desert of Canada. But we are having a good fortune analogous to the gold rush of '49. For nothing that has so far happened in Canada has done so much to dispel the myths of the north as the rich discoveries of minerals in Northern Ontario and Northern Manitoba.

Vilhjalmur Stefansson, Arctic explorer, address, "Abolishing the Arctic," Toronto, 25 October 1928, The Empire Club of Canada.

I think the future of the North lies in something much more permanent than plunder. I think it lies in the presence of the land largely untouched and its history.

Pierre Berton, author, address, "The Future of the North," Toronto, 11 October 1973, The Empire Club of Canada.

Remember, the North really is our last frontier; after we have passed this frontier, there is no other frontier beyond.

Thomas Berger, justice, Supreme Court of Canada, address, "Northern Frontier, Northern Homeland," Toronto, 19 May 1977, The Empire Club of Canada.

North is a philosophical, even an emotional, stance. It is an ineluctable geographic condition. It means, perhaps, a sense of being at the top of the world—or near enough to smell twenty kinds of snow.

John Ferguson, architect, "Northern Lights," *Wild Culture: Specimens from* The Journal of Wild Culture (1992), edited by Whitney Smith and Christopher Lowry.

Why is being lost in the frozen North—and going crazy there—still alive and kicking as a Canadian theme, even though most Canadians now live in cities?

Margaret Atwood, author, introduction, *Strange Things: The Malevolent North in Canadian Literature* (1995).

In the North, for the North, and by the North.

Motto of the University of the Arctic, established by the circumpolar countries on 12 June 2001, with co-ordinating office at Rovaniemi, Finland. Athabasca University, from its campus at Athabasca, Alta., is fostering its online service and developing its distance-learning programs. It attracts "Students with Latitude."

I feel Canadian in the act of going north. North is this abstraction which is so much a part of the Canadian personality.

Robert MacNeil, broadcaster and author, quoted in *Maclean's*, 14 July 2003. Born in Montreal, raised in Halifax, based in New York, MacNeil became a U.S. citizen in 1997 and still praises Canadian values and spends the summer in Nova Scotia.

In the Yukon, where I spent my childhood and much of my teens, the old-timers had a phrase for those who had been held captive by the North. "He's missed too many boats," they'd say.

Pierre Berton, author, *Captives of the North* (2004).

The North is a vast and sparsely populated wilderness whose residents are heavily subsidized by vast sums of money from the south. For that matter, there are fewer indigenous Canadians living in the North than in downtown Toronto.

Margaret Wente, columnist, *An Accidental Canadian: Reflections on My Home and (Not) Native Land* (2004).

NORTH AMERICA *See also* America; Continentalism

God does not like the present name of our continent. It is not America [*sic*] who planted the cross on the soil of the New world, but Christopher Columbus. And the divine will is that this continent be called "Beautiful Columbia" in honour of the good Christian and great man who discovered it.

Louis Riel, Métis leader and mystic, diary entry, 17–18 October 1885, *The Diaries of Louis Riel* (1976), edited by Thomas Flanagan.

Did you know that Canada just joined North America? It's a big story up north.

Rick Mercer, television comedian, "Talking about *Talking to Americans*," *Elm Street*, February–March 2001.

We are really North Americans first and Quebeckers second.

Louise Beaudoin, Quebec minister of International Relations, address, Beverly Hills, California, in Doug Saunders, "Quebec Expanding Missions in the U.S.," *The Globe and Mail*, 20 May 2002.

NORTH AMERICAN FREE TRADE AGREEMENT (NAFTA) *See also* America; Free Trade

There are thousands of pages of rules to protect corporate and business rights, over 20,000 pages of them in the most recent General Agreement on Tariffs and Trade (GATT), but no rules to protect human rights or the quality of the environment.

John McMurtry, philosopher, referring to NAFTA, "The Contradictions of Free Market Doctrine," prepared for the Westminster Institute Conference, London, Ont., May 1995.

NORTH POLE *See also* Arctic Regions; North

It is clear enough that in order to take part in such a North Pole expedition one must, if he lives in Europe, first leave Europe, his home.

The parsons will take advantage of this. Naturally, they will easily see that the number of persons who really undertake the dangerous and difficult North Pole expedition will be exceedingly small, and that so small a number will not suffice to provide a livelihood for a legion of parsons with their families. The thing to do therefore is to transform the "North Pole Expedition" into "an endeavour in the direction of such a North Pole expedition," and then to jabber men into the vain belief that all—the millions—are also endeavouring in the direction of such a North Pole Expedition.

Søren Kierkegaard, philosopher, "Yet the Endeavours," 2 July 1855, in Walter Lowrie, *Kierkegaard,* Volume II (1938, 1962). In a letter written to a friend, the Danish religious thinker satirized the way church pastors deal with mankind's religious struggles in terms of a hypothetical expedition to the North Pole (which would not be accomplished for 50 years) by minimizing the effort required and by suggesting that everyone is already part of the endeavour.

It is averred in Occultism that the land, or island, which crowns the North Pole like a skull-cap, is the only one which prevails during the whole Manvantara of our "Round." All the central continents and lands will emerge from the sea bottom many times in turn, but this land will never change.

H.P. Blavatsky, theosophist, referring to the cradle of humanity at the North Pole, known as the "Sacred Imperishable Land," *The Secret Doctrine: A Synthesis of Science, Religion and Philosophy,* Volume II (1888; 3rd ed., 1902).

Now when I was a little chap I had a passion for maps.... At that time there were many blank spaces on the earth, and when I saw one that looked particularly inviting on a map (but they all look that) I would put my finger on it and say, When I grow up I will go there. The North Pole was one of these places, I remember. Well, I haven't been there yet, and shall not try now. The glamour's off.

Thoughts of the narrator Marlow recalling his youth in **Joseph Conrad**'s novella *Heart of Darkness* (1902).

A few toes aren't much to give to achieve the Pole.

Attributed to **Robert E. Peary**, Arctic explorer, in 1898, who attained the North Pole on 6 April 1909, by Helen O'Neill, "Explorers Finding Corners of Earth Still Undiscovered," Associated Press, website, 21 May 2000.

Afterwards he will go to the North Pole, which is inhabited by Christians, who will be of service later in the great Crusade. And soon.

William Bolitho, author, paraphrasing the late-in-life ruminations of Christofero Colombo, the Italian navigator who was related to the Counts of Cuccaro, who believed he would "attain" the North Pole, "Christopher Columbus," *Twelve against the Gods: The Story of Adventure* (1929).

"Well, for this reason we this time decided to send our ship for mooring to what is called the 'North Pole,' where their ships have as yet no possibility of going."

Speech of the alien being named Beelzebub, referring to his spaceship *Occasion* as well as to man-made airplanes, in **G.I. Gurdjieff**'s philosophical epic *All and Everything: Ten Books, in Three Series, of Which This Is the First Series* (1950).

We live in a bad place in the universe—near the North Pole.

P.D. Ouspensky, Russian-born philosopher, talk, 9 January 1935, *A Record of Some of the Meetings Held by P.D. Ouspensky between 1930 and 1947* (1951, 1992).

We are like Amundsen in his airship over the North Pole, whose compass pointed in all directions and nowhere in particular.

A.R. Orage, English literary critic, referring in 1924 to the bearings of Roald Amundsen, the Norwegian explorer who determined the position of the North Magnetic Pole in 1903–1906 and in 1926 disappeared during a flight over the Arctic, in C.S. Nott, *Teachings of Gurdjieff* (1961).

I have quoted somewhere or other a remark of Chekhov's, which, since it is to the point, I venture to quote again. "People don't go to the North Pole and fall off icebergs," he said, "they go to the office, quarrel with their wives and eat cabbage soup." That is unduly to narrow the scope of the realistic novel. People do go to the North Pole, and if they don't fall off icebergs, they undergo adventures as formidable.

W. Somerset Maugham, novelist, quoting the Russian writer **Anton Chekhov**, "In

Conclusion," *Ten Novels and Their Authors* (1954).

Hapgood presented evidence to demonstrate, in the same way, that the North Pole moved from the Yukon district to the Greenland Sea about 80,000 years ago, then from the Greenland Sea to Hudson Bay about 50,000 years ago, and from Hudson Bay to its present position about 17,000 to 12,000 years ago. In other words, the most recent crustal movement began about 15,000 B.C. and ended about 10,000 B.C.

These movements of the Pole were not gentle and steady, and as far as human beings were concerned this shift from Hudson Bay to its present position probably involved many shocks, some of them cataclysmic, such as the crustal movement in the La Brea area of California around 11,000 B.C., which killed off a dozen species in twenty-five years.

Rand Flem-Ath and **Colin Wilson**, librarian-researcher from Ladysmith, B.C., and Cornwall-based popular author, *The Atlantis Blueprint* (2000). The reference is to Charles H. Hapgood's *The Path of the Pole* (1958, revised 1970).

In fact, the North and South Poles experience only one day and one night a year, each 179 days long.

Christopher Dewdney, poet and author, *Acquainted with the Night: Excursions through the World after Dark* (2004).

NORTHERN LIGHTS

At times, the intensity of their motion produces flashes like the Northern Lights in the Aurora Borealis. The sight is so marvellous, that, as the Seer gazes into this inner world, and feels the scintillating points shoot past him, he is filled with awe at the thought of other, still greater mysteries, that lie beyond, and within, this radiant ocean.

H.P. Blavatsky, theosophist, *The Secret Doctrine: The Synthesis of Science, Religion and Philosophy*, Volume I (1888; 3rd ed., 1902).

For Inuit everywhere the two basic physical properties of the aurora, in addition to its luminosity and movement, are the sounds it makes when active, and the fact that its display can occur close to the ground, if not actually at ground level. While most atmospheric scientists reject these opinions, typically dismissing anecdotal reports of auroral sound as "ice cracking on lakes," and low-level occurrences of aurorae as optical illusions, it is noteworthy to find that a number of European and American explorers, on the basis of their experience with the aurora, shared the Inuit view on these points.

John MacDonald, researcher, Igloolik Research Centre, *The Arctic Sky: Inuit Astronomy, Star Lore, and Legend* (1998). In an endnote, MacDonald adds, "However, some investigators have been willing to consider the possibility of auroral sound, attributing the cause to such mechanisms as 'very-low-frequency electromagnetic waves' or 'coronal discharge.' These mechanisms and their possible links to aurora sound are explained in *The Aurora Watcher's Handbook*," written by Neil Davis (1992).

The power of the aurora's charged particles is extraordinary and it has been estimated that a single display can generate a million megawatts of power, one hundred times greater than the few thousand megawatts of power generated by Niagara Falls.

Christopher Dewdney, poet and author, *Acquainted with the Night: Excursions through the World after Dark* (2004).

NORTHWEST PASSAGE *See also* Discovery; Exploration

To the memory of Sir John Franklin, born April 16, 1786, at Spilsby, Lincolnshire: died June 11, 1847, off Point Victory, in the Frozen Ocean, the beloved chief of the crews who perished with him in completing the discovery of the North-west Passage.

Inscription beneath the bust of **Sir John Franklin**, Arctic explorer, in Westminster Abbey, London, as noted by Pierre Berton, *Captives of the North* (2004).

NORTHWEST TERRITORIES *See also* Nunavut

The land of feast and famine.

Evocation of the Barren Lands of the North West Territories in the 1920s, associated with **John Hornby**, English explorer, by Pierre Berton, *The Mysterious North* (1959).

It is impossible to describe the country, for it is built on a scale outside that of humanity.

John Buchan, Governor General Lord Tweedsmuir, response to the country around Great Slave Lake, at Fort Providence, N.W.T., September 1937, in Janet Adam Smith, *John Buchan* (1965).

Tomorrow's Country.

Slogan associated with the Centennial of the Northwest Territories, celebrated on 1 July 1970.

Within reach, yet beyond belief.

Tourism slogan of the Northwest Territories, *Canada's Northwest Territories: 1992 Explorers' Guide* (1991).

NOVA SCOTIA *See also* Atlantic Provinces

Ciad Mile Failte / 100,000 Welcomes.

Traditional Gaelic greeting, associated with Nova Scotia and especially Cape Breton Island.

"Thank you" is excellent, but formal and English in effect. "Thanks a million" is excellent, but it has an American extravagance which is unbecoming in Canadian mouths. What would you think of "Thanks a hundred thousand"? It seems to me to strike the right Canadian note.

Robertson Davies, novelist, *Samuel Marchbanks' Almanack* (1967).

I'm going to Nova Scotia ... 'cause I got a gal in Boston and another in New York ... I'm going there for the smoked salmon.

Approximate words breathlessly delivered by the Pan-like character Banjo (played by Jimmy Durante) in the movie *The Man Who Came to Dinner* (1942), written by **Julius J. Epstein** and **Philip G. Epstein** and directed by William Keighley, based on the 1939 stage play of the same name by George S. Kaufman and Moss Hart.

Gentlemen, a new era is in store for Nova Scotia ... we are no longer an isolated peninsula on the East Coast of Canada ... the determination of our people, along with the far-sighted programs which we are implementing, is going to catapult us into this new era of potential and ultimate prosperity. In the words of the great Joseph Howe, "You don't need a big field to raise a big turnip."

Gerald A. Regan, Nova Scotia premier, address, "A Future for the Maritimes," Toronto, 13 January 1972, The Empire Club of Canada.

Your village touched us by not knowing how.

First line of American poet **James Merrill**'s poem "Overdue Pilgrimage to Nova Scotia," *A Scattering of Salts* (1995).

You're a Nova Scotian to the second generation, at least, so I've been visiting the relatives myself, ever since.... (Nova Scotians go in for genealogy. The first aim of a conversation with any of them is to find out, not only whether you're related, but also how.)

Margaret Atwood, author, both of whose parents came from Nova Scotia, "At Home among the Bluenosers," *The New York Times Magazine: The Sophisticated Traveller*, 16 November 2003.

NOVELTY

The entire economic system in which we live seems to have become completely dependent upon an incessant craving for the new—new music, new fashion, new everything. The paradox of modern culture today is that it is both inclined to change rapidly and yet highly predictable in the way it changes.

Marcel Danesi, semiotician, *Forever Young: The "Teen-Aging" of Modern Culture* (2003).

NUCLEAR WARFARE *See also* Arms Race; War; Weapons

The hydrogen bomb is history's exclamation point. It ends an age-long sentence of manifest violence.

Marshall McLuhan, communications theorist, quoted in *Instant Quotation Dictionary* (1969), compiled by Donald O. Bolander et al.

It would be an act unprecedented in human history for two nations with profound unresolved differences to agree to set aside a large portion of their weaponry. "Our differences remain," they would be saying, "but we shall, because we must, settle them without resort to such weapons."

John C. Polanyi, scientist and peace activist, address, Governor General's Conference, Calgary, 30 May 1987.

A single night below freezing is enough to destroy the Asian rice crop. A 2 to 30 degree average local temperature drop is sufficient to destroy all wheat production in Canada, and 3 to 40, all grain production.

Carl Sagan and **Richard Turco**, scientists, referring to the effects of "nuclear winter," *A Path Where No Man Thought* (1990).

Claiming nuclear energy production is "clean" is like dieting but stuffing yourself with food between meals.

Rosalie Bertell, anti-nuclear and peace activist, "Radioactivity: No Immediate Danger?" *Ms.*, September–October 1991.

He who lives by the sword will die by the bomb.

Mavor Moore, theatre personality, aphorism, 22 December 2002.

NUDITY

The stripper puts on her audience by taking off her clothes.

Marshall McLuhan, communications theorist, *Take Today: The Executive as Dropout* (1972), with Barrington Nevitt.

NUNAVUT *See also* Northwest Territories

At a time when people are attempting to dismantle Canada, the people of Nunavut are trying to complete it.

The Nunavut Implementation Commission, quoted in *The Canadian Global Almanac, 1996* (1995).

Our collective agreement is far more than a simple exercise in cartography. It is, at its core, an important act of nation-building.

Brian Mulroney, prime minister, signing the agreement to transfer title to much of the Eastern Arctic to its Inuit inhabitants and thereby create the Territory of Nunavut by the year 1999, Iqualuit, 25 May 1993, in *Toronto Star*, 26 May 1993.

O

John Gray, playwright, *Lost in North America: The Imaginary Canadian in the American Dream* (1994).

OBESITY *See also* Diets; Food & Drink; Weight

It's not the CAT scans, MRIs that are the most important pieces of medical equipment in 1996. It's the bathroom scale. Obesity kills more people than heart disease and cancer. Today our medical system is in a financial mess, but if people could maintain a weight they would never go over, the Minister of Health could fire half the doctors and close half the hospitals.

Kenneth Walker, physician and columnist (aka Dr. Gifford-Jones), address, "The Healthy Barmaid, The New Minister of Health?" Toronto, 11 April 1996, The Empire Club of Canada.

If you weigh twenty per cent more than your ideal weight for your height and age, you are technically obese. It's not the weight that's the problem; it's the health condition that usually accompanies that weight.

Sarah Rosenthal, health specialist, *Women of the '60s Turning 50* (2000).

OCEANS *See also* Water

I am not the queen of the oceans, but I might be a mermaid.

Elizabeth Mann Borgese, academic, Dalhousie University, Halifax, N.S., and promoter of the 1970 conference "Peace in the Oceans" on the law of the sea, playfully disregarding the honorific, noted in her obituary by Allison Lawlor, "Crusader Was the 'Queen of the Oceans,'" *The Globe and Mail*, 20 February 2002.

If you hold Canada to your ear, you can hear the ocean.

John Gray, playwright, *Lost in North America: The Imaginary Canadian in the American Dream* (1994).

Blood, sweat, and tears are portions of the primordial ocean that cradled our ancestors. That physical link to the ocean means that, in a sense, what goes on within the oceans goes on within us. Perhaps that is why, as Carl Jung theorized, dreams of water must be dreams about our unconscious selves. The creatures within us that haunt the vast, twilight ocean depths of our own unconscious minds are cousins to the denizens of the abyss.

Christopher Dewdney, poet and author, *Acquainted with the Night: Excursions through the World after Dark* (2004).

OCTOBER CRISIS *See also* Canada & Quebec; Separatism; Terrorism

Trudeau: Yes, well there are a lot of bleeding hearts around who just don't like to see people with helmets and guns. All I can say is, go on and bleed, but it is more important to keep law and order in the society than to be worried about weak-kneed people who don't like the looks of …

Ralfe: At any cost? How far would you go with that? How far would you extend that?

Trudeau: Well—just watch me.… Yes, I think the society must take every means at its disposal to defend itself against the emergence of a parallel power which defies the elected power in this country, and I think that goes at any distance.

Impromptu interview with Prime Minister **Pierre Elliott Trudeau** conducted by reporter **Tim Ralfe**, Parliament Hill, Ottawa, 13 October 1970, and telecast by CBC-TV that evening. The text was reproduced by the *Toronto Star*, 14 October 1970. The government invoked the War Measures Act on 16 October 1970.

We believe that a group of prominent Québécois is plotting to replace the province's duly elected government. The conspirators include René Lévesque, Jacques Parizeau, Marcel Pepin, and Claude Ryan. This move toward a parallel power must be stopped.

Marc Lalonde, Prime Minister Trudeau's principal secretary, addressing Peter C. Newman and Christina McCall Newman in his East Block office, 23 October 1970, in Newman, *Here Be Dragons: Telling Tales of People, Passion, and Power* (2004). This was the origin of the notion that a "provisional" or "parallel government" was to replace the duly elected Bourassa administration in order to negotiate with the *Front de libération du Québec* (FLQ) terrorists. Newman was dubious about the story until later that day Trudeau phoned him to confirm the plot. Newman concluded it was "the story of the decade" and wrote it up for the *Toronto Daily Star*. Eight days later Trudeau dismissed it as "rumours and unconfirmed speculations." This seemed to be Lalonde and Trudeau's brutal way of discrediting Claude Ryan (and belittling Newman).

I acted because of everything I knew since I was three years old. The fact that the insurrection did not occur did not mean that it could not have been apprehended. Rather, it was precisely because we apprehended it—and acted—that it did not occur. The defence of democracy is the first defence of civil liberties.

Pierre Elliott Trudeau, former prime minister, explaining the need for the War Measures Act given the absence of evidence of a conspiracy by public officials for an "apprehended insurrection" or "parallel government" during the October Crisis of 1970, in a conversation some years later, as recalled by Minister of Justice Irwin Cotler, "How Trudeau Drove Charter Fight," *Toronto Star*, 25 April 2005. It seems that Trudeau was an early study.

OFFICES *See also* Information Technology

People used to think technology would mean the end of office space. People would be working from home. This is not the case at all. The office building is the factory of the information age.

Philip Reichmann, real-estate developer, address, shareholders' meeting, Toronto, 28 June 2000, in Dana Flavelle, *Toronto Star*, 29 June 2000.

OIL INDUSTRY

Dear Mr. Pocklington: Could you please advise me on the following problem. I am twenty-five years of age and have two brothers. One is working for Petro-Can and the other is serving a nine-year sentence in Stony Mountain for murder and arson. My two sisters are on the street and my father is living off their earnings. My mother is a psychic. Recently I met a charming girl, a single ex-prostitute and mother of three children. My problem is this: should I tell her about my brother who is working for Petro-Canada? Signed, Confused.

Mock letter read by **Peter Pocklington**, address, "Let's Make Canada Great Again," Toronto, 4 November 1982, The Empire Club of Canada.

Meanwhile, here in the "advanced world," we keep alive the dream of freedom—the dream that some day we'll be able to drive 18-wheelers that accelerate like racing cars.

Linda McQuaig, investigative journalist, final sentence, *It's the Crude, Dude: War, Big Oil and the Fight for the Planet* (2004).

OLYMPIC GAMES *See also* Sports

The Montreal Olympics can no more have a deficit than a man can have a baby.

Jean Drapeau, Montreal mayor, announcing the "self-financing" Olympic budget of $310 million, press conference, Montreal, 29 January 1973. It took 25 years to pay off the Olympic debt.

Cities made up exclusively of greedy, vulgar, hard-drinking, cigar-chewing, cowboy, capitalist oilmen do not win the right to host Olympic Games.

Ralph Klein, Calgary mayor, speech, Canadian Club, Burlington, Ont., 10 February 1982, referring to Calgary's growth and prosperity during his period in office, noted in "King of Candour Rarely, if Ever, Runs Short of Bon Mots," *The Globe and Mail*, 15 March 2001.

I sincerely hope that when one of our athletes climbs up on the podium and you see the maple leaf rising to the strains of "O Canada," you remember that moment, savour that moment, that pride that one of "ours," a product of Canadian society, has realized a goal, a dream, and we can all share in it. I also want you to remember that these victories will have a profound effect on thousands of young children right across the country. They will be inspired. They will start to dream their own dreams, establish their own goals, and we can't let them down.

Ken Read, skier, address, "The Importance of the Olympics to Canada," Toronto, 20 January 1994, The Empire Club of Canada.

If one of our Canadian athletes wins a gold medal halfway around the world, he or she can choose to wait for the sportscast, the evening news or morning papers or find out immediately, with just a keystroke. Swifter, higher, stronger indeed!

Jean C. Monte, Bell Canada Enterprises executive, address, "Competing in the Internet Economy," Toronto, 28 September 2000, The Empire Club of Canada.

A bronze is as good as gold.

Dominique Bosshart, winner of the bronze medal in Taekwon-Do, Summer Olympics, Sydney, Australia, interview, CBC Radio, 30 September 2000.

You see yourself on the [medal] podium. There are some nights when I can't fall asleep because that's all I think about.

Jamie Salé, half of the figure-skating pair Jamie Salé and David Pelletier, visualizing high achievement in competition, quoted in *TV Guide*, 9 February 2002.

Sometimes a Silver Medal is won by a Gold Medal performance.

David Pelletier, champion figure skater, interview, CBC Radio, 12 February 2002. Pelletier and Jamie Salé were awarded the silver medal in the pairs figure-skating competition at the Olympic Games in Salt Lake City, Utah, 11 February 2002. In a controversial decision, they lost the gold to Russian contenders. A later decision awarded them their gold.

You know what the problem is? It's the exchange rate. Gold in Canada is only Silver here.

Jay Leno, host of the *Tonight Show*, 12 February 2002. He was interviewing David Pelletier and Jamie Salé, who received the silver medal for pairs figure-skating at the Olympic Games at Salt Lake City, Utah, in a controversial decision.

We're on a high because we skated great. Sure, we're disappointed we didn't win, but when we finished skating that was probably the best moment we'll ever experience. So we're not bitter. We're so proud of what we've done. Today we're happy people.

Jamie Salé, on her and figure-skating partner David Pelletier's accepting the loss (later reversed) of the Olympic pairs gold medal to Russian skaters Elena Berezhnaya and Anton Sikharulidze, in Scott Taylor, *Winnipeg Free Press*, 13 February 2002. Salé and Pelletier were married at the end of December 2005.

The whole world wants us to lose.

Wayne Gretzky, hockey superstar, organizer of Team Canada at the Salt Lake City Olympic Games, press conference, 18 February 2002, in Roy MacGregor, "'The Whole World Wants Us to Lose,'" *National Post*, 19 February 2002. Gretzky and Team Canada's coach Pat Quinn accused the Czech Republic players of "dirty hockey." Getzky sounded off against the media: "They don't like us. They love beating us. I'm tired of people taking shots at Canadian hockey. If we do something like that, we're hooligans. Nobody wants us to win but our players and our loyal fans. We're very proud—I guarantee you we'll be standing at the end. They should remember that there's payback in this game, and it won't be pretty."

It was an awesome game and we're so proud of you. All of Canada is cheering at this moment.

Jean Chrétien, prime minister, congratulating Wayne Gretzky, executive director of Team Canada in Salt Lake City, by telephone following the 5-to-2 victory of Team Canada against the U.S. team, 24 February 2002. This marked Canada's first Olympic gold medal in men's hockey since 1952, in David Shoalts, *The Globe and Mail*, 25 February 2002.

Nevertheless, the Canadians screamed bloody murder and demanded an inquiry and, mirabile dictu, Salé and Pelletier got the gold medal, although the Russians were allowed to keep theirs, too.

Adam Gopnik, columnist, "There Is No End to the Kick-ass Canucks," *National Post*, 2 March 2002.

When they did get their gold, he said, "I do hope we get the bronze, too, so we can get the entire collection."

Adam Gopnik, columnist, quoting David Pelletier at the Salt Lake City Olympic Games, "There Is No End to the Kick-ass Canucks," *National Post*, 2 March 2002.

I'd also like to say how sorry I am about Canada winning the gold medals in Olympic hockey. Not so much for what we did but the way we did it. In women's hockey, particularly. I can't imagine how humiliating it must be for American players to go through life explaining how they had a power play for 59 minutes but still lost the gold medal.

Colin Mochrie, actor-comedian, "A Canadian Apologizes," routine posted on a website, 8 June 2002. Mochrie's routine took the form of a mock letter addressed to U.S. President George W. Bush.

And who would have thought laid-back Vancouver would get its act together? The Marilyn Monroe of cities (beautiful, but not known for brains or business acumen) mounted a bid that even Type-A Toronto couldn't have improved on.

Margaret Wente, columnist, "Counterpoint," *The Globe and Mail*, 3 July 2003. The International Olympic Committee awarded Vancouver sponsorship of the Summer 2010 Olympic Games on 2 July 2003.

ONTARIO

On the old Ontario strand, my boys / Where Victoria evermore shall stand; / For has she not stood since the time of the flood / On the old Ontario strand.

Chorus of "On the Old Ontario Strand" (1886), the college song beloved of generations of students of both Queen's University in Kingston and Victoria College of the University of Toronto in Toronto, as noted by Lennox Irving, *The Queen's Alumni Review*, August 1933.

Ontario was our most permanent home. We continued to be struck dumb by her variety of scenery, her fertile agricultural land, and the dainty charm of the countryside in the Niagara Peninsula.

Susan Buchan, compiler of *John Buchan by His Wife and Friends* (1947), describing the province in the late 1930s.

If it were not for the riches of Ontario, I don't know what would happen to the rest of the Dominion.

Mitch Hepburn, Ontario premier, address, "Present Day Problems," Toronto, 15 December 1938, The Empire Club of Canada.

Give us a place to stand / And a place to grow / And call this land / Ontario.

Chorus of the theme song "Ontar-i-ar-i-ar-io" rousingly sung in the documentary film *A Place to Stand*, directed by Christopher Chapman for the Ontario Pavilion at Expo 67. **Richard Morris** wrote the catchy words, **Dolores Claman** the lively tune.

Ontario has a third of the population and half of everything else.

Identified as "an old Canadian cliché" by **Geoffrey Stevens**, "Ontario," *The Canadian Voter's Guide: Election 79* (1979), edited by Fraser Kelly.

Most of the people who have arrived here have thought they were somewhere else—an island created by magical creatures, the east coast of China, a mysterious kingdom where gold lay on the ground like gravel, a blank place that could be easily turned into a new France or a new Britain. Gradually they began to understand that they had arrived in a land thick with stories.

John Bentley Mays, author, *Arrivals: Stories from the History of Ontario* (2002).

Ontario has been—and Ontario remains—the heart of Canada. Just as it is fair to say that Canada is the soul of Ontario.

Dalton McGuinty, Ontario premier, address, "Ontario," Toronto, 24 March 2005, The Empire Club of Canada.

OPERA *See also* Music

When audiences fail to shudder at the terrible doom of Don Giovanni, when they are unmoved by the final choked "Mimi!" of *La Bohème*, when they sit placidly through the "*Liebestod*" of Tristan, and when they no longer feel the primitive terror of Azucena's wild jeremiads in *Il Trovatore*, then opera will be old-fashioned indeed and ready to make way for a more advanced form.

Edward Johnson, opera singer and manager, remark made in 1948, in Ruby Mercer, *The Tenor of His Time: Edward Johnson of the Met* (1976).

When people ask me what I think of opera in Maple Leaf Gardens I reply we only hope ice hockey will look as well in the Metropolitan Opera House.

Rudolf Bing, general manager, Metropolitan Opera, referring to the Met's performance in Maple Leaf Gardens, address, "The Business of Opera," Toronto, 28 March 1957.

Name a great city that does not have a great opera house.

Barton Myers, architect, address, "A Great City and Its Institutions," Toronto, 18 February 1988, The Empire Club of Canada.

I have been careful to locate the operas in Wetzlar or Windsor or wherever they are supposed to take place, as one cannot depend on today's aberrantly deconstructionist directors not to transfer the action of any opera to a World War II battleship. (Let's hope that such produceritis will soon go the way of the dodo.)

M. Owen Lee, opera commentator, on the setting and staging of opera performances, *The Operagoer's Guide: One Hundred Stories and Commentaries* (2001).

OPINION POLLS *See also* Opinions

Polling is to sociology what the daily news is to history.

Michael Adams, consultant, *Fire and Ice: The United States, Canada and the Myth of Converging Values* (2003), with Amy Langstaff and David Jamieson.

A story on polls is only news when it confirms what the editors want to hear.

Peter C. Newman, journalist and memoirist, *Here Be Dragons: Telling Tales of People, Passion, and Power* (2004).

OPINIONS *See also* Opinion Polls

Do you wish to know what public opinion is? It is the opinion of those who are against us.

Maurice Duplessis, Quebec premier, in Pierre Laporte, *The True Face of Duplessis* (1961).

A man's reputation is the opinion people have of him; his character is what he really is.

Jack Miner, pioneer naturalist, *Wild Goose Jack* (1969).

We all have opinions, but some of us happen to be right.

Louis Dudek, poet and aphorist, *Epigrams* (1975).

OPPORTUNITY

Every crisis is an opportunity.

Harry Browne, investment adviser, *You Can Profit from a Monetary Crisis* (1974).

You miss one hundred percent of shots you don't take.

Attributed to hockey personality **Wayne Gretzky** in an interview in June 1996.

Opportunities are problems waiting to happen.

Chris Gudgeon, author, *You're Not as Good as You Think You Are: A Demotivational Guide* (1997).

OPPOSITION

Opposition creates the illusion that there is good policy and bad policy, and that political life is simply a matter of choosing the good over the bad, in a relatively painless way. Rhetorical dragons are slain with rhetorical swords, and even drowned in a flood of eloquent wounds.

Bob Rae, former Ontario premier, *From Protest to Power: Personal Reflections of a Life in Politics* (1996).

OPTIMISM *See also* Hope; Pessimism

In recent times there has been a curious reluctance to dwell upon the future possibilities of Canada. I still recall, as a youngster in British Columbia at the turn of the century, being thrilled by the orators who rhapsodized about the future of Canada. The fashion receded. Wars and their consequences helped to breed a cynicism and uncertainty that made it almost "bad form" to be confident about the future. There is need now to revive the glowing inspiration of the pioneering period. There is, however, one consideration that should be kept in mind always. Some element of risk is indispensable to progress. And this applies especially to Canada.

Gladstone Murray, broadcaster, address, "The Plague of Pessimism," Toronto, 6 April 1950, The Empire Club of Canada.

The only thing incurable about me is my optimism.

Robert Hunter, activist and ecologist, referring to his cancer, characteristic remark, in Terry Weber, "Bob Hunter, Environmentalist and Writer, 1941–2005," *The Globe and Mail*, 3 May 2005.

ORDER *See also* Governance; Law

It shall be lawful for the Queen, by and with the Advice and Consent of the Senate and House of Commons, to make Laws for the Peace, Order, and good Government of Canada.

Key section of the British North America Act, which came into effect on 1 July 1867. It is part of the Constitution Act, 1982. Historians are wont to contrast the Canadian objectives of "peace, order, and good government" with the American aims of "life, liberty, and the pursuit of happiness."

Not life, liberty, and the pursuit of happiness, but peace, order, and good government are what the national government of Canada guarantees. Under these, it is assumed, life, liberty, and happiness may be achieved, but by each according to his taste.

W.L. Morton, historian, influential paragraph based on differences between the Declaration of Independence, 1776, and the British North America Act, 1867, *The Canadian Identity* (1961).

Novelty, opportunity, order, generosity define for me this vast country. But perhaps of all its aspects, it is the illusion of a democracy that attracts me most to Canada. I say an illusion because we believe in it but are not quite there yet, perhaps never will be.

Alberto Manguel, Canadian author born in Argentina, "Destination Ithaka," *Passages: Welcome Home to Canada* (2002), with a preface by Rudyard Griffiths.

For some truly mysterious reason, our mind requires that there be order within apparent disorder. The search for order has been the central motivating force of human history. And it will continue to be so as long as humans are around.

Marcel Danesi, semiotician, *The Puzzle Instinct: The Meaning of Puzzles in Human Life* (2002).

OTTAWA

On the whole, therefore, I believe that the least objectionable place is the city of Ottawa. Every city is jealous of every other city except Ottawa.

Sir Edmund Head, governor general of British North America, "Confidential Memorandum … Containing Reasons for Fixing the Seat of Government for Canada at Ottawa," October 1859, reprinted by James A. Gibbon, *Canadian Historical Review*, December 1935.

Ottawa is a small town, with incongruously beautiful buildings crowning its insignificance.

Lady Dufferin, wife of Governor General Lord Dufferin, *My Canadian Journal* (1891).

Ottawa is a sub-arctic lumber-village converted by royal mandate into a political cockpit.

Goldwin Smith, historian, widely quoted opinion, noted by William Buckingham, *The Hon. Alexander Mackenzie: His Life and Times* (1892).

The problem with Ottawa is that it is inhabited by only three types of people: civil servants, who have no interests; politicians, who have no principles; and journalists, who have no manners.

Allan Fotheringham, columnist, *Fotheringham's Fictionary of Facts and Follies* (2001).

Before I came to Ottawa, I had a real job and I lived in the real world.

Allan Rock, Liberal Cabinet minister, interviewed by Peter Mansbridge, CBC-TV's *One on One*, 28 October 2001.

Could I allow myself to make a wish—that your beautiful capital of Ottawa be, some day, declared a bilingual city.

Jean-Pierre Raffarin, prime minister of France, responding to a toast, National Gallery of Canada, Ottawa, 21 May 2003, in Graham Fraser, "Canada Praised as Model for 21st Century," *Toronto Star*, 22 May 2003.

Ottawa is one square kilometre surrounded by reality.

Chuck Strahl, Member of Parliament, "Strahl on the Art of Poo," *National Post*, 24 June 2003.

There's something about the spirit of the great city of Ottawa that attracts the cream of Canada's high-school hallway monitors.

Emo Philips, U.S. comedian, from his website, characteristic remark, 12 November 2003.

The cardinal rule of Ottawa is simple: power is measured by proximity to power.

Peter C. Newman, journalist and memoirist, *Here Be Dragons: Telling Tales of People, Passion, and Power* (2004).

Hugh Brody, author, introduction (1988), *Maps and Dreams: Indians and the British Columbia Frontier* (1981, 1988).

P

PACIFICISM *See also* War

I take my place with the children.

J.S. Woodsworth, Co-operative Commonwealth Federation leader, House of Commons, 9 September 1939. A lifelong pacifist and a Methodist clergyman, Woodsworth cast the sole dissenting vote against the bill to ratify Canada's entry into World War II.

Pacificism, the naive or cowardly efforts to extricate ourselves from our common North American destiny in a world of powerful totalitarianism, is a guaranteed road to war.

Josef Škvorecký, essayist and novelist, "Are Canadians Politically Naive?" (1983), *Talkin' Moscow Blues* (1988), edited by Sam Solecki.

PACIFIC OCEAN

I have it on good authority / that west of this / cloud-bound coast / there are islands / beyond the islands.

Lines from the untitled poem datelined "Vancouver, 1975" that ends **Theodore Roszak**'s *Unfinished Animal: The Aquarian Frontier and the Evolution of Consciousness* (1975).

PAIN & SUFFERING *See also* Health; Medicine

Once or twice in the last year of his life he said to me, "I am like a Red Indian; I am in constant pain and don't show it."

Susan Buchan, wife of the Governor General Lord Tweedsmuir, describing his health in the late 1930s, *John Buchan by His Wife and Friends* (1947).

If we refuse to acknowledge the past, we conceal the nature of suffering, and therefore cannot understand demands in the present.

Hugh Brody, author, introduction (1988), *Maps and Dreams: Indians and the British Columbia Frontier* (1981, 1988).

She would find it intolerable that in Canada 50 per cent of cancer patients die in pain. She would urge doctors to use heroin which was legalized for medical use in 1984. If they refused to do so when other painkillers had failed, families should sue both the doctor and the hospital. Malpractice occurs when a surgeon amputates the wrong leg. It's also malpractice when patients are allowed to die in severe pain when it can be prevented.

Kenneth Walker, physician and columnist (aka Dr. Gifford-Jones), referring to the caring physician as a barmaid, address, "The Healthy Barmaid, The New Minister of Health?" Toronto, 11 April 1996, The Empire Club of Canada.

To hear somebody talk about why they hurt is not small talk. It's a form of intimacy.

Marni Jackson, author, interviewed by Ellen Vanstone, "Outing Pain," *The Globe and Mail*, 1 June 2002.

No brain, no pain.

Thought of a character in **Margaret Atwood**'s novel *Oryx and Crake* (2003).

The pain that brings me to my knees also lifts me up with possibility. It has cut to the core of my being where pain, excitement, sadness and joy live in such close proximity to one another that they can be felt in the same day, the same hour, the same moment.

Silken Laumann, athlete, "Starting Over: Rebuilding a Life after Divorce," *Chatelaine*, September 2003.

PARENTING *See also* Family

Toast to parents: They didn't give me everything I wanted but they gave me everything I needed.

Hugh Arscott, aphorist, *Hugh's Views: Volume 4* (2000).

Few of us explore our philosophy of parenting before we become parents. Then, after we have our children, when we are tired and worn out, we tend to parent the way we were parented.

Barbara Coloroso, consultant, *Kids Are Worth It* (2002).

Parenting is not easy. Everyone struggles.

Marie Adams, educator, advice to parents, *Our Son, a Stranger: Adoption Breakdown and Its Effects on Parents* (2002).

Remember that some children who had the worst parents have turned out to be marvellous people. It is not strictly cause and effect.

Marie Adams, educator, advice to parents, *Our Son, a Stranger: Adoption Breakdown and Its Effects on Parents* (2002).

As with other animals, rearing is something that comes instinctually to human beings. It is simply foolish to believe that society's behavioural and social scientists can replace the family in matters of rearing.

Marcel Danesi, semiotician, *Forever Young: The "Teen-Aging" of Modern Culture* (2003).

PARIZEAU, JACQUES *See also* Separatism

By Jove!

Characteristic expression of **Jacques Parizeau**, former Quebec premier, as noted by columnist Andrew Coyne, "Jacques Parizeau's Long Shot," *National Post*, 18 August 2004.

Jacques Parizeau's most charming habit as a politician has always been his proclivity for having one of his feet firmly planted in his mouth.

Peter C. Newman, columnist and author, "The Great Lobster Revolt," *Defining Moments: Dispatches from an Unfinished Revolution* (1997).

Him again.

Reference to Jacques Parizeau, former Quebec premier, in a column in *Le Devoir* by **Michel David**, who covered the 2003 TV leadership debates between Quebec Premier Bernard Landry and Liberal leader Jean Charest, as noted by L. Ian MacDonald, "Parizeau Just Won't Go Away Quietly," *National Post*, 7 February 2005. Like a popinjay, Parizeau popped up and made pejorative remarks earlier that day that Landry had to disavow, assuring Charest an easy victory in the debates.

PARKS

Please Walk on the Grass.

Wording on signs in Toronto's public parks (introduced in 1960) that attracted international commendation for the "hands-on" approach. It was the inspiration of **Tommy Thompson**, parks commissioner (1955–1981), and the words are inscribed on his tombstone, as noted by Mike Filey, *Mount Pleasant Cemetery: An Illustrated Guide* (1999).

He intended to cross the mountains at Kicking Horse Pass and spend the night beside the Columbia River, but after a hundred miles he decided to stop amid the beauties of Banff, where Queen Victoria had ordered a large area reserved for future generations to bathe themselves in the hot mineral springs that gush from the mountains.

Narration from actor and writer **David Niven**'s novel *Go Slowly, Come Back Quickly* (1981).

In addition to "Please walk on the grass," we want to make signs that read "Please swim in the lake."

Advertisement for the City of Toronto's Waste and Water Education program, *The Globe and Mail*, 7 June 2002. "Please walk on the grass," the widely noted slogan of the city's Parks and Recreations department, was created by its first director, **Tommy Thompson**.

It is a Parks Canada principle: Leave this campsite cleaner than you found it.

Graham Fraser, columnist, "Intervention Hope Kept Alive by Chrétien," *Toronto Star*, 20 July 2003.

PARLIAMENT *See also* Government; House of Commons; Senate

If witnessed frequently enough by earnest members of the public, it can destroy their faith in Parliament, politicians, and democracy more rapidly than any other political experience.

Preston Manning, politician, leader of the Reform Party and later of the Canadian Alliance, describing Question Period in the House of Commons, *Think Big: Adventures in Life and Democracy* (2002).

Mr. Speaker, I apologize to you and the House for touching the mace, a symbol of democracy in the House. The government House leader mentioned the issue of proper, legal and judicious affronts to the House. There is only one great affront: the violation of democracy that took place today with the government's motion.

However, I apologize to the House for touching the mace. I did so in the heat of the moment and to try to make the point that democracy was violated, four years of work was destroyed and people's lives were at stake. I did it to make a point. I should not have done it and I apologize to the House.

Keith Martin, Member of Parliament, House of Commons, 17 April 2002. In a moment of either pique or calculation, Martin seized and brandished the mace during a session of the Commons. He transgressed the parliamentary rule that the sole member of the Commons permitted to wield the mace is the Speaker of the House. The Canadian Alliance member had been upset that his private member's bill to decriminalize the possession of marijuana was amended and effectively dismissed: "On Wednesday, I broke that tradition and hoisted the Mace into the air, declaring, 'Parliament is not a democracy any more,'" he wrote; "Undemocratic," *National Post*, 19 April 2002.

Parliament is showbiz for ugly people.

Carolyn Parrish, Member of Parliament, in Ray Conlogue, "Loose Cannon," *Saturday Night*, March 2005.

PARTI QUÉBÉCOIS *See also* Canada & Quebec; Political Parties; Quebec; Separatism

I never thought I could be as proud to be a Quebecker as I am tonight ... We're not a minor people. We're maybe something like a great people.

René Lévesque, leader of the Parti Québécois and premier designate, election victory party, Montreal, 15 November 1976. These words were not lost on his arch-rival, **Pierre Elliott Trudeau**, who addressed the nation following the pro-federalist outcome of the first Quebec referendum on sovereignty-association, Ottawa, 20 May 1980: "I never thought I could be as proud to be a Quebecker and a Canadian as I am tonight."

Their platform has two plans only: referendum and separation.

Jean Charest, federal Conservative leader, agreeing to contest the Quebec provincial Liberal leadership, address, Sherbrooke, 26 March 1998, in *Toronto Star*, 27 March 1998.

How will I explain that in Boston?

Attributed to Quebec Premier **Lucien Bouchard** at a party meeting by an unnamed Parti Québécois official on 8 December 2000 to explain Bouchard's rejection of demands by language extremists that attendance at French-language community colleges be made mandatory for all non-francophone student immigrants, in Rhéal Séguin, "PQ Showdown Looms as Internal Rift Grows," *The Globe and Mail*, 2 January 2001.

PASSION *See also* Love; Lust; Sex

I was once asked what my novels were about. I said I was recording the passionate inner life of the Canadian. Well, the laughter at that nearly brought down the roof. No one believes Canadians have an inner life.

Robertson Davies, man of letters, in George Gamester, *Toronto Star*, 13 August 1976.

PAST *See also* Future; Heritage; Tradition

A wise nation preserves its records, gathers up its muniments, decorates the tombs of its illustrious dead, repairs its great public structures, and fosters national pride and love of country, by perpetual references to the sacrifices and glories of the past.

Joseph Howe, statesman, address, Framingham, Mass., 31 August 1871, *Poems and Essays* (1874).

We cannot understand the present without some knowledge of the past, and few studies possess more interest than that which relates to human development.

David Boyle, archaeologist, "Canadian Folk-Lore," *The Globe*, 19 March 1898.

THE RECORD OF NATURE THROUGH COUNTLESS AGES / THE ARTS OF MAN THROUGH ALL THE YEARS.

Inscriptions in stone that flank the grand entrance to the Royal Ontario Museum, Toronto, credited to **C.T. Currelly**, the ROM's first curator, in 1932.

The past & the future are the two great enemies, of tyranny & mystery respectively, yet so much in them is essential that the problem of breaking off from them is not so easy.

Northrop Frye, cultural critic, aphorism, "Notebook 3" (1946–1948), *Northrop Frye Newsletter*, fall 2000.

As all historians know, the past is a great darkness, and filled with echoes. Voices may reach us from it; but what they say to us is numbed with the obscurity of the matrix out of which they come; and try as we may, we cannot always decipher them precisely in the clearer light of our own day.

Thoughts of Professor Pieixoto at an address at the University of Denay, Nunavit, 25 June 2193, in **Margaret Atwood**'s novel *The Handmaid's Tale* (1985).

The past can only be managed. With remembrance, with accountability, with justice—however frail, however inadequate, however imperfect.

Erna Paris, author, final lines, *Long Shadows: Truth, Lies and History* (2000).

Your past was perfect. It got you where you are. I did not say that you had a perfect past.

Peter Urs Bender, business motivator, characteristic remark, 20 May 2000.

PATRIOTISM *See also* Canada; Nationalism

During the recent election in England, a candidate for parliament in the North of England began his nightly spell-binding by pointing to the Union Jack and saying: "I was born an Englishman, I have lived an Englishman; and I hope to die an Englishman." Whereupon a Scotchman at the back of the hall said: "Hoot man, hae ye no ambitions." (Laughter.)

Arthur Stringer, novelist, address, "The Interpreters of Canada," Toronto, 7 April 1932, The Empire Club of Canada.

Canada is not an easy country in which to be a patriot.

Peter C. Newman, columnist and author, in response to political commentator Dalton Camp following Newman's publication of *Renegade in Power* (1963), noted in *Here Be Dragons: Telling Tales of People, Passion, and Power* (2004). In answer Camp "explained that Canada is not a land of patriots, but of loyalists."

It's not enough to love Canada like a mistress, and whisper about her in the back alleys. If you're going to love this country, you should shout about it—like a wife you're proud to take out in the daylight. Bring out your thoughts.

Ben Wicks, London, U.K.–born cartoonist, address, "Up the Empire," Toronto, 9 November 1978, The Empire Club of Canada.

It's said that to describe our love of land, / A minute is too long, a lifetime not enough, / That if we love in many joyful ways, we'll keep our heritage intact, / Though time be short and we are wracked by doubts about our worth. / What good is done if we have served mankind and failed ourselves?

Lines of verse written by **Charles Lynch**, journalist, and recited by him, address, "How Stands Our Native Land?" Toronto, 9 April 1981, The Empire Club of Canada.

Throughout my life I have found it difficult to feel patriotic about Canada. Perhaps, as Lawrence Durrell suggested, the duty of every artist is to hate his own country creatively.

R. Murray Schafer, composer, preface, *Patria: The Complete Cycle* (2002).

PATRONAGE *See also* Corruption; Crime

Good patronage.

Maurice Duplessis, Quebec premier in the 1940s, recalled by Pierre Sévigny in 1975, who added, "The noun was seldom heard without the qualifying adjective."

If you hear of somebody who is very young and talented, pick them up and give them that little assistance to make sure that they get to the professional stage. It is terribly important and very necessary. Very few performers' relatives or parents can afford to see them through that stage of their lives.

Maureen Forrester, opera singer, address, "Out of Character," Toronto, 30 October 1986, Toronto, The Empire Club of Canada.

You call who you know.

Jean Chrétien, prime minister, dismissing charges during the federal election campaign that he had repeatedly phoned the president of the Business Development Bank of Canada to lobby on behalf of one of his constituents who wanted to buy a hotel partly owned by Chrétien; in James Brooke, "One Battle More for Canada's Old Warrior," *The New York Times*, 26 November 2000.

PEACE *See also* Pacificism; Peacekeeping; War

I, Dekanahwideh, and the Confederated Chiefs, now uproot the tallest pine tree, and into the cavity thereby made we cast all weapons of war. Into the depth of the earth, deep down into the underwater currents of water flowing to unknown regions, we cast all weapons of strife. We bury them from sight and we plant again the tree. Thus shall the Great Peace be established.

Stirring words of **Dekanahwideh**, the semi-mythological Iroquois statesman who, in league with the Ojibwa chief Hiawatha, founded the Great League of the Iroquois (the Five—later, the Six—Nations Confederacy), near the present-day site of Kingston, Ont. Paul A.W. Wallace, *The White Roots of Peace* (1946), reproduces the traditional words of the Great Peace as well as Dekanahwideh's final words to his people: "If the Great Peace should fail, call on my name in the bushes, and I will return."

To shirk work is to abbreviate labour. To shirk argument is to settle controversy. To shirk war is to cherish peace.

Stephen Leacock, humorist, *Essays and Literary Studies* (1916).

The grim fact, however, is that we prepare for war like precocious giants and for peace like retarded pygmies.

Lester B. Pearson, former president of the UN General Assembly and future prime minister, accepting the Nobel Prize for Peace, Oslo, Norway, 11 December 1957. The address is published in Pearson's *The Four Faces of Peace and the International Outlook* (1964).

Canada is not a big enough country to be really significant in world affairs, but we are big enough to set the pace in this field of peace research. Canadians can indeed help start a world-wide programme for peace research institutes. We are more affluent than most countries. We are a democratic country where such an idea can be brought to a state of vitality. The mass media in Canada, in fact, have already shown great enthusiasm. Scientific peace research may be the place where Canadians can take world-wide initiative.

Norman Z. Alcock, founder of the Canadian Peace Research Institute, address, "Can the Scientist Win the Peace?" Toronto, 8 February 1962, The Empire Club of Canada.

We have a voice that is calling / Telling all free men we're willing / To show them how to live in peace, / For that's what Canada is. // We have peace in our valleys, / We're happy and contented, / We have peace in our cities, / And our boundaries know no chains.

Verses of the song "Canada Is," an unabashed paean of praise composed and sung in the 1990s by **Roger Whittaker**, the U.S. singer-songwriter.

Despite a stellar record in four 20th-century wars, we are a decidedly unmilitary-minded community, proudly parading about as the free world's most peaceable kingdom.

Peter C. Newman, "The Day the War Began," *Maclean's*, 24 September 2001.

Peace is not the absence of war but the absence of fear, which is the presence of justice.

Ursula Franklin, scientist and peace activist, address, receiving the Canadian United Nations Association's Pearson Peace Medal, in Michael Valpy, *The Globe and Mail*, 19 January 2002.

Exporting peace, order and good government should be the core of a disciplined foreign policy that shares the Canadian dream with the rest of the world.

Michael Ignatieff, commentator, address, biennial policy conference of the Liberal Party, Ottawa, 3 March 2005, excerpted as "A Generous Helping of Liberal Brains," *The Globe and Mail*, 4 March 2003.

PEACEKEEPING *See also* Canadian Armed Forces; Holidays: Remembrance Day; Peace

Countries that have soldiers in charge seem, more often than not, to be the ones where democracy is but a flickering candle sitting in an open window with a forecast of rain.

Lewis MacKenzie, retired major general, UN chief of staff for peacekeeping in Sarajevo, August 1992, letter concerning his retirement, *The Globe and Mail*, 21 January 1993.

If blessings at home dictate responsibilities abroad—and I believe they do—Canada has a big bill to pay.

Lewis MacKenzie, retired major general, "There's No Risk-Free Way to Keep Peace," *The Globe and Mail*, 14 September 2000.

There are times when the best medication and therapist simply can't help a soldier suffering from this new generation of peacekeeping injury.

Roméo Dallaire, former commander, UN Assistance Mission in Rwanda, letter to the CBC, expressing thanks for the corporation's coverage of his nervous collapse, 3 July 2000, "Bystanders to Genocide: Why the United States Let the Rwandan Tragedy Happen," *Atlantic*, September 2001.

And then, finally, there is Roméo Dallaire. It is both paradoxical and natural that the man who probably did the most to save Rwandans feels the worst.

Samantha Power, commentator, "Bystanders to Genocide," *Atlantic*, September 2001. She is referring to the former commander, UN Assistance Mission in Rwanda, at the time of the massacre of 1994. She noted that officials at the United Nations, in common with the United States and other governments, withheld the military assistance that would have permitted him to accomplish his mission successfully and contain the slaughter.

PEARSON, LESTER B.

When Lester Pearson won the Nobel Peace Prize in 1957 for preventing World War II, he said, "Gee thanks." (A Pearsonian lisp embellishes this accurate story, but I am unable to master it.)

Peter Gzowski, host of CBC Radio's *Morningside*, *The Private Voice: A Journal of Reflections* (1988).

Treat those two imposters, triumph and disaster, just the same.

Words from the once-popular "If" by **Rudyard Kipling**, British Imperial poet, in *Rewards and Fairies* (1909), inscribed above a doorway at Oxford University where Lester B. Pearson had studied and which he recalled the night in 1958 when John G. Diefenbaker's Conservatives routed his Liberal Party, in Peter Dempson, *Assignment Ottawa: Seventeen Years in the Press Gallery* (1968).

No one has greater affection for Mr. Pearson than myself, except perhaps Mrs. Pearson.

Barney Danson, Member of Parliament, on preserving historic sites, including the homes of prominent politicians, House of Commons, 7 December 1973.

The great Canadian novelist Robertson Davies used to tell of the response at a reception in British Columbia when the news came that Lester Pearson, later the Prime Minister of Canada, had been awarded the Nobel Peace Prize. "Well!" someone said. "Who does he think he is!"

Calvin Trillin, essayist, "Paper Baron," *The New Yorker*, 17 December 2001.

PENSIONS *See also* Employment

At a job interview, a Canadian will ask about the pension plan before inquiring about the starting salary.

Richard Stengel, journalist, "The Canadians," *Spy*, February 1988.

PERCEPTION *See also* Canadian Identity; Existence; Ideas; Imagination; Impressions

Very few people can perceive in a new way, and very few of those who can perceive in a new way can bring it into reality, can actualize it. Of those who can, some of them may be great and others probably not.

Tom Daly, producer and director, "Running Past Our Habit Patterns," *Pot-Pourri* (National Film Board), September 1973.

It's not what you think you are; it's what you think … you are!

Denis S.J. Shackel, management communications, Richard Ivey School of Business, London, Ont., 17 October 2005.

PERFECTIONISM *See also* Excellence

To strive for perfection is to kill love because perfection does not recognize humanity.

Marion Woodman, analyst and author, *Addiction to Perfection: The Still Unravished Bride* (1982).

"The world is as sharp as a knife" is a philosophy of perfectionism—a constant striving for the knife-edge perfection, which can be shown nowhere more perfectly than in art.

Wilson Duff, anthropologist, specialist in Haida art, random observation, quoted in *Bird of Paradox: The Unpublished Writings of Wilson Duff* (1996), edited by E.N. Anderson.

PESSIMISM *See also* Optimism

Pessimism is a form of intellectual laziness.

Jean Drapeau, long-time Montreal mayor, aphorism directed against critics of the Montreal Olympics, July 1975.

PETS *See* Animals; Cats; Dogs

PHARMACOLOGY *See also* Drugs & Drug Trade; Hallucinogenics; Medical Care; Medicine

Ths issue is that Canada isn't a drugstore for the U.S. It's been sustainable up to now, but who knows how long that will last?

Ujjal Dosanjh, federal minister of Health, defining Canada's position with respect to mail-order and internet pharmacies selling low-cost Canadian drugs to purchasers in the United States, quoted by Brian Laghi, "Canada Isn't Drugstore for U.S., Dosanjh to Say," *The Globe and Mail*, 10 November 2004.

Antipsychotics.

"The pharmaceutical term *antipsychotic* may not have been coined by Dr. **Heinz E. Lehmann** at the Verdun Protestant Hospital outside Montreal, who is renowned for the introduction into the Western Hemisphere of the antipsychotic medication chlorpromazine and is identified with it. Yet he published the key scientific paper on its effects in the *Archives of General Psychiatry*, February 1954. He certainly popularized the term *antipsychotic* to replace the term *tranquilizer* shortly after July 1958." Explanation from an unpublished paper "Heinz Lehmann and Psychopharmacology" (1999) by Thomas A. Ban.

Psychopharmacology in a strict sense means the study of the differential response to drugs, using medications as a pharmacological torch to delineate new disease entities. In a wider sense, it means simply studying the clinical response to medication.

Edward Shorter, medical historian, introduction, *A Dictionary of Psychiatry* (2005).

PHILANTHROPY *See also* Charity; Gifts & Giving

Anyone can give money, but it must be accompanied by the sweat and tears of its donor if it is to be from the heart.

Louis B. Mayer, New Brunswick–raised Hollywood mogul, credo, in Charles Foster, *Stardust and Shadows: Canadians in Early Hollywood* (2000).

Philanthropy is all about making a positive difference in the world by devoting your resources and your time to causes you believe in. In my case, I like to support causes where "a lot of good comes from a little bit of good," or, in other words, where the positive social returns vastly exceed the amount of time and money invested.

Jeff Skoll, Montreal-born Toronto-educated co-founder of the internet trading company eBay, philanthropist, referring to the Skoll Foundation, which he founded in 2000 in California's Silicon Valley, webpage of the Skoll Foundation, 20 December 2004. The foundation's motto is "Uncommon Heroes. Common Good."

Nobody cares how much you know until they know how much you care.

David Burgoyne, management specialist, characteristic observation, Richard Ivey School of Business, London, Ont., recalled by Denis S.J. Shackel, 17 October 2005.

PHILOSOPHY *See also* Belief; Civilization; Cruelty; Ethics; Good & Evil; Humanity; Ideas; Ideologies; Life; Luck; Principles; Values; Virtue & Vice

To carry in one's mind an abiding sense of the futility of human endeavour and the absurdity of human desire is a sure protection against the malignant narrowness that marks the men endowed with fixed convictions and positive ideas.

Stephen Leacock, humorist, *Essays and Literary Studies* (1919).

Lives are like snowflakes. Individually we are all different, but together all the same.

Hugh Arscott, aphorist, *Hugh's Views: Volume 4* (2000).

The philosopher has to be banished from the poet's republic: perhaps the *Symposium* says so.

Northrop Frye, cultural critic, aphorism, "Notebook 3" (1946–1948), *Northrop Frye Newsletter*, fall 2000.

For every philosopher, in every age, the first question must be: just what is philosophy?

Francis Sparshott, philosopher, "Speculation and Reflection," *Looking for Philosophy* (1972).

This book is about you. And me. And every other creature that ever measured itself in the mirror of consciousness. More broadly still, it is about every creature that ever swam, or walked, or flew over the face of the Earth.

Paul M. Churchland, philosopher, introduction, *The Engine of Reason, the Seat of the Soul: A Philosphical Journey into the Brain* (1995).

That key philosophical questions have gone unsolved—not unanswered, but unsolved—is something that chases many away, once they find that they will not find ready solutions to life's common quandaries. However, it is just this perennial, unyielding character of some philosophical questions that gives them that much more appeal for some, myself included.

F. Michael Walsh, collector and benefactor of philosophical texts, *Philosophy & Bibliophily: An Exhibition of the Walsh Philosophy Collection* (2004), The Thomas Fisher Rare Book Library, University of Toronto.

PHOTOGRAPHY *See also* Arts & Artists; Existence; Perception

You can even make a roaring lion stand still to be photographed.

Winston Churchill, British wartime leader, to Yousuf Karsh after the Ottawa portrait photographer snatched the cigar from Churchill's mouth during the latter's sitting for his portrait, Speaker's Chamber, Centre Block, Parliament Buildings, Ottawa, 30 December 1941. Karsh recalled the retort in CBC-TV's *Karsh: The*

Searching Eye, 23 January 1986. The photographic session resulted in the famous portrait of Churchill that inspired millions during World War II.

To make enduring photographs, one must learn to see with one's mind's eye, for the heart and the mind are the true lens of the camera.

Yousuf Karsh, portrait photographer, quoted on the dust jacket of *Karsh Portraits* (1976).

For me the kind of still picture which you can look at indefinitely without a time limit is an image of a moment of rest of some kind, an eternal moment.

Tom Daly, producer and director, "It's the Mind That Moves," *Pot-Pourri* (National Film Board), summer 1977.

Photography is the great folk art of the twentieth century. It is not an elitist art-form—therein lies its strength and appeal.

Lorraine Monk, photography editor, proposal for the creation of Image Canada: A Canadian Centre for Photography, *Canadian Photography*, February 1978.

You make photographs with your body. Your eyes have feet.

Geoffrey James, photographer, interviewed on CBC Radio's *Sunday Morning*, 3 March 2002.

To me, his work is more important than the flag.

Lorraine Monk, photography specialist, tribute to Richard Harrington and his portraits of Eskimos, quoted by John Goddard in "Richard Harrington: 1911–2005," *The Toronto Star*, 13 October 2005.

PHYSICIANS *See* Doctors

PHYSICS *See also* Research; Science

One of the chief results of experiments such as those which my colleagues and myself have done over the years and which are now conducted by a large number of people is confidence. Because you're getting at the very roots, the guts of the theories that you used in conceptualizing and talking. We talk about atoms, don't we? We talk about the electrons, the holes and the electrons in semiconductors, and all these things. If you have experimental methods, you get at the very things themselves and do not have to rely on enormous calculations from a theoretical base for whatever you observe in real life or in the laboratory. So it's this confidence which is one of the chief products.

Bertram Brockhouse, physicist and Nobel laureate, address, "Nobel Prize Winning Work on Neutrons," Toronto, 19 January 1995, The Empire Club of Canada.

If you look back through history, every industrial revolution has come from a breakthrough in theoretical physics.

Mike Lazaridis, CEO of Research in Motion (which launched the BlackBerry, the handheld wireless-email device), and leading founder of the Perimeter Institute, a community for theoretical physicists dedicated to extending theories of space, time, and matter, in Ben Worthen, *CIO Magazine*, 1 October 2002.

PIONEERS *See also* Settlers

I have learned to feel a great admiration for your pioneer people with their warm-hearted enthusiasm and their fresh minds. They are still so close to nature as to love her open spaces and her wide prairie lands. The invigorating climate of the cold north has kept their blood warm with human perfection and I welcome with hopefulness their eager efforts to fashion a new world.

Rabindranath Tagore, Bengali sage, farewell message delivered to the Southam newspaper chain, Fourth Triennial Conference of the National Council of Education, Vancouver, 8–13 April 1929, quoted in "Tagore," *The Canadian Theosophist*, May 1929.

This memorial was erected to honour the memory of the men and women in this land throughout their generation who braved the wilderness, maintained the settlements, performed the common task without praise or glory and were the pioneers of political freedom and a system of responsible government which became the corner stone of the British Commonwealth of Nations.

Inscription on the Niagara Falls Pioneer Memorial Arch, unveiled by Prime Minister Mackenzie King in 1937 to mark the 100th anniversary of the Rebellion of 1837 and dismantled in 1968; *Fifty-third Annual Report of the Niagara Parks Commission 1938 and 1939* (1940).

PITY

Pity is never wholly free of contempt.

Robin Skelton, poet and aphorist, characteristic observation, May 1990.

PLACES *See also* Canadian Identity; Cities & Towns; Place Names

Are there no places in this country that have their stories? Are we yet too young a nation (outside of Quebec) to possess anything of this sort?

David Boyle, archaeologist, "Canadian Folk-Lore," *The Globe*, 11 December 1897.

Where is here?

Northrop Frye, literary critic, "Haunted by Lack of Ghosts," *The Canadian Imagination: Dimensions of a Literary Culture* (1977), edited by David Staines. Frye elaborated: "The Canadian problem of identity seemed to me primarily connected with locale, less a matter of 'Who am I?' than of 'Where is here?'"

We can walk between two places and in so doing establish a link between them, bring them into a warmth of contact, like introducing two friends.

Thomas A. Clark, poet, "In Praise of Walking," *Wild Culture: Specimens from* The Journal of Wild Culture (1992), edited by Whitney Smith and Christopher Lowry.

How did he get here? What is he doing here? As the Canadians say, Where is here?

Self-questioning of the main character, Oskar, a German-Jewish Holocaust survivor and long-time Toronto resident, in **Rick Salutin**'s novel *A Man of Little Faith* (1988). "Where is here?" is Northrop Frye's formulation of Canadian identity in terms of geography and culture.

We need to imagine foreign places in order to feel at home.

Alberto Manguel, traveller and writer, "Breakfasts of the Poor," *The Times Literary Supplement*, 27 July 2001.

The only way to know Ontario, or any place, is to look at the ground under one's feet and start thinking about it.

John Bentley Mays, author, *Arrivals: Stories from the History of Ontario* (2002).

PLACE NAMES *See also* Cities & Towns; Places

Place names had always been the most permanent things in the short little human story.

Observation of a character in **Hugh MacLennan**'s novel *Voices in Time* (1980).

You would like it here for we have some beauties which originated in the minds of homesick surveyors—Albion, Caledon, Asphodel and the like. They sit strangely on the Canadian landscape but are much more to my taste than Moose's Gut, Wolf's Cave and Bear's Grease and Indian names meaning all sorts of strange things. Our aboriginal people insist that these are part of what they call Our Heritage. Not my heritage, dammit, and now and then I long for Wales.

Robertson Davies, man of letters, letter, 17 July 1989, *For Your Eye Alone: Letters, 1976–1995* (1999).

Arcola, Sask.

Movie Town 1976 / There are no strangers here: / Only friends you haven't yet met.

Message on badges worn in Arcola, the Saskatchewan town where *Who Has Seen the Wind* was filmed in 1977.

Banff, Alta.

The hotel, a huge baronial edifice that would not have been out of place in Bavaria, was echoing with out of season emptiness, but his room was warm and comfortable with a magnificent view of cataracts at the bend of the river below and the summit of Cascade Mountain pink-sugared where the setting sun kissed the first dusting of snow.

Narration from actor and writer **David Niven**'s novel *Go Slowly, Come Back Quickly* (1981).

Canso, N.S.

The constitution of the universe will radiate from these islands of Canada.

Maharishi Mahesh Yogi, India-born spiritual leader and promoter of Transcendental Meditation, dedicating two islands for a school and conference centre near the town of Canso, N.S., October 2005, quoted by James Keller, "Indian Guru Who Taught the Beatles Sets Sights on Canada," *The Globe and Mail*, 17 October 2005. Past projects include an international spiritual theme park for Niagara Falls and the Natural Law Party and its "yogic flyers," which ran candidates in the 1993 federal election.

Climax, Alta.

Climax / Do Come Again.

Wording on the sign on Highway 18 on driving west from the southern Alberta town of Climax, said to have been in place in the 1950s.

Cobalt, Ont.

For we'll sing a little song of Cobalt. / If you don't live there it's your fault.

Refrain of "The Cobalt Song" (1910), in J.B. Macdougall, *Two Thousand Miles of Gold* (1946).

Dawson City, Y.T.

Up the Pole! I went to Dawson City to open it. It's day and night. All night all day. I can't stay awake all day at night! When I got back to New York, I couldn't sleep when it was dark!

Beatrice Lillie, comedienne, recalling the invitation extended by Bert Lahr, friend and comedian, to accompany him to Dawson City to open the musical *Foxy* in 1964, as noted by Bruce Laffey, *Beatrice Lillie: The Funniest Woman in the World* (1989).

Fort McMurray, Alta.

Fort McMurray's lively (read: rowdy) expat community (read: highly paid rig workers) has transformed this remote, landlocked city into one of the largest Newfoundland communities outside St. John's. Newfoundland, in turn, can be considered an outpost of Iceland ... and on it goes.

Will Ferguson, travel writer, "On the Road with Will," *Maclean's*, 15 October 2004.

Hamilton, Ont.

There's something very, very strange and striking about it.

Werner Herzog, Austrian film director, referring to Hamilton, Ont., interviewed in Toronto by Susan Walker, "Herzog Finds Poetry in Buddhism," *Toronto Star*, 25 April 2003.

Hull, Que.

"Papa," I asked, "is it true Hull is wicked?"

"Not in the part where they play baseball," my father assured me.

Dialogue from "Got Hit a Home Run," *The Happy Time* (1945), a memoir set in Ottawa, by **Robert Fontaine**.

Kananaskis Park, Alta.

Big enough for a group photo, but small enough that nine would be a crowd.

Description of Kananaskis Park, a small provincial park located in the Rocky Mountains between Calgary and Banff, Alta., selected as the site of the Group of 8 summit meeting scheduled for 2002, as quoted by Bruce McCall, "Unreachable? It's an Ideal Summit Site!" *The New York Times*, 29 July 2001.

Kingston, Ont.

A mirage, like all of Kingston. A soft-voiced mirage; nothing brash about the townsfolk. It is the capital of an imaginary country, that old Loyalist Canada that, despite achieving self-consciousness, never actually happened.

David Warren, columnist, "Kingston: Larger Than Life and Twice as Quiet," *National Post*, 2 August 2003.

Kitchener, Ont.

Kitchener is big enough to have two clocks.

W.L. Mackenzie King, prime minister, address delivered from the steps of Kitchener's City Hall in the mid 1940s, where one of the city's two public clocks lacked hands.

Lachine, Que.

I am here as a kind of testimony to the fact that it's possible for a child from Lachine to do some things which have been called—not by me but by others—extraordinary. It also fits very well with my own resistance to that deterministic philosophy that tells you that the place you come from makes you absolutely; it does not. The human soul has its own way to declare its freedom and to develop itself, and it is not true to say, "Show me where you came from and I'll tell you what you are."

Saul Bellow, novelist born in Lachine, Que., address, dedication of the Saul Bellow Municipal Library, Lachine, Que., 12 June 1984, in James Atlas, "Last Days of a Ladies' Man," *Saturday Night*, 14 October 2000.

Un grand écrivain né à Lachine, conscient de ses origines et orienté vers la compréhension humaine; America's greatest urban novelist, Lachine-born, slum-raised, streetwise kid, Chicago-made, world-renowned writer.

Wording on the bilingual plaque unveiled in the presence of Lachine-born Chicago-formed novelist Saul Bellow at the dedication of the Saul Bellow Municipal Library, Lachine, Que., 12 June 1984, in James Atlas, "Last Days of a Ladies' Man," *Saturday Night*, 14 October 2000.

Lake of the Woods, Ont.

These islands are books in themselves … you could think of the lakes as libraries.

Louise Erdrich, Minnesota-based author born of an Ojibwe-French mother, writing about the collections of glyphs and books in the region, *Books and Islands in Ojibway Country* (2003).

London, Ont.

Zurich is … the size of London, Ontario, but a great, international hub.

Tyler Brûlé, Winnipeg-born marketing consultant based in London, England, and responsible for the newly named airline "Swiss," interviewed by Anne Kingston, "Poised for the Next Big Thing," *National Post*, 6 July 2002.

Medicine Hat, Alta.

In Hollywood, about twenty years ago, I met Hedda Hopper, who was so influential she could make or break a career by just leaving a name out of her column. Later, she wrote, "All my life I've wanted to meet someone who actually came from Medicine Hat! Now one of my life's ambitions is realized!"

Roloff Beny, globe-trotting photographer, born in Medicine Hat, address, "What Is Wrong with Loving Canada?" Toronto, 27 October 1983, The Empire Club of Canada.

Moose Jaw, Sask.

It's going to be the biggest social event Moose Jaw has seen in years.

Line spoken by Lou (Burt Lancaster) to Sally (Susan Sarandon) about the delivery from Atlantic City of six dozen roses to a funeral in Moose Jaw in the movie *Atlantic City* (1980), directed by **Louis Malle**.

Opeongo Lake, Ont.

Now that the boys are dead and gone / And grim old age is mine, / A phantom team and teamster start / From Renfrew, rain or shine—// Aye, dreaming, dreaming, I go teaming / On the Opeongo Line.

Anonymous fragment composed by a former teamster on the Opeongo Line, a colonization road extending nearly 100 miles from Farrell's Landing on the Ottawa River to Lake Opeongo, Renfrew County, Ont., opened in 1854, reproduced by N. Brian Davis, *The Poetry of the Canadian People, 1720–1920* (1976).

Peterborough, Ont.

A few years later Gerald Robinson, a Toronto architect, applied the superellipse to a parking garage in a shopping centre in Peterborough, a Toronto suburb.

Martin Gardner, columnist and polymath, uncharacteristically uncertain of his geography, "Piet Hein's Superellipse," *Mathematic Carnival* (1957).

Porcupine, Ont.

Rings on my fingers, corns on my toes, / God up in Porcupine, everybody knows. / Put on your snowshoes, and hit the trail with me, / For P-o-r-c-u-p-i-n-e—that's me!

Verse of the traditional "Porcupine Song," *Canada's Story in Song* (1965), edited by Edith Fowke and Alan Mills.

Red Deer, Alta.

Red Deer, you are beautiful and you always will be.

Stockwell Day, newly elected leader of the Canadian Alliance, celebrating his electoral victory in Red Deer, Alta., 8 July 2000, in Daniel Girard, *Toronto Star*, 9 July 2000. Day first won the Red Deer North riding in the Alberta legislature in May 1986 and was re-elected three times.

Resolute Bay, N.W.T.

Welcome to Resolute Bay Hotel / Reasonable Rates / In the Heart of Canada's North Land / Surrounded by Miles and Miles of Nothing but Miles and Miles.

Sign in the hotel at Resolute Bay, N.W.T., noted by Leonard Brockington in 1954.

Saint John, N.B.

The city of Saint John, New Brunswick, has boasted on many occasions that Walter Pidgeon was born there, but at the time of writing nobody in authority had chosen to name a street or perhaps a square or park after this gracious star, who brought nothing but credit to the city in which he started life. If anyone out there is listening, perhaps it is still not too late to make amends.

Charles Foster, biographer, referring to Hollywood star Walter Pidgeon (1898–1984), native of Saint John, *Once Upon a Time in Paradise: Canadians in the Golden Age of Hollywood* (2003).

Strathroy, Ont.

There was acre upon acre of farmland, and all we could see—though I pressed my forehead against the cold window—all we could see were little lights here and there. And I was wondering: What kind of people live in those houses? And what kind of people worked in this part of Canada? And lived and loved here?

Pierre Elliott Trudeau, prime minister, musing about a train trip made through Strathroy earlier that evening, which he mentioned to reporters at the airport at London, Ont., 13 October 1983. One recalls Ontario Premier John Sandfield Macdonald's question in 1871: "What the hell has Strathroy done for me?"

Wadena, Sask.

For me, the centre of the universe will always be Wadena, Saskatchewan.

Pamela Wallin, broadcaster, *Since You Asked* (1998). The town's main street is named "Pamela Wallin Drive."

Waterloo, Ont.

Re "Canada's Physics Shangri-La" (April 10): As an erstwhile resident of Waterloo, Ont., I take exception to the depiction of my home-town as a "cultural vacuum." Surely, you have confused Waterloo with Kitchener.

Rob Woolstencroft, resident of Oakville, Ont., Letters to the Editor, *The Globe and Mail*, 14 April 2004.

PLANNING *See also* Cities & Towns; Innovation

When schemes are laid in advance, it is surprising how often the circumstances fit in with them.

Sir William Osler, physician, "Internal Medicine as a Vocation," *Aequanimitas* (1932).

They are now working towards a solution which will dissatisfy everybody. That is the Canadian way of getting complete agreement.

Observation made in the CBC Radio's "The Man from Number Ten," a play in the "Stage 50" series directed by **Andrew Allan**, fall 1950.

It is not good enough to be on the side of the angels when the devil is in the details.

Chantal Hébert, columnist, "Fools Rush in Where Angels …," *Toronto Star*, 6 December 2002.

Zoning rules and tools neglect performances that outrage people. What are actually needed are prohibitions of destructive performances.

Jane Jacobs, urban planning critic, *Dark Age Ahead* (2004).

I have no plan to have plans.

Attributed to **William (Bill) Davis**, former Ontario Conservative premier, by Murray Campbell, "Queen's Park," *The Globe and Mail*, 19 October 2004.

POETRY *See also* Authors; Literature; Writers & Writing

You do not translate your poetry into words, but into deeds. In a young country it is better to make poetry in actions than in words. I have seen your great powerhouses at Niagara Falls. Great simple buildings where all that energy is translated. They are very beautiful. Very impressive. The turbines! There you have revolving poetry … you are building up a young country; do not worry too deeply about interpreting it. You are expressing yourself in another medium than literature, but you are expressing yourselves.

Paul Claudel, French poet and ambassador to Washington, D.C., accepting an honorary degree from the University of Toronto, interviewed by Merrill Denison, *Toronto Daily Star*, 7 November 1928, as noted by Greg Gatenby, *Toronto: A Literary Guide* (1999).

A poet on a platform reciting his verses, with suitable growls and making passes in his hair, is behaving like an ape. They would recognize and welcome him on the Congo.

Stephen Leacock, humorist, *How to Write* (1943).

The singing has not made me less alone / Nor will it you.

Concluding lines of **Philip Child**'s poem "To a Future Poet," *Victorian House and Other Poems* (1951).

Poetry is the most highly developed and sensitive form of language there is. In finding out how to read poetry we find out certain things about poetry without which we can scarcely read it.

George Whalley, scholar, commencement address, Rothesay College School, N.B., 1959, *George Whalley: Remembrances* (1989), edited by Michael D. Moore.

Poets are supposed to liberate the words—not to chain them in phrase. Who told poets they were supposed to think? Poets are meant to sing and to make words sing.

Brion Gysin, artist and writer, "Cut-Ups Self-Explained" (1964), *Back in No Time: The Brion Gysin Reader* (2001), edited by Jason Weiss. Gysin was born in London, England, and died in Paris, France, and spent his youth in the 1920s in and around Edmonton, Alta. He developed the "cut-up" technique with the American writer William S. Burroughs.

This is the first world conference of poets since Homer. Let's hope it will be the last until another Homer comes along.

Irving Layton, poet, addressing a session of the Expo World Poetry Conference 1967, in John Robert Colombo, "Poetry at Expo," *The Canadian Forum*, October 1967.

I say the best Canadian poet is Phil Esposito, and that is not a joke.

Yevgeny Yevtushenko, Russian poet, after watching a hockey game in Maple Leaf Gardens, in John Fraser, *The Globe and Mail*, 6 December 1973.

Wherever a poem comes from, it's not from good intentions.

Dennis Lee, poet, postlude, *Alligator Pie* (1974).

It is the destiny of Montreal to show the country from time to time what poetry is.

Louis Dudek, poet and aphorist, in André Farkas and Ken Norris, introduction, *Montreal: English Poetry of the Seventies* (1977).

In a traditional culture, a bard is the reciter of the identity of the past. I have tried to change it to make the bard the invoker of the identity of the future.

William Irwin Thompson, theorist, "Mind Jazz," *Wild Culture: Specimens from* The Journal of Wild Culture (1992), edited by Whitney Smith and Christopher Lowry.

We could make forays down streets called Australia, Canada (a short street that), New Zealand, India....

Michael Schmidt, anthologist, giving reasons why his anthology of English-language poetry does less than justice to countries other than the United Kingdom and the United States, *Lives of the Poets* (1998).

Poetry is a kind of content, or a quality of content, and verse is a kind of form.

Robert Bringhurst, scholar and poet, *A Story as Sharp as a Knife: The Classical Haida Mythtellers and Their World* (1999).

The irony of the situation is that if most writers of poetry & other dabbles would think entirely of the benefit to them & not at all of publication, the publishable merit of what they produce would be greatly & constantly increased.

Northrop Frye, cultural and literary critic, aphorism, "Notebook 3" (1946–1948), *Northrop Frye Newsletter*, fall 2000.

There are far more writers of bad poetry than there are readers of good.

Pauline Michel, Poet Laureate of Parliament, in Natasha Gauthier, "An Athlete of the Soul," *National Post*, 17 December 2004.

POLICE *See also* Governance; Law; Order; Royal Canadian Mounted Police

How can the police be expected to do a good job when people leave their doors unlocked making them a temptation to criminals?

Complaint of a chief constable of Toronto, Report of 1895 (unpublished), as in Maureen Jennings, "To Protect and Serve: Policing in Victorian Toronto," *BoucherCon 2004: Murder among the Maples, 7–10* Oct. 2004.

The cop's a nasty fellow / He grabs you with a curse. / He doesn't make life better / But he stops it getting worse.

Unpublished verse "Observation" (1975), by **F.R. Scott**, poet and lawyer.

In backward countries, the police execute the criminals; in progressive ones, the criminals execute the police.

Richard J. Needham, columnist, *The Wit and Wisdom of Richard Needham* (1977).

Advanced cultures are usually sophisticated enough, or have been sophisticated enough at some point in their pasts, to realize that foxes shouldn't be relied on to guard hen houses.

Jane Jacobs, urban planning critic, *Dark Age Ahead* (2004).

POLITENESS

Certainly it did not appear to me that courtesy to strangers could be numbered among the Canadian virtues.

Ida Pfeiffer, Austrian traveller who visited Montreal in 1854 and was refused accommodation at a hotel and was snubbed when she asked people in the street for directions because she was a woman travelling alone, *A Lady's Second Journey around the World* (1856).

A real saving grace for me has been not wanting to sacrifice my Canadian politeness. It really has been a major part of the way I approach my success and the challenges of this part of my life.

Michael J. Fox, Canadian-born film star, on facing health problems, interviewed by David Rakoff, "The Next Chapter," *The New York Times Magazine*, 31 March 2002.

Being polite can be deadly.

Frank Ogden, futurist, with specific reference to reticence before medical specialists, characteristic remark, 15 January 2003.

POLITICAL CORRECTNESS *See also* Censorship; Freedom of Expression

Virtually everyone except Anglo-Saxon, able-bodied, middle-aged, heterosexual, male, middle-class Ontarians is now the officially recognized bearer of a subventionable grievance.

Conrad Black, publisher and historian, *A Life in Progress* (1993).

Here, now, is the latest law / That Ottawa's declared: / Ghosts must be referred to / As "Dimensionally Impaired."

Emo Philips, U.S. comedian, characteristic remark, from his website, 2003.

Increasingly, we are becoming an oversensitive and sissified bunch who are reluctant to speak plainly ourselves and are even aghast at the sound of anyone else doing it in our presence.

Christie Blatchford, columnist, referring to the departure of hockey commentator Don Cherry from CBC-TV, "Last of the Curmudgeons," *The Globe and Mail*, 1 May 2004.

POLITICAL PARTIES *See also* Bloc Québécois; Canadian Alliance; Conservative Party of Canada; Government; Liberal Party; New Democratic Party; Parti Québécois; Politics; Progressive Conservative Party; Reform Party

This is always the way with parties. "Socialist parties" become bourgeois as they have in France, "labour parties" quit work and wear evening dress and "clerical parties" go to the devil.

Stephen Leacock, humorist, *My Discovery of the West: A Discussion of East and West in Canada* (1937).

Canadian political parties operate like secular arms of the Unitarian Church. The only faith they require is attendance.

Robert Fulford, columnist, *Maclean's*, 8 July 1963.

We, in Canada, must be considered by the rest of the world, if they consider us at all, as a nation of a certain fixed irresolution. Our parties are models of piety, full of ritual, liturgy and platitude, timid about change, standing forever in the shadows of history, reluctant to embrace the true spirit of the party system, free speech, open debate, the clash of ideas, and hesitant before the rising spirit of democracy.

Dalton Camp, national president, Progressive Conservative Association of Canada, address, "Opportunity for Reform," Toronto, 20 October 1966, The Empire Club of Canada.

If None of the Above were an organized party, it could be in opposition.

Rick Mercer, television comedian, "The Election Has 22 Minutes," *Time*, 16 June 1997. This observation was made before the formation of the Canadian Alliance.

Conservatives falsify the past, socialists falsify the future, and Liberals falsify the present.

J.L. Granatstein, historian, *Who Killed Canadian History?* (1998).

I'm from North Winnipeg, remember, where the right wing votes NDP and the left wing votes Communist.

Avrom Isaacs, art dealer, referring to his birthplace in the 1930s, in Sarah Milroy, "Goodbye to All That, One More Time," *The Globe and Mail*, 26 May 2001.

We have been described as the world's first postmodern nation. Certainly we are the most diverse and pluralistic and fragmented, all of which are postmodern qualities. Maybe we are on the way to becoming the world's first post-party democracy.

Richard Gwyn, columnist, "Home and Away," *Toronto Star*, 21 June 2001.

Don't give up on government. It's the only thing that you own.

Attributed to **Dalton Camp**, political theorist, by columnist Silver Donald Cameron, 14 April 2002.

Liberals tend to fish from rented rowboats, while Tories prefer casting off docks, letting the fish come to them. Conservatives also favour sleeping in twin beds, while Grits preferred doubles, which explains why there were more Liberals.

Peter C. Newman, journalist and memoirist, *Here Be Dragons: Telling Tales of People, Passion, and Power* (2004).

POLITICIANS *See also* Government; Politics

"In Canada," has it been said, "there is more politics to the square foot than there is in any other country under the sun." If the fruits of confederation are not overdrawn, it must be said that in Canada there is more political rascality to the square foot than anywhere this side of St. Petersburg or Constantinople.

Unidentified American reviewer of **Goldwin Smith**'s *Canada and the Canadian Question* (1891), *The Atlantic Monthly*, August 1891.

We have had good men at Ottawa and bad—and some of the pages of history they have made for us we would gladly wipe out—but when the last word of censure is said, it still remains true that in the main, for the most part, most of our public men have cared a lot for the common good. Those who hold differently betray ignorance and malice and certainly invite peril.

Grattan O'Leary, newspaper editor, address, "The Public and the Politicians," Toronto, 30 March 1933, The Empire Club of Canada.

I was surprised the other day in passing by one politician friend's office where I noticed a somewhat cynical sign on his wall that read: "Old age and treachery will triumph over youth and idealism every time." I won't say what party he was with, but it was a revealing commentary on his thoughts.

Knowlton Nash, journalist and broadcaster, address, "Television News," Toronto, 26 June 1986, The Empire Club of Canada.

Americans worry about political jokes. We go out and vote for them.

Dave Broadfoot, comedian, in Sid Adilman, "Eye on Entertainment," *Toronto Star*, 5 October 2002.

You know, in politics it's very dangerous to have a philosophy. In a democracy you should have politicians who settle the problems that exist, not set out to prove philosophical ideals.

Daniel Johnson, later premier of Quebec, in conversation in Quebec City in the 1960s with Peter C. Newman, "Adieu to Separatism?" *Maclean's*, 12 May 2003.

In our culture, people who make a living pretending to be other people have the most credibility.

Paul Watson, environmental activist, interviewed by John F. Schumaker, "Earth Warrior," *The CCPA Monitor*, December 2003–January 2004.

I've always believed as a politician that you find out where the parade is going and get out in front of it.

Ralph Klein, Alberta premier, interview, Council of the Federation, Niagara-on-the-Lake, Ont., 29 July 2004, in Murray Campbell, "Klein Takes Centre Stage—Again," *The Globe and Mail*, 30 July 2004.

In reality, what politicians say is totally uninteresting and unimportant: it's what they do, and more to the point, fail to do. That's what counts.

Peter C. Newman, journalist and author, "Going Strong," *Maclean's*, 8 November 2004.

POLITICS *See also* Corruption; Elections; Government; Nepotism; Patronage; Political Parties; Politicians; Revolution

The reputation of the Canadian politicians is not the most savoury in the world; and from time to time rumours have been wafted across the border which have led us to think that, in the little capitals of the Provinces and in the general capital of the Dominion, there may be concentrated more political iniquity than that existing in the Augean stables which sporadically defile our own land.

Unidentified American reviewer of **Goldwin Smith**'s *Canada and the Canadian Question* (1891), *The Atlantic Monthly*, August 1891.

Let me begin at the beginning. Everybody in Mariposa is either a Liberal or a Conservative or else both.

Stephen Leacock, humorist, *Sunshine Sketches of a Little Town* (1912).

Put into the plainest prose, we are saying that the government of every country ought to supply work and pay for the unemployed, maintenance for the infirm and aged, and education and opportunity for the children.

Stephen Leacock, humorist, *The Unsolved Riddle of Social Justice* (1920).

Secret of political success in Canada—that of keeping Scottish Presbyterians and French Canadians in the same party.... [1949]

Harold Adams Innis, social scientist, *The Idea File of Harold Adams Innis* (1980), edited by William Christian.

What the masses want are monuments.

Jean Drapeau, Montreal mayor, observation made in the 1970s, in Brian McKenna, "Jean Drapeau," *The Canadian Encyclopaedia* (1988).

Bland works.

William (Bill) Davis, Ontario premier, replying to a reporter who asked him why he presented so bland a public personality, in Claire Hoy, *Bill Davis: A Biography* (1985).

I was reminded once again of something that a prairie politician said during the 1930s. He was talking about politics in Canada by region. It was written a long time ago and I think it's still quite apropos. He said, "In Atlantic Canada, politics is a way of life. In Quebec, it's a religion. In Ontario, it's a business. On the Prairies, it's a cause, and in British Columbia, it's entertainment." Now how did he know that, how could he look fifty years ahead?

Maude Barlow, chair, Council of Canadians, address, "Canadian Sovereignty in a Global Economy," Toronto, 19 November 1990, The Empire Club of Canada.

Politics at every level seemed to me a theatre in which conjurors of interchangeable stripes manipulated the public through its own gullibility.

Mavor Moore, theatre personality, *Reinventing Myself: Memoirs* (1994).

In short, we need to move away from the priorities of politics and toward the reality of global economics. Therein lies the promise of prosperity.

Frank Stronach, manufacturer, Magna International, address, "Operating within a Global Economy," Toronto, 10 February 1994, The Empire Club of Canada.

I love Canada because the politics are so dull. When politics are exciting, the guns soon drown out the speeches.

George Feyer, Hungarian-born cartoonist, quoted in *Maclean's*, 7 May 1960, as recalled by Terry Mosher, "A Felt Pen Always at the Ready," *Maclean's*, 14 October 2002.

When one person said to her, "You don't write political novels," she said, "Politics is what one person does to another." I thought that was pretty sharp.

Carol Shields recalling an exchange between a reader and Margaret Atwood, in Noah Richler, "Every Person Is a Novel," *National Post*, 2 November 2002.

It must not be forgotten, however, though it often is, that the things which Canadians value most, like health care and an orderly and humane society, are the result of political action, not of litigation over rights.

Robert Ivan Martin, law professor, *The Most Dangerous Branch: How the Supreme Court of Canada Has Undermined Our Law and Our Democracy* (2003).

Moreover, in an era of identity politics and the politics of recognition, a monocultural multiculturalism inflicts a disservice on the human experience.

Augie Fleras, sociologist, "Racializing Culture / Culturalizing Race," *Racism, Eh? A Critical Inter-Disciplinary Anthology of Race and Racism in Canada* (2004), edited by Camille A. Nelson and Charmaine A. Nelson.

Terrorism is a form of politics that aims at the death of politics itself.

Michael Ignatieff, essayist, *The Lesser Evil: Political Ethics in an Age of Terror* (2004).

Once, politics was about doing good, and it still is for many; increasingly, however, it is about doing well—an arena for the ambitious to pursue personal quests for wealth, status, or power.

Norman Spector, columnist, afterword, *A Secret Trial: Brian Mulroney, Stevie Cameron, and the Public Trust* (2004), by William Kaplan.

Another reason why there were more Liberals was that they had few qualms about counting the ballots of dead voters.... It was Mike Pearson who tipped me off to that bizarre practice when I saw him shortly after he had returned to Ottawa from campaigning in Newfoundland. "It was a cool afternoon," he told me. "Premier Joey Smallwood and I were being driven in the back of an open car through the streets of St. John's, waving to the people. When we went through a cemetery, I put my hands in my coat pockets to keep warm, but Joey nudged me, and said, 'No, Mike. Keep waving. This is our best district.'"

Peter C. Newman, journalist and memoirist, *Here Be Dragons: Telling Tales of People, Passion, and Power* (2004).

POLLUTION *See also* Acid Rain; Environmentalism; Kyoto Accord

Love has to become a stronger power than the poisons of self-interest and powerlessness or else we will all perish.

Anastasia M. Shkilnyk, sociologist, conclusion, *A Poison Stronger Than Love: The Destruction of an Ojibway Community* (1985).

To live is to pollute.

John Dales, economist, in Patrick Luciani, "Environmental Crisis? What Rot!" *National Post*, 15 July 2000.

Even if fully implemented, with the United States participating, Kyoto would delay global warming by a mere fraction of a degree in the coming century. Given how marginal Kyoto's benefits, and how great the cost, we should probably be grateful that none of the protocol's signatories were actually serious about honouring their commitments.

Editorial, "Kyoto's Actuaries," *National Post*, 15 February 2005.

I am a Canadian, and I am polluted. Polluted by dozens of toxic chemicals. Chemicals that are all around us, every day, and that accumulate in our bodies.... The reckless pollution of our environment and Canadian people must stop now.

Robert Bateman, artist and naturalist, volunteer for the Toxic Nation project sponsored by the Environmental Defence group, "A Canadian Artist's Lament," *Toronto Star*, 15 November 2005.

PORNOGRAPHY *See also* Sex

Nevertheless, only 12% of Canadian adults polled said that they regard pornography as a problem in their communities, with 59% seeing it either as a small problem or no problem at all.

Reginald W. Bibby and **Donald C. Posterski**, sociologists, *The Emerging Generation: An Inside Look at Canada's Teenagers* (1985).

Our society has many intellectual difficulties in coming to terms with pornography; but this is not because the issue is a complicated one, rather because we are not very smart.

David Warren, editor and columnist, "Moral and Aesthetic Squalor," *The Idler*, September–October 1989.

Child pornography and pedophilia. Two topics for which 98 per cent of my constituents have no tolerance. And neither do I.... Also, by extension, Goddard must also believe it is fine for a teacher to possess child porn. Perhaps even pictures of one of his own students, as long as he got the photos or videos from someone else.

Stockwell Day, Alberta Member of Legislative Assembly, provincial treasurer, lay pastor, and administrator of a Pentecostal Christian school, Letters to the Editor, *Red Deer Advocate*, 7 April 2000, that defamed lawyer Lorne Goddard, who was defending a teacher accused of possessing child pornography, in Jill Mahoney, "Is It the End of Day?" *The Globe and Mail*,

13 January 2001. The libel suit attracted national attention when it was settled out of court at the expense of Alberta taxpayers for an undisclosed amount on 22 December 2000.

Canada's increasing tolerance of content offensive to some viewers contrasts with the growing power of conservative religious minorities in the U.S. to influence advertisers and broadcast regulators to ban material deemed to be offensive. Incidentally, most of these same censors are staunch supporters of the right of Americans to bear arms, but in opposing bare arms they reveal their views on violence and nudity to be roughly opposite those of most Canadians.

Michael Adams, consultant, *Fire and Ice: The United States, Canada and the Myth of Converging Values* (2003), with Amy Langstaff and David Jamieson.

POST-MODERNISM *See also* Modernity

In fact, it has become apparent to me that Canadians are at the forefront of a fascinating and important social experiment: we are coming to define a new sociological "post-modernity" characterized by multiple, flexible roles and identities while Americans, weaned for generations on ideals of freedom and independence, have in general not found adequate security and stability in their social environment to allow them to assert the personal autonomy needed to enact the kind of individual explorations—spiritual, familial, sexual—that are taking place north of the border.

Michael Adams, consultant, *Fire and Ice: The United States, Canada and the Myth of Converging Values* (2003), with Amy Langstaff and David Jamieson.

The greatest danger of postmodernism is that it takes us away from the possibility of any kind of shared understanding based on science and its accumulated body of knowledge. Instead, it encourages a mushy-headed kind of moral relativism.

Neil Boyd, criminologist, Simon Fraser University, *Big Sister: How Extreme Feminism Has Betrayed the Fight for Sexual Equality* (2004).

POVERTY *See also* Charity; Food Banks; Homelessness; Hunger

The Victorians let the poor starve and shed tears over their graves; we swear at them and feed them.

Stephen Leacock, humorist, *My Discovery of the West: A Discussion of East and West in Canada* (1937).

You can never have international peace as long as you have national poverty.

Stephen Leacock, humorist, *Last Leaves* (1945).

The poor do not choose poverty. It is at once their affliction and our national shame.

David Croll, chair, Senate Committee on Poverty, 1971, in Thomas S. Axworthy, "Our Rights Revolutionaries," *National Post*, 5 March 2005.

The data show that the richest Canadians are not as well off financially as equivalent Americans, while the poorest Canadians are infinitely better off than their counterparts south of the border. All of which proves, at least in terms of income, that it's better to be poor in Canada and rich in America.

Michael Adams, consultant, *Fire and Ice: The United States, Canada and the Myth of Converging Values* (2003), with Amy Langstaff and David Jamieson.

If birds, with the brains they have, feed their young, how is it that there are still people who don't feed their children?

Bernard Landry, Quebec premier, asking a rhetorical question of representatives of poverty groups and indicating a small cranium with his fingers, Quebec City, 14 February 2003, in Alexander Panetta, "Bird-brained Comment Dogs Quebec Leader," *Toronto Star*, 20 February 2003.

The richest 25 million Americans have an income equal to that of almost 2 billion of the world's poorest. For the half of the world's population that lives on less than $2.00 a day, it would be better to be a European cow that receives $2.20 daily in subsidies from the European Community taxpayer.

John C. Polanyi, Nobel Laureate and peace activist, address, "World at the Crossroads: Law or War?" *University of Toronto Magazine*, spring 2003.

The poor and disabled are always the first to alert us to social breakdowns. If their plight worsens or their numbers increase, it is prudent for cushioned members of a culture to take notice.

Jane Jacobs, urban planning critic, *Dark Age Ahead* (2004).

POWER *See also* Atomic Energy; Authority; Electrical Power; Energy; Leadership; Nuclear Warfare; Supreme Court of Canada

Till power is brought to pooling / And outcasts share in ruling, / There will not be an ending / Nor any peace for spending.

F.R. Scott, lawyer and poet, "Dedication," *The Collected Poems of F.R. Scott* (1981).

Power has direction: it is always exercised downwards, towards the weak.

Jean Vanier, founder of L'Arche movement, *Becoming Human* (1998).

I believe in the power of One. If you want to do something, and you're determined, you will achieve it despite the obstacles.

Judy Feld Carr, humanitarian, in Sam Orbaum, "What One Woman Can Do," *Eskimos of Jerusalem and Other Extraordinary Israelis* (2001).

Hard power dissuades; soft power persuades.

Matthew Fraser, journalist and author, *Weapons of Mass Destruction* (2003).

If absolute power corrupts absolutely, so does powerlessness on the international stage.

Norman Spector, columnist and former diplomat, "Canada's Global Decline," *Ottawa Citizen*, 15 March 2003.

Prime Minister Paul Martin, we depend on you and expect you to change the laws and give the courts real power. Give the police real power. Take the power away from the Supreme Court and give it back to the House of Commons. We are a good country.

Colleen Myrol, mother of slain RCMP member Brock Myrol, part of the statement made on behalf of all the members of the Myrol family of Mayerthorpe, Alta., 4 March 2005, "Mother Pleads for a 'Stand on Evil,'" *National Post*, 5 March 2005.

PRAIRIES *See also* Alberta; Manitoba; Saskatchewan; Western Canada

I think we have a singular opportunity; I think Canada stands in a position of unique advantage. We have, as the world has never seen it before, a country that was born rich, I mean our western plains. Men are almost born rich out there. We have that heritage at our hand, and we have the rare spectacle of seeing the wealth of the west coming to meet the wealth of the east, just as the civilization of the west comes to meet the civilization of the east. I think that is going to give us a wonderful progress, the climax and outcome of which the most sanguine do not dream.

R.E. Knowles, Presbyterian clergyman and later interviewer, address, "Two Tokens of National Progress," Toronto, 27 February 1913, The Empire Club of Canada.

Half the trouble of the Prairie Provinces is that they feel cut off from the rest of the world.

John Buchan, Governor General Lord Tweedsmuir, letter of August 1936, in Janet Adam Smith, *John Buchan: A Biography* (1965).

The beer parlours on the Prairies are sacred places; they organize the landscape as the cathedrals organize Europe.

Robert Kroetsch, novelist, "The Plains of My Youth," *Weekend Magazine*, 9 July 1977.

A curious thing: on the prairie one can feel infinitely small, and at the same time infinitely uplifted.

Gabrielle Roy, novelist, *The Fragile Lights of Earth: Articles and Memories, 1942–1970* (1982), translated by Alan Brown.

The Westerner doesn't have a point of view. He has a vast panorama; he has such tremendous space around him.

Marshall McLuhan, media theorist, interviewed by Danny Finkleman, *Speaking of Winnipeg* (1974), edited by John Parr.

The grandeur of the place strikes me as unresolved, as if it too never quite achieves liftoff, but sinks back always under the sheer hugeness of everything.

Jan Morris, Anglo-Welsh traveller and essayist, commenting on "that infinite horizon" that lies over prairie cities, "Suddenly Saskatoon," *Saturday Night*, July–August 1990.

The Indians were the only inhabitants of this continent, and they were doing stuff that was changing nature. They were sculpting the prairies. Everywhere we look in nature we see processes like that going on.

William Irwin Thompson, theorist, "Mind Jazz," *Wild Culture: Specimens from* The Journal of Wild Culture (1992), edited by Whitney Smith and Christopher Lowry.

PRAYER *See also* Belief

We're all like two-year-olds when it comes to prayer.

Betty Jane Wylie, author, *No Two Alike* (1980).

PREDICTION & PROPHECY *See also* Destiny; Luck

If at any time through the negligence and carelessness of the lords, they fail to carry out the principles of the Good Tidings of Peace and Power and the rules and regulations of the confederacy and the people are reduced to poverty and great suffering, I will return.

Messianic prophecy attributed to **Dekanahwideh**, semi-mythical Native statesman, "The Traditional Narrative of the Origin of the Confederation of the Five Nations" (1900), in Arthur C. Parker, *Parker on the Iroquois* (1968), edited by William N. Felton.

The time will be when the white man will come and take all the land, the rivers and the forests, and there will be unhappiness among my people. I go North to make for all Indians a Happy Hunting Ground in which no white man may enter.

Messianic prophecy attributed to **Glooscap**, semi-mythical Native statesman, as noted by Roland H. Sherwood, *Atlantic Harbours* (1972).

Many things are yet to happen before others begin.

Oracular pronouncement of the psychic Mr. Yahi-Bahi in **Stephen Leacock**'s burlesque *Arcadian Adventures with the Idle Rich* (1914).

Prophecy consists of carefully bathing the inevitable in the eerie light of the impossible, and being the first to announce it.

Robertson Davies, man of letters, *Samuel Marchbanks' Almanack* (1967).

What about Canada? "Canada will be split up. It will divide. But the people won't feel it much."

Prophecy made by the **Zima** (identified only as a college-educated "witch"), Russian psychic, in Moscow in July 1968, as recorded by Sheila Ostrander and Lynn Schroeder, *Psychic Discoveries behind the Iron Curtain* (1970).

There's an old Newfoundland saying. He who lives by the crystal ball must learn to eat ground glass.

Michael Walker, Newfoundland-born director of the Fraser Institute, in Judy Steed, *The Globe and Mail*, 2 October 1981.

It is easier to write of the future if one is prepared to be a good sport about things, and predict a new and better world. Optimists are generally forgiven when they are proved wrong. People tend to be unforgiving of doomsayers, even when they are right.

Dalton Camp, columnist, "New Year Will Be No Worse Than the Old One," *Toronto Star*, 2 January 2002.

The world of 2050 is utterly beyond our predictive abilities. With the accelerating rate of change, any year-2000 guess as to what 2050 would be like is almost certainly going to be as far off base as a guess Christopher Columbus might have had about what 2000 would be like.

Robert J. Sawyer, science-fiction author, "The Future Is Already Here" (2004), *Relativity: Stories and Essays* (2004).

PREJUDICE *See also* Anti-Semitism; Race & Racism

It is easier to smash an atom than a prejudice.

Dick Beddoes, sports columnist, *The Globe and Mail*, 1 October 1979.

Jews, Blacks, Italians (and many others), Welcome. No Artists or Canadians.

Facetious wording of an advertisement for accommodation in the October issue of the community newspaper for the town of Kerhonkson, N.Y., as noted by Jordan Heath-Rawlings, "Making Peace the Canuck Way," *Toronto Star*, 7 December 2004.

PREMIERS *See also* Federal–Provincial Relations; Government

During my four years as premier, I've dealt with the people who organize these demonstrations. They are forceful. They are well-financed. They are well-organized. They know what they want and when they want it. As premier, you must always be prepared to listen to all viewpoints, not just the loudest or the most threatening. And you must make decisions which you know at the end of the day will benefit all the people of Ontario.

Mike Harris, premier of Ontario, address, "Strong Leadership for a Strong Ontario," Toronto, 12 May 1999, The Empire Club of Canada.

I was once seated next to Allan MacEachen at a dinner party. The former Liberal kingpin from Atlantic Canada told me that no provincial premier has ever become prime minister of Canada. "Really," I said. "Why do you think that is?"

He leaned in close, his eyes flashing. "Because provincial politicians learn to think small."

Edward Greenspon, columnist, "The Nation," *The Globe and Mail*, 14 September 2000.

Interestingly enough, you never hear the provincial premiers talking about transferring some of their powers to the municipalities or to the cities that badly need them.

Mel Hurtig, publisher and nationalist, *The Vanishing Country: Is It Too Late to Save Canada?* (2002).

PRIME MINISTERS *See also* Government

The Canadian political system is so jurisdictionally fragmented and the population so regionally fractious, the federal prime minister's role consists chiefly of endless debates with his provincial analogues.

Conrad Black, publisher, *A Life in Progress* (1993).

How important it is to have a prime minister who can be absolutely depended upon at all times to speak for Canada.

Michael Bliss, historian and columnist, "Joe Clark for P.M.? Get Serious," *National Post*, 16 June 2001.

Prime ministers are high-wire acrobats, swinging between opportunism and pragmatism, exercising the art of making possible the necessary.

Peter C. Newman, columnist, "Back in the Limelight," *National Post*, 11 May 2002.

A good man, Mr. Clark, but perhaps it was just as well that, with Arthur Meighen and John Turner and Kim Campbell, he goes down in Canadian history as one of our coffee-break prime ministers.

Michael Bliss, historian and columnist, "Clark: Never a Winner," *National Post*, 7 August 2002.

We have permitted a culture to arise that has been some thirty years in the making, one that can best be summarized by the one question that everyone in Ottawa believes has become the key to getting things done: "Who do you know in the PMO?"

Paul Martin, former minister of Finance, Liberal leadership contender, referring to the Prime Minister's Office (PMO) as it evolved under Jean Chrétien and his predecessors, address, Osgoode Hall, York University, Toronto, 22 October 2002, in Susan Delacourt, "Martin Vows to Make PM Less Mighty," *National Post*, 21 October 2002.

Since we don't have a resident monarch or pope, prime ministers become our role models.

Peter C. Newman, journalist and author, "Going Strong," *Maclean's*, 8 November 2004.

You cannot name a Canadian prime minister who has done as many significant things as I did, because there are none.

Brian Mulroney, prime minister, in Peter C. Newman, *The Secret Mulroney Tapes: Unguarded Confessions of a Prime Minister* (2005).

PRINCE EDWARD ISLAND

Truly, truly, something wonderful has happened in Charlottetown.... Small towns are best for arts festivals—especially if they are hard to get to, have no cultural tradition whatever, and are administered by artistic directors with bees in their bonnets—Bayreuth, Salzburg, Spoletto, Cannes, Tanglewood, Stratford....

Nathan Cohen, drama critic, referring to the establishment of the Charlottetown Festival, *Toronto Daily Star*, 21 August 1965, quoted by Mavor Moore in *Reinventing Myself* (1994).

Perhaps we should relegate the notion of "central Canada" to the scrap heap. We must strive to build a country that resists simplification, one that takes its strength from its diversity. It should be every Canadian's dream, and right, to become a "central Canadian," regardless of where they live, not by "going down the road" to Toronto, but rather by finding meaning and livelihood in their own community. This is the only idea of Canada which makes sense to me, and the only one worthy of our national destiny.

Joseph C. Ghiz, Prince Edward Island premier, address, "Canada: A View from the Regions," Toronto, 28 September 1989, The Empire Club of Canada.

Still, there does seem to be something evil about the place. Have you noticed that the number of letters in each word of Prince Edward Island is 666?

Allan MacEachen, historian, "If P.E.I. Didn't Exist, We'd Have to Invent It," *The Globe and Mail*, 24 October 2002.

PRINCIPLES *See also* Ethics; Integrity; Philosophy

The Alliance of which both Canada and the Czech Republic are now members is waging a struggle against the genocidal regime of Slobodan Milosevic. It is neither an easy struggle nor a popular one, and there can be different opinions on its strategy and tactics; but no person of sound judgment can deny one thing: this is probably the first war ever fought that is not being fought in the name of interests but in the name of certain principles and values.

Vaclav Havel, president of the Czech Republic, joint session of the Senate and the House of Commons, 30 April 1999.

When issues are matters of principle, there's no room for negotiation.

Lucien Bouchard, Quebec premier, resignation speech, National Assembly, Quebec City, 11 January 2001, in Sean Gordon, "A Dream Unfulfilled," Montreal *Gazette*, 12 January 2001. Bouchard was referring to the "comparative quantification of the suffering of the Jewish people" with that of Quebeckers within Canada.

You've got to stand up for what you believe in, even if you have to do it sitting down.

Barbara Turnbull, journalist, address, Unique Lives & Experiences lecture series, Toronto, 21 January 2001, in Dale Anne Freed, "Triumph of the Spirit," *Toronto Star*, 22 January 2001. At the age of 18 in 1983, she was shot by the robber of a convenience store where she worked part-time. She has been paralyzed from the neck down ever since.

History taught me that it is not just what you stand for, it is what you stand up for.

Rosalie Abella, justice, Ontario Court of Appeal, address, "Anti-Semitism: A Battle That Never Ends," *The Globe and Mail*, 5 July 2003.

In any great organization it is far, far safer to be wrong with the majority than to be right alone.

John Kenneth Galbraith, economist and author, in Kate Harries, "Scotch Hangover Subsidies," *Toronto Star*, 12 October 2003.

PRINTING *See also* Design; Typography

Good printers have much else to teach their clients, and the best typographer can always find something to learn. But the path from the editor's desk to the press-room floor remains a journey often fraught with danger and surprise.

Robert Bringhurst, author and typographer, *The Elements of Typographic Style* (2nd ed., 1996).

PRISONS *See also* Crime; Law

Our penal system—does this sound startling?—is psychologically worse than the callous European transportations of two hundred years ago. It is worse than the reviled practice of sending convicted men to Siberia in the Russia of the Czars.

Hugh MacLennan, novelist, foreword, Gertrude Katz, *The Time Gatherers: Writings from Prison* (1970).

Nothing is worse in prison than the consciousness of one's innocence.

Nicholas Catanoy, poet, "Notes from a Prison Wall (Fragment)," *Canadian Literature*, summer 1989.

It is in prison that one really comes to realize how precious a thing freedom is and that it's worth fighting for.

Frank Cotroni, Montreal Mafia boss who spent much of his adult life in prison, interview with a Quebec journalist in 1991, in Adrian Humphreys, "Mafia Boss 'The Big Guy' Dead at 72," *National Post*, 18 August 2004.

Solitary felt better than anything I ever had that was supposed to be closeness. In solitary the walls never laugh at you.

Statement made by an ex-convict who had served time in solitary confinement in **Catherine Gildiner**'s novel *Seduction* (2005).

No, I don't think I will ever be free. There are different kinds of prisons. There are prisons made of concrete and there are interior prisons. I think I will always be in an interior prison.

Karla Homolka, convicted murderer implicated in the deaths of three teenage girls, interviewed in French by Joyce Napier on Radio-Canada within hours of her release following a 12-year prison sentence, 4 July 2005, "Television Interview Transcript," *National Post*, 5 July 2005.

PRIVACY *See also* Confidentiality; Freedom; Mysteries; Secrets; Security & Intelligence

You are only what you are when no one is looking.

Bob Edwards, publisher, *Calgary Eye Opener*, 11 May 1918.

There's no place for the state in the bedrooms of the nation.

Pierre Elliott Trudeau, minister of Justice, addressing reporters on the bill he had just introduced into the House of Commons to revise the Criminal Code, 21 December 1967. This celebrated statement is variously quoted. What follows is a verbatim transcript of Trudeau's remarks at the scrum.

Take this thing on, uh, on, um, homosexuality. I think the, the view we take here is that, uh, there's no place for the state in the bedrooms of the nation, and I think that, uh, you know, what's done in private between adults, uh, doesn't concern the Criminal Code. When it becomes public, this is a different matter.

Pierre Elliott Trudeau, minister of Justice, answering reporters' questions about legislation that he had just introduced in the House of Commons, 21 December 1967. This verbatim transcription of the scrum was called "Quibbling over Quotes" by Blair Shewchuck, CBC News Online, 4 May 2004. Trudeau acknowledged at a later date that he had paraphrased journalist **Martin O'Malley**'s unsigned editorial in *The Globe and Mail,* 12 December 1967. O'Malley wrote: "Obviously, the state's responsibility should be to legislate rules for a well-ordered society. It has no right or duty to creep into the bedrooms of the nation." Trudeau's version is frequently quoted as "The state has no business in the bedrooms of the nation." Shewchuck observed, "It's worth noting that even highly articulate speakers appear less so when editors are unkind enough to include all the uhs, ums and false starts of natural, unscripted speech."

Whenever I visit a tourist attraction that has a guest register, I always sign it. After all, you never know when you'll need an alibi.

Robert J. Sawyer, science-fiction author, "Privacy: Who Needs It?" *Maclean's,* 7 October 2002.

For, as the silence from the stars attests, not only is an unexamined life not worth living, it may be that unexamined lives are too dangerous for us to allow them to be lived. The very future of humanity may depend on giving up the outmoded notion of privacy, rather than fighting to retain it.

Robert J. Sawyer, science-fiction author, arguing the benefits of disclosure, "Privacy: Who Needs It? (2002), *Relativity: Stories and Essays* (2004).

PROGRESS *See also* Change; Future; Growth; Improvement

We cannot continue as we are. In the history of every nation, as of every man, there is no such thing as standing still. There is no pause upon the path of progress. There is no stagnation but the hush of death.

Stephen Leacock, economist and humorist, address, "Education and Empire Unity," Toronto, 19 March 1907, The Empire Club of Canada.

The melancholy lesson is being learned that the path of human progress is arduous and its forward movement slow and that no mere form of government can aid unless it is inspired by a higher public spirit of the individual citizen than we have yet managed to achieve.

Stephen Leacock, economist and humorist, *The Unsolved Riddle of Social Justice* (1920).

Now has come to Canada in this generation a still greater pioneer work in human progress. For the debris of the dead past has to be cleared away in human life, the wild, untamed forces in human nature have yet to be overcome, the moral progress of humanity itself has to be pioneered by cutting down all social inequalities and by bridging over the gulfs between rich and poor and also between the different races of mankind. To this higher service of humanity I would venture to beckon this present generation in Canada before I leave her shores. For she has that unbounded moral energy and high enthusiasm of purpose which are most deeply felt when the heart of a people is young.

Rabindranath Tagore, Bengali sage, farewell message delivered to the Southam newspaper chain, Fourth Triennial Conference of the National Council of Education, Vancouver, 8–23 April 1929, quoted in "Tagore," *The Canadian Theosophist,* May 1929.

A bird smell of extinction follows *Homo sapiens* around the world.

Ronald Wright, author, Massey Lectures, *A Short History of Progress* (2004).

Like most things in life, progress comes in two kinds: good and bad. The invention of nuclear weapons (a brilliant feat technically) was the worst kind of progress because it may yet kill us all. But the invention of Viagra was good, it seems to me, because it softened the market in rhino horn, seal penises, and other supposedly aphrodisiac bits of wildlife.

Ronald Wright, essayist, "What Price Progress?" *The Globe and Mail,* 4 May 2005.

The lesson of ancient ruins is that economic limits can never exceed natural ones—or not for long. Jobs "created" at the cost of nature are merely stolen from the future, from our grandchildren. It is the duty of our leaders to know the difference between good progress and bad, and to err on the side of caution when they don't.

Ronald Wright, essayist, "What Price Progress?" *The Globe and Mail*, 4 May 2005.

PROGRESSIVE CONSERVATIVE PARTY

See also Canadian Alliance; Conservative Party of Canada; Conservatism; Political Parties

"PC" now stands for neither "progressive" nor "conservative" but simply the "Party of Clark."

Preston Manning, leader of the Canadian Alliance, address, "Think Big," Toronto, 9 March 2000, The Empire Club of Canada.

Founded 133 years ago, the Conservative Party today constitutes governments in five provinces representing almost 65 per cent of Canada's GDP.

Brian Mulroney, former prime minister, address, Conservative Party gathering, Markham, Ont., 9 June 2000, published in *The Globe and Mail*, 10 June 2000.

PROHIBITION

See also Alcohol; Food & Drink

It's easy, boy. The first question should be "Are you in favour of the New Temperance Act?" and the second "Are you in favour of the Old Prohibition Act?" People will vote for the first option because it is first, because it is new, and because it is temperance.

Advice of an elderly statesman to James **William MacKinnon**, novice deputy minister of Prince Edward Island, unsure how to draft a question for a plebiscite on the abolition of prohibition, as noted by Mary MacKinnon, "Lives Lived," *The Globe and Mail*, 4 August 2000.

PROMOTION

See also Advertising; Markets & Marketing

Canadians haven't been good at promoting ourselves. We've worked very hard on building the better mousetrap, but not telling people how we did it.

Alan Middleton, marketing mentor, Schulich School of Business, York University, Toronto, on being inducted into the Marketing Hall of Legends, in Tony Wong, "Drive and Charisma Define First Inductees," *Toronto Star*, 28 January 2005.

PROPERTY

See also Conservatism; Foreign Ownership; Free Trade; Land

Fundamentally, my property is mine, my work is mine, and the fruits of my work, the result of the efforts of my brain and my industry—that is mine and there is no other system of running society and there never will be—none, none, none! (Applause.)

Stephen Leacock, economist and humorist, address, "The Riddle of the Depression," Toronto, 16 February 1933, The Empire Club of Canada.

PROPHECY

See Prediction & Prophecy

PROSTITUTION

See also Sex

There is more white slave trafficking in Hamilton than any other city its size in the whole of America—not Canada, but America.

Ernest Bell, evangelist, referring to Hamilton, Ont., *Fighting the Traffic in Young Girls, or War on the White Slave Trade: A Complete and Detailed Account of the Shameless Traffic in Young Girls* (1911).

You know what I think Oshawa needs? A good brothel.

Xaviera Hollander, author and former madam known as "the Happy Hooker" and sometime Toronto resident, in David Cobb, *Toronto Life*, July 1973.

I guess that means we can say Flora MacDonald is one of the finest women ever to walk the streets of Kingston.

Quip at the expense of Flora MacDonald, popular Conservative member for Kingston and the Islands, dating from 1974, attributed to **John G. Diefenbaker**, disgruntled Conservative leader, by Sean O'Sullivan, *Both My Houses* (1986), written with Rod McQueen.

We don't sell our bodies. Housewives do that. What we do is *rent* our bodies for sexual services.

Valerie Scott, Toronto prostitute by choice, who prefers the term "whore," spokesperson for the Canadian Organization for the Rights of Prostitutes (CORP), in Rosie DiManno, *Toronto Star*, 27 November 1989.

PROVINCES

Canada's states are called provinces for a good reason: provincialism.

Bruce McCall, Canadian-born New York humorist, "O Canada! That Fractured, Frosty Land," *The New York Times*, 21 November 2004.

PSYCHIATRY *See also* Depression; Madness; Medicine; Mental Illness; Therapy

In Europe, people go to the psychiatrist because of a symptom, in America because of a problem.

Henri F. Ellenberger, psychiatrist and historian, "A Comparison of European and American Psychiatry," *Bulletin of the Menninger Clinic*, Volume 19 (1955), as noted by Edward Shorter, *A History of Psychiatry* (1997).

A lady afterwards said that Europeans might dream of sleeping with their mothers but Canadians were different. Canadians, she said, respected their mothers even when they were asleep.

Passage from **Anthony Burgess**'s novel *The End of the World News* (1983). It concerns the reaction of a lady who attended an address in Winnipeg on the subject of the Oedipus complex, beloved of psychoanalysts, delivered by Sigmund Freud's disciple Ernest Jones, a one-time Toronto resident.

For a person who does not want to be locked up, it hurts no less if it is done by a psychiatrist who smiles than by a constable who growls.

A. Alan Borovoy, general counsel, Canadian Civil Liberties Association, *When Freedoms Collide: The Case for Our Civil Liberties* (1988).

Academic psychiatry has found itself floating in the air. The teaching of the treatment of mental illness has slipped out of their hands. I wonder for how long it will be possible to preserve and teach a psychiatric theory, which has nothing to do with the effective treatment of mental illness at the clinic.

Thomas A. Ban, Toronto-based psychiatrist, interviewed by David Healy, "They Used to Call It Psychiatry," *The Psychopharmacologists* (1996).

Thus, the discipline is subject to faddism—anything could be true, nothing can be disproven. During the years, time and again psychiatry has been held hostage by trendy new ideas that cannot be invalidated on the basis of scientific evidence but that must either be the objects of disbelief or of sectarian enthusiasm.

Edward Shorter, medical historian, introduction, *A Dictionary of Psychiatry* (2005).

This may not be true, but learn it.

Joel Paris, professor and chair, Psychiatry, McGill University, handing psychiatry residents a copy of *DSM-IV*, the diagnostic and statistical manual of mental disorders, address, "The Marriage between Psychiatry and Industry," *Social Sources of Psychopharmacology*, University of Toronto, 28 April 2005.

PSYCHICAL RESEARCH *See also* Belief; Ghosts

R.S. (Rex) Lambert, adviser on art & education: ex-editor BBC *Listener*, old crony of Murray's. Would like Grannan's job or bigger, but knows he's too old & too English. Also a warlock: speaks intimately about everything from libel laws to poltergeists.

Mavor Moore, broadcaster, letter to Merrill Denison, May 30, 1943, about personnel in CBC Radio in Toronto, including writer and psychical researcher R.S. Lambert, in Moore, *Reinventing Myself: Memoirs* (1994).

Every psychic I know or have heard of is an absolute fraud.

Henry Gordon, magician and skeptic, *Extra-Sensory Deception: ESP, Psychics, Shirley MacLaine, Ghosts, UFOs…* (1987).

PSYCHOLOGY *See also* Belief; Psychiatry; Therapy

The problem of understanding behaviour is the problem of understanding the total action of the nervous system, and vice versa.

D.O. Hebb, psychologist at McGill University and founder of cognitive psychobiology, *The Organization of Behaviour: A Neuropsychological Theory* (1948).

In the course of the development of the individual there are critical phases which have the character of change points, or periods of rapid transition. Less familiar perhaps, though nonetheless real, are the crises which occur around the age of 35—which I shall term the mid-life crisis—and at full maturity around the age of 65. It is the mid-life crisis with which I shall deal in this paper.

Elliott Jaques, Toronto-born psychologist, psychoanalyst, and social scientist, introducing the concept of the "mid-life crisis" in the scholarly paper "Death and the Mid-life Crisis," *International Journal of Psycho-Analysis* (1965), pp. 502–14. The concept of "the mid-life crisis" was subsequently popularized by the American writer Gail Sheehy in her best-selling book *Passages* (1975), as noted by Stuart Lavietes, "Elliott Jaques, 1912–2003," *The Globe and Mail*, 29 April 2003. Elsewhere, Jaques refers to the mid-life crisis as "contemplative pessimism," likens it to menopause, and calls it "the adult encounter with the conception of life to be lived in the setting of an approaching personal death."

PUBLIC HEALTH *See* Health Care

PUBLIC LIFE

When Dr. Smith was merely the president of Toronto University, he was even then a legend in Nova Scotia. They used to say of Dr. Smith, that, at the age of four, he used to row a boat one mile to get to school. Since his elevation to the Canadian Government, the legend now is that Dr. Smith, at the age of one, used to row a boat four miles to get to school. Nothing, Mr. Chairman, makes a legend grow like public office.

Robert L. Stanfield, Nova Scotia premier, referring to Sydney Smith, address, "Nova Scotia in the Canadian Scene," Toronto, 7 November 1957, The Empire Club of Canada.

PUBLIC OPINION *See* Opinions; Opinion Polls

PUBLIC SERVICE *See* Bureaucracy; Government

We need in Canada more of the spirit of the Englishman who, whenever he writes a letter to a civil servant, ends with: "You have the honour to be, Sir, my obedient servant."

Eugene Forsey, constitutional specialist, *The Globe and Mail*, 7 September 1954, in J.E. Hodgetts, *The Sound of One Voice: Eugene Forsey and His Letters to the Press* (2000).

PUBLIC SPEAKING *See also* Language; Speech

Mr. President and Gentlemen: It is told of Daniel that when he found himself in the lion's den he went over to the most ferocious-looking of the lions and whispered something in his ear, whereupon the lion went into a corner and began to tremble violently. It is said that what Daniel whispered in the ear of the lion was that after luncheon he would be expected to make a few remarks. On occasions such as this I always sympathize with that lion. (Laughter.)

Grattan O'Leary, publisher, editor, *The Ottawa Journal*, address, "Democracy Limited," Toronto, 1 April 1937, The Empire Club of Canada.

Mr. Chairman and Gentlemen: It always strikes me as funny that a newspaper man can sit down and dash off words of wisdom, of infinite wisdom, to half a million readers at any hour of the day or night; but the minute he has to stand up and face even fifty or a hundred of his fellow mortals he gets a cramp in his intelligence and his courage vanishes.

Gregory Clark, foreign correspondent, address, "London to Paris to Rome," Toronto, 4 April 1949, The Empire Club of Canada.

People need political and social leaders who can define policies, articulate problems, and express the aims and ideals of their society for those who cannot express them for themselves, though they may feel them very deeply. But the evidence is overwhelming that voters in a democracy want, and expect, bumble and burble from their leaders, and seem to be disturbed, if not upset, by the impact of articulate speech.

Northrop Frye, literary critic, address, "The Authority of Learning," Toronto, 19 June 1984, The Empire Club of Canada.

The human rear can only endure so much reality.

Margaret Atwood, author, "Concerning Franklin and His Gallant Crew," *Strange Things: The Malevolent North in Canadian Literature* (1995).

Well, friends, I once ended a speech by saying, "To make a long story short ..." and somebody from the back of the hall said, "Too late for that, Roy."

Roy Romanow, Saskatchewan premier, address, "Prairie Agriculture," Toronto, 4 February 2000, The Empire Club of Canada.

PUBLISHERS & PUBLISHING See also Authors; Books; Editors & Editing; Newspapers; Writers & Writing

Belford Bros., Canadian thieves.

Mark Twain's depiction in 1876 of the Toronto-based printer and publisher, headed by Alexander Belford, which pirated an edition of *The Adventures of Tom Sawyer*, as noted by Taylor Roberts, "Mark Twain in Toronto, Ontario, 1884–1885," *Mark Twain Journal*, fall 1998. Their act of piracy so incensed the American author that he swore "if I can make a living out of plays, I shall never write another book." Twain visited Toronto and Montreal to secure British copyright for his books. "Yes, of course I will go to Toronto, if necessary; but I don't hanker after it," he wrote in a letter to a friend on 27 October 1881.

I have a theory about publishers which explains their curious temperament: I think they tend to be undiagnosed schizophrenics. They are people of dual personality, and both of their personalities are directed at different sides of their business. They tend to be friendly, literate, agreeable men with a genuine enthusiasm for literature and a cultivated taste in it; they like authors and are nicer to them than most people because I may tell you that authors are not usually very pleasant companions, being often egotistical, or dishonest, or childish, or drunken and sometimes all four. Publishers often lend authors money, or buy them out of jail. I sometimes think that there is a saint-like streak in the best publishers, because the more detestable and troublesome an author is, the better they like him.

Robertson Davies, man of letters, address, "How the Author Reaches His Public," Toronto, 2 March 1972, The Empire Club of Canada.

Gutenberg made everybody a reader. Xerox makes everybody a publisher.

Marshall McLuhan, communications theorist, *The Guardian Weekly*, 12 June 1997.

One reads from that one book, so that people can say, "Oh, I like it," and buy the book. This is the way to eventually exhaust the market. This is the goal of a book: it must exhaust its potential market. This is a lesson I learned from Gaston Miron.

Antonio D'Alfonso, poet and publisher, in conversation with Pasquale Verdicchio, *Duologue: On Culture and Identity* (1998). He is referring to publishing French, English, and Italian editions of Quebec poet Gaston Miron's *The Other Shore* (1986).

What he meant by this was that even if we reduced literature to *samizdat*, to Xeroxes passed from hand to hand, that would be preferable to the lie that official CanLit had become.

View of **William Hoffer**, the antiquarian bookdealer, who held outspoken views on the baleful influence of the Canada Council on contemporary Canadian writing, as recalled by his friend, book collector, and critic-editor John Metcalf, *An Aesthetic Underground: A Literary Memoir* (2003).

Guernica requires complete patience on the part of the Author. / The author will publicly thank the publisher in recognition of combined work accomplished. / By signing this contract the Author accepts to be patient when difficulties associated with any aspect of the Work are encountered along the way.

Sentences from a contract employed by Guernica, a Toronto-based publisher of literary books, April 2003.

If the truth were told, he was tired of writers, period: tired of their emotional neediness, their whining about money, their childish vanities.

Thoughts of literary book editor Daniel Fielding in **Richard Wright**'s novel *Adultery* (2004).

PUZZLES *See also* Mysteries

Buried deeply within the imagination is the belief that if we were to solve all the puzzles of the world we could bring about change in that world, because we would have discovered the mystical structures that it conceals.

Marcel Danesi, semiotician, *The Puzzle Instinct: The Meaning of Puzzles in Human Life* (2002).

Thus, in a fundamental sense, puzzles provide a means of "comic relief," so to speak, from the angst caused by the unanswerable larger questions.

Marcel Danesi, semiotician, *The Puzzle Instinct: The Meaning of Puzzles in Human Life* (2002).

q

QUALITY *See also* Excellence; Mediocrity

I am convinced that Canada will continue to accomplish great things if we work together for a better quality of life—for our own population and for all humanity. Our country is vast and it is blessed with a wealth of colours and the varied music of its tongues and accents.

> **Michaëlle Jean**, governor general, installation address, Ottawa, 27 September 2005, quoted in the *National Post*, 28 September 2005.

QUALITY OF LIFE

Well, it's still a good place to live, but that's all Canada is now—just a good place to live.

> **Donald G. Creighton**, historian, observation made in 1979, the year of his death, to Charles Taylor who quoted the lamentation in *Radical Tories* (1992).

In 2001, the United Nations ranked Canada third on the Human Development Index, a comprehensive measure of quality of life factors, trailing only Norway and Australia. Canada is, in fact, usually ranked first, holding the title for seven years in a row before slipping back two spots in 2001. This reflects the solid healthcare and education system, strong economy, low crime rates, and great cities of this nation.

> **Leonard Brody** et al., entrepreneurs, *Innovation Nation: Canadian Leadership from Java to Jurassic Park* (2002).

QUEBEC *See also* Canada & Quebec; Continentalism; Quebec, Conquest of; New France; Two Nations; Two Solitudes

Je me souviens.

> Motto of the Province of Quebec since 1978, the year it replaced the previous motto *La Belle Province.* Recalled, apparently, are the glories of the *Ancien régime*—the language, laws, and religion of Quebec before the Conquest of 1759. Yet the motto, selected to be inscribed beneath the coat of arms of the National Assembly in Quebec City, 9 February 1883, comes from a three-line poem of unknown origin found by architect **Eugène Taché**: "*Je me souviens / Que né sous le lys, / Je crois sous la rose.*" It translates: "I remember / That while under the fleur de lys [of France], / I grow under the rose [of England]."

Consider, for instance, the French of Lower Canada. Equality of conditions is more universal there than in the United States, for the whole people, without exception, are in easy circumstances, and there are not even that considerable number of rich individuals who are to be found in all the great towns of the American republic. Yet do we find in Canada that go-ahead spirit—that restless impatient eagerness of improvement in circumstances—that nobility, that shifting and fluctuating, now up now down, now here now there—that absence of classes and class-spirit—that jealousy of superior attainments—that want of deference for authority and leadership—that habit of bringing things down to the rule and square of each man's own understanding—which M. de Tocqueville imputes to the same cause in the United States. In all these respects the very contrary qualities prevail.

> **John Stuart Mill**, English philosopher, commenting on Alexis de Tocqueville's failure in *Democracy in America* (1835–1839) to recognize that equality is at odds with liberty, as noted by Garry Wills, "Did Tocqueville 'Get' America?" *The New York Review of Books*, 29 April 2004.

In this land of Quebec naught shall die and naught change....

> Theme of the novel *Maria Chapdelaine* (1916), famous description of life in the farming communities in the Lac-Saint-Jean region of Quebec by the French traveller **Louis Hémon**; translated by W.H. Blake in 1921.

French Canadians have a great respect for tradition and there is an enchanting mixture of old and new in the Province of Quebec. Montreal has all the modernity of a busy North American city, while in the city of Quebec, and the surrounding country, lingers the grace of old France.

Susan Buchan, compiler of *John Buchan by His Wife and Friends* (1947), describing the province in the late 1930s.

Canada or Quebec, wherever the French-Canadian nation finds its freedom, there will be its *patrie.*

Daniel Johnson Sr., Quebec premier, *Egalité ou Indépendance* (1965), in William Johnson, "Is There a Master in the House?" *The Globe and Mail*, 14 April 2001.

Vive le Québec! Vive le Québec libre! Vive le Canada français! Vive la France!

Charles de Gaulle, president of France, balcony of Montreal's City Hall, 24 July 1967. He deliberately incurred the wrath of federalists and curried favour with separatists by employing their slogan "*Québec libre.*" He never did visit Ottawa. The most stylish response was made by **Pauline Vanier**, widow of Governor General Jean Vanier; she had the following terse communiqué conveyed to the general: "1940."

In my years in Quebec, what most impressed me about Quebec nationalists was that I never met one who could conceive of the idea that there was such a person as a Canadian who felt as patriotically about Canada as he felt about Quebec. Quebec's problem with Canada today is not grievances but lack of respect, and who can blame Quebec for that, given Canada's political record in recent years.

Conrad Black, newspaper magnate, address, "Post-election Prospects in Canada," Toronto, 2 November 1993, The Empire Club of Canada.

The French Canadians form a nation. But the Quebeckers do not form a nation.

Léon Dion, political economist, remark made in 1995, in William Johnson, "Is There a Master in the House?" *The Globe and Mail*, 14 April 2001.

The battle at Quebec gained Canada for Britain, but it set in motion a series of events that ultimately lost America.

Paul K. Davis, historian, *100 Decisive Battles from Ancient Times to the Present* (1999).

Quebec is not, and cannot be, unilingual French. It is bilingual and that is our strength. It is time we recognized it and rejoiced.

Monique Nemni, linguist, "Nurturing Linguistic Insecurity," *Cité libre*, summer 2000.

Quebec is neither the spoiled child nor the victim of the federation.

Stéphane Dion, minister of Intergovernmental Affairs, address, Ottawa, 2 March 2001, in Justine Hunter, *National Post*, 3 March 2001.

Our attitude is closer to the European one, less Anglo-Saxon, if I may say so.

Francine Lalonde, Bloc Québécois Member of Parliament, distinguishing between the approaches of Quebec and the rest of Canada to assisting the United States following the World Trade Center disaster, in Hugh Winsor, "The Power Game," *The Globe and Mail*, 19 September 2001.

Mr. Landry's First Rule of Nations is you can't belong to two of them. You can't be Québécois and Canadian.

Paul Wells, columnist, referring to the outspoken Quebec premier, "Let Bernard Landry Explain It All for You," *National Post*, 26 November 2001.

Mr. Dumont, said to be the sort of man every mother wants for a son, was liked and trusted, and that seemed enough.

André Pratt, columnist, referring to Mario Dumont, Action démocratique du Québec leader, and his "Adéquistes," "Quebec's Quiet Counter-revolution," *The Globe and Mail*, 7 November 2002.

I miss a country that is not far; / I miss a country that doesn't exist; / I miss a country that will be.

Lines from an unidentified poem composed by **Gilles Vigneault** and read by entertainer

Louise Portal, conceding the defeat of the Parti Québécois, Théâtre du Capitole, Quebec City, 14 April 2003, as quoted in the *National Post*, 15 April 2003.

Less and less distinguishes Quebec from the mainstream of North America. Except for French.

Mark Abley, author, *Spoken Here: Travels among Threatened Languages* (2003).

Quebec has much more complex issues with the rest of Canada (and in particular Ontario) than, say, Alberta or Manitoba. But there's no inferiority complex attending its frustrations and demands. The province knows it's the coolest thing going in Canada. Toronto? Toronto is a cultural backwater full of people not cool enough to live in Montreal.

Marzena Czarnecka, columnist, "Sleeping with the Enemy," *Lexpert Magazine*, June 2003.

QUEBEC CITY *See also* Quebec

Never have I beheld anything so beautiful and magnificent as the site of the city of Quebec; none better could have been chosen for that which it must one day become—the capital of a great empire.

Le Comte de Frontenac, governor, letter of 3 November 1677, in David B. Knight, *Choosing Canada's Capital: Jealousy and Friction in the 19th Century* (1977).

It was with added pleasure and pride that for the first time I set foot in Quebec, the Capital of French Canada. What better feature could you have to represent the genius of the British Empire, than this large, powerful, thriving French community with their own traditions, their own history, their own language, dwelling happily and in perfect freedom within the confines of a British dominion.

Winston Churchill, British statesman, address, *The Ottawa Morning Journal*, 16 August 1929, in David Dilks, *"The Great Dominion": Winston Churchill in Canada 1900–1954* (2005).

Only nature, at Quebec, is American—superlatively so. The harbor is unbelievably spacious. It is a great gateway, yes, to the "great open spaces" beyond. In that respect Quebec is a truer and more natural portal to the American Scene than is the structural phantasmagoria of the city of New York.

Wyndham Lewis, English author, one-time Toronto resident, *America, I Presume* (1940).

The only problem in Quebec is choosing the best restaurant.

Brian Mulroney, prime minister, explaining why Quebec City was chosen as the site of the so-called Shamrock Summit with U.S. President Ronald Reagan, which opened on St. Patrick's Day, 17 March 1985.

QUEBEC, CONQUEST OF *See also* Quebec

So much the better: I shall not see the English in Quebec.

Attributed to the **Marquis de Montcalm**, Quebec commander, on being assured that his wound was mortal, Quebec, 13 September 1759, in Samuel Arthur Bent, *Familiar Short Sayings of Great Men with Historical and Explanatory Notes* (6th ed., 1887).

Gentlemen, I would rather have written those lines than take Quebec tomorrow.

Major-General **James Wolfe**, commander of the British forces at Quebec, on board his ship the night before he led the famous assault of 13 September 1759. At the time, it is said, Wolfe was reciting Thomas Gray's poem "Elegy Written in a Country Churchyard" (1749), and that he paused over the fourth line of the following verse: "The boast of heraldry, the pomp of power, / And all that beauty, all that wealth e'er gave, / Awaits alike the inevitable hour. / The paths of glory lead but to the grave." Eighteen hours later he lay dead on the Plains of Abraham. Francis Parkman tells the story in *Montcalm and Wolfe* (1884). Its genesis is discussed in *Colombo's All-Time Great Canadian Quotations* (1994).

They mourn Quebec; for Wolfe our sorrows flow; / Victors and vanquish'd felt the twofold blow. / To both perpetual let each loss remain; / If Quebec be restored, Wolfe fell in vain.

Anonymous verse on the Conquest of Quebec and the death of General James Wolfe, cited in "General Wolfe," *Notes and Queries*, 24 April 1852.

MORTEM VIRTUS COMMUNEM
FAMAM HISTORIA
MONUMENTUM POSTERITAS DEBIT.

Latin inscription, Wolfe and Montcalm Monument, Governor's Garden, Quebec City, dedicated 8 September 1828. Composed by journalist John Charlton Fisher, the inscription translates: "Valour gave them a common death / History a common fame / Posterity a common monument." The inspired inscription honours the two commanders, the victorious General James Wolfe and the vanquished Marquis de Montcalm, both of whom fell during and following the Battle of the Plains of Abraham, 13 September 1759.

I must myself be part of this labouring class, since never in my life have I given the least thought to the defeat on the Plains of Abraham, even though Victory-Lévy Beaulieu and Bernard Landry gripe about it all day long. Much good may it do them. The people still don't go along with it. They must be either stupid or colonized, or both at the same time. That's why one feels sorry for them or looks down on them, or both at the same time.

Daniel Poliquin, commentator and novelist, referring to the Quebec novelist and the Quebec premier and the "defeat" of the French in 1759, *In the Name of the Father: An Essay on Quebec Nationalism* (2001), translated by Don Winkler.

QUEBEC CULTURE *See also* Culture

Québécois art doesn't exist: only Québécois artists exist. / *L'art québécois n'existe pas: il n'existe que des artistes québécois.*

Statement dripping with irony that was added to the text of the preface "*Un stratégie* / The Strategy" for the exhibition catalogue *Québec 75* (1975), to qualify for federal funding, as noted by Ray Conlogue, "Spectator," *The Globe and Mail*, 3 April 2002. Montreal's Musée de l'art contemporaine sponsored the exhibition, which featured the work of 74 francophone artists and one anglophone artist to represent the years from 1970 to 1975.

Quebec culture is influenced by intellectual life in Paris (we share the same language) and by the creative energy of New York (we are almost neighbours).

Jacques Godbout, writer and filmmaker, "In Quebec Culture, a Deep Skepticism of Tradition," *The New York Times*, 16 September 2001.

QUESTIONS *See also* Interviews

For your information, let me ask you a question.

Marshall McLuhan, media philosopher, address, National Association of Educational Broadcasters, Omaha, Nebraska, 1958, in Judith Fitzgerald, *Marshall McLuhan: Wise Guy* (2001).

Capture accidents. The wrong answer is the right answer in search of a different question. Collect wrong answers as part of the process.

Bruce Mau, designer, author of "Incomplete Manifesto for Growth," in Sarah Scott, "Shock of the New," *Globe and Mail*'s *Report on Business*, August 2002.

I've heard everything. There are no stupid questions.

Sue Johanson, straight-talking sex therapist on television, in Vinay Menon, "Sunday Sex Lady Makes Men Blush," *Toronto Star*, 18 October 2003.

When appointed to the federal Science Advisory Board for Health Canada, all but one of my colleagues were scientists or physicians or both—at the first meeting when directly asked my role, I answered: "To ask uninformed questions."

Leslie Millin, writer and consultant, "Idols of the Cave—My Career as a Misfit," *Queen's Quarterly*, spring 2005.

QUIET REVOLUTION *See also* October Crisis; Quebec; Revolution

Many have laid claim to the paternity of the Quiet Revolution. Analyze the DNA—the real father is Pierre Trudeau.

Roch Carrier, essayist and author, referring to Trudeau's work in opposing Quebec's Duplessis-ism, "The Thinker Whose Ideas Will Endure," *The Globe and Mail*, 30 September 2000.

QUOTATIONS *See also* Language; Words

Epigram: a half-truth expressed in such a way as to be annoying to those who believe the other half. [1950]

Harold Adams Innis, social scientist, *The Idea File of Harold Adams Innis* (1980), edited by William Christian.

Look it up in Colombo.

Lorne Parton, journalist, reviewing *Colombo's Canadian Quotations* (1974), recommending that these words be a "line for a future printing," Vancouver *Province*, 22 November 1974.

I know it is supposed to be dreadful to fake references, but when people insist on quotations that do not already exist, what is an author to do?

Robertson Davies, man of letters, 13 August 1979, confessing in a letter to his Danish translator that he had invented the term "Fifth Business" and to lend it respectability had attributed it to the Dutch theatre critic Tho. Overskou, a fabrication uncovered by the Dutch translator of the novel; *For Your Eye Alone: Letters, 1976–1995* (1999).

The art of the quoter is to know when to stop.

Line from **Robertson Davies**'s novel *What's Bred in the Bone* (1985).

But I have never been able to shake the habit altogether. My later essays are often garnished with others' epigrams, and now that my own appear in books of Canadian quotations I have taken to stealing from myself.

Mavor Moore, theatre personality, *Reinventing Myself: Memoirs* (1994).

Being quotable is always good, provided that which is quoted does not make the speaker appear an idiot.

David A. Fram, solicitor, email to consulting lexicographer, 14 May 2003.

r

RACE & RACISM *See also* Anti-Semitism; Diversity; Ethnicity; Hate; Multiculturalism; Prejudice

Let me sketch the situation. The human races are, roughly speaking, divided, like all Gaul that we used to read about many years ago, into three parties. First there are the uncivilized races, including the blacks of Africa, the tinted peoples on the Pacific Islands, the red man of America and other aborigines scattered everywhere. The second is the civilized, non-Christian races, including the yellow races of Eastern Asia, the brown races of India, and shades of skin and of thought in Western Asia. Thirdly, there are the civilized and so-called Christian races, principally white, and foremost among them the Anglo-Saxons, whose energy and strength would dominate the world; whose energy, if harnessed to righteousness, could recreate this world, but, harnessed to militarism, has turned it in a different direction.

C.S. Eby, church minister, address, "The True Inwardness of the Yellow Peril," Toronto, 10 October 1907, The Empire Club of Canada.

She will have to solve, for the salvation of men, the most difficult of all problems, the race problem, which has become insistent with the close contact of communities that had their isolation for centuries in their geographical and cultural exclusiveness.

Rabindranath Tagore, Bengali sage, "Farewell to Canada," 13 April 1929, *Education and Leisure: Addresses Delivered at the Fourth Triennial Conference on Education Held at Victoria and Vancouver, Canada, April 1929* (1929), edited by S.E. Lang. He refers to Canada as a "she" and the "race problem" refers to the fate of the Sikhs aboard the Komagata Maru, who were refused entry into the country in 1914, an incident that much exercised Tagore.

Colour discrimination exists because people refuse to think. The pigmentation of men's skins differentiates them from one another in nothing but colour. What causes them to differ in behaviour and character is their antecedents and education. What the world needs today, black and white alike, is to rid itself altogether of the habit of thinking in terms of colour, and to judge a man, whether he be black or white, brown or yellow, or just a mixture of all four, solely by this character and capacity.

Roy Thomson, chairman, Thomson Newspapers Limited, address, "The Winds of Change in the New Nations," Toronto, 7 January 1963, The Empire Club of Canada.

When people are left to their own devices they will often discriminate against groups, whites against blacks, blacks against whites or East Indians, Catholics against Protestants, and my people, Jewish females, against any man who won't marry us. But the great lesson that we learned about racism we learned from the institutionalized racism of Hitler's Third Reich, and from the institutionalized racism of the United States which limited the rights of blacks up to the Civil Rights Act of 1964. That lesson is that the best a society can do to minimize and prevent racism is to see that the state itself is non-discriminatory, that so long as our society does not have laws discriminating against whites, blacks, Jews or gentiles, we have the best chance for a decent society.

Barbara Amiel, journalist, address, "How Canada Does It and Other Social Diseases," Toronto, 4 February 1982, The Empire Club of Canada.

Whatever happened to those nice old Arabs who used to fold their tents and silently steal away?

Barry Mather, writer, letter, 1 July 1979.

To be black and female, in a society which is both racist and sexist, is to be in the unique position of having nowhere to go but up.

Rosemary Brown, NDP leadership candidate, in Allan Fotheringham, *Saturday Night*, July–August 1975.

You don't need the Klan here. You have the Orange Lodges.

Attributed to **R.C. Snelgrove**, U.S. organizer of the Ku Klux Klan, referring to Orange Lodges in Alberta in 1929, promoters of "racial purity," as noted by Bill Baergen, "The Mail," *Maclean's*, 2 October 2000.

Racism is as Canadian as *Hockey Night in Canada*.

Attributed to **David Ahenakew**, first elected national chief of the Assembly of First Nations (1982–1985), in Margaret Wente, "Counterpoint," *The Globe and Mail*, 17 December 2002.

A "mythology of racelessness" and "stupefying innocence"—these would appear to be the twin pillars of the Canadian history of race.

Constance Backhouse, scholar, *Colour-Coded: A Legal History of Racism in Canada, 1900–1950* (1999).

We can just go to British Columbia in Prince George, where crosses are being burned on lawns as we speak. I know of this because I was contacted immediately that the incidents occurred by the mayor of Prince George.

Hedy Fry, secretary of state for Multiculturalism, House of Commons, 21 March 2001. Fry, a B.C. member of Parliament, was referring to the cross-burning activities associated with the Ku Klux Klan on the International Day for the Elimination of Racism. As Daniel LeBlanc and Robert Matas noted in *The Globe and Mail*, 23 March 2001, Mayor Colin Kinsley immediately denied the statement: "This reference to cross-burnings in the city of Prince George is false." Fry apologized to the House on 23 March 2001: "Yesterday I mistakenly linked the city of Prince George with a specific hate activity. I regret that. And I apologize to the people of Prince George."

Thank God I'm not an Arab. Let me say it again in case any of you didn't quite understand. Thank God I'm not an Arab. Offended, hurt, shocked? Are your politically correct sensibilities dented and bruised? Tough. Because you shouldn't be surprised at all.

Michael Coren, author and broadcaster, "Thank God I'm Not an Arab," *All Things Considered: Collected Columns and Essays* (2001). Coren is referring specifically to Western media treatment of its Arab population.

The state will not destroy racism, the law will not destroy racism and politically correct intrusions will not destroy racism. We will destroy racism.

Michael Coren, author and broadcaster, "Only You and I Can Destroy Racism," *All Things Considered: Collected Columns and Essays* (2001).

Perhaps we will learn from it a truly terrifying truth: that anti-racism is worse than the disease it claims to cure.

Robert Fulford, columnist, referring to the racist imprecations characteristic of the UN-sponsored conference on racism held at Durban, South Africa, "From Delusions to Destruction," *National Post*, 6 October 2001.

Data on race and crime may be collected to prove racial profiling, but not to prevent it.... Simple statistical disparities are not sufficient grounds to discriminate against individuals on the basis of race. They are sufficient grounds to accuse the police of doing the same.... Police must not draw inferences from data on race and crime in deciding who to arrest. But the courts must draw inferences from the same data in deciding who to punish.... The higher incidence of crime among blacks shows they are less deserving of punishment. The lower incidence of crime among women shows they are less in need of punishment.

Andrew Coyne, columnist, ironically offering "four principles" on racial profiling as it affects the police, the courts, and the public, "Do Not Take Race into Account. No, Do," *National Post*, 5 March 2003.

I have always been called the Gandhi of the right. I have always been against violence.

Ernst Zundel, German-born Toronto-based Holocaust denier, testifying at a refugee-status hearing, "'I Have Never Been a White Supremacist,' Zundel Tells Hearing," in Estanislao Oziewicz, *The Globe and Mail*, 10 May 2003.

Race represents a socially defined construct rather than a reflection of biological reality. Human races do not exist except as artificial categories that are subject to racialized definitions and exclusions. Nor is there such a thing as race relations; more accurately, there are relations between groups that have been racialized by those with the power to impose and enforce such impositions.

Augie Fleras, sociologist, "Racializing Culture / Culturalizing Race," *Racism, Eh? A Critical Inter-Disciplinary Anthology of Race and Racism in Canada* (2004), edited by Camille A. Nelson and Charmaine A. Nelson. The author discusses the matter under the heads "Racism as Race" and "Racism as Culture."

Recourse to race appears to have lost what little discursive muscle it once flexed in Canada.

Augie Fleras, sociologist, "Racializing Culture / Culturalizing Race," *Racism, Eh? A Critical Inter-Disciplinary Anthology of Race and Racism in Canada* (2004), edited by Camille A. Nelson and Charmaine A. Nelson.

But being black in Canada has taught me the central lesson of racism: It rarely has anything to do with the individual. In all the times I've had things yelled at me from a passing car or have received a hostile look, not once was it the result of someone thinking, "There's Anthony Stewart." Rather, each incident was simply the depersonalised observation of skin colour.

Anthony Stewart, professor of English, "Pen and Teller Magic," in *Racism, Eh? A Critical Inter-Disciplinary Anthology of Race and Racism in Canada* (2004), edited by Camille A. Nelson and Charmaine A. Nelson.

It suggests that all "we" need is an encounter with an "Other" to set us on an unencumbered and more enlightened path. Until we are ready to interrogate positions of privilege as well as oppression, we will only be hearing one side of the story.

Michele Byers, sociologist, "Race In / Out of the Classroom," concluding sentences of a study of CBC-TV series *Degrassi Junior High* in terms of race, *Racism, Eh? A Critical Inter-Disciplinary Anthology of Race and Racism in Canada* (2004), edited by Camille A. Nelson and Charmaine A. Nelson.

Racism, Eh?

Canadians are inheritors of this colonial legacy. Although we often proudly discuss and glorify our national origins as the history of two European forces—British and French—we rarely address or confront the inherent racism of their imperial projects, nor the colonial logic that allowed them to disavow the legitimate presence of First Nations peoples, enslave and import black Africans, and selectively manage immigration for "desirable" racial populations. The language of race is carefully policed in Canada.

Camille A. Nelson and **Charmaine A. Nelson**, lawyer and teacher, editors, introduction, *Racism, Eh? A Critical Inter-Disciplinary Anthology of Race and Racism in Canada* (2004).

When everything is racism, nothing is racism.

Karen Mock, Candian Race Relations Foundations, quoted in the editorial "Time to End 'Racist' Name-calling," *National Post*, 7 May 2005.

I don't like that term. I don't see myself that way. I'm a black woman of Haitian origin—which is perfect—and a full-fledged Quebecker. But I don't see myself as a visible minority.

Michaëlle Jean, Quebec TV journalist, born in Port-au-Prince, speaking at the Montreal press conference to announce her appointment as Adrienne Clarkson's successor as governor general of Canada, in Ingrid Peritz, "Outspoken Journalist Admits to an 'Interior Fire,'" *The Globe and Mail*, 4 August 2005.

RACING

There's a little larceny in every man—but you notice it more around a race track.

Robert James Speers, thoroughbred racing enthusiast, in Jim Coleman, *A Hoofprint on My Heart* (1971).

RADIO *See also* Broadcasting; Canadian Broadcasting Corporation; Communications

It is appalling, and it will remain so while radio broadcasting material is subject entirely to commercial motives and to commercial rewards.

Arthur Meighen, former prime minister, "commenting upon the Radio situation," address, 11 April 1929, *Education and Leisure: Addresses Delivered at the Fourth Triennial Conference on Education Held at Victoria and Vancouver, Canada, April 1929* (1929), edited by S.E. Lang.

You were a slob in Moose Jaw and you're still a slob over here!

Familiar line from BBC Radio's *Breakfast with Braden*, a popular morning program in the early 1950s, starring **Bernard Braden** and his wife, Barbara Kelly, both born in Vancouver; in Ed Gould, *Entertaining Canadians: Canada's International Stars, 1900–1988* (1988).

Tonight, Canada enters the world radio arena. As we undertake this new service, let us resolve that, in peace as in war, we will be true to the values you are so valiantly upholding—ideals which have made our country a nation. The unity of Canada belongs not only to Canada, it belongs to mankind.

W.L. Mackenzie King, prime minister, inaugural broadcast over CBC Radio's International Service, addressing Canadian forces overseas in particular, 25 February 1945, in James L. Hall, *Radio Canada International: Voice of a Middle Power* (1997).

We already had at our disposal the world's most extensive radio network. There was in the air—and we were on the air—an Arthurian sense of having been given a sword with which to seize the day.

Mavor Moore, theatre personality, recalling the esprit de corps among radio broadcasters in Toronto in the late 1940s, *Reinventing Myself: Memoirs* (1994).

The radio is the subtlest attack on human peace of mind yet made, and constitutes a major obstacle, perhaps in many cases an insuperable one, to it.... I suppose radios incarnate the semiconsciousness of others, and of course increase the mental disturbance they're turned on to soothe.

Northrop Frye, cultural critic, aphorism, "Notebook 3" (1946–1948), *Northrop Frye Newsletter*, fall 2000.

It is an offence to have a wireless on too loud these still summer evenings. It can annoy your neighbour. An even better way is to throw a dead cat on his lawn....

Characteristic humour (possibly contributed by **Eric Nicol**) from the BBC Radio series *Breakfast with Braden*, as noted by Bernard Braden, *The Kindness of Strangers* (1990).

It's four elements: speech, music, sound, and silence. That's it. There are no other colours on your palette. And it's a much more verbal medium than TV or film—it allows you to flex the writerly muscles.

Silver Donald Cameron, in Philip Moscovitch, "The W Files," *Canadian Screenwriter*, fall 2001.

Radio means you invite a person into your morning—or afternoon or Saturday night.

Shelley Ambrose, radio producer, in Edna Barker, *Remembering Peter Gzowski: A Book of Tributes* (2002).

Today, I like to think that every time someone in the world turns on a radio plugged into the wall, they are—in a small way—paying homage to my dad, his innovation and his vision. With enthusiasm and optimism, he always believed "the best is yet to come," and I have long echoed those sentiments.

Ted Rogers, broadcast executive, referring to his father, Edward Rogers Sr., the Toronto wireless pioneer who invented the vacuum tube that made it possible to operate a radio from a wall socket rather than a battery, "'Dad Was a True Visionary," *Maclean's Special Commemorative Issue 100*, October 2004.

RAILWAYS

Stand fast, Craigellachie!

Command cabled by **George Stephen**, president of the Canadian Pacific Railway, in London to raise last-minute capital, to his cousin, Donald Smith, Lord Strathcona, in Montreal, November 1884. The message signalled that Smith was not to lose faith and that the needed capital would be raised in the nick of time. Craigellachie is the name of a rocky prominence in northern Scotland; in Gaelic, the word means "the rock of alarm."

At home in Canada our politics turn on such things as how much money the Canadian National Railways lose as compared with how much they could lose if they really tried; on whether the Grain Growers of Manitoba should be allowed to import ploughs without paying a duty or to pay a duty without importing the ploughs.

Stephen Leacock, humorist, *My Discovery of England* (1922).

The Canadian National Railway represents, perhaps, as fine an expression of co-operative effort as will be found in the industrial world. (Hear, hear and applause.)

Sir Henry Thornton, CNR president, address, "Problems of the Canadian National Railways," Toronto, 10 October 1929, The Empire Club of Canada.

Yet it seems strange to recall that only two decades ago the Canadian National was regarded as the problem child of the nation—a foundling that had been left on the doorstep and was starting to eat Canadians out of house and home. If someone in those days had designed a coat of arms for the C.N.R. it would certainly have contained a bar sinister in token of its questionable parentage.

Donald Gordon, chairman, Canadian National Railways, address, "Talking Shop," Toronto, 21 March 1951, The Empire Club of Canada.

Indeed, in the middle of Birmingham, there was a Canadian Pacific branch office, and in the window were displayed models of its ships and trains. I regularly dreamed of travelling on them; but I never did. For my first visit to any part of what had been the British Empire did not take place until I went to Canada in 1973.

David Cannadine, English historian, *Ornamentalism: How the British Saw Their Empire* (2001).

RCMP *See* Royal Canadian Mounted Police

READING *See also* Books; Writers & Writing

I learned to read in Canada.

Martin Gilbert, English historian and biographer, interviewed in Toronto by Judy Stoffman, "Prolific Historian Fondly Recalls T.O. Childhood," *Toronto Star*, 13 February 2002. He was three years old when he was evacuated from London; he spent the period 1940–1943 in Toronto before being taken back to England.

I once wrote an essay about books and reading named "A Call to the Clerisy," and I defined that unusual and almost obsolete word like this: "The clerisy are those who read for pleasure, but not for idleness; who read for pastime, but not to kill time; who love books, but do not live by books." The clerisy are not professional critics or scholars, tirelessly assessing books, or bound by their work to read a lot of books that give them no pleasure. The clerisy are those who seek, and find, delight and enlargement of life in books. The clerisy are those for whom reading is a personal art.

Robertson Davies, man of letters, "Folio Is Addictive," circa 1980s, an essay written and printed as a brochure to draw attention to the publications of the Folio Society, England's leading publisher of finely produced books since 1947.

Reading: an exercise in forgetting.

Line from the prose poem "On Writing" from **Antonio D'Alfonso**'s *The Other Shore* (1988).

Paper as dense as prayers, and as mute. Paper that you will find or burn. All around walls of paper you cannot climb, with only one window to look out of. Language has put there for you to stare at the world without windows.

Lines from the prose poem "You Refuse to Write" from **Antonio D'Alfonso**'s *The Other Shore* (1988).

To call reading a pleasure is an understatement. For me, reading is the source of all pleasure, colouring all experience, making it somehow more endurable, more reasonable.

Alberto Manguel, man of letters, foreword, *The Pleasure of Reading* (1992), edited by Antonia Fraser.

But, then, as Laurence Sterne so aptly put it, "I think there is a fatality in it—I seldom go to the place I set out for." As a writer (and as a reader), I believe that this, somehow, must have always been my motto.

Alberto Manguel, writer and reader, *Reading Pictures: A History of Love and Hate* (2000).

I find great joy in reading. It was the most wonderful gift my parents gave me.

Robert Adams, reader, public speaker, and writer, *A Love of Reading: Reviews of Contemporary Fiction* (2001).

Finally, beyond reason there is indeed irrationality. But of greater importance, there is non-rationality.

John Ralston Saul, philosopher, *On Equilibrium* (2001).

Hockey is a cold country's means of escape.

Well, reading is the same. It is to the mind what hockey is to the body. The ordinary limits are forgotten. The reader moves through time and space as lightly as Guy Lafleur moved from one blue line to the next. Imagine a nation supreme in hockey and reading. The rest of the world would choke on its envy.

Editorial, "Here's to a New Goal: Most Literate Nation," *The Globe and Mail*, 31 December 2004.

The death of print, of course, has been on its way since the invention of the radio, talkie films, television and, most recently, the Internet. But somehow the printed word refuses to lie down anywhere but on the page.

Roy MacGregor, columnist, "This Country," *The Globe and Mail*, 17 March 2005.

REALITY *See also* Authenticity; Truth

Indeed, we mustn't live in a wonderland as though it were real life, but instead we should live life as though it were a wonderland. Still, there will always be those who prefer the circus to the forest.

Pierre Perrault, filmmaker, "Film and Reality," expressing a preference for documentary over dramatic films, *How to Make or Not Make a Canadian Film* (1968), edited by André Pâquet.

You can go through a red light but you can't go through a red truck.

Louis Dudek, poet and aphorist, *The Tamarack Review*, winter 1976.

You can't wed the reality of childhood with the unreality of adulthood. It'd be like gravity and anti-gravity colliding. It would rip a hole in the fabric of the universe for sure.

Rob McKenzie, columnist, "Commentary," *National Post*, 19 August 2004.

REBELLION *See also* Revolution; Violence

Canada is a little bit like the kids who never rebelled, but when they turn forty, they start smoking pot.

Naomi Klein, author, interviewed by Deborah Solomon, "Countercultural Canada," *The New York Times Magazine*, 6 July 2003.

RECYCLING *See also* Environmentalism

If Canada had a state religion, it would be recycling. If you doubt this, ask your kids. They may not have picked up much readin', 'riting and 'rithmetic in school, but from their tenderest years they've had pounded into them the three r's that really count: reduce, reuse, recycle.

Margaret Wente, columnist, "Recycle, or Else! You've Been Warned," *The Globe and Mail*, 7 August 2004.

RED TORY *See also* Conservatism; Socialism

The Red Tory part means that I am a socialist. Thus, I do not support private ownership of the means of production and [I] believe that economic and political power should be in the hands of ordinary people.... The Tory part means that socially, culturally, and intellectually I tend to be conservative. I believe that all citizens should be treated as legal and political equals.

Robert Ivan Martin, law professor, *The Most Dangerous Branch: How the Supreme Court of Canada Has Undermined Our Law and Our Democracy* (2003).

REFERENDA ON QUEBEC SOVEREIGNTY *See also* Canada & Quebec; Separatism; Sovereignty; Sovereignty-Association

NOUI.

Neologism to suggest the attitude of Quebeckers to both federalism and separatism, according to a CROP-*L'Actualité* poll, a combination of *non* and *oui*, coined or at least popularized by **Jean Paré**, "Noui au Canada, Non à Ottawa," *L'Actualité*, 15 March 1995.

Are you happy? It was because of you immigrants that the No has won, and a whole bunch of you had voted No.... Why is it that we open the doors to this country so you can vote No?

Bernard Landry, Quebec deputy premier, addressing Anita Martinez, a Mexican-born night clerk at the InterContinental Hotel in Montreal, following the defeat of the second referendum on the status of Quebec, 30 October 1995, reported by Rod Macdonell and William Marsden, "Hotel Workers Claim Landry Ranted about Immigrants," Montreal *Gazette*, 3 November 1995. This happened within hours of Quebec Premier Jacques Parizeau's blaming the defeat on "money and the ethnic vote." A resident in Canada for 25 years, Martinez summoned a security guard. Landry denied that the incident had taken place as reported until presented with a security videotape of the incident; he then apologized. Another witness stated that Landry angrily said, "*Maudits ethnics*" (damned ethnics). Landry later said, "It's true that the immigrant community massively voted No, to my great sadness. And I wonder about the cause of this phenomenon, but I don't blame anybody."

The next time there is a referendum in Quebec we will support the separatists.

Unidentified U.S. State Department official, addressing a threat to Canada's ambassador Raymond Chrétien in 1997, as recalled by James Bartleman, *Rollercoaster: My Hectic Years as Jean Chrétien's Diplomatic Adviser* (2005). The threat following publication of Prime Minister Jean Chrétien's indiscreet remark made (into an open microphone) to the leaders of Germany, Belgium, and Spain, at the 1997 NATO meeting in Madrid: "In your country and in mine, all the politicians would be in prison because they [Americans] sell their votes. They sell their votes! You want me to vote on NATO, then you have to vote to build me a new bridge in my constituency."

It was magnificent, to be brought so close to the goal of the Quebec people. The people will go forward again, and very soon.

Lucien Bouchard, Quebec premier, announcing his resignation, National Assembly, Quebec City, 11 January 2001, translated and published in the *Toronto Star*, 12 January 2001.

It is said that if you oppose two mirrors with an intervening object you manufacture an infinity of regressing images. And since there are an infinite number of images it would take an eternity distinctly to look at each of them. The intervening object which multiplies to infinity in our political case is called a referendum. Staring into the double mirror is that peculiar coma we know in this country as constitutional reform.

Rex Murphy, broadcaster, address, "Canada after September 11," Toronto, 6 December 2001, The Empire Club of Canada.

I will not hold a losing referendum.... I will be happy to hold one before 2005 when the militants and the citizens who support sovereignty have mobilized people to the cause.

Bernard Landry, Quebec premier, deflecting criticism that he and the Parti Québécois lack a firm commitment to the independence of Quebec, in Rhéal Séguin, "Landry Rejects Bégin's Accusations," *The Globe and Mail*, 30 October 2002.

You know, at fifty plus one, I was not about to let go the country.... You don't break your country because one guy forgets his glasses at home.

Jean Chrétien, prime minister, responding to the close shave of the Quebec referendum on sovereignty, to Paul Martin, as quoted by Lawrence Martin, *Iron Man: The Defiant Reign of Jean Chrétien, Volume Two* (2003).

Historically, we've never had a referendum with a Conservative government. Conservative governments have a philosophy of federalism that Quebecers are more comfortable with.

Stephen Harper, Conservative Party leader, interviewed by the editors of *Maclean's*, 9 May 2005. The two Quebec referenda took place while Liberals held the federal reins.

Quebecers will vote overwhelmingly to separate. They will vote yes not because they have anything in particular to gain economically or politically, but simply because they are really tired of referendums. They have already been through two, and despite deciding twice to stay, the argument has gone on and on. It is driving them crazy.

Joey Slinger, columnist, "Viewpoint," *Toronto Star*, 9 June 2005.

REFORM PARTY *See also* Canadian Alliance; Political Parties

The West Wants In!

Slogan and tocsin of the Reform Party of Canada, coined by **Ted Byfield**, Conservative spokesperson and magazine publisher, used by Preston Manning at his Western Assembly in Vancouver in spring 1987, which led to the creation of the Reform Party four months later in Winnipeg, as noted by Lorne Gunther, *National Post*, 11 November 2005. Reform morphed into the Canadian Alliance in 2000 and, merging in 2003 with the rump of the Progressive Conservative Party of Canada, emerged as the Conservative Party of Canada.

Quebec wants out of Confederation; we want in.

Slogan of the Reform Party of Canada and its founding leader Preston Manning, in "Nice Country, Nice Mess," *The Economist*, 29 June 1991.

REFUGEES *See also* Emigration; Exile

I dream of a great statue below Quebec City on the Île d'Orléans, with its arms outstretched in welcome to immigrants as they first see the Canadian heartland. On that statue I would inscribe these words: Leave all your hates behind. Bring us only your love.

Gregory Clark, newspaperman, remark made following the arrival of Hungarian refugees in the late 1950s, in David Maclellan, *Canadian Geographical Journal*, February–March 1977.

Today, one Canadian in ten is a refugee.

Val Ross, journalist, *Maclean's*, 27 October 1980.

For me, there is a unifying idea of the Canadian experience. We are the debris of history. We are the children of the expelled, the persecuted, the abandoned and the marginal. We are the remnants of empires and the refugees of lost causes. It's not blood that unites us, it's the experience of refuge. That's how we recognize each other in foreign places.

Mark Starowicz, TV producer, "The Death of History," *The Globe and Mail*, 20 September 2000.

I came to Canada as a refugee. Forty-five years later, for me, Canada is a refuge still.

Joe Schlesinger, correspondent, testimonial, museum, Pier 21, Halifax, in Myriam Shechter, "Stepping Back in Time," *Toronto Star*, 8 January 2005.

A lot of people say if you want to go abroad and get a visa or Canadian citizenship and be a millionaire, get yourself raped.

Pervez Musharraf, president of Pakistan, interviewed in New York City by the editors of *The Washington Post*, 13 September 2005, as quoted by Tim Harper, "U.N. Summit," *Toronto Star*, 16 September 2005. Prime Minister Paul Martin bearded Musharraf for the remark. Amnesty International deemed it offensive. Musharraf denied making it, though he did brand his country's rape victims as attention-seekers.

REGINA

The best way to see Regina is through a double martini from 35,000 feet.

Sentiments attributed to prairie-based painter **Ronald Bloor** in the 1950s, according to Stephen Brook, *Maple Leaf Rag: Travels across Canada* (1987).

Reginans—and this is surely a sign of maturity and witness of grace—are content to live with and be themselves.

Edward McCourt, writer and traveller, *Saskatchewan* (1968).

If you can say "Regina" without giggling, give yourself 12 points.

Quiz question set by **William Ferguson** and **Ian Ferguson**, *How to Be a Canadian (Even if You Are One)* (2001).

REGIONALISM *See also* Communities; Economics; Federal–Provincial Relations

We are, furthermore, a country of regions, whose right to *remain* as regions we hold dear. (I never did figure out what was wrong with Joe Clark's "community of communities.")

Peter Gzowski, broadcaster and author, *The Private Voice: A Journal of Reflections* (1988).

Canada may be the most decentralized country in the world but, the most naturally divided, it must be.

Ken Dryden, hockey personality, lawyer, and author, address, Charles R. Bronfman Lecture in Canadian Studies, University of Ottawa, "The Canadian Way," *Maclean's*, 13 November 2000.

REGRETS

Regrets are killers, yet they're impossible not to have, except when you feel good, or well, as they say in French, which is the way you sometimes beat regret. It slips aside because everything led to this well state, so what's to regret?

Thoughts of the narrator of **Rick Salutin**'s novel *The Womanizer* (2002).

REGULATIONS *See also* Government; Law

We are constantly forming societies for the suppression of war, for the suppression of alcohol, for the suppression of industrial conflicts, and various other things, but in the main our activities both as individuals and in these organizations are directed to demanding that the government shall step in and regulate something or other, or enact something or other which we want enacted. (Applause.)

B.K. Sandwell, professor of English, address, "On Being Sorry for Ourselves," Toronto, 24 January 1924, The Empire Club of Canada.

RELIGION *See also* Belief; Buddhism; Catholicism; Christianity; Church; Faith; Ghosts; Gods; Islam; Judaism; Spiritualism

Thou shalt go to Upper Canada and shalt find a prepared people and they shall receive thee.

Hebert C. Kimball, elder in the newly formed Mormon church in upstate New York, April 1836, dispatching Elder Parley P. Pratt to carry the church's mission to Toronto. John Taylor, one of his converts, became the church's third president, following the death of Brigham Young, the second prophet, in 1877. The sentence above comes from the plaque on the Mississauga Stake of the Church of Jesus Christ of Latter-day Saints, Black Creek area of Toronto, August 2000.

About the only people who don't quarrel over religion are the people who haven't any.

Bob Edwards, publisher, *Calgary Eye Opener*, 15 October 1910.

The beliefs of savages are a veritable chaos. Not only do they vary from one place to another so that, for instance, along the shores of British Columbia scores of different religious systems can be found over a distance of a few hundred miles, but within the same tribe even various individuals will give widely divergent views on religious subjects. Within the mind of the same native even the most varied and contradictory opinions live together. It seems extremely probable that this diversity in space is paralleled by a similar diversity in time.

Denis Saurat, Anglo-French critic, *A History of Religions* (1934).

Religion developed to spare men against their consciences. [1950]

Harold Adams Innis, social scientist, *The Idea File of Harold Adams Innis* (1980), edited by William Christian.

The Bible is not a committed book. It is an anthology of poems.

François Hertel (pseudonym of Rodolphe Dubé), poet, addressing a session of the Expo World Poetry Conference 1967, quoted by John Robert Colombo, "Poetry at Expo," *The Canadian Forum*, October 1967.

When we flew over Otto Fjord it occurred to me that probably all the churches and cathedrals man has ever built to the glory of God would fit into this fjord which is only a portion of the Arctic. This land and its great unspoiled beauty is at times terrifying, and at other times makes you cry. I feel like I have just returned from the greatest church on earth.

Eli Bornstein, sculptor, on Otto Fjord on Ellesmere Island, N.W.T., "Notes on Art and Nature" (1986), *Eli Bornstein: Art toward Nature* (1996), edited by Jonneke Fritz-Jobse.

There was a religious schism in our family, as my mother was an agnostic and my father was an atheist.

Conrad Black, publisher, recalling his formative years, *A Life in Progress* (1993).

In our three cases we observe one of the wonders of humanity: the way that humankind articulates systems of belief so that we can manage to survive the rawness of a world that is so harsh as to be almost beyond belief.

Donald Harman Akenson, historian, *Surpassing Wonder: The Invention of the Bible and the Talmuds* (1998).

Everyone thinks he or she is right. I have never heard anyone ever say, "I think I'm in the wrong religion."

Peter Urs Bender, motivational speaker, characteristic remark, 11 May 2000.

Quebec has evolved into the most postmodern region on this continent, a status that is at least partially explained by the fact that only 29 per cent of Quebecers now believe in the Devil and fewer still, 26 per cent, believe in Hell, the lowest proportions, by far, of any region on the continent—the 3 per cent differential apparently being made up of those who think the Devil is with us, not in the afterlife.

Michael Adams, consultant, *Fire and Ice: The United States, Canada and the Myth of Converging Values* (2003), with Amy Langstaff and David Jamieson.

The oldest message and the only one that is in every religion in the world: "Do unto others as you would have them do unto you." Not because you are going to heaven or because you might go to hell, but because it's the right thing to do. Live your life as if this is all there is.

Art Linkletter, game-show host born in Moose Jaw, Sask., referring to American self-help author Norman Vincent Peale, in Barry Shainbaum, *Hope & Heroes: Portraits of Integrity & Inspiration* (2003).

Religion explains everything—except why.

Peter C. Newman, journalist and memoirist, *Here Be Dragons: Telling Tales of People, Passion, and Power* (2004).

REMEMBRANCE DAY *See* Holidays: Remembrance Day

REPUTATION

Reputation is your character minus what you have been caught doing.

Seymour Schulich, business executive and philanthropist, slightly adapted from an interview by Peter C. Newman, address, "Titans," Toronto, 10 November 1998, The Empire Club of Canada.

RESEARCH *See also* Medical Research; Psychical Research; Science; Technology

National Research Laboratories / Great is Truth, and Mighty above All Things: / It Endureth, and Is Always Strong: / It Liveth and Conquereth for Evermore. / The More Thou Searchest, the More Thou Shalt Marvel.

Words carved in stone above the main entrance to the old and imposing National Research Laboratories on Sussex Drive, Ottawa, in late 1935, earlier chosen by Prime Minister **W.L. Mackenzie King**, as noted by Boris Stoicheff, *Gerhard Herzberg: An Illustrious Life in Science* (2002). The words are described as "apocryphal statements from the book of Esdras."

[I] think it to be most important that the young man or woman undertaking a research career should be imbued very early with the intense if not burning desire to extend the frontiers of knowledge, and this should be his or her paramount thought.

J.B. Collip, medical researcher, notes for an address (1948), in Alison Li, *J.B. Collip and the Development of Medical Research in Canada: Extracts and Enterprise* (2003).

Someday there will be no war, no famine, no illness, no crime, no exploitation, no alienation. And then what? Will that be the end of our need for research and development? No, for we shall still have the flame hidden in our hearts. There will still be painting and chemistry, sculpture and physics, music and mathematics and ultimately in Utopia that is what NRC will be all about.

Larkin Kerwin, president, National Research Council, address, "And Now the Good News," Toronto, 12 November 1981, The Empire Club of Canada.

I decided to follow a byway, rather than the highway. It is a procedure I have subsequently recommended to beginning scientists in this country, where research strategy is best modelled on that used by Wolfe at the Plains of Abraham.... British General James Wolfe defeated the French defending Quebec in 1759 after scaling a cliff for a surprise attack.

John C. Polanyi, physicist, describing his early, underfunded experiments in "reaction dynamics," address, "A Scientist and the World He Lives In," Toronto, 27 November 1986, The Empire Club of Canada. Polanyi was addressing an audience of businessmen, not scientists or historians.

As we landed, a flag already flew over the Moon.

Cryptic admission of British cosmologist **Joao Magueijo** who with physicist Andreas Albrecht published their paper "Time Varying Speed of Light as a Solution to the Cosmological Problems" in *Physical Review D* in 1998, only to discover that John Moffat, a theoretical physicist at the University of Toronto, had taken scientific precedence, *Faster than the Speed of Light: The Story of a Scientific Speculation* (2003).

A biologist can walk into a room full of lay people and say, "Tse-tse flies are hermaphrodites," and not many people will demur. But if I walk into a room and say, "At the beginning of the twenty-first century, Canadians are more autonomous people than Americans," a tide of challenge and dissent rises immediately.

Michael Adams, consultant, *Fire and Ice: The United States, Canada and the Myth of Converging Values* (2003), with Amy Langstaff and David Jamieson.

RESOURCES *See also* Forests; Geology; Lumber & Lumbering; Mining; Technology; Water

"Rich by nature, poor by policy," might be written over Canada's door.

Goldwin Smith, political economist, well-known assessment of the social and economic conditions made in his *Canada and the Canadian Question* (1891).

Often we read that Canada is blessed with immense natural resources. Canada is blessed with cheap power. Sometimes I think it may not have been so much of a blessing. It is like the rich man's son who never learns to work. We have been blessed with riches, but I am not sure that we have been the most intelligent stewards. The time to do something about it is now.

Ursula Franklin, scientist, address, "The Conserver Society," Toronto, 30 March 1978, The Empire Club of Canada.

Let us recognize that Canada's greatest natural resources do not lie buried deep in the ground, but in the skills and talents of those who walk upon it.

Paul Martin, finance minister, Budget Speech, House of Commons, 18 February 1997.

Hewers of wood and drawers of water we began in the seventeenth century. Hewers of wood and drawers of water we continue to be in the twenty-first, at least while supplies last.

John Fraser, essayist, "Strange Journey," *The Walrus*, February 2005.

RESPONSIBILITY *See also* Accountability

Be attentive, be intelligent, be reasonable, be responsible.

Bernard J.F. Lonergan, Catholic philosopher, popular formulation of his "four transcendental precepts," as noted by Hugo A. Meynell in the entry "Bernard J.F. Lonergan (1904–84)," *The Oxford Companion to Canadian Literature* (2nd ed., 1997), edited by Eugene Benson and William Toye.

RETIREMENT *See also* Pensions

I went home, discussed it with the boys, put them to bed. I walked until midnight in the storm, then I went home and took a sauna for an hour and a half. It was all clear. I listened to my heart and saw if there were any signs of my destiny in the sky, and there were none—there were just snowflakes.

Pierre Elliott Trudeau, prime minister, announcing his decision to retire from public life, press conference, Ottawa, 29 February 1984. His "went for a walk in the snow" decision is celebrated each leap year.

Retired from earning but not from learning.

Motto of the website of geologist **Peter Fitzgerald-Moore**, on retiring in 1998 from the University of Calgary, in Lynn Gaudet, "Lives Lived," *The Globe and Mail*, 16 August 2004.

Canada is a great place to retire—if you're poor or work for the government.

Jonathan Chevreau, journalist, "The Big Squeeze Crimps Retirement," *Financial Post*, 26 May 2001.

REVOLUTION *See also* Politics; Rebellion; Violence

Every revolution is started by a crank, exploited by a politician, and terminated by a soldier.

Thoughts of a character in **Hugh MacLennan**'s novel *Two Solitudes* (1945).

The bourgeois has been the only revolutionary class in history. That thought crucifies me.

Irving Layton, poet and aphorist, *The Whole Bloody Bird (obs, aphs & pomes)* (1969).

No, if Canadians decided to have a real political revolution it would probably be like the 1993 federal election—unpredictable (no one guessed that the governing Conservatives would go from 169 seats in 1988 to two seats in 1993), contradictory (what other country would elect a separatist Opposition to its federal parliament?), and organized from the bottom up (both the Bloc and Reform ran "populist style" campaigns). Any revolution, to be truly Canadian, would also have to be "extremely moderate."

Preston Manning, politician, leader of Reform Party and later the Canadian Alliance, *Think Big: Adventures in Life and Democracy* (2002).

RICHLER, MORDECAI

Mordecai Richler is the Salman Rushdie of Canada.

Sam Orbaum, Montreal-born columnist, "Make 'em Mad, Mordecai Richler!" *The Jerusalem Post Magazine*, 6 November 1992.

Richler is as odd as a black polar bear: He is a Canadian who has not sought to live elsewhere to succeed internationally, and has succeeded anyway. He is a Jew who persecutes the anti-Semites. He is not afraid of what "they" will say, about him, his books, the Jews, the Québécois. He is a worldwide celebrity so completely unpretentious that he wore a wrinkled shirt to an ambassadorial reception in his honour. He is thoroughly politically incorrect. And in all the time I have heard him speak, he has never, not ever, punctuated a phrase with "eh?" Canadians must really hate him.

Sam Orbaum, Montreal-born columnist, "Make 'em Mad, Mordecai Richler!" *The Jerusalem Post Magazine*, 6 November 1992.

Forget about the family tree. Next they'll say Mordecai Richler's Mordecai *Richelieu*.

Approximate wording of the complaint about common ancestors made by one old French Canadian to another in the comic movie *La Florida* (1993).

Richler was, though he would disdain the term, Quebec's greatest writer.

Jacques Godbout, writer and filmmaker, "In Quebec Culture, a Deep Skepticism of Tradition," *The New York Times*, 16 September 2001.

RIDING

Inside every woman there's a little girl who wants to see the ponies.

Advertisement for "Checks' Day Out" at Woodbine Racetrack, Toronto, jointly placed by Woodbine and radio station Country 95.3 FM, *National Post*, 21 November 2003.

RIEL, LOUIS

I know that through the grace of God I am the founder of Manitoba.

Louis Riel, Métis leader, defence speech, Regina, Sask., 31 July 1885, "The Prisoner's Address," *The Queen vs. Louis Riel, Accused and Convicted of the Crime of High Treason* (1886).

They killed my brother Riel.

Attributed to **Honoré Mercier**, Quebec premier (1886–1892), referring to "les Anglos," as noted by Donald Rudin, "Not Quite the Birth of a Nation," *The Globe and Mail*, 17 March 2005. The phrase was adapted as "They Killed My Brother Richard" by André Laurendeau, in *Le Devoir*, following the riot over the suspension of hockey star Maurice Richard in Montreal on 13 March 1955.

It is all too easy, should disturbances erupt, to crush them in the name of law and order. We must never forget that, in the long run, a democracy is judged by the way the majority treats the minority. Louis Riel's battle is not yet won.

Pierre Elliott Trudeau, prime minister, address, unveiling of the Louis Riel monument, Regina, 2 October 1969.

RIGHT & WRONG *See* Ethics; Good & Evil; Principles; Values; Virtue & Vice

RIGHTS *See also* Aboriginal Rights; Abortion; Animal Rights; Charter of Rights and Freedoms; Communications; Free Speech; Freedom; Freedom of Expression; Human Rights; Women's Rights

In my belief, rights are rights are rights. There is no such thing as inside rights and outside rights. No such thing as rights for the tall and rights for the short. No such thing as rights for the front and rights for the back, or rights for East and rights for West. Rights are rights and will always be rights. There are no partial rights. Rights are fundamental rights. Rights are links in a chain of fundamental values that bind all individuals in a society that wants to be equitable, and just, and fair. Rights are bridges that unite people in a society through a set of fundamental values, and the minute you deny those rights, you withdraw that bridge, and create a gap between members of that society by denying those fundamental rights that bind them together.

Clifford Lincoln, defender of minority rights, resigning from the Quebec cabinet in 1988 over the decision to invoke the notwithstanding clause regarding Quebec's sign law, recalled by Jane Taber, "One M.P.'s Emotional Stand on Same-sex Marriage," *The Globe and Mail,* 22 August 2003.

Canadians have good reasons to love their country, and I would argue that our rights culture is one of them ... the essential distinctiveness of Canada itself lies in the fact that we are a tri-national community, trying to balance individual and collective rights without sacrificing the unity and equality of our citizenship. If you ask me what I love about my country, this is it.

Michael Ignatieff, commentator, *The Rights Revolution* (2000).

Deference ends where the constitutional rights the courts are charged with protecting begin. The rule of law can be shallow without proper mechanisms for its enforcement.

Majority report of the Supreme Court of Canada to the effect that it has the power to police the enforcement of its orders in appropriate cases to prevent government inaction when it violates constitutional rights; drafted by Justices Frank Iacobucci and Louise Arbour, in Kirk Makin, "Supreme Court Says Judges Can Ride Herd on Politicians," *The Globe and Mail,* 7 November 2003. It was a 5-to-4 decision in a case instigated by parents demanding French-language instruction in certain school districts in Nova Scotia.

RISKS

We can't smell roses unless we are willing to handle thorns.

Reg Hartt, film exhibitor, email, 18 August 2003.

RIVERS *See also* Water

In France it would have seemed a mighty stream, but, coming fresh from the vastness of the St. Lawrence, their eyes were used to great sheets of water.

Observation made about the Richelieu River in Quebec by a French-Canadian character in **Sir Arthur Conan Doyle**'s novel *The Refugees: A Tale of Two Continents* (1892).

The ripples begin when I begin: they wash up on that large circle, the world. / ... the Bow River, the gentle green river which has always flowed, / flowed larger than the Rockies have stood as the sentinels of time we believe them to be, / flowed always on the western edge of the small green world I have always called home.

Lines from a poem by **John Whyte** reproduced in green lettering on a window of the Whyte Museum of the Canadian Rockies, Banff, Alta., July 2001.

ROCKY MOUNTAINS *See also* Mountains

For all those numberless gigantic ruins which are discovered one after the other in our day, all those immense avenues of colossal ruins that cross North America along and beyond the Rocky Mountains, are the work of the Cyclopes, the true and actual Giants of old.

H.P. Blavatsky, theosophist, *The Secret Doctrine: The Synthesis of Science, Religion and Philosophy,* Volume II (1888; 3rd ed., 1902).

I lived there for about ten years of my life in all the hours of dreamland.

Sir Arthur Conan Doyle, writer and traveller, describing "my old familiar Rockies" after seeing them in Alberta in 1914, according to Christopher Redmond, "Sherlock Holmes from Sea to Sea," *Lasting Impressions: The 25th Anniversary of the Bootmakers of Toronto, The Sherlock Holmes Society of Canada* (1997), edited by George A. Vanderburgh.

The magnificence of the Rockies made beauty a weak word.

Elsa Gidlow, memoirist, passing through the Rockies by train in 1916, "I Come with My Songs" (1986), included by George Fetherling in *The Vintage Book of Canadian Memoirs* (2001).

But the talk always drifted to the valley of the South Nahanni River, which is one of the mystery spots in the North.

There used to be a tale of a valley in the Northern Rockies where hot springs produced a kind of tropical vegetation, and where, it was rumoured, strange prehistoric beasts were still alive. This pleasing story has been disproved by Dr. Camsell's flight in 1935.

But the mystery of the South Nahanni remains.

Sir Shuldham Redfern, secretary to Governor General Lord Tweedsmuir, account of his journey to the Arctic in 1937, noted by Susan Buchan, *John Buchan by His Wife and Friends* (1947).

The mountains are all right, I guess, but they sure do block the view.

Peter Berglund, retired Saskatchewan farmer living in Kelowna, B.C., quoted in 1958 by *Time's* correspondent Ed Ogle.

Well, if you still want your Rocky Mountains, keep them!

René Lévesque, separatist, addressing Yves Michaud, Quebec parliamentarian and federalist in 1967, in Peter Desbarats, *René: A Canadian in Search of a Country* (1977).

Nos belles Rocheuses....

Catchphrase ("Our beautiful Rockies") identified with federal politician **Jean Chrétien**, who particularly during the 1980s, frequently reminded his fellow Quebeckers that their nation was Canada, that Canada was much larger than Quebec, and that Canada included the Rocky Mountains, as recalled by Daniel Sanger, "Why It's Time for Us to Dump the Monarchy," *Saturday Night*, summer 2002. Between 1968 and 1984, he often exclaimed, "The Rockies are my Rockies. They were discovered by the *voyageurs* Radisson, des Groseilliers and La Vérendrye. I want them for my children and grandchildren."

I remember waking up and seeing the Rockies, with snow on them. I said, "Screw it, I'd rather starve here than live in Toronto." The Rocks have been doing that to people for 150 years.

Ian Tyson, folksinger and rancher, *I Never Sold My Saddle* (1994), with Colin Escott.

ROMAN CATHOLICISM *See* Catholicism; Religion

ROWING *See also* Sports

In rowing, fear is sitting at the starting gate and knowing that ten years of work all boils down to seven minutes. I could fail by being so terrified and so overwhelmed that I'm incapable of performing.

Silken Laumann, champion rower, in Barry Shainbaum, *Hope & Heroes: Portraits of Integrity & Inspiration* (2003).

ROYAL CANADIAN MOUNTED POLICE *See also* Crime; Police

The famous force is another of our Canadian links with the days of chivalry. Like knights of old, only a thousand times more thrilling, they ride abroad to protect the weak. The uniform, the riders, their glorious record, the countless stories of danger and success that are told of them all, make immediate appeal to the children, and not to the children only.

Instructions to teachers on reading a poem about the Mounted Police, appendix, *The Canadian Poetry Book: A Book of Modern Verse* (1922), edited by D.J. Dickie.

Oh, Rose-Marie, I love you! / I'm always dreaming of you.

Couplet from one of the most famous love duets of modern times, identified with the Mounties, from the operetta *Rose-Marie,* the hit of the 1924 Broadway season, with music by Rudolf Friml and lyrics by **Otto Harbach** and **Oscar Hammerstein II**. In 1935, it was filmed as *Rose-Marie* by Hollywood with Jeanette MacDonald and Nelson Eddy.

The story you are about to hear was taken from the files of the Royal Canadian Mounted Police ... or as they say in Hull, Quebec ... doz buggers.... The story was taken from

Mountie files, and until now, has not been missed. "I was sitting in my lonely log cabin, on the fourteenth floor of Mountie headquarters, with my incredible dog Cuddles, and so on and so on…

Dave Broadfoot, comedian, address, "Dave Broadfoot's Canada," Toronto, 9 March 1978, The Empire Club of Canada.

We like to believe that the motto of the R.C.M.P. is still "Give us the charge and we will find the man." The official policy of the K.G.B. in the U.S.S.R., on the other hand, is simpler: "Give us a man and we will find him a charge."

Morris Shumiatcher, Regina advocate, *Man of Law: A Model* (1979).

Actually, the Mounted Police were formed to protect the Indians from the wild settlers.

Pierre Berton, historian, disagreeing with Hollywood's version of the opening of the West, in Margo Goodhand, *Winnipeg Free Press*, 20 May 2000.

One is often left wondering whether Dudley Doright is a cartoon or a documentary.

William Kaplan, advocate and author, referring to the Force's handling of the Airbus inquiry, *A Secret Trial: Brian Mulroney, Stevie Cameron, and the Public Trust* (2004).

To wear the uniform of the RCMP is to dedicate oneself to feats of courage and to nobility of purpose. It is to carry one of Canada's greatest traditions into a future of unyielding change.

Paul Martin, prime minister, tribute, Edmonton, 10 March 2005, published in the *Toronto Star*, 11 March 2005. It was delivered at the memorial service held in Edmonton for the four officers slain near Mayerthorpe, Alta.

ROYAL COMMISSIONS

A chance remark by somebody coming out of a bank or a supermarket might tell the man of the future a lot more about the 1970s than a whole shelf of Royal Commission reports.

Andrew Allan, radio producer, "On Writing Memoirs," *Andrew Allan: Self-Portrait* (1974).

After all, people will be reading the poems and aphorisms of F.R. Scott, Irving Layton, and Louis Dudek long after the reports of Royal Commissions have been relegated to the stacks of all but the largest reference libraries.

John Robert Colombo, editor, preface, *Colombo's All-Time Great Canadian Quotations* (1994).

ROYAL FAMILY *See* British Monarchy

ROYAL TOURS *See also* British Monarchy

I need not tell you how deeply I have been touched by the wonderful welcomes which have been given me in every city, town and hamlet, which I have visited in the great Dominion. These welcomes have been quite overwhelming, and I can never be sufficiently grateful to Canadians for the warmth with which they have received me, nor can I ever forget it.

Edward, Prince of Wales, address, "An Address," Toronto, 2 November 1919, The Empire Club of Canada.

As you know, my right hand has been out of action for nearly two months. When asked why I shake hands with my left hand, I always reply that my right hand was "done in" in Toronto. Though painful at the time, I shall always look back on that as a great compliment.

Edward, Prince of Wales, address, "An Address," Toronto, 2 November 1919, The Empire Club of Canada.

The Prince gets here on Tuesday. Prince Charming, the Ambassador of Empire, the fair haired bugger.

Ernest Hemingway, journalist and future novelist then a Toronto resident, letter written from that city to Ezra Pound, 6 September 1923, included by Carlos Baker in *Ernest Hemingway: Selected Letters* (1981). It refers to the arrival of the Duke of York, the future Edward VIII.

The King, the Queen and Mr. King have now arrived at the city hall and Mr. Queen is on the steps to meet them.... The King is now shaking hands with Mr. Queen and now the Queen is shaking hands with Mr. Queen, and now Mr. King is shaking hands with Mr. Queen.... And now the King and Mr. Queen and the Queen and Mr. King are moving into the reception hall ... And now the King and Mr. Quing, I mean Mr. Keen and the Quing, I'm sorry, I mean, oh sh—.

An unnamed CBC radio announcer thus covered the royal visit and the arrival of Their Majesties King George VI and Queen Elizabeth at the city hall, Winnipeg, 24 May 1939. In addition to Their Majesties and their host Prime Minister Mackenzie King, the cast of characters included Mayor John Queen and Mrs. Queen. The transcript appears in Tom MacDonnell, *Daylight upon Magic: The Royal Tour of Canada—1939* (1989).

Although it is hard to believe she would harbour any real affection for Canada, she does appear to have some bemused fondness for our fractured selves.

John Fraser, columnist, referring to Queen Elizabeth II, "In Between Two Portraits," *National Post*, 5 June 2002.

Neil Wadhvana: All these people that are around you, they come from different parts of the world. But we all live together in peace and harmony. Thank you for coming today. I hope some day I can come and visit you at your royal castle. If you need my help, call me any time.
Queen Elizabeth: You will be a politician some day.

Unplanned exchange between **Neil Wadhvana**, a lively six-year-old Canadian boy, and an amused **Elizabeth II** on her Jubilee visit, Copps Coliseum, Hamilton, Ont., 10 October 2002, in Rob Faulkner, "'Call Me Any Time,'" *Toronto Star*, 11 October 2002.

During a previous visit thirty-two years ago I said that "I want the Crown in Canada to represent everything that is best and most admired in the Canadian ideal. I will continue to do my best to make it so during my lifetime, and I hope you will all continue to give me your help in this task." I would like to repeat those words today as, together, we continue to build a country that remains the envy of the world.

Elizabeth II, Queen, Speech from the Throne, delivered to mark the centennial of Alberta, Alberta Legislature, Edmonton, 24 May 2004, in Jason Markusoff, David Howell, and Elizabeth Withey, "Queen Makes History at Legislature," *National Post*, 25 May 2004.

The Queen, it's assumed, will never visit Canada again, and that's a good thing. She does bring out the worst in us. And perhaps she will be the last monarch ever to visit Canada, in a ceremonial capacity at any rate. That would be a good thing, too. Unaccountably, they endure. But why, dear god, do we?

Margaret Wente, columnist, referring to Queen Elizabeth's visit to Alberta to mark the province's centennial, "Your Majesty: Here's Your Hat, What's Your Hurry?" *The Globe and Mail*, 26 May 2005.

RUNNING

If you remember where you were the day Ben got caught: 1 point.

Quiz question set by **William Ferguson** and **Ian Ferguson** in *How to Be a Canadian (Even if You Are One)* (2001). It refers to sprinter Ben Johnson who on the day to remember—Monday, 26 September 1988—ran the 100-metre event in 9.79 seconds at the Seoul Olympics. Two days later the Olympic committee stripped "the fastest man in the world" of his gold medal for a drug infraction.

RUSSIA *See also* Communism

Life there, from what I can gather at a distance of six thousand miles,—which is all I propose to gather—seems in some way—how shall I say it, restrained, what one might call unhomelike.

Stephen Leacock, humorist, *Over the Footlights* (1923).

Canada and Canadians want very much to be able to look to the north, as they have looked to the south, and see friends in each direction.

Pierre Elliott Trudeau, prime minister, address in the Soviet Union in 1971, in Ian Urquhart, *Maclean's*, 20 February 1978.

Ladies and gentlemen, the world is presently at a crossroads. Tomorrow may never come. In the words of John [Kenneth] Galbraith, "All ashes are very similar." Whether they are from different systems, from the forces of Good or Evil, from believers or atheists, soldiers or children, geniuses or plain workers and farmers. We are representatives of different political systems, different civilizations, but we are linked by life itself—we must live together or die together.

Alexander Yakovlev, U.S.S.R. ambassador to Canada, address, "Idols and Dangers of Our Complex World," Toronto, 3 February 1983, The Empire Club of Canada.

The distance between the continents should not be measured by the minutes of flight of ballistic missiles, but by the closeness of our human values, the most basic of which is life itself.

Mikhail Gorbachev, member of the Soviet Politbureau, first foreign visit, addressing Parliament's foreign-affairs committees, May 1983, in Christopher Shulgan, "The Walk That Changed the World," *Saturday Night*, April 2003.

Gorbachev: In Russia, we won't have factories this advanced for a hundred years.
Yakovlev: See? I told you so.

Exchange between Politbureau member **Mikhail Gorbachev** and Soviet Ambassador **Alexander Yakovlev** during a tour of the Heinz tomato factory in Leamington, Ont., May 1983, overheard by Ottawa official James Wright, and quoted by Christopher Shulgan, "The Walk That Changed the World," *Saturday Night*, April 2003. So it seems that the Cold War began and ended in Ontario—with the defection of Igor Gouzenko in Ottawa in September 1945 and with this conversation in Leamington in May 1983 and that the seeds of *glasnost* and *perestroika* were planted and would grow like the tomatoes of the Heinz 57 varieties.

Another project is the Arctic Bridge, which is designed to shift the main flow of goods between the two countries to northern routes with the use of sea ways. In Russia this area of activity is fairly effective and some success was developed back in Soviet times. I am convinced that with the development of the Arctic junction our countries will become much closer to each other, and on this northern theme we have a whole package of long-term projects.

Vladimir Putin, president, Russian Federation, address, "Political and Economic Events in the Russian Federation," Toronto, 19 December 2000, The Empire Club of Canada.

You may have seen something in the papers about the movement in Quebec to seek independence and become a country on its own. It won't work, I am ready to bet, because Washington would not put up with a fragmented Canada to its North. They have not yet ridded themselves of a dread that the Russkies are going to come over the Pole, squash Canada in seven minutes (they call us Seven Minutes in the Pentagon) and attempt to subdue the great republic and put its free citizens into peonage. Opium dream though this is, it has astonishing strength.

Robertson Davies, man of letters, letter, 1 August 1994, *For Your Eye Alone: Letters, 1976–1995* (1999).

Note: Second-largest country in world (after Russia); strategic location between Russia and U.S. via north polar route.

Editors, *The CIA World Factbook* (1995–1996), in Wayne Grady, *Chasing the Chinook* (1998).

I gave ten years of my life to Canada. I carefully studied Canadian life. It was a simple, pragmatic life, based on common sense. I wondered why we in the Soviet Union refused to give up our dogmas. My instructions from

Moscow—to criticize Canada to promote our propaganda—seemed so silly to me.

Alexander Yakovlev, Russian statesman, Soviet ambassador to Canada (1973–1983), writing in his memoirs *Maelstrom of Memory*, quoted in Geoffrey York, "Why Father of Glasnost Is Despised in Russia," *The Globe and Mail*, 9 March 2001.

RWANDA *See also* Africa; Genocide

Rwanda, that's somewhere in Africa, isn't it?

Roméo Dallaire, lieutenant-general, recalling his response in 1993 to the order issued by Major-General Armand Roy, military area commander for Quebec, to head a peacekeeping mission to the troubled African country, in *Shake Hands with the Devil: The Failure of Humanity in Rwanda* (2003).

S

SAINT JOHN, N.B.

How dare you claim to come from my home town. Get out of my office. We don't want frauds at MGM.

Louis B. Mayer, Hollywood mogul (1885–1957), addressing actor Walter Pidgeon, both one-time residents of Saint John, N.B., in Charles Foster, *Stardust and Shadows: Canadians in Early Hollywood* (2000). Pidgeon convinced Mayer that Saint John was his hometown too.

As Canadian cities go, Saint John is old; but when compared with European cities it's only a coastal settlement. The real Saint John is only just beginning to be built, and that's true of most Canadian cities.

Alden Nowlan, poet and essayist, "Alden Nowlan's Canada," *Maclean's*, June 1971.

ST. JOHN'S, NFLD.

St. John's is the oldest continuously inhabited settlement of the Western Hemisphere. From the year 1498 St. John's has not continually, but continuously, populated the oldest white man's settlement of the New World, and continuously British, the first of Britain's overseas, of Britain's most ancient and, we say, most loyal colony ... the first place on earth where the British flag was planted outside the British Isles ... the rendezvous of every seaman, of every Captain of every ship, of every adventurer that ever left Europe ... for two whole centuries, the rendezvous of them all. Wherever they might be going, St. John's is where they came first.

J.R. (Joey) Smallwood, Newfoundland premier, address, "Newfoundland," Toronto, 19 November 1959, The Empire Club of Canada.

The harbour could—if it were like the old harbour at Marseilles, for example—be very nice. One imagines clapboard houses, clean restaurants beyond a pleasant quayside framing the water. Actually there is a huge Esso oil refinery and several factories on the side opposite the town....

Stephen Spender, English poet, journal entry, St. John's, Nfld., 27 March 1975, *Journals, 1939–1983* (1985), edited by John Goldsmith.

ST. LAWRENCE RIVER

We held to the St. Lawrence (it is astonishing how the old water-ways still pull us children of the air), and followed his broad line of black between its drifting ice-blocks, all down the Park that the wisdom of our fathers—but every one knows the Quebec run.

Narration of the pilot of a General Post Office "coach," an airship administered by the "Aerial Board of Control" in the year 2000, en route from Athabasca over Quebec along the St. Lawrence River and then across the Atlantic to England, in **Rudyard Kipling**'s prophetic story "With the Night Mail: A Story of 2000 A.D." (1905), *Actions and Reactions* (1909).

The dream of the commercial empire of the St. Lawrence runs like an obsession through the whole of Canadian history; and men followed each other through life, planning and toiling to achieve it. The river was not only a great actuality: it was the central truth of a religion.

Donald G. Creighton, historian, *The Empire of the St. Lawrence, 1760–1850* (1937, 1956).

The traditional sights of Egypt are well worth a view, though for someone accustomed to the St. Lawrence, the lower Nile is an absurdly slow and narrow course of torpid brown fluid.

Conrad Black, publisher and historian, *A Life in Progress* (1993).

SALESMANSHIP *See also* Markets & Marketing; Merchandising

It was that well known, and not entirely uncommunicative Torontonian, Roy Thomson, who once told me the only difference between rape and rapture is salesmanship. I admit I'm rapturous about Bermuda. Just come and see for yourselves.

Sir Edwin Leather, Ontario-born governor of Bermuda, address, "Bermuda Calling," Toronto, 12 December 1974, The Empire Club of Canada.

The best salesman hasn't been hired yet.

Jim Pattison, entrepreneur, in Russell Kelly, *Pattison: Portrait of a Capitalist Superstar* (1986).

People buy your ideas because they like you.

Peter Urs Bender, motivational speaker, characteristic remark, 11 May 2000.

SAME-SEX MARRIAGE *See also* Marriage

So far, the debate has been among lawyers. It is time for there to be a debate in Canadian society as a whole.... If same-sex marriage receives the approval of Parliament, then what?

Aloysius Ambrozic, Roman Catholic cardinal, archbishop of the Diocese of Toronto, "An Open Letter: Why the Rush on Same-Sex Marriage?" *The Globe and Mail*, 19 January 2005.

But same-sex marriage doesn't breed polygamy. Same-sex marriage breeds nothing, by definition. If polygamy comes to Canada, it'll come because Canada no longer has the courage of its culture.

George Jonas, columnist, "Readers of Multicult vs. Amazons of the Status Quo," *National Post*, 24 January 2005.

Toronto is the gay marriage capital of North America. More same-sex couples have tied the knot here than anywhere else on the continent: at press time, 2,233 since June 10, 2003, when Ontario expanded the province's definition of marriage to include gay and lesbian unions. Adam and Steve can now officially wed in seven provinces and one territory. And a final parliamentary vote could make Canada the third country in the world—along with Belgium and the Netherlands—to enshrine gay marriage in statute law.

Sara Wilson, journalist, "The Marriage Question," *Toronto Life*, June 2005.

Corruption is not a Canadian value; marriage is a Canadian value.

Stephen Harper, Opposition leader, address to protestors on Parliament Hill, linking the corruption that gave rise to the Gomery Inquiry with Bill C-38 (which legalizes same-sex unions), in David Krayden, "Counterpoint," *National Post*, 8 June 2005.

Prime Minister Martin should be given credit for inspiring the grassroots of Canadian politics. Nobody has energized so many Canadians as he has in opposition to same-sex marriage.

Adapted from a remark attributed to Senator **Anne Cools** by David Krayden, "Counterpoint," *National Post*, 8 June 2005.

SARS *See* Severe Acute Respiratory Syndrome (SARS)

SASKATCHEWAN

Her population is about five million souls. Her Valley of the Saskatchewan alone, it has been scientifically computed, will support eight hundred millions. In losing the United States, Britain lost the *smaller* half of her American possessions; the Colony of the Maple Leaf is about as large as Europe.

William D. Lighthall, editor and nationalist, introduction, *Songs of the Great Dominion: Voices from the Forests and Waters, the Settlements and Cities of Canada* (1889).

The Land of Living Skies.

Slogan of Tourism Saskatchewan, chosen from submissions to its 1997 contest, won by Becky Pritchard of Tisdale, Sask. These five words were added to the province's automobile licence plates in January 1998.

Saskatchewan and Ontario. Saskatchewan so bitter, tenacious, aware. Ontario so careless and immune. An affair between two landscapes and two histories no less real, and no less ongoing than are certain romances between people.

Passage from **Elizabeth Hay**'s novel *A Student of Weather* (2000).

The little town was a lost city, three hours' rail ride out of Winnipeg in the middle of a thousand-mile snowfield, and Justin walked in it determinedly, avoiding the gaze of rare passers-by.

Description of an imaginary community said to be located in Saskatchewan in **John le Carré**'s novel *The Constant Gardener* (2000).

Has Saskatchewan suddenly become cool? We're too old, too small, too rural, too boring, too cold, too dry and too flat. Suddenly it has become very hip to be square ... or, more accurately put, rectangular.

Murray Mandryk, columnist, on his native Saskatchewan, in Roy MacGregor, "Saskatchewan Turns One Hundred," *The Globe and Mail*, 24 December 2004.

The Great Plains are a land for visionaries, they induce visions, they are themselves visions, the line between fact and dream is so blurred. What other landscape around the world produces the mystic psyche so powerfully? Sky and land, that is all, and grass, and what Nature leaves bare and the human psyche fills.

Sharon Butala, author, *Perfection of the Morning: An Apprenticeship in Nature* (1994), in Roy MacGregor, "Saskatchewan Turns One Hundred," *The Globe and Mail*, 24 December 2004.

We are many and we are one. / Lift your voice and sing Saskatchewan. / We are many and we are one. / 'Cause we love this place, Saskatchewan.

Chorus of "Saskatchewan, We Love This Place!" composed by **Stan Garchinsky** and the winner of the province's Centennial song contest, January 2005, in Lana Haight, "Saskatchewan Has a Song in Its Heart," *National Post*, 29 January 2005.

Saskatchewan is not only a province with a hundred years of heart. We are a province now with a song in our hearts.

Lorne Calvert, Saskatchewan premier, referring to the winning centennial song, Stan Garchinsky's "Saskatchewan, We Love This Place!" in Lana Haight, "Saskatchewan Has a Song in Its Heart," *National Post*, 29 January 2005.

This is the province that is the hardest to spell but the easiest to draw.... We revel in being geographically challenged. Our great town of North Portal is in the deep south, South End is in the North, Eastend is in the West. And West Bend is in the East.

Ralph Goodale, minister of Finance, address in Regina, May 2005, in Jane Taber, "Ottawa Notebook," *The Globe and Mail*, 27 August 2005.

SASKATOON

Where on Earth is Saskatoon, Saskatchewan?

Gerhard Herzberg, 29-year-old scientist in Darmstadt, Germany, reacting to a letter dated 29 March 1933 from Dr. John W.T. Spinks, chemist at the University of Saskatchewan, suggesting there might be a position available in chemistry at the Saskatoon campus. "They looked for it in their atlas and found that such a place actually existed, in the vast western prairies of Canada. That this tiny dot on the map of a far-off, unknown country would within two years provide them with a safe haven from a turbulent Germany and a welcome home was of course unforeseen by them." So writes Boris Stoicheff in *Gerhard Herzberg: An Illustrious Life in Science* (2002).

It's good to be here ... in Saskatoon, Saskatchewan ... Saskatoon, Saskatchewan. If you say that often enough, you don't need dental floss.

Bob Hope, comedian, routine performed in that city in the 1960s, as recalled on his hundredth birthday, CBC Radio, 29 May 2003.

Only someone standing with one foot in a pail of boiling water and the other frozen into a pail of ice can truthfully say: "On average Saskatchewan is very comfortable."

Hugh Arscott, aphorist, *Hugh's Views: Volume 4* (2000).

Saskatoon has more people than the entire province of Prince Edward Island.

Will Ferguson, columnist, "Mythic Isle," *Maclean's*, 12 August 2002.

We discovered from our round table with the writers why Saskatoon is a very good place to be a writer. Because it's "one of the few places where a poet can buy a house."

Adrienne Clarkson, governor general, address, "Challenging Cities in Canada," McGill Institute for the Study of Canada, 12 February 2003, "The Making of Good Cities," *Toronto Star*, 28 February 2003. Two of the writers present were Guy Vanderhaeghe and David Carpenter.

SASQUATCH *See also* Monsters

Are the vast mountain solitudes of British Columbia, of which but very few have been so far explored, populated by a hairy race of giants—men—not ape-like men? ... "The strange people, of whom there are but few now—rarely seen and seldom met—" said the old hunter, "are known by the name of Sasquatch, or, 'the hairy mountain men.'"

J.W. Burns, Indian agent, "Introducing B.C.'s Hairy Giants," *MacLean's Magazine*, 1 April 1929. (The monthly publication later became *Maclean's* magazine.) Burns first used the Salish word *sasquatch* to refer to the "hairy mountain men" said to inhabit the remote interior regions of British Columbia. The term Bigfoot (or Big Foot) did not appear in print until 5 October 1958, when Andrew Genzoli, editor of the *Humbolt Times*, coined it to describe the plaster cast of a large hominid footprint found in the mud of Bluff Creek Valley, California. The American media immediately adopted the new name. Yet there is a difference between the American creature and the Canadian creature: the Sasquatch is a human being, however primitive, while Bigfoot is an animal.

I'm a big, rough, tough Sasquatch from back of beyond, / I'm not a monster from a prehistoric pond, / I'm a semi-human being, and surely it's no crime / If I want to leave my footprints in the sands of time. / Many people have seen me vanish in the woods, / And they maintain I was absconding with stolen goods, / But all I did was steal away, get out of sight: / At the approach of man, I took to the hills in flight. / I'm a big, rough, tough Sasquatch, I am indeed, / And I can disappear with most uncanny speed. / So whenever people say that they've seen me around, / The only proof they can show is footprints on the ground.

Percy Maddux, versifier, "I'm a Sasquatch," *Innisfail Province* (Alta.), 11 February 1975.

SCIENCE *See also* Belief; Future; Medicine; Research; Technology

The future belongs to science. More and more she will control the destinies of nations. Already she has them in her crucible and on her balances. In her new mission to humanity she preaches a new gospel.

Sir William Osler, physician, introduction to R. Vallery-Radot, *The Life of Pasteur* (1911).

I knew Rutherford well as we were colleagues at McGill for seven years. I am quite sure that he had no original intention of upsetting the foundations of the universe. Yet that is what he did, and he was in due course very properly raised to the peerage for it....

Stephen Leacock, humorist, referring to Sir Ernest Rutherford, who established the principle of radioactivity at the Cavendish Laboratories, McGill University, *Last Leaves* (1945).

However, I happen to believe that in science heresy is a virtue and reaction often a necessity, and that in no field of science are heresy and reaction more desirable than in evolutionary theory.

William R. Thompson, entomologist, introduction to the Everyman Library edition of Charles Darwin's *On the Origin of Species* (Dent, 1956), reprinted as a booklet, *New Challenging "Introduction" to* The Origin of Species (Revolution Protest Movement, 1967).

We are but children, wondering, bemused children. Let us see ourselves in perspective amidst this maze of concrete and steel and radioactive fallout and placid chlorophyll.

Evan Shute, physician and theorist, *Flaws in the Theory of Evolution* (1961).

Science is thus worth pursuing solely as an artistic process, that like our great artists progressively reveals to us the endless marvels in a truly marvellous world. Our culture needs scientists and technicians as it does cellists, poets and sculptors, because in every case the thing done is both intrinsically worth doing and a unique embodiment of truth. It is good for a sculptor to sculpt and good for us to see his sculpture. It is good for an engineer to plan and good for us to use the fruits of his planning. It is in beautiful activities that we are truly human.

Larkin Kerwin, president, National Research Council, address, "Now the Good News," Toronto, 21 November 1981, The Empire Club of Canada.

Science is the glory as well as the terror of mankind. Our respect for ourselves as a people requires that we, as a prosperous and civilized nation, contribute to this central strand in twentieth-century culture.

John C. Polanyi, chemist, address, "A Scientist and the World He Lives In," Toronto, 27 November 1986, The Empire Club of Canada.

Today I am convinced that the double-blind experiment is a "dud" method, used only by clinicians and administrators who have a lot of money and little imagination. It is a method which has never been validated, an emperor without clothes. I have been pointing this out for many years, but few see the naked emperor—the retrospective, double-blind, placebo-controlled experiment. I suspect that it is useful only after one already knows that a compound works, and that it is employed today mainly in order to get published and to satisfy funding agencies when one applies for grants.

Abram Hoffer, biochemist, "The Introduction of Megavitamin Therapy for Treating Schizophrenia," *The Rise of Psychopharmacology and the Story of CINP* (1998), edited by Thomas A. Ban, David Healy, and Edward Shorter.

Now it happens that inconsistencies and puzzles in science are like oxygen to my blood! My entire philosophy of science is predicated on the motto that anomalies are gateways to discovery.

Rand Flem-Ath, researcher, *The Atlantis Blueprint: Unlocking the Ancient Mysteries of a Long-Lost Civilization* (2000), with Colin Wilson.

The task of the liberal today is what it has always been: shaping a world without war or want. What is new, and science has something to do with it, is that we live in a time of runaway change in which we are being forced to implement that dream. Fostering creativity has never been more important.

John C. Polanyi, scientist, address, The New Liberalism Conference, Toronto, published as "Fostering Better Science," *Toronto Star*, 30 September 2002.

To science, not even the bark of a tree or a drop of pond water is dull or a handful of dirt banal. They all arouse awe and wonder.

Jane Jacobs, urban planning critic, *Dark Age Ahead* (2004).

I don't think there's any question, including the most basic philosophical conundrums of where did we come from, why are we here, what does it all mean, and, indeed, the biggest of them all, is there a God, that cannot be most effectively addressed through the application of the scientific method, especially with its absolute requirement that if an idea—such as the superstition of astrology—is disproven, then it must be willingly discarded.

Robert J. Sawyer, science-fiction author, "The Future Is Already Here" (1999), *Relativity: Stories and Essays* (2004).

SCIENCE FICTION *See also* Aliens; Space; Writers & Writing

I was … living in Toronto, near what is now the corner of 25th Street and Second Avenue.

Line from the futuristic disaster-scenario novel *The Storm of '92: A Grandfather's Tale* (1889), by **W.H.C. Lawrence**. It tells the story of a fishing dispute that provokes the United States into declaring war on Canada, which in turn is defended by the British and the Australian governments. A footnote to the sentence above reads: "Before the bombardment and fire, the city had no numbered streets or avenues, but in the re-building a more modern plan was adopted." Apparently, Yonge Street was renamed Sixth Avenue, King Street became Fifth Street, etc. By 1932, Canada's cities are "adorned with the stateliest triumphs of architecture and replete with all that wealth can create, or refinement approve." Noted by Karen Bennett in "Fantastic Toronto: Toronto in Science Fiction & Fantasy," *TorCon3: 61st World Science Fiction Convention, Toronto—August 28 to September 1, 2003* (2003).

But I do wonder whether some people might prefer at least a quiet and dignified obscurity to one involving publication with spaceships on the cover. And I wonder whether those people might include me.

Andrew Weiner, science-fiction writer, noting the diverse readerships of science fiction and mainstream literature, "SF—Not!," *The New York Review of Science Fiction*, May 1993.

The job of the science-fiction writer is to be profoundly ambivalent about changes in technology.

William Gibson, science-fiction novelist, in Robert J. Sawyer, "The Future Is Already Here" (1999), *Relativity: Stories and Essays* (2004).

Science Fiction is like taking a mirror and looking at the back of your head.

Attributed to Darko Suvin, literary critic, by novelist **Ursula K. Le Guin**, in Donna Bailey Nurse, "She Gives Sci-Fi a Good Name," *National Post*, 19 October 2000.

Okay, science fiction failed to deliver passenger service to Luna City, anti-gravity belts, or benign planetary government. But it did promote, worldwide, an awareness that a benign planetary government would be a good thing to have, and that's a start.

Spider Robinson, science-fiction author, "Forward—Into the Past!" *The Globe and Mail*, 1 January 2002.

Science fiction, I suspect, is now dead, and probably died about the time that Judy closed her anthology and left to found her memorial library to the genre in Toronto. I remember my last sight of her, surrounded by her friends and all the books she loved, shouting me down whenever I tried to argue with her, the strongest woman in a genre for the most part created by timid and weak men.

J.G. Ballard, British author, writing about science-fiction personality Judith Merril, foreword, *Better to Have Loved: The Life of Judith Merril* (2002), with Emily Pohl-Weary.

If there is a message science fiction can promulgate for the 21st century—a message that the world needs to hear—it is this: the rational, scientific worldview is the only perspective that effectively deals with reality.

Robert J. Sawyer, science-fiction author, "The Future Is Already Here" (1999), *Relativity: Stories and Essays* (2004).

Indeed, the appeal of mystery fiction for many readers isn't the intellectual puzzle of figuring out whodunit. Rather, it's the emotional lives of the characters, which are brought to the surface by the extreme circumstance of having someone close to them die. I'm looking for that same sort of laying bare of inner feelings in my science-fiction writing.

Robert J. Sawyer, science-fiction author, "Autobiography" (2004), *Relativity: Stories and Essays* (2004).

SCOTLAND

The designs of FIVE HUNDRED HIGHLANDERS who … were so audacious as to attempt an escape from theire lawful lords and masters whose property they are by emigrating from the lands of Mr. McDonald of Glenary to the wilds of CANADA, in search of that fantastic thing—LIBERTY—

Excerpts from the dedication by **Robert Burns**, the Scots poet, to the satiric poem "Address of Beelzebub" (1786 but facetiously dated "Anno Mundi 5790"), *Burns: Poems and Songs* (1968), edited by James Kinsley.

Go not to Glengarry if you be not a Highlandman.

Warning of a publication for prospective Scottish emigrants in 1829, referring to the district in Upper Canada that is today's Glengarry County, Ont., in Arthur Herman, *How the Scots Invented the Modern World* (2001).

There is not a college or university in Canada, where at least one "son of the heather" is not to be found in some high capacity.

Arthur Herman, historian, quoting a commentator in 1896, *How the Scots Invented the Modern World* (2001).

The Scot is very rarely discomfited. It is his amazing self assurance and complacency that gives the greatest laughter to other people. For instance, I can demonstrate that by the story of the head of the clan, MacGregor, who was giving a lecture on family tradition to his family and he said, "This history of the MacGregors is contained in five large volumes and in the middle of the second part of the third volume there is a wee marginal note which says, 'It was about this time that the world began.'" (Laughter.)

H. Napier Moore, editor, address, "The Melancholy of Laughter," Toronto, 7 February 1935, The Empire Club of Canada.

I have no Scotch in me except what I put in.

Stephen Leacock, humorist, *Here Are My Lectures and Stories* (1937).

Canada, in one sense, is simply Scotland writ large.

John Buchan, Governor General Lord Tweedsmuir, address in Winnipeg, St. Andrew's Day, 1936, in Arthur C. Turner, *Mr. Buchan, Writer* (1949). Someone else—not Lord Tweedsmuir—once said with respect to England, "Canada is Scotland's revenge."

The Scotch in Ontario may brood a little too darkly on sins material and immaterial, especially after the merriment of Hogmanay, but the habit of introspection is beneficial. It gives us a little perspective and a sense of a new beginning. The only trouble with it is that it doesn't last very long and it doesn't extend very far into the wider relations of states and nations.

Arthur Hays Sulzberger, president, *The New York Times*, address, "Power and Responsibility," Toronto, 12 January 1952, The Empire Club of Canada.

There are millions of Scots. Only one of them has marked the history of humanity in a decisive way. His name is Adam Smith.

Bernard Landry, Quebec premier, addressing a delegation of Scottish parliamentarians, Quebec City, "last month," according to Diane Francis, "How Landry Gets Away Scot-free," *Financial Post*, 1 December 2001.

SCULPTURE *See also* Arts & Artists

After landing in Montreal, I had to register at the immigration office. The young man at the desk asked me, "What is your 'trade'?" I did not know what he meant, so I said, "I am a sculptor." The pencil stopped in his hand. After a long pause, he looked at me and asked, "How do you spell it?" Not only had he never met one, he didn't even know the word. To simplify matters, I said that I carved little animals from wood. "Oh, that is wonderful, congratulations, and welcome to Canada!"

Dora de Pédery-Hunt, sculptor and medallist, quoted in the brochure *Dora de Pédery-Hunt / Retrospective Exhibition: 1949–1999* (1999).

SEAL HUNT *See also* Animals; Hunting

It's an anachronism. The Canadian seal hunt is like sending little boys up chimneys, stuffing hummingbirds for ladies' hats, and baiting badgers.

Richard Adams, author of *Watership Down* and vice-president of the Royal Society for the Prevention of Cruelty to Animals, quoted in *Maclean's*, 26 February 1979.

The Canadian seal "hunt" currently entails the biggest ongoing destruction of large, wild mammals anywhere in the world.

Farley Mowat, author, *The Farfarers: Before the Norse* (1998).

The commercial harvesting of seals on Canada's East Coast is more tightly regulated than ever before; humane practices are strictly enforced, with penalties for violations among the toughest in the world. Seals are an abundant, renewable resource. The harp seal population is one of the healthiest mammal populations in the world. It is a resource that allows people in our coastal communities to pursue their livelihoods with dignity. It provides a significant resource for aboriginal people.

John Efford, minister of Fisheries, Labrador and Newfoundland, address, "The Sealing Industry," Toronto, 22 January 1998, The Empire Club of Canada.

SEASONS *See also* Autumn; Spring; Summer; Winter

Now, when I am in England I say to my English friends, "There is an honesty about the very seasons in Canada. In the winter it is cold. In the summer it is hot."

Beverley Baxter, political commentator, address, "From the Heart of Things," Toronto, 9 September 1937, The Empire Club of Canada.

For it's forty below in the winter, / And it's twenty below in the fall. / It just rises to zero in summer, / And we don't have a springtime at all.

Lines from the refrain of the song "Forty Below," a four-verse parody of the folk song "Red River Valley," written by journalist **Christopher Dafoe** and published in his column "Coffee Break by Wink," *Winnipeg Free Press*, 39 May 1959. In the same vein, Marie-Lynn Hammond wrote "Canadian Love" (1980), which begins, "Oh Canadian love, Canadian love; / it's either 40 below or it's 90 above."

SECRETS *See also* Mysteries; Privacy

Canadian society is deficient, not in respect for law but in respect for liberty. And the fundamental function of secrecy in Canadian government practice is not concealment but the cultivation of docility.

Edgar Z. Friedenberg, political scientist, *Deference to Authority: The Case of Canada* (1980).

If you want to keep something secret, put it in print, like Hansard. The irony is that there's so much material that people become overwhelmed....

David Ben, magician and historian of magic, in Sylvia Fraser, "The Mogul and the Magician," *Toronto Life*, April 2001.

Secrecy becomes a greater evil—a danger to democracy itself—when it is used to prevent the process on which constitutional liberty depends, the adversarial justification of lesser evils.

Michael Ignatieff, essayist, *The Lesser Evil: Political Ethics in an Age of Terror* (2004).

SECURITY & INTELLIGENCE *See also* Freedom; National Interests; Privacy

Collective bluffing cannot bring about collective security.

Attributed to **W.L. Mackenzie King**, former prime minister, in a speech in the House of Commons in the 1930s by U.S. Secretary of Defence Donald Rumsfeld during a Pentagon briefing, 15 January 2003, as noted by Paul Koring, "Rumsfeld Conjures Up Mackenzie King Quote," *The Globe and Mail*, 16 January 2003. While Rumsfeld had in mind King's response to the failure of the League of Nations to act when Italy was threatening Abyssinia in 1935, the statement is atypical of King, who consistently cautioned inaction over action.

I am well aware that Canadian politics has long and systematically advanced the principle of security of the human being, which you deem equally important as that of security of the State, if not even more important. Let me assure you that this Canadian ethic enjoys a profound respect in my country. I would wish that we are not merely allies in a formal or institutional sense as members of the same defence alliance, but also as partners in promoting this worthy principle.

Vaclav Havel, president of the Czech Republic, joint session of the Senate and the House of Commons, 30 April 1999.

To keep your edge, you have to feel insecure.

Guy Laliberté, co-founder, Cirque du Soleil, in Sarah Scott, "Shock of the New," *Globe and Mail's Report on Business*, August 2002.

We Canadians always assume that we live in God's country and that we will always be secure and safe, well protected in our prosperity. But the world is still a dangerous place—after September 11, who can doubt it? At some point, Canada's national interests will require us to be prepared to fight to protect our security, and it won't help us much then to prattle about our values and principles to those who would do us harm. We need a capable Canadian Forces to fight for us, and it is only sensible today to prepare for whatever the future may bring.

J.L. Granatstein, historian, "We Must Begin Rebuilding Our Military—Now," *National Post*, 7 February 2004.

"Lie, deny, and then act surprised."

John Farrell, ex-CSIS agent, suggesting a motto for the Canadian Security Intelligence Service, testimony before Ernst Zundel's deportation hearing, in Kirk Makin, "CSIS Intercepted Zundel's Mail, Ex-Agent Says," *The Globe and Mail*, 17 September 2004.

True "security," most Canadians would argue, is achieved when people's basic needs and rights are met through decent jobs, a clean environment, universal health-care and education, cultural diversity, and peaceful co-existence.

Tony Clarke, founder of the Polaris Institute, "National Insecurity," *The CCP Monitor*, February 2005.

In the world's failed and failing states, the most urgent human need is security. People at the mercy of tyrants and gunmen need protection first of all.

Michael Ignatieff, commentator, address, biennial policy conference of the Liberal Party, Ottawa, 3 March 2005, excerpted as "A Generous Helping of Liberal Brains," *The Globe and Mail*, 4 March 2005.

SENATE

See also Government; House of Commons; Parliament

In the Upper House, the controlling and regulating, but not initiating branch, we have the sober second thought in legislation.

Sir John A. Macdonald, statesman, defining the role of the Senate, 6 April 1865, in Sir Joseph Pope, *Confederation* (1895). Pope also quotes Macdonald saying, less elegantly, "The Senate is the saucer into which we pour legislation to cool."

The only thing worse than a dormant Senate would be an active one.

Attributed to **Lester B. Pearson**, diplomat and prime minister, by Charles Lynch, "Reports Useless," Montreal *Gazette*, 21 January 1972.

The proposal for a "triple E" Senate (equal, elected, effective) includes provision for six senators from every province. That alone is enough to prove that it is just flailing the air, whistling in the wind, blowing soap bubbles.

Eugene Forsey, constitutional specialist, letter, *The Globe and Mail*, 25 April 1987, in J.E. Hodgetts, *The Sound of One Voice: Eugene Forsey and His Letters to the Press* (2000).

We need to abolish the Senate and replace it with a new chamber of democratically-elected citizens. These new citizen members would be people elected by their fellow voters from a list of candidates randomly chosen in the same way we select juries. Citizen representatives would hold the balance of power under this new arrangement, thereby depoliticizing our Parliament. This will allow government to focus more on the fundamental problems of the country rather than on short-term political solutions.

Frank Stronach, manufacturer, Magna International, address, "Operating within a Global Economy," Toronto, 10 February 1994, The Empire Club of Canada.

A lot of people think Senators are entirely preoccupied with protocol, alcohol and Geritol.

Ernest Manning, former Alberta premier, in Brian Brennan, *Alberta Originals: Stories of Albertans Who Made a Difference* (2001).

I find our Parliament a mockery of democracy. The Senate is a joke. The Senate is a scandal. What democratic country allows 25 per cent of its seats to be decided by a 19th-century appointment system? When the old Soviet Union was breaking up and those democrats were coming over here to learn about democracy I used to wonder where we should take them in Ottawa to show them how it works. We sure shouldn't take them to the Senate.

Preston Manning, contender for leadership of Canadian Reform Conservative Alliance, address, "Why I Want the Job of Being Your Next Prime Minister," Toronto, 19 June 2000, The Empire Club of Canada.

Man proposeth, God disposeth, and the Senate reposeth.

Eric Nicol, humorist, *Canadian Politics Unplugged* (2003), with Peter Whalley.

Senate appointments are taskless thanks.

Attributed to **Hugh Segal**, political commentator known to be critical of Senators if not the Senate, recalled by reporters when he himself was summoned to the Red Chamber. Interviewed by Gloria Galloway, "Segal's New Post Raises Eyebrows," *The Globe and Mail*, 4 August 2005. Segal then attempted to shift responsibility for the phrase "taskless thanks," adding, "I've used it. But I think it was a Liberal who first used it [perhaps as long ago as 1974]."

SEPARATISM

See also Bloc Québécois; Canada & Quebec; Ethnicity; October Crisis; Parti Québécois; Quebec; Sovereignty; Sovereignty-Association

English Canada will not make concessions—and we are not even sure of that—unless it has a knife at its throat.

Léon Dion, law professor, Laval University, constitutional specialist, and adviser to the Robert Bourassa administration, statement, Bélanger–Campeau Commission on the Future of Quebec, 12 December 1990, in Rhéal Séguin, *The Globe and Mail*, 13 December 1990.

I doubt that Quebec, unless it is oppressed or rejected in some unimaginable manner, has any real interest in independence if it costs anything and there is no version of independence that won't be costly.

Conrad Black, publisher and historian, *A Life in Progress* (1993).

One of the problems is that Quebeckers see their future quite differently than we do. We say: "Well, either you are in or you're out." There was a recent book called *The Six Degrees of Separation* and six degrees of separation in Quebec are separation, independence, sovereignty, sovereignty association, autonomy and special status. These things are all different to them and we have to respect that. We can't just say that you have to be in or out. We have to give them a chance to be understood.

Peter C. Newman, author, address, "The Canadian Revolution," Toronto, 30 November 1995, The Empire Club of Canada.

If Quebec insists on becoming a foreign country, we can negotiate that. It will not be easy. It will not be pleasant. It will impoverish us all, spiritually as well as materially. It will be a tragedy. But it can be done.

Eugene Forsey, constitutional specialist, "No Surrender," *Toronto Star*, 24 February 1991, in J.E. Hodgetts, *The Sound of One Voice: Eugene Forsey and His Letters to the Press* (2000).

I accept my full responsibility for not having succeeded in reviving the flame and in making citizens sensitive to the seriousness of the situation.... I only regret not having done better and more and above all not having been able to realize my dream for our collective future, to achieve the new Quebec nation.

Lucien Bouchard, Quebec premier, referring to the cause of Quebec's sovereignty, announcing his resignation, National Assembly, Quebec City, 11 January 2001, translated and published in the *Toronto Star*, 12 January 2001.

Faith can move mountains. In Quebec, it can relocate a whole province.

William Johnson, columnist, "Pit Bill," *The Globe and Mail*, 17 January 2001.

In Quebec, say the nationalists, all the real patriots have white hair. (It's true. I once attended a debate between sovereigntist writers, which was more like a round table, and the average age of the participants was unsettling.)

Daniel Poliquin, commentator and novelist, *In the Name of the Father: An Essay on Quebec Nationalism* (2001), translated by Don Winkler.

Quebec is imprisoned in a political debate without issue, between an undesired sovereignty and an impossible reform of federalism.

Alain Dubuc, editorialist for *La Presse*, LaFontaine-Baldwin Lecture, published in *The Globe and Mail*, 10 March 2001.

The Quebec question will haunt Quebec men and women until it is resolved. Resolving the national question means joining the United Nations.

Bernard Landry, Quebec premier, remarks to journalists following a PQ Cabinet meeting, La Malbaie, Que., 23 August 2001, in Kevin Dougherty, "Mourning Loss of 1995 Referendum Over: Landry," *National Post*, 24 August 2001.

The project for political sovereignty, it seems, has succeeded only on the personal level. Our national culture aspires to be international, and Quebec, which is still only a symbolic country, regularly showcases its arts abroad.

Jacques Godbout, writer and filmmaker, "In Quebec Culture, a Deep Skepticism of Tradition," *The New York Times*, 16 September 2001.

Quebec (whose official motto is "I Remember"), remains one of Canada's ten provinces and may continue to do so for a long time to come, from one referendum to the next. No matter. If boredom grows out of uniformity, our French presence on this continent is a factor for diversity.

Jacques Godbout, writer and filmmaker, "In Quebec Culture, a Deep Skepticism of Tradition," *The New York Times*, 16 September 2001.

Face the facts. Quebec separatists are mostly rednecks who speak French.

Diane Francis, columnist, "How Landry Gets Away Scot-free," *Financial Post*, 1 December 2001.

We have to rapidly rally a majority of our fellow citizens around a sovereignty project, not in twenty years, not in ten years, but in 1,000 days, in 2005.

Bernard Landry, Quebec premier, address to P.Q.'s National Council, Gatineau, Que., 7 September 2002, in Rhéal Séguin, "Parti Québécois Reneges on Promise of Referendum," *National Post*, 9 September 2002.

I say again to our friends in the rest of Canada: You have said too many times, separatism is dead. I agree, in a sense. Separatism is dead; welcome to sovereignty.

Bernard Landry, Quebec premier, news conference, Quebec City, 23 April 2003, in Rhéal Séguin, "Delaying Retirement, Landry Will Remain Opposition Leader," *The Globe and Mail*, 24 April 2003. Landry's reference to "sovereignty" recalls René Lévesque's call for "sovereignty-association" (in lieu of "separation"), yet what Landry promoted was his own nebulous notion of a "confederal union" of Quebec and Canada as achievement of Quebec's sovereign-nation status—which in turn echoed Robert Bourassa's musings about "an economic superstructure like the European Common Market").

In the end, what turned the tide against separatism in Quebec was the successful functioning of the federal system itself, which has allowed Quebec sufficient political autonomy to protect its language, culture, and economy.

Michael Ignatieff, essayist, *The Lesser Evil: Political Ethics in an Age of Terror* (2004).

Sovereignty is a concept that is outmoded. We see a resurgence of nationalism and patriotism everywhere in the world. But, for me, it's like a dying person where there is a bit of a revival just before death.... We have achieved it [sovereignty] in our minds. We have it in our hearts. We are Québécois and we have already come a long way. But for me, the legal status of a country called Quebec is no longer necessary. We are Québécois ... and nobody can take that away from us.

Yvon Deschamps, Quebec comedian and prominent sovereigntist, interviewed by Mario Langlois on Montreal Radio CKAC, quoted by Rhéal Séguin, "Sovereignty a Dying Concept, Quebec Entertainer Declares," *The Globe and Mail*, 6 May 2004.

The Clarity Act of 2000 permits any province to hold a referendum on separating, and if a clear question elicits a clear response then Ottawa is bound to negotiate a parting of the ways in good faith.

Michael Bliss, historian and columnist, referring specifically to Newfoundland and Labrador, not Quebec, "A Country of Their Own," *National Post*, 8 January 2005.

To me it seems simple: under the Liberals / Quebec and Ottawa are blades of a scissors: / One cuts the roots of the Fleur de Lys, / The other meddles with our services.

First two lines from the sing-along protest song "*Liberez-nous des Liberaux*" (Liberate Us from the Liberals), an ad hoc anthem composed by the rap group **Loco Locass** in 2003 and embraced by the Bloc Québécois, the Parti Québécois, unions, strikers, etc., as noted by Marty Patriquin, "Separatists Get a Theme Song," *National Post*, 4 June 2005.

It may be that a French Quebec can survive without Canada as well as a fish can survive on a snooker table, but we are not our brother's keeper. We won't even be our brother's brother any more. Frère Jacques will be an only child. Dormay voo.

Joey Slinger, columnist, "Viewpoint," *Toronto Star*, 9 June 2005.

SEPTEMBER THE ELEVENTH *See* Terrorism

SERVICE

The service we render to others is really the rent we pay for our room on this earth.

Sir Wilfred Grenfell, medical missionary, *A Labrador Logbook* (1938).

True service is unseen and unheard but never unnoticed.

Line from an advertisement for the Four Seasons Hotel and Resorts in the brochure *Festival of Festivals: 13th Toronto International Film Festival* (1988).

To turn, to love, to share the pain, / This is my life, my song, and its refrain.

Catherine de Hueck Doherty (1896–1985), founder of Madonna House, a centre dedicated to Our Lady of Combermere, Ont., characteristic assertion, website, June 21 2005.

SETTLERS *See also* Pioneers

Horrible experience had taught the Canadians what the English settlers had yet to learn, that in a land of savages it is a folly to place isolated farm-houses in the centre of their own fields.

Observation made by a Canadian character in **Sir Arthur Conan Doyle**'s novel *The Refugees: A Tale of Two Continents* (1892).

SEVERE ACUTE RESPIRATORY SYNDROME (SARS)

The majority of cases in the SARS outbreak in the greater Toronto area were related to hospital exposure.... Although SARS is associated with significant morbidity and mortality, especially in patients with diabetes and other comorbid conditions, the vast majority (93.5%) of patients in our cohort survived.

Christopher M. Booth with 20 other specialists, "Clinical Features and Short-term Outcomes of 144 Patients with SARS in the Greater Toronto Area," *Journal of the American Academy of Medicine*, 6 May 2003. The first SARS outbreak was reported in China's Guangdong Province.

This Friday, order the most expensive thing on the menu, buy the best seats in the house, give your plastic a workout, and don't crawl home before 2 a.m. Consider it your civic duty.

Text of large-size advertisements placed in Toronto's daily newspapers by the "Go Out Toronto Night" alliance of public and private interests launching a campaign to ease fears of SARS and minimize the warning of the World Health Organization about travel to and from the city. In smaller type it says, among other clichés, "We all know the Toronto economy has taken a real hit recently. We can either sit at home, or we can get out and do something about it.... Be a model citizen. Go out and get a little T.O. this Friday. In fact, get a lot." "'Go Out Toronto Night,'" *The Globe and Mail*, 2 May 2003.

This is the biggest party in Toronto's history, right? We're here, you're here, Toronto's back and it is booming.

Mick Jagger, lead singer of the Rolling Stones, addressing an enthusiastic audience of 450 000 youth, Molson Canadian Rocks Toronto Festival, Downsview Park, Toronto, "SARStock" (SARS relief combined with Woodstock), 30 July 2003, in Francine Dubé and Siri Agrell, "'Toronto's Back,'" *National Post*, 31 July 2003.

SEX *See* Abortion; Abuse: Sexual; Acquired Immune Deficiency Syndrome; Adultery; Homosexuality; Love; Lust; Marriage; Men & Women; Pornography; Prostitution; Same-sex Marriage; Women's Rights

Any ordinary reader would gather Freud advocates Free Love, removal of all restraints and a relapse into savagery.

C.K. Clarke, head of the department of psychiatry, University of Toronto, June 1910, as noted by Ernest Jones, a member of Clarke's department and an early proponent of psychoanalysis, recalled by Vincent Brome, *Ernest Jones: Freud's Alter Ego* (1983). Brome called this "as wildly inaccurate an account of the lectures as unbridled prejudice could produce." He added, "The impermeability of Canada to the rapidly growing new approach to psychological medicine, sex and mortality, which had begun far back in the 1880s with the work of Krafft-Ebing and Havelock Ellis, was remarkable."

The attitude in Canada towards sexual topics has I should think hardly been equalled in the world's history: slime, loathing and disgust are the only terms to express it.

Ernest Jones, psychiatrist and psychoanalyst, letter written from Toronto to Sigmund Freud in Vienna, 1911, in Vincent Brome, *Ernest Jones: Freud's Alter Ego* (1983).

Society is going to have to accept ... that premarital sex isn't always a bad thing; what is bad is the sense of guilt, shame and sin which keeps young people at arm's length from their parents and in a state of constant emotional tension. Furthermore we must make much less fuss about virginity and continence and realize that, while they're okay for some people, they are not necessarily okay for all.... At this point I fancy I hear a Greek chorus of well-intentioned old women carolling their slogan: "Would you want your daughters, etc...? ... Well, I have several daughters, mesdames, and I must tell you that this is not a question that haunts my slumber.... Indeed I would rather have them indulge in some good, honest, satisfying sex than be condemned to a decade of whimpering frustration brought on by the appalling North American practice called "petting."

Pierre Berton, columnist, "Pierre Berton's Page," *Maclean's*, 18 May 1963. This column was subtitled "It's time we stopped hoaxing the kids about sex." Such was the tenor of the times that officials of the United Church and other Christian congregations objected to Berton's expression of opinion. They pressed the publishers of *Maclean's* and the regular column was cancelled.

Sexuality is a scary thing. It cuts to the core of who we are and how we see the world.

Allan Gould, author, *What Did They Say about Gays?* (1995).

The gladiator on the cover of *Sports Illustrated* is the symbolic warrior, the ideal male. The sex worker on the cover of *Penthouse* is his symbolic lover—his reward. The women in the *Sports Illustrated* annual swimsuit issue look very much like those in *Playboy* and *Penthouse* and in *Cosmopolitan, Glamour,* and *Elle.*

Varda Burstyn, cultural critic, *The Rites of Men: Manhood, Politics, and the Culture of Sport* (1999).

If a man doesn't get an erection when he sees a heron, then he's not functioning. Flesh and spirit are one.

Attributed to **Scott Symons**, writer, as adapted by Sarah Hampson in an interview, "CanLit's Bad Boy Is Back," *The Globe and Mail*, 8 June 2000.

Casual sex may have always been an oxymoron, but now it is an anachronism.

Irena F. Karafilly, aphorist, characteristic observation, 7 November 2000.

English Canadians: puritanism touched by orgy. / French Canadians: orgy tainted by puritanism.

William Ferguson and **Ian Ferguson**, writers, *How to Be a Canadian (Even if You Are One)* (2001).

Some of them specifically requested Canadians, perhaps charmed by their accent, so subtle that it was hard to know if it came out of old France or England....

Passage from *The Past Recaptured*, a section from **Marcel Proust**'s *Remembrance of Things Past* (1913–1927), which describes the clients of Baron de Charlus' pederastic bordello, as noted by Daniel Poliquin, *In the Name of the Father* (2001).

The more sophisticated the circles in which one moves, the more it is taken for granted that a woman's promiscuity is no more a reflection on her general morality than a man's.

Barbara Amiel, columnist, in Peter C. Newman, *Here Be Dragons: Telling Tales of People, Passion, and Power* (2004).

Having sex with a woman is not unlike riding a bicycle. You never forget how, even though you may choose to ride a motorcycle.

Lines from **Edward O. Phillips**'s novel *A Voyage on Sunday* (2004)

The best sexual aphrodisiac is your partner's pleasure.

Frank G. Sommers, psychiatrist and sexologist, interviewed on SexTV's *Sexual Secrets*, 3 January 2004.

When it comes to sex, there's no right or wrong answer. For centuries people have been trying to make it a black-and-white issue—you're either a virgin or a whore. The truth is, it's all the shades of grey that make life interesting.

Ellen Kate Friedrichs, health educator, "Saint or Slut?" *Shameless: For Girls Who Get It*, fall 2004.

SEXUAL ABUSE *See* Abuse: Sexual

SHIPS & SAILING *See also* Water

The wood that can beat the *Bluenose* ain't been planted yet.

Angus Walters, captain of the *Bluenose*, the last of the great clipper ships, launched in Lunenburg, N.S., in 1921, in David MacDonald, "Unbeatable Bluenose," *Canada—This Land, These People: A Reader's Digest Collection* (1968).

Please put me back in the water. I am Paddle-to-the-Sea.

Message on the toy boat launched in Lake Nipigon, Ont., that makes its way to France in the popular children's book *Paddle-to-the-Sea* (1941), by the American author **Holling C. Holling**.

The Bluenose is more than a name—a ship or a service. It contains in its eight letters something of the heart and life that flows by the waters of Minas, Fundy and the restless Atlantic. It designates a people—and lives in their blood.

Henry D. Hicks, Nova Scotia premier, in Will R. Bird, *These Are the Maritimes* (1959).

It is the ship that stays afloat that gets to port.

Sir Samuel Cunard, Maritime-born shipbuilder and operator, in John S. Crosbie, *The Incredible Mrs. Chadwick: The Most Notorious Woman of Her Age* (1975).

SHOPPING *See also* Consumerism; Markets & Marketing; Merchandising

Attractive presentation of products is a very romantic business. If we ever took away from people, for one month, the privilege of going shopping, many of them would go out of their minds!

Ed Mirvish, merchandiser, address, "When Is the Right Time to Retire?" Toronto, 26 February 1981, The Empire Club of Canada.

SIGNS *See also* Language

Customer Service is like making love to a gorilla. You don't stop when you're satisfied; you stop when the customer is satisfied.

Sign over a cash register in a store in Yahk, south of Cranbrook, B.C., 1994, as noted by correspondent Stan French.

James L. Outhouse / Law Offices

Sign, main street, Digby, N.S., 1994, as noted by correspondent Stan French.

Shoplifters Will be Stabbed and Tomahawked / Then Burned at the Stake. / Those That Survive Will Be / Prosecuted and Then Scalped. The Management

Warning engraved on a wooden plaque at the Moccasin and Gift Shop, Rama Reserve, Orillia, Ont., June 2001.

Indian Weather Rock / Rock Dry—Sunny / Rock Wet—Rain / Rock Swinging—Windy / Rock White—Snow / Rock Gone—Tornado!

Lines engraved on a rock at the Moccasin and Gift Shop, Rama Reserve, Orillia, Ont., June 2001.

You Park / You Preach! / Reserved / for the / Minister / 24 hours/day / 7 days a week.

Sign at a parking space, St. James–Bond United Church, Toronto, May 2002.

SILENCE

Silence is a pocket of possibility. Anything can happen to break it.

R. Murray Schafer, composer, *Ear Cleaning* (1967).

If you cannot understand my silences, how can you begin to understand my words?

Toller Cranston, skater, in Elva Oglanby, *Toller* (1975).

SIN *See also* Good & Evil; Virtue & Vice

Mary Mother, we believe / That without sin you did conceive; / Teach, we pray thee, believing, / How to sin without conceiving.

"The Maiden's Prayer to the Virgin" was quoted in a private letter from Hugh John Macdonald to James Coyne, 15 December 1871, as noted by P.B. Waite, *Macdonald: His Life and World* (1975).

Many people think that sin is just an acronym for their social insurance number.

Betty Jane Wylie, author, *All in the Family: A Survival Guide for Living and Loving in a Changing World* (1988).

SINGERS & SONGS *See also* Music, Popular

American woman, stay away from me! / I don't want your war machine, your ghetto scenes.

Two lines from the perennially popular protest song "American Woman" from the Guess Who's album *American Woman* (1970). The song began as a riff performed during a tune-up at a curling rink in Kitchener, Ont. The object of the Vietnam-protest song is the Statue of Liberty, not American womanhood, according to **Randy Bachman**, who wrote it with **Burton Cummings**, **Garry Peterson**, and **Jim Kale**, as noted by Lisa Ladouceur in "Songs That Stick with Us," *Words & Music*, spring 2005. Randy Bachman added, "That is the big Guess Who song, the one that puts everyone over the edge. When we do it live and I start that riff, it's the same reaction as when I first played it. It's so unbelievably simple, it could only be done on stage, tuning up a guitar. I wouldn't sit down and try. Well, I do now sit down and try to play stuff that simple and it just doesn't work. It has to come out without thinking about it."

Lear jet up to Nova Scotia, to see the total eclipse of the sun.

Line from **Carly Simon**, American singer and songwriter, in song about a former lover, "You're So Vain" (1972), in Anne Kingston, "The Value of Keeping a Secret," *National Post*, 9 August 2003.

Women like me because I'm a fun-loving, food-loving Arab.

Paul Anka, Ottawa-born popular singer of Syrian ancestry, in Leslie Scrivener, *Toronto Star*, 11 August 1974.

Sometimes my voice can make *me* cry.

Leonard Cohen, poet and singer-songwriter, in Christopher Jones, *Now*, 3 November 1988.

Canada is the Rocky Mountains / Canada is Prince Edward Island / Canada is a country made for love / Canada is La Belle Province / Canada is the Yukon mine / Canada is a country full of faith.

Refrain of the song "Canada Is," an unabashed paean of praise composed and sung by the U.S. performer **Roger Whittaker** in the 1990s.

Was it Gordon Lightfoot who sang "The Wreck of the *Edmund Fitzgerald*" or Edmund Fitzgerald who sang "The Wreck of Gordon Lightfoot"?

Rhetorical question asked by the character Elaine of Jerry Seinfeld in the episode "The PTA Disbands" of the U.S. TV series *Seinfeld* during the 1998 season.

If Gene MacLellan hadn't written "Snowbird," Anne Murray might still be teaching in Summerside.

Remark attributed to folksinger **John Allan Cameron** by Silver Donald Cameron, "The Pathfinder," *The Sunday Herald* (Halifax), 20 November 2002.

Song is an extremely effective way of passing a culture down through the generations. As we all recognize, memorable songs and poems that we learn when we are young stay with us into old age. The emotional powers of the arts—authentic arts, not official propaganda—are obviously central to every culture.

Jane Jacobs, urban planning critic, *Dark Age Ahead* (2004).

SKATING *See also* Olympic Games

If you hear the name "Elvis" and immediately think of figure skating, give yourself 1 point.

Quiz question set by **William Ferguson** and **Ian Ferguson**, *How to Be a Canadian (Even if You Are One)* (2001).

I love to skate. I'm happiest when I'm on the ice. I don't want this to end.

Jamie Salé, one half of the figure-skating pair Jamie Salé and David Pelletier, in Scott Taylor, *Winnipeg Free Press*, 13 February 2002. Salé and Pelletier were married at the end of December 2005.

SKEPTICISM

One special advantage of the skeptical attitude of mind is that a man is never vexed to find that after all he has been in the wrong.

Sir William Osler, physician, "The Treatment of Disease," *Canadian Lancet*, Volume 42, 1909.

SKIING

I've been introduced to you as a "Crazy Canuck." I get a lot of people asking me exactly where the name came from. Well, if you've spent any time on the ski slopes up at Blue Mountain you would realize that "Crazy Canuck" is a very good description of how most Canadians ski.

Ken Read, skier, referring to the slopes at Collingwood, Ont., address, "The Importance of the Olympics to Canada," Toronto, 20 January 1994, The Empire Club of Canada.

SKY

Get in the habit of looking at the sky. It is the source of light and art.

Aphorism associated with the Group of Seven, "The New Canadian Art," *The Daily Intelligencer* (Belleville, Ont.), 27 September 1919.

Inuit returning to Igloolik from visits to southern Canadian cities have remarked how different and unfamiliar the sky seems to be in "the south."

John MacDonald, researcher, Igloolik Research Centre, *The Arctic Sky: Inuit Astronomy, Star Lore, and Legend* (1998). Igloolik is an Inuit centre in the Eastern Arctic.

No—to be born a North American is to want to climb up out of shadowed places toward the sky, to live in brightness.

Marjorie Spock, student of anthroposophy, "North America under a Light Sky," *The Golden Blade* (1971), edited by Adam Bittleston.

SLAVERY

Some low fellows, they say, say to him, "Tom, why don't you make tracks for Canada?"—"Ah, master trusted me, and I couldn't!"

Words of Uncle Tom, hero of **Harriet Beecher Stowe**'s influential novel *Uncle Tom's Cabin; or, Life among the Lowly* (1852). The character of Uncle Tom was based on Josiah Henson, who erected his cabin near Chatham, Ont., now a museum.

I'm on my way to Canada / Where everyone is free, / So goodnight, Old Master, / Don't chase after me.

Verse from "Slave Song," in **Brion Gysin**, *To Master—A Long Goodnight: The Story of "Uncle Tom," A Historical Narrative* (1946).

Canada is not merely a neighbour of Negroes. Deep in our history of struggle for freedom Canada was the North Star. The Negro slave, denied education, dehumanized, imprisoned on cruel plantations, knew that far to the north a land existed where a fugitive slave if he survived the horrors of the journey could find freedom.

Martin Luther King, Jr., civil liberties leader, Massey Lectures, *The Trumpet of Conscience* (1967).

SLEEP

It's no coincidence that Thomas Edison, the creator of the incandescent light that has done so much to eradicate sleep, was himself an unrepentant, nay willful, insomniac.

Christopher Dewdney, poet and author, *Acquainted with the Night: Excursions through the World after Dark* (2004).

Sleep may have become a "waste of time" for our adrenalized civilization but, biologically speaking, it is still time well wasted.

Christopher Dewdney, poet and author, quoting Thomas Edison, who considered sleep a waste, *Acquainted with the Night: Excursions through the World after Dark* (2004).

SMALLWOOD, JOSEPH R. (JOEY)

I have claimed, over many a dinner table, to have been the first to describe Joseph Smallwood as "the only living father of Confederation." I recall saying so in the course of an address delivered in Newfoundland on the occasion of an annual meeting of the Newfoundland Progressive Conservative Party. I also recall that when I said it, my audience appeared to be hearing it said for the first time, which was early in the '60s.

Dalton Camp, columnist, "Trust Me, I Discovered a Lot of Things," *Toronto Star*, 11 October 2000.

SMOKING

No, thank you, I never indulge in any non-cooperative vices.

Lister Sinclair, writer and broadcaster, reply to an offer of a cigarette in the 1940s, in Andrew Allan, *Andrew Allan: A Self-Portrait* (1974).

I can't quite twist my mind around the logic of a society that persecutes people who smoke a legal product from which the government derives considerable tax revenue.

Barbara Amiel, columnist, *Maclean's*, 12 December 1988.

SNAKES

"The Khan" waxes wroth over the hoop-snake yarns, vowing that "there is no really talented liar in Canada who would think of leaving out the hoopsnake when giving an exhibition of his powers." "He will tell you," continues the Khan, "that this here snake doesn't travel like other snakes, he has a sharp pointed tail ful of 'pizen,' and when he wants to take after a man or a critter he takes the end of his tail in his mouth, forms himself into a hoop and revolves after his victim at the rate of a mile a minute. He can only travel, however, in a straight line, and if a man will make a beeline for a tree and then duck sidewise the snake will strike his forked and 'pizened' tail into the tree, and the tree will die."

David Boyle, archaeologist, "Canadian Folk-Lore," *The Globe*, 13 November 1897. Boyle is quoting the colourful speech of Robert Kirkland Kernighan, a poetaster who called himself "The Khan" and wrote from "The Wigwam," Rockton, Ont. Kernighan wrote *The Khan's Book of Verse* (1925).

SNOW *See also* Ice & Icebergs; Winter

Mon pays ce n'est pas un pays c'est l'hiver.

Opening line of **Gilles Vigneault**'s ever-popular song "Mon Pays," *Avec les Vieux Mots* (1975): "My country is not a country it's winter."

Mixing your Arabic and Inuktitut metaphors, however, it is certainly true that the "Inuit have many words for snow but no word for camel."

John MacDonald, Culture and Linguistic Section, Indian and Northern Affairs, personal communication concerning whether the Inuit have 23 words for snow just as the Arabs have 100 words for camel, 21 January 1981.

Until I came to Canada I never knew that "snow" was a four-letter word.

Attributed to **Alberto Manguel**, Buenos Aires–born author and anthologist, April 1988.

Upon these premises Crispin propounds / And propagates. His colony extends / From the big-rimmed snow-star over Canada, / To the dusk of a whistling south below the south, / A comprehensive island hemisphere.

Lines from the American poet **Wallace Stevens**'s poem "From the Journal of Crispin: IV, The Idea of a Colony," *Opus Posthumous* (expanded edition, 1989). Crispin serves as the poet's alter ego.

Snow, that indispensable element of Inuit material culture—which in its various forms quenches thirst, provides shelter, and gives swift access to distant hunting grounds—is also the basis of the Iglulingmiut's most used and most trusted navigational key.

John MacDonald, researcher, Igloolik Research Centre, *The Arctic Sky: Inuit Astronomy, Star Lore, and Legend* (1998).

The Inuit really do have twenty words for snow; Canadian mariners and ice scientists have many more designations for different kinds of ice.

Wayne Grady, author, *Chasing the Chinook: On the Trail of Canadian Words and Culture* (1998).

The Eskimos of the frozen North have forty words for snow and only one word for sex. College students in sunny southern California have forty words for sex, and none for snow. Each society develops a specialized vocabulary that suits the specific demands of its environment and culture.

William Ferguson and **Ian Ferguson**, authors, *How to Be a Canadian (Even if You Are One)* (2001).

SNOWBIRDS

Snowbirds embody what has become yet another distinctly Canadian ritual: purchasing sunshine from the Americas.

Philip Preville, "Marginalia: Snowbirds," *Saturday Night*, March 2003. Snowbirds are "Canadians who migrate south, mostly to Florida, in search of warmer climes."

SOCIAL CREDIT

Douglas's Social Credit system (or a partial form of it) was tried out by Alberta, Canada, in the inter-war years and was so successful that Social Credit Governments have not only continued to be returned there ever since but have consistently added to their majorities in the provincial legislature. Major Douglas was appointed chief reconstruction adviser to the Social Credit Government of Alberta in 1935, but he was never in favour of the precise steps taken to apply Social Credit there, regarding the limited powers of a provincial legislature as unfavourable to a proper "try out" of his system, and he resigned the following year. Later British Columbia also adopted a modified form of Douglas Social Credit.

Hugh MacDiarmid, poet, Scots nationalist, and Communist, *The Company I've Kept* (1966). He refers to Major C.H. Douglas, founder of the Social Credit movement.

... The Social Credit philosophy, which in its early years was a mix of pre-Keynesian economics, social resentment, and untutored hope.

Preston Manning, politician, referring to the Social Credit movement of Alberta founded by William "Bible Bill" Aberhart (1878–1943) and continued by his father, Ernest Manning (1908–1996), *Think Big: Adventures in Life and Democracy* (2002).

Through my formative years, Ernest Manning was a premier from Monday to Friday, a lay preacher on Sunday, and a dairy farmer on Saturday.

Preston Manning, politician, referring to the Social Credit movement of Alberta founded by William "Bible Bill" Aberhart and continued by his father, Ernest Manning, *Think Big: Adventures in Life and Democracy* (2002).

SOCIAL PROGRAMS

Yes, Canada can solve her problems of social need and assistance, entirely to the extent that she will face them with intelligence, knowledge, courage and determination as the factors which condition the lives of millions of individuals and the ultimate destiny of the Dominion that is the greatest overseas unit in that venture of the partnership of free nations that we call the British Empire. (Applause.)

Charlotte Whitton, member, Imperial Order Daughters of the Empire, address, "Canada's Problems in Relief and Assistance," Toronto, 19 March 1936, The Empire Club of Canada.

We defined ourselves as a nationality through social programs. I believed and often wrote that these would lead to a painful day of social and fiscal reckoning, that they encouraged underachievement and envy, and that they dampened individualism.

Conrad Black, Lord Black of Crossharbour, publisher and historian, address, Fraser Institute, Vancouver, 15 November 2001, published in the *National Post*, 16 November 2001.

Canada now spends 45 per cent of its gross domestic product on government services, which is close to the average for the countries of the European Union. The United States, by contrast, spends 35 per cent—including double the amount spent by the entire European Union on defence.

Michael Adams, consultant, *Fire and Ice: The United States, Canada and the Myth of Converging Values* (2003), with Amy Langstaff and David Jamieson.

SOCIAL SCIENCE

Social scientists in Canada must have a sense of humour. [1946]

Harold Adams Innis, social scientist, *The Idea File of Harold Adams Innis* (1980), edited by William Christian.

SOCIALISM

See also Capitalism; Conservatism; New Democratic Party

You may say to me this is all very difficult. So it is. I see in the Toronto morning paper that Mr. Duplessis had produced a suggestion that Canada has three enemies, Communism, Socialism and Bolshevism. With all apologies, I can't think of any more mischievous notion. I happen to be a Socialist.

G.E.G. Catlin, professor, referring to Quebec Premier Maurice Duplessis, address, "The Role of Canada in the Challenge of the East to the West," Toronto, 9 October 1947, The Empire Club of Canada.

Socialists are liberals in a hurry.

Louis St. Laurent, prime minister, catchphrase from a speech of April 1949, according to Dale C. Thomson, *Louis St. Laurent* (1967).

My family doesn't play Monopoly. We play Collective.

Stephen Lewis, Ontario NDP leader, distinguishing between competitive and non-competitive types of play for the benefit of reporters, election campaign, September 1975.

When one's left wing is not working, one tends to fly around in circles a great deal.

Bob Rae, Ontario NDP leader, remark made 16 December 1981, *The Globe and Mail*, 28 December 1981.

My notion of socialism is class-based and aggressively rejects what passes for the left in Canada today, namely a grand coalition of victim groups.

Robert Ivan Martin, law professor, *The Most Dangerous Branch: How the Supreme Court of Canada Has Undermined Our Law and Our Democracy* (2003).

There's nothing Canada loves more than a dead socialist.

Attributed to **T.C. "Tommy" Douglas**, CCF founder, by Ted Byfield, "Our State Religion Is Secularism," *National Post*, 27 June 2003.

SOCIETY *See also* Aristocracy; Class System; Collectivity; Family; Virtue & Vice

Every society is an invention, an imaginary construct based on the agreement between individuals who have decided to live together under common laws. These laws are a belief system: Lose faith in the system and the notion of society disappears, like water in water.

Alberto Manguel, Argentine-born man of letters, "No Money, No Vision, No Faith," *The Globe and Mail*, 27 December 2001.

We must return to a more traditional vision of politics in which the voluntary authority of a free, national, and hierarchical civil society is upheld as prior to abstract individual rights manipulated for egalitarian reasons.

William D. Gairdner, athlete, academic, businessman, author, and commentator, *The Trouble with Democracy: A Citizen Speaks Out* (2001).

The world today is a bewildering mosaic of cultural winners, groups of people sunk into old or recent Dark Ages and downward spirals, groups in the process of climbing out, and remnants of pre-agrarian cultures, as well as remnants of declined empires. Even within countries, mosaics of modern, ancient, and Dark Age cultures exist.

Jane Jacobs, urban planning critic, *Dark Age Ahead* (2004).

What lesser evils may a society commit when it believes it faces the greater evil of its own destruction? This is one of the oldest questions in politics and one of the hardest to answer.

Michael Ignatieff, essayist, *The Lesser Evil: Political Ethics in an Age of Terror* (2004).

We have been social entities far longer than we have been technological entities, and social interactions ultimately, fundamentally, at the core of our beings, interest all of us, and, ultimately, it is the social that has a bigger impact on our life.

Robert J. Sawyer, SF author, "Science Fiction and Social Change" (2004), *Relativity: Stories and Essays* (2004).

SOLDIERS *See also* Canadian Armed Forces

Ahh, soldiers. You know, soldiers are very unusual people. On the outside, they are the hardest, most demanding, severe people, but underneath that, they are the most human, the most feeling, the most emotionally attached people who exist.

Words of "a fat, old priest who was a retired army padre" to the youthful **Roméo Dallaire**, recalled by Dallaire, *Shake Hands with the Devil: The Failure of Humanity in Rwanda* (2003).

SOLITUDE *See also* Two Solitudes

People in search of solitude are flocking here from the four corners of the world.

Leo Rosten, author, found in a "Canadian Hotel Prospectus," *Carnival of Wit* (1994).

SOULS *See also* Belief; Spirit

Souls have a bad name in the world of atomic energy.

Spoken by a character in **Robertson Davies**'s novel *The Lyre of Orpheus* (1988).

SOUTH AFRICA *See* Africa

SOVEREIGNTY *See also* Independence; Separatism; Sovereignty-Association

Sovereignty is the right to say no. This is as it must be. But we must use a national interest calculus when we make decisions that may shape our future course and not an irrational, emotional anti-Americanism.

J.L. Granatstein, historian, "Defence Freeloading Imperils Sovereignty," *National Post*, 22 February 2002. Granatstein is discussing the U.S. initiative of the Northern Command then being formed to defend the North American continent against terrorism.

Sovereignty, it has been said, is what you can get away with.

Andrew Coyne, columnist, "Jacques Parizeau's Long Shot," *National Post*, 18 August 2004.

Canadians want to exercise as much sovereignty as we can. But we adamantly oppose the U.S. exercising as much sovereignty as it can, which, clearly, is a whole lot more.

Richard Gwyn, columnist and essayist, "Surviving Survivalism," *Literary Review of Canada*, December 2004.

SOVEREIGNTY-ASSOCIATION *See also* Canada & Quebec; French Canadians; Independence; Quebec; Separatism; Sovereignty

Quebec won't separate if we can live in Canada as a group.... Unless Quebecers can live in Canada as a group, we will separate!

Daniel Johnson, Quebec premier, circa 1966, in Peter C. Newman, "Adieu to Separatism?" *Maclean's*, 12 May 2003. When Johnson unexpectedly beat Jean Lesage's reformist regime in 1966, he began promoting the idea of Canada as "two equal brother nations." He would meet nervous bond dealers in Toronto or New York City and reassure them with the former statement. Then he would fly to Quebec City and make the latter assertion. Journalists would subtract one statement from the other, end up with zero, and Johnson would attack them for misinterpreting his position.

The truth is that sovereignty-association in any form is a horse that can't run.... There is no way to negotiate dry water, boiling ice, sour sugar or stationary motion.... I am not interested in a Canada that would just be a splash on the map, with a six-letter word scrawled across it.

The only Canada I want to preserve is a Canada that can do something; for its own people, for the hungry two-thirds of the world, for the survival of the planet; not a phantom that can only watch helplessly as we all tumble down a steep place to destruction.

Eugene Forsey, constitutional specialist, "No Surrender," *Toronto Star*, 24 February 1991, in J.E. Hodgetts, *The Sound of One Voice: Eugene Forsey and His Letters to the Press* (2000). These were Forsey's final thoughts on the national question. The article appeared posthumously.

SPACE *See also* Astronomy; Earth; Stars; Universe

In the wide awe and wisdom of the night / I saw the round world rolling on its way, / Beyond significance of depth or height, / Beyond the interchange of dark and day.

Lines from **Sir Charles G.D. Roberts**'s poem "In the Wide Awe and Wisdom of the Night" (1893), *Selected Poetry and Critical Prose* (1974), edited by W.J. Keith.

But while flight to the moon may be conceded as theoretically possible it is doubtful if some of the difficulties, from a practical standpoint, are fully realized.... There are many other practical problems, and while it is always dangerous to make a negative prediction, it would appear that the statement that rocket flight to the moon does not seem so remote now as television did less than one hundred years ago is over-optimistic.

J.W. Campbell, astronomer, University of Alberta, "Rocket Flight to the Moon," *The Philosophical Magazine: A Journal of Theoretical, Experimental and Applied Physics*, January 1941.

Canada and the great Northwest were obscured by cloud, a vast low-pressure area that spread across the continent. It shone with an even more satisfactory dazzling white than the polar caps.

Description of the northern reaches of North America from the porthole of the spaceship that ferried D.D. Harriman from the Earth to the Moon in **Robert A. Heinlein**'s classic short story "Requiem," *Adventures in Time and Space* (1946), edited by Raymond J. Healey and J. Francis McComas.

When the planet was suddenly enveloped by a man-made artifact, "Nature" flipped into art form. The moment of Sputnik was the moment of creating Spaceship Earth and/or the global theatre. Shakespeare at the Globe had seen all the world as a stage, but with Sputnik, the world literally became a global theatre with no more audiences, only actors.

Marshall McLuhan, media philosopher, address, "The End of the Work Ethic," Toronto, 16 November 1972, The Empire Club of Canada.

You wish everybody could see this beautiful planet. You will feel much more protective of the civilization and how much we mean to each other and how much we need to take care of each other.

Roberta Bondar, astronaut, on the view of Earth from orbit, address, "The Adventure of Space," Toronto, 22 September 1992, The Empire Club of Canada.

Well, what's it like in space? I've been asked that maybe two hundred times and I try to answer it each time. It's fun, when you get over all the other stuff you have to deal with; it's kind of neat to be able to fly around. Here I am wearing a T-shirt that I had prepared before the flight, pictures of my family on the back of it.

Roberta Bondar, astronaut, address, "The Adventure of Space," Toronto, 22 September 1992, The Empire Club of Canada.

The perspective of Earth we gained from space made us begin to understand the fragility of our biosphere. Now we must understand that there is an ethnosphere, and it too is fragile—and irreplaceable.

Wade Davis, explorer and author, referring to the ethnosphere or psychological sphere that parallels the earth's biosphere, "A Dead End for Humanity," *The Globe and Mail*, 28 December 2000.

Oh man! What a view. That takes your breath away.

Chris Hadfield, astronaut, first Canadian to walk in space, 22 April 2001, in Chris Sattie, "1st Canadian Spacewalker," *National Post*, 23 April 2001. Colonel Hadfield, responding specifically to the sight of the coast of Africa, spent seven hours on his space walk, 400 kilometres above the surface of the Earth, transferring the construction crane Canadarm2 from the Space Shuttle *Endeavour* to the new International Space Station.

If Canadians want to visit an icy, desolated place, they'll go to Winnipeg.

Adapted from a remark during his monologue by **Conan O'Brien**, American talk-show host, *Late Night with Conan O'Brien*, Elgin Theatre, Toronto, 11 February 2004, in Vinay Menon, "Conan Diary," *Toronto Star*, 12 February 2004.

SPECULATION

A certain amount of free, in the sense of irresponsible, speculation is a good thing, because it's part of the wise process of letting things come & not forcing or cramping or repressing them. That's what Goethe told Schiller, anyway.

Northrop Frye, cultural critic, aphorism, "Notebook 3" (1946–1948), *Northrop Frye Newsletter*, fall 2000.

SPEECH *See also* Language; Public Speaking

The English make an art of small talk. I find it charming, perhaps because I've become a little tired of a certain school of writing that despises small talk and fashions characters who convey paragraphs with a grunted monosyllable. I admire it, but it somehow depicts its people as living continuously at high tension. To me, people who actually do live at high tension, and appear not to, are still more admirable.

Bernard Braden, actor and broadcaster, *These English* (1949).

I shall never forget the uproar at a Canadian voice conference I attended in French-speaking Montreal when a Parisian voice coach bluntly asserted that "no Canadian actor could speak the plays of Racine and Molière because they sounded so coarse." So we are instantly known to others by our voice and dialect, and we are actually censored from having the right to speak certain things. You may not believe it is true but there is such a thing as "vocal imperialism."

Patsy Rodenburg, English voice coach, *The Right to Speak: Working with the Voice* (1992).

Canadians are noticeably inclined to turn a statement into a question by means of a rising intonation: this expresses hope that there are no objections, and simultaneously requests a sign from the listener that the statement has been understood.

Margaret Visser, cultural commentator, *The Way We Are* (1994).

We have freedom of speech until we speak.

Paul Watson, environmental activist, interviewed by John F. Schumaker, "Earth Warrior," *The CCPA Monitor*, December 2003–January 2004.

SPIRIT

We worship the Spirit that walks unseen / Through our land of ice and snow: / We know not His face, we know not His place, / But His presence and power we know.

Refrain of **Thomas D'Arcy McGee**'s poem "The Arctic Indian's Faith," *The Poems of D'Arcy McGee* (1860).

The life of the spirit demands imagination (a sense of the reality of things) and inventiveness (the willingness to grow and change).

George Whalley, scholar, commencement address, Rothesay College School, N.B., 1959, *George Whalley: Remembrances* (1989), edited by Michael D. Moore.

SPIRITUALISM *See also* Belief

We Spiritualists, or Spiritists—we call ourselves both, or either—never ask anybody to believe us. If they do, well and good. If not, all right. Our attitude simply is that facts are facts. There they are; believe them or not as you like. As I said the other night, in conversation with Aristotle and John Bunyan and George Washington and a few others, why should anybody believe us?

Stephen Leacock, humorist, *Frenzied Fiction* (1919).

This will probably sound like a lot of superstitious humbug but when I sit down at my Talking Table I know when I am in harmony and just which Deepsters are present. I have three that constitute a sort of Board and I call them Rigonally, Faxton and Kardova.

Stewart James, master puzzle-maker, in Sylvia Fraser, "The Mogul and the Magician," *Toronto Life*, April 2001. The reclusive deviser of illusions admitted to magic-minded mogul J. Allan Slaight that he consulted "imaginary companions" for help with his magical effects at his house, Aberystwyth, at Courtright, Ont.

SPIRITUALITY *See also* Belief

We do not want to trust a wild doctor or surgeon. But we must.

Chogyam Trungpa Rinpoche, eleventh Trungpa tulku or incarnation, Tibetan Buddhist teacher, one of the unorthodox spiritual leaders who re-established his ashram from Boulder,

Colorado, to Halifax, N.S., *The Myth of Freedom and the Way of Meditation* (1976).

I find that we cannot grow spiritually if we ignore our humanness, just as we cannot become fully human if we ignore spirituality....

Jean Vanier, founder of L'Arche movement, *Becoming Human* (1998).

In the adventure of transcendence, we cannot go back; we can only go forward into the unknown.

Peter C. Emberley, political scientist, final sentence, *Divine Hunger: Canadians on Spiritual Walkabout* (2002).

SPONSORSHIP & ADVERTISING SCANDAL

See also Corruption; Government; Liberal Party; Patronage

Once again, I will get the government that many of you desire.

Christie Blatchford, columnist, "Ire over Scandal, Unfortunately, Will Not Persist," *The Globe and Mail*, 17 February 2004. The lively columnist is noting the lethal and lingering effects of Adscam.

Ladies and gentlemen, Paul Martin says he saw nothing; he heard nothing.... The truth is, he did nothing.

Stephen Harper, Conservative Party leader, press conference, Ottawa, 23 May 2004, campaigning, Brockville, Ont., in Brian Laghi, "Federal Election 2004," *The Globe and Mail*, 24 May 2004.

It's been so cold in Ottawa I actually spotted a Liberal with his hands in his own pockets.

Stephen Harper, Conservative Party leader, election campaign, Smiths Falls, Ont., 24 May 2004, quoted in "Federal Election 2004," *The Globe and Mail*, 27 May 2004.

Je me souviens pas.

Motto cynically suggested for the Gomery Commission Inquiry into charges of Liberal Party patronage in Quebec, aka Adscam, appointed in December 2004, headed by Quebec Justice **John H. Gomery**, as of April 2005. It recalls that *Je me souviens* (I remember) is the motto of the Province of Quebec.

If some people acted in bad faith for personal gain, they betrayed the prime minister, the government, and the country.

Jean Chrétien, former prime minister, testimony before the Gomery Commission's inquiry into corruption (aka Adscam Scandal), Ottawa, 8 February 2005, in Susan Delacourt and Les Whittington, "Defiant Chrétien Scolds His Critics," *Toronto Star*, 9 February 2005.

The other day, the Montreal *Gazette* had an article on [ad-executive Jean] Lafleur, big banner headline, "I Worked Hard for My Millions," Sprung recalls angrily. "That's it! That's the kind of feeling of entitlement to taxpayers' money. In fact, when I saw that line, I immediately put it into the play.

Guy Sprung, theatre director and author of the play *Death and Taxes*, in interview with J. Kelly Nestruck, "Canada: A People's History of Moral Decay," *National Post*, 17 March 2005.

There was no doubt in my mind. My understanding was that these amounts were destined for the Liberal Party of Canada.

Jean Brault, advertising executive, admitting Groupaction's participation in a kickback scheme involving $1 million between 1996 and 2002, Gomery Commission Inquiry, in Hubert Bauch, "Adman Says He Paid Liberals' Salaries," *National Post*, 8 April 2005. The admission was made a few days earlier in closed testimony.

I don't want to be mean, but she's a poor girl who doesn't have a husband that I know of. She has the stress of being a single mother who has economic responsibilities. Basically, I find that she deserves pity.

Jean Pelletier, chair of VIA Rail, dismissing the criticism and the person of Myriam Bédard, two-time biathlete gold medallist at the 1994 Olympics, who in a letter to Prime Minister Paul Martin, 13 February 2004, recalled that as early as 2001, while employed by VIA Rail as a marketing adviser, she was fired by Pelletier for questioning the size of commissions paid to Quebec advertising agencies for sports sponsorships—the Sponsorship Scandal in the making. Bédard's accusation and Pelletier's reaction appeared in *La Presse,* 27 February 2004. Pelletier's response was outrageous as well as factually incorrect, and his attempt to apologize the following day was dismissed. He was fired publicly by the prime minister on 1 March 2004. In Elizabeth Thompson, "VIA Boss Fired for Olympian Error," *National Post,* 2 March 2004.

Perhaps there were a few million dollars that might have been stolen in the process, but how many millions of dollars have we saved because we have re-established the stability of Canada by keeping it a united country?

Jean Chrétien, prime minister, on the Sponsorship Program, May 2002, in "Quotes," *The Globe and Mail,* 13 February 2004.

It's like the battle of Coke and Pepsi. If, suddenly, Coke decides not to put its name everywhere, and Pepsi is everywhere, everybody will go to Pepsi. It's as simple as that with mass media information.

Jean Pelletier, former PMO chief of staff and former chair of VIA Rail, statement before the Parliamentary inquiry into the Advertising and Sponsorship Scandal, 6 April 2004, in Daniel LeBlanc, "Pelletier's Denial Spurs Martin to Soften Attack," *The Globe and Mail,* 7 April 2004. Pelletier refers to political involvement in the authorization of federal funds to reserve billboard space in Quebec to promote the federalist cause before Quebec's 1995 referendum on its status.

If this game is worth playing, this game is worth winning.

Ken Dryden, Liberal Member of Parliament and former hockey star, before a non-confidence vote (following upon revelations of the Gomery Commission Inquiry) in the House of Commons, 19 May 2005, in "Martin Breathes Huge Sigh of Relief," *The Globe and Mail,* 20 May 2005.

Le Canada est des voleurs.

Graffiti on the Jordi Bonet Bridge, Mont-Saint-Hilaire, Que., May 2005. Translation: "Canada is Thieves."

I recall as clearly as yesterday ... minister Dingwall got up from his chair, walked around his desk towards me, extended his hand and said, "Welcome aboard. You won't rat on them, you won't rat on us."

Chuck Guité, government official, addressing the Gomery Inquiry, referring to federal Cabinet minister David Dingwall, who appointed him to the post that oversaw the Sponsorship program, as quoted by Margaret Wente, "More Than One Way to Milk a Cash Cow," *The Globe and Mail,* 8 October 2005.

SPORTS *See also* individual sports; Olympic Games

A sportsman is a man who, every now and then, simply has to get out and kill something. Not that he's cruel. He wouldn't hurt a fly. It's not big enough.

Stephen Leacock, humorist, *My Remarkable Uncle* (1942).

Commercialized sports is to real sports what pornography is to literature. In both cases, the entrepreneur wants to please the base instincts of the crowd in order to make money.

Gérard Fillion, editor of *Le Devoir,* criticizing the business of hockey, following the Maurice Richard riot in Montreal on 13 March 1955, in Donald Rudin, "Not Quite the Birth of a Nation," *The Globe and Mail,* 17 March 2005.

Sport is a perfect example of neo-liberal economics and neo-conservative culture—a commercialized, gendered cultural enterprise, subsidized by the state, that encroaches on and finally occupies and defines public space.

Varda Burstyn, cultural critic, *The Rites of Men: Manhood, Politics, and the Culture of Sport* (1999).

The rituals of sport engage more people in a shared experience than any other institution or cultural activity today.

Varda Burstyn, cultural critic, *The Rites of Men: Manhood, Politics, and the Culture of Sport* (1999).

SPRING *See also* Seasons

He reached Montreal in the filthy weeks when the spring thaw begins—the worst sample of weather to be found on the globe.

Line about the English remittance man Jim Hallward in **John Buchan**'s story "Ship to Tarshish," *The Runagates Club* (1928).

STARS *See also* Astrology; Astronomy; Belief; Heaven; Space

Even the stars, through their reflected light, contribute significantly to their own dimming.

John MacDonald, researcher, Igloolik Research Centre, *The Arctic Sky: Inuit Astronomy, Star Lore, and Legend* (1998). Star-gazing in the Arctic is made difficult by the reflected light of the stars brightening the snow-covered landscape.

The glittering pageant of the stars conveys a profound sense of our insignificance in a universe that is incomprehensibly huge.

Christopher Dewdney, poet and author, *Acquainted with the Night: Excursions through the World after Dark* (2004).

STOCK MARKET *See also* Finance

The stock market used to be thought of as a casino but that's no longer true because casinos have rules and the stock market doesn't. It's a crapshoot.

Peter C. Newman, journalist, address, "Titans: How the New Canadian Establishment Seized Power," Toronto, 10 November 1998, The Empire Club of Canada.

STORIES *See also* Literature; Myths & Mythology; Writers & Writing

There's only one story—the story of your life.

Northrop Frye, cultural and literary critic, St-Jovite, Que., 12 May 1964, offering insights about the myth of the Minotaur for NFB's *Labyrinth* pavilion at Expo 67, as recorded by film producer Tom Daly, and quoted by D.B. Jones, *The Best Butler in the Business: Tom Daly of the National Film Board of Canada* (1996). Frye also noted, "The walls of the labyrinth are the walls that wall you off from yourself. The Minotaur has to be something you created yourself. The Monster is externalization."

And stories, whether mythical or historical, timeless or temporal, never exist in isolation. They are linked to other stories, forming a timeless or temporal web.

Robert Bringhurst, scholar and poet, *A Story as Sharp as a Knife: The Classical Haida Mythtellers and Their World* (1999).

Stories are the R&D of the soul, and the pride Canadians feel in the truths of our history, and our achievements, is passed from generation to generation fundamentally through the written word.

Scott McIntyre, publisher, Douglas & McIntyre, "Literary Life Support," *Maclean's*, 3 June 2002.

I am fond of reminding my colleagues that "two points make a hypothesis but three points make a story."

Michael Adams, consultant, *Fire and Ice: The United States, Canada and the Myth of Converging Values* (2003), with Amy Langstaff and David Jamieson.

Any story you don't have to retract is a great story.

Peter C. Newman, journalist and memoirist, *Here Be Dragons: Telling Tales of People, Passion, and Power* (2004).

STRATFORD FESTIVAL *See also* Arts & Artists; Theatre

Tom Patterson had seen opera in Italy.

Tyrone Guthrie, first artistic director of the Stratford Festival, characteristic remark to explain why quite alone among the natives of Stratford, Ont., Patterson was committed to the arts, *A Life in the Theatre* (1959). As Patterson later admitted, "He was, alas, quite mistaken. Indeed, I had never made it to Italy until many years after the Stratford Festival was established."

Stratford was special. It was my home town. I wanted to see it done. And I did. But closing night of the first festival I was so broke I couldn't buy milk for the baby.

Tom Patterson, founder of the Stratford (Shakespearian) Festival, launched the evening of 13 July 1953, in Lotta Dempsey, *Toronto Daily Star*, 18 June 1966.

Caldwell: "Dost thou not see my baby at my breast?" … Your behaviour is extremely inappropriate and totally unacceptable. You now have two choices. Either you will sit quietly or we will consider the play finished immediately. Adult voice from the audience: Miss Caldwell, please accept our apologies and please continue.

Interruption of a student matinée performance of the Stratford Festival's production of *Antony and Cleopatra* in 1967, starring **Zoë Caldwell** as the Egyptian queen who would no longer endure ridicule as he placed the poisonous asp to her breast, as recalled by Marilyn Lightstone, who played the woman who handed her the snake, "Theatre Manners," *Standing Naked in the Wings: Anecdotes from Canadian Actors* (1997), compiled by Lynda Mason Green and Tedde Moore. Lightstone continued, "Without missing a beat she went right back into her dying speech and we finished the play."

The Stratford Festival is proud to welcome our founder, the man whose dream is now our reality, Mr. Tom Patterson.

Announcement made to the audience before the performance in September 2004 of the Stratford Festival's production of *Henry VIII*, as noted by John Allemang, "Tom Patterson, Matinée Idol," *The Globe and Mail*, 25 September 2004. In the audience in a wheelchair was the 84-year-old Patterson, the newspaperman who had, almost single-handedly, established the festival in his hometown of Stratford, Ont., 53 years earlier.

STRESS

I have defined stress as "the nonspecific response of the body to any demand made upon it." Today, stress is so defined in virtually every textbook of medicine or psychology, but at first it was quite difficult to convince people that the body can respond in the same manner to things as different as a painful burn or the news that you won the jackpot of the Quebec lottery.

Hans Selye, medical specialist, address, "How to Cope with Stress," Toronto, 29 October 1970, The Empire Club of Canada.

It is quite possible to refuse all the coercion, violence, property, triviality, to simply walk away.

Thomas A. Clark, poet, "In Praise of Walking," *Wild Culture: Specimens from* The Journal of Wild Culture (1992), edited by Whitney Smith and Christopher Lowry.

STRIKES *See also* Unions

I don't have to remind you of Canada's record in terms of industrial conflict. We are normally in the top five; we are seldom out of the top ten in the world league of strikes and lost time. The only country that we can't beat is Italy. We have tried!

John Crispo, professor of industrial relations, address, "The Public Interests in Collective Bargaining," Toronto, 25 May 1979, Empire Club of Canada.

STROKES *See also* Health

In 1945 the three most powerful leaders in the world met at Yalta to determine the boundaries of the New World order that would prevail after the Second World War, Franklin Delano Roosevelt, Winston Churchill and Josef Stalin. Their doctors were worried with good reason. Each of the world leaders was suffering from high blood pressure. Roosevelt, Stalin and Churchill would all die from a stroke. No medical treatment then available could have saved them. The most powerful leaders in the world were no match for stroke.

Frank Silver, physician and stroke specialist, address, "Prevention and Treatment of Strokes," Toronto, 23 March 2000, The Empire Club of Canada.

STYLE

Abstraction and realism work best together.

Ken Danby, artist, characteristic observation, 6 July 2005.

SUCCESS *See also* Achievement; Failure

Nothing succeeds like one's successor.

C.M. Hincks, founder and director of the Canadian Mental Health Association, remark made to his successor as director, Dr. J.D.M. Griffin, in 1951, in Cyril Greenland, "In Memoriam," *Canadian Journal of Psychiatry*, September 2001.

It all started when I finished my law degree at McGill University in 1950 with a $1,500 loan from my mother to buy a small weekly newspaper. She insisted that in every event of my life, I should aim to be a winner. That is why I enjoy so much the story of the American general who, in an up-and-up restaurant, ordered a fried lobster. The waiter brought him a lobster with a broken claw. The general inquired, how come the claw was broken. You know, said the waiter, lobsters fight one against the other when they are in a common pool. It so happened that this lobster got a licking and had one of his claws broken. The general looked at the waiter, and said, "Bring me the winner." So, I tried to follow my mother's advice—her command, I should rather say—because she was really "a little general."

Pierre Péladeau, publisher, address, "The Quebecor Success Story," Toronto, 25 February 1988, The Empire Club of Canada.

Some people have the crazy idea that if they are successful, they will be happy. The truth is, if they are happy, they will become successful.

Leslie Bendaly, motivational speaker, *Winner Instinct: The 6 New Laws of Success* (1999).

Peale taught me that things turn out best for the people who make the best out of the way things turn out.

Art Linkletter, game-show host born in Moose Jaw, Sask., referring to American self-help author Norman Vincent Peale, in Barry Shainbaum, *Hope & Heroes: Portraits of Integrity & Inspiration* (2003).

SUFFERING *See* Pain & Suffering

SUICIDE *See also* Euthanasia

Suicide is a thing that ought not to be committed without very careful thought. It often involves serious consequences, and in some cases brings pain to others than oneself.

Stephen Leacock, humorist, *Sunshine Sketches of a Little Town* (1912).

Who owns my life?

Sue Rodriguez, victim of ALS (amyotrophic lateral sclerosis), video presentation to the House of Commons justice subcommittee, November 1992, quoted by Deborah Wilson, *The Globe and Mail*, 5 December 1992. The Supreme Court of Canada subsequently denied Rodriguez's request for a physician-assisted death.

Only magic could have saved me, and I can no longer rely on magic.

H.S. Bhabra, author, note addressed to his friend Vee Ledson, 1 June 1999, the day of his suicide in Toronto, in Curtis Gillespie, "Last Exit," *Saturday Night*, 16 December 2000.

All of us—patients, their families, doctors, and also bio-ethicists, and certainly Canada's "ethical canary," Margaret Somerville—need to be educated about choosing or rejecting treatment, and choosing to die. Then, one hopes, as Canadians embrace a new knowledge of death, we may be able to afford universal health care.

Audrey Andrews, correspondent from Calgary, "The Cost of Health Care," *The Walrus*, February 2005.

SUMMER *See also* Seasons

Operas, speeches, movies, meetings, sermons, monologues, dinner parties, car trips, airport waits, supermarket checkout lines, hockey playoffs, answering-machine messages, TV series, apologies, farewells and all too many conversations. Everything in life, I have come to conclude, is about fifteen minutes too long. Except for summer. In Canada at least, summer never begins early enough and always ends too soon.

Peter Gzowski, journalist and broadcaster, "Gzowski's Canada," *Canadian Living*, August 2000.

Summer nights wouldn't be summery without the sound of crickets, as any Hollywood ambient-sound technician knows.

Christopher Dewdney, poet and author, *Acquainted with the Night: Excursions through the World after Dark* (2004).

SUNRISES

Are sunrises the mirror images of sunsets? I've often speculated that you could take photographs of sunsets and claim that they were sunrises and no one would be the wiser.

Christopher Dewdney, poet and author, *Acquainted with the Night: Excursions through the World after Dark* (2004).

SUPREME COURT OF CANADA *See also* Government; Law; Power

It is legitimate to ask whether it is still possible and accurate to call the Supreme Court a court. This question can be raised from two perspectives. First, the Supreme Court has trespassed to an extraordinary extent on the proper constitutional role of the legislature and, second, it no longer seems to feel constrained to behave like a court.

Robert Ivan Martin, law professor, *The Most Dangerous Branch: How the Supreme Court of Canada Has Undermined Our Law and Our Democracy* (2003).

If Supreme Court decisions have one common characteristic, it is that they are unprincipled.

Robert Ivan Martin, law professor, *The Most Dangerous Branch: How the Supreme Court of Canada Has Undermined Our Law and Our Democracy* (2003).

The reality in Canada is that our constitution confers certain powers on unelected bodies, notably the courts. To start from the assumption that any exercise of governance power, other than by elected officials, is illegitimate, is to ignore the reality of our democracy as defined by our constitution.

Beverley McLachlin, chief justice, Supreme Court of Canada, in Bruce Garvey, "Judicial Activism Won't Be Thwarted," *National Post*, 10 December 2004.

In a complex society with increasingly involved rules and inter-relationships, it is no longer acceptable for courts to foist the entire responsibility of lawmaking upon the legislature.

Claire L'Heureux-Dubé, retired justice, Supreme Court of Canada, in Bruce Garvey, "Judicial Activism Won't Be Thwarted," *National Post*, 10 December 2004.

Deference cannot lead the judicial branch to abdicate its role in favour of the legislative branch or the executive branch.

Beverley McLachlin et al., Justices of the Supreme Court of Canada, Joint Reasons for deciding against the Quebec law that bans private medical insurance, 9 June 2005.

SURVIVAL

This above all, to refuse to be a victim. Unless I can do that I can do nothing.

Thoughts of the narrator of **Margaret Atwood**'s novel *Surfacing* (1972).

If the country is in fact going to exist forever, and on the whole it is in pretty good shape, then we no longer need to expend time and energy on worrying about it and on thinking up ways and devices to ensure that it continues to exist. This is to say, we have not merely survived. We have survived survivalism.

Richard Gwyn, columnist and essayist, "Surviving Survivalism," *Literary Review of Canada*, December 2004.

SWIMMING

If you hear the name "Marilyn" and immediately think of swimming Lake Ontario: 5 points.

Quiz question set by **William Ferguson** and **Ian Ferguson**, *How to Be a Canadian (Even if You Are One)* (2001). The reference is to marathon swimmer Marilyn Bell, who crossed Lake Ontario in 1954.

SWITZERLAND

When in Switzerland, though, I was forcibly struck by an example that carries a great lesson for us Canadians. Within Switzerland, there is apparently a spirit of real national unity. When you consider that this country is composed mainly of three racial entities—German, French and Italian—in both world wars, although they were not active participants, they did not remain insensitive or indifferent. The races constituting the main population of Switzerland were on opposite sides in two conflicts, but they still remained a united country.

George McCullagh, newspaper publisher, address, "Testing Time," Toronto, 20 May 1949, The Empire Club of Canada.

In many ways, Switzerland is the model for a peaceful and co-operating Europe, and Canada, ringed around with the world's great powers, is a kind of global Switzerland. Politically, it is constantly falling apart and being patched together by ad hoc compromises; economically, it has been trampled over by exploiters from three continents. But somewhere in its literature, its universities, its scholarship staggering and limping under budget cuts, there may be buried the model vision of a new world, where nightmare visions of tyranny and destruction have vanished as even the worst dreams do.

Northrop Frye, literary critic, address, "The Authority of Learning," Toronto, 19 June 1984, The Empire Club of Canada.

The Swiss banking system is governed by two overriding principles: security and security.

William Kaplan, advocate and author, *A Secret Trial: Brian Mulroney, Stevie Cameron, and the Public Trust* (2004).

What's wrong with neutrality? Why shouldn't Canada be the Switzerland of the Western hemisphere? Aren't we, too, protected by our geography? No doubt, latitudes, longitudes and oceans shield Canada, just as mountains shield Switzerland. (At least against invaders—climate and terrain offer little protection against infiltrators.) In any event, whatever may be good or bad about neutrality, the Swiss haven't relied on the Alps to protect theirs. They've relied on crack troops equipped with state-of-the-art weaponry embedded in Alpine strongholds.

George Jonas, columnist, "A Lesson from the Swiss," *National Post*, 2 May 2005.

SYMBOLS *See also* Motto; National Anthem; National Emblems; National Flag

It has been said that Canada is a patch-work of imported ideas—French, English, Scottish or American ... There are Canadian customs, ... suggesting this country and no other. It is perhaps not too juvenile to try to make a list of some of these—a catalogue of "Canadiana."... A constable of the Royal Canadian Mounted Police—and Canada has no better symbol; a sheaf of Marquis wheat; Canadian landscape painting; a beaver-pelt; a silvered church spire in French Canada; a bar of nickel; a bush-pilot; a pair of moccasins; the Wolfe–Montcalm monument at Quebec; a tube of insulin; a totem pole; a calèche; a cake of maple sugar; a Hudson's Bay blanket; the song "Alouette"; a hockey stick; the Canadian Boat Song; a pair of snow-shoes; a roll of birch-bark; a silver fox; a canoe; a Canada goose; a grain elevator; a lacrosse stick; a boom of logs; a buffalo; the Quebec Citadel; a maple tree; the opening of Parliament in winter.

Vincent Massey, statesman and future governor general, *On Being Canadian* (1948).

I think of the Secretary of State who is in charge of the Great Seal of Canada who in a statement made not long ago said this: "We have been accused of suppressing the Canadian Coat of Arms and it really doesn't matter. We could put Schenley's Coat of Arms on government buildings and no one would know the difference. These symbols do not mean a thing in the twentieth century."

John G. Diefenbaker, former prime minister, address, "The Things We Treasure," Toronto, 9 March 1972, The Empire Club of Canada.

Let me tell you what we Americans think.... Let people know the beaver has fangs. Cover your Maple Leaf in computer chips.

Jay Jaffe, Washington-based business-development consultant, on rebranding Canada and its business products, in Miro Cernetig, "Canada Isn't Working," *The Globe and Mail's Report on Business*, May 2001.

SYMPATHY

I have sympathy for things that are sat upon.

Norman McLaren, documentary filmmaker, quoted by director Don McWilliams on the liner notes of the video *Creative Process: Norman McLaren* (1991).

TALENT *See also* Abilities

You might be tempted to think that talent rules. The problem with talent is that it runs hot and cold. Talent is inconsistent that way. If you have no talent but you have a system you will always start with poor results. But with a system you will be consistent and improve over time. It may be frustrating and slow at first, but you will grow.

George Torok, motivational speaker, address, Ontario Junior Achievement, conference, Hamilton, Ont., 5 February 2000, *The Hamilton Spectator*, 14 February 2000.

Well, I lived in Canada long enough to know that the country abounds in talent, out of all proportion to its population. The trouble is that its own people don't recognize it ... and in my far from humble opinion they won't in your lifetime. I'd stay where you are ... but don't take success for granted. Nothing is quite so fleeting as fame.

Gilbert Harding, rude English radio personality and one-time Toronto resident, offering advice to Bernard Braden, Vancouver-born performer who settled in London in 1949. There he and his wife, Barbara Kelly, enjoyed a string of hits, as noted by Braden, *The Kindness of Strangers* (1990).

TAXES *See also* Finance; Goods & Services Tax

He had never paid taxes. All he had from the taxpayers were grants, subsidies, tax concessions, and tax exemptions. But he wouldn't pay taxes. That's why he's worth $8 billion today.

Louis J. Robichaud, N.B. premier (1960–1970), referring to capitalist K.C. Irving, recalled by Sandra Martin, "Obituary," *The Globe and Mail*, 7 January 2005.

The most interesting tax haven is the Cayman Islands. It has a population of only 25,000 but is the world's fourth-largest financial centre. There are 550 banks on this little island 32 kilometres long because of course there are no taxes. The only daily paper in the Caymans incidentally is the *Cayman Compass* which has a regular column on teaching your parrot to talk and guess who owns it? Conrad Black.

Peter C. Newman, journalist, address, "Titans: How the New Canadian Establishment Seized Power," Toronto, 10 November 1998, The Empire Club of Canada.

SMOG E. COLI / Your Tax Cuts at Work.

Sticker on an automobile, Toronto, September 2000. It refers to dirty air and toxic water in Ontario communities at a time of provincial tax cuts and rebates.

A tax refund is almost as satisfying as a stolen kiss.

Irena F. Karafilly, aphorist, characteristic observation, 7 November 2000.

There are three levels of government but only one level of taxpayer.

Barney Danson, former minister of State responsible for Urban Affairs, House of Commons, recalled, personal communication, 20 July 2003.

But taxes are the price we pay for civilization. If you do not like government and taxes, try Somalia.

Robert Bateman, artist and naturalist, "I Am a Conservative, I Conserve," *The Globe and Mail*, 13 December 2003.

I think the Liberals are going to run on the slogan, "Tax me; I'm Canadian. Waste my money; I'm Canadian."

Stephen Harper, Conservative Party leader, campaigning, Cornwall, Ont., 24 May 2004, in Campbell Clark and Heather Scofield, "Harper, Martin Speak on Taxes," *The Globe and Mail*, 25 May 2004.

The Liberals will tax you to death, and the NDP will tax the corpse.

Stephen Harper, Conservative leader, campaigning in Richmond, B.C., in Tonda MacCharles, "Harper Lambastes Martin over 'Rot,'" *Toronto Star*, 30 May 2004.

TEACHERS & TEACHING *See also* Education

It goes without saying that no man can teach successfully who is not at the same time a student.

Sir William Osler, physician, "The Student Life," *Aequanimitas* (1932).

Salaries of teachers are probably often too good at beginning—but far too small with development. I think mine, at Upper Canada, was a little less when I quit than when I began.

Stephen Leacock, humorist, discussing salaries, including his own as a young teacher at Upper Canada College, interviewed by R.E. Knowles, "Leacock Says Sir A. Currie Most Distinguished Pupil," *Toronto Daily Star*, 16 February 1933.

This course has been an experiment. Some independence of effort is called for. There is the necessity of going out fearlessly into the world. You must try to say what you think. In Canada, there is a need of originality … a necessity of being alive.

Harold Adams Innis, political scientist, address on the last day of his class as recalled by his student Kenneth D. McRae, 3 April 1946, *The Best Teacher I Ever Had: Personal Reports from Highly Productive Scholars* (2003), edited by Alex Michalos.

TEARS

If I cry it means I am sad. It doesn't mean I am weak. It takes strength to be able to cry.

Henry Morgentaler, pro-choice activist, addressing a family member on a painful subject, in Catherine Dunphy, *Morgentaler: A Difficult Hero* (1996).

TECHNOLOGY *See also* Communications; Computers; Genetic Engineering; Global Village; Information Technology; Research; Resources

The question is simply whether a society gains more from its M.I.T.'s or from its Institutes of Mediaeval Studies.

George P. Grant, philosopher, "Philosophy," *Royal Commission Studies: A Selection of Essays Prepared for the Royal Commission on Natural Development in the Arts, Letters and Sciences* (1951).

Yet Canada, abundantly rich in resources, is technology-poor. We act like a giant Kuwait! We have come to believe that we can dig it up, cut it down, or pump it out, endlessly. We have depended for years, for our economic well-being, on our abundant natural resources and whatever secondhand technology our branch plants and a protected domestic economy have brought with them. We've been the victims of good fortune and complacency.

Douglas T. Wright, president, University of Waterloo, address, "Technology and the Competitive Challenge," Toronto, 28 November 1985, The Empire Club of Canada.

Each technology makes new environmental demands on our lives. As we use technologies, they also use us.

Frank Zingrone, theorist, *The Media Symplex: At the Edge of Meaning in the Age of Chaos* (2001).

Most traditional people are lost, spiritually lost, when it comes to space exploration, genetic engineering, genetically modified food, computers…. [Our movement is] the most fanatically pro-science of all religions … the best adapted to the new century. Science and technology are beautiful, but if you don't link it to spirituality, you can easily become unbalanced or depressed and go to drugs and suicide. When you realize, on the other hand that technology is not only technology but an extension of our spiritual life, it changes everything.

Claude Vorhilon, aka Raël, Quebec-based founder of the Raëlian movement, which supports the research group Clonaid to further the cloning of human beings, in Margaret Talbot, "A Desire to Duplicate," *The New York Times Magazine*, 4 March 2001.

What we have and enjoy today is a result of physics discoveries. Maxwell's equations are an example of physics discoveries that have been commercialized. Marconi invented wireless transmissions from Maxwell's discoveries.

Mike Lazaridis, co-founder of Research in Motion, referring to English physicist James Clerk Maxwell and Italian inventor Guglielmo Marconi, quoted by Scott Tyler Shafer, "Top Ten Technology Innovators," InfoWorld, website, 27 February 2002. The trademarked slogan of RIM, creator of the BlackBerry, is "Always On, Always Connected."

Technology that has a close affinity with human nature is capable of creating tremendous social changes, on a global scale. It could radically improve our lives and those of our children and grandchildren.

Kim Vicenti, professor of engineering, *The Human Factor: Revolutionizing the Way People Live with Technology* (2003).

Bill Gates is the world's current technological leader—a futurist if ever there was one—and he, of course, is the same man who once said that no one would ever need a computer with more than 640K of memory.

Robert J. Sawyer, science-fiction author, "The Future Is Already Here" (2004), *Relativity: Stories and Essays* (2004).

We are the undisputed leaders of technological change. But with our abundance of talent and resources, we also have the opportunity to be the pioneers of social change and, ultimately, this may be our greatest contribution.

Jeff Skoll, Montreal-born Toronto-educated co-founder of eBay, the internet trading company, and philanthropist, referring to the Skoll Foundation, which he founded in 2000 in California's Silicon Valley. The foundation's motto is "Uncommon Heroes. Common Good"; webpage of the Skoll Foundation, 20 December 2004.

TELEPHONE *See also* Communications

It may have been fanciful, but I could not help feeling a breath of home, as from a flap or flutter of St. George's Cross, when I first sat down in a Canadian hostelry, and read the announcement that no such telephonic or other summonses were allowed in the dining-room. It may have been a coincidence, and there may be American hotels with this merciful proviso and Canadian hotels without it; but the thing was symbolic even if it was not evidential. I felt as if I stood indeed upon English soil, in a place where people liked to have their meals in peace.

G.K. Chesterton, author and traveller, contrasting the practice of "paging" guests in dining rooms in American but not Canadian hotels, "A Meditation in a New York Hotel," *What I Saw in America* (1922). What would Chesterton have made of the ubiquity of cellphones?

TELEVISION *See also* Advertising; Broadcasting; Canadian Broadcasting Corporation; Communications

The first image that appeared on Canadian TV was an upside-down CBC logo. Fortunately I wasn't responsible. I was in too much of a panic to even notice.

Norman Jewison, floor director and later movie director, 8 September 1952, *This Terrible Business Has Been Good to Me: An Autobiography* (2004).

A TV licence is a licence to print money.

Roy Thomson, Lord Thomson of Fleet, boasting to fellow businessmen following the award to his company Scottish Television Limited of the licence to operate a national television service, 19 June 1957. As Thomson admitted in his memoirs *After I Was Sixty* (1975), "Perhaps this remark was injudicious but it was entirely right."

The high spots of Canadian television are not the chat shows or the old films or the endless quizzes, but the weather reports. These are by far the most dramatic, the most expert.

Robert Morley, British actor in Toronto on tour, "Confessions from a Hospitable City," *London Observer*, 24 December 1972.

It has often been said that Britain has the best television in the world. Milton Shulman ... believes that this assessment is smug and inaccurate. The most he will concede is that Britain's television is the "least worst" in the world.

Wording on the jacket of the influential book *The Least Worst Television in the World* (1973), by **Milton Shulman**, Toronto-born London-based journalist, drama critic, and TV producer. This statement rivals Lord Thomson of Fleet's remark about a TV franchise being a licence to print money as the most widely known observation about the medium.

All TV networks should end with the letters BS.

Louis Dudek, poet and aphorist, *Epigrams* (1975).

English-speaking Canada is the only industrialized country where domestic television is not—by a long shot—the primary source of supply for viewers of all ages.

Robert J. Lantos, CEO, Alliance Communications, born in Hungary, address, "Beyond Cultural Imperialism," Toronto, 16 February 1998, The Empire Club of Canada.

I've made movies and television shows in Canada. I've worked for the most part in Toronto, and also Montreal a couple of times. I liked those cities very much. I've never worked in Vancouver, which is sort of astounding. Every time I've worked in Canada, it's been Canada doubling for the United States. If we go to Canada, we'll shoot it as Canada, and that will be the difference.

Tim Daly, actor on the TV sitcom *Wings*, referring to the possibility of shooting his new TV series *The Fugitive* in Canada, in Kevin Dickson, *TV Guide*, 7 October 2000.

When I first did the show and saw it on the air, it shocked me because it looks like a 1950s television show. Red Green is like a Jack Benny or something. I think there's an innocence to it. I think the young kids see it and relate to it because they share that innocence now, and the old guys miss it. They're nostalgic for it.

Steve Smith, comic, on his CBC-TV comedy series *The Red Green Show*, in Randall King, *Winnipeg Free Press*, 12 April 2002.

Well, King, this case is closed.

Traditional final line of each episode of the radio and TV serials *Sergeant Preston of the Yukon*, with the lead Mountie played by Dick Simmons, who died in 2003, as noted by Roy MacGregor, *The Globe and Mail*, 28 January 2003.

There are more TV sets in the world than indoor toilets.

Moses Znaimer, TV executive and visionary, in Pearl Sheffy Gefen, "A Prophet Steps Down," *Maclean's*, 10 February 2003.

TV stations are gigantic advertising machines there to be filled with product.

Israel (Izzy) Asper, television and publishing executive, in Margaret Wente, "Counterpoint," *The Globe and Mail*, 9 October 2003.

The remote is a ballot that instantly executes the mandate of the thumb.

Robert Priest, poet and columnist, referring to the remote TV control, "Click! I'm Obsessed," *Now*, 3 February 2005.

The human condition is not served by our technical ability to transmit a televised image around the world—if that image is totally inane.

Ken Danby, artist, characteristic observation, 6 July 2005.

TERRITORIES

See North; Northwest Territories; Nunavut; Yukon Territory

TERRORISM

See also America; Border, Canada–United States; Canada & United States; Defence; Iraq War; October Crisis

With perhaps the single exception of the United States, there are more international terrorist groups active here than any other country in the world.

Ward Elcock, director of the Canadian Security Intelligence Service, observation offered in 1998, as noted by Stewart Bell, *Cold Terror: How Canada Nurtures and Exports Terrorism around the World* (2005), reprinted as "The Jihadis in Our Midst," *The Globe and Mail*, 18 April 2005.

When does the Canadian army march on Kabul?

Eric Margolis, correspondent and commentator, TVOntario's *Studio 2*, 12 September 2001. Margolis, as a member of a regular discussion panel, asked this rhetorical question to illustrate the futility of a militiary response by Canada, a NATO member, against Afghanistan for harbouring Arab terrorists believed to have perpetrated the World Trade Center disaster, the Pentagon disaster, and the crash of the hijacked plane in Pennsylvania, all of which had taken place within one hour on the previous morning.

Halifax sat on the invisible periphery of a New York epicentre, with 45 planes, mostly chock full of poor strangers from strange lands, arrayed in two lines on the tarmac, and holding 9,000 passengers to house, feed and, especially, to comfort.

Stephen Jay Gould, paleontologist and author, "An Ode to Human Decency," *The Globe and Mail*, 20 September 2001. Gould and his family had their Milan–New York City flight diverted to Halifax on 11 September 2001 where a local family hosted them.

Sometimes the mouse must thank its stars that it isn't the elephant.

Joey Slinger, columnist, referring to the World Trade Center disaster, "America under Attack," *Toronto Star*, 13 September 2001.

We're all Americans now.

Margaret Wente, columnist, referring to the World Trade Center disaster, "We're All Americans Now," *The Globe and Mail*, 13 September 2001. Michael Adams, in *Fire and Ice* (2003), says the remark, which has become "We are all Americans now," may be seen as "post-traumatic political rhetoric, but not as a statement of social scientific fact."

Mr. Ambassador, as your fellow Americans grieve and rebuild, there will be no silence from Canada. Our friendship has no limit.

Jean Chrétien, prime minister, addressing U.S. ambassador Paul Cellucci and an estimated 75 000 mourners assembled on Parliament Hill to mark the Day of National Remembrance, 14 September 2001, *The Globe and Mail*, 15 September 2001.

We have just witnessed the opening battle of the Third World War.

Peter C. Newman, "The Day the War Began," *Maclean's*, 24 September 2001.

Dual allegiances are complex: A newly minted Canadian citizen who would not dream of assassinating a fellow citizen from some oppressor group does not hesitate to fund assassinations in the old country.

Michael Ignatieff, commentator, "Immigration: The Hate Stops Here," *The Globe and Mail*, 25 October 2001.

If nineteen men, with limited means but strong convictions and infinite ingenuity, were able to shake the economy and change the world order, imagine what one hundred Quebecers, even just half as determined, could do to shake the Canadian empire.

Raymond Villeneuve, convicted FLQ terrorist and president of the Mouvement de Libération Nationale du Québec, article, October 2001, MLNQ's newsletter *Le Tempête*, in Graeme Hamilton, "Police Probe Alleged Threats by FLQ Bomber," *National Post*, 17 January 2002. The suggestion is that the 19 hijackers whose actions brought about the September 11 disaster should inspire FLQ-style terrorism in Quebec.

The world is more likely to be a place of noise and pain and threat than it is likely to be one of calm and ease and harmony. We have been for such a long interval exempt from the predominant miseries of life on the planet that we have forgotten the exceptionalism of our condition. We on this swatch of the globe have been awakened to the contingent nature of our exemption from the dirty side of history.

Rex Murphy, broadcaster, address, "Canada after September 11," Toronto, 6 December 2001, The Empire Club of Canada.

The world of 10 September 2001 was a much different place from the one that emerged on the 11th, when hideous, concentrated destruction and murder shattered all our concepts of a civilized society. Virtually nothing was secure any longer.

Barney Danson, politician, *Not Bad for a Sergeant: The Memoirs of Barney Danson* (2002).

States like these, and their territorial allies, constitute an axis of evil, arming and threatening the world.

George W. Bush, U.S. president, State of the Union address, Washington, D.C., 28 January 2002. He refers to "rogue states" such as Iraq, Iran, and North Korea that commit acts of terror or harbour known terrorists following the disaster of 11 September 2001. The phrase "axis of evil" is notable. The word "axis" recalls the "axis" powers, Germany, Italy, and Japan, during World War II; the word "evil" in this context recalls U.S. President Ronald Reagan's words "evil empire" (borrowed from the *Star Wars* movies) to characterize the Soviet Union. Coining the term "axis of evil" is attributed to Toronto-born former journalist and White House speechwriter David Frum, as noted by Glen McGregor, "Frum Hailed, Blamed for 'Axis of Evil' Line," *The Globe and Mail*, 7 February 2002. In an unguarded moment, Frum's wife and fellow writer, Danielle Crittenden, sent an email to a friend in which she boasted, "I realize this is very 'Washington' of me to mention this, but my husband is responsible for the 'Axis of Evil' segment. It's not often a phrase one writes gains national notice." John Ibbitson quoted the email, "Speechwriter Frum Quits White House," *The Globe and Mail*, 26 February 2002, and went on to quote Frum as stating that what he wrote was "axis of hate" and that Bush himself had changed "hate" to "evil." There are other claimants of the dubious honour. Whoever wrote the phrase, Bush will long be identified with it. Its bellicosity alarmed his allies; its effect on the "axis" remains undetermined.

Regardless of where they come from, every single Muslim on the planet is the worse off because of 9/11. So much for the master planners' fanatical scheme of "advancing the Muslim cause."

Mohamed Elmasry, professor of engineering, national president, Islamic Congress, "Islam," *Toronto Star*, 7 September 2002.

That place is a complete haven for international terrorists. Even their own retired security guys say it's a complete haven. We … need lectures from some people, not from Soviet Canuckistan.

Pat Buchanan, American ideologue and broadcaster, cable-TV program *Buchanan and the Press*, 31 October 2002, quoted in the *Toronto Star*, 1 November 2002. Buchanan was ridiculing the fact that the Department of Foreign Affairs had protested the U.S. border authorities' newly instituted practice of photographing and fingerprinting Canadian passport-holders with Arab backgrounds.

Why did your governments ally themselves with Americans to attack us in Afghanistan, and I cite in particular Great Britain, France, Italy, Canada, Germany and Australia?

Osama bin Laden, terrorist leader, audiotape message broadcast on the Arabic-language TV channel Al-Jazeera, 12 November 2002, in Stewart Bell, "Terror Tape Says Canada Target," *National Post*, 13 November 2002.

When democracies fight terrorism, they are defending the proposition that their political life should be free of violence. But defeating terror requires violence. It may also require coercion, deception, secrecy, and violation of rights. How can democracies resort to these means without destroying the values for which they stand? How can they resort to the lesser evil, without succumbing to the greater?

Michael Ignatieff, essayist, *The Lesser Evil: Political Ethics in an Age of Terror* (2004).

Terrorism is a violent form of politics, and it is because terrorism is political that it is dangerous.

Michael Ignatieff, essayist, widely quoted aphorism, *The Lesser Evil: Political Ethics in an Age of Terror* (2004).

What if Mohamed Atta had been raised on soul-stretching questions instead of simple certitudes?

Irshad Manji, television personality and proponent of the Islamic tradition of *ijtihad* (questioning), referring to an infamous Islamist and terrorist, *The Trouble with Islam: A Muslim's Call for Reform in Her Faith* (2004).

The real terrorism is not going to be from airplanes. It's going to be in the air we breathe and the water we drink.

David Schindler, scientist who specializes in the effect of acid rain on freshwater lakes, in Brian Bergman, "It's Cleanup Time," *Maclean's Special Commemorative Issue 100*, October 2004.

Somehow, Canada, which prided itself as an international champion of peace, had become a source of international terrorism, an operational base for world terror—a country where the planet's deadliest religious, ethnic and political extremist movements had set up shop to recruit, raise money, spread propaganda, buy weapons and plan their operations. According to a classified 2003 report by the Canadian Security Intelligence Service (CSIS), "Virtually all of the most notorious international terrorist organizations are known to maintain a network presence in Canada."

Stewart Bell, researcher, *Cold Terror: How Canada Nurtures and Exports Terrorism around the World* (2005), reprinted as "The Jihadis in Our Midst," *The Globe and Mail*, 18 April 2005.

These are detestable murderers and scumbags, I'll tell you that right up front. They detest our freedoms, they detest our society, they detest our liberties.... We're not in the public service of Canada, we're not just another department. We are the Canadian Forces, and our job is to be able to kill people.

Rick Hillier, chief of Defence Staff, referring to Muslim terrorists, interviewed by Daniel Leblanc, "JTF2 to Hunt al-Qaeda," *The Globe and Mail*, 15 July 2005. General Hillier's official biography notes that "LGen Hillier enjoys most recreational pursuits, but, in particular, runs slowly, plays hockey poorly and golfs not well at all."

THANKSGIVING *See* Holidays

THEATRE *See also* Actors & Acting; Stratford Festival

I chose the theatre as the subject of my few words to you not only because it is my profession but because I know that to Canadians and Torontonians particularly the theatre is a very cherished institution.

Raymond Massey, Toronto-born actor, address, "The Future of the Theatre," Toronto, 8 February 1934, The Empire Club of Canada.

I know there is a live public here and you have got in your midst a little theatre which is going to do things in the world, little Hart House which is going to show something of what life has thought and felt and discovered and expressed here in Toronto, something Toronto can give to the world, as what no other city in the world can give, something we in London, in Wales, wherever we are, have got, something to contribute, and we get nothing if we sit back without effort and don't participate.

Dame Sybil Thorndike, actor, address, "The Theatre," Toronto, 21 February 1935, The Empire Club of Canada.

The second day I was in Toronto I was walking down the street and I met a very old friend of mine who had been in the army with me. He said, "Good Heavens, what are you doing in Toronto?" I said, "I am acting at the theatre." He said, "Where is the theatre?" This, to me, especially after the Knowledge Test, was another very, very severe shock.

Sir Cedric Hardwicke, touring British actor, address, "The Theatre as We Know It," Toronto, 13 October 1938, The Empire Club of Canada.

One summer at Dora Mavor Moore's little barn beside her house in Toronto, the Village Players did an obscure comedy of Federico García Lorca's called *The Shoemaker's Prodigious Wife*. I was cast as an eight-year-old boy (I was an ungainly twenty-two at the time) and succeeded in getting the best review of my career. The program neglected to mention that I was playing an eight-year-old and Rose MacDonald in the *Toronto Telegram* wrote, "Donald Harron was perfect as the idiot."

Donald Harron, actor, circa 1964, "Idiot Reviews," *Standing Naked in the Wings: Anecdotes from Canadian Actors* (1997), compiled by Lynda Mason Green and Tedde Moore.

I walked on to enormous applause, which threw me a little, and during the pause allowed by audience reaction, something flashed into my mind and I said, "Well, what do you know? A Canadian at the Palladian." It wasn't very funny, particularly since Paul Carpenter was also a Canadian, but it brought the house down. From then on I could do no wrong. It just hadn't occurred to me that I'd reached a point through radio where whatever I said sounded funny.

Bernard Braden, comic actor, pinch-hitting for the compère (or M.C.) at the London Palladium in 1950, as recalled by Braden, *The Kindness of Strangers* (1990).

Frank, give me the bottom line. I know you guys are very content with your life in Canada but, you know, if you come to the States, you will … you will … become … truly … international stars! Your careers will … will flourish! … You know, there's more to life than happiness!

Marty Kummer, New York–based agent for MCA Talent Agency, trying in 1968 to convince Johnny Wayne and Frank Shuster, stars of *The Ed Sullivan Show* and contented Torontonians, to relocate in the United States, as recalled by Shuster, "There's More to Life Than What?" in *Standing Naked in the Wings: Anecdotes from Canadian Actors* (1997), compiled by Lynda Mason Green and Tedde Moore.

They were immensely kind and lived, one gathered, pleasant, detached lives in pleasant, detached houses.

Robert Morley, British actor in Toronto on tour, "Confessions from a Hospitable City," *The London Observer*, 24 December 1972.

In any country, no matter how thinly populated, no matter how widely scattered across a continent, people must eventually produce their own theatre, as objects produce their own shadows.

Herbert Whittaker, theatre personality, in Joe Fiorito, "Theatre Critic Turns Tribute into Call to Arms," *National Post*, 22 September 2000.

The audience focuses on the magic; the magician focuses on the trick.

Mavor Moore, theatre personality, aphorism, characteristic observation, 22 December 2002.

THERAPY *See also* Psychiatry; Psychology

My advice is: never—NEVER—put yourself in the hands of an analyst whom you do not feel certain is at least of equal intellectual and moral and spiritual stature with yourself. The profession is crowded with self-seeking, duplicitous peewees.

Robertson Davies, man of letters, letter, 27 December 1994, *For Your Eye Alone: Letters, 1976–1995* (1999).

THOMSON, ROY

If this were a formal dinner in London, on some great ceremonial occasion, … some official would … in a loud sonorous voice proclaim: "My Lords, Ladies and Gentlemen, pray silence please for the Right Honourable Sir Roy Herbert Thomson, First Baron Thomson of Fleet and of Northbridge of the City of Edinburgh, … etc., etc., ad infinitum." But to those of us here in Toronto, who know and love Roy Thomson best, who remember those cold wintry evenings when one would often see, long after business hours, our guest walking home with a bag full of work under one arm and a bundle of newspapers under the other, the best salutation I can offer is to present to you our very dear and very old friend, Roy Thomson.

Henry N.R. Jackman, spokesman, introducing the speaker, Lord Thomson of Fleet, Toronto, 6 January 1972, The Empire Club of Canada.

THOMSON, TOM *See also* Arts & Artists; Group of Seven

Foreign-taught painters of Canadian landscape have we, Canadian-taught painters of foreign landscapes, but an artist with the spirit of Canada's youth in his heart—wild, strong, free, untrammelled by convention, where is he?

Sid Howard, commentator, tribute "The Red Gods Called" (1904), in a booklet *In Memoriam Neil McKechnie, June 14, 1904* (1904). The curators of the major Tom Thomson retrospective at the Art Gallery of Ontario in May 2003 recalled the passage.

Through the story of painting in Canada there stalks a tall, lean trailsman with his sketch box and paddle, an artist and dreamer who made the wilderness his cloister and there worshiped Nature in her secret moods.

Blodwen Davies, essayist, *Paddle and Palette: The Story of Tom Thomson* (1930).

THOUGHTS *See also* Ideas

We have it on the very best authority that "we are fearfully and wonderfully made," and although the statement is generally understood to apply to our bodily structure it is quite as true regarding our habits of thought.

David Boyle, archaeologist, slightly paraphrasing Psalm 139, "Canadian Folk-Lore," *The Globe*, 4 December 1897.

Few men think for themselves. The thoughts of most of us are little more than imitations and adaptations of the ideas of stronger minds.

Stephen Leacock, humorist, *The Unsolved Riddle of Social Justice* (1920).

But, Daddy, I just can't fall asleep, my head is too full of thinks!

Goldie Josephy, activist, recalling why as a child she was unable to sleep, in Lisa Rainford, "Bloor West Columnist Remembered," *The Villager* (Toronto Community News), 7 June 2002.

TIBET

So, finally I much appreciate people here. I think very attentively that you listen. So I much appreciate. So as a human, brothers and sisters, we Tibetans are really passing through a most difficult period. This moment we need your help. Thank you very much.

Dalai Lama, spiritual leader of Tibet, born Tenzin Gyatso, closing words, address, "A Peace-loving Nation Takes a World View," Toronto, 28 September 1990, The Empire Club of Canada.

We hope Canada, which has its own problem with Quebec, will understand our position.

Statement issued by the Chinese embassy in Ottawa, 12 April 2004, objecting to the decision of Prime Minister Paul Martin to meet with the Dalai Lama, in Graham Fraser, "China Issues Warning on Meeting Dalai Lama," *Toronto Star*, 14 April 2003. China branded the Tibetan political and spiritual leader a "splitist"; Martin agreed to meet him as a humanitarian leader.

TIME

To be here at this moment when the human mind has begun to expand into the universe is a privilege beyond anything that earlier generations could have imagined.

Harold Horwood, author, last sentence of *Among the Lions: A Lamb in the Literary Jungle* (2000).

In Iowa I spoke with Americans about Canada's 20-hour clock. As all Canadian readers are well aware, Canada operated on the 20-hour clock for centuries. Let's face it, if we each had a dollar for every time we had to tell an American that a Canadian hour was actually 75 American minutes, and that if your bus is leaving at 5:00 P.M., that actually means quarter to 6:00, we'd all be rich.

Rick Mercer, television comedian, "Talking about *Talking to Americans*," *Elm Street*, February–March 2001.

If, by some impossible twist of fate, a man crossed paths with the child he used to be, and they both recognized each other, they would both crumble to the ground, the man in despair, the child in terror.

Remark made by the actor in **Wajdi Mouawad**'s monologue *Alphonse*, translated by Shelley Tepperman, directed for Theatre Direct by Lynda Hill and Alon Nashman, in Robert Cushman, "Theatre Review," *National Post*, 12 November 2002.

TOBACCO *See* Smoking

TOONIE *See* Money

TORONTO *See also* Architecture; Cities & Towns; Design

We Toronto people think there is no such place under the sun as our own City and Country.

Timothy Eaton, merchandiser, letter to an American associate in 1893, in Leon B. Litvack, "Timothy Eaton: Canadian Capitalist, Irish Saint," *Boswell's Children: The Art of the Biographer* (1992), edited by R.B. Fleming.

Ottawa, March 18—The Senate spent most of the afternoon discussing the proposed Canadian Historical Exhibition to be held in Toronto on the four hundredth anniversary of the discovery of Canada by Cabot.

Several features of the bill were objected to, and the committee reported progress whilst having passed all the clauses. Some hard things were said about Toronto.

Senator Power said he had heard the city called "Hogtown" and the bill showed that name well fitted the Ontario capital.

This is the first known reference to Toronto as "Hogtown": "Calls Us Hogtown / Senator Power Apes the 'Wit' of Jealous Hamilton," *The Evening Star* (Toronto), 19 March 1896. Place-name specialist Alan Rayburn traced it to the report of an address by **L.G. Power** of Nova Scotia in the Senate.

Toronto is the friendliest place on earth for the man who knows how to make himself at home there. There were plenty to help him if he had looked for them, for nowhere will you find more warm-hearted people to the square mile.

Thoughts of the narrator about the English remittance man Jim Hallward in **John Buchan**'s story "Ship to Tarshish," *The Runagates Club* (1928).

Mr. President, Your Honour, and Gentlemen, here in Toronto I feel in one of the vital nerve centres of the British Empire. (Applause.) Here is a stronghold of the United Empire Loyalists. Here too are many of those who have cherished affection and affinities with Northern Ireland, with Ulster. I have had many ups and downs with Ulster. I remember in the bitter party struggles which in Great Britain preceded the Great War, that I had a quarrel with Ulster, but I have been forgiven. (Laughter.) I have renewed a friendship with Ulster that I might have inherited from my father, and I know that when Ulstermen make friends, they make them for a long time.

Winston Churchill, statesman, address, "British Imperial Interests," Toronto, 13 August 1929, The Empire Club of Canada.

Toronto,—I come from there myself, so I have the right to insult it,—Toronto is a village and always will be, if it spreads out a hundred miles wide....

Stephen Leacock, humorist, *My Discovery of the West: A Discussion of East and West in Canada* (1937).

Toronto, though unlovely, has a great deal of life of a sort—of an American sort.

Wyndham Lewis, English author, one-time Toronto resident, *America, I Presume* (1940).

Toronto in 1961 was no Camelot. But to be realistic, knowing what we know now, I suspect that even Camelot—King Arthur's Camelot—was no Camelot.

Judith Krantz, later novelist and city resident in 1960–1961, *Sex and Shopping: The Confessions of a Nice Jewish Girl* (2000).

Toronto—gateway to Mississauga.

Bob Hope, comedian, convulsing an audience at the Canadian National Exhibition, Toronto, regarding the former bedroom community next door to Ontario's largest city, during one of his five appearances there (1957, 1965, 1969, 1976, 1978), noted by John McKay, "Hope Played the Ex Five Times," *Toronto Star*, 29 July 2003.

Perhaps the reason I put up with Toronto's foul climate, smelly air, unshovelled snow, grey flatness, is that it comes as close as I can get to a World City, and that, for me, perhaps more than any other part of Canada, it represents the national open and hang-loose and people images.

Judith Merril, science-fiction personality, writing in 1968, *Better to Have Loved: The Life of Judith Merril* (2002), with Emily Pohl-Weary.

It is a lonely city, a drugstore city, where the cheap counter food is munched by sad, lonely women already preparing at six in the evening for bed and television. The television is terrible, worse, if that is possible, than in the United States, a constant stream of advertisements for laxatives. The uptight city of all uptight cities, I told myself, before I knew it a little better.

Robert Morley, British actor in Toronto on tour, "Confessions from a Hospitable City," *The London Observer*, 24 December 1972.

Toronto has a way of turning everyone into a Presbyterian.

Don Cullen, actor and producer, bon mot, 1 July 1975.

Toronto has a vitality and centrality to the meaning of Canada that is possessed by no other city. It is the cultural capital of this country. How you, the citizens of this city, support it, treat it, use it and love it will in large measure reflect Canada's interest in its own cultural life, its cultural strength and its cultural future.

Isaac Stern, violinist, address, "The Concert Hall as an Artistic Instrument," Toronto, 5 November 1979, The Empire Club of Canada.

Toronto is a kind of New York operated by the Swiss.

Peter Ustinov, theatre personality and frequent visitor to the city, interviewed by John Bentley Mays, *The Globe and Mail*, 1 August 1987.

"Why do you think he stopped believing in magic?"

"I don't really know. It could have been the move to Canada. I told you he was Irish, didn't I? We met in Dublin when I was studying at Trinity. Perhaps Toronto killed that part of him. It's not a magical city."

Dialogue from the fantasy novel *Falling Out of Time* (1989), by **O.R. Melling** (pseudonym of Geraldine Whelan).

It's an American city plus memory, a British city plus hope. It's class *sans classe*, the gamble in North America for quality. It's all these things and more, live in the heat. Or it's a void, a destiny squandered!

Scott Symons, author, "Glitz City" (1990), *Dear Reader: Selected Scott Symons* (1998), edited by Christopher Elson.

The efficient, ordered feel of the Yellow Pages sprung to life in three dimensions, peppered with trees and veined with cold water.

Description of Toronto in **Douglas Coupland**'s novel *Generation X* (1991).

Toronto is a progressive, avant-garde city. It's so far advanced over anything I've seen in the States.

Philip Johnson, U.S. architect and designer of the CBC Broadcast Centre, with its Glenn Gould Studio, Toronto, 1992, recalled by David Olive, "Architect Built for Real Life," *Toronto Star*, 30 June 2005. The studio was officially opened 25 September 1992.

Surrender her pronto, or we'll level Toronto.

Ultimatum issued by the U.S. president (played by Alan Alda) in the satiric movie *Canadian Bacon* (1994), written and directed by **Michael Moore**. The Americans launch a Cold War on Canada, but Canadian forces are holding an American celebrity named Honey (Rhea Perlman) hostage.

The monolithic Toronto depicted on TV is not the vibrant Toronto we live in: ours is more interesting. No wonder people hate Toronto.

Antonio D'Alfonso, poet and essayist, "Introduction," *In Italics: In Defense of Ethnicity* (1996).

How can we be a great city? All we do is covet the title and the skyline. But not the contents.

Scott Symons, novelist and essayist, "A City of Pirates," *National Post*, 16 December 2000.

As a friend of mine once said, "There are a million things not to do in Toronto."

Peter Brown, broadcaster, quoting his editor friend Julian Mills about the city, CBC Radio's *Radio Active*, Edmonton, 21 December 2000.

Toronto has what I've come to call "social beauty." It's a city that has flourished because of the stuff that goes on in it, between the people who live there.

Blake Gopnik, art critic, comparing and contrasting Toronto and Venice, "I'm in a Venice State of Mind," *The Globe and Mail*, 31 January 2001.

Here, I thought, was all Manhattan's software without its hard drive.

Pico Iyer, traveller and writer, "Mongrel Beauties," *Saturday Night*, 31 March 2001.

It struck me that in some ways all Canadian roads lead to Yonge Street and that there is history in that road, stories about Canada, untold stories, stories about life, about the way we live.

Ken Wiwa, journalist, "Yonge and Restless," *The Globe and Mail*, 4 August 2001. He is referring to Yonge Street, the 1986-kilometre-long "street" and highway that (in effect) runs from Toronto to Rainy River, Ont.

This will be my 25th Toronto festival. Every year I feel a sense of *déjà-vu* as I return. For years, I thought that was because of all my memories of past festivals. Now I realize it is because I recognize the locations from all of those movies about Chicago.

Roger Ebert, U.S. movie critic, on the opening of the 26th annual Toronto International Film Festival and the use made of Toronto locations by American directors, "In Autumn, Thoughts Turn to Film," *National Post*, 6 September 2001.

The World within a City.

Slogan for the City of Toronto popularized by Tourism Toronto, in use in January 2002.

I was struck by the cultural diversity of the city, and how everyone is allowed to conserve their national … brand.

Edoardo Ponti, movie producer, referring to Toronto, where he filmed *Between Strangers*, which starred his mother, Sophia Loren, in Katrina Onstad, "Movies," *National Post*, 4 October 2002.

I love Toronto. It's cosmopolitan. There's all sorts of different kinds of people everywhere you go in Toronto.… It's a real melting pot in every sense of the word.

Prince, popular singer-composer, interviewed in Jacksonville, Florida, by Lee-Anne Goodman, "Prince Is Back on His Throne," *The Globe and Mail*, 29 April 2003. He married a Canadian and purchased a residence in the exclusive Bridle Path neighbourhood of the city.

Toronto was at that moment, and will be again, an absolute centre for the studies of letters and humanities.

George Steiner, literary critic, conversing at the Living Literacies Conference, York University, Toronto, November 2003, as noted by Philip Marchand, "It's Half the City It Used to Be," *Toronto Star*, 20 December 2003. Steiner recalled an earlier visit to the city during which he met Northrop Frye and Marshall McLuhan at the University of Toronto's Massey College and felt the city was "the centre."

You know, one of the last times I was here they tried to arrest me. That wasn't very nice … but I'm a good girl now.

Madonna, U.S. performer, aka The Material Girl, Esther, etc., interviewed in Toronto and quoted by Shinan Govani, *Toronto Star*, 24 July 2004.

Toronto Unlimited.

Slogan adopted by Tourism Toronto for "branding" and tourism purposes, announced 23 June 2005, as noted by John Spears, "Look Out World, Here We Are," *Toronto Star,* 24 June 2005.

Torontonians live in a city where the beginning is forgotten and the end is unknown, and so whatever happens can only surprise and surpass.

Erik Rutherford, writer, "The Unfinished City," *uTOpia: Towards a New Toronto* (2005), as in *Toronto Star,* 13 November 2005.

TORTURE

The history of our little human race would make but sorry reading were not its every page imprinted with the fact that human ingenuity has invented no torment too great for human fortitude to bear.

Stephen Leacock, humorist, *Essays and Literary Studies* (1916).

Canada, Canada, Canada.

Dying screams of **Shidane Arone**, Somali youth, intruder on the Canadian Forces base near Belet Huen, Somalia, who was tortured and beaten to death by commandos from a subunit of the Canadian Airborne Regiment, 16 March 1994, in Brian Bergman and Luke Fisher, *Maclean's,* 28 March 1994. "Somalia will never die," observed Peter Desbarats, commissioner of the Commission of Inquiry, convened and prematurely concluded the following year.

Legalization of physical force in interrogation will hasten the process by which it becomes routine. The problem with torture is not just that it gets out of control, not just that it becomes lawless. What is wrong with torture is that it inflicts irremediable harm on both the torturer and the prisoner.

Michael Ignatieff, essayist, *The Lesser Evil: Political Ethics in an Age of Terror* (2004).

TOTEM POLES

The stuff we offer tourists in B.C. is shameful. Cheap dirty little souvenirs such as Jap-made totem poles are a detriment to us.

Jack Shadbolt, artist, addressing the Rotary Club of New Westminster, B.C., in "Cross-Canada 'Chit-Chat,'" *Liberty,* December 1954.

I call these poles my silent teachers.

Norman Tait, traditional Nisga'a carver, referring to the old Tsimshian poles that stand in the University of British Columbia's Museum of Anthropology in Vancouver, in Vickie Jensen, *Totem Pole Carving: Bringing a Log to Life* (1992).

Wil Sayt Bakwhlgat.

Traditional words of dedication at the naming of a newly raised totem pole, meaning "You will walk straight," as noted by Vickie Jensen, *Totem Pole Carving: Bringing a Log to Life* (1992). "According to Nisga'a belief, now that the pole has been named, it awakens from its dormant state and is considered a living being."

TOURISM *See also* Travel

How do you spell CN Tower? / Is Cirque du Soleil an astronomer? / Do you celebrate Christmas? / Does the currency rate fluctuate with the change in the seasons? / How do you drive in Toronto? / Is Canada considered part of the United States? / Is there a dress code in downtown Toronto? Can you wear shorts?

Tourists' questions asked of guides in 2001, reported by Tourism Toronto, as noted by **Wallace Immen**, "No, Virginia, Canada Is Not Part of the U.S.," *The Globe and Mail,* 21 January 2002.

I'm sure it will be part of my job to tell the world what an incredible country this is.

Paul Anka, singer and songwriter, in Sarah Schmidt, "Anka Signs on to Sell Canada," *National Post,* 26 April 2002. Born in Lebanon, raised in Ottawa, and based in Los Angeles, Anka was appointed an "ambassador" for one year by the Canadian Tourism Commission, succeeding previous "ambassadors" Jann Arden and Pinchas Zukerman. As music critic Mike

Usinger of B.C.'s *Georgia Strait* noted, "Come to Canada. We're nice and bland and won't offend you. Paul Anka is the watered-down vanilla of pop music."

Tourism is about difference.... Indeed, the quest for difference is a fundamental aspect of modern Western tourism; so much so that the designation "tourist" has become a term of embarrassment, something almost everyone is but no one wants to be.

Karen Dubinsky, historian, "Local Colour: The Spectacle of Race at Niagara Falls," *Racism, Eh? A Critical Inter-Disciplinary Anthology of Race and Racism in Canada* (2004), edited by Camille A. Nelson and Charmaine A. Nelson.

This is my first time to Canada, yes, and I only get to see things related to Denmark.

Prince Joachim, second son of Queen Margrethe and Prince Henrik of Denmark, on opening the "SuperDanish" exhibit at Harbourfront, Toronto, in Sarah Hampson, *The Globe and Mail*, 9 October. 2004.

Canada. Keep Exploring.

Advertising slogan for "Brand Canada" adopted by the Canadian Tourism Commission, May 2005. It replaces the slogan "Discover your true nature" adopted seven years earlier. "We may very well end up with a campaign that has mountains, Mounties and moose in it, but they're going to be portrayed in a very different way," explained Steve Wright of the advertising agency DDB Canada, as noted by Keith McArthur, "A Brand New Canada," *The Globe and Mail*, 1 June 2005. International slogans used in the past: "Canada the World Next Door," "The World Needs More Canada," "Where Worlds Meet," "Rediscover Canada." Domestic slogans used in the past: "No Place like Home," "I Can, Canada," "Go Far Stay Close."

A northern community. Cold. Pristine. Natural. Mountains. Mounties. Multicultural. Clean. Relaxation. Safety. Vast. Nature. Inclusiveness. Tolerance. Peace. Order. Good government. Peacemaker.

Traits associated by foreign tourists with Canada, as determined by market researchers commissioned by the Canadian Tourism Commission, announced May 2005. This led to a new slogan: "Canada. Keep exploring." New brand statement: "Canada is a catalyst for self-expression." New brand promise: "Come to Canada. Create extraordinary stories all your own." New reward: "Proof of a life less ordinary." New vision: "Canada will be the premier four-season destination to connect with nature and experience diverse cultures and communities." These concepts were noted in "Canada's Extreme Makeover," *The Globe and Mail*, 1 June 2005. Perhaps they pale in comparison with Australia's bright slogan: "See life in a different light in Australia."

TRADE

See also Business; Canada & the World; Economics; Free Trade; North American Free Trade Agreement

I can foresee the day when Sydney or Vancouver will be far more eligibly situated than London for transacting the business of the world.

Surmise of Mr. Ebenezer Wakefield, "a Canadian Statesman," in **John Buchan**'s novel *A Lodge in the Wilderness* (1906). The reference is to Sydney, Australia, not Sydney, Nova Scotia, or Sidney, British Columbia.

No minister in Canadian history has ever led a trade mission to Norway in January.

George Bain, columnist, "Bain," *The Globe and Mail*, 1 February 1982.

I want to see us pursue policies that make Canada a "Northern Tiger"—a country that is a magnet for investment and for skilled knowledge workers.

John Manley, minister of Finance, address, House of Commons Finance Committee, Ottawa, June 19, 2002, in Alan Toulin, "Manley Goal: A 'Northern Tiger,'" *National Post*, 20 June 2002. The reference is to the burgeoning economies of the countries of Southeast Asia.

We can further our partnership in international trade because we believe there should not be more barriers between Quebec and Ontario than there are between Quebec and New York State.

Mario Dumont, Action Démocratique du Québec leader, speech, Canadian Club, Toronto, 23 September 2002, published in the *Toronto Star*, 24 September 2002.

TRADITION *See also* Heritage

Our faith is in steam and electricity, our love of wealth and all that is external has done many things, not all for the best. We may some day realize, to our regret, that modern progress has, in spots, given us stones rather than bread. We are forsaking matters which are quite as important as material gain, that is, matters of the mind and the heart—the traditions and past ideals of our race. (Applause.)

Marius Barbeau, folklorist, address, "Folk Songs of French Canada," Toronto, 9 April 1925, The Empire Club of Canada.

Inuit traditional knowledge is characteristically personal, its acquisition and application, in varying degrees, specific to communities, families, and individuals.

John MacDonald, researcher, Igloolik Research Centre, *The Arctic Sky: Inuit Astronomy, Star Lore, and Legend* (1998).

TRAFFIC *See also* Automobiles

You know what it's like to drive there? It's so boring, it's dangerous. All the roads are straight, everyone drives safely, nobody goes too fast. It's hard to stay awake, unlike here, where you have to be constantly alert even when your car is parked.

Sam Orbaum, Montreal-born columnist, "I'd Rather Live in Israel," *The Jerusalem Post Magazine*, 13 July 2001.

Traffic flow holds the secret to many mysteries, in his view. It's a totally scientific matter of physics and math, yet it's one hundred per cent about psychology and choice. It is, in other words, like economics.

Thoughts of the narrator of **Rick Salutin**'s novel *The Womanizer* (2002).

TRAINING *See also* Education

You will be glad to know that the training is in only three subjects—science, art, and the knowledge of men—of equal importance one with another.

Sir William Osler, physician, "The Reserves of Life," *St. Mary's Hospital Gazette*, Volume 13, 1907.

TRAINS *See* Railways

TRANSCENDENCE

The immanent source of transcendence in man is his detached, disinterested, unrestricted desire to know.

Bernard Lonergan, theologian, *Insight: A Study of Human Understanding* (1953) in *The Lonergan Reader* (1997), edited by Mark D. Morelli and Elizabeth A. Morelli.

TRANSFER PAYMENTS *See also* Federal–Provincial Relations

In addition, since it was necessary to implement the myths of egalitarianism, that all people everywhere should enjoy the same services and standards of living, whether they were in the subsistence agricultural economy of Newfoundland or the rich industrial heartland of Ontario, we initiated absurd systems of transfer payments and lunatic projects to turn areas of our country more appropriate to the farming life of the Hebrides into little Detroits or Calgarys. We penalized success and wealth since we decided that success could only come about at the expense of someone else's exploitation.

Barbara Amiel, journalist, address, "How Canada Does It and Other Social Diseases," Toronto, 4 February 1982, The Empire Club of Canada.

Surely Canada can build a future where the short-term prosperity of whole regions does not depend on unfair transfers that severely damage others and could ultimately impoverish all Canadians. But we must build toward this future now.

Lawrence Martin, columnist, "It's Time for Our Very Own Manifest Destiny," *The Globe and Mail*, 17 February 2005.

Canada has been built on the basis of a series of one-off, one-time agreements between the federal government and the provinces. So much geography, such incredible disparities, such different problems. Fairness can't be one size fits all.

Paul Martin, prime minister, conversing with the *Toronto Star*'s editorial board about federal transfers to favoured provinces, in Susan Delacourt, "P.M. Moves to End Cash Feud," *Toronto Star*, 26 April 2005.

TRANSLATION *See also* Language

A generation ago in the Arctic Quebec community of Kangiqsualujjuaq a government development officer was explaining the virtues of hard work and efficiency to a rather polite Inuit audience. During his talk the enthusiastic official used the expression "time is money" and the interpreter, confused but compliant, translated this gem of capitalistic wisdom as "a watch costs a lot!" Inuktitut indeed has no word for time, not, at least, in the abstract, regimented sense commonly understood in Western industrial society.

John MacDonald, researcher, Igloolik Research Centre, *The Arctic Sky: Inuit Astronomy, Star Lore, and Legend* (1998). Apparently in Inuktitut the suffix *-vik* means "place" and "time" together.

TRANSPORTATION *See also* Automobiles; Aviation; Railways; Travel

My purpose was a run to Quebec in "Postal Packet 162 or such other as may be appointed," and the Postmaster-General himself countersigned the order.

Line of narration from **Rudyard Kipling**'s predictive work of fiction titled "With the Night Mail: A Story of 2000 A.D." (1905), *Actions and Reactions* (1909). It chronicles the transatlantic flight of a General Post Office "coach," an airship under the administration of the "Aerial Board of Control."

The only transportation mode that doesn't require public investment is pogo sticks.

Lecia Stewart, executive, Bombardier Inc., in Katherine Macklem, "Is There a Fast Train Comin'?" *Maclean's*, 24 February 2003.

I don't like passengers. They complain too much. I prefer cargo.

Surjit Babra, founder with Walter Arbib of SkyLink Aviation Inc., Toronto-based private airline that specializes in high-risk cargo flights, in Peter C. Newman, "The New Canadian Establishment," *Maclean's*, 29 August 2005.

TRAVEL *See also* Automobiles; Aviation; Journey; Railways; Tourism; Transportation; Walking

I prefer to think there is something different about the low rolling ground which I see in the early dawn when I look from the window of my berth, that a voice calling an order on the station platform carries a familiar note, that there is a pattern about the villages, even that there is something in the air which says to me: "Young fellow, you have come home again."

Thomas B. Costain, novelist, address, "A Glance at the Future," Toronto, 8 May 1951, The Empire Club of Canada.

To those who travel, all routes are circuitous.

Wayne Grady, author, *The Bone Museum: Travels in the Lost Worlds of Dinosaurs and Birds* (2000).

There is so little time between having to travel with your parents and having to travel with your children.

Hugh Arscott, aphorist, *Hugh's Views: Volume 4* (2000).

Canada is one of the in-between places where foreigners congregate.

Pico Iyer, traveller and essayist, "The Last Refuge," *Harper's*, June 2002.

GO CANADIAN.

Wording on a T-shirt manufactured by U.S. online-clothing giant t-shirtking.com (name of both company and website). The T-shirt comes with a kit that also includes a maple-leaf flag, lapel pin, sew-on patch, and short dictionary of Canadianisms, *How to Speak Canadian, Eh?* The kit—a novelty item selling for US $24.95—was introduced following the U.S. federal election of 2 November 2004 that returned George W. Bush to the White House.

TREES *See also* Forests; Lumber & Lumbering; Nature

Look, those were elms! Long vanished from our world. / Elms, by whose goblet stems distance itself / Taken between two fingers could be twirled, / Its bouquet breathed.

Lines from **James Merrill**'s poem "Overdue Pilgrimage to Nova Scotia," *A Scattering of Salts* (1995).

We give rights to corporations so why shouldn't trees have standing before law?

Paul Watson, environmental activist, interviewed by John F. Schumaker, "Earth Warrior," *The CCPA Monitor*, December 2003–January 2004.

There's a great proverb that says: "One generation plants the trees; another gets the shade."

Maude Barlow, chair, The Council of Canadians, "One Generation Plants the Trees," *Canadian Perspectives*, winter 2005.

My life is endlessly involved with the paper that comes from our forests. The fibre I write upon was once a tree. My life is as intimately involved in the pulp and paper industry as anyone I know.

Patrick Lane, poet, "The Forest's Edge," *The Walrus*, May 2005.

TROUBLE

Don't meet trouble halfway. It is quite capable of making the entire journey.

Bob Edwards, publisher, *Calgary Eye Opener*, 17 July 1920.

If you have trouble, you are the trouble.

Lord Martin Cecil, English-born nobleman and leader of the Emissaries of Divine Light, headquartered at 100 Mile House, B.C., *Being Where You Are* (1974).

TRUDEAU, PIERRE ELLIOTT

In 1968, when Trudeau was first running, we couldn't even find out his age! Was he forty-nine or forty-seven? He wouldn't tell us and we couldn't find out. Some people thought he lost those years in the war! We were so mesmerized by this man that we never looked at him.

Peter Worthington, editor, *Toronto Sun*, address, "Blame the Media," Toronto, 8 March 1979, The Empire Club of Canada.

Fuddle-duddle.

Pierre Elliott Trudeau, prime minister, House of Commons, 16 February 1971. Accused of directing "a four-letter word" at two Conservative members, Trudeau denied the charge as "an absolute untruth." Later, outside the House, asked by CTV's parliamentary reporter Max Keeping if he had told the Tory members of Parliament to "fuck off," Trudeau replied, "No, it was fuddle-duddle." That led **M.T. McCutcheon**, M.P., to quip, "Mr. Trudeau wants to be obscene but not heard."

When he said in his address to the Liberal Convention in April 1968, "*Maîtres chez nous mais pour tout le Canada*," it was the most brilliant political formulation I had ever heard in that country.

Conrad Black, publisher and historian, referring to Trudeau's extension of the Quebec separatist slogan "*Maîtres chez nous*," *A Life in Progress* (1993).

Trudeau won because if Expo 67 had been a person, that person would have been Trudeau.

Richard Gwyn, columnist, referring to Trudeau's electoral victory in 1968, in Peter C. Newman, *Here Be Dragons: Telling Tales of People, Passion, and Power* (2004).

More importantly, he chose to marry into a younger generation which, despite its present flat tummies, high, firm breasts and wholesome expressions, has few inner resources and whose particular ethos puts no premium on duty, loyalty or sacrifice at the expense of self-fulfillment.

Auberon Waugh, columnist, referring to the marriage of Pierre Elliott Trudeau and Margaret Sinclair, "Found under a Stone," *Spectator*, 19 March 1971.

Trudeau was asked the other day by a reporter if it was true that he was born in a log cabin. He replied, "No, you must be thinking of Abe Lincoln. I was born in a manger." I'm not saying he has a high opinion of himself, but the other day he was out for his morning stroll—and nearly got hit by a motor boat. I was reading the classified ads in the *Globe*, and I noted that there was one which read: "Pierre Trudeau supporter wishes to meet another Trudeau supporter. Object: to find out if there is another Trudeau supporter."

Peter Pocklington, capitalist and sports promoter, address, "Let's Make Canada Great Again," Toronto, 4 November 1982, The Empire Club of Canada.

Trudeau came to the leadership of the Liberal party like a stone through a stained-glass window. Suddenly he was there. He wasted no time crying in the wilderness like Diefenbaker or in the marble halls like Pearson. He had been wandering around sharpening his mind and body like an ancient Greek athlete for no apparent purpose other than the exercise itself.

Gordon Donaldson, author, celebrated description of the political advent of Pierre Elliott Trudeau, *Fifteen Men* (1969), later expanded as *Eighteen Men* (1985).

He haunts us still.

Celebrated opening sentence of the foreword to Volume 1 of the two-volume study *Trudeau and Our Times: The Magnificent Obsession* (1990) and *The Heroic Delusion* (1994) by **Stephen Clarkson** and **Christina McCall**. It is said that editor-publisher Douglas Gibson shifted the position of the adverb from its customary place before the verb to its position as the last word in the sentence. The closing words of the conclusion of Volume 2 state that the subject is "the most compelling and controversial Canadian of his times."

Never once in his long tenure did Pierre Trudeau fail to captivate the country with the illusion of change.

J.L. Granatstein, historian, *Pirouette: Pierre Trudeau and Canadian Policy* (1990), with Robert Bothwell, in Christopher Moore, "Writers of History: The Organized Man," *The Beaver*, April–May 1991.

His incitement of ethnic, occupational, regional, and sexual groups debased public policy and ultimately almost bankrupted the country. He, more than anyone, turned Canada into a people of whining politically conformist welfare addicts.

Conrad Black, publisher and historian, *A Life in Progress* (1993).

Clearly then, Pierre Elliott Trudeau has left an indelible mark on our institutions and our political culture. Today's Canada is Trudeau's legacy: a Canada of free and equal citizens, open to cultural diversity.

Max Nemni, political scientist, "Trudeau's Canada," *Cité libre*, fall 2000.

There cannot be one among us who does not feel older today than yesterday.

Roy MacGregor, columnist, the celebrated opening sentence of the column he wrote when it became known that former Prime Minister Pierre Trudeau, aged eighty-one, was terminally ill, "An Elitist Who Empowered Populism," *National Post*, 8 September 2000.

As a Quebec sovereigntist I cannot help but recognize in him a certain idea of Canada which, even if I don't share it, has left its mark on the evolution of the country. But we must recognize as well that Quebec doesn't have a place in it.

Gilles Duceppe, Bloc Québécois leader, tendering a barbed tribute to the late Pierre Trudeau, "Tributes to Greatness," *The Globe and Mail*, 29 September 2000. It recalls the celebrated—and controversial—opening sentence of Charles de Gaulle's memoirs, "I have a certain idea of France."

He was a giant of a man. He had a transforming impact on the country.

Joe Clark, Opposition leader, "Tributes to Greatness," *The Globe and Mail*, 29 September 2000. It is said that he added, "He was the type of man who would build a railway."

He was perhaps the last Canadian nationalist to be a politician.

Dalton Camp, columnist, on the death of Pierre Trudeau, "Tributes," *National Post*, 29 September 2000.

History will remember him as a man of will and intelligence.

Lucien Bouchard, former premier of Quebec, "Tributes to Greatness," *The Globe and Mail*, 29 September 2000.

Even the big guys have to go: some weeks ago, Maurice Richard; yesterday, Pierre Elliott Trudeau. If the Rocket was Quebec's body, Pierre Trudeau was its brain.

Roch Carrier, essayist and author, "The Thinker Whose Ideas Will Endure," *The Globe and Mail*, 30 September 2000.

A terrified Mr. Pearson sent Mr. Gordon—the only man in Ottawa brave enough to do it—to face Mr. Trudeau with the rumours. In effect, confirm or deny. Mr. Trudeau, those famous mesmerizing eyes blazing, replied: "Show me the man who will say that and leave me with his wife in a room for an hour."

Allan Fotheringham, columnist, *The Globe and Mail*, 30 September 2000. Fotheringham was writing about the former prime minister, Lester B. Pearson; former minister of Finance Walter L. Gordon; Pierre Trudeau, then the minister of Justice and leadership contender; and the rumour in 1968 that the unmarried minister was homosexual. The incident and the reply are apocryphal: "a total crock," fellow columnist John Fraser wrote in the *National Post*, 11 October 2000. In a subsequent column in the *Globe*, 21 October 2000, Fotheringham responded to Fraser's charge by citing his source: Christina McCall's book *Grits* (1982). Fraser checked that source in his column "For the Benefit of Dr. Foth," *National Post*, 25 October 2000, and noted that McCall had written: "Coldly furious, Trudeau gave what he later developed into his standard response to this charge, a sarcastic statement to the effect that whoever said that about him should leave him alone in a room with his wife for a couple of hours and what transpired there would provide his rebuttal."

But he won't be coming back any more. It's all up to us, all of us, now. The woods are lovely, dark and deep. He has kept his promises and earned his sleep. *Je t'aime, papa....* Pierre Elliott Trudeau. The very words convey so many things to so many people. Statesman, intellectual, professor, adversary, outdoorsman, lawyer, journalist, author, prime minister. But more than anything to me he was dad. And what a dad. *Je t'aime, papa.*

Justin Trudeau, eldest son and representative of the family, "A Son's Eulogy," Notre-Dame Basilica, Montreal, 3 October 2000. Aired on CBC-TV and published in *The Globe and Mail*, 3 October 2000.

Oh, you look at the Indian in him! Oh, was he one of our elders!

Margaret Trudeau, former wife of the late Pierre Trudeau, commenting on Rod MacIvor's photographs of the man, TVOntario documentary, in John Gray, "Margaret Trudeau on Pierre," *The Globe and Mail*, 5 January 2001.

Black's observation came in the course of recounting a conversation he'd once had with Pierre Elliott Trudeau, who was discussing his own tall-poppy problems and remarking, according to Black's account, that Canada was difficult to govern partly because French-speaking Canadians boo the loser and English-speaking Canadians boo the winner.

Calvin Trillin, essayist, referring to the ubiquitous Conrad Black, "Paper Baron," *The New Yorker*, 17 December 2001.

It's like giving Dracula's name to a blood bank. This is pure provocation on the part of the Chrétien government ... it's taking Quebecers for fools.

Gilles Rhéaume, president, Mouvement souverainiste du Québec, reacting to the decision of the Chrétien administration to rename Montreal–Dorval International Airport the Pierre Elliott Trudeau Airport to honour the memory of the late prime minister, a native Montrealer, in Michelle MacAfee, "Outrage over 'Trudeau Airport,'" *Toronto Star*, 22 August 2003. The new name, announced 21 August 2003, became official on 9 September 2003. Separatist critics of Trudeau suggested that a more suitable honour would be attaching his name to the money-losing Mirabel airport north of Montreal.

As an obsessive Trudeau watcher, I gradually realized that his essence was not that difficult to divine: Pierre Trudeau was an emotional cripple with a sliver of ice in his heart.

Peter C. Newman, journalist and memoirist, *Here Be Dragons: Telling Tales of People, Passion, and Power* (2004).

He was the only truly magical leader we have had in my lifetime, a man of indefinable intensity, pent-up power and hidden dimensions.... In politics, Pierre Trudeau ... magicked us.

Peter C. Newman, journalist and author, "Going Strong," *Maclean's*, 8 November 2004.

I suppose if you're Pierre Trudeau it must be kind of difficult to get up in the morning and look in the mirror and know you've seen perfection for the last time all day.

Brian Mulroney, former prime minister, in Peter C. Newman, *The Secret Mulroney Tapes* (2005), as published in *Maclean's*, 19 September 2005.

TRUTH *See also* Authenticity; Honesty; Integrity; Lies

She [Canada] must dream of the introduction of honesty even in politics, which is the self-interest of the nation, knowing that such interest can only have its sure foundation in truth, justice, and sympathy in international relationships.

Rabindranath Tagore, Bengali sage, "Farewell to Canada," 13 April 1929, *Education and Leisure: Addresses Delivered at the Fourth Triennial Conference on Education Held at Victoria and Vancouver, Canada, April 1929* (1929), edited by S.E. Lang.

As all newspaper writers are aware, truth can be an error of judgment.

John Kenneth Galbraith, economist and author, email to journalist Kate Harries, "Scotch Hangover Subsidies," *Toronto Star*, 12 October 2003. He is referring to the fact that farm folk in Elgin County, where he was born and raised, still smart from his descriptions of them in his affectionate and witty memoir, *The Scotch* (1964).

Truth was what made sense within the tale you were telling, and tales were about something other than truth—they were about lessons, lessons that gave you insight into how the world worked, how things fit together. If little truths did not fit under the big "real" truth, then they had to be cut or dropped to satisfy the need at hand.

Janice Dickin McGinnis, lawyer and historian, "Aimee Semple McPherson: Fantasizing the Fantasizer? Telling the Tale of a Tale-Teller," *Boswell's Children: The Art of the Biographer* (1992), edited by R.B. Fleming.

Be careful when you tell the truth. You may be found out.

Hugh Arscott, aphorist, *Hugh's Views: Volume 5* (2001).

What is true we believe will outlive the sun.

John Polanyi, scientist, concluding sentence, address about human values and research, Bach Festival, Toronto, 13 January 2004, published as "Peaceable Kingdoms of Science and Music," *The Globe and Mail*, 13 January 2004.

TUQUE

The tuque is as Canadian as hockey itself, or maple syrup, the beaver, the red maple leaf or, for that matter, yellow snow—yet it has never before been celebrated. In all the books of quotations of great Canadian sayings, there doesn't seem to be an entry for what has been the traditional hat since the first voyageur began paddling.

Roy MacGregor, columnist, "This Country," *The Globe and Mail*, 1 December 2003.

TWENTIETH CENTURY

The twentieth century belongs to Canada.

Sir Wilfrid Laurier, prime minister, address, Canadian Club of Ottawa, 18 January 1904. According to the printed text, he said, "The nineteenth century was the century of the United States. I think we can claim that it is Canada that shall fill the twentieth century." The sentiment soon assumed the form of the words above. The famous remark has been seen as a touchstone of national aspiration measured against national achievement. In the 1900s it was regarded as prophecy; in the 2000s, as irony. About three dozen variations appear in *Colombo's Canadian Quotations* (1974), *Colombo's Concise Canadian Quotations* (1978), *Colombo's New Canadian Quotations* (1987), *The Dictionary of Canadian Quotations* (1991), *Colombo's All-Time Great Canadian Quotations* (1994), and *Famous Lasting Words* (2000).

I remember a Toronto in which the admirably true phrase—the 20th century was to be Canada's—was accepted as the general watchword; only nobody had begun to realize what a rotten century the twentieth was going to be. (Laughter.)

B.K. Sandwell, professor of English, address, "On Being Sorry for Ourselves," Toronto, 24 January 1924, The Empire Club of Canada.

The 21st century will not belong to Canada, just as the 20th century did not. Belonging suggests ownership, and no country will own the world, not even the United States.

Jeffrey Simpson, columnist, *Star-Spangled Canadians: Canadians Living the American Dream* (2000).

In 1904, Prime Minister Wilfrid Laurier declared that the 20th century would belong to Canada. He was wrong. Canada wasn't big enough or strong enough for an age of power. But Laurier may have spoken 100 years too soon. This century will not belong to Canada, but it will belong to the attitudes, values, and understandings that are our legacy.

Ken Dryden, hockey personality, lawyer, and author, address, Charles R. Bronfman Lecture in Canadian Studies, November, University of Ottawa, "The Canadian Way," *Maclean's*, 13 November 2000.

I feel that while the 20th century was the century of nation states, the 21st century will be the century of city states and we are not going to be very important in that context. We don't have enough critical mass, either in population or [in] technology. The question isn't so much whether the 21st century will belong to Canada, but whether Canada will belong to the 21st century.

Peter C. Newman, journalist and author, "Going Strong," *Maclean's*, 8 November 2004.

TWENTY-FIRST CENTURY *See also* Millennium; Y2K

The 21st century, I believe, will be a "find a way" century. Ideologies will matter less. Naked power will have less impact.... The 21st century will belong to the conciliators. To the listeners. To the learners. To people who know that whatever they are sure of today will not be right tomorrow.

Ken Dryden, hockey personality, lawyer, and author, address, Charles R. Bronfman Lecture in Canadian Studies, November, University of Ottawa, "The Canadian Way," *Maclean's*, 13 November 2000.

The 21st century has made its decisions. It imposes on us protection of the environment, it imposes decentralization, integration, cultural diversity. It has made its choice for new technology, for controlled imagination. The values of the 21st century are already there; the 21st century has already chosen its first country: Canada.

Jean-Pierre Raffarin, prime minister of France, responding to a toast, National Gallery of Canada, Ottawa, 21 May 2003, in Graham Fraser, "Canada Praised as Model for 21st Century," *Toronto Star*, 22 May 2003.

TWO NATIONS

You know that these two nations have been at war over a few acres of snow near Canada, and that they are spending on this fine struggle more than Canada itself is worth.

Voltaire, French man of letters, casting a cold eye on his country's foreign adventures, notably its struggle with the English for mastery of Quebec, *Candide, ou l'Optimisme* (1759), as translated by Robert A. Adams in 1966. The satiric novel appeared the year of the English Conquest of Quebec.

I expected to find a contest between a government and a people. I found two nations warring in the bosom of a single state. I found a struggle, not of principles, but of races; and I perceived that it would be idle to attempt any amelioration of laws or institutions until we could first succeed in terminating the deadly animosity that now separates the inhabitants of Lower Canada into the hostile divisions of French and English.

Lord Durham, English commissioner inquiring into the causes of the Rebellion of 1837, *Report on the Affairs of British North America* (1839). The words "two nations warring in the bosom of a single state" retain their sting and relevance to this day. So do the words he used to describe the French in Lower Canada: "They are a people with no history, and no literature."

No wonder the Canadians never liked Lord Durham. He came in a Pique, and went off in a Huff, say they. He did something more: he told the truth about them.

Unidentified American reviewer of **Goldwin Smith**'s book *Canada and the Canadian Question* (1891), *The Atlantic Monthly*, August 1891.

I thought of Durham's report on the state of Quebec when he arrived there after the Rebellion of 1837–38, and said he found two nations warring in the bosom of a single state. That would be the case in Canada, as applied to Canada as a whole, unless the whole question of conscription from now on is approached with the utmost care.

W.L. Mackenzie King, prime minister, diary, referring to the conscription crisis in 1942, in Ramsay Cook, "The Triumph and Trials of Materialism, 1900–1945," *The Illustrated History of Canada* (1987), edited by Craig Brown.

TWO SOLITUDES *See also* Canada & Quebec; Quebec

Two solitudes.

Hugh MacLennan, novelist, *Two Solitudes* (1945). MacLennan introduced these words into Canadian political discourse to refer to the mutual isolation of the French and the English in Montreal, in Quebec, and in Canada. He in turn had found them in a letter written on 14 May 1904 by Rainer Maria Rilke, the German poet, and published in *Letters to a Young Poet* (1934), translated by M.D. Herter Norton. MacLennan's novel is set in Montreal and defines its theme in these words, giving a psychological dimension to the expression of Canadian dualism.

At the same time, those of us who care about the future of Canada must not allow the two solitudes of the past to become the twin lassitudes of the present.

Peter C. Newman, columnist, referring to the legendary indifference of English Canadians to French Canadians in the aftermath of the election of Quebec Premier Jean Charest, "Adieu to Separatism?" *Maclean's*, 12 May 2003.

The time of the "two solitudes" that for too long described the character of this country is past. The narrow notion of "every person for himself" does not belong in today's world, which demands that we learn to see beyond our wounds, beyond our differences for the good of all.

Michaëlle Jean, governor general, installation address, Ottawa, 27 September 2005, *Toronto Star*, 28 September 2005. Gerald Owen, in "Two Solitudes: A Short History," *National Post*, 1 October 2005, noted that the governor general's newly issued coat-of-arms reads "*Briser les solitudes*" (French for "to break the solitudes" or "breaking down the solitudes"). Owen recalled that *Two Solicitudes* was the title of a book of conversations between Margaret Atwood and Victor-Lévy Beaulieu (1995).

TYPOGRAPHY *See also* Design; Printing; Publishers & Publishing

The typographer gives outward and visible form to the text's intrinsic, invisible order.

This determines, in large part, who will read the text and how.

Robert Bringhurst, author and typographer, *The Elements of Typographic Style* (2nd ed., 1996).

For type designers are, at their best, the Stradivarii of literature: not merely makers of saleable products, but artists who design and make the instruments that other artists use.

Robert Bringhurst, author and typographer, *The Elements of Typographic Style* (2nd ed., 1996).

Typographic history is just that: the study of the relationships between type designs and the rest of human activity—politics, philosophy, the arts, and the history of ideas. It is a life-long pursuit, but one that is informative and rewarding from the beginning.... Typography is an ancient craft and an old profession as well as a constant technological frontier.

Robert Bringhurst, author and typographer, *The Elements of Typographic Style* (2nd ed., 1996).

U

UFOS *See* Unidentified Flying Objects

UNDERSTANDING

Thoroughly understand what it is to understand, and not only will you understand the broad lines of all there is to be understood but also you will possess a fixed base, an invariant pattern, opening upon all further developments of understanding.

Bernard Lonergan, theologian, "The Original Preface to *Insight*" (1949–1953) in *The Lonergan Reader* (1997), edited by Mark D. Morelli and Elizabeth A. Morelli. (This passage is italicized in the original.)

UNEMPLOYMENT *See also* Employment; Labour; Welfare; Work

We have more than a million unemployed. For me, it is more than economics. It is very much a matter of human dignity for human beings to have the right to work. Human beings do not want to collect welfare; they do not want to collect unemployment insurance.

Ed Broadbent, New Democratic Party leader, address, "The Choice for Canada," Toronto, 11 May 1979, The Empire Club of Canada.

UNIDENTIFIED FLYING OBJECTS *See also* Aliens; Space; Universe

Later events proved that it was not the end of a journey and my studies would continue many years into the future, for it was only the tiny thread that linked to a far greater voyage, through knowledge, to the infinite reaches of the universe.

H. Albert Coe, American contactee, referring to his accidental meeting with the mysterious alien being from a flying saucer (or UFO) who called himself Xretsim (read it backwards) at Trout Lake, near the Mattawa River, Ont., June 1920, and published in *The Shocking Truth* (1969), with illustrations by Thomas Lulevitch.

I was so far north they have ice circles instead of crop circles.

Frank Ogden, futurist, remark made on 20 March 2001, following a trip to the Yukon Territory, where circles of ice on the lakes resembled crop circles investigated by ufologists.

Perhaps UFOs are an answer to our existential loneliness as a species. On some deep, collective level we are desperately alone, and when we realized the vastness of the universe four hundred years ago, our concomitant inconsequentiality made us even lonelier. We want company.

Christopher Dewdney, poet and author, *Acquainted with the Night: Excursions through the World after Dark* (2004).

UNIONS *See also* Labour; Strikes

If collective bargaining goes down the drain, everything else goes with it. I say to you that all you are going to lose is your freedom of contract and your freedom of property. I hope that after listening to me you will understand why I happen to believe that's nothing compared to what I'll lose, and that's my freedom of speech.

John Crispo, professor of industrial relations, address, "The Public Interests in Collective Bargaining," Toronto, 25 January 1975, The Empire Club of Canada.

Who promotes the adversary system? Who benefits from it? Certainly not organized labour. Certainly not the workers that we represent. If anyone thinks that a strike is a romantic experience, I suggest that you get involved in one on a practical basis.

Dennis McDermott, Canadian director, United Auto Workers, address, "Canada's Adversary System," Toronto, 3 March 1977, The Empire Club of Canada.

There is nothing I like better than to be standing on a street corner, passing out leaflets, because it is how you come to understand what people are about.

Lea Roback, union organizer, interviewed by Sophie Bissonnette for the documentary film *Des Lumières dans la Grande Noirceur* (1991), as quoted by Judy Rebick, "Trailblazer," *Elm Street*, November 2000.

UNITED KINGDOM *See* British Character; Canada & United Kingdom; England; Ireland; Scotland

UNITED NATIONS *See also* Canada & the World; Foreign Affairs; Foreign Aid; Globalism & Globalization; International Affairs; World

Today it's LeCorbusier's United Nations Headquarters in Manhattan that shelters the architects of the next Holocaust.

George Jonas, columnist, "It's Time for Kofi to Get out of Town," *National Post*, 29 January 2003.

Canada cannot conceive of a world succeeding without the United Nations. But make no mistake: The UN needs reform.

Paul Martin, prime minister, address, UN General Assembly, 16 September 2005, in Steven Edwards, "Martin Lashes UN for 'Empty Rhetoric,'" *National Post*, 17 September 2005.

UNIVERSE *See also* Astronomy; Exploration; Space; Stars

With it goes out in extinction all that was thought of as matter, and with that all the framework of time and space that held it, and the conscious life that matched it. All ends with a cancellation of forces and comes to nothing; and our Universe ends thus with one vast, silent unappreciated joke.

Stephen Leacock, humorist, *How to Write* (1943).

You are a child of the universe no less than the trees and the stars; you have a right to be here. And whether or not it is clear to you, no doubt the universe is unfolding as it should.

Widely quoted lines from "Desiderata," a prose poem composed in 1927 by **Max Ehrmann**, the American writer (1872–1945). The expression of sentiment found a sympathetic response in the 1960s when it was mistakenly believed to be an anonymous inscription on an old church wall. Widely reproduced without authorship on posters, the homily came to the attention of Pierre Trudeau, who mused on it and quoted these lines on a number of public occasions in 1972, 1974, 1975, and notably on 22 May 1979, when he conceded electoral defeat.

After all, the same cosmic night in which the galaxies swirl is inside all substance, inside us, an eternal, brilliant night within and beyond all matter, for all time.

Christopher Dewdney, poet and author, concluding sentence, *Acquainted with the Night: Excursions through the World after Dark* (2004).

UNIVERSITIES & COLLEGES *See also* Education; Learning

A great university has a dual function, to teach and to think.

Sir William Osler, physician, "Teaching and Thinking," *Aequanimitas* (1932).

University—centre where one has the right and duty not to make up one's mind. [1946]

Harold Adams Innis, social scientist, *The Idea File of Harold Adams Innis* (1980), edited by William Christian.

I believe that the function of a university is to be counter-technical, subversive, iconoclastic; that it sets out to shatter assumptions and prejudices.

George Whalley, scholar, commencement address, Rothesay College School, N.B., 1959, *George Whalley: Remembrances* (1989), edited by Michael D. Moore.

If Canadian universities are underfunded so badly that they can no longer function effectively, Canada would disappear overnight from modern history and become again what it was at first, a blank area of natural resources to be exploited by more advanced countries. This is not empty rhetoric: it is a verifiable fact, though I should not care to become known as the person who verified it. What is connected with the universities is what is really happening: the political and economic charades also going on are what are called pseudo-events, created for and blown up by the news media to give us the illusion of living in history.

Northrop Frye, literary and cultural critic, address, "The Authority of Learning," Toronto, 19 June 1984, The Empire Club of Canada.

Forty thousand students at York! Get it down to 10,000 and you could have a good university.

J.L. Granatstein, historian, referring to York University, Downsview, Ont., interviewed by Christopher Moore, "Writers of History: The Organized Man," *The Beaver*, April–May 1991.

The *tout ensemble* symbolized all the contradictory things I loved about the University. The scale and classical façade of Convocation Hall spoke about the national aspirations of Canada's oldest university. The aggressively Victorian mien of University College announced the weight the founders gave to its secular leanings, which opposed the church-affiliated colleges that made up the rest of the University. Every outrageous gargoyle and buttress proclaimed Darwin and Spencer. Hart House's graceful arches showed the Oxbridge loyalties that had shaped the university's intellectual aspirations, and the overcrowded and nondescript library announced the wave of expansion that had swept over the university in the baby boom years. I never looked at them all without an affectionate pleasure for the three-dimensional representation they provided of the frustrations and challenges of running part of this large and untidy institution.

Jill Ker Conway, historian, memoirist, and vice-president of the University of Toronto, offering a remarkable, impressionistic panorama of the main campus of one of the country's earliest of universities, November 1973, *A Woman's Education* (2001).

A university without controversy is probably doing something wrong.

John Lorinc, journalist, "School of Hard Knocks," *Saturday Night*, September 2002.

Credentialing, not educating, has become the primary business of North American universities. This is not in the interest of employers in the long run. But in the short run, it is beneficial for corporations' departments of human resources, the current name for personnel departments.

Jane Jacobs, urban planning critic, *Dark Age Ahead* (2004).

V

VACATIONS

The best part of a vacation is thinking of your colleagues back at the office.

Irena F. Karafilly, aphorist, characteristic observation, 7 November 2000.

What Canadian wouldn't love to vacation at the Mediterranean sea? What Israeli would want to vacation at Baffin Bay?

Sam Orbaum, Montreal-born columnist, "I'd Rather Live in Israel," *The Jerusalem Post Magazine*, 13 July 2001.

VALUES *See also* Ethics; Government; Philosophy; Principles; Virtue & Vice

My voice is certainly not a lone voice, but it sometimes amuses me that when I speak of nothing but holding up the best values and institutions of the Western world, equality of opportunity, due process of law, defence of liberty and individual rights; when I speak out in favour of the virtues of our society—not its vices, not its faults, not its errors, but its virtues—I should be such a minority voice.

Barbara Amiel, journalist, address, "How Canada Does It and Other Social Diseases," Toronto, 4 February 1982, The Empire Club of Canada.

Yes, I bring a vision and a sense of values to an issue. However, I believe it is still an age of miracles, the glass is half full and the world is a wonderful place.

Stuart McLean, CBC-Radio personality, quoted in *Metropolis*, 2 November 1989.

Multiculturalism has been government policy for only three decades, hardly long enough to be pronounced immutably Canadian. The yet-to-be-achieved goal of gender equality has been in place for even less time, flexible federalism is a swear word to some Canadians, and Canada's good governance is not quite the model for the world we might wish it to be. Values that are not long-lived and widely cherished by the Canadian people may seem more as government propaganda than as expressions of the popular will.

J.L. Granatstein, "The Importance of Being Less Earnest," *National Post*, 22 October 2003.

They're about the only ones who still believe in it all, the Canadians.

Attributed to **John le Carré**, novelist, with respect to decent values by columnist John Ivison, "Another Scot Follows a Grand Tradition," *National Post*, 30 June 2005.

VANCOUVER

Little Vancouver was born in the west, / The healthiest baby on Canada's breast. / Motherly Canada nursed the wee youth, / And brought it a railroad to cut its first tooth. / And soon it grew out of its swaddling bands, / To slip from the lap and the old nurse's hands.

Couplets from the verse "Little Vancouver" (*c.* 1894) by **E. Pauline Johnson**, in Charlotte Gray, *Flint & Feather: The Life and Times of E. Pauline Johnson, Tekahionwake* (2002). Gray calls the verse "possibly the worst piece of poetry that Pauline ever wrote."

Vancouver is a wonder city. There will be a million people in it in twenty years. It has the combined excellence of nature's gift and man's handiwork. God did a lot for Montreal, but man didn't add to it.

Stephen Leacock, humorist, *My Discovery of the West: A Discussion of East and West in Canada* (1937).

I gather films are still being made in Vancouver, but with a few noble exceptions, most of the voices which reach me now echo as from a morgue.

Allan King, filmmaker, "Canadian—Cinema—Vancouver," looking back on a period of CBC-TV film production on the West Coast, *How to*

Make or Not Make a Canadian Film (1968), edited by André Pâquet.

We hope to move to Vancouver one day.... I loved it up there, but I missed my friends here.

Philip K. Dick, science-fiction writer, letter to John Brunner, 2 February 1974, written in Fullerton, Cal., about a brief trip to Vancouver in 1972, *The Selected Letters of Philip K. Dick* (1974), edited by Paul Williams.

I think we should franchise ourselves and put Vancouver all around the world—it's actually not a bad idea.

Douglas Coupland, author, *City of Glass: Douglas Coupland's Vancouver* (2000).

So this book arises from both love and laziness: love, because I spent my twenties scouring the globe thinking there had to be a better city out there, until it dawned on me that Vancouver is the best one going; and laziness, because I thought I was going to go mental explaining dim sum, the sulphur pits and Kitsilano for the umpteen-hundredth time.

Douglas Coupland, author, *City of Glass: Douglas Coupland's Vancouver* (2000).

Vancouver is Regina with hills.

Attributed to **William Thorsell**, former editor-in-chief of *The Globe and Mail*, discussing Douglas Coupland's *The City of Glass* (2000), which evokes the spirit and architecture of Vancouver.

Vancouver is like Winnipeg, only boring.

Characteristic remark attributed to **Larry Zolf**, wit and raconteur and a native of Winnipeg, December 2000.

I don't think they collect art there.

Attributed to **Andy Warhol**, American artist, in a diary entry dated 1976 by Douglas Coupland, "Critical Mass," *The Globe and Mail*, 12 May 2001.

Vancouver is one of Earth's youngest cities, uncursed with much European history and its ultimate gestalt as yet unattained. Vancouver's landscape is awe provoking but never far from a mall, and its citizens deeply aware and deeply suspicious of the global economy's penchant for erasing personal and regional voice.

Douglas Coupland, author and artist, "Critical Mass," *The Globe and Mail*, 12 May 2001.

Vancouver is the only city in the world where you don't buy a picture. You put in a window.

Attributed to **Alvin Balkin**, art critic, by publisher Scott McIntyre, Vancouver, July 2001.

I do not want to live in a city that puts Glenn Gould's death on page five.

Attributed to **Keith Spicer**, journalist and commissioner, by Allan Fotheringham, "The Way of the World," *The Globe and Mail*, 5 July 2001. Spicer lived in Vancouver in 1982 when pianist Glenn Gould's death received page-five prominence in *The Vancouver Sun*. Thereupon Spicer moved to Ottawa and then to the south of France.

Vancouver is a good city. I think it would be a good place for the Olympics and we would never oppose your holding the Olympic Games here.

Fidel Castro, president of Cuba, impromptu press conference, Vancouver, during a stopover between Japan and Cuba, 4 March 2003, in Jason Proctor, "Leader Muses on Baseball, Salmon, War and Health," *National Post*, 5 March 2003.

VANCOUVER ISLAND *See also* Victoria

The story of Boy Niven who lured seven or eight able-bodied seamen and marines into the woods of British Columbia used to be a legend of the Fleet.

Line of dialogue from **Rudyard Kipling**'s story "Mrs. Bathurst" (1904), *Traffics and Discoveries* (1904).

But as I was saying, Vancouver Island with the city of Victoria that lies at the foot of it, represents the last word in charm of climate and in beauty. Beyond it, till we reach another world, it is nothing.

Stephen Leacock, humorist, *My Discovery of the West: A Discussion of East and West in Canada* (1937).

Vancouver Island has everything that makes life pleasant. The scenery is exquisite; nearly everyone grows flowers and there is an abundance of fruit. Life moves there a little more slowly than in the rest of Canada, and the English lark sings there, which is perhaps symbolic.

Susan Buchan, compiler of *John Buchan by His Wife and Friends* (1947), describing conditions in the province of British Columbia in the late 1930s.

If you ever go on the ferry from Vancouver Island to Schwartz Bay, or Vancouver to Victoria, the ferry boat goes right by. If you wave a handkerchief, I can see you from my house, and I'll wave back to you if it is a red handkerchief.

Robert Bateman, artist, address, "My Art and My Life," Toronto, 13 November 1986, The Empire Club of Canada.

VICE *See* Virtue & Vice

VICTIMS & VICTIMHOOD *See also* Abuse: Sexual; Crime; Law; Violence

The ever-increasing popularity of the victim and the new role for the victim obscures the role of the state, attempts to legitimate personal revenge as a justification for public punishment, and tends to overshadow the primary focus of the criminal trial—the legalized attempt by the state to deprive the individual of his liberty. There are other forums for redress of the violence done to victims. The legitimacy of the violence we do to an individual accused of a crime can only be determined in a criminal trial.

Edward L. Greenspan, advocate, address, "The Role of the Defence Counsel," Toronto, 19 November 1987, The Empire Club of Canada.

Do not be intimidated by social workers, teachers, or judges. Do not accept the role of scapegoat.

Marie Adams, educator, offering advice to parents, *Our Son, a Stranger: Adoption Breakdown and Its Effects on Parents* (2002).

To turn people into victims is to deprive them of their humanity and their citizenship.

Robert Ivan Martin, law professor, *The Most Dangerous Branch: How the Supreme Court of Canada Has Undermined Our Law and Our Democracy* (2003).

If definitions of reality are simply power relationships, as many postmodernists would have it, any individual can fairly assert a claim that he or she has been victimized: if you think you were abused and if you feel you have been victimized, you probably were.

Neil Boyd, criminologist, Simon Fraser University, *Big Sister: How Extreme Feminism Has Betrayed the Fight for Sexual Equality* (2004). Boyd neatly summarizes this attitude: "If you think you are a victim, you are."

VICTORIA *See also* Vancouver Island

The place itself appears a perfect Eden in the midst of the dreary wilderness of the Northwest coast, and so different is its general aspect from the wooded, rugged regions around that one might be pardoned for supposing it had dropped from the clouds.

Sir James Douglas, later governor of Vancouver Island, letter written in 1842, in Henry Gregson, *A History of Victoria, 1842–1970* (1977).

We reached Victoria in Vancouver Island (which is as big as England) by a beautiful voyage in a perfectly appointed ship through an archipelago of delicious inlets. Victoria is English with a splendid climate thrown in. Sentiment, vegetation, manners, all revive the best in England.

Winston Churchill, British statesman, letter to his wife, 12 September 1929, in David Dilks, *"The Great Dominion": Winston Churchill in Canada 1900–1954* (2005).

I remember, however, when one of us was sounding the praises of the Victoria climate, Sir John agreed, but added as an aside, "The day was always in the afternoon."

Sir Joseph Pope, biographer, referring to Prime Minister Sir John A. Macdonald in Victoria, in William Toye, *A Book of Canada* (1962).

VICTORIA DAY *See* Holidays

VIETNAM WAR *See also* War

If we learned nothing from Vietnam we should have learned how little helicopters, armies, weapons and those walls count if they are not backed by the spirit of determination and a belief among the people that they are fighting for a worthwhile cause.

Barbara Amiel, journalist, address, "How Canada Does It and Other Social Diseases," Toronto, 4 February 1982, The Empire Club of Canada.

It was in summertime. The very light clothes I had on instantly disappeared, and my body caught fire. I was so scared. I kept running and running until I had to stop from exhaustion. One of the soldiers gave me some water to drink. I was screaming, "Too hot! Too hot!" Trying to help, he poured water over my body. But the napalm burned under my skin, so pouring water on it just made it worse. To give you an idea of how hot it was: The temperature of boiling water is 100 degrees Celsius, and napalm is 800 to 1,200 degrees Celsius.

Kim Phuc, nine-year-old Vietnamese girl, describing how her entire body was burnt with napalm when her village in Vietnam was bombed, 8 June 1972. The image of her running toward Nick Ut's camera is a landmark image of the Vietnam war and of wartime atrocities. Ut took her to a hospital; she recovered. She now lives near Toronto, where she established the Kim Foundation to provide aid to children in war-torn countries; in Barry Shainbaum, *Hope & Heroes: Portraits of Integrity & Inspiration* (2003).

VIOLENCE *See also* Abuse: Sexual; Crime; Murder; Revolution; Victims & Victimhood; War; Women's Rights

Violence against women is seen as the consequence of social, economic and political inequality built into the structure of society and reinforced through assumptions expressed in the language and ideologies of sexism, racism and class.

Sentence from *Final Report: Changing the Landscape: Ending Violence—Achieving Equality* (1993), produced by the Canadian Panel on Violence against Women, in Robert Ivan Martin, *The Most Dangerous Branch: How the Supreme Court of Canada Has Undermined Our Law and Our Democracy* (2003). Martin adds, "Why, one might ask, did the panel bother conducting any research at all? It could simply have stated the conclusions it had evidently reached before it began its inquiry and saved the Canadian people a lot of money."

A civilizing process of socialized repression inhibits the display of violence.

Elliott Leyton, anthropologist and criminologist, *Men of Blood: Murder in Everyday Life* (1995, 1996).

A man is more than the worst thing he has ever done.

Sentence from the seven-page, handwritten suicide note left by **Ralph Hadley**, the postal worker who stalked and then murdered his estranged wife and himself, sparing their 11-month-old son, 20 June 2000, Pickering, Ont., in Renée Huang, "Fatal Attractions," *The Globe and Mail*, 23 June 2000.

There's nobody more dangerous to a woman than a weak and vengeful man with a fist, or a club, or a gun.

Margaret Wente, columnist, "Counterpoint," *The Globe and Mail*, 22 June 2000.

A bomb is a vote.

Attributed to **Ted Honderich**, the Ontario-born London-based philosopher, by a broadcaster on the BBC World Service. Honderich noted in *Philosopher: A Kind of Life* (2001) that what he had written in *Three Essays on Political Violence* (1977) was: "If some bombs are like votes, they also maim and kill." He secured a retraction.

Given the kind of democracy we have, mass civil disobedience is a rational and necessary supplement to it.

Ted Honderich, Grote professor of mind and logic, University College London, born in Baden, Ont., *Philosopher: A Kind of Life* (2001).

Canadians are an ambivalent lot: one minute they're peacekeepers, next minute they punch the hell out of each other on the ice rink.

Ken Wiwa, journalist, "First of July," *The Globe and Mail,* 1 July 2001.

VIRTUE & VICE *See also* Crime; Ethics; Good & Evil; Law; Right & Wrong; Society; Values

There can be no moral framework, and therefore no true community, without a judicious public intolerance. In other words, there can be no public sense of virtue without a public sense of vice.

William D. Gairdner, athlete, academic, businessman, author, and commentator, *The Trouble with Democracy: A Citizen Speaks Out* (2001).

VISION *See also* Destiny; Dreams; Future; Idealism; Ideologies; Perception; Philosophy

It is all a reminder that theoretically driven utopian visions, with their promises of a better world, can all too easily reproduce the same injustices that they were designed to combat.

Neil Boyd, criminologist, Simon Fraser University, *Big Sister: How Extreme Feminism Has Betrayed the Fight for Sexual Equality* (2004).

The vision I waited for I hoped would in some way transform my life. The vision never came. Instead there arose in me a deep sense that all of the things I experience—the joyful and the painful, light and dark, courage and fear, kindness and meaning—are all part of me.

Bob Kull, Vancouver-based student of solitude, referring to one year he spent in self-imposed exile on an island off the coast of Chile, in Leslie Scrivener, "Solitude," *Toronto Star,* 13 March 2005.

We do not see with our eyes, but through them.

Ken Danby, artist, characteristic observation, 6 July 2005.

WAITING

So much of life is waiting, isn't it? Waiting for inspiration, for love, for a cab, for the toast to pop up in the morning.

Brent Carver, actor, interviewed by Richard Ouzounian, "Carver No Stranger to Death's Shadow," *Toronto Star*, 17 October 2004.

WALKING *See also* Exercise; Travel

I have been walking ever since I could walk.

Attributed to Toronto conservationist **Charles Sauriol**, who even in his nineties found delight and instruction in walking the trails and river-banks of the city's Don Valley, recalled at the time of his death, 17 December 1995.

Early one morning, any morning, we can set out, with the least possible baggage, and discover the world. / A journey implies a destination, so many miles to be consumed, while a walk is its own measure, complete at every point along the way. / The most distant places seem accessible once one is on the road. / In the course of a walk we usually find out something about our companion, and this is true even when we travel alone. / A day, from dawn to dusk, is the natural span of a walk.

Thomas A. Clark, poet, "In Praise of Walking," *Wild Culture: Specimens from* The Journal of Wild Culture (1992), edited by Whitney Smith and Christopher Lowry.

WAR *See also* Afghan War; Arms Race; Canadian Armed Forces; Conscription; Defence; Disarmament; Gulf War; Iraq War; Land Mines; Nuclear Warfare; Pacificism; Peacekeeping; Vietnam War; Violence; War of 1812; War Dead; Weapons; World War I; World War II

I have no reply to make to your general other than from the mouths of my cannon and muskets.

Comte de Frontenac, defender of Quebec, to Major Thomas Savage, envoy of Admiral Sir William Phips, the commander of the English forces, who was demanding the surrender of Quebec, 15 October 1690. Phips was forced to withdraw, as noted by W.J. Eccles, *Canada under Louis XIV* (1964).

Ready, aye, ready.

Traditional British response to the call to arms as well as the motto of the Marlborough family (from whom Winston Churchill was descended), voiced by Sir Wilfrid Laurier, Opposition leader, special war session, House of Commons, 19 August 1914. Arthur Meighen, later Opposition leader, echoed the words in a Toronto address, 22 September 1922, at the time of the Chanak affair. The belief that Canada would follow Britain's lead received a near-mortal blow when the Dominion issued its own declaration that a state of war existed between Canada and Germany on 9 September 1939.

PEACE CERTAIN IF NO WAR. / WAR CERTAIN IF NO PEACE.

Headlines on different newspapers held aloft by two neighbours who turn into enemies and then into murderers in the 8-minute, 10-second film *Neighbours* (1952), produced, directed, and animated by **Norman McLaren**, as noted by Maynard Collins, *Norman McLaren* (1976).

The bad side of the Space Age was heralded by the V2 attacks on Great Britain; the bad side of the Nuclear Age had its lurid baptism of fire in that monumentally inhuman error, the dropping of the Atomic Bomb over Hiroshima.

Sir Robert Watson-Watt, inventor of radar and resident of Richmond Hill, north of Toronto, address, "The Dangers of the Nuclear Age," Toronto, 15 January 1959, The Empire Club of Canada.

We no longer tolerate fights between individuals, tribes or cities. Thus we are at the last rung of the ladder. The only anarchy that remains is between nations. In the process of achieving peaceful settlements between individuals and groups within a nation we have not changed basic human nature; we have simply restrained and regulated it. This remains to be done in the field of international conflicts. It must be done, for today weapon technology has made war as obsolete as a means of settling international disputes as duelling in the street is obsolete.

Norman Z. Alcock, Canadian Peace Research Institute, address, "Can the Scientist Win the Peace?" Toronto, 8 February 1962, The Empire Club of Canada.

The wars fought by Canadians in the twentieth century were not fought for the purpose of uniting Canada, but the country that emerged was forged in the smithy of sacrifice. We will not forget that.

Adrienne Clarkson, governor general, "Eulogy for Canada's Unknown Soldier," Ottawa, 28 May 2000.

I don't see any difference between American and Canadian bombs.

Slobodan Simic, biologist based in Serbia, complaining about U.S.-led bombing of Bucharest to his brother Goran Simic, who had immigrated to Canada, noted by Goran Simic, "Gone, but Not Forgotten," *The Globe and Mail*, 2 April 2001.

There is not an ounce of that land that is without blood. Think of the wars, one after another.

Tomson Highway, Cree playwright, born at the Lac Brocher Reserve, northern Ontario, and one-time resident of France, referring to the scent of dried human blood that he detects whenever he lands in France, in Sandra Martin, "Finding Joy beyond the Rage," *The Globe and Mail*, 3 October 2001.

I suppose that if human history has taught us anything, it is that, in the end, everybody invades everybody. And one day Canada will be invaded. If not next year, then in the 2384. We simply might not be here to watch the first volley of lasers.

Douglas Coupland, novelist and essayist, "Strong and Free," *Maclean's*, 25 November 2002.

We can't fight the enemy with speeches.

Attributed to **Charles Philippe Beaubien**, senator, speaking on behalf of conscription during World War II, quoted in "In Brief," *The Globe and Mail*, 17 January 2003.

The first signs of the winds of war these days are usually those little gusts caused by military ad men shuffling through thesauruses looking up new words for murder.

Robert Priest, poet and columnist, "Shock and Awe," *Now*, 30 March 2003.

The weak must have the right to fight dirty; otherwise the strong will always win. If you oblige the weak to fight clean, injustice will always triumph.

Michael Ignatieff, essayist, discussing "a tactical argument in favour of asymmetrical warfare," *The Lesser Evil: Political Ethics in an Age of Terror* (2004).

War is always good for making it seem that something is being done.

Paul Watson, environmental activist, interviewed by John F. Schumaker, "Earth Warrior," *The CCPA Monitor*, December 2003–January 2004.

I want to know why there is always so much money for war and so little for the human condition.

If we launch a war on Iraq, the world will find \$7 billion, \$8 billion, \$10 billion, a month for bombing, but there's always a huge shortage of funds required to fight AIDS, malaria, tuberculosis.

Stephen Lewis, special UN representative to Africa, in Mel Hurtig, *Rushing to Armageddon* (2004).

I do not want anyone but the best to lead my nation into war; I want none but the ablest to take my grandchildren into battle. This standard should matter to all Canadians, and it is not good enough for you and me to turn away or to say we will never be threatened.

J.L. Granatstein, historian, "We Must Begin Rebuilding Our Military—Now," *National Post*, 7 February 2004.

WAR OF 1812 *See also* War

Push on, brave York Volunteers!

Dying command of **Sir Isaac Brock**, commander of the British and militia forces in the War of 1812. He addressed the militia brought to the Niagara Peninsula from York, Upper Canada, today's Toronto, and pressed them into the Battle of Queenston Heights, 13 October 1812. Minutes later he was fatally wounded by a sniper's bullet, as noted by C.P. Stacey, "Brock's Muniments," *Books in Canada*, August–September 1980.

They wanted this iron fist to command them.

Arthur Wellesley, **Duke of Wellington**, introducing the words "iron fist" into the language for military discipline, in a letter written about the need for order among the English troops dispatched to the Canadian frontier during the War of 1812, dated 8–9 November 1840, in Philip Henry, Earl of Stanhope, *Notes of Conversations with the Duke of Wellington* (1888).

WAR DEAD *See also* War

Yes, it is a wonderful thing to think of all those men that have gone, and to think of those cemeteries out there, as well as the men who have come back, more or less maimed, and to think of the wonderful sacrifice which has won us this peace.

F.G. Scott, canon and senior chaplain during the Great War, address, "Personal Reminiscences of the War," Toronto, 27 October 1919, The Empire Club of Canada.

On all the oceans / White caps flow. / We do not see crosses / Row on row, / But they who sleep beneath the sea / Rest in peace / Because our country / Is Free.

Inscription on the cenotaph to commemorate the lives of 2024 Canadian naval personnel lost on active service, World War II, Spencer Smith Park, Burlington, Ont. The cenotaph was erected by the Royal Canadian Naval Association and dedicated on 14 May 1995. The lines recall the imagery of John McCrae's elegiac poem "In Flanders Fields."

In honouring this unknown soldier today, through this funeral and this burial, we are embracing the fact of the anonymity and saying that because we do not know him and we do not know what he could have become, he has become more than one body, more than one grave. He is an ideal. He is a symbol of all sacrifice. He is every soldier in all our wars.

Adrienne Clarkson, governor general, "Eulogy for Canada's Unknown Soldier," Ottawa, 28 May 2000.

The grass grows on your tomb Gilles and the sand creeps up / And the nearby sea feels the pull of your death / You live on in us as you never could in yourself / You are where we will be … you open the road for us.

Lines from **Jacques Brault**'s poem *"Suite Fraternelle,"* written on the death of his brother in Sicily in World War II, recited by Governor General Adrienne Clarkson, "Eulogy for Canada's Unknown Soldier," Ottawa, 28 May 2000.

We will never know him. But we come today to do him honour as someone who could have been all these things and now is no more. We who are left have all kinds of questions that only he could answer. And we, by this act today, are admitting with terrible finality that we will never know those answers.

Adrienne Clarkson, governor general, "Eulogy for Canada's Unknown Soldier," Ottawa, 28 May 2000.

Today, we are gathered together as one, to bury someone's son. The only certainty about him is that he was young. If death is a debt we all must pay, he paid before he owed it.... Did he read poetry? Did he get into fights? Did he have freckles? Did he think nobody understood him?... In giving himself totally through duty, commitment, love and honour, he has become part of us forever. As we are part of him.

Adrienne Clarkson, governor general, "Eulogy for Canada's Unknown Soldier," Ottawa, 28 May 2000.

A monument of this scale is an enduring message to children yet unborn, and to the hundreds of thousands of citizens of other nations who will enter it. It will speak of the past, but most of all, it will speak of those who erected it. It must honour, across the centuries, with whatever vigorous scholarship it takes, and with generosity, every name and community of people who fought, even if they fought each other, so that we could now have the blessed luxury of reflecting on the values we cherish.

Mark Starowicz, producer of CBC-TV's *Canada: A People's History*, defining the parameters of a proposed new war museum in Ottawa, "Remembrance," *The Globe and Mail*, 9 November 2001.

WAR MEASURES ACT *See* October Crisis

WASTE DISPOSAL *See also* Environmentalism; Recycling

On some dark level, I appreciate the irony of Canadians being able to dump their crap on America. You have had to suffer for God knows how many decades from our crap—the air you breathe and what you're forced to watch on TV.... Many are willing to dig large holes in the ground and accept garbage from Canada ... because they need the jobs and money flowing in.

Michael Moore, filmmaker, addressing the Recycling Council of Ontario, meeting in Markham, Ont., via a 10-minute teleconference call from California, 6 May 2004, in Leslie Ferenc, "Filmmaker Talks Trash to Toronto," *Toronto Star*, 7 May 2004.

WATER *See also* Food & Drink; Great Lakes; Lakes; Oceans; Rivers

Most Canadians will be shocked to learn that our government has not supported the right to water at the United Nations. Canada was the only country to vote against a 2002 resolution by the UN Committee on Human Rights to appoint a Special Rapporteur to promote the right to water, stating "Canada does not accept that there is a right to drinking water and sanitation."

Maude Barlow, chair, The Council of Canadians, "Water Is a Human Right," *Canadian Perspectives*, winter 2005.

As you know, Canada is a unique place. Our country is blessed with vast quantities of fresh water. *Twenty percent of all fresh water in the world rests inside our borders.* Unfortunately, the threats to this pristine resource are real and growing.

Leslie J. Muir, president, Sierra Legal Defence Fund, "Water Warning," fundraising literature, 15 April 2005.

WEAKNESSES

In exchange for His strength, I offer Him my weakness.

Georges P. Vanier, governor general, prayer upon taking the oath of office, Ottawa, 15 September 1959, quoted by his son Jean Vanier in his biographical study of his father, *In Weakness, Strength* (1969).

Let us not put our sights too high. We do not have to be saviours of the world! We are simply human beings, enfolded in weakness and in hope, called together to change our world one heart at a time.

Jean Vanier, founder of L'Arche movement, *Becoming Human* (1998).

WEALTH *See also* Money; Poverty

If we do not take stock of what it means when one country has not enough and another country is throwing away and in that country that is throwing away it is deeply divided amongst the hundreds of thousands who have no work, those that are despised and those that are handicapped, those that are shut up in hospitals; we must take stock of this. This new era is going to show us something fantastic in the years to come and if we, who are in part the makers of our society do not take stock of this and act, the tidal wave which is taking its movement already will eventually arise at its plentitude and overwhelm us.

Jean Vanier, humanitarian, address, "A World in Violence: Eruption to Hope?" Toronto, 11 February 1971, The Empire Club of Canada.

The rich spend their money; the wealthy live on the interest; the filthy rich make do with the interest paid on the interest.

Peter C. Newman, journalist and memoirist, *Here Be Dragons: Telling Tales of People, Passion, and Power* (2004).

Bill Gates won't be the richest person in the world two decades from now; rather, everyone will have unlimited wealth.

Robert J. Sawyer, science-fiction author, "The Age of Miracle and Wonder" (1999), *Relativity: Stories and Essays* (2004).

WEAPONS *See also* Arms Race; Crime; Disarmament; Firearms; Justice; Land Mines; Law; Murder; Violence; War

I am well aware that scepticism is rife throughout the world. I picked up a paper in Montreal yesterday morning when I arrived and I found in it some quip by some unknown writer who said that every new disarmament plan seemed to bring a little hope to the manufacturers of armaments.

Philip J. Noel-Baker, British diplomat of Canadian background, address, "Disarmament," Toronto, 27 March 1934, The Empire Club of Canada.

Three bacterial warfare chemists at Toronto were suspended for emotional instability; they announced that they would carry their cases to the High Court.

Passage describing future weaponry in **Robert A. Heinlein**'s futuristic novel *Stranger in a Strange Land* (1961).

Where failing states possess nuclear weapons, we must prevent them from failing.

Michael Ignatieff, essayist, *The Lesser Evil: Political Ethics in an Age of Terror* (2004).

If Guns Are Outlawed, Only Outlaws Will Have Guns.

Ambiguous statement about the legality (or illegality) of gun ownership on signs for (or against) the need for a federal gun registry; noted by Jane Taber, "M.P. Targets Gun-Registry Vote," *The Globe and Mail*, 6 December 2004.

WEATHER *See also* Climate; Environmentalism; Seasons

The Northern weather so far shows no sign of improvement.

Line of narration from **Rudyard Kipling**'s predictive work of fiction "With the Night Mail: A Story of 2000 A.D." (1905), *Actions and Reactions* (1909). It chronicles the transatlantic flight of a General Post Office "coach," an airship under the administration of the "Aerial Board of Control."

Most important of all is the temperature, given right through the day and night on the hour. It is a temptation for the visitor who may search in vain for the action to believe that in this land of theirs, vast cataclysms overwhelm the Canadian geese, and a man who is not sufficiently briefed with the weather forecast may boil or suddenly freeze to death in downtown Hamilton, but this I understand very rarely happens. No, the explanation is more prosaic. The weather service is complementary, along with the second cup of coffee, and the television station takes a brief halt from customer bashing to try to persuade itself that it cares.

Robert Morley, British actor in Toronto on tour, "Confessions from a Hospitable City," *The London Observer*, 24 December 1972.

For two days and nights, whirling in the wind that blew off Lake Ontario, muffling the trees and ravines of Toronto … it was followed by what the weather forecasters called "a frigid blast of Arctic air," which spread a murderous coating of ice over streets and sidewalks where the snow had been cleared. Most of the schools closed down, and a great many offices.

Description of Toronto in winter in **Susan Cooper**'s children's novel *The Boggart* (1993).

That night, New York, for the sake of variety, had shaken off its sticky humidity. Canadian air descended in a solid wall from the stratosphere to the crushed beer cans and began to blow a fresh wind through the tired metaphors of Manhattan—that is, through the stone canyons, or maybe through the stone labyrinth.

Passage of rococo writing from Russian-American writer **Vassily Aksyonov**'s novel *The New Sweet Style* (1999), translated from the Russian by Christopher Morris.

Don't knock the weather. Nine-tenths of the people couldn't start a conversation if it didn't change once in a while.

David Phillips, climatologist, *The 2001 Canadian Weather Trivia Calendar* (2000).

When my parents took me to Toronto in 1962 I was eight years old, exiled to an austere foreign town where the shops closed on Sunday and the weather actually hurt.

Robert Charles Wilson, California-born novelist and Toronto resident, afterword, *The Perseids and Other Stories* (2000).

Sex, religion and politics are passé. In Canada, the real emotional energy and resulting passionate debate revolve around the weather (and when we say weather, we mean, of course, "winter").

William Ferguson and **Ian Ferguson**, writers, *How to Be a Canadian (Even if You Are One)* (2001).

Complaining about the weather is a Canadian thing, probably because we get so much of it, of all kinds, everything from heat waves to blizzards, gentle breezes to hurricanes (Hurricane Hazel hit Toronto hard in 1954).

Karen Bennett, science-fiction fan, "The Speculative Torontos of Robert Charles Wilson & Robert J. Sawyer," *TorCon3: 61st World Science Fiction Convention, Toronto—August 28 to September 1, 2003* (2003).

I always say there are 31 million weather experts in this country.

David Phillips, climatologist, interviewed by Stephen Strauss, "Canada's Mr. Weather," *The Globe and Mail*, 13 September 2003.

Someone else might get up and think, "Ugh, what a grey day." But I get up and think, "What a perfect day for hockey."

Michael Budman, co-founder of Roots and amateur hockey enthusiast, in Amanda Lang, "Hockey Night in Forest Hill," *The Globe and Mail*'s *Report on Business*, April 2005.

WEIGHT *See also* Diets; Food & Drink; Obesity

Fatness, not sex, is a taboo in our culture; and fatness has taken on evil and moral overtones.

Marion Woodman, analyst and author, *The Owl Was a Baker's Daughter: Obesity, Anorexia Nervosa and the Repressed Feminine* (1980).

We are obsessed with overeating because gluttony is the last sin left. In a world where politicians steal, where promiscuity is sanctioned, and where youth and beauty are revered, gluttony is the sin we can *see.*

Janet Polivy, researcher into the psychology of eating and dieting, Clarke Institute of Psychiatry, Toronto, in Cynthia Wine, *Homemaker's Magazine*, January–February 1980.

WELFARE *See also* Homelessness; Labour; Liberalism; Poverty; Unemployment

We are responsible for each other, but we are not responsible to each other.

Michael Ignatieff, commentator, *The Needs of Strangers* (1985).

In 20th-century liberalism, as practised in Canada and elsewhere, the responsibility for well-being rests with either the individual or the family, or with both. Simultaneously, there is a clear acceptance that capitalist economies are not self-regulating but require significant levels of state intervention to achieve stability.

Allan Moscovitch, professor of social work, "Welfare State," *The Canadian Encyclopedia* (2nd ed., 1988).

The cost of corporate welfare amounts to many times that of social welfare. It is not a question of fiscal responsibility, it is a question of ideology.

Robert Bateman, artist and naturalist, "I Am a Conservative, I Conserve," *The Globe and Mail*, 13 December 2003.

WENDIGO *See also* Monsters

So let us begin with the figure of the Wendigo—or is it a figure? Perhaps it is also a verb, a process; it can certainly be used as such.

Margaret Atwood, author, "Eyes of Blood, Heart of Ice: The Wendigo," *Strange Things: The Malevolent North in Canadian Literature* (1995).

Fear of the Wendigo is twofold: fear of being eaten by one, and fear of becoming one.

Margaret Atwood, author, referring to the Algonkian spirit of solitude and cannibalism, "Eyes of Blood, Heart of Ice: The Wendigo," *Strange Things: The Malevolent North in Canadian Literature* (1995).

Over the years, the belief in and fear of Weendigoes has diminished. There is no longer the sense, as there once was, that malevolent beings are nearby, just out of sight, ever present, waiting to turn humans into Weendigoes. The Weendigoes may or may not roam the north in winter any longer as they were once believed to do, but their spirit and the ideas they embody live on in the modern world.

Basil Johnston, elder, *The Manitous: The Spiritual World of the Ojibway* (1995). The Weendigo (plural "Weendigook") or Windigo (plural "Windigoes") are cannibals or ever-hungry giant beings who feast on villagers and wanderers in winter.

Actually, the Weendigoes did not die out or disappear; they have only been assimilated and reincarnated as corporations, conglomerates, and multinationals. They've even taken on new names, acquired polished manners, and renounced their cravings for raw human flesh in return for more refined viands. But their cupidity is no less insatiable than that of their ancestors.

Basil Johnston, elder, *The Manitous: The Spiritual World of the Ojibway* (1995).

WESTERN CANADA *See also* Alberta; British Columbia; Manitoba; Saskatchewan

Oh, take me back to the Land of Promise, / Back to the land of the ice and the snow. / There you and I once more together will wander, / Down lovers' lane, where the maple trees grow. / Skating, baseball and canoeing, / That's the place to do your billing and cooing. / Oh, take me back to the land I love best, / Back to my little grey home in the West.

Lyrics sung by **Beatrice Lillie** in the touring variety show *Cheep* in April 1917 in London, England, as noted in her memoir *Every Other Inch a Lady* (1972). She explained, "I recollect that the idea of a young dandy aching to return to the Golden West was an accepted tradition of the time which nobody considered out of place. So, with a tweak of the tie and a twirl of the tails, I sang about the glories of Canada.... Believe me, this was good, serious stuff, and the audience accepted it as such."

The Western provinces are like the outposts of the nation, held by most gallant and enterprising outpost troops, who are continually pushing forward into the No Man's Land of the great Northwest. Ontario and the east is still the main body of the nation and the main line of resistance, and I congratulate you on the way in which your fine position is organized.

Edward, Prince of Wales, address, "An Address," Toronto, 2 November 1919, The Empire Club of Canada.

Canada improved in interest as we went West.

Winston Churchill, British statesman, letter to his wife, 12 September 1929, concerning points west of Ontario, in David Dilks, *"The Great Dominion": Winston Churchill in Canada 1900–1954* (2005).

I just think you Westerners should take over this country if you are so smart.

Attributed to **Pierre Trudeau**, former prime minister, after his government's National Energy Program was introduced on 28 October 1980. It angered Albertans and other Westerners and was dismantled by the Progressive Conservatives in 1984.

OUT EAST IT'S PROBABLY EXPENSIVE; / OUT WEST IT'S PROBABLY RAINING.

Slogans on black-and-yellow billboards in Winnipeg from the advertising campaign launched by the Winnipeg Chamber of Commerce, 6 September 2001.

WHALES *See also* Oceans; Wildlife

The whale was not alone in being trapped. We were all trapped with her.

Farley Mowat, naturalist and author, describing the outporters' reaction to the beaching of a whale near Burgeo, Nfld., in *A Whale for the Killing* (1972).

Baby Beluga in the deep blue sea, / Swim so wild and you swim so free. / Heaven above and the sea below, / And a little white whale on the go.

First verse of "Baby Beluga," popular children's song composed and sung by **Raffi**, *Baby Beluga Book* (1983).

Well, if we could stop killing the whales, maybe we could stop killing each other.

David McTaggart, ecologist and activist, quoted by Ted Turner and interviewed by Ned Martel, "The Radical Do-Gooder," *The New York Times Magazine*, 30 December 2001.

WHEAT

A bargain in wheat never made a nation great. It may be profitable but it never made anyone great. Your souls have to have something, too, that you find nowhere else as in the north country.

Grey Owl, author and conservationist, address, "A Plea for the Canadian Northland," Toronto, 12 November 1936, The Empire Club of Canada.

WILDLIFE *See also* Animal Rights; Animals; Birds; Environmentalism; Fish & Fisheries; Fishing; Hunting; Ice Fishing; Nature; Seal Hunt; Snakes

Sometimes an eagle screaming in the sky, sometimes a lion / Stalking upon the mountains, & sometimes a whale, I lash / The raging fathomless abyss; anon a serpent folding / Around the pillars of Urthona, and round thy dark limbs / On the Canadian wilds I fold....

Lines from **William Blake**'s "Preludium" in his epic poem *America: A Prophecy* (1793), in Denis Saurat, *Blake and Modern Thought* (1929).

I used the beaver as the thin edge of the wedge to gain the interest of the public in wild life. To hear the beaver talk it sounds like people from another planet talking in a tongue we do not understand, like little children. I can tell a hundred stories of the childlike appeal of the beaver. They have inspired most of my work. I am not a writer yet, I don't intend to be, but I intend to get some stuff on paper before it is impossible to get it.

Grey Owl, author and conservationist, address, "A Plea for the Canadian Northland," Toronto, 12 November 1936, The Empire Club of Canada.

We are all creatures of the wilderness, children of the frontier, even though the frontier has been pushed back into the mists of the North, even though the wilderness has given way to concrete. Wild and mysterious, savage and forbidding, this is the cyclorama against which the drama of our past has been staged; for better and for worse it has helped to fashion us into our distinctive Canadian mould.

Pierre Berton, media personality and historian, preface, *The Wild Frontier: More Tales from the Remarkable Past* (1978).

The living world is dying in our time.

Farley Mowat, author, *Sea of Slaughter* (1984).

WINE *See also* Alcohol; Food & Drink

Perhaps it is not a bad thing that Canadian wines have yet to be discovered. That means the best that we produce still remains within our borders for our own delectation and delight.

Tony Aspler, oenophile, *Tony Aspler's Vintage Canada* (2nd ed., 1991).

When I began writing about wine in 1975, the term "Ontario wine" was an oxymoron. You may remember Ontario wines then were mainly enjoyed by gentlemen who did most of their entertaining standing up in doorways, drinking out of brown paper decanters. The Ontario products they favoured were sweet, highly-alcoholic beverages. Along Parliament Street they were known as "block and tackle wines." You drank a bottle, walked a block and you could tackle anyone. Come alive for "a dollar five." Remember that?

Tony Aspler, wine consultant, address, "The Ontario Wine Industry," Toronto, 4 March 1993, The Empire Club of Canada.

WINNING & LOSING

You don't play a game to lose. You go out and you give your best to win.

Bobby Hull, hockey star, quoted in *The Canadian*, 7 September 1974.

You don't have to win the race to have done well in the race.

Paul Martin, Sr., statesman, on losing the Liberal leadership to Pierre Elliott Trudeau in 1968, CBC-TV, 14 July 1975.

WINNIPEG

Hannay: How far is it from Winnipeg to Montreal?
Mr. Memory: Ah, a gentleman from Canada. You're welcome, sir. [Applause from the audience.] Winnipeg, the fair city of Canada and the capital of the Province of Manitoba. Distance from Montreal? 1,454 miles? Am I right, sir?
Hannay: Quite right!

Dialogue from **Alfred Hitchcock**'s thriller *The 39 Steps* (1935), which Charles Bennett and Alma Reville adapted from **John Buchan**'s popular novel *The Thirty-nine Steps* (1915). Richard Hannay was played by Robert Donat, and the vaudeville mnemologist "Mr. Memory" by Wylie Watson. In the film, Hannay is a Canadian; in the novel, he is a South African mining engineer footloose in London. The reference to Winnipeg is unique to the movie.

Those who love Winnipeg,—and they all do,—explain that though it is cold it is "dry," and that being dry, you don't feel the cold. People always defend their home town in this way....

Stephen Leacock, humorist, *My Discovery of the West: A Discussion of East and West in Canada* (1937).

The people I was with were talking about wanting to go to England. Nobody wanted to stay in Winnipeg. That seemed strange to me, because I had just arrived, and I wanted to make a life there. I was determined to love it—even if it killed me. I wanted to get going, to create something.

John Hirsch, Hungarian-born co-founder (with playwright Tom Hendry) of the Manitoba Theatre Centre in 1958, referring to his late teens spent in Winnipeg, in Martin Knelman, "Hirsch Missed Now More Than Ever," *Toronto Star*, 7 May 2005.

In January, the zero isotherm goes from the southeast corner of Manitoba westward to Peace River. It passes across Winnipeg, the largest city in the world with such a low temperature.

Environment Canada, *The Climate of the Prairie Provinces* (1972), in Douglas J. Johnston, "The Fabled City of Cold," *Maclean's*, 4 March 2002. Johnston explained, "What this means to climate-watchers is that Winnipeg in January has an average daily mean temperature of 0 degrees Fahrenheit, or -17 degrees C (the mean is the midpoint between high and low). But what it means to us is that when winter is at its frigid acme, no comparable city anywhere else in the world is as cold as ours—not in Scandinavia, not in Russia, not in Alaska."

Bob Hope, Bing Crosby, Al Jolson and many more performed at the Walker Theatre—the vaudeville stage in Western Canada in the early part of the last century. It was a favoured testing ground for new productions. "If you can make it in Winnipeg, you can make it anywhere." Success in Winnipeg meant the shows went on the road.

Jordan Wheeler, columnist, "First Take," *Winnipeg Free Press*, 10 September 2000.

In the end, what I find amazing about Winnipeg is not the facade but the heartbeat of its people and the secret of its simplicity. For a city that often has to bear minus 30 degrees, its personality is one of the warmest I know.

Evelyn Hart, ballerina, "My Town," *National Post*, 23 July 2001.

WINTER *See also* Seasons

The Canadians are the luckiest of people. They wear earmuffs half the year.

Christopher Morley, man of letters, writing as the character Jane Nightwork in the 1940s, as noted by Christopher Redmond, "Sherlock Holmes from Sea to Sea," *Lasting Impressions: The 25th Anniversary of The Bootmakers of Toronto, The Sherlock Holmes Society of Canada* (1997), edited by George A. Vanderburgh.

The winters of my childhood were long, long seasons. We lived in three places—the school, the church, and the skating rink—but our real life was on the skating rink.

Opening sentences of **Roch Carrier**'s well-loved short story "The Hockey Sweater," *The Hockey Sweater and Other Stories* (1980).

There is a sense in Canadian literature that the true and only season here is winter: the others are either preludes to it or mirages concealing it.

Margaret Atwood, author, *Survival: A Thematic Guide to Canadian Literature* (1972).

"Quebeckers love snow but they hate winter," says a friend of mine. The remark probably applies to all Canadians who—except for the blessed West Coast residents—spend about a fourth of the year fighting the cold when they're not trudging through the slush. But who doesn't want a white Christmas?

Lysiane Gagnon, columnist, "Inside Quebec," *The Globe and Mail*, 20 January 2003.

I began trying to persuade Canadians that they weren't put on this earth merely to outlast cold winters.

Peter C. Newman, journalist and memoirist, *Here Be Dragons: Telling Tales of People, Passion, and Power* (2004).

WISDOM *See also* Knowledge; Learning

For every single thing in the world, had we but the eyes to see through it, can be a doorway to the profoundest thoughts that the human mind can compass.

Ernest Raymond, attendee, Conference Sermon at Christ Church Cathedral, Victoria, B.C., 7 April 1929, *Education and Leisure: Addresses Delivered at the Fourth Triennial Conference on Education Held at Victoria and Vancouver, Canada, April 1929* (1929), edited by S.E. Lang.

Wisdom consists in discovering patterns.

Attributed to **H.S.M. Coxeter**, geometer, by broadcaster Lister Sinclair, CBC Radio's *Ideas*, 29 October 2001.

WIT *See* Humour

WOLVES *See also* Animals

Any man that says he's been et by a wolf is a liar.

J.W. Curran, publisher and polemicist, *Wolves Don't Bite* (1940).

There is no authentic report of wolves ever having killed a human being in the Canadian North; although there must have been times when the temptation was well-nigh irresistible.

Farley Mowat, naturalist and author, *Never Cry Wolf* (1963).

WOMEN *See also* Feminism; Mankind; Men & Women; Motherhood; Women's Rights

A married woman with children must draw a government salary for being a married woman with children, just as at present an old maid, an old one, without children, draws a salary for being an old maid without children.

Stephen Leacock, humorist, *Last Leaves* (1945).

Women probably cannot expect an easier life, but they can rather be expected to shoulder a larger share of responsibility as citizens in an increasingly complex world.

Ellen L. Fairclough, secretary of state, address, "Canadian Women as Citizens," Toronto, 12 December 1957, The Empire Club of Canada.

Whenever I see a woman who is soft on the outside, I look for a jungle within.

John Reeves, photographer, interviewed by Eve Rockett, "Conversations with Five Men about Women," *Homemaker's Magazine*, May 1979.

Women have begun to see other men, especially their husbands (and to a lesser extent their doctors)—instead of other women—as their main allies. Female bonding, if my argument is right, has thus been vanquished both by improvements in health and by the companionate marriage.

Edward Shorter, historian, *A History of Women's Bodies* (1982).

If pioneer women could build and bake and give birth and shoot bears, then the pioneering working woman can overextend herself too, composing office memos in her head while she breastfeeds the baby.

Marni Jackson, journalist, "Hormones or History?" *Wild Culture: Specimens from* The Journal of Wild Culture (1992), edited by Whitney Smith and Christopher Lowry.

Something interesting starts happening to Canadian female protagonists around the middle of the twentieth century. Instead of going off into the woods to be with a man, they start going off into the woods to be by themselves. And sometimes they're even doing it to get away from a man.

Margaret Atwood, author, "Linoleum Caves," *Strange Things: The Malevolent North in Canadian Literature* (1995).

She was the type who would crumple up. She thought she had totally left behind the Canadian farm girl but she hadn't really. I'd watch her watching the news; she'd say, "All this killing and for what? If women ran the world there'd be no more war." How do you talk to someone who thinks that way, who knows nothing of grudges and grievances that go back centuries, of tribal conflicts that will remain until the end of time? Why can't we all just love each other? she asked of the nightly news. I don't know, I really don't, I wish I did.

Thoughts of the American husband of a Canadian-born farm girl in Liverpool, England, in **Linda Grant**'s novel *Still Here* (2002). The thoughts recall those of Carl Jung on Canadian women who "lack Europe's sham politeness."

Think like a man, act like a lady, and work like a dog.

Hazel McCallion, feisty long-time mayor of Mississauga, Ont., advice to a conference of young women, in Tess Kalinowski, "Mutual Admiration at Girl Event," *Toronto Star*, 15 October 2003.

WOMEN'S RIGHTS

See also Feminism; Law; Rights; Women

I shall not consent to be tried under a law which my sex had no voice in making.

Pearl Hart, so-called Bandit Queen, defence speech, Arizona, May 1899, in Ed Butts, *She Dared: True Stories of Heroines, Scoundrels, and Renegades* (2005). Born in Ontario, Hart was one of the few women to rob stagecoaches. She and her sidekick Joe Boot made history when they conducted one of the last such robberies of the Old West in Arizona. Her spirited defence failed to convince the court of the justice of her cause. In prison she promoted women's causes.

Their Lordships are of opinion that the word "persons" in s. 24 does include women, and that women are eligible to be summoned to and become members of the Senate of Canada.

Lord Sankey, Lord Chancellor of the Privy Council of Great Britain, decision in the case *Henrietta Muir Edwards and Others* v. *Attorney General for Canada*, 18 October 1929. The five women who pressed for a decision in the celebrated Persons case were from Alberta: Emily Murphy, Nellie L. McClung, Louise McKinney, Irene Parlby, and Henrietta Muir Edwards.

There will be no emancipation for women anywhere on this planet until the Western domination of this planet is ended.

Sunera Thobani, academic, speech, Women's Resistance Conference, Ottawa, 15 October 2001, quoted by Mary Vallis and Mark Hume, "Thobani 'Rant' Called Hateful," *National Post*, 17 October 2001.

I will tell you I'm insulted, absolutely insulted, to be called a minority. We are in the majority as women ... we have a problem because we don't have something between our legs.

Bethany Thorne Dykstra, New Brunswick delegate, objecting to setting quotas for female representation, Liberal Party Convention, Ottawa, 4 March 2005, in Joan Bryden, "Liberals Defeat '50% Women' Resolution," *Toronto Star*, 5 March 2005.

WONDERS *See also* Miracles

We grow to one world / Through enlargement of wonder.

Lines from **F.R. Scott**'s poem "A Grain of Rice" (1952), *The Selected Poems of F.R. Scott* (1981).

Everything has its astonishingly, wondrous aspect if you bring a mind to it that's truly your own....

Observation made by a character in **Robertson Davies**'s novel *Fifth Business* (1970).

We live in an empty place filled with wonders.

Peter C. Newman, author, *Maclean's*, October 1973.

WORDS *See also* Language

Beware of words—they are dangerous things. They change colour like the chameleon, and they return like a boomerang.

Sir William Osler, physician, in W.S. Thayer, "Osler the Teacher," *Osler and Other Papers* (1931).

And then there are the words that are left unsaid / And the undetectable words used in their stead.

Concluding couplet of **Robert Finch**'s sonnet "Words," *Poems* (1946).

Before we can learn the words necessary to live, it is already time to learn to die.

Lines from **Jean-Guy Pilon**'s prose poem "The Needs of the Land!" *Recours au pays* (1961), translated by Louis Dudek, *Poetry of Our Time* (1965), edited by Louis Dudek.

Oh Lord, help my words to be gracious and tender today, for tomorrow I may have to eat them.

Inscription in a briefing book owned and carried by **Pierre Trudeau**, prime minister (1968–1969, 1980–1984), in Roy MacGegor, "Continentalism Is Back," *National Post*, 4 October 2001.

Scientists have dubbed humankind variously: *Homo sapiens*, the knowing human; *Homo ludens*, the playful (creative) human. An anthropologist suggested *Homo denominator*, the naming human, for we are the only creatures who label a word in order to know it.

Bill Casselman, writer and broadcaster, *Casselman's Canadian Words: A Comic Browse through Words and Folk Sayings Invented by Canadians* (1995).

A widespread and ancient Inuit greeting, *chimo!* may be accompanied by a gesture of salutation as well, namely moving the left hand in a circle on the area of the chest over the heart ... today *chimo* is exclusively a warm greeting and is used in our North as a toast before drinking.

Bill Casselman, writer and broadcaster, *Casselman's Canadian Words: A Comic Browse through Words and Folk Sayings Invented by Canadians* (1995).

My pet annoyance is a word of bamboozlement entirely Canadian in origin, "nordicity," used by no less a master of plain speech than Joe Clark. I take *nordicity* into the word morgue and apply a scalpel to its pompous corpus.

Bill Casselman, writer and broadcaster, *Casselmania: More Wacky Canadian Words & Sayings* (1996). Paraphrasing Louis-Edmond Hamelin, Casselman notes, "Nordicity is an index of northern-ness that calculates and quantifies certain polar values, criteria acronymed as VAPO.... VAPO is an acronym of French origin, from the initial letters of ***VA**leur* ***PO**laire*. 'Polar value.'"

The first thing man learned to recycle was words.

Hugh Arscott, aphorist, *Hugh's Views: Volume 5* (2001).

In a basic sense, every single word devised by human beings is an anagram for a fragment of knowledge, since it alludes to the presence of something real or imagined in the world.

Marcel Danesi, semiotician, *The Puzzle Instinct: The Meaning of Puzzles in Human Life* (2002).

Power does not lie just in bank accounts and gun barrels. Power lies in the words that govern behaviour.

Mark Abley, author, *Spoken Here: Travels among Threatened Languages* (2003).

Words cannot stop a bullet; but a person who hears them, and ponders, may.

Susan McMaster, editor, preface, *Waging Peace: Poetry and Political Action* (2003).

WORK *See also* Business; Commerce; Employment; Offices; Retirement; Unemployment; Unions

We are beginning to admire the lazy loafer who will not work, the man who would rather live upon a dole than make an effort to save himself; and we are beginning to look with suspicion on anything that seems to spell effort and success; and there, I tell you, we are wrong. (Applause.)

Stephen Leacock, economist and humorist, address, "The Proper Limits of State Intervention," Toronto, 6 March 1924, The Empire Club of Canada.

We know that the people of Canada are independent, freedom-loving folks who are willing to work for the things they would like to have. Canada has great natural resources, and its people have the spirit and ability to develop them.

Charles E. Wilson (nicknamed "Engine"), president, General Motors Corporation, address, "Essentials for Labour Peace," Toronto, 4 January 1951, The Empire Club of Canada.

For me, work is more fun than fun.

Peter Gzowski, broadcaster and journalist, in conversation with June Callwood on CBC-TV's *National Treasures* in 1992, recalled by Michael Enright, CBC Radio's *Sunday Morning*, 27 January 2002.

There will be lots of work, very interesting work, but it will be done in task forces. It will be done by people who take on a task and then move out, the way the original cathedrals were built. There was never a cathedral builder. There were people who came in and did the glass work, the carpenters, the stone layers, and then they moved on to other jobs. This is the way it is going to be. There are five million Canadians now working out of their homes and that is the trend of the future. So, yes, there will be work, but there will not be jobs. And this is going to cause a great revolution in the way people live.

Peter C. Newman, author, address, "The Canadian Revolution," Toronto, 30 November 1995, The Empire Club of Canada.

I've been one of the most fortunate people in the world. I've always loved what I did. I've never awakened in the morning and felt, oh God, I can't face that job and put the blanket over my head. One of my morals has been if it's easy, do it. If it's not easy, don't do it.

Adrienne Clarkson, governor general, interviewed by Christopher Guly, "Class Act at Rideau Hall," *Forever Young*, July 2003.

My weekend includes Thursday, as they say in Montreal.

Remark noted by **Jacob Richler**, commentator, "Too Many People, Too Little Time," *National Post*, 5 July 2003.

I have a lot of thank-yous. I don't have any IOUs. My conscience is clear.

Julian Fantino, chief of Toronto Police, whose contract was not renewed by the Toronto Police Services Board, final statement, in Rosie DiManno, "Secret-vote Fantino Ouster Has the Feel of a Messy Coup," *Toronto Star*, 25 June 2004.

The burden of far, far too many of us these days is what I call List A. That's the one with "Items that must be done immediately or things will fall apart, possibly tomorrow." When that list grows too large, List B simply never gets its due. That one contains "Items I'd love to do for pleasure but must sacrifice to duty or necessity or things will fall apart, possibly tomorrow." Damn, I'm on the most intimate terms with the tension between these two lists, the latter of which is constantly being eclipsed by the former, by their very natures.

Varda Burstyn, author, personal communication, 21 April 2005.

For those who care to connect the dots it should come as no surprise that a workforce made up of increasing numbers of self-employed is also a workforce where people work harder and smarter in the face of adversity and change and aren't likely to lay themselves off.

Angus Reid, consultant and pollster, foreword, *Everything I Needed to Know about Business … I Learned from a Canadian* (2005), by Leonard Brody and David Raffa.

WORLD *See also* Canada & the World; Globalism & Globalization; International Affairs; United Nations

As a nation I believe in Canada's destiny. I believe we have a job of work to do that can be done by no other nation. I believe we have a contribution that can be made by no other nation. I feel that our whole history has brought us to this place where we can make this contribution to the prosperity and unity of one world. In all sincerity I pray, "God grant that we shall make it."

Robert B. McClure, medical missionary, address, "Canada's Place in the Pacific Basin," Toronto, 20 March 1947, The Empire Club of Canada.

The world is a dumbbell.

Characteristic remark based on a Yiddish expression used by **Gershon Iskowitz**, artist, in Toronto in the 1960s.

The world is as sharp as the edge of a knife.

Old Haida saying in Robert Davidson, *Northwest Coast Indian Artists Guild: 1977 Graphics Collection* (1977).

There is a proverb widely known on the Northwest Coast, though you will hear it much more often now in English than in Haida or Tlingit or Nishga. In southern Haida it is this: *tlgaay higha ttlabju'waaga*; in English: the world is as sharp as a knife. That, at any rate, is now the standard English form, which came by way of a German translation from Tlingit, made in the early 1890s by Franz Boas. If you translate the Haida literally, the saying seems a little less dramatic but a little more precise. *Tlgaay*, "the earth" (or the ground, or the place); *higha*, "straight up"; *ttlabju'waaga*, "is shaped like a woodcutter's wedge or the head of an axe."

Robert Bringhurst, scholar and poet, *A Story as Sharp as a Knife: The Classical Haida Mythtellers and Their World* (1999).

Merely varying your dimensional scale creates new worlds.

William Illsey Atkinson, science writer, *Nanocosm: Nanotechnology and the Big Changes Coming from the Inconceivably Small* (2003).

WORLD WAR I *See also* War

In Flanders fields the poppies blow / Between the crosses, row on row…. / If ye break faith with us who die / We shall not sleep, though poppies grow / In Flanders fields.

Familiar lines from the famous 15-line poem "In Flanders Fields" composed during the Second Battle of Ypres, Belgium, 3 May 1915, by Major **John McCrae**, First Brigade surgeon, Canadian Field Artillery. It was published anonymously in *Punch*, 8 December 1915. McCrae died in France on 28 January 1918 and never lived to hear his elegy recited as part of the official Armistice Day program on 11 November 1918. The text appeared in *In Flanders Fields and Other Poems* (1919), edited by Sir Andrew Macphail. "In Flanders Fields" must be the most widely reprinted of Canadian poems, yet even it is not to everyone's taste. Jon Silkin wished to exclude it from his edition of *The Penguin Book of First World War Poetry* (1979, 1981) but decided to reprint it (though with an asterisk) on the principle that "no anthology as far as I know has tried to *limit* itself to excellence. Even so, there are certain poems that have embedded themselves in our consciousness…." In all, he asterisked as non-excellent works the following poems: Wilfred Grenfell's "Into Battle," John McCrae's "In Flanders Fields," Alan Seeger's "I Have a Rendezvous with Death," Charles Hamilton Sorley's "All the hills and vales along," and Wilfred Owen's "Anthem for Doomed Youth." There is no accounting for tastes.

If you want a monument of the English of this generation, and when I say English I include of course Canadians, for there were Canadians among them, if you want a spiritual monument of the life of England in the years of the great war, you cannot find a greater and finer or more immortal monument than the poems which her soldiers wrote, and in which they commemorated their own sacrifice and their own belief in the fundamental faith of the nation in which they were born. (Loud applause.)

Sir Henry Newbolt, poet, referring to the English-language poets of the Great War, address, "Songs of the Fleet," Toronto, 22 February 1923, The Empire Club of Canada.

The troops with the worst reputation for acts of violence against prisoners were the Canadians (and later the Australians). The Canadians' motive was said to be revenge for a Canadian found crucified with bayonets through his hands and feet in a German trench.

Robert Graves, English memoirist and novelist, *Goodbye to All That* (1929, rev. 1957). He is referring to the Great War atrocity legend of the "crucified Canadian."

Vimy Ridge is the place where Canadian history meets French geography.

Adapted from a sentence by **Brian Bethune**, writer, "Monumental Obsession," *Maclean's*, 16 April 2001. The Canadian Corps launched its assault on Vimy Ridge, northern France, on Easter Monday, 9 April 1917. Walter Allward's monument to Canada's 60 000 Great War dead, dedicated in 1936, stands on 100 hectares of land deeded in perpetuity to Canada by the French government.

WORLD WAR II *See also* Conscription; Fascism; Hitler, Adolf; War

Only twice in Canada did I see the light go out of his eyes: once when endorsing a death warrant; and when signing Canada's declaration of war.

Alastair Buchan, son of Governor General Lord Tweedsmuir, John Buchan, recalling how his father at Rideau Hall signed the declaration that a state of war existed between Canada and Germany, Ottawa, 9 September 1939, in Susan Buchan, *John Buchan by His Wife and Friends* (1947).

When I warned them that Britain would fight on alone, whatever they did, their generals told their Prime Minister and his divided cabinet, "In three weeks England will have her neck wrung like a chicken." Some chicken! Some neck!

Winston Churchill, prime minister of Great Britain, addressing a joint meeting of the Senate and the House of Commons, 30 December 1941. In this famous speech, certainly the most significant ever delivered on Canadian soil, Churchill refers to the German occupation of parts of France. An hour later he sat in the Speaker's Chambers to pose for Yousuf Karsh, who created the celebrated "bulldog" photographic portrait, certainly the most memorable ever taken on Canadian soil. Karsh later wrote: "I said, 'Forgive me, sir,' and plucked the cigar out of his mouth. By the time I got back to my camera, he looked so belligerent he could have devoured me. It was at that instant that I took the photograph. The silence was deafening."

I hate war and I think killing is madness, but seeing those German dead, I am very happy.

Fred Griffin, war correspondent, describing with high emotion the "charnel fields" of Normandy and the dead of the German 7th Army, widely reprinted dispatch to the *Toronto Daily Star*, 24 August 1944.

This is the second time in the lifetime of most of us that the Germans have forced war upon the world. It is the second time that Canadians have crossed the Atlantic, leaving the fishing boats of British Columbia and Nova Scotia, the farms on the prairies, and the villages and towns of Ontario, and, if it is not the last, I think we shall all have to bear a certain amount of responsibility. When the war is over we shall talk about the bitter glories of the war, the deeds of heroism, the contribution of a whole people, but we shall, I am afraid, unless history fails to repeat herself, very quickly forget the cost of the war, the waste of treasure, waste of life, the maimed, the crippled, the blind, the widows, the fatherless, and above all the deep legacy of hatred which any war leaves. And the hatred which this war is going to leave, I think, will be bottomless.

Gilbert Harding, British broadcaster, address, "Postwar Treatment of Germany," Toronto, 19 October 1944, The Empire Club of Canada.

KAPUT

One-word headline on front page of the "Special Victory Edition" of *The Maple Leaf*, the four-page weekly paper published "For Canadian Forces in Action," 9 May 1945, edited by **J. Douglas MacFarlane**, as noted by Richard MacFarlane, *Canada's Newspaper Legend: The Story of J. Douglas MacFarlane* (2000).

During the war, I once asked a famous Englishman what single fact had impressed him most during the air raids in London. He told me that as far as he could find out (and he had made many inquiries), no taximan had ever disobeyed a traffic light while the bombs were falling.

Leonard W. Brockington, orator, address, "St. George and Meerie England," Toronto, 22 April 1954, The Empire Club of Canada.

Who will Mulroney apologize to next—the German soldiers Canadians killed in World War II?

J.L. Granatstein, historian, referring to Prime Minister Brian Mulroney's penchant for offering apologies for alleged injustices committed in the past, "Writers of History: The Organized Man," *The Beaver*, April–May 1991.

Without Canadian pilots, the Battle of Britain might well have been lost. Without Canadian sailors, the Battle of the Atlantic surely would have been.

Niall Ferguson, British historian, *Empire: The Rise and Demise of the British World Order and the Message for Global Power* (2002).

If the Japanese had been privy to the July 16, 1945, A-bomb test explosion in Alamogordo, New Mexico, I doubt they would have needed to be surprised by bombs dropping on Hiroshima and Nagaski before surrendering.

Robert J. Sawyer, science-fiction author, arguing the benefits of disclosure, "Privacy: Who Needs It?" (2002), *Relativity: Stories and Essays* (2004).

War is a dirty thing. I hope we will never see the like of those days again.... [We fought] because no one man can ever rule the world and a lot of people were dying because one tried.

Philip Favel, grand chief of the Cree, war veteran, laying a wreath to commemorate the Cree who helped keep Canadian communications secure by sending and receiving radio messages in their own language, Juno Beach, D-Day ceremony, 7 June 2004, interviewed by Neil Tweedie and Michael Smith, *The Daily Telegraph*, 8 June 2004.

Much has been said about the significance of the battle of Vimy in the First World War as a defining moment in Canadian history, a milestone along Canada's road to nationhood, because Canadian troops won victory there as an identifiable army. So it has also been said that Canada took its place in the world on June 6, 1944, when its soldiers came ashore in Normandy as full partners in the Allied breaching of Hitler's Atlantic Wall. Both claims may be true.

Ted Barris, broadcaster and historian, *Juno: Canadians at D-Day, June 6, 1944* (2004).

Don't forget the Canadians.

John Keegan, English military historian, one of five historians who personally advised U.S. President Bill Clinton in the White House, May 1994, before Clinton's drafting and delivering his address to mark the fiftieth anniversary of D-Day, foreword, Ted Barris, *Juno: Canadians at D-Day, June 6, 1944* (2004). Keegan added, "I explained that, of the five D-Day beaches, two had been British, two American, and one Canadian, Juno. I said that it had been an extraordinary achievement for a country of Canada's modest population to provide a force large enough to assault so large a sector, to take it and to advance inland, and that the achievement was a source of enormous Canadian national pride. The president nodded, noticed my advice, and, when in France, paid generous tribute."

WORRY

Worrying helps you some—it seems as if you were doing something when you're worrying.

Thoughts of Anne Shirley, the principal character in **L.M. Montgomery**'s novel *Anne of Green Gables* (1908).

We spend our lives preparing for delights which don't come, and recovering from disasters which do.

Richard J. Needham, columnist, "A Writer's Notebook," *The Globe and Mail*, 25 May 1971.

WRITERS & WRITING *See also* Authors; individual writers; Language; Literature; Poetry

I would say that *Huckleberry Finn* is the greatest story ever written by an American author. The funny thing about it is that the States at first failed to recognize Twain's genius. The book I named was first acclaimed in England—they detected Mark Twain's genius before his own countrymen did.

Stephen Leacock, humorist, interviewed by R.E. Knowles, "Leacock Says Sir A. Currie Most Distinguished Pupil," *Toronto Daily Star*, 16 February 1933.

As William Wallace Cook in his heyday was known as the deforester of Canada, so H. Bedford-Jones followed in his track as the best paid, and most widely read pulp paper writer.

H. Bedford-Jones, Canadian-born contributor to pulp magazines, writing about the productivity of a fellow pulp writer and himself in the third person, "I Began Again," *Writer's Digest*, December 1931.

Writing is fifty years behind painting. I propose to apply the painters' techniques to writing; things as simple and immediate as collage or montage.

Brion Gysin, artist and writer, "Cut-Ups Self-Explained" (1964), *Back in No Time: The Brion Gysin Reader* (2001), edited by Jason Weiss. Gysin was born in London, England, and died in Paris, France, but spent his youth in the 1920s in and around Edmonton, Alta. He developed the "cut-up" technique with William S. Burroughs.

If publishers are schizophrenics, writers are paranoids. He is sure the critics hate him, and want to destroy him; in this he is never more than half-right. If a critic gave him a good review last time, he shrinks from meeting the man, lest he should appear to be cultivating him in hope of future favours.... And it is true that critics are capricious people and pick on things in a book that an author never thinks about. When my last novel was published a critic called attention to the fact that none of the beautiful women in it were Canadians.

Robertson Davies, author, address, "How the Author Reaches His Public," Toronto, 2 March 1972, The Empire Club of Canada.

We All Began in a Little Magazine.

Title of a short story about the small-press launchings of literary careers in the 1940s and 1950s in **Norman Levine**'s collection *Thin Ice* (1979).

I set the story at Hobbema, Alberta, not because I knew anything about the place.... Until I'd written about twenty of these stories I didn't even know the residents of Hobbema were Cree.

W.P. Kinsella, author, quoted in *The Oberon Reader* (1991), edited by Michael Macklem. "Illianna Comes Home" was the first of Kinsella's controversial "Hobbema stories"; it was written in Vancouver in 1971 and included in *Dance Me Outside* (1977).

To a real writer the only Creative Writing Course is life itself and it goes on for 24 hours a day.

Robertson Davies, man of letters, letter, 8 February 1991, *For Your Eye Alone: Letters, 1976–1995* (1999).

If discipline sounded half as good as inspiration, there would be twice as many writers.

Irena F. Karafilly, aphorist, characteristic observation, 7 November 2000.

Life-writing is the general term whose specifics include autobiography (about one's public self), memoir (frequently about others but with oneself as a thread), diary (a day-by-day record), and journal (a discontinuous and often more private or intense product of the same impulse to record).

George Fetherling, editor, preface, *The Vintage Book of Canadian Memoirs* (2001).

Armchair travellers read travel narratives to transport themselves to places they're unlikely to visit in any other way. Similarly, people read literary memoirs to travel inside the luggage of somebody else's life.

George Fetherling, editor, preface, *The Vintage Book of Canadian Memoirs* (2001).

On average, Canadian writers have an annual income equivalent to a McDonald's cook. Yet together we have transformed the Canadian imagination.

Scott McIntyre, publisher, referring to writers and publishers, "Literary Life Support," *Maclean's*, 3 June 2002.

I used to think I was just writing as a witness. But I guess I think of fiction as redemption in some way. It's about looking at the otherwise possibilities or the unless possibilities that make one life different from another life. The novel is in fact a far more subversive and capacious vehicle than I ever thought.

Carol Shields, novelist, in Noah Richler, "Every Person Is a Novel," *National Post*, 2 November 2002.

The state of fiction at the moment—and I do say this with deep respect in the country of Alice Munro, of Robertson Davies, of Margaret Atwood and many others—nevertheless, I pick up new novels and after five pages I drop them because of their infantilism, their cliché-ridden monotony.

George Steiner, critic, interviewed by Eleanor Wachtel, *Original Minds* (2003).

My best advice to writers is get yourself born in an interesting place.

Pierre Berton, writer and historian, born in Whitehorse, Y.T., interviewed by Sarah Hampson, "The National Dream Weaver," *The Globe and Mail*, 24 May 2003.

There is a treadmill quality to being a writer: if you don't keep producing new books at a good clip, your readers will go off and find someone else to read.

Robert J. Sawyer, science-fiction author, "Autobiography" (2004), *Relativity: Stories and Essays* (2004).

In a way, it was more important to find clear thinkers than great writers; good writing, after all, comes down to clear thinking made visible.

Peter C. Newman, journalist and memoirist, discussing hiring writers for *Maclean's, Here Be Dragons: Telling Tales of People, Passion, and Power* (2004).

It was the quality of one's writing that won one an audience and influence. I never departed from that belief. The writing—about which I'm hearing from you favourable comment of almost adequate proportion—I have counted as important as the economics itself.

John Kenneth Galbraith, economist, on the importance of the quality of his prose in advancing his economic thought, interviewed by John Geddes, "'The Frailty of Judgment,'" *Maclean's,* 31 January 2005.

X

Strangely enough, the letter *X* crops up far more often than those words that begin with *X.* We see the letter *X* everywhere….

Bill Sherk, logophile, *Brave New Words* (1979).

y

Y2K *See also* Computers; Information Technology; Millennium

We've finally broken the back of the Y2K problem.... Have we "solved" Y2K? No, not entirely. But we have avoided the doomsday scenarios. The next twelve months or so are going to be fascinating to watch. But it will not, contrary to the ravings found in some of the media reports and in many places on the internet, be TEOTWAWKI.... Through hard work and effort, we've broken the back of Y2K.

Peter de Jager, computer specialist, "Doomsday Avoided," 1 March 1999, website, 3 November 2000. The acronym means "The End Of The World As We Know It."

I'm officially unemployed.

Peter de Jager, business speaker based in Brampton, Ont., expert on the Y2K (Year Two Thousand) computer problem, aboard a transatlantic flight, midnight, 31 December 1999–1 January 2000, in Christopher Shulgan, "The Sky Fell on Him," *National Post*, 23 December 2000.

YOUTH *See also* Adolescence; Age; Children; Family

The barriers of religion and morality, the barriers of law, have disappeared. The young question all forms of authority and the rich and the wise are distressed and feel that the young are rebellious and not good. Yet in the hearts of the young a fantastic call exists, a desire for peace, a desire for tolerance, an openness, and a compassion. Undoubtedly frequently lacking a structure, undoubtedly there is a mixed motivation, but it is so easy for the smug to criticize and condemn as laziness and abusive action.

Jean Vanier, humanitarian, address, "A World in Violence: Eruption to Hope?" Toronto, 11 February 1971, The Empire Club of Canada.

I am convinced that the time has come to dispel the romantic myth of "young is good, old is bad" that fuels virtually all the engines of our market economy.

Marcel Danesi, semiotician, *Forever Young: The "Teen-Aging" of Modern Culture* (2003).

YUKON TERRITORY *See also* Klondike

Meals $75 to men with full sacks. Meals gratis to men with no sack at all.

Sign at the Do-Drop-Inn, Bonanza, Y.T., advertisement, *The Yukon Nugget*, 30 July 1898, in Russell A. Bankson, *The Klondike Nugget* (1935).

The Yukoners are made up of people from all quarters of the earth but the Yukon. The population consists of but two classes—the men who dig, and the men who get it after it is dug.

Eugene C. Allen, editor of *The Yukon Nugget*, 3 May 1899, in Russell A. Bankson, *The Klondike Nugget* (1935).

Yukon.

The name *yukon* was proposed for the subatomic particle, subsequently named *meson*, the existence of which was predicted in 1934 by **Hideki Yukawa**, the Japanese theoretical physicist. "The particle was supposed to be named, after him, the 'yukon,' but those responsible for scientific nomenclature feared that it would be confused with the northwest region of Canada. Thus the meson was born." Nevertheless, Yukawa was awarded the Nobel Prize for Physics in 1949, according to *The People's Almanac No. 2* (1978).

This territory has 1 city, 3 towns, 4 villages, and 3 hamlets. All are included except the hamlet of Elsa, which has a population of fewer than 10.

Alan Rayburn, place-name specialist, explaining some principles of inclusion, introduction, *Dictionary of Canadian Place Names* (1997).

Z

ZED

We have built a society that both expresses what we are and *is* what we are. Saying *zed* rather than *zee* does not make us different.

Richard Gwyn, columnist, "Cultural Sovereignty: Myth or Reality?" *Proceedings of the 28th Annual Seminar on Canadian-American Relations, University of Windsor, 5–7 Nov. 1986* (1987), edited by James Chako.

"Zed" is not a Canadianism; "zee" is an Americanism.

Wayne Grady, author, noting that "zed" is pronounced as such in most English-speaking countries except the United States, *Chasing the Chinook: On the Trail of Canadian Words and Culture* (1998).

ZEN *See also* Buddhism

Zen trying to define itself is not Zen.... True transmission is about recognizing the spirit, not the totem.

Maurine Stuart, Canadian-born *roshi* in the Rinzai movement of Buddhism and a student of piano in Paris, resident of Cambridge, Mass., quoted by Helen Tworkov, *Zen in America* (1989), in Andrew Rawlinson, *The Book of Enlightened Masters: Western Teachers in Eastern Traditions* (1997).

ZNAIMER, MOSES

Moses discovered the G-Spot of television.

Jacques de Souze, TV producer, referring to impresario Moses Znaimer, CHUM Television's tribute *MosesTV*, CITY-TV, 5 January 2005. More specifically the CBC executive producer Slawko Klymkiw subsequently noted that Znaimer introduced television that was at once popular, cool, and local.

In a certain sense he's the CPR of music.... He really stretched the rail from one end of the country to the other.

Leonard Cohen, singer-songwriter, referring to Znaimer's continent-wide contribution to popular music, CHUM Television's tribute *MosesTV*, CITY-TV, 5 January 2005.

I want TV to look like the subway.

Moses Znaimer, TV impresario, quoted by lawyer Michael Levine in CHUM Television's tribute *MosesTV*, CITY-TV, 5 January 2005.

I read recently a little maxim and it's unattributed, anonymous. But it says, "First secure an independent income. Then practise virtue."

Moses Znaimer, TV impresario, interviewed by Vinay Menon, "Ex-boss Znaimer Blasted, Loved," *Toronto Star*, 5 January 2005.

ZOOS *See also* Animals; Wildlife

We commonly say in the trade that the most dangerous animal in a zoo is Man. In a general way we mean how our species' excessive predatoriness has made the entire planet our prey. More specifically, we have in mind the people who feed fish-hooks to the otters, razors to the bears, apples with small nails in them to the elephants and hardware variations on the theme....

Thoughts of the narrator, whose father is a zookeeper, in **Yann Martel**'s *The Life of Pi: A Novel* (2002).

ZZEDWYEXIAN

Zzedwyexian, *noun.*

A person who can recite the alphabet backwards as quickly as forwards.

Noun coined by **Bill Sherk**, logophile, as the last entry in *Brave New Words* (1979).

Index

The letter *a* or *b* that follows the page number indicates that the quotation can be found in either the left-hand column (a) or the right-hand column (b) on the page. Unattributed quotations appear under the heading Anonymous.